T3-BSK-250

# John Žižka

AND THE HUSSITE REVOLUTION

# John Žižka
## and the Hussite Revolution

BY FREDERICK G. HEYMANN

PRINCETON, NEW JERSEY
PRINCETON UNIVERSITY PRESS
1955

London: Geoffrey Cumberlege, Oxford University Press

L. C. Card 55-5005

The publication of this book was aided by a grant from
the Committee for the Promotion of Advanced Slavic Studies

Title-page decoration: *Žižka Leading His Troops*,
woodcut from an early edition of Aeneas Sylvius,
*Historia Bohemica*

Printed in the United States of America
By Princeton University Press, Princeton, New Jersey

*To Winifred Bryher*
*in lasting gratitude*

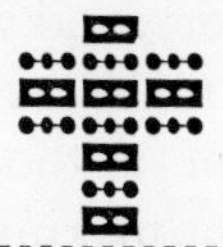

# PREFACE

THIS BOOK, I believe, is the first full-scale monograph to appear in this country on any single phase of the history of the Kingdom of Bohemia, the old land of the Czech nation. This, at least, was the task which I set myself—to present not just a biography of Žižka, but beyond it an adequate account of that short but extraordinary period of Czech history of which he was the leading figure. The question may be asked why so much space was given to this seemingly limited subject when, for all the rest of the history of the Czechs and Slovaks, the English-speaking reader is still largely dependent on one-volume works. But I felt—and for this decision I found welcome encouragement from many—that there was good reason to turn the light of a rather detailed historical observation on the Hussite Revolution and especially on its decisive earlier phase. This is a subject that has already received attention—as a true turning point of history—from historians writing in Western languages, men like Ernest Denis and Count Lützow, in books which, while now out of date and out of print, did pioneer work. Yet the true significance of the Hussite Revolution has not been sufficiently recognized outside the circle of those scholars who have specialized in Slavic or Central and Eastern European studies. Those, indeed, who relied on German historiography were none too well served; for, with some notable exceptions, German medievalists as well as German historians of Protestantism have until recently been somewhat less than objective or generous in their treatment of the Bohemian Reformation.

It is the underlying thesis of this book—presented in the second part of Chapter I, which serves as an introduction—that the birth of Protestantism, with most of its later facets, occurred in Bohemia a century before Luther. For this view I can claim no originality. Indeed it was presented, about a century ago, outside Bohemia itself by the Protestant theologian L. Krummel as well as by the Catholic historian C. von Hofler. Both considered the Hussite Reformation as an earlier part rather than as a forerunner of "the" Reformation. If eventually this view should be accepted as essentially correct, then a more general reevaluation of this phase of history, and with it of the prehistory of Protestantism, seems needed. To make any valid contribution to such a reevaluation, nothing short of a thorough monographic treatment seemed appropriate, a treatment making the fullest use of all accessible sources.

For the help I received for this study I owe a manifold debt of gratitude. First of all I was enabled to take time off, especially in a series of long academic summers, when the Eugene F. Saxton Foundation granted me, in the fall of 1950, a fellowship for the completion of this book. Only now, with its publication, can I adequately thank the trustees for their favorable decision. Further financial help, intended directly to support publication, was given by the Committee for the Promotion of Advanced Slavic Cultural Studies.

To those scholars who read part or all of the manuscript, gave me advice on special aspects or helped me with the loan of books from their personal libraries, I shall ever be thankful. But beyond this I am particularly indebted to Professor Otakar Odložilík, formerly of the Charles University in Prague, now of Columbia University. I shall always consider it a high privilege that I was permitted to discuss with him, at length, many aspects of this work. His patient guidance in the early phases of my research and his continued interest and advice throughout the growth of the work have encouraged and helped me immeasurably.

I have found much friendly support from librarians. This was most important as the project depended on the use of book loans from a large number of libraries all over the country. But I owe special thanks to the Harvard College Library, the Slavonic Department of the New York Public Library, and most of all to the Czechoslovak Department of the Webster Branch of the New York Public Library, whose head, Mrs. Ludmila Matulková, has shown the liveliest interest in the project and was indefatigable in her efforts to provide material which was sometimes difficult to locate.

Finally I wish to thank my son Frank Heymann, who drew the maps in this book, and my wife Edith who has shared the worries and hopes connected with the work, who has carried an enormous burden in the process of collecting research material in three languages, of tirelessly typing and retyping the manuscript and—together with my daughter Ruth and with Mrs. Emmy Bloch—of proofreading and indexing.

F.G.H.

August, 1954

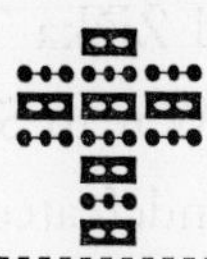

# CONTENTS

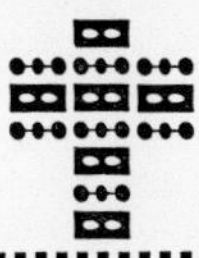

# ILLUSTRATIONS



## MAPS

# John Žižka

## AND THE HUSSITE REVOLUTION

Names of places, rivers, mountains, etc., within Bohemia or Moravia, are given in Czech regardless of their nationality character in 1419 or at any later time, and for places in present day Slovakia (then Northern Hungary) the Slovak names are used. Exceptions are those few places where another than the Czech form has become English usage:

Prague for Praha
Pilsen for Plzeň
Budweis for Budějovice
Tabor for Tábor

Familiar first names are used in the English form:

Ambrose for Czech Ambrož
Ernest for Arnošt
George for Jiří
Henry for Jindřich
John for Jan
Lawrence for Vavřinec
Nicholas for Mikuláš
William for Vilém

Names of origin are generally given in the form used by their bearers. Where, however, these names (mostly those of castles) are clearly German, the German spelling is used instead of the slight Czech deviations. Thus Wartenberg and Lichtenburg instead of Vartenberk and Lichtenburk.

The pronunciation of Czech words is, in the general character of vowels, similar to that of German and Italian. Vowels are short except where they carry a lengthening accent (′ or °). Among consonants c is like ts in tsar, ch is like kh or like ch in German nicht, č like ch in chair, ě like ye in yellow, ň like ni in onion, ř like rsh in harsh (as pronounced by a Scotsman), š like sh in short, ž like zh (or like j in French jour). All Czech words have the stress on the first syllable.

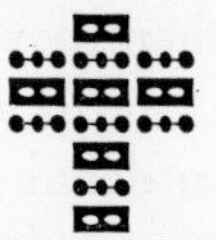

# CHAPTER 1

## THE VERY PRETTY CHRONICLE OF JOHN ŽIŽKA THE SERVANT OF KING WENCESLAS[1]

WHEN it was the year one thousand four hundred and ten after the birth of the Son of God, there arose Master John Hus, and he began to preach, and to castigate the people for their sinful life. And the clergymen praised him very highly, and they said that the Spirit of God Himself spoke through the Master's mouth. But then he began to preach also against the sinfulness of the clergy, sparing neither the Pope on his throne nor the lowliest priest, and he preached against their haughtiness and their greed, against simony and concubinage, and he said that priests should not wield worldly power nor worldly estates, and he also preached that in the Holy Communion the Body of Christ and also the Blood of Christ should both be given to the common people.[2] And now the clergy grew furious against him, and they said that the Devil himself entered into him and that he was a heretic. And this came to pass in the Kingdom of Bohemia, when Wenceslas, son of the Emperor Charles, was King, and the priest Zbyněk was Archbishop in Prague.

And when it was the year one thousand four hundred and fifteen, the council of the highest priests summoned Master John Hus, that he should come to them, under safe conduct, to Constance. And he went, together with the Master Jerome, under the safe conduct of King Sigismund, the Hungarian King. And when he came to Constance and with him some Czech lords, then they arrested him there in Constance, and they deprived him of his priesthood, and the highest priests

[1] *Kronika velmi pěkna o Janovi Žižkovi, celedinu Krále Václava.* Edition used here by V. Novotný, Prague 1923. Some rather monotonous reports on the conquest of towns, castles, and monasteries and a somewhat odd interlude on the disinterment and reburial of King Wenceslas IV have been omitted. The chronicle was written in the fifteenth century, probably between 1434 and 1436, but there is some controversy on the exact dating.

[2] Hus did not originate the Communion in both kinds, he only approved of it in one of his last messages from Constance. See below, Chapter 10.

sentenced him to death. And when they sentenced him the King Sigismund sat on the judgment seat, and it was he that had given safe conduct to Master Hus. And they ordered him to be burned at the stake, and also Master Jerome, but him only in the year after. And that came to pass when the priest Conrad was Archbishop in Prague.

And when such things came to pass, the Czechs and Moravians were filled with wrath and many priests in Prague and elsewhere in many towns in Bohemia and Moravia began to give the Body and Blood of Christ, in both kinds, to the common people. And they raised the host in the monstrance, and it became the custom for crowds of men to walk behind the host, praising the Lord. And when the common people partook in the Holy Communion in both kinds, Body and Blood of Christ, then some abused them, calling them Husses, or else Wigleffs, or even heretics. And so then the people divided themselves, both clerics and laymen, into two parties. And of the two parties of priests, one was followed by many, and the other also by many. And these began to abuse each other and struggle until the King could no longer do anything about it.

And when the King went away from Prague to the New Castle, it came to pass that priests with the host and with a great crowd following went from the Church of St. Stephen and passed the town hall of the New Town of Prague. Then someone hurled a stone from the town hall down upon the priest, and the crowd that followed him was infuriated, and they cried: There they throw stones against the Body of God and against our priest! And they stormed the town hall and forced the entrance, and they threw the councilors out of the window and slew them.

Then when the King learned that this had occurred, he was, through great exasperation, hit by a heavy stroke, and thus died King Wenceslas.

And in Prague the people got very infuriated against some priests and monks and against the Germans, and they drove them out of the town, and others fled on their own account. For at that time it was common for Germans to be on the council and in the town offices.

And thus because of the great uproar the lords could not conduct the dead King Wenceslas through the city of Prague, and so they carried him secretly up to the castle of Saint Wenceslas.[3] And there he lay unburied for some time, for he had ordered that he be buried in the monastery of Zbraslav. Then the lords sent him, again secretly during the night, to Zbraslav, and there the monks buried him.

[3] "The Castle of St. Wenceslas" is the present Hradčany Castle.

After that the Hungarian King Sigismund, the brother of King Wenceslas, came to Brno, and he sent for the lords of Bohemia and Moravia, for the Praguers and for the others who adhered to the Law of God. And when they came thither, he asked them: What is it you stand for, that you are in such uproar? And the Czechs and Moravians answered the King together and spoke: We stand for the Four Articles: first, that the Body and Blood of God both be given everywhere to the common people; second, that all notorious sins be suppressed; third, that the Word of God be freely preached; fourth, that priests may not wield worldly power nor possess worldly goods. Then the King spoke on the Body and Blood of God and said: Thus as it has been at the beginning, thus it shall be again.[4] And he asked the Praguers, and said: When I come to Bohemia, will you let me in the city of Prague? So the Praguers said to the King: If you do not want to enter through the gates, so will we make a breach in the wall to shame ourselves, so you may enter as our lord. Then said the King: Remove all chains, with which you blocked the streets and from the Old Town take them up to the castle of Saint Wenceslas, and from the New Town to the Vyšehrad. This the Praguers did.

Then in the same year the Pope declared against the Czechs, that they are heretics, because they take both the Body and Blood of Christ; and he gave indulgences, whosoever slew such a Czech or took his life this way or the other, then he that did this was rid of all sin and punishment. And they began to slay the people and to take their lives in manifold forms of death.

Then one Czech stood up from the ranks of the knights, a man most brave, one-eyed, named Žižka, by the grace of God, and he stood up grimly and took the field to fight against those who did not take the Body and Blood of Christ in both kinds. Those he took for his enemies, and he also held them to be heretics.

Thus one party fell out with the other, and whichever party held more power, that party killed and burned cruelly and without mercy, or took the lives of their enemies in manifold ways. And he whom God Himself in His grace wanted to save, he alone remained alive. And above all the Germans sought the lives of the Czechs, and the Czechs of the Germans. And that war went on cruelly for fourteen years.

And Žižka and other Czechs lay afield in Bohemia and other lands all the time, fighting for the Law of God. So they conquered Sezimovo

[4] In reality Sigismund never expressed himself in favor of the return to the old ways, i.e. the Communion in the two kinds.

Ústí and from there went on and conquered Hradiště and occupied the castle and the hill, and upon it they built a town which they called Tabor. And Žižka marched through the land with his soldiers, conquering castles and towns. And many battles he fought with strong enemies, and yet he never lost a battle.

And then the Hungarian King Sigismund marched from Hungary into the lands of the Bohemian crown, and he came to Breslau. There he commanded one citizen of Prague to be dragged by horses, and he commanded that likewise should be done to other Czech heretics. When the Praguers learned this, then wherever there had been one chain before to barricade the streets, they put two, and they locked themselves up against him.

And the King laid garrisons of many knights on the castle of Vyšehrad and the castle of Saint Wenceslas against the Praguers. And when Žižka heard this, he forthwith occupied and fortified the hill of Vítkov against the King, and the people gave this fortress the name Žižkov. . . .

And then there came the Duke of Austria, and the Margraves of Meissen, and many other princes with masses of knights to help the King. And the King marched on and laid his armies before Prague. And there they crowned the King up on the castle of Saint Wenceslas. And at that occasion many Germans were dubbed knights.

After that[5] they marched in strength to Žižka's fortress to conquer it. And they undertook to storm it. And when Žižka was in great distress, a priest came out of the city with the Body of Christ. And the Germans were struck by panic, and they tried to flee with their horses, and they plunged down from the hill and broke their necks.

After that, when the Germans got hold of a Czech, even if he was of their own party in his creed, they did not even ask him about that, but as soon as they laid eyes on him they took him and burned him. And this went on until even those Czechs who were of the King's own party grew indignant against him. . . .

And when the King had sent the foreign armies home from this land, Žižka took the field and marched through the land, and he burned the monasteries and drove the monks out of the country, and he ordered the burning of the priests who kept giving the Communion to the common people in one kind only.

And the Praguers with other lords besieged the castle of Vyšehrad, and there were many knights in that castle. And they defended them-

[5] The sequence is wrong. The battle described in this paragraph took place before Sigismund's coronation.

selves bravely, but they had great hunger, for as they had nothing left to eat they ate their horses. And in the morning of All Saints' Day the King approached with a great army hoping to save the Vyšehrad. And there of the Lords of Bohemia and Moravia who held with the King many were killed. And the King suffered great damage of brave men, and he was beaten. Then the Praguers occupied the Vyšehrad and destroyed the castle. . . .

Then the Hungarian King marched against Žižka with a strong might. And he besieged some of Žižka's people at Kladruby. And the King lay there himself, and he was armed with strong siege guns. And Žižka gathered his troops and marched into the Pilsen land to save his people at Kladruby. And when Žižka was still six miles from Kladruby the King retreated and went away from Bohemia to Hungary. . . .

And Žižka went on to Prague. And at that time they gave the castle of Saint Wenceslas up to the Praguers.

Then from Prague Žižka went to Český Brod with strong troops. And there the Germans closed the gates against him, and he took the town by storm. And some Germans fled up into the church tower. Then they put fire to the church below their feet. There a few Germans died in the flames and some jumped down from the tower. And those who did not break their necks they slew with their flails.

Then the other towns gave themselves up: Kouřim, Nymburk, Kolín, Kutná Hora, Čáslav, Chrudim, Litomyšl, Polička, Dvůr Králové. But the town of Jaroměř they had to conquer by storm, for the defenders trusted that the town was strong enough to resist them. And so all these towns and many others adhered to the Law of God.

After that Žižka marched on and laid siege to the castle of Rabí. And there his second eye was shot out of him. And he was completely blind and barely saved his life. . . .

Then after some weeks the German Electors invaded the land with a very strong army, and with them there were many princes, counts, bishops, and also the Margrave of Meissen. And they committed many cruelties, and whenever they got hold of a Czech, they killed or burned him every time.

And they marched before Žatec with all their might, and they laid close siege to the town. And while they lay there they stormed thrice, and yet they could not conquer the town, and many of the attacking people were killed. And the Electors suffered great damage and shamefully and humbly they left the country. . . .

Then the Hungarian King came with a vast army to Bohemia, having with him Turks and Wallachians, Croatians and Hungarians, Cumans and Yassyans, Germans and other people from many different countries.

And Žižka with his army marched against him to Kutná Hora. And the King, when he learned that Žižka was at Kutná Hora, marched to that town, for he hoped he would catch him there. Then Žižka marched out of Kutná Hora to fight the King, and he built his encampment with his war wagons in the field before Kutná Hora and there they battled all day long. And when evening came, the King invested that encampment but he stayed just out of shot of Žižka's troops. Then when it was five o'clock at night, Žižka moved against the King's army. And there he fought his way straight through that army, for there was no other way he could go with his troops. And he marched less than a quarter mile, till day came, and again he commanded his war wagons to be put in defense position. But the King did not move to join battle, but he waited for reinforcements, for he knew that they were near. And so Žižka commanded to march to Kolín. And there he gathered still more soldiers, for he was still resolved to give battle to the King.

And the King who had occupied Kutná Hora had ordered his army to camp near the town. And his soldiers went around raping women and virgins till they died. And everywhere the King ordered people to be burned.

But when Žižka had gathered more soldiers, he quickly moved on to Kutná Hora to give battle to the King. And when the two armies lay opposite each other, then the King commanded, at three o'clock at night, that Kutná Hora be burned. And he retreated before Žižka toward Německý Brod, and Žižka pursued him. And when the King's army had passed the village of Habry, Žižka caught up with them, and he beat them and destroyed them while they fled to Německý Brod. And many drowned when they crossed the river with their horses and the ice broke under them. And Žižka captured all their wagons with rich booty.

And on the next day Žižka ordered the storming of the town. And they stormed all day, yet they could not conquer it for the defenders fought bravely. And on the day after that, they conquered the town and they killed all the defenders, but the Lord Zawisza from Poland and the Lords Borovský and Mrtvice, those three knights they took as prisoners. And Žižka returned with his army. . . .

And at that time there came one prince [Korybut of Lithuania] with knightly attendance, and he had with him an army of about four thousand horse. And he was received in Prague and the city given over to his rule. And Žižka called him "my son," and he called Žižka "my father."

At the same time the Praguers besieged the castle of Karlstein. And the prince besieged Opočno, and this they could not conquer. And at that time the Taborites went to Prague with a strong force and laid themselves in the New Town. . . . And the people of the Old Town, who were on their watch, threw some out of the houses and some hundred of them they took prisoners and the others they drove shamefully out of the town.

And when the Prince did not want to take the Communion in both kinds, then the Praguers deserted him and so did Žižka.[6] And the Prince returned to Lithuania. Later he came back, and he thought he would be received as he was the first time. But this was not so.

After that, trouble broke out between the Praguers and Žižka. And when Žižka went to Kostelec on the Elbe, the Praguers marched toward him with a powerful army. And he, when he saw how great their army was, marched off and the Praguers followed him. And when he arrived near Malešov, then Žižka turned around and fought with them and beat them. And because of that battle there were many widows and orphans in Prague and elsewhere in the land.

After that Žižka marched with his army to the Hospital Field near Prague. And there he made peace with the Praguers.

After that Žižka marched to Moravia and besieged Přibyslav. And already the Taborites had much hate for Žižka, mostly because Žižka's priests held the mass in the proper way, in full ornate with tonsure and surplice, and they held the Body of Christ in the monstrance. Therefore the Taborites called Žižka's priests linen weavers, and Žižka called the Taborite priests cobblers. For the Taborite priests held the mass in simple garb without tonsure and some had even grown beards. And in this, too, they were different.

Then it came to pass that there at Přibyslav Žižka was overcome by the plague. And thus died Žižka, and they took him to Hradec Králové and buried him, and there he lies.[7]

[6] Here the old chronicler is quite wrong. Prince Korybut held faithfully the Communion in both kinds and left Bohemia only because he was recalled by his uncle, Grand Duke Witold of Lithuania. For the treatment of Korybut's role, see below, Chapter 20.

[7] Žižka's body did not rest long at Hradec Králové but was disinterred and reburied at Čáslav, probably sometime between 1434 and 1437. See below, Chapter 28.

Then his soldiers called themselves Orphans, and thus they have been called ever since.

And the people of Hradec Králové ordered Žižka to be painted on their banner, mounted on a white horse, in knightly armor, holding his battle club, as he looked when he was alive. And whenever the people of Hradec Králové went into battle under this banner, they were invincible.

And then the people of Hradec Králové elected themselves a captain, whoever they thought was best. But the priest Prokůpek was in command most of the time. Also the Taborite people raised a large army, and this army was to serve in the field all the time. This field army was under the command of the Priest Prokop the Bald. And in battle he always was at the head of his army in his heavy coat.

And the two armies took the field at all times, and they fought in Bohemia and Moravia, in Austria and in Hungary, in Thuringia, in the Marches of Brandenburg and in Lusatia. And far and wide marched the Czech soldiers, and they came to Ruthenia and to Prussia, and they lay in the Prussian lands and in Denmark, and they watered their horses in the far sea.

And every time when they returned, they had earned fame and honor. In the end, however, many found their doom when, between Český Brod and Kouřim,[8] they fought against Czechs.

---

This little chronicle is the first attempt ever made to describe in its historical context the life of that strange, great man and soldier John Žižka. True, there are many phases of his life and of the Hussite wars on which more detailed and more reliable contemporary reports are preserved. None of them, however, tries, as our old author did, to gain a general perspective of this great struggle and of Žižka's role in it. There is little sophistication in this simple tale, written in the vigorous Czech of his time. The chronicler's prime intention was to tell a war story, without any attempt at weakening or extenuating the cruel truth. Yet just those parts that go beyond the mere battle reports point to some of the essential facts of that great revolution of which the chronicler must have witnessed at least the final phases.

It was one of the great, almost elementary events in history, one

[8] At the battle of Lipany, fought in 1434 between Taborites and Orphans on the one side, the lords and Praguers on the other. See below, Chapter 30.

which shook Europe's Christian society to its very depths. It was the moment when for the first time "the people divided themselves, both clerics and laymen, into two parties." It was, in other words, the birth of the Protestant Reformation. For the majority of the Czechs in Bohemia and Moravia the Law of God[9] had been rediscovered by Master John Hus. The "Four Articles of Prague," which, as the chronicler tells us, were what the Lords and Praguers stood for in their meeting with Sigismund, and especially the Communion in the two kinds (the cup to the laity), were, at an early stage, the rallying point for the reform party. They did not think of themselves as innovators, as creators of a new form of religion and society, but as restorers of the old ways of God, as the direct successors of the people of Israel, true to the covenant, true to Christ who had died for them and whom the fanatics among them expected soon to return.

The frightful word heretics that was hurled against these first Protestants was bound to arouse fierce resentment, for it implied not only the worst of all sins, but eternal damnation. There was only one answer: It is we, the followers of Master Hus, who are obeying the Law of God, we who are the true followers of Christ. Those, therefore, who oppose us, oppress us, kill us, are themselves heretics, trying to thwart the Will of God. Out of this deep, passionate conviction was born the determination not to yield, not to surrender, but to challenge, if need be, all the forces of the religious and political order which had dominated medieval Europe for nearly a thousand years, to fight it out against odds the like of which have seldom been seen in history.

In the forefront of the "enemies of God," however, stood the Germans. German patricians had, as the chronicle correctly tells us, held a dominant position in the councils of many of Bohemia's cities and towns, and being conservative, owing to their privileged social position, very few of them would join the reformation. Sigismund, to whom in accordance with Hussite usage our chronicle refers only as the Hungarian King, was also King of the Romans, that is German King and later Emperor. It was in the Hussite wars and on the basis of this struggle against Germans that the Czechs learned to think of themselves as a nation very nearly in the modern sense of the word, and in their

[9] The expression "Law of God" which plays a great role in all Hussite literature is understood as the basic teachings of the Bible. (In Czech the word for law, "zákon," also stands for the Biblical meaning of the word "testament".) In the course of the theological discussion, however, it became almost synonymous with the Four Articles of Prague which are quoted by the Chronicle, in somewhat unusual sequence, in the report on the discussions between Sigismund and the Praguers at Brno.

attempt to organize their national resistance they began forming what was to be one of the first nation-states in history. Thus the birth of Protestantism, a hundred years before Luther and Calvin, and of modern Nationalism—years before Jeanne d'Arc called the French up under the banner of defending their fatherland—both occurred in Bohemia in those early days.

There is more that makes the Hussite movement one of the decisive turns of European history. Among the social forces which stood behind the Bohemian Reformation, the group that had been on top of the social ladder for hundreds of years—the high nobility—was the most reluctant, the least reliable. Many of them felt this great earthquake to be a danger to their position altogether, whereas others were loath to throw off the bonds of feudal loyalty which tied them to Sigismund, the only surviving man of Bohemia's royal dynasty.

As there was no acknowledged king, nor an aristocracy which could have supplied a firm leadership, other forces had to take over. The strongest of them were the towns—first and foremost Prague, which had always been privileged among the royal towns. For a considerable time the capital city, presented by its elected officials and largely inspired by the masters of its famous University, ruled supreme, calling national diets, dispatching ambassadors to foreign rulers, deposing and imposing governors and burgraves in the country's towns and castles, and even directing the war effort. This role of a city which was not an expanding city state but the ancient capital of a fairly large country, was again a new development, foreshadowing the leading role which was later played by London during the Puritan era, or by Paris during the great French Revolution.

Yet this leading position had its limits and challenges. Not only were most of the nobles reluctant to bow to the rule of people who were just townsmen, but there arose in the country, from below, strange and unknown forces, organizing themselves in little theocratic communities, drawing their population largely from peasants whose farms had been burned by war or abandoned on the notion that the last days were near and Christ's return imminent. Taking names from Biblical mountains like Tabor and Oreb, these communities grew strong and, under the leadership of priests and some captains who mostly belonged to the lower nobility, they maintained a virtual independence in their political, ideological, and military existence. Their creed, even more than that of other Hussite parties, was stern, puritan, old-testamentarian, often fanatic in its determination to purge this world from all sins and sinners by fire and sword.

It was as captain of the Taborite community that Žižka gained his leading position. His rise to an almost unassailable power was in itself an extraordinary event. Only a thorough revolution could shake the social order of the time to the extent that a poor squire without any background or means except his character and genius could rise to those heights. His enemies could not express enough amazement that a man, so low born, was allowed a role that at times was almost tantamount to national rule.[10]

Under the circumstances it was to the work of organizing and directing the war that he had to devote most of his tremendous strength. Out of the raw bands of peasants he formed effective field armies, ruled with sharp discipline and employed with high tactical skill. He developed technical means by which this infantry—for they had few horses—was able to withstand and beat the huge armies of mounted and armored knights which, again and again, were sent against them. In the five years in which Žižka led these troops they acquired the fame of invincibility which they succeeded in upholding for ten more years after his death in 1424—and even then these field armies were only beaten by other Czech forces whose leaders had themselves fought under Žižka and learned from him the art of war.

Žižka really revolutionized warfare. At least as much as the famous mercenary infantry of the Swiss, and perhaps even more effectively, it was Hussite forms of military organization, Hussite methods of fighting, and the development of the recently invented fire weapons by the Hussites under Žižka which led to the eclipse of the knightly cavalry of the Middle Ages. To this day we use weapons whose names—howitzer from the Czech word *houfnice*, and pistol, from the Czech word *pišťala*—betray their Czech-Hussite origin.

The Hussite movement was the first in that chain of great upheavals which together destroyed the caste structure of the Middle Ages, liberated the individual from the embrace and burden, but also from the mental security represented by the omnipresent Church, and finally reorganized Europe and its child America in the form of modern na-

[10] Thus Eberhard Windecke, Sigismund's contemporary biographer (*Denkwürdigkeiten zur Geschichte des Zeitalters Kaiser Sigmunds*, ed. W. Altmann, Berlin 1893, quoted hereafter as Windecke), tells us of the King's anger that the lords of Bohemia "liessent zu Behem einen solichen snöden man von bubenart regieren." The wording expresses contempt of Žižka's social standing rather than hostility.

tions in which the idea of personal freedom found its concrete expression in the reality of Western democracy.

It is the first years of all these movements which, though usually the fiercest, are also the decisive, the most productive, and therefore historically most interesting. This can be said also of the Hussite movement. True, some of its greatest military triumphs—the far-flung campaigns into Germany and Hungary—fall into those later years. But otherwise much that happened then was a mere repetition of earlier happenings. The first five years—the years of Žižka's leadership—are the decisive ones. It was those years that saw some of the most daring experiments in the military as well as in the political sphere. In the field of foreign policy the scene was dominated by the vacillating relationship to Poland-Lithuania, where the Czechs hoped to find not only support but a new ruler as well. In the religious life of the nation, which had so suddenly—and largely against all original reforming intentions—broken loose from the universal Church, a welter of differing streams and groupings developed, each fighting for recognition, some in a cautious, probing, rather rational way, others with the furious pleading of fanatics, some trying to convince by argument and well-ordered theological disputation, others by the reckless and merciless use of fire and sword. Between the extremes there were many shades of transition, many attempts at a compromise.

In all these activities, fights, reconciliations, in all those painful attempts to create a new unity out of the revolutionary chaos, Žižka was permanently involved. This was not only because all these problems concerned him very deeply, but also because, being the leader of what was the strongest, most permanent and most alert military force in the country, his personal decision was bound to carry a tremendous weight. His role was in many ways central and representative even though he, who has more than once been compared to Cromwell, never sought nor achieved the official position as head of the Hussite commonwealth. There is no lack of important leaders, interesting characters, and even creative thinkers in the early phase of the Hussite revolution, but somehow their position in the movement is determined by their relationship —their friendship or hatred—for the old leader of the Taborite armies.

Indeed the Hussite Revolution with its ups and downs, its hopes and disappointments, its outbursts of the highest and purest religious sublimation coupled with outbursts of hatred and carnage, cannot even be sketched without constantly looking at Žižka. Yet the writer who undertakes to draw such a sketch is gravely handicapped. Sources are often scarce or inadequate, as many of the original documents have disappeared, partly because of the destruction wrought by the Hussite wars themselves, partly by the Thirty Years' War and its aftermath, when Habsburg officials and Jesuit teachers tried to remove or destroy as radically as possible the traditions of a Protestant revolution in the richest of the Habsburg Kingdoms.

There is, in addition, the usual indifference of the medieval mind toward the individual personality. There was no lack of alert and attentive chroniclers in the Bohemia of the early fifteenth century, and some of them displayed enough vision, interest, and responsibility to deserve to be called historians, but they hardly ever tried to study Žižka as a personality, or to find out much about his past, his youth and early manhood. To most of his contemporaries he was, it seems, not so much an individual character as a great and frightful natural phenomenon: a terrific power, sent by God to save the Law of God and to punish the sinners; or, to his enemies, a great scourge of humanity, but even so: sent by God. That it was God indeed, who made him do what he did, was the firm conviction of Žižka himself.

We are fortunate, within all those limitations, that at least a small part survives of what must have been a fairly large number of letters and messages of Žižka. They, at least, give us some insight into his personal thoughts and motivations which, in many other cases, have to be deduced from his actions and reactions. They appear, most of them here for the first time translated into English, in an appendix to this book, and they are given great weight in our evaluation of Žižka's personality. For they are the only medium through which this man, one of the first pioneers of that reforming, questioning, impatient age which is still ours, can talk to us over the immense stretch of more than five centuries.

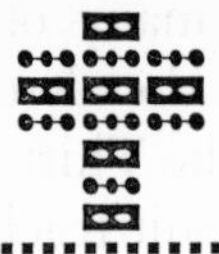

CHAPTER 2

# ŽIŽKA'S LIFE BEFORE THE REVOLUTION

JAN ŽIŽKA Z TROCNOVA, John Žižka of Trocnov: this is the name under which the greatest of Hussite leaders was known through most of his life. "Of Trocnov" he was, not only because this was his birthplace but also because the hamlet of Trocnov, a small freehold estate, belonged to his family. It lay in the southern corner of diamond-shaped Bohemia, in a clutter of hamlets and villages spread out at or near one of the oldest roads of the country, which connected Prague and Vienna, largely using the valley of the Vltava (or Moldau) River. The nearest important town, some twelve miles to the northwest of Trocnov, is Budějovice, better known as Budweis. There the people of Trocnov would go if they had to do any important business. Budweis was one of the royal towns, having no lord but the king. It was rich and busy and it was to play a role in Žižka's life. Some fifteen miles upstream in the Vltava valley lies another fortified town of venerable age which also served as an important regional center: Krumlov (or, in German, Krummau). This place, of spectacular medieval beauty to this day, was the residence of the lords of Rosenberg, the richest and most independent of the great Bohemian barons.

Krumlov and the land to the south of it was mostly inhabited by people of German descent, and so was the land to the southeast of Trocnov. Trocnov itself and its neighboring communities were Czech. In Budweis, as in many Bohemian towns of the time, a considerable part of the burghers were Germans, and German patricians dominated and ruled the city. Thus from the village of his birth Žižka had before his eyes the phenomenon of two nationalities living together in one state. He lived at what later came to be called the "language frontier."

This frontier was, through centuries, a moving one. For a considerable time it had crept toward the plains of Central Bohemia, slowly widening the ring of German settlements along most of the country's borderlines. It was to be one of Žižka's achievements to reverse this trend. After the Hussite wars most of the territory lost in the preceding two centuries had been regained by the Czechs.

The landscape which formed the background of Žižka's early youth is not spectacular. The valley of the Vltava to the west of Trocnov is lovely, with the river winding through strongly wooded hills. But to the east of it the land is heathlike. If it has any beauty it is of a harsh and reserved kind. It is fairly high ground (approximately 1,500 feet). It also is one of the few regions where Bohemia is rather open to the outer world, where there is a breach in the natural fortress formed by its border mountains. From the high plain around Trocnov the land declines softly toward the plains of the Danube in Lower Austria.

High and heathlike, the country of Trocnov was poor land, too, poor certainly compared with the extraordinarily rich soil of the northern part of the country. It is no accident that a little to the northeast of Trocnov, in the region of Třeboň, we find many fish ponds, some of them as large as fair-sized lakes. They somehow prove the poverty of the soil, which gave richer reward covered by water than plowed.[1]

This is the scenery which Žižka had before his eyes in the years of his growth. Unfortunately very little is known about his youth and his early manhood. He had passed through the greater part of his life when the searchlight of history fell upon him. To his contemporaries those earlier years were no object of curiosity. Of the historians of his time the one who knew him best, the one also who has proved our most reliable guide, Lawrence of Březová, one of the town secretaries of Prague,[2] introduces him in his *Hussite Chronicle* simply as "regis Bohemiae familiaris,"[3] expecting that he was well enough known to everybody who read his book. Among all contemporary or near contemporary writers only one bothered to find out a little more about Žižka's past: Aeneas Sylvius, later Pope Pius II, whose *Historia Bohemica* treats the Hussite wars in great detail and devotes no less than six chapters to Žižka's role in it.[4] He tells us that the Czech war leader came from a family of the gentry, that he was born in Trocnov ("Trosnovia"), that

[1] Though some of the great fish ponds of Bohemia date back to the time of Charles IV most of the great ponds of southern Bohemia are more recent, having been built by the Rosenbergs in post-Hussite times. See *Československá vlastivěda*, I, 165, and *Masarykův Slovník*, VI, 251.

[2] *Vavřince z Březové kronika husitská*, ed. Jaroslav Goll, in *Fontes Rerum Bohemicarum*, V, Prague 1893. Quoted after this as Březová.

[3] Březová, p. 345.

[4] *Aeneæ Sylvii Historia Bohemica*, printed in many editions; the one used here published by J. G. Steck, Frankfurt 1687. Quoted hereafter as Aeneas Sylvius.

his family was financially rather badly off, that in his youth he was brought up at the Royal Court, that he soon gained experience in warfare, and that, long before the Hussite wars, he had lost one eye in a stalwart fight.[5] On this last fact Aeneas Sylvius, in two prior statements, gives us also slightly different and more precise information: the fight in which Žižka lost his eye took place during his boyhood when he was playing with other boys of his age.[6]

Meager though this information seems, it was a beginning in the long process which, mainly through documentary research in the nineteenth and twentieth centuries, has thrown some light on the earlier life of Žižka. And this later evidence has confirmed all of Sylvius' statements, with the exception of one which is still subject to doubt: the claim that the Hussite leader was brought up at the Royal Court of Prague. But even here only the period is in question. That Žižka became a servant of King Wenceslas IV at an early stage of his life seems fairly well established.

Yet there remains a disappointing list of things we should like to know and in all likelihood will never have any means of knowing. We do not know the names nor anything else about the lives of Žižka's parents. We do not know the exact date of his birth. We do not know anything about his childhood. In his adult life there is a long period of almost two decades, roughly from the middle of his twenties to the middle of his forties, when we lose every track of his existence with the exception of one short glimpse, even that not quite free of doubt.

And it seems that this list of blanks is final. The archives, the church books, the court and land registers of Prague, of Budweis, of Krumlov, and all other places where new facts might have turned up, have all been sifted and scanned and reexamined by Czech historians, professional and amateur, for more light on the man whom the Czechs consider as one of their greatest. The chances for additional finds have grown even less likely since 1924 when the celebrations of the quincentenary of Žižka's death brought about an immensely heightened interest in his life.

The earliest documents in which Žižka appears give us only very modest clues. The first one, dated April 3, 1378, presents his signature as witness in the marriage contract of a young squire from the neighbor-

[5] Aeneas Sylvius, chapter 38, pp. 78, 79.

[6] In a letter to Cardinal Carjaval, see Josef Pekař, *Žižka a jeho doba* (Žižka and his time), Prague 1927-1933, II, 120, 249. Quoted hereafter as Pekař.

hood.[7] A second document, of July 10 in the same year, shows him, together with two friends of similar station, confirming a small debt, to the value of a few hundred dollars, borrowed from two Jewish women at Budweis. The conditions were stiff not only in stipulating the high rates of interest usual in those times but in invoking, in the case of failure to repay in time, very hard reprisals.[8] The document also says that the debt may be collected with the help of "the Lord," doubtlessly meaning Lord Peter of Rosenberg, first of the magnates of Bohemia, whose main residence was the great castle of Krumlov. The reference to him may indicate that the debtors were, at the time, in that baron's service. This becomes even more likely when we see Žižka's name once more, less than three weeks later, as witness in the sale of a small estate whose owner lived at Krumlov and who appears to have been one of the Lord's servants or officials.[9]

So far we can only conclude that in 1378 Žižka was a young man, already able to be a witness in a business transaction of this minor kind, with a number of more or less close friends among the squires of his district, and probably in the service of the Lord of Rosenberg. We can also conclude that his pay was poor enough to make him go into debt. That he was able to get a loan at all was, however, due to the fact that he was a squire in his own right; in other words that he still owned some land, free of bonds, inherited from his father. Thus we have reason to believe that Žižka's father died before his son reached manhood.

The land Žižka owned consisted of two parts: one at Trocnov, another one at the village of Čerejov, just a couple of miles to the south. On the history of this property we are, from documentary entries, rather well informed.[10] The estate of Trocnov consisted of two parts or "hides," of about equal size. The whole estate appears, from later entries in the ground register, to have comprised about 150 acres of which 33 were woods, the rest arable land. In 1378 Žižka held only half of this small estate, one "hide" of it, and by 1380 he had sold it to another squire, one William Pucek. A year later we learn from the documents of a law suit involving the death of one Nicholas (Mikeš) of Trocnov. The inheritance, that is the remaining half of the estate, was claimed by one John (Ješek) of Trocnov who is almost certainly identi-

[7] A. Sedláček, "Doklady k otázce o Žižkově staři" (Documents relating to the question of Žižka's age), *Český časopis historický*, Prague 1913, p. 457, quoted hereafter as *Č.Č.H.*

[8] Pekař, II, 200, 201.

[9] Sedláček, *op.cit.*, p. 462, and F. M. Bartoš, *Čechy v době Husově*, Prague 1947, p. 227.

[10] The documentary material has been most carefully assembled and treated by Sedláček, *op.cit.*, pp. 446-480. See also Pekař, II, 5-8, 198-200, and Bartoš, *loc.cit.*, with bibliography in footnote.

cal with our Žižka. Objections were raised, however, by one Peter of Trocnov who maintained that he had been co-owner of the land and was entitled to its possession. Peter won, and thus all the land remaining to Žižka after 1380 was the hide at Čerejov, smaller than the grounds at Trocnov, but with somewhat better land. Even with this, however, Žižka parted soon after. In 1384 he sold the last of his possessions to two brothers from the neighboring village of Jedovary. The entries on this transaction give us another important piece of information: by this time Žižka was married, to a woman whose first name was Catherine. What family, what place she came from is unknown. She seems to have played a small role in his life and was dead before the eyes of his contemporaries were focused upon him. But she bore him one child: a daughter. It is not at all unlikely that Catherine died, as did so many women of her time, in her first childbed.

Whether Žižka, at that time, still lived near Trocnov seems doubtful. An entry, dating from the sixteenth century, by a Rosenberg archivist[11] says that already after the sale of his Trocnov estate to Pucek, probably in 1380, Žižka went away to serve Wenceslas IV, who had succeeded his father, Charles IV, two years earlier as King of Bohemia and "King of the Romans." It seems quite possible that Žižka, then, had no further interest in maintaining a property in the south which gave him only a very small income, especially if he had had to incur some initial expense for his court service, for which he could pay with the proceeds from the land sale.

How did the little country squire from the south get into the King's service? Perhaps a family connection helped. A cousin of his seems to have been one of the King's food purveyors.[12] But it is just as possible that the connection was older: that Žižka, as Aeneas Sylvius says, had spent part of his childhood at court. This would imply that his father had already been in the royal service. Perhaps Žižka returned to the place of his birth only as a young man in his late teens when, after his father's death, the Trocnov and Čerejov estates became his property. That he had left this region by 1385 can hardly be doubted. There is no certain trace of him there for the next twenty years.

But before we try to follow him into the years of his manhood one question remains: the year of his birth. The dates of his first appearance give us a clue. He could, in 1378, hardly have been younger than eighteen. Having lost his father before and being in rightful possession by

[11] V. Březan, "Rosenberské kroniky kratky výtah," *Časopis musea českého*, 1828.
[12] Pekař, IV, 202.

inheritance of a free estate, he could, even at that age, have been allowed to serve as a witness. And if, in 1380, he was twenty he could, according the custom of his time, dispose of his property without interference from another side. It seems very unlikely that he could have been any younger. But of course he could have been much older. We still have to find a basis for the other margin.

Let us first look at those of Žižka's close relatives of whom we have any knowledge. He seems to have had two brothers. One of them, so we hear, met an early and violent death. As member of a band of mercenaries disturbing the peace of the land, he was beheaded at Budweis probably in one of the early years of the fifteenth century. Before this, however, he had procured an altar for the monastery church of Borovany near Trocnov, and it is a later entry into the register of the Borovany monastery which tells us of his fate. Another brother was Jaroslav or Jaroš of Trocnov.[13] He was mentioned occasionally by contemporary sources, became one of the officers in Žižka's Taborite army, followed him faithfully till his end, was one of the Taborite field commanders as late as 1427 and, according to a later but quite credible source,[14] was killed at the siege of the castle of Bechyně in the fall of 1428. By that time he must have been an elderly man even if he was considerably younger than his brother. The older we expect Žižka to be, the stranger appears the military activity of his brother half a century after Žižka's first appearance.

There are two more of Žižka's kinfolk of whom we have precise knowledge: a sister Agnes (Anežka) of Trocnov, and an aunt, Anna. The latter was given a house by the city council of the New Town of Prague in 1429, when she must have been a very old woman, in express recognition of her close relationship to the famous general.[15] After her death the house fell to Žižka's sister Agnes who possessed it until November 1434 when, partly for political reasons, the house was taken away from her. We have, then, certain knowledge that Žižka's sister was still alive by the end of 1434.

[13] See Mareš, *Bratr Žižkův Jaroslav z Trocnova,* in *Časopis musea českého,* 1899, p. 75. It seems strange that the aforementioned entry in the register of the monastery of Borovany also call the other brother who was beheaded at Budweis Jaroslav. It was an obvious error, probably resulting from the fact that the name of Jaroslav as that of Žižka's brother was by that time (it was after 1472) vaguely familiar to many people in that region. It cannot, of course, be quite excluded that the whole entry is based on a wrong identification, perhaps by confusing Jaroslav with a member of the Trocnov family who was not Žižka's brother at all.

[14] Zacharias Theobald in his *Hussiten-Krieg* (Nürnberg 1620), chapter 16. Theobald had some sources of his own which have since been lost.

[15] Tomek, *Jan Žižka,* Prague 1879, pp. 209, 210.

Žižka was probably the eldest of those four since he was the one to inherit Trocnov and the land at Čerejov from his father. Even so, unless we surmise that all the members of his family (with the exception of one brother) and also his aunt reached an exceptionally great age, we have reason to think that in the year of his first appearance, in 1378, he can hardly have been older than eighteen or twenty. Thus the year of his birth must be put at somewhere toward the end of the sixth decade of the fourteenth century, 1358 to 1360. He then was nearly sixty when, in 1419, he began his leading role at the outbreak of the Hussite revolution.

Some Czech historians have suggested that the Žižka whom we find in 1378 was not the Hussite leader at all but his father.[16] They put Žižka's birth somewhere between 1375 and 1378 which would make him a man in his forties at the time of the outbreak of the revolution, and still under fifty at his death. Tempting though this hypothesis may seem,[17] many facts are against it. There is first of all Aeneas Sylvius, who says twice that in 1424 Žižka was an old man.[18] The reader will also recall the statement in *The very pretty chronicle* that Žižka used to call the Polish-Lithuanian Prince Korybut, then regent of Bohemia and a man in his thirties, "my son" whereas the prince called him "my father."[19] It seems most unlikely that even a powerful military leader could have addressed a prince of royal blood, a man whom he had just recognized as supreme ruler of the land, in this condescending way if the latter had not been considerably younger. The most telling argument against the theory of a much younger Žižka, however, is the fact that the documents of 1378 speak not merely of John of Trocnov, but of Žižka. His brother was called Jaroslav of Trocnov, his sister Agnes of Trocnov. The name "Žižka" was his alone. Its origin is not quite beyond dispute. The word had later the meaning "one-eyed."

[16] Especially Tomek and F. M. Bartoš. See e.g. Tomek, *Žižka*, pp. 2, 3, and Bartoš, "Sporné otázky Žižkova života" (Disputed questions in Žižka's life) in *Žižkova doba*, Prague 1924, IX, 13-18. See on the other hand J. Šusta, *K otázce stáří Žižkova*, in *Úvahy a drobné spisy*, Prague 1934.

[17] In 1910 part of the skull of a man deemed to be slightly below 50 at the time of death, with one damaged but long cicatrized eye socket, was found near the place in the parish church of Čáslav where Žižka's body was supposed to have rested until the grave was destroyed in 1631. This find seemed to lend some support to Tomek's theory, but the circumstances of the discovery and the diagnosis of the skull's age and lesion were such that the majority of Czech historians received it with the utmost caution and distrust. (See Pekař, II, 19, and Bartoš, *Sporné otázky*, pp. 19, 20.)

[18] Chapters 44 and 46.

[19] See above, toward the end of *The very pretty chronicle*. Also Stáří letopisové čeští (Old Czech Annalists), *Scriptores Rerum Bohemicarum*, III, 52. Quoted hereafter as "Old Annalists."

Some people suggested that it might have acquired this meaning only in memory of Žižka who, as everybody knew, had been one-eyed. Today it is almost generally accepted that the word actually had the meaning "one-eyed" even before Žižka's time. It was certainly something of a nickname, a very usual thing in Bohemia then as well as later.[20] Thus it could hardly have been carried over from father to son unless we accept the rather absurd notion that Žižka's father, too, had been one-eyed.[21]

We left Žižka when, probably soon after 1380, he sought service at the Court of King Wenceslas IV. It is there indeed that, after a long pause, we find the next significant trace of him.[22]

In 1392 an entry in the royal accounts shows an order to pay a year's salary to "Siska, venator domini regis" at the little town of Zahořany, some forty miles south of Prague.[23] This place was very near the royal castle of Orlík, and it is there that Žižka must, at that time, have occupied the post of the King's hunter, if we accept the name Siska (one of the various spellings occurring in Latin texts) as sufficient identification. The job of a hunter was certainly quite congenial to Žižka. It assured him of an outdoor life, a life on horseback, and gave him the certainty of the congenial occupation in the woods which, at the time, fairly teemed with bear, wolf, wild boar, and red deer. But this occupation gave him the more important opportunity of frequently meeting the King. With Wenceslas IV hunting was even more of a passion than with most other medieval kings: he indulged in it for weeks on end, often to the detriment of his obligations as a ruler. Since one of the King's best qualities was his complete affability and friendliness with people of every station, it is not hard to imagine that for all the difference in rank something like familiarity and friendship arose between the two men, who were probably of almost equal age. This relationship —and here we are again on very firm ground—was to become one of

[20] We shall come across several examples in the course of our story, but perhaps the most striking is the name of Hus himself which is derived from "husa" (goose), though in connection with the name of the place where he came from: Husinec.

[21] K. Titz, in a monograph *O původu jména Žižka* (On the origin of the name Žižka), Brno 1924, tries to prove that the name was actually derived from Sigismund (in Czech: Zikmund). But in a more recent article by V. Mrtl (*Naše Řeč*, XI, 128) this theory has been refuted.

[22] For the years 1388 and 1402 Sedláček has found mention of a citizen of Budweis by the name of John Žižka who owned a house in that town. It seems uncertain whether this was our Žižka. (*Č.Č.H.*, 1913, p. 452, and Pekař's remarks, *Žižka*, II, 203.)

[23] *Archiv český*, XXXI, 132.

the determining factors of Žižka's later life. The time was to come when he needed and received the King's help and protection.

To explain how this need arose we shall borrow, as it were, from our next chapter and devote some space to the general political and social background of the time. Under Charles IV Bohemia had achieved a political consolidation and internal stability rare for any European country throughout the Middle Ages. Even though the King-Emperor's great law reform, contained in the code known as Maiestas Carolina, was not accepted in its entirety by the Estates because it gave too much centralized power to the crown, many of its important features had, one after the other, been put through to the extent that law enforcement was strict, private feuds were markedly reduced, and internal as well as external trade could consequently develop to an astonishing degree. This happy state did not long survive the man who had mainly been responsible for it. Rather soon after young Wenceslas had succeeded his father in 1378, at the age of seventeen, conditions began to deteriorate. True it took the unruly nobility of Bohemia some years to realize how far they could go in resisting the new King and asserting their rights of independent action with and against each other. But in 1395 a league of the great lords, under the leadership of Henry of Rosenberg, went to the length of keeping the King in captivity for several months. Wenceslas' position became even shakier by the fact that two other members of the house of Luxemburg—his younger brother Sigismund, King of Hungary, and his cousin Jost, Margrave of Moravia and later Brandenburg[24]—supported the revolt of the magnates. Two other Luxemburg princes took Wenceslas' side. One was Wenceslas' and Sigismund's youngest brother John, Duke of Görlitz,[25] who was most instrumental in securing the King's release from captivity in 1395, but who died the year after at the age of twenty-six. The other was Jost's brother Prokop, who had followed Jost as Margrave of Moravia and who stepped in as an active, ingenious, and rather unscrupulous supporter of Wenceslas, especially when the struggle between the two royal brothers flamed up again in 1399.[26]

[24] Brandenburg as well as Lusatia and Silesia were at the time (together with Bohemia and Moravia) dependencies of the Bohemian crown. Jost, who had been Margrave of Moravia before being enfeoffed with Brandenburg in 1397, is more generally known as "Jost of Moravia." On his role in this struggle see Bartoš, *Čechy v době Husově*, Prague 1947, pp. 120-139.

[25] The duchy of Görlitz (Zhořelec) formed part of Lusatia. On John see Bartoš, *op.cit.*, pp. 123ff.

[26] Prokop was, for a while, regent of Bohemia. See Bartoš, *ibid.*, pp. 159ff.

Even before that time the fraternal strife had been reflected in the forming of parties among the nobility, somewhat comparable to what happened sixty years later in England's War of the Roses. Against the group of magnates led by Rosenberg and supported by Sigismund stood other nobles who, either genuinely concerned about the growing disorder or expecting a personal reward for proved loyalty, sided with King Wenceslas and Margrave Prokop. The nobles, on both sides, began what soon developed into small-scale war—organized feuds in which, besides their personal retainers, they employed little bands of mercenary soldiers, led mostly by members of the lower nobility, knights, and squires. Many of these were only too glad to escape the drabness and comparative poverty of their peaceful existence by taking to a more dangerous but also more rewarding life of guerilla warfare. Thus the strife that began to rend Bohemia and Moravia, and increased rather than decreased during the early years of the fifteenth century, was actually fought out on three levels: the personal and political struggle between the two kings and the two margraves of the House of Luxemburg; the feuds of the barons, who supported one or the other side; and finally the guerilla warfare of the mercenary bands employed by the barons.

These bands, once formed, became a real plague to the country. The borderline between legitimate warfare, properly begun with a letter of challenge to the prospective adversary, and pure brigandage became more and more fluid. In one case as in the other, war was waged first and foremost against the material possessions of the enemy.

That the men who lived and fought in these bands were, most of the time, in the service of some of the lords was, of course, quite generally known. Their leaders were therefore not subject to any general moral or social disapproval. Yet those who were the principal sufferers, and especially the Lord of Rosenberg and his officials and retainers, loathed the guerilla bands who did much damage to his tremendous holdings all over southern Bohemia. If the Rosenberg bailiffs got hold of one of their members they would put him to torture so as to gain as much information as possible on the personnel and the whereabouts of the band. This done, the prisoner would, as a rule, be subjected to a summary court procedure and, having confessed under torture, be put to death.

The intelligence collected by the courts of the Rosenberg administration was carefully preserved in records which became known as "the

Court Books of the Lords of Rosenberg,"[27] and it is from these that we have a rather detailed knowledge of the guerilla fights, and of the people involved in them, starting with 1389 and covering, with some interruptions, the next twenty years. They are supplemented by court records kept by the town of Jihlava, an important mining town in western Moravia.[28] In both books we find fairly frequent mention of Žižka, and it is through them that we know that he returned to the region of his origin—southern Bohemia—in 1405 or 1406.

When or why exactly he left the King's service to join in the guerilla fights is anybody's guess. The particular band which he joined was one commissioned, at least at the beginning, by noblemen who belonged to the King's party, and one of their main targets was and remained the domains of Henry of Rosenberg. Whether Žižka turned to his activity on the King's wish, or in order to please the King, is not clear. As far as the conflict between the King and the Lord of Rosenberg was concerned, Žižka very probably was for the King, who was liked by his lower-born subjects and employees. A certain degree of general resentment of the lower nobility against the magnates may also have played a role.[29] Yet this can hardly have been the dominant motive, as Žižka had close friends among some of the great lords all through his later years. Indeed it is very likely that even during his years as royal hunter he met some of the very people who, soon after, appear in the court records of the Rosenberg administration as the backers of the brigand bands.

Among these people we find members of some of the greatest baronial houses of the country.[30] The troop to which Žižka belonged was led by another squire, called Matěj Vůdce (Matthew the Leader), but it was directly backed by the Lords of Lichtenburg. One of their relatives, Hynek Krušina, was to play a major role in the Hussite wars. More important for Žižka's future, however, was his connection with another family, the Kunštats, a great and rich clan, owning towns and

[27] "Popravčí knihy pánů z Rosenberka," ed. F. Mareš in *Abhandlungen der kgl. böhmischen Gesellschaft der Wissenschaft*, Prague 1878.

[28] Ed. Millauer, in *Abhandlungen der kgl. böhmischen Gesellschaft der Wissenschaft*, Prague 1824.

[29] Some Czech historians (Toman, Prokeš) put forward the version that the feud arose because the great lord Rosenberg had robbed the poor squire's (Žižka's) land. There is little basis for this assumption. For a somewhat more substantial conjecture, see Bartoš, *op.cit.*, p. 228, n. 2.

[30] For a treatment of these feuds and raids, and of the men known to have participated in them, see Pekař, II, 21-58, as well as Bartoš, *op.cit.*, *passim* in chapter IV.

castles both in Bohemia and Moravia. One of them, Boček, owned among other domains the great castle of Poděbrady on the Elbe, from which his three sons later adopted their name. They became leaders in the Hussite wars, and two of them, Victorin and Hynek, became close friends of Žižka. Victorin especially remained one of Žižka's most faithful followers to the end, and Žižka is said to have been godfather to his son George of Poděbrady, later to be King of Bohemia.

But in the years from 1406 to 1409 the idea that any of those great nobles would ever feel compelled to follow, and serve under, a poor squire like Žižka would have seemed absurd. Žižka was not even the leader of that troop which was in the pay of those men, and if they showed any special interest in him at all it can only have been because they saw in him a useful subaltern officer. This thought, indeed, seems to have occurred originally to still another member of the Czech aristocracy: a Moravian nobleman by the name of John Sokol of Lamberg. Sokol had in the years even before the turn of the century become renowned as an unusually gifted and brilliant soldier. He was also a man of culture, used to moving around in the court circles of more than one country. When, in the last years of the fourteenth century, open fighting broke out between the Luxemburg princes, the main actors in this drama openly vied for the favor of Sokol. He, too, was by no means above cooperating with bands like that of "Matthew the Leader." It seems likely that Sokol had met Žižka early, probably during the latter's service as royal hunter at one of the King's great hunting parties. But it is beyond doubt that the two men remained in touch through the years in which Žižka lived and fought with Matthew's band.

In those years after 1405 or 1406 the original line-up—the King and Prokop against Sigismund and Jost—had actually lost its validity. In 1405 Prokop had died, Wenceslas had entered into a working agreement with his cousin Jost and also with Henry of Rosenberg, which resulted in the dissolution of the old League of the Lords. Sigismund, on the other hand, was kept too busy by his Hungarian affairs to interfere effectively in Bohemia. Sokol, no longer paid as a condottiere by Prokop, entered the service of Jost and, in 1407, with Jost's agreement, was taken on by Duke Leopold of Austria in the personal war which this Habsburg Prince fought against his own brother, Duke Albert. The guerilla struggle in southern Bohemia thereby became connected, in a rather muddled way, with the internal struggle in Austria. Thus it is that not only Sokol's but also Žižka's activities at this time extended to both regions: southern Bohemia and the northern fringes of lower Austria. It was still the Rosenberg domains together with some of the land subject to Albert of Austria that presented the main object of attack, but occasionally royal towns, especially Budweis (which had always had intimate economic ties with the Rosenberg dominion) were also among the sufferers. The combined efforts of the Rosenberg administration and the cities allied with it eventually proved a serious danger for the guerillas, whose troops found it increasingly difficult to keep out of the nets laid to trap them. The head of Žižka's own band, Matthew the Leader, was taken prisoner in 1409, was subjected to the torture at Budweis, and was doubtless put to death afterwards. We have already mentioned the report which indicates that a like fate overtook one of Žižka's brothers. An inglorious death of this sort might well have cut short Žižka's career, too, had he not found help from the highest place when he needed it most. Like a real *deus ex machina* in a Renaissance play, King Wenceslas himself interfered on Žižka's behalf and thereby insured his return into the society of honorable gentlemen.

This help was given in two letters, dated April 25 and July 27, 1409, in which Wenceslas directed his town of Budweis to make peace with Žižka.[31] The first is couched in rather general terms, but the second tells the people of Budweis that "we have received in grace our faithful, dear Jan Žižka of Trucnov [*sic*] forgiving him all single excesses committed against the King and the Crown of the Bohemian Kingdom, and have handed him a special letter confirming this." The message continues with instructions to the city council to give Žižka an open letter confirming the royal amnesty.

Letters of amnesty of this type were not unusual. The King in his rather weak position had to use such means to win back to his side or to rehabilitate people whom, for one reason or another, he considered as potential supporters of some consequence. Also the formula "our faithful, dear . . ." is normal in reference to any of the King's free subjects.[32] Yet the whole action seems incongruous in its application to a little squire turned soldier or brigand or something in between. It would sound quite impossible if we could not be sure that the man in question was well known to the King and liked by him. This, of course,

[31] Printed in Tomek's study: *O rodu a počátcích Jana Žižky* (On the family and early years of John Žižka) in *Časopis musea českého*, 1876, footnotes on pp. 199 and 200.

[32] More examples of such royal letters of amnesty are listed by Pekař, II, 40, 41, who also thinks that the King must have written a similar letter to Žižka's other important adversary, the Lord of Rosenberg.

does not exclude the possibility that some powerful influence had drawn Wenceslas' attention to the plight of his former hunter. If there was such it was most likely exerted by Sokol of Lamberg.[33] For it is in Sokol's military attendance that we find Žižka, only a few months after the letter.

The enterprise for which Žižka was hired, an expedition to help the King of Poland against the Teutonic Knights, was of great importance; Sokol had reason to make his troop as strong and efficient as possible. So it seems that apart from all personal regard, he must have thought highly of Žižka as a soldier. This judgment he can hardly have based on anything but the impressions he got from his cooperation, in the years before, with Matthew's little band. Indeed there can be no doubt that in those guerilla fights Žižka had learned much and had had good opportunities to show his mettle. Here for the first time he had, if only on a small scale, grown to be a leader of men. In these little wars he had learned to make the best possible use of the terrain in attack and defense—and this was to be one of the abilities for which he was most admired after he became the leader of armies. Those led by him were little men—peasants who had lost their homesteads in similar raids, some members of the lower gentry—people, in general, who had never had much and had little to lose. They were the same people for whom, in later life, he proved to have an extraordinary appeal, people who would flock to his colors from all parts of the Kingdom, listen to his stern, puritan talks, and follow him through all adversities of war.

There had been several wars in which the Prussian Order had fought against Poland; others, even more frequent, in which it had fought against the country which recently, through personal union, had become a huge and essentially autonomous dependency of Poland: Lithuania. Fighting against the Lithuanians, the last remaining heathen nation in Europe, had long been the main *raison d'être* for the Order. In all those fights the Prussian Knights, acting under the order of the Pope, had found the willing and most effective support of the Kings of Bohemia, whereas the relationship between Bohemia and Poland had mostly been (though with some important interruptions) one of friction and competition. Wenceslas IV had been the first Bohemian ruler whose foreign policy had been one of fairly constant friendship with Poland. In 1386, Lithuania had been joined in personal union with

[33] Pekař thinks of Boček of Kunštat, but Sokol's word had at least as much weight with the King, and in addition he had a direct interest in Žižka's rehabilitation.

Poland, and her Grand Duke Jagiello, on becoming King of Poland, accepted Christianity with his whole nation. Thus the old purpose of the Order, fighting against the heathens, had lost its validity, and Wenceslas did not see any need for supporting the Knights against their former enemies.

Though the King's friendship for Poland had lately become rather cool, the general feeling in Bohemia and Moravia was, in the war of 1409-1411, all in favor of Poland. For the first time the sense of attachment between the two nations, whose languages were so much alike, had some real influence upon their historical development. Both felt menaced by the same foe: the Germans. This feeling is clearly expressed in a letter in which John Hus, then rector of Prague University, congratulated King Władysław on the great victory which Slav arms achieved over the Prussian Order at the battle of Grünwald-Tannenberg in 1410.[34] But it also emerges from the military participation of the Czechs. The Prussian Knights, too, had made strong efforts to gain military support by hiring Czech military leaders and soldiers, who at the time were considered to be superior to most others anywhere in central and eastern Europe. But the number of King Wenceslas' subjects, even mercenaries, who were ready to go to the Order's help was modest, and most of them were people of German language and descent.[35]

On the Polish side, on the other hand, the participation of Bohemians and Moravians was considerable.[36] Of the fifty banners in which the Polish army was formed at the battle of Grünwald on July 15, 1410, two consisted entirely of Czechs, three at least in part.[37] Poland's chronicler Dlugosz tells us that Sokol of Lamberg was so highly regarded by King Władysław that he offered the Czech nobleman the supreme command of his whole large army. Sokol, of course, politely refused.[38] In the course of the battle he stayed with the King, but some of the Czech warriors whom he had enlisted distinguished themselves in the fight, especially those of the fourth banner which consisted entirely of men from Bohemia and Moravia. Among them was a young knight, Wil-

[34] See among other editions the latest: *Listy dvou Janů*, ed. Císařová-Kolářová and Daňhelka, Prague 1949, p. 39.

[35] Some more help came to the Order from Silesia and Lusatia. Details on this question gives Jaroslav Goll, *Čechy a Prusy ve středověku* (Bohemia and Prussia in the Middle Ages), Prague 1896, pp. 118 and 123. This book contains what is probably still the best account of the role played by Bohemia in the war of 1409 (pp. 115-134).

[36] Joannes Dlugosz, *Historia Polonica*, lib. XI, in "Opera omnia," ed. A. Przezdziecki, Cracow 1877ff., XII, 38ff.

[37] Goll, *op.cit.*, pp. 119, 120.

[38] See Bartoš, *Čechy v době Husově*, pp. 340, 341.

liam Kostka of Postupice, who was to show later, in the Hussite wars, that he could make good use of the experience gained in Prussia. No mention is made of Žižka in the contemporary reports on the battle, and it is therefore uncertain whether he stayed with Sokol in the King's headquarters or was among the first line fighters.

The battle of Tannenberg ended with an overwhelming victory for the Polish-Lithuanian troops. The army of the Knights was utterly routed and the way opened for the Poles to march on the Order's capital, Marienburg on the Vistula. Marienburg was able to hold out, but another strong castle, Radzyń, near the Vistula east of Chełmno, fell on September 23 after a siege by Władysław's army, and was garrisoned by a mixed Czech-Polish troop under Sokol's command. The Poles then retired from the Vistula and a new army of the Knights, who had managed a rather unexpected recovery after the defeat of Tannenberg, laid siege to the castle soon afterwards.

It is here now that we find specific records of Žižka as one of the Czech officers who under Sokol's command took part in the defense of Radzyń against the German Knights.[39] The defense was entirely successful. Radzin, the westernmost position the Poles had gained, was held till the end of the war. Sokol himself died before the end of the year, suspectedly of poison. The command of the fortress was now taken over by Polish officers, but Žižka seems to have stayed with the defenders till, early in 1411, the Peace of Thorn returned Radzyń to the Prussian Order.[40]

Sokol's death was mourned greatly, not only by his Czech friends but also by the Poles. King Władysław ordered a solemn funeral and offered to have Sokol's two young sons, Nicholas and Jaroslav, educated at his own expense at Cracow University. They had both been with their father during the war, and probably they knew Žižka well. Later both joined Žižka's party, the party of Tabor, during the Hussite wars, and Nicholas in particular became a worthy successor to his valiant father.

In Sokol's death Žižka lost more than an influential patron: if any man can be said to have been Žižka's teacher in the arts of war, it was Sokol. It was with him that he was able to discuss the various moves of

[39] Dlugosz, *op.cit.*, XIII, 92. The second mention in the same book (p. 237) reading: "Johannes Zischka, qui superiori tempore apud Poloniae Regem in Prussia bellis assiduis exercitatus fuit . . ." seems to prove that Žižka's experience in the war went far beyond the defense of Radzin. Dlugosz was well informed about this war in which his father took an active part.

[40] For a good modern treatment in English of the war and its consequences see the *Cambridge History of Poland*, I.

the great battle in which they had been engaged, and the way in which Sokol managed to defeat the onslaught of the Knights against Radzyń may have set Žižka thinking about the ineffectiveness of the knightly cavalry in encounters with a strongly entrenched enemy. The best teacher, however, was the reality of the war itself, when the pupil was a man of Žižka's open and realistic mind. Surely he returned from Poland with a greatly enriched outlook on the military and political realities of his time. He had now experienced the movement of large bodies of troops in full-scale war. He had seen the use of fire weapons, and though their role was still very modest it was at least larger than at any battle ever fought before. Even the train of wagons used by both sides to carry supplies and posted in the rear of the armies during the battle may have been the starting point for important changes which Žižka later wrought in the art of war.

Politically, too, the campaign in Prussia taught Žižka an important lesson. In his homeland he had seen the national antagonism that had developed internally. In the Prussian campaign, now, the conflict was a clear-cut issue of foreign policy. The German who, in Bohemia and Moravia, had been a competitor and, to some extent, an internal oppressor was now in Poland encountered as an external enemy. At the same time the ally, the brother in arms, was a Slav, spoke a language which it was easy to understand. Though it would probably be wrong to overestimate the weight of these new impressions it would be equally wrong to deny the Slav-nationalist element in Žižka's later policy. It is clearly expressed in some of his preserved letters. The experiences of the Prussian war must have helped him to shape his ideas in this direction.

The issue, though, which was destined to be the decisive motivating force in the life of the country as well as in Žižka's life, the religious issue, does not seem to have confronted him yet, at least not in any controversial sense. It is, of course, quite possible that he, as so many others, had taken offense at the sight of the overluxurious life of part of the Bohemian clergy. But so far he had had little chance to give this criticism any vigorous expression. In general he probably conformed to the laws and customs of the Roman Church as did everybody else. At any rate, the greater part of his life, so far, had been spent far away from those centers of learning and discussion, especially at and around Prague University, where the seeds were growing for the great reformatory movement of Hussitism. There is a story that in his youth Žižka had sworn vengeance to the monks because one of them had raped his sister.[41] No confirmation can be found for it in the sources. It surely is one of those later legends with which friend or foe tried to adorn or tarnish his memory. For all we know he had not started on the path of nonconformist thought and action during his first fifty years. But all this was bound to change radically when he returned, richer in experience, to his native land sometime in 1411.

Of this date, though, we cannot be absolutely sure. Some Czech mercenaries stayed in the service of Poland even after the war had drawn to its close—enough, indeed, to worry Sigismund of Hungary, who, in his dignity as King of the Romans, gave the full backing of his authority to the Prussian Order. In a letter to his brother Wenceslas he admonished him urgently to call all his subjects back from Poland and thus to prevent them from giving any further comfort to a nation supposedly allied with heathens.[42] This admonition made little impression, for already in 1414, when war broke out anew between the Order and Poland, we again find contingents of Czechs serving with the Poles (among them the aforementioned William Kostka), whereas the Order, this time, could not get any Czech help worth mentioning.

Žižka, this time, was not among the Czech auxiliaries. We have proof that he was then in Prague. In this year of 1414 an entry in the court register of the New Town of Prague lists the purchase by Žižka of a house in the street which to this day bears the name "Na Příkopě" (At the Moat), near what had once been the wall of the Old Town.[43] (In modern times it actually became the "Wall Street" of Prague where all the great banks of Czechoslovakia were located.) The house must have been substantial, considering the price which Žižka paid: fifty threescores of Bohemian groše, a sum corresponding in purchasing power to several thousand dollars. It seems likely that this money came from the pay he had received for his service in the Prussian war. In the court register he is now called "portulanus regius," but it would hardly be correct to translate this as "doorkeeper." Rather was he an officer of the Palace guard, as the office of "portulanus regius" was reserved to members of the gentry.[44] Žižka's house was not far from the modest city palace which Wenceslas preferred as his residence to the splendor of the royal castle, then called the Castle of St. Wenceslas, high up on Hradčany Hill. In 1416 Žižka sold this house and bought another

[41] Especially George Sand, in her interesting but semifictional book *Jean Zyska*, made ample use of this purely personal, psychological explanation of Žižka's later actions.

[42] Janssen, *Frankfurts Reichscorrespondenz*, I, 238.

[43] See Tomek, *Žižka*, p. 12.

[44] *ibid.*

one, still nearer the King's residence, in the northern part of the Old Town.[45] In this purchase he is no longer named as "portulanus" but as "cliens de curia domini regis." The word "cliens" covered every sort of officialdom in the service of a ruler or lord, and court positions were, of course, not yet very clearly defined as to office and function. But it makes sense that Žižka, the veteran officer, returning from the great war in Poland and applying to the King for a court position, was given a function which was, at least, semi-military.

As an officer of the palace guard or bodyguard at the King's city palace Žižka would, of course, be in regular contact again with both the King and the Queen. Lawrence of Březová, our most reliable witness, repeatedly calls him "regis Wenceslai familiaris," which would indicate a relationship of a courtier. But this contradicts in no way the assumption that he was, as a member of the bodyguard, responsible for the royal couple's safety. There is, among some doubtful stories about his relationship to the King, one report which deserves to be believed. It is contained in an old chronicle of memorabilia of the Church of the Bohemian Brethren and says that Queen Sophia, at her regular visits to the Chapel of Bethlehem, where Master Hus used to preach, was often accompanied by John Žižka.[46] This would confirm two facts which, otherwise, we could only conjecture: first, that Žižka entered the royal service soon, if not immediately after the Prussian war; for by June 1412 Hus retired, on the King's pleading, to a castle (Kozí Hrádek) far from Prague, and this ended the Queen's visits to hear his sermons; second: that Žižka himself had the opportunity to hear Hus preach, and that he met him personally.

This last fact at least is perfectly credible. We know that at that time Hus had his most faithful and most determined adherents among the King's courtiers. It was for this reason that the Church of Rome and the Council of Constance made Wenceslas responsible for the rise of the Hussite heresy. Later this same group of courtiers, with Žižka in their front, openly revolted when the King tried to suppress the movement. There is no doubt that Žižka later fought for what he believed to be Hus's tenets, though we may be much less certain whether Hus, had he lived, would have approved of Žižka's fierce ways.

It is sad that we have no way of reliving this meeting of the greatest religious reformer with the greatest soldier of the fifteenth century. There must have been a sequence of experiences in Žižka's mind the

[45] See for this and future references to Prague localities the map on page 134.

[46] Ms. in the archives of Herrnhut, discovered by Goll and quoted by Tomek, *op.cit.*, 9, 10.

depth and strength of which we cannot measure—a mental awakening worthy of the pen of a great poet or novelist. The historian must remain silent about what was perhaps the personally decisive event in Žižka's life. What he can and must do, though, is to supply the material without which the historical importance of this event cannot be fully gauged: the general development of the political, social, and religious forces of Bohemia that led up to this meeting and consequently to the Hussite revolution.

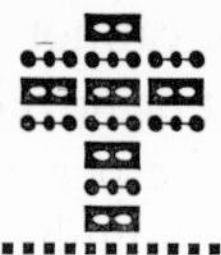

CHAPTER 3

# RISING PRESSURES

THE YEARS of Žižka's youth—the sixties and seventies of the fourteenth century—coincided with that period in which Bohemia's "Golden Age" reached its fullest flowering. It is the second half of the reign of Charles IV. A combination of favorable economic, political, and social trends had been fully used and reinforced by this great ruler, a man as shrewd and calculating in his ways and means as he was conscientiously devoted to his high tasks. The first in the long line of Bohemian kings to bear the imperial crown of the Holy Roman Empire, he did much for the vast regions under his sovereignty, and the judgment that he was the Empire's "archstepfather" has long been discarded. Yet it is true to say that his special love belonged to the country of his birth, that he was proud of being, through his mother, a descendant of the old Slavic royal house of Přemysl, and that under him the country, and especially its capital, rose to be the political and cultural center of Europe north of the Alps. None of the great cities of the Old World shows to this day the stamp of a fourteenth century ruler as impressively as Prague shows the stamp of Charles. From the great St. Vitus Cathedral on Hradčany Hill across the beautiful stone bridge which bears his name to the New Town, his building and planning can be traced, and long before his death the University, founded by him in 1348, had begun to equal in fame such older places of learning as Bologna, Paris, and Oxford. With Brandenburg added to its dependencies, the Crown of Bohemia ranked, at this time, as one of the strongest of Europe's powers. Though technically it still formed part of the Holy Roman Empire its role in the ancient super-state was practically limited to the identity of the ruler. It was not as Emperor that Charles ruled over Bohemia, rather was he the King of Bohemia who had been elected to rule the Empire as well.[1] And in comparison with the widely

[1] While Bohemia had been made a hereditary kingdom in 1156, its character as fief of the Empire had all but disappeared when the Golden Bull, granted in 1212 by Frederick II to Přemysl Otakar I, renounced the right of the Emperor to confirm the election of the King and freed the Kingdom from all financial obligations toward the Reich. Only the fact that

unsettled conditions in most of Germany, the Bohemian state presented a picture of order, prosperity, and cohesive strength.

This situation changed considerably when, at the age of only seventeen, Wenceslas IV followed his father in 1378. The inexperience, personal incompetence, and inconsistency of this ruler contributed much to the weakening of the royal power and with it to the resumption of those domestic struggles which Charles' stronger hand had been able to suppress almost completely. In the Empire the ineffectiveness of Wenceslas' rule led to his deposition by the electors in 1400, in Bohemia to the rise of the League of Lords, to the repeated imprisonment of the King, and to the unwelcome interference in the affairs of the Kingdom by other Luxemburg princes, especially Sigismund of Hungary and Jost of Brandenburg. We have discussed these struggles briefly in the preceding chapter.

It would, however, be wrong to hold Wenceslas' deficiencies as a ruler responsible for all the troubles or conflicts which began to beset Bohemia during his reign. To a considerable extent their roots go deeper into past history. They can well be described as the growing pains of a young and vigorously developing society, a society which was exposed to unusual problems and challenges and eventually reacted in equally unusual ways. A mere record of events during the rule of Wenceslas would contribute but little to an understanding of them.[2] It seems more helpful to attempt to analyze, as clearly as it is possible in the space of a short chapter, the structure of Bohemian society and the basic tendencies of its development in the last decades before the outbreak of the great storm of 1419.[3]

---

Bohemia's kings kept insisting on their role as the ranking temporal electors of the Empire (with the hope of acquiring for themselves the imperial dignity) prevented the complete separation between Bohemia and the Empire.

[2] The most recent treatment of the general history of the period from 1378 to 1415 is contained in F. M. Bartoš, *Čechy v době Husově*, Prague 1947 (Part II, vol. 6, of the great history of Bohemia, edited by Novotný and Krofta). The most detailed treatment of the government of Wenceslas IV, but with more emphasis on Germany than Bohemia, is T. Lindner's *Geschichte des deutschen Reiches unter Koenig Wenzel*, 1875-78. The period is, of course, rather fully covered in every standard history of Bohemia. A concise but excellent account is given by O. Odložilík in *Československá Vlastivěda*, Prague 1932, IV, 114-162.

[3] There is, as yet, no comprehensive social history of Bohemia in pre-Hussite times except for the rather obsolete work by J. Lippert, *Social-Geschichte Böhmens*, Prague 1896-1898. Also slightly obsolete in some of its conclusions but very valuable in regard to the basic material represented is Z. Winter's *Dějiny řemesel a obchodů v Čechách v XIV a v XV století* (History of the trades and the commerce in Bohemia in the 14th and 15th centuries), Prague 1906. The main work on the history of the Czech peasantry is still Krofta's *Dějiny selského stavu* (History of the peasant class), first published in 1919 and recently revised, Prague 1949. In the field of the economic and social development of the cities and towns much valuable spade-work has been done by Bedřich Mendl, mostly in series of articles in *Č.Č.H.: Hospo-*

We are accustomed to thinking of the whole part of late medieval Europe belonging to the Church of Rome as something like a unit, and usually describe its social structure as feudal. Regional differences, however, were considerable and highly significant. Thus the degree of stratification which society had reached in western Europe even before the fourteenth century was nowhere attained in the east, and the main reason for this lesser rigidity of the social texture can probably be found in the fact that all through the thirteenth century the eastern countries of the Roman-Christian world, especially Poland, Bohemia, and Hungary, were still in the process of lively colonizing activities. There were still empty spaces to be filled, forests to be cleared, new settlements to be founded. By far the most active (though not, as it is sometimes assumed, the only) national group engaged in these activities were, of course, the Germans. In Bohemia especially German colonization, favored both by the royal power and the Church, had proceeded unchecked during the rule of the late Přemyslide kings. Early in the fourteenth century, however, this process came to a halt, having lost its original drive as well as the possibilities for new settlement. The end of the colonizing period led to stronger competition and friction, not only between the two nationalities but also between the main strata of society regardless of ethnological origin.

There were other elements in this process making for more differentiation as well as for increasing tendencies toward stratification. Population as a whole was growing again, soon after the years of the Black Death (1348-1350) had temporarily—and rather mildly in the case of Bohemia and Moravia—checked this development. And the balance of social forces existing in the twelfth and thirteenth centuries had been shaken, with gains for some and losses for other groups, by the impact of a budding merchant capitalism and a money economy which, though still primitive in its methods, at least in comparison to Italy, had already spread through the whole of society.

All these changes, however, and the dynamic forces responsible for them, have to be seen against the background of an overwhelmingly

---

*dářské a socialní poměry v městech Pražských v letech 1378-1434* (The economic and social conditions in the towns of Prague), vols. 1915-1916; *Sociální krise a zápasy ve městech čtrnáctého věku* (The social crisis and the internal struggles in the cities of the fourteenth century), vols. 1924-27; and *Počátky našich cechů* (The beginnings of our guilds), vol. 1927; also a special study, *Z hospodářských dějin středověké Prahy* (From the economic history of medieval Prague), Prague 1925. A short social history of the Czech people, generally using most of the recent research, is M. Volf, *Sociálni a politické dějiny československé v hlavních obrysech*, Prague 1948. For special documentation see later notes.

agricultural society. The distribution of the soil was and remained the predominant factor in determining the relative strength of each social group. And here again we are faced by a significant difference between the situation in Bohemia and that in most other European countries.

The Church was a very great landowner everywhere in Europe, but it seems unlikely that in any other country the proportion of Church-held land was quite as huge as in Bohemia. The clerical estate, the Archbishop of Prague and the bishops, the chapters and especially the monasteries, owned together no less than one half of all the land.[4] (In other countries this proportion was probably nearer one third.) Against this tremendous collective wealth we find, as the greatest single owner, the King with about one sixth of the total soil, a good deal of it forest land. All other social groups—high nobility, lower nobility, towns, and free peasants—had to share the remaining third.

Among these last-named groups the greatest landowners were still the lords, not only individually but also collectively. Yet compared with earlier times they had lost much, while the Church had gained. Split inheritance, combined with the need for cash caused by an ever-increasing personal standard of living, had been among the main causes for this development. Consequently, the number of vast baronial holdings, such as had still been frequent in the twelfth and early thirteenth century, had shrunk considerably. Hardly more than half a dozen of the great clans were still rulers of extended domains, each holding large numbers of villages, several castles, and a few dependent towns. Most or all of these we shall encounter in the course of the revolutionary years: The Rosenbergs and the Wartenbergs, the Lords of Dubá, Kolovrat and Sternberg, the Kunštats and the Lichtenburgs. (The predominantly German names, taken from their main castles, are only the reflection of the fashion of an earlier time to give German names to those castles. The men themselves were very conscious of belonging to the Czech nation, the "lingua bohemica.") Apart from those leading families few lords owned more than one or two castles and ten villages, and one castle with five to eight villages can be considered the average baronial holding of the late fourteenth century.[5]

The reduction in the property status of the high nobility strengthened the tendency of that group toward exclusion and rigid stratification. In earlier times the borderline between higher and lower nobility had been distinct but not impassable. In the late fourteenth and early fifteenth

[4] J. V. Šimák, *Hus a doba před ním* (Hus and the time before him), Prague 1915, p. 29.
[5] *ibid.*, p. 28.

century, on the other hand, few if any members of the lower nobility succeeded in rising to the higher class even if—for instance, due to the favor of the King—they had been able to amass a considerable landed property or to occupy an office of high standing. Nor did the barons permit any political influence to be wielded by the gentry as a class. Though they were represented in the great diets of the Kingdom their role there was strictly secondary, as was generally that of the towns as well. How much any decision of the diet was considered as a decision by the barons emerges very clearly from reports written during the Hussite wars. Even though in reality the two other estates were then no longer politically weak, some chroniclers still talked of "the barons" when they wanted to refer to the diet as a whole.[6]

If, inside the baronial caste, a degree of differentiation had developed between the few very rich and powerful houses and the main body of the class, the same was true to a much stronger degree of the lower nobility. Indeed, we can almost say that this term (the gentlemen or vladyky) includes not one but two social classes or groups: the knights (rytíři), and the squires (zemané). Generally the status of knight, as social rank, implied the ownership of a "castle," which however might be a fairly modest building. (The Czech language contains a special word "tvrz," for the small, not necessarily stone-built castle.) In addition knightly families would hold one or two villages, some very well-to-do ones even a slightly larger number.[7] The ordinary squire would, on the other hand, just own one village or hamlet and not infrequently would even have to be content with sharing this small property with another member of his class. This increasing differentiation was, to some extent, due to the same reasons which had led to the relative impoverishment of part of the high nobility: split inheritance and needs for cash money which could not be fully satisfied by the sale of agricultural produce.

The poor squire would thus hardly differ in his economic position from any well-to-do freeholder. But whereas there is no clear or rigid dividing line between the knights and the squires, the line between the poorest squire and the richest peasant of "ignoble" origin is drawn with the greatest strictness. The squire has his coat of arms which also appears on his seal—an important instrument of personal identification at a time when even noblemen could not all be counted upon to know how to write. No social contact, especially no intermarriage, was pos-

[6] See Březová, pp. 485ff.
[7] Šimák, *loc.cit.*

sible between noblemen and those below them. The line was thus much stricter than that between the lords and the gentry, where it was still possible though unusual for a baron to marry the daughter of a squire without loss of rank.[8]

It was, as we have seen, from the rank of the squires that Žižka emerged. And in his case we can well observe the fate of the economically weakest members of this estate, men who had lost or were about to lose their old basis of existence and station, their land, under the pressure of the economic changes of the time. He was only one of many who had to look for a different living, lawful if possible, in the service of one of the lords or perhaps of the king or, if there was an opportunity, of a foreign ruler who needed experienced soldiers; unlawful, that is as brigands, if no other employment seemed available. This widespread impoverishment was bound to create dissatisfaction and resentment among the lower gentry, and in the case of Žižka—where we find a very poor squire living in the shadow of the richest baron of the country—it seemed tempting to see something like a class struggle in the historically documented early fight between the former squire of Trocnov and the Lord of Rosenberg. We have earlier expressed our doubts concerning such an interpretation, and even if an element of such feelings should have been present in Žižka's actions in the early years of the fifteenth century it would still have been more a personal than a class reaction. In general the economic troubles of the gentry were different in degree rather than in substance from those of the higher nobility, and what antagonism there was between the two classes had a political rather than a strictly socio-economic character, though a rise in the legal and political stature of the gentry would, of course, be looked upon as a chance for safeguarding or improving its economic position. In the course of the Hussite revolution the gentry had ample opportunity to strengthen itself. It emerged from the struggle with very solid gains, both economic and political, and with its special status recognized by its representation in the diet as a separate "curia" or house. In a way, thus, the miraculous career of the squire of Trocnov can be said to have symbolized (and to some extent to have directly influenced) the fate of his class. But to understand how this was possible we shall have to watch the whole gigantic struggle itself.

[8] A case in point is the marriage of Žižka's daughter to Henry of Duba. See Chapter 25 below and the literature quoted by F. M. Bartoš, *op.cit.*, footnotes on pp. 227, 228. Pekař (II, 17, 18) makes the somewhat unconvincing attempt to prove that Žižka's son-in-law could not possibly have been a member of the high nobility.

The masses of people living in rural areas were, of course, peasants. Without the rich manpower derived from the villages of Bohemia, Žižka could never have built up his revolutionary armies which were to prove superior to the great international crusades sent against them from west and east. The peasants, streaming to the banners of Tabor in the early years of the Hussite wars, were, at this stage, a revolutionary class, even though none of their better known leaders derived from peasant origin. Should we conclude from this knowledge that Bohemia's peasants, in the period before the outbreak of the Hussite revolution, were especially badly off, that they had been oppressed or exploited beyond endurance? This somewhat primitive notion about the causes of revolutions has been discarded quite generally, and it would be just as mistaken in reference to the Bohemian Revolution of the early fifteenth century as it is in reference to the French Revolution of the late eighteenth century.

It can probably be said that at no time before, and at no time again until the early nineteenth century, Bohemia's peasants were as relatively well off as in the period preceding the Hussite wars. Slavery—a common institution in eastern Europe during the early Middle Ages—had disappeared in Bohemia in the course of the twelfth century. The Bohemian peasants of the fourteenth century were personally free and were not bound to the land as were the serfs of western Europe under the manorial system. They could move and, in the period concerned, made ample use of this right.

The proportion of freeholders, on the other hand, was very small. Quite generally duty-free ownership of the land by peasants was the exception rather than the rule. More frequent was an institution called *Lhota* in which land was given to peasants for clearing and free use on a temporary basis. After a fixed (but locally different) number of years this status could be terminated by either side or could be made permanent with the land either to be paid for by the tenant over a certain period or to be rented by him for a fixed annual rent.[9] In the second case the relationship between peasant and landlord approached the status which was prevailing in Bohemia in the fourteenth century: that of a hereditary tenant farmer with limited duties both in payment of rent and in services, and with the right to the full and free use of the soil. This advantageous position of the peasants of Bohemia had at least partly been due to the introduction, in the late twelfth and early

[9] See Krofta, *Dějiny selského stavu*, 2nd ed., p. 32. The frequency of the institution can be gauged from the large number of villages which, to this day, are named Lhota or Lhotka.

thirteenth centuries, of the "German Law," that is those legal advantages by which it had been possible to induce German settlers to come to Bohemia.[10] The need to keep the peasant on his farm against the competition of other landlords—first among them the Church[11]—made it necessary to meet the general demand of the peasants for equally good conditions, especially with the help of written contracts. The duties, under these circumstances, were not overly heavy. True the barons could try to exert pressure as, in most cases, they had the right of jurisdiction over the peasants on their estates. But Charles IV limited the punishment they could inflict, and, more important, the peasants could appeal against baronial decisions to the royal courts.[12]

All this, of course, does not mean that the peasants had no complaints. It rather meant that they were far enough advanced to voice their complaints with determination. And it is characteristic of the general mood prevalent in the late fourteenth century that those complaints found considerable support among those men who had begun to think first and foremost in terms of religious reforms. Thus one of Hus's "forerunners," Thomas of Štítný, accused some of the lords of putting heavier taxes on the peasants than they themselves had to deliver to the King,[13] and Hus himself described as atrociously unfair the fact that the compensation (apart from punishment) to be paid for the killing of a lord was as much as ninety-five threescores of groše whereas for a peasant it only amounted to five threescores.[14] There was special resistance to the "odúmrt," that is, the claim of the lord to have the land whose tenant died without leaving a direct heir in his house revert to him. (It had its parallel in the French "mortmain".) The demand for its abolition was also taken up by the religious reformers.[15] There was, thus, an early tradition of social conscience which would make the reform movement attractive to the peasants long before any thought of revolution could have entered the heads of either the reformers or the peasants. Indeed neither Hus nor his friends ever considered any radical change in the structure of society, at least not in regard to the temporal estates.

The way, however, in which the peasants could try to help themselves most effectively in cases of real hardship was to make use of their

[10] Krofta, *op.cit.*, p. 43. The "German Law" was, incidentally, by no means the prevailing legal status of the peasantry in Germany. Conditions were different in different regions and in some of them manorial serfdom was no longer unknown.

[11] *ibid.*, pp. 30, 42. [12] *ibid.*, pp. 87-88. [13] *ibid.*, p. 89.

[14] F. Hrubý, *Z hospodářských převratů českých v st. XV a XVI*, *Č.Č.H.*, 1924, p. 212.

[15] Krofta, *op.cit.*, p. 92.

freedom of movement. The way of collective departure and resettlement was hardly open any longer, but for the individual there was always the chance to go into one of the royal cities. His fate there might be doubtful, and it was not too easy for the recent immigrant from the rural areas of the country to acquire the rights and advantages of citizenship. Yet considerable numbers of peasants flocked to the cities, some driven by pressure, others lured by the expected advantages of town life.[16] There, eventually, they contributed to the growth of the "chudina," the masses of the people with little or no property, dependent on whatever wage labor was available at the time. In Prague especially this group of people was large and was to have some influence on the development of the Hussite movement, especially during the earlier years of the revolution.

The overwhelming importance of the towns in changing the social structure of European society in the late Middle Ages has long been recognized, but the main examples which come to mind when this fact is stressed are the cities of Italy, France, the Netherlands, and the Hanseatic towns of Germany. The degree to which Bohemia and Moravia had become an important town region is less well known. Here again it is the reign of Charles IV, the years from 1346 to 1378, which saw the full flowering of a development which had started long before. Toward the end of his life Bohemia (without Moravia or any of her other dependencies) counted about a hundred walled towns, thirty-five of them royal cities. Under Wenceslas IV this number increased still further, though not very considerably.[17] But more important than the increase in the number of towns was the increase of their economic and political strength.

Some of these towns were, of course, very small communities of a couple of thousand or even less, and dependent in the main, on agricultural pursuits. But in the majority of the royal towns the trades, and with them the guilds, were very fully developed in the fourteenth century, and in the greatest of them agriculture had already ceased to be of paramount importance for the main body of the citizenry, except those people living in the suburbs outside the town walls.[18] Cities like Hradec Králové, Pilsen, Žatec and many others had not only become markets and trading centers by the end of the fourteenth century but also seats of

[16] Hrubý, *loc.cit.*

[17] Z. Winter, *op.cit.*, p. 122. See also Frederick G. Heymann, "The Role of the Towns in the Bohemia of the Later Middle Ages," *Journal of World History*, II, 1955.

[18] Mendl, "Socialní krise . . . ," *Č.Č.H.*, 1926, p. 274.

a highly diversified manufacture. In a class by itself was Kutná Hora (as well as the Moravian town of Jihlava) because of its highly productive silver mines. The role which Bohemia's silver production played for the rapid economic development of the country has probably not yet been quite fully evaluated.[19] It did then, and in a lesser way, for Bohemia what the bullion of the New World did in the sixteenth century for Western Europe. It accelerated the replacing of older forms of trading and of payment for services by money transactions. It made possible the importation of goods beyond the capacity of the country to export, even though Bohemia's export was growing and included such items as linen and woolen cloth, ceramics, leather, knives, beer, wine, and various agricultural products.[20] Bohemian silver, which paid for the balance, was used all over the neighboring countries, especially in Germany.[21] The income from the silver mines made the King less dependent on the readiness of the estates to grant him additional taxation and thus, by strengthening royal power, helped in the pacification and unification of the country under Charles IV. It was on the basis of silver that Kutná Hora became the second city of the Kingdom, but once this position had been achieved it flourished in many ways, its guilds were highly diversified, building proceeded in an impressive way, and the Hussite wars confirmed the city's importance by the many actions fought for its possession.

But even Kutná Hora's prosperity paled when compared to that of Prague, Bohemia's old, immemorial capital. Castle, market, and seat of the early Bohemian dukes in the ninth century, seat of a bishop in the tenth, it was, before the end of the first millennium, a busy trading center with many churches and with some houses of stone.[22] From early times the settlement included two boroughs, the Small Town (Small Side) lying on the left bank of the Vltava under the protection of the royal castle on Hradčany Hill, and the Great Town, later Old Town, across the Vltava in the bend formed by the river. By the middle of the twelfth century the two towns were connected by a stone bridge which lasted for almost two hundred years. The succeeding structure was built early under Charles IV. Its grave and solid beauty has survived six centuries and does not show any signs of decrepitude.

The time of Charles was the great era for Prague. The city's growth was spectacular. The building of the New Town, in which the King

[19] J. Slavík, *Husitská revoluce*, Prague 1934, p. 48. See also Z. Winter, *op.cit.*, pp. 378ff.

[20] Winter, *op.cit.*, p. 364. [21] Mendl, Socialní krise, *Č.Č.H.*, 1924, p. 49.

[22] See the report by the Spanish Jew Ibrahim ibn Jakub from his visit to Prague in 973. (Frequently quoted, e.g. by O. Schürer, Prag, 4th ed., Munich 1940, p. 27.)

Emperor took a very personal part,[23] constituted one of the most impressive feats of late medieval town planning. It just about doubled the area of the city, which from now on consisted of three autonomous boroughs. Before Charles' death the New Town contained a population roughly equal to that of the two other boroughs. The capital as a whole had, by that time, approximately 40,000 inhabitants[24] which made her one of the largest cities of Europe, roughly on a par with London and the leading Flemish cities and outranked only by Paris. But the intensive side of its growth was even more amazing. Prague was now, beyond dispute, the cultural hub of central and eastern Europe. The development of learning,[25] powerfully supported by the King and the University, was equaled by a magnificent flowering of the arts, with architecture in the lead and painting not far behind.[26] And while, under Wenceslas, Prague too began to feel the beginnings of the social and political crisis, the arts continued to prosper. We have a report from a Milanese ambassador who visited the city just at the turn of the century. This man who knew the wonders of Italy's early Renaissance was deeply impressed by the magnificence of the northern capital which, so he said, approached the beauty of Rome.[27] And all this splendor reflected not only, and perhaps not even in the first place, the copious patronage of a great ruler but also the pride of the citizens who, in their own churches, city halls, and many of their private houses, exhibited their individual and collective wealth.

But the wealth was, of course, not truly collective or general. On the contrary the social and economic differentiation which characterized Bohemia's development in the fourteenth century was nowhere as distinct and even extreme as it was in the cities, more especially in the capital. Three classes are fairly clearly discernible there, and the differences in their social status are almost as great, in their economic status even greater than those between the classes in rural areas.[28] The predominant position, economic as well as social and political, was held by the old patrician families of the great merchants. Their wealth can be gauged from the fact that many of them acquired considerable

[23] See J. Šusta, *Karel IV* (*České dějiny* II, 4), pp. 58ff.

[24] During the Hussite wars the population decreased (mainly through the ejection of Germans) by about one fourth. See Mendl, *Č.Č.H.*, 1916, p. 436. Earlier estimates which compute something like 100,000 inhabitants (see e.g. Winter, *op.cit.* p. 122) are surely much exaggerated as they base their count on an average population of 25 per house.

[25] See S. Harrison Thomson, "Learning at the court of Charles IV," *Speculum*, xxv, 1950, no. 1.

[26] Schürer, *op.cit.*, pp. 72-84. [27] *ibid.*, p. 89.

[28] Mendl, *op.cit.*, *Č.Č.H.*, 1925, p. 561, and 1926, p. 258.

landed property and had little difficulty in gaining acceptance (and intermarriage) at least with the lower nobility.[29] In their hands had long been the government of the cities, and only relatively late in the fourteenth century could the urban middle class, the craftsmen and artisans, gain a foothold in the city councils. The separate government of the New Town was more accessible to them as it was this social group which constituted the majority of the full citizens of that borough. They were, of course, backed by their great professional organizations, the guilds.

The fight of the guilds for more influence in the town governments is a feature of the contemporary town history all over Europe. In Bohemia and Moravia it was conducted with considerable vigor. Charles IV still supported the patricians against the claims of the guilds, going at times so far as to order some of the latter to be dissolved.[30] But in the seventies and eighties of the fourteenth century they were gaining strength again. In 1378 we find them, in Brno, openly rebelling against the patrician rule, and in the following decades various similar moves followed. Wenceslas IV, unlike his father, tolerated this strengthening of the guilds if he did not favor it outright.[31]

This large class of craftsmen and artisans was to become the leading group during the subsequent struggle, and the German chronicler Andrew of Ratisbon was hardly wrong when he accused the guilds of Prague of having given strong support to the Hussite revolution.[32] Yet we should not think of this class, either before or during the Hussite movement, as a fully homogeneous and politically united social body. They acted in unison only as long as they shared their antagonism against the great patrician families, an antagonism, as we shall soon have to discuss, in national and religious as well as in social terms. But once their common adversary was removed their unity disintegrated. The richest, most firmly established layer of this middle class actually took the place of its former social superior and, having acquired a strong vested interest in forms similar to those of the older town aristocracy, turned conservative and anti-revolutionary. Cooperating closely with the more conservative leaders of the academic clergy and also with the high nobility, it obtained, after the first years of revolution, the upper

[29] Slavík, *op.cit.*, p. 44.

[30] Mendl, "Počátky naších cechů," *Č.Č.H.*, 1927, pp. 317ff.

[31] *ibid.*, p. 341. Wenceslas' attitude becomes especially clear in his mild reaction to the guild revolt of 1418 in Breslau, the same which two years later was bloodily revenged by Sigismund. See Chapter 7 below.

[32] *ibid.*, p. 345, and Höfler, *Geschichtschreiber der husitischen Bewegung*, I, 339.

hand in the Old Town and eventually in the whole city. The rest of the middle class—numerically weaker—was much less inhibited in its revolutionary tendencies. It was more open to influences from radical sectarianism and provided, in the early years of the Revolution, the decisive backing for the greatest and perhaps the most interesting among the radical clerics of the Hussite movement, Priest John Želivský, formerly a monk at the Premonstratensian monastery of Želiv.

It is hardly surprising that, in following the leadership of this gifted and fascinating orator and politician, the lower middle class found itself accompanied and reinforced by the third and lowest social stratum, the masses of the "proletarians" of the city, the people without any possessions and without any guild standing, especially the day laborers. In the contemporary sources they appear as "the poor people," the "chudina." Many of them had been recent immigrants from the rural areas, people who still had their roots in the country and could perhaps go back to their villages if opportunities for employment became scarce (for instance if the building activity slackened) or if the wage level fell. For others this possibility no longer existed. It is obvious that, in an increasingly revolutionary situation, these people could follow the line that seemed to promise them an approach to better living conditions under a more egalitarian society. Thus they did, at times, provide something like an increased dynamism to the revolutionary movement.[33] At no time, however, did they play an independent role or assume any leadership of their own. All the men who under the guidance of John Želivský later appeared as spokesmen of the revolutionary masses belonged, as far as their names are known, to the craftsmen who were organized in the guilds and who probably had acquired in those organizations the experience necessary for political leadership. In this way the role of the city "proletariat" in the Hussite movement was quite similar to that of the peasants, who had equally to rely on their social superiors—the squires—for leadership in the common struggle.

[33] This lowest stratum of the Bohemian cities, and especially of Prague, is the subject of a recent study by F. Grauss: *Městská chudina v době předhusitské*, Prague 1949. The book tends to prove that this class was stronger than had generally been presumed and it presents interesting material about the employment and the development of the wage level of the dependent workers. However, I do not believe Grauss to be right in attributing to the *chudina* a leading role in the initial stages of the revolution and in considering (on pp. 147-173) John Želivský as the specific leader of this class as opposed to the middle class and the guilds. Witness the names and professions of his most influential followers such as the brothers Charvát whose father had built one of the streets of the New Town which was called after him, George "the glover" or Jerome Šrol whose father was a master in the furriers' guild. (Tomek, *Dějepis města Prahy*, 2nd ed., IV, 233, 238.) John Želivský's personality and historical role will be discussed more specifically below.

We have tried so far—in what was necessarily a very cursory presentation—to show that, in the course of the later fourteenth century, Bohemia had developed in its social and economic structure into one of the most progressive, most differentiated, and most dynamic societies of late medieval Europe. Yet many of the features discussed can be found elsewhere, and even the looseness and weakness of the government of Wenceslas IV, which failed to discourage internal strife and thus let social frictions develop rather freely, was paralleled in other countries, for example, in the France of Charles VI, without leading to open revolution. In England, it is true, the great peasant revolt of 1381, supported as it was by part of the citizenry of London, testified to the increasing force of the social tensions of the time, and it can well be argued that even earlier movements like the peasant revolt which started in Flanders in 1324 or the great French Jacquerie of 1358 were, as phenomena of social history, basically of the same nature as the revolution which followed, just a century after the Flemish outbreak, in the land of John Hus.[34] But all those movements were limited in scope and were quickly and completely defeated. The very different course and outcome of the Hussite movement would remain inexplicable if it were to be understood as a purely socio-economic development. Its scope and success was largely due to the fact that the social forces and tensions were reinforced and largely directed by the two other great elements which are manifested all through its course: the Czech nationalism which had begun to be a strong and effective force rather early in the fourteenth century, and the movement for religious reform which, though acquiring its elementary strength only at the beginning of the fifteenth century, was to overshadow all other issues once the struggle had become an open clash. The question how those three elements—the social, the national, and the religious—influenced and reacted upon one another is intricate, largely debatable, and beyond the scope of this study. In this context we may say that the social and the national tendencies which led up to the revolution were very intimately interwoven at an early stage, whereas the trend for religious reform seemed originally to have different sources, partly even foreign, and to be fairly independent from the other two trends.

Czech national feelings are expressed quite unmistakably as early as at the beginning of the twelfth century in the first great and coherent

[34] The basic similarity between these earlier movements and the Hussite revolution, and the social determinants of this revolution, have been most strongly emphasized by Jan Slavík in his book *Husitská Revoluce*, Prague 1934, pp. 27-37.

attempt at writing the history of Bohemia: in the Latin Chronicle of Cosmas of Prague. Even then it finds its basis in a defensive attitude against the Germans. Cosmas writes of "the innate arrogance of the Germans, who in their puffed-up pride always hold in contempt the Slavs and their language." It is a sentence which might well have been used by Czechs eight centuries after Cosmas wrote—so constant has been the resentment against German encroachments throughout Bohemian history.[35] But German influence in Bohemia, exerted with varying intensity all through the high and late Middle Ages, was far from having only negative results for Bohemia. We have mentioned before the improvement in the life of the peasants due to the introduction of the "German Law." The German settlers in the cities whose immigration had been favored especially by the later Přemyslide kings in the thirteenth century contributed greatly to the development of commerce and of the trades and crafts in the country. Even in the "Golden Age," the time of Charles IV, much of the great cultural progress was due to German participation, though French and Italian influence was far from negligible. The active role of the German element in the country thus proved a constant challenge to the Czech population. The need to compete with the older and more varied experience of the immigrants resulted in strong and highly successful efforts on the side of the Czechs to meet the challenge, to match the achievements of the foreigners. It was in this hard school of national competition that Czech craftsmen, Czech artisans, but also Czech artists and Czech scholars developed their abilities and became as competent in all these endeavors as any of the townsmen in the great civilizations of late medieval Europe. But with the increased ability of the Czechs to cope with all the technical, economic, and cultural tasks of a steadily progressing society there arose, understandably, the desire for a role of social and political equality. And here they came up against the strongly entrenched groups of Germans who, on their side, tried to keep the most important as well as the most profitable positions to themselves. This was true in the Church where many of the leading prelates were Germans, among them the holders of some of the richest abbacies. It was just as true in the cities where the ruling patrician families were almost exclusively German. It is characteristic that up to the early fourteenth century few Czechs succeeded in entering the closed rank of the city councilors. Then, however, things began to change. By the middle of the century

[35] This trend up to the Hussite time is reviewed by Krofta in his lecture "Hnutí husitské po stránce sociální a národní," reprinted in *Duchovní odkaz husitství*, Prague 1946, pp. 102ff.

small numbers of Czech councilors were to be found in several cities, for example in Pilsen and Žatec, and before 1400 Czechs were already in the majority in a number of important city governments, such as Hradec Králové, Louny, and Beroun.[36]

Most grimly contested, however, were the governing positions in the capital. True the New Town which, from the beginning, was settled almost exclusively by Czechs, had a majority of Czech councilors as early as 1356. The Small Side followed somewhat later. But in the Old Town, still economically as well as politically the most important of the three boroughs, there were seldom more than two or three Czechs among the councilors until the early years of the fifteenth century, although the Germans constituted rather less than one third of the population.[37] Only in 1413, when Czech nationalism in close connection with the religious reform movement had already assumed a highly militant character, was the proportion of Czechs in the council, by order of King Wenceslas, determined to be at least one half. The measure was not accepted without considerable resistance which even led to some bloodshed.[38]

It is understandable that this slow and only grudgingly accepted progress did not really satisfy the Czechs. And the struggle for full recognition of the nation in its own national affairs became more and more allied to and interwoven with the social struggle of the urban middle class against the rich patricians. To identify completely the relationship between patricians and urban middle class with that between Germans and Czechs would be an oversimplification. There were some Czechs among the richest of the citizens of Prague,[39] and there were many Germans among the craftsmen and artisans, at least in the Old Town. Yet for the Czechs in the lower social groups the German patrician, lording it over the city, was clearly and increasingly the object of social as well as of national antagonism. And this resentment was fanned into even stronger hostility when the twofold adversary eventually proved also to be the enemy of the great religious reform movement.

Here again the identification of Germans with enemies of the reform movement was hardly anything basic or innate. Indeed the very first of the many clergymen who preached the need for moral reform and religious revival in Bohemia was a German: Conrad Waldhauser, the

[36] Z. Winter, *op.cit.*, p. 233. [37] *ibid.*, p. 235.
[38] Tomek, *Dějepis*, III, 549. [39] Winter, *op.cit.*, p. 232.

Augustinian whom Charles IV had called from Vienna to Prague in 1358, hoping thus to counteract the clerical corruption which the King-Emperor, for all his benevolence to the clergy, could not fail to perceive. Waldhauser's immediate successor, Milič of Kroměříž, was a Czech from Moravia, but his sermons (he preached in both Czech and German) found an equally enthusiastic audience among members of both nations. The Czech character of the reform movement in Bohemia is more clearly expressed in the following generation by the great reform preachers of the last quarter of the fourteenth century, foremost among them Thomas of Štítný and Matthew of Janov. But their emphasis upon writing and preaching in Czech, though a conscious deviation from custom, was directed against the monopoly of Latin rather than German and expressed the idea that religious life had to be more than a ritual performed in a language which the common people could not understand. In this sense, trying to open up the sources of full religious experience to the masses of the people, the growing reform movement had truly democratic implications which were also inherent in Matthew of Janov's insistence upon the frequent, if possible daily, partaking of the Holy Communion by all the people. It was in this spirit of creating free access to religious experience for everybody that two wealthy Czech citizens of Prague founded in 1391 the Chapel of Bethlehem, to be used exclusively for Czech preaching. And this church became the center of the reform movement when its pulpit was occupied by a man whose mental stature, moral fiber, and reformatory zeal surpassed in creative strength that of all his predecessors and contemporaries: John Hus.

Hus was so great a man, and his role in the history of his country and of the Western church was of such vast dimensions, that any attempt at an adequate description or evaluation within the framework of this chapter would seem hopeless. Fortunately both his personality and his work have been covered by rather extensive studies and writings in English.[40] There is no special need to go into the difficult and intricate questions of Hus's contributions to the development of Christian theology and dogma. The claim, once made by an influential scholar,[41] that Hus was not much more than a popularizer of the teachings of

[40] The great standard work on Hus is in Czech: Novotný a Kybal, *M. Jan Hus, život a učení*, Prague 1919-1931. In English we have among others: Count Lützow's *The Life and Times of Master John Hus*, London 1909; Otakar Odložilík, *Wiclif and Bohemia*, Prague 1937; Matthew Spinka, *John Hus and the Czech Reform*, Chicago 1941; Krofta's article on Hus in *Cambridge Medieval History*, VIII, 1936, and all Church histories, best among them in its treatment of Hus probably Mandell Creighton, *History of the Papacy during the Period of the Reformation*, I, London 1882. Hus's letters are translated into English by Workman.

[41] J. Loserth, *Hus und Wiklif*, Prague 1884, revised edition 1926.

Wiclif, has been quite definitely refuted. But theological speculation was not in the center of Hus's thinking. "He never stresses doctrinal reconstruction for its own sake, but always in connection with some effort at moral reform or religious awakening."[42] Wiclif's writings provided him with much help and inspiration, and he thought highly of the great Oxonian. Yet there was also much in Wiclif's doctrines that he felt he had to reject, and he gave his life not for the truths of Wiclif but for the truth of Christ and the Scriptures as he understood them.

Perhaps it was partly this stronger emphasis upon the religious practice which enabled Hussitism even in its early stages to achieve, within Bohemia, the universality which none of the earlier reform movements, including Lollardy in England, had been able to reach: The struggle for religious reform in Bohemia became a great general upsurge which received and absorbed many of the social and national strivings which we tried to describe earlier in this chapter. And though the later Hussite revolution, especially in its more radical developments, surely went beyond what Hus personally ever had advocated or would have welcomed, nevertheless Hus himself must quite largely be credited with, or made responsible for, the wide scope of the reform movement. True he never consciously advocated any basic change in the stratified structure of society. But his passionate defense of the common people, the little ones and poor ones, and his whole insistence upon the active role of the lay population within the Church as an all-inclusive community, gave his activities the democratic tinge which was just as strongly felt by his friends and adherents as it was understood and decried by his enemies.[43] Like Luther after him, he vitalized the religious services of his country, drawing in all his congregation by developing the religious song.[44]

Hus's social credo was based still more on the general demand for moral decency and the humane ethics commanded by Christ and the Scriptures than on any program for a better society.[45] It was revolutionary only to the extent that the actual practices of the rulers of his society, and of the Church in particular, were incompatible with those principles of Christian ethics. Yet some of Hus's bitterest conflicts with

[42] Spinka, *John Hus*, p. 8.

[43] Slavík, *Husitská revoluce*, pp. 39ff. Slavík, it seems to me, somewhat overemphasizes the social-revolutionary character of Hus's teachings.

[44] See Z. Nejedlý's great work: *Dějiny husitského zpěvu* (History of the Hussite Song), Prague 1913.

[45] Krofta, *Duchovní odkaz husitství*, p. 92.

the great power structure of the Roman Church arose over issues which had economic significance, such as the question of simony on which Hus wrote one of his most impressive and militant books,[46] and the sale of indulgences in 1412 by a papal emissary (incidentally a German prelate by the name of Thiem) to which Hus reacted with a determination not surpassed by Luther in his much more famous quarrel with Tetzel a century later. In the fight against indulgences Hus went so far as to declare that believing Christians did not have to obey the Pope if his commands went against the Law of Christ. To the adherents of Papal supremacy this was clearly an act of brazen rebellion.

That anyone who still considered himself a faithful son of the Church could take so audacious a stand against the Pope can only be fully understood against the background of the Great Schism which had, by then, lasted for thirty-four years and had discredited the institution of the Papacy in the eyes of many otherwise fully orthodox people.[47] The purpose for which John XXIII had ordered the sale of indulgences actually grew out of the Schism. With them he wanted to finance a crusade against King Ladislas of Naples who supported the older Roman rival-Pope, Gregory XII (in addition to whom there was still a third Pope, Benedict XIII, residing at Avignon).

The Great Schism had, even earlier, provided causes for national friction inside Bohemia and had thus, indirectly, caused Hus to become something like the spiritual leader of his nation. In 1408 a struggle had broken out between the conciliar party, which hoped to heal the great breach by calling a church council to Pisa, and the party which fully recognized the Roman Pope Gregory XII against his Avignonese rival. The latter group was supported by Archbishop Zbyněk of Prague, whereas King Wenceslas supported the calling of the council. When the matter was brought before the University as the highest authority in ecclesiastical law the majority of that institution decided against the King. The vote had to be taken in "nations" of which there were (as at Paris) four: the Bohemian, Bavarian, Saxon, and Polish. The majority was formed by the three last-named, most of them actually Germans. Only the Bohemian "nation" voted, in agreement with the King, for the conciliar solution.

[46] *O svatokupectví*, ed. Novotný, in *Světová Knihovna*, nos. 604-606. An English translation of this work is to be found in Matthew Spinka, ed. and tr., *Advocates of Reform*, Philadelphia and London, 1953.

[47] As the rest of this chapter contains, in the main, a rapid summary of the events leading up to the Hussite revolution, a documentation of single facts seems pointless.

The Czech members of the University had long complained about the fact that they could be outvoted by foreigners, and under the impact of the decision on the issue just described, King Wenceslas decided to heed their demand for a change. By the Decree of Kutná Hora, issued on January 18, 1409, the King granted three votes to the Bohemian nation against one to be held by the three foreign nations.

The Decree of Kutná Hora, enforced by the King against the fierce protest of the Germans (with the Rector von Baltenhagen at their head), had highly important consequences. It led to the exodus of large numbers of German masters and students (who, in their majority, subsequently founded the University of Leipzig). It changed the character of the University from an international into a national institution. And while it harmed the prestige which the school had had all over Europe, it established all the more firmly its position as the spiritual center of the Czech nation.

The rectorship (presidency) of the University which Herr von Baltenhagen had to lay down was now taken over by Hus. Though not all of the masters followed his leadership it can be said that, from now on, the University became both the spiritual testing ground and the increasingly firm platform on which the reform movement could develop. And just as the University had become a national institution so the reform movement became ever more clearly a national movement. The social implications inherent in it, at least as far as they tended to divide the Czechs internally, were temporarily forgotten or at least overshadowed by the common enthusiasm for a cause in which, religiously and nationally, Czechs of all stations could unite. The King himself seemed to approve of it, at least to the extent of backing Hus against the increasing hostility of the Papal party and of Archbishop Zbyněk. Queen Sophia quite openly sided with Hus, often visited the Chapel of Bethlehem to listen to him (where, as we have heard before, she was sometimes accompanied by Žižka) and even made the great reformer her confessor. Among the members of the Royal Court, among the high nobility and the gentry, Hus found an ever-growing number of friends and adherents, and the masses of the Czech city population of Prague began to look to him as their Godsent leader and almost a saint.

During the years 1410 and 1411 the struggle centered around the issue of Wiclif's writings, seventeen of which had been declared heretical by the Curia, whereas the University, under Hus's leadership, contested this ban. Archbishop Zbyněk demanded that all of Wiclif's writings then in the personal possession of members of the University be handed in to him for inspection. When this demand had generally been complied with, he had them summarily burned. Energetic protests on the side of Hus and his adherents were answered by Zbyněk with temporary excommunication of Hus and his friends, but Hus kept preaching.

The conflict became still more bitter in 1412 through Hus's intervention, mentioned earlier, against the sale of indulgences which drove him to challenge openly the Pope's right to demand general obedience. This time Pope John XXIII not only confirmed Hus's excommunication but demanded the demolition of the Church of Bethlehem as a "nest of heretics," and laid the interdict upon Prague. To alleviate the situation, following an appeal from the King, Hus went in the summer of 1412 into a sort of voluntary exile which lasted for two years. He spent them in the south, dwelling part of the time in the castle of Kozí near Bechyně where he produced some of his most important writings.[48] But at least as consequential was his continued preaching activity. His listeners, now, were mostly peasants who came from all over the country to hear his sermons, delivered often under the open skies. The seed of this activity was to grow until eventually the rural masses, especially in south-central Bohemia, became the active and enthusiastic supporters of the great sectarian movement of Tabor.[49] And the wide adherence of the peasantry to the reform movement completed, as it were, the truly national support which Hus could count upon when early in November 1414, equipped with a safe conduct from the Roman King Sigismund, he arrived at Constance to justify himself before the greatest and most significant church council to have assembled for centuries.

Hus's trial for heresy before the Council of Constance is one of the famous court procedures in history, and its course and outcome represents one of those truly moving tragedies by which reality has sometimes challenged the art of the dramatist. There seems little doubt that, for all the personal enmity which Hus encountered, especially among some of his Bohemian accusers, the majority of the assembly would have been glad to see him revoke and thereby save his life. It is equally clear that Hus was not, as it has sometimes been asserted, the stubborn

[48] R. W. Seton-Watson, *A History of the Czechs and Slovaks*, London 1943, p. 48., points out the similarity between Hus's voluntary exile at Kozí Hrádek and Luther's retirement to the Wartburg, both periods having been used for important literary production.

[49] Slavík, *op.cit.*, p. 49, infers from the influence which Hus's preaching exerted upon the Czech peasants that these people must have had a high standard of mental alertness and understanding. This may have been true, but the conclusion seems hardly compelling, as the attraction was, in all probability, emotional rather than intellectual.

dogmatist who, for his own major glory, consciously sought the crown of the martyr. He often declared that he would be glad to revoke any error that should be proved to him out of the Scriptures. But this insistence on the Bible as the supreme authority challenged the basic claim of the Church to be the sole judge of divine truth and therefore had to be rejected if the Church was to retain its indisputable mastery over the religious life of the Christian world. To this extent, then, compromise seemed from the first well-nigh hopeless. But in addition to those differences touching upon the very basis of the struggle, it can hardly be denied that Hus was never given the opportunity for a proper and unfettered self-defense, however little this might have helped him. The demands of the council to revoke such theses of Wiclif's as Hus himself had never held[50] were, in the eyes of the Czech reformer, so many demands for him to deviate from the truth by self-accusations which would have been lies before God. The letters which he wrote home from Constance, especially those written in prison at a time when he knew himself to be doomed, movingly express the greatness and purity of this noble soul, the sublime idealism which motivated him, and the deep love for his people to whom he had given a new, strong, and dynamic understanding of Christianity.

Many attempts have been made to justify not only the sentence of the Council but even the breach of the safe conduct by which Sigismund, as protector of the Council, had assured Hus of free and unmolested return to Bohemia. But there surely is no excuse for this breach short of the fantastic claim that no Christian need keep faith with a heretic, and Sigismund himself acknowledged the flagrant wrong he felt compelled to do, not only by violently blushing when the sentence was pronounced and Hus looked at him, but also by his earlier attempts at stalling when Hus was first arrested. The accusation that he was guilty for the death of Hus followed Sigismund through most of his life and seems to have burdened his conscience, as he made considerable efforts, throughout the following years, to prove his innocence.

Hus died at the stake on July 6, 1415. When the news arrived in Bohemia it caused an outcry of fierce indignation all through the country. A diet of the estates of Bohemia and Moravia was called to Prague which, on September 2, addressed a note of protest to the Council of Constance couched in the strongest language. The diet protested the innocence and excellence of Master John Hus and declared that any-

[50] Especially the theory of remanence. See also Krofta, *op.cit.*, p. 54.

one claiming that there was heresy in Bohemia "speaketh lies as a treacherous enemy of our kingdom and our nation, being himself a malicious heretic, and even a son of the Devil, who is the father of lies." Immediately afterwards the majority of the lords present at the diet, under the leadership of Čeněk of Wartenberg, Lacek of Kravaře, and Boček of Poděbrady, concluded a covenant to last for six years by which they obliged themselves to defend the freedom of preaching on all their estates, to obey the bishops only as long as those acted according to the Scriptures, and to acknowledge the University of Prague as the highest authority in disputed matters of faith. The document received the signatures of 452 lords and knights, the overwhelming majority of Bohemia's nobility. A Catholic counter-league, based on the promise of obedience to the King, the Church of Rome, and the Council of Constance, achieved the adherence of only fourteen lords.

The violent reaction of the majority of the Czech people did not serve as a warning to the Council. Sigismund had some difficulty in preventing the Council from indicting his brother King Wenceslas and Queen Sophia. The 452 signatories of national covenant, together with some of the prominent followers of Hus among the masters of the University, were summoned to Constance to undergo a trial for heresy. They never considered following the summons, of course, but one of Hus's foremost clerical friends, Jerome of Prague, who had gone to Constance to testify on Hus's behalf, was now subjected to a procedure similar to that accorded to Hus. At one stage, cowed by the fear of death, he revoked completely, but while still in prison repented his weakness and strongly protested Hus's innocence and his own agreement with him. Therefore, as one relapsing into heresy, he was burned on May 30, 1416.

The thunder from Constance made no impression upon the majority of the people of Bohemia, except perhaps in stiffening their attitude. Their defiance of the Council's commands was most clearly expressed in the rapid spread of the custom, first practiced by the eminent master of the University, Jacobellus of Stříbro, to dispense the Holy Communion in both kinds to laymen of both sexes, though the Council had only in June 1415 solemnly condemned this practice, maintaining that only priests were allowed to partake of the wine. The new custom (in reality a return to the oldest form of the Eucharist) had been approved by Hus in one of his last letters from Constance. It now became so crucial to all adherents of the reform that in many places all over the country those priests who were not prepared to adhere to it were driven from their churches. On March 10, 1417, the University of Prague approved of the custom, declaring the Communion in both kinds as indispensable for salvation. From now on the chalice was the official symbol of the reformed Church of Bohemia, and its adherents became known as Calixtines or (from the Latin form for "in both kinds," sub utraque parte) Utraquists.

But even in this early stage of its development the Hussite movement showed the tendency almost necessarily inherent in any such movement once it starts deviating from the firm basis of an established dogmatic structure: the tendency toward further splitting into differing groups. There was, for instance, some disagreement among the masters of the University on whether Jacobellus of Stříbro did not go too far in demanding the Communion, always in both kinds, also for children right from the time of their baptism. Deeper, however, went the difference between the views of the Utraquists as represented by the University of Prague, and large sectarian groups which had arisen in some of the rural areas, especially in the south of Bohemia not far from the centers where Hus had done his preaching in the years from 1412 to 1414. The most important of these sectarian groups was, at an early stage of the Hussite revolution, to become known as Taborites from the Biblical name of Mount Tabor, and though we cannot be sure when this name was first used by them we can, for the purpose of identification, apply this denotation even now in talking of those religious radicals. They were chiliasts and expected the coming of Christ at an early date. And whereas the Utraquists were determined to discard all those parts of the ritual which seemed to be incompatible with the Scriptures, the Taborites went a great step further, discarding everything that could not directly and unmistakably be inferred from the Bible.

The Taborite radicalism—we shall later have to discuss it in much more detail[51]—soon worried the University, and a declaration issued by the masters in February 1418 warned against them. In September of the same year a synod called to Prague tried, for the first time, to lay down the religious principles of the Utraquists in twenty-three precise points, among them the prescription that all those beliefs and rituals of the Roman Church which did not directly contradict either the Scriptures or the moral principles were to be upheld.

For all the deep changes that had occurred in the religious life of the nation, the political situation within Bohemia during the first three years after the death of Hus did not yet show any clear signs of the

[51] See below, especially Chapters 5 and 10.

impending storm. The Council of Constance had, to the last moment, clamored for radical measures against the Hussite movement. But in April 1418 the great assembly dissolved after having achieved at least one of its main tasks: the liquidation of the Great Schism. After the resignation of Gregory XII and the deposition of John XXIII and Benedict XIII the Council elected Cardinal Colonna who, under the name of Martin V, inherited the difficult task of dealing with the greatest heretical movement that had ever arisen within the framework of the Western Church. The opportunities to eradicate the heresy largely depended on the attitude of King Wenceslas, and for the time being the King seemed determined not to yield. As late as June 1418 he issued an order forbidding his subjects to follow any summons before an ecclesiastical court outside the Kingdom. But the tensions inside as well as the pressure from outside were still growing, and some months later his constancy waned. And with it waned the precarious peace which so far had been maintained in Bohemia.

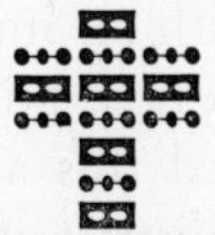

## CHAPTER 4

# THE OUTBREAK OF THE REVOLUTION

EARLY in 1419 the situation in Bohemia was fast approaching a stage in which it became ever more difficult to prevent open clashes of a serious nature. The long religious antagonism had created bitterness on all sides. Only strong, clear-minded leadership could have kept the incipient chaos from growing into a civil war. But Wenceslas IV was indecision personified. Torn between the personal influence of his Hussite courtiers and the tremendous pressure of the whole Catholic world he began seriously to fear for his throne. At last Queen Sophia seems to have spoken the decisive word. She had long been a fearless and constant defender of Hus himself and his tenets, but under the growing threat of direct interference from outside she now felt that it was necessary to give way.

At the end of February the King restricted permission for holding Hussite services to only three of the many Prague churches. They were, of course, quite insufficient to supply the needs of the large Hussite population. Some Hussite priests now left Prague and joined the Taborite movement.

They were soon followed in this move by a man whose personality and qualities of leadership did much to change the character of the movement. It was Nicholas of Pístny, usually called Nicholas of Hus after a castle in southern Bohemia of which he had been burgrave early in the century.[1] He, like Žižka, belonged to the most determined supporters of the Hussite cause. When the King ordered most of the Hussite churches closed, Nicholas stepped forward in a long and heated argument with his royal master which ended in Wenceslas threatening to have him strangled. Nicholas, in consequence, left Prague and went to the country where he became, as the first layman of any stature, active in the Taborite movement.[2]

[1] Ironically the castle of Hus, while under Nicholas's burgravate, had in 1408 been the object of a planned attempt at conquest on the side of the guerilla band of which Žižka had been a member. See Bartoš, *Čechy v době Husově*, p. 230.

[2] Aeneas Sylvius, our main source for this event (chapter 35, p. 76) reports that Nicholas, who

A brave and able soldier, with an impressive, dominant personality, ambitious and highly self-possessed, Nicholas was, above all, an effective organizer. He soon applied this ability in his dealings with the Taborite peasant masses of the district of Bechyně in southern Bohemia. It was in this region that John Hus had dwelt during his voluntary exile from Prague in 1412 and after, and the religious fervor which he had kindled among the simple people of this district had never since subsided but had rather strengthened and spread. Even in Hus's time assemblies in open fields and on hills had replaced the services in the narrower confines of church buildings. This had, in the meantime, become more and more the custom. Slowly a tradition had evolved for the way in which the brethren and sisters convened, preferably on hills. We cannot be sure when, for the first time, the Biblical name "Tabor" was adopted for those high places of assembly and worship. But this name was used when on July 22 a meeting was held which attracted unusual attention. Supposedly more than 40,000 people, some of them from faraway districts, assembled on a hill near the town of Bechyně. This meeting of which Nicholas was the main organizer was, as yet, a purely religious occasion. No threats were uttered, no political plans discussed or propagandized. Yet the presence of so many thousands worshiping in a way which had no longer the blessing of the powers of government was, in itself, a political fact. Before long, similar meetings were to assume a more activist character. But the spark that set off the flames did not spring up in those rural regions. Revolutions, almost invariably, are city-born, and this was true, too, of the Hussite revolution.

Soon after the strict limitation of Hussite churches in Prague, the interdict which had prevented regular Catholic services was raised, and one after the other the churches regained for the older creed were put into service after having been solemnly reconsecrated. But this process did not go on undisturbed. On June 18, when the Church of St. Nicholas in the Old Town was to be reconsecrated, a strong crowd of Hussites prevented the celebration from starting, and themselves took possession of the church. Certainly many of those people came from the New Town and belonged to the followers of John Želivský, the former monk who was now preacher at St. Mary's in the Snow, one of the two Huss-

encountered the King at the head of a large and unruly crowd, addressed him in a very demanding and unrespectful way. He also hints that he had designs upon the royal crown, and that the King, knowing this, got so angry as to threaten him with execution.

ite churches in the New Town that had remained open. Of all Hussite leaders in the capital he was the most outspoken, in his theological sermons as in his fierce attacks upon all enemies of the "Law of God." A brilliant orator who had a deep influence especially upon women, he became the self-appointed but rather widely acknowledged leader of the "little people" in the New Town, the Czech craftsmen, artisans, and workers. Just as the Taborite peasants in some regions of central and southern Bohemia, so the masses of the unprivileged or underprivileged townsmen of the Prague New Town became enthralled and intoxicated by sermons promising them an entirely new and better world, provided the Law of God could be made to rule freely and its enemies destroyed.[3]

It was against the more radical Hussite masses of the New Town that King Wenceslas felt he had now to proceed. On July 6 he ordered Bechyně of Lažany, the royal subchamberlain of Bohemia, to purge the government of the New Town of all persons suspected of Hussite leanings, and to replace them by energetic and reliable Anti-Hussites. The new city councilors tried to break up the Hussite movement by elaborate police methods. They also ordered all the parochial schools which, with their churches, had been used to educate children in the Hussite spirit, to be closed or returned to strictly Roman teaching. All through July this new restrictive policy made itself felt, and with it rose the resentment of the people against whom it was directed.

John Želivský now decided to act. He prepared himself, not without circumspection, for a major clash, procuring the help of a man in whom he could trust in case open fighting should result. This man, still at this time a member of the royal household, was John Žižka of Trocnov.[4]

On July 30, 1419, one of the usual crowded services took place at the Church of St. Mary in the Snow. John Želivský in his sermon fiercely attacked the new city council and its oppressive police methods. After the service he called upon the crowd to follow him, and he had made sure that among them would be people with arms in their hands. Preceded by a priest, probably John Želivský himself, who carried, visible to all, the sacred host, the crowd marched to the Church of St.

[3] A collection of sermons found by Truhlář, dating from 1417 to 1419, are very likely those of John Želivský (*Č.Č.H.*, 1903, pp. 198-200). See Pekař's commentary (III, 13, and note 2).

[4] For the following events see Old Annalists, especially in text Sa which, so far, has not been fully published, but whose account of the First Defenestration is printed in Pekař (IV, 14); further Březová, *Fontes Rerum Bohemicarum*, V, p. 345 and Aeneas Sylvius, chapter 37, p. 77.

Stephen. This church which had not yet been reconsecrated, was forced open, a service held there, and mass was celebrated, with the Communion given in the two kinds. From there the procession went on, the crowd growing steadily while it wormed its way through the streets of the New Town, back toward the Church of St. Mary in the Snow. But on the way the crowd stopped in front of the New Town city hall, a large building with a tall tower at the northern end of the wide Cattle Market, today's Charles' Square. The leaders of the procession called on the town councilors to admit some of their speakers and to release from prison all those who had lately been arrested because of their Hussite creed. The members of the council: burgomaster, town councilors, and magistrates, tried to parley with the crowd, talking to them out of the window, but the main demand, that of releasing the prisoners, they refused to discuss. Meanwhile the crowd, down on the street, grew more and more excited, and suddenly shouts went up from among the people claiming that a stone had been hurled down from one of the windows at the priest who was carrying the host. Whether this was true or only the imagination of one of the excited participants, the effect was the same: it released the fierce rage of the crowd against the "enemies of God" at the town hall. They threw themselves against the bolted doors, forced them open and rushed up the stairs.

Some of the members of the council barely escaped through back stairs and exits, but the others were taken and thrown out of the window onto the street. Those who survived the fall were slain by the furious demonstrators. After that the town hall was occupied by armed men from the crowd and, so concludes one of the most detailed reports we have, "John Žižka, King Wenceslas' most personal attendant, was present at the slaying of the councilors."[5] It was probably he who took charge in the final occupation and garrisoning of the town hall.

This earliest outbreak in the history of the Hussite movement has become known as "the First Prague Defenestration," as distinct from the second similar act which, two centuries later, led to the outbreak of the Thirty Years' War.

What, actually, was Žižka's position at this important moment? It was, first of all, the event which brought him to public attention. From now on he was, and remained for the rest of his life, in the public eye. We shall still be faced with certain periods of his life, when for weeks and even months our sources dry up—like a river that for stretches of

[5] Old Annalists, *loc.cit.* and similarly the other sources quoted before.

its course runs hidden and then comes to the surface again. But generally we have from now on a fairly good picture of his acts and whereabouts.

This is not true for the time immediately before the events just told, and we are still faced with the problem how, out of Žižka the soldier and Žižka the courtier, developed Žižka the revolutionary leader, fully ready for his historical role. This change cannot have been easy, for by participating in the revolt of July 30 he committed an act of grave disobedience toward the king in whose service he still was, to whom he owed much and to whom, for all we know, he had been a loyal servant throughout the long years in which he belonged to the royal household.[6]

There can however be little doubt about the motives for his decision. He was the victim of what might be called conflicting loyalties: the duty to the King and the duty to the Law of God. But in the decisive moment he had no choice or doubt. To serve the Law of God was to him the supreme duty. "Legis Christi zelator praecipuus," an extraordinarily zealous defender of the Law of Christ, thus he is characterized by the chronicler who knew him best: Lawrence of Březová.[7] There was no law higher than this. As long as the King seemed to protect it, or at least not to stand in its way, he could still serve him. Once the King had decided against it, Žižka had to decide against him. "Those who did not take the Body and Blood of Christ in both kinds," said *The very pretty chronicle*, "those he took for his enemies." It was, indeed, as simple as that.

The outbreak of the revolt in the Prague New Town caught all those off guard whose office it should have been to deal with it. A small troop of royal horsemen under the command of the subchamberlain had, at the news of the outbreak, tried to proceed to the city hall, but perceiving

[6] On Žižka's role immediately before the revolution two stories have survived, both however first appearing in print more than a century after the event. (Kuthen, *Historia Bohemica*, written in 1539, ed. of 1817, p. 306, and Z. Theobald, *Hussiten-Krieg*, Nürnberg 1621, p. 137.) The first one says that King Wenceslas, finding Žižka deeply depressed after the death of Hus and Jerome, told him: "My dear John, what can we do about this? If you know of any way, go ahead, we shall not be in your way." This supposedly Žižka took as a permission to avenge the death of the martyrs of Constance. The second tale, somewhat less incredible, shows Žižka reacting to an order by the King (presumably early in 1419) that all Prague citizens should give up their arms. He advised the Praguers to appear before the King fully armed, and, putting himself at their head, asked the King which enemy he wanted them to fight. They would, of course, fight for the King's honor to the last. The King, rather perplexed, praised their loyalty and sent them home without any reference to his original demand, but soon after left Prague, never to return there.

[7] *op.cit.*, p. 362.

the enormous number of people in the demonstration they quickly retired. The revolutionaries themselves did not lose any time in stabilizing their gains. They called an election for another city council of the New Town, which contained, this time, a large number of reliable Hussites. They also mobilized and armed a considerable number of citizens and appointed several captains of whom Žižka became the first in rank.[8]

When the news of the revolt reached the royal court at the New Castle it caused tremendous excitement. The King flew into a fierce rage, swore vengeance on the guilty ones, reproaching at the same time all his entourage, and when one of his courtiers remarked that, on the basis of the King's recent policy an event like this could have been foreseen, he threw himself upon the man and would have run him through with his dagger if the other people present had not prevented him. Then suddenly he collapsed, hit by a stroke which partly paralyzed his left side.

When, in the following days, he seemed at least partially restored to health he was again the vacillating, irresolute man he had always been. On the one hand, feeling that he had been deserted by every one of his friends, including even the Queen, he decided to seek help from Sigismund. He dispatched a messenger to Hungary, asking for speedy action. But immediately after this he was again ready for compromise. Through the mediation of councilors of the Old Town an arrangement was reached by which the New Town asked the King's forgiveness and promised him to be loyal and keep law and order, whereas the King, in return, recognized and confirmed the new city council. There might have been a chance now for things to calm down. But this hope was thwarted when, on August 16, the King suffered a second stroke, much more severe than the first one. "Roaring like a lion" with pain, as Březová tells us,[9] he died the same night.

For all the weakness that had characterized Wenceslas' rule his disappearance from the scene at this critical moment was decidedly unsettling. Even in his last stages the King personally had not been an object of hatred to the masses of the Czech people, especially not in Prague where his affability and personal friendliness toward the "little

[8] Tomek (*Žižka*, p. 21) thinks that Žižka remained in the service of the royal court even after July 30, but this claim has no foundation in the available sources. Also Pekař's conjecture that Žižka personally, like the New Town in general, may have sought and found the King's forgiveness (III, 18), is merely a guess.

[9] *op.cit.*, p. 346.

man" had made him popular. Now, with him out of the way, important inhibitions to open revolutionary action disappeared as well.

What made matters worse was that there was no legitimate and active heir, ready to take over the royal power. Wenceslas had died without any children of his own, and so, before him, had his younger brother John and his cousins Soběslav, Prokop, and Jost. Of the proud and flourishing dynasty of Luxemburg which, at the death of Charles IV, had seemed so firmly established, no one was left but Sigismund. He, according to the laws of primogeniture, was now the natural heir and king. Yet from the beginning it was clear that he was not going to take possession of his heritage without great difficulties.

In the first place Sigismund was not on hand, nor was he likely to be for some time. Dwelling at Buda in his Hungarian kingdom he was busy preparing for war against the Turks who, under their powerful ruler Mohammed I, had recently resumed their westward expansion. Sigismund's involvement in Hungarian problems had prevented him from fulfilling many of his obligations as Roman (or German) King. For Bohemia too, he would be an absentee ruler most of the time.

This fact alone, however, would not disqualify him in the eyes of those who had a feeling of strong feudal loyalty to the "natural king." To them, probably, belonged at this time the larger part of the higher nobility, though many of them had disapproved of his attitude towards his brother Wenceslas, and had resented his role at the trial and death of Hus and Jerome. But Sigismund's candidature was bound to meet sharp resistance on the side of the more radical Hussites. For them the Hungarian king was treachery personified. They did not delude themselves, as some of the more moderate people did, that Sigismund could be prevailed upon to intercede with the Holy See for the freedom of worship in the Hussite way. On the contrary they felt sure that, if Sigismund ever gained power over the Kingdom, their own survival and that of their religious movement was doomed.

This view had many adherents among the men who were now in control of the New Town of Prague. It was in these terms that John Želivský described the King in his powerful sermons. Some years before Sigismund had established the Order of the Dragon, as the highest decoration to be given to a limited number of noblemen. This gave the great orator his cue: Sigismund, so he said, was really the Great Red Dragon which, in St. John's Revelation, was cast out of heaven. "The accuser of our brethren is cast down, which accused them before our God day and night. And they overcame him by the blood of the

Lamb, and by the word of their testimony; and they loved not their lives unto the death."[10] For his audience who knew their Scripture and were wont to take it as literally as possible, the significance of these lines was not hidden. They themselves were the brethren who would overcome Sigismund, the apocalyptic dragon, "by the blood of the Lamb," that is by taking the chalice, and they would not "love their lives" but fight this enemy unto death. It was only one of the many allusions for which John Želivský could make use of the great apocalyptic poem, and at a time of deep excitement, when everyone expected great and unusual things to happen, these sermons kept the masses of his hearers poised for action.

Žižka, too, was ready for action, though perhaps we are justified in crediting him with a somewhat less intoxicated, more sober attitude. His religious feeling was deep and fervent, and, as his letters testify, he knew well how to express it. Yet nowhere in his writing or thinking do we find any proof that he let himself be carried away completely by the chiliastic phantasmagories which became, at this time, so characteristic of certain groups among the radical Hussites, especially some of the Taborite priests. Even so his religious belief, which will emerge more clearly in later stages, made him into a "radical," that is an irreconcilable enemy of Sigismund and his supporters, and thereby Hussite radicals like John Želivský became his natural allies.

The domestic adversary against whom both Žižka and John Želivský could unite easily at this moment was the monastic clergy. The monasteries had been the object of fierce criticism for a long time. They formed a solid body of economic wealth which made them, for that reason alone, an object of envy for large parts of the people from the high nobility down to the peasants. True, the great buildings of chapters and churches which they had erected added no little to the fame and beauty of the country, eliciting from as competent a judge as Aeneas Sylvius the recognition that no other kingdom in all Europe could compare with Bohemia in the wealth, size, and beauty of its churches and monasteries.[11] But to the puritan outlook of the reformers, who wanted the original poverty of Christ's church reestablished, the elaborate beauty of the monastery buildings was scandalous to behold, just as the abundance of paintings and sculptures which adorned them was, in their eyes, a flagrant violation of the Second Commandment.

In the face of this enmity the monastic orders themselves, strong and influential as they were, naturally felt endangered, and as the general

[10] John 12:10, 11. [11] Březová, pp. 74, 75.

discontent rallied more and more around Hussite teachings they, on the other hand, became the most prominent centers of resistance against a movement which threatened their very existence. In addition many of the monks, even of monasteries in purely Czech districts, were of German origin, which isolated them from the people and exposed them to their steadily growing nationalism and anti-Germanism.

The monasteries, then, became the "natural" object of the riots which shook the capital on August 17, the day following the King's death. The first attack went against the great chapter house of the Carthusian order at Smíchov, a suburb just to the south of the Small Side. One of the most luxurious of monastic buildings in the region, its monks were almost all Germans, and some of their clerics had, for some years, been prominent in fighting the Hussite doctrine. The people, with Žižka at their head,[12] ordered the monks to leave, and under the guard of armed men they were taken, over the Charles Bridge, to the city hall of the Old Town. As yet no personal harm was done to them—the councilors of the Old Town had them soon after escorted to the sanctuary of the monastery of Sedlec—but the magnificent buildings, symbol of Romanist pride and oppression in the people's eyes, went up in flames.

The feeling of antagonism against the Germans was not limited to clerics. Some of the rich German patricians of Prague were, for the first time, made to feel that their power and safety were now on shaky ground, and though, in these days, they suffered little harm except threats, there started a trickle of emigration of Germans from Prague which soon was to grow into a stream. On the other hand the Jews, usually the first victims whenever in a medieval town the masses of the people got out of control, remained completely unmolested—a remarkable fact, especially if one considers the religious fervor underlying the movement and remembers that the Jews were then often considered the servants of Antichrist. But the Jews had at least one thing in common with the reformers: their ways of life were, in general, just as austere and puritan as those followed by the adherents of the new creed.

[12] The only one of the contemporary chroniclers to know of Žižka's presence at this occasion is Bartošek of Drahonice (ed. Goll in *Fontes Rerum Bohemicarum*, v, 591), according to whom the people responsible for the storming of the monastery were "Ziska cum suis complicibus." Tomek (*Žižka*, p. 18) doubts the truth of this report, pointing to the fact that in Březová's chronicle Žižka's presence at Smíchov is not mentioned. Pekař, on the other hand, (II, 104, and III, 18), sees no reason to doubt Bartošek's report. I think he is right, as all through his later life Žižka regarded the destruction of monasteries as one of his important tasks. Žižka's participation is also stressed by Aeneas Sylvius (chapter 38, p. 79) who, of course, may have known Bartošek's chronicle.

The puritan character of the movement expressed itself most eloquently in another outbreak of popular wrath, directed against the numerous brothels. They had been most odious to the virtuous Hussites, they had soiled the good name of Prague which, in the sermons of some of the Hussite priests, had more than once been likened to the "great whore Babylon." Now all these houses were closed, and to wipe out the shame, most of them were leveled to the ground.

The events in Prague were soon followed by similar happenings in several provincial towns, first among them Písek, followed by such important centers as Pilsen, Hradec Králové, Žatec, and Louny. This whole first wave of unrest, stormy as it was, was as yet remarkably bloodless. In Prague, in particular, the councilors of the Old Town did all in their power to restore calm and order, and felt strong enough to punish some excessive acts of vandalism. And they were by no means alone in their attempt to stabilize the situation.

Toward the later part of August the capital and other parts of the Kingdom seemed to have returned to a somewhat more sober mood. People went about their business again, and the Queen, who at first had not dared to expose the embalmed body of her husband to a conduct through the streets of Prague, could on August 21 at least order him to be taken (though still at night) from the Vyšehrad to the chapel of St. Wenceslas in the St. Vitus Cathedral on the Hradčany. (His solemn burial, at the prepared tomb in the monastery church of Zbraslav, did not take place till September 12.)

Before August was over an important measure was taken to tighten the reins of government in the Kingdom. In agreement with the Queen, Čeněk of Wartenberg who, as Lord High Burgrave of Prague, was the foremost official in the kingdom, called a general diet. It addressed a long series of demands to the heir to the throne, King Sigismund of Hungary. This document[13] throws some light on the political situation of Bohemia at that moment. It consists of two parts: general demands put forward by the whole diet, barons, gentry, and towns; and an addition listing special demands put forward by the City of Prague. There, for the first time, we find a documentary expression of the highly autonomous and, at the same time, leading role which the capital was playing.

The message to Sigismund is a decidedly Hussite document: it shows that the majority of the Czech nobility adhered at this moment to the

[13] *Archiv český*, ed. Palacký, III, 206-208.

Hussite creed and that the anti-Hussite minority, though it had probably voted against part of the message, did not, for that reason, break away from the assembly which represented the estates of the Kingdom.

Of the sixteen points contained in the general document, the first and most important ones are purely religious. The King is asked to grant the freedom of God's word (meaning the freedom of preaching the Hussite doctrine), and the freedom to give the chalice to the laity. He should acknowledge that the Communion in the two kinds is in accord with the Law of God, as was done before (here the document is on rather unsafe ground) by King Wenceslas. He should also safeguard the Hussite creed in general and the memory of Hus and Jerome in particular against the reproach of heresy. He should intercede with the Pope on behalf of the freedom of Hussite worship, and should see to it that the Holy See, too, stops denouncing the Czech nation as heretic.

The following demands have a more political character. They try to limit the political and economic power of the Church by prohibiting priests from holding any temporal office, from receiving any temporal income, and from practicing simony. Papal bulls against Bohemia should not be considered valid until a final arrangement between Sigismund and the estates of Bohemia was concluded. Other demands refer to financial questions such as safeguards against certain forms of taxation, and general guaranties that the laws of the land be respected by the prospective ruler. But perhaps the most striking demands, apart from those on religion, show the degree to which the nationalist feeling had developed. None of those who had been exiled under King Wenceslas (referring mostly to Germans) should be allowed to hold any office. No foreigner should be entrusted with any office, either spiritual or temporal. And, so the message continues in point 9: "especially no Germans should be allowed to hold offices in the towns where Czechs could, and would be able to, administer them; in all the courts of Bohemia indictments and sentences should be given in the Czech language, and Czechs should everywhere have the foremost voice in the Kingdom of Bohemia and throughout its towns."

The nationalist character of these demands not only reflects the general mood of the time, it also betrays the distrust which the majority of the diet must have felt in its dealings with Sigismund, the man whom the Hussites all through the coming years were to call only "the Hungarian King," and who, though born and reared in Prague as a Bohemian prince, had long before become completely identified with the interests of foreign nations: Hungarians and Germans.

That the message was sent at all showed, it is true, that the diet had decided on the way of negotiating with Sigismund. Many of the Czech nobles still cherished the hope of gaining from the King the concessions which the Hussite majority considered indispensable. This in particular was the expectation of those who, like Čeněk of Wartenberg, were genuinely devoted to the Hussite creed but just as genuinely opposed to revolutionary methods.

Yet in reading the diet's message one feels strongly that at least some of its authors must have counted on a negative or evasive answer. For the message demanded nothing less than a complete reversal of Sigismund's church policy. Could the man who, until now, had shown the greatest zeal in conforming with and implementing the resolutions of the Council of Constance directed against Hus's teachings, suddenly turn into their faithful defender and advocate? Could the man largely responsible for the burning of Hus as a heretic now be ready to defend the reformer's posthumous fame, thereby acknowledging Hus as a martyr and accusing himself indirectly as the author of a judicial murder? It should have been clear that Sigismund, even if at best he would not say no, could not say yes either. And the more radically minded among the members of the diet would not regret a negative answer, as they felt that they could never trust him if he came forward with what might seem a conciliatory attitude.

This more radical wing was, as yet, only weakly represented among the members of the nobility. It had, of course, its representatives among the delegates of Prague. We do not know who they were and have no special reason to assume that either John Želivský or Žižka personally participated in the meeting of the diet. Nor can their influence be clearly discerned in the city's eight demands added to the diet's general message. They mainly appear as an attempt to achieve, from Sigismund, the same concessions that shortly before his death had been granted by Wenceslas: he should "not remember" the acts of revolt and should confirm the legality of all measures taken by the city councils since Wenceslas' death.[14]

[14] Other demands refer to the free use of Czech in Prague churches, the continued suppression of prostitution, the regulation of securities for money borrowed from Jews, and a rather interesting paragraph referring to religious heresies. Anyone found guilty of such (of course heresies from the point of view of Hussite teachings) should receive corrective teaching from the masters of the University. Only if the culprit was not ready to take such instruction should any punishment be inflicted. This demand, probably suggested by the University, shows how utterly impossible it seemed to the leading Hussite spirits that they, themselves, could be in error. But it is also a proof for the tendency, on the side of the masters of Prague University, to deal with religious offenders (in this case probably people with Pikhart leanings) in a rather humane way.

Much now depended on Sigismund's action. Had he followed the advice of Queen Sophia who repeatedly urged him to betake himself, with all speed, to Prague and had he then shown moderation and wisdom in his treatment of the difficult religious question—perhaps the old distrust against him might have vanished and he might have rallied a strong enough part of the nation behind such attempts at a constructive and peaceful solution. Yet in fairness one has to admit that even with the best of intentions such a solution was difficult. Sigismund decided to do as little as possible, and above all not to act in a hurry. In his answer to the Bohemian diet, which is not preserved in the original wording but can be reconstructed from a message sent to the City of Prague,[15] he tried to avoid any commitment. He merely told them that as soon as he came to Bohemia—which, he hoped, would be soon—he would discuss all impending questions with the estates and on that basis make his decisions.

Surely this was as conciliatory an answer as the Czechs could expect. And optimism as to a positive outcome might draw additional comfort from his only practical decision: he vested the regency, for the time of his absence, in the hands of the Queen, and confirmed as her chief adviser Čeněk of Wartenberg, Lord High Burgrave, foremost among the Czech nobles who adhered to the Chalice. He went even further: to Čeněk, a man who on the basis of strict church doctrine was as heretic as any other Hussite, but whose influence upon the Czech nobility was very strong, he awarded his highest decoration, the Order of the Dragon, therewith making him "the king's cousin."[16] This, of course, was an attempt at bribery, but it also showed that the King was ready to go to great lengths to win the friendship and support of the dominant Hussite nobles.

The one thing that he would not do, very much against the recommendations of his Bohemian advisers and of Queen Sophia, was to go to Bohemia. His Hungarian counselors were adverse to any postponement of the expedition against the Turks. In following their advice Sigismund could ban from his mind, for a while at least, the disagreeable Bohemian business. Trying to settle quickly at least one of his major problems as Roman King, the old dispute between Poland and the Prussian Order, he visited on September 12 King Władysław at

[15] *Archiv český*, III, 209.

[16] It is at this stage that Palacký puts the award of the decoration but Sigismund's counselor and biographer Windecke reports this event as having occurred early in 1420 when Wartenberg attended the King's court at Breslau. See Windecke, p. 130. The same chapter contains a detailed description of the Order of the Dragon, its insignia and functions.

Nowy Sącz and persuaded the Polish ruler to submit the unsolved question of Samogitia to his (Sigismund's) arbitration. Soon after he proceeded toward the Balkans and at Niš, in Serbia, his army won on October 4 a victory which, for the moment at least, removed the Turkish danger. By the end of October or early in November he was back in Hungary. But not till the year was almost out did he decide to tackle the thorniest of all his problems: that of Bohemia.[17]

By then, four months had passed since the Bohemian diet had first tried to open negotiations with Sigismund. His absence throughout these months naturally weakened those who tried to uphold law and order in the name of a faraway king, and strengthened those who wanted to proceed in creating a new religious society according to their own creed. The growth, in particular, of the Taborite movement went on unchecked.

[17] For the whereabouts and moves of Sigismund then as later, compare the itinerary in H. Aschbach, *Geschichte Kaiser Sigmunds*, Hamburg 1841ff.

## CHAPTER 5

# PILGRIM'S STAFF OR SWORD?

WE HAVE SEEN that Taboritism, in its origins, was largely a rural movement, flourishing most vigorously in the south-central region of Bohemia, especially around Bechyně and Sezimovo Ústí at the lower course of the Lužnice River. Hus had spent much of his time there after leaving Prague in 1412. Sooner perhaps than most other rural parts of Bohemia this region had been won for the reform movement. Yet it was here, too, that the movement first developed forms of fanaticism never dreamed of, let alone advocated by Hus.

This was a world of people who had suddenly, and against the strong resistance of the established clerical hierarchy, rediscovered the very sources of Christianity: the Holy Scripture. The true spiritual force of the great book had long been hidden from the mass of the people by the exclusive use of the Latin Vulgate. Now it was revealed to them by the translations and sermons of Hus and his followers, who, whenever they preached, would quote long passages from the Bible in the Czech vernacular. This practice was continued by the steadily growing number of Hussite priests. But these men who, as did all the later reformatory movements, preached the return to the original church, the *ecclesia primitiva*, stood under the impression that they lived in an extraordinary time. Their religious zeal was strengthened by one of the most passionate waves of chiliasm that ever shook medieval man. Astrological prophecies contributed to the belief that, early in 1420, Christ would return to this earth to establish His Kingdom. For those who looked for the signs that would indicate "the end of all things" they were not too difficult to find. Had there not been great wars? And it was said: "Nation shall rise against nation, and Kingdom against Kingdom."[1] Had there not been famines and plagues? And it was said:

[1] Of this and the following quotations from the Bible not all can be fully documented as having been used by the Taborite preachers, but it is known that Matthew 24 and corresponding chapters on the promised return of Christ in the other synoptic gospels; further, Revelation and large parts of the prophets, especially Isaiah, were constantly used and most extensively quoted by them.

"there shall be famines and pestilences . . . in divers places." (Matthew 24:7) Had not their leaders, Hus and Jerome, been taken and killed by men of many nations, and their people called heretics? And it was said: "Then shall they deliver you up to be afflicted, and kill you: and ye shall be hated of all nations for my name's sake." (Matthew 24:9) Thus they would argue, and go on saying: "So likewise ye, when ye see these things come to pass, know ye that the Kingdom of God is nigh at hand. Verily I say unto you, This generation shall not pass away, till all be fulfilled." (Luke 21:31, 32)

The coming of Christ was often described in the fearful, mystical, and tempestuous terms of the Revelation: "And I saw heaven opened, and behold a white horse; and he that sat upon him was called Faithful and True, and in righteousness he doth judge and make war. His eyes were as a flame of fire. . . . And he was clothed with a vesture dipped in blood. And out of his mouth goes a sharp sword, that with it he should smite the nations; and he shall rule them with a rod of iron: and he treadeth the winepress of the fierceness and wrath of Almighty God." (19:11-13, 15)

This, indeed, was the dominating note of the chiliastic idea: the time when Christ would come down to earth, amidst fierce thunderstorms and convulsions of heaven and earth, was not, or not yet, the time of love: it was the time of vengeance. All things which were written, mainly by the prophets of the Old Testament, would be fulfilled. The wrath of God would turn against the cities, the hotbeds of sin. "That day is a day of wrath . . . a day of clouds and thick darkness, a day of trumpet and alarm against the fenced cities. . . ." (Zephaniah 1:15, 16) They all "shall be devoured by the fire of His jealousy." "As God overthrew Sodom and Gomorrah and the neighbor cities thereof, saith the Lord; so shall no man abide there, neither shall any son of man dwell therein." (Jeremiah 50:40) "For, behold, the day cometh, that shall burn as an oven; and all the proud, yea, and all that do wickedly, shall be stubble: and the day that cometh shall burn them up, saith the Lord of hosts, that it shall leave them neither root not branch." (Malachi 4:1)

But how, then shall they act who are righteous and faithful, the true successors of the children of Israel? "Then let them which are in Judea flee to the mountains." (Luke 21:21) And had not Isaiah asked the children of Israel: "Bring all your brethren for an offering unto the Lord out of all nations upon horses, and in chariots and litters, and upon mules, and upon swift beasts, to my holy mountain Jerusalem."

(66:20) All those who go to the mountains might be saved, and the righteous ones should not wait, nor let themselves be held up or prevented from going by other members of their own family.

Yet, so some of the Taborites said, not all cities will be destroyed. For, as Isaiah said: "In that day shall five cities in the land of Egypt speak the language of Canaan, and swear to the Lord of hosts . . ." (19:18), so five towns in Bohemia will escape the general destruction. All of them will be in the western part of the country: Pilsen, Žatec, Louny, Slaný, and Klatovy; all towns where Hussitism, or even Taboritism, had gained a strong, early foothold.

Taborite sectarianism was, however, not satisfied with the preaching of those adventist ideas. Out of them and other scriptural discoveries developed a comprehensive set of creeds as well as religious practices, many of which went beyond the tenets held by the great center of Hussite theological teaching: the University of Prague. While some of them were the outgrowth of uninhibited chiliastic fanaticism it would be utterly wrong to pass sentence in these terms on the whole movement, its theology and practice. There was much in it that was to form part of the substance of Protestant thought.[2]

The insistence on a pure life, a life without sin, was basic and common to all Hussitism, but it was still more strongly emphasized in the Taborite camp and there especially it led to a puritanism with which Calvin would have been in thorough agreement. In accord with Wiclif the Taborites taught that no priest in deadly sin can give any sacraments or perform any other religiously valid acts. This was a belief which the Roman Church could not tolerate, a heresy with which Hus had been charged at Constance but which he had never admitted. An even stronger attack against the spirit and structure of the Catholic Church was the insistence, built upon the strict understanding of the Second Commandment, that no one but God in each form of His trinitarian appearance was a legitimate object of worship. The existence of saints (and of sainthood as such) was not denied, and the Taborites continued to use their names in the daily calendar. But to build them churches, paint, carve, or worship their likeness, worship relics of saints, pray to them for intercession with God, all this was considered idolatry.

[2] For the general description of early Taborite creeds one of the richest sources is the long list of theses, 92 in all, with which the representatives of the Taborite clergy were charged, as being partly erroneous, partly heretical, by the masters of Prague University at the great disputation held on December 10, 1420, in the house of Lord Peter Zmrzlík in Prague. See *Archiv český*, III, 218ff., and Březová, pp. 452ff. Another source is the special appendix No. 3 in the Old Annalists, pp. 476ff.

These churches, paintings, or sculptures, therefore, were insults to God, things to be destroyed without any regard to their artistic beauty or value.

Ostentatious and ceremonial clothing, too, was sin in the puritan eyes of Tabor. This issue gained, in the course of the revolution, an importance which it did not deserve, and later the wiser among the Taborite priests sought to minimize the "struggle over the ornates."[3]

Much nearer to the substance of religious life was the question of the books. Many of the Taborite priests were men of the highest education.[4] Yet, especially during the early phase of the movement, book learning was often attacked and the reading of theological books, except for the Scripture, was discouraged. Nothing in the field of religion was or could be true that was not to be found in the Bible, for "if any man shall add unto these things, God shall add unto him the plagues that are written in this book." (Revelation 22:18) This attitude tended, as it were, to delete with one stroke the rich and complex tradition of theological thought of the Middle Ages, a step which the Calixtines, led by Prague University, were never ready to follow. Though somewhat attenuated in later phases this was, perhaps, the most revolutionary of all Taborite innovations. Freeing the mind from this theological tradition meant, on the one hand, the possibility of an entirely new, fresh approach to all religious problems, a wonderful freedom of individual research for the presence and essence of God. Yet this step also contained grave dangers, as it seemed to license self-appointed prophets to go to almost any length in deviation. Indeed splits in doctrine, splits leading to the formation of subsects, was a natural weakness of Hussitism and Taboritism just as to some extent it was a weakness of later Protestantism. An especially important issue on which the Taborites soon were split among themselves was the question of transubstantiation. This struggle went so deep because the sacrament to which it referred, the Holy Communion, held a central place in the religious symbolism of all Hussite groups.

Hardly less revolutionary was the break with another venerable tradition: the continuity of priesthood through ordination. Here the difference between Taboritism and moderate Utraquism appeared most clearly. For the latter the monopoly of the Roman episcopate in ordain-

[3] The reader will remember the somewhat naïve reflection which this struggle has found in *The very pretty chronicle.*

[4] This fact was admitted even by Aeneas Sylvius who met some of the Taborite leaders (especially Koranda and Nicholas of Pelhřimov) on a personal visit to Tabor. See also Pekař, I, 161.

ing a priest was still binding and the borderline between priests and laymen a strict one. Tabor, on the contrary, felt that the role of a priest was purely one of ministry, of service to the community. Priests could, and actually did, elect their own bishop, who then could ordain as priests those considered worthy of the office. Among all Hussites only the Taborites permitted their priests to marry. It was consistent with this new understanding of priesthood that Tabor, followed by later forms of Protestantism, abolished auricular confession. Each man should confess to God, as God alone could absolve him from his sins.

Some Taborite tenets touched, in a revolutionary way, the state of society. Especially during the first, chiliastic phase some Taborite priests described the coming Kingdom of Christ as a state in which there would be no rulers or nobles and Christ alone would be King. The Taborite communities themselves never tried to abolish caste differences, but at least in the religious field all were brethren, and for a short time a sort of primitive socialism was practiced at Tabor the significance of which was, by some contemporary and later critics, greatly exaggerated. Essentially the role of the Levelers in the Hussite revolution was no greater than it was, 220 years later, in the Puritan revolution in England.[5]

Yet equality in the religious field coupled with vague expectations for a better life in the Kingdom of Christ held, of course, a strong magnetic force just for the least privileged among the Czech people. This factor was strengthened by the use, at all religious occasions, of the Czech language. While Utraquism demanded, and obtained in its own realm, the freedom to use the vernacular during church services, Taboritism banned Latin from its services altogether. Therein, too, lay a strong democratic appeal: the language of the common people was to be the language of the church that served them. And their burning religious zeal found full satisfaction in a religious community life where everyone could fully understand everyone else.

Chiliasm was understandably strongest at the beginning of the movement, especially before the prophecies referring to certain dates (early in 1420) had proved wrong. It was in this early phase that the meetings on the hills gained such importance. We have already mentioned the first of those mass meetings which was directly connected with the

[5] Březová (p. 438) describes the disappointment of the peasants in the Taborite districts who had believed themselves to be rid of all feudal dues but then were faced with the demand, vigorously enforced, that those dues had now to be paid to the government of Tabor.

revolutionary movement: the congregation which Nicholas of Hus organized on July 22 on the hill called Tabor near Bechyně. It was followed, on September 17, by another great meeting, this time on a hill called Bzí, near Pilsen. Its dominating personality besides Nicholas of Hus was Wenceslas Koranda, priest at the parish church of Pilsen, one of the most fiery and uncompromising representatives of the Taborite spirit. Even so this meeting, as had the first one, remained a purely religious occasion.[6] But each succeeding meeting attracted larger numbers of people and took place a little nearer the capital. The third one was called to a hill called Na Křížkách (At the Crosses) near Benešov, only some twenty-five miles from Prague. There the people arrived in large crowds even on the eve of the appointed day (September 30). Thousands came from the south, thousands from Prague, some even from far Moravia. An especially strong delegation came from Pilsen, led by Wenceslas Koranda. The citizens of Rokycany, on the direct route from Pilsen to Benešov, were so frightened by their very number (and perhaps the rumors current about their fanaticism) that they closed their gates against the unarmed host and thereby forced them to take a long detour.[7]

The revolutionary character of the movement now revealed itself more clearly than ever before. It was most strikingly expressed by Koranda. He warned the people to be ready to defend their creed against the servants of Antichrist. "God's vineyard," he said, "is flourishing wonderfully; but the goats are nearing, who want to gnaw off all grapes." And so he continued: "The time to wander with the pilgrim's staff is over. Now we shall have to march, sword in hand."

This appeal to revolutionary activity was addressed to an audience which, this time, was no longer limited to peasants but contained large numbers of active, alert Prague citizens. Among them were the two leaders, both formerly of the King's court: Nicholas of Hus and John Žižka.[8] At this occasion, presumably, occurred the first meeting between Žižka and Koranda, between the pious soldier and the belligerent priest, which, at least for some time, bound them together in close cooperation.

Contact was established on this day not only between the leaders. The new mass friendship of Prague and Tabor was expressed by a strange gesture: when the Praguers returned to their city, other participants, many thousands of them, men, women, and children, went along with

[6] See *Archiv český*, p. 29. [7] Old Annalists, p. 29.
[8] Aeneas Sylvius, chapter 38, p. 79.

them in a sort of giant escort. Marching through the precinct of the castle on the Vyšehrad, where the royal garrison failed to stop them, the crowd arrived late at night in the New Town. There they had a joyous reception. Church bells were rung, and large torch-light processions formed, welcoming the brethren and sisters and escorting them to the monastery of St. Ambrose and other buildings which the city council requisitioned as lodgings for the multitude of unexpected guests.

Next day the leading men from both sides convened to deliberate and plan for the way ahead. From the course of these discussions[9] it seems clear that again Nicholas of Hus functioned as the guiding spirit, pressing, as far as he could, for action, supported by Žižka, Koranda, and John Želivský. The Taborite group urged the representatives of Prague to elect, in the name of the Law of God, a bishop—an act which would mean that all ties with the Church of Rome would voluntarily be cut by the Hussite community. The representatives of Prague, especially the masters of the University, refused. They still considered themselves as faithful sons of the true Church. Their objections blocked, at this stage, any action on such radical lines. Still less hopeful were proposals to elect somebody like a Roman "dictator" (*ducem saecularem*), a role for which Nicholas of Hus must have been the foremost or only candidate.

This conference thus ended without any practical results. Indeed it may have helped to make both sides more conscious of the differences between them. In addition the influx of Taborite elements in Prague led to some unwelcome incidents. Prague's magnificent churches excited the puritan iconoclasm of the Taborite peasants—men who had never seen such pomp and had been told that it was the mark of Romanist perversion, if not of Antichrist. They destroyed many paintings and statues in the Old Town church of St. Michael, whose parish priest was Christian of Prachatice, one of the most highly regarded Hussite priests, a master of the University and an old personal friend of Hus. Although the Taborites left the city soon afterwards, their visit ended on a less harmonious note than it had begun.

Even before the end of the meeting "at the Crosses" it had been decided to call another great mass meeting, with representatives from all parts of the Kingdom, in Prague itself for November 10. But dreading renewed unrest, the Queen and her chief adviser Čeněk of Wartenberg

[9] The course of the meeting is described in the report given by the Czech delegation to the Council of Basel in 1433, and is contained in Monumenta Conc. Basil. I, 387.

decided that no such meetings should be allowed in future. And in his attempt to safeguard "calm and order" the Lord High Burgrave went much further. He organized a conference of members of the high nobility—Calixtine and Romanist—together with representatives of the Old Town. At this occasion, on November 6, a formal alliance was concluded whose signatories undertook to help the Queen against anyone who tried to gain power in the state by force—presumably this was said in reference to Nicholas of Hus—or who disturbed the peace of the country.[10] To implement this program of internal pacification, Wartenberg took military precautions. He increased the royal guard by hiring large numbers of mercenaries, among them many Germans. He reinforced the garrison of the royal castle on Hradčany Hill by several hundred men, and on October 17 he occupied a number of strategic points, such as monastery buildings and other large houses, thus completely dominating the Small Side, that is the left bank of the Vltava, as well as the main artery between Prague and the west: the Charles Bridge. The Old Town, too, strengthened its military forces by hiring soldiers. Finally, strict orders were issued by the High Burgrave to prevent by force any Taborites from entering Prague for the planned meeting of November 10.

For the men in control of the New Town, and especially for Žižka as the city's captain, these measures sounded ominous. A force dominating the Old Town as well as the left bank of the river was, in itself, hard to resist. The order not to admit any Taborites into the town had also gone to the garrison of the other royal castle, the Vyšehrad, which geographically dominated the New Town. It could be expected that this strong fortress was the next to be reinforced, and that then the days of the present city council of the New Town, and with it of the determined reform movement in the capital, would be numbered. Žižka, in agreement with the New Town councilors, decided to prevent this. On October 25, at the head of a troop of New Town militia, he took the Vyšehrad. The garrison, as yet small and commanded by some of King Wenceslas' old courtiers, people whom Žižka knew well, ceded the stronghold without any resistance.[11]

[10] Among the signatories of this document (*Archiv český*, III, 208) was also Lord Victorin of Kunštat-Poděbrady, son of Lord Boček whom Žižka knew from the time of his activities in Matthew's guerilla band. Soon afterwards Victorin turned toward the Hussite side and became one of Žižka's closest friends.

[11] Tomek (*Žižka*, pp. 21, 22) thinks that Žižka, right up to this moment, had stayed in the royal service and only now, after the conquest of the Vyšehrad, joined the forces of the New Town. But this version is almost certainly based on a misinterpretation of Březová, whose report on this event (p. 348) is, indeed, unusually laconic and scanty. That Žižka led the

The occupation of the Vyšehrad was a stroke most characteristic of Žižka. It showed his presence of mind, his ability to act with dispatch. But it also showed his clear strategic vision. The Vyšehrad in the hands of the New Town largely compensated for the occupation by strong royal garrisons of the Hradčany and the Small Side. Now the New Town had its rear to the south and east free of all threats and could face any danger from the west with increased confidence.

With both sides thus poised for a showdown the date approached for the great Taborite meeting in Prague: November 10. In the west people from Pilsen, Domažlice, Klatovy and Sušice established a common route for their march. With this army of pilgrims, some 4,000 strong,[12] went one of the few barons who, so far, had joined the Taborite movement: Lord Břeněk Švihovský of Skála, a member of the great family of Riesenberg. To his armed retinue belonged two young knights: the brothers Chval and Kuneš of Machovice. Their escort enabled those pilgrims to reach Prague safely.

But not all the pilgrims were so lucky. Another, smaller group came from the south, from the town of Sezimovo Ústí. While they moved through the narrow Vltava valley, they were ambushed near Živohoust' by a superior force under Lord Peter of Sternberg, one of the Catholic nobles in the pay of Sigismund. Only after having suffered heavy casualties did part of this group reach Prague. Sternberg made many prisoners whom he sent to one of the centers of Anti-Hussitism: to Kutná Hora.

The news of this attack reached Prague on November 4 and caused fierce excitement. Storm bells were rung, and people crowded together in front of the city halls. The people of the Old Town were just as angry as those of the New Town, and it was to them that now Nicholas of Hus offered his services. They were accepted. Thus the troops of both Prague towns, under the leadership of Nicholas of Hus and Žižka, took up the challenge,[13] and went into action to open up free access to the city for all Taborite groups expected from the west.

---

attack upon the Vyšehrad is known to the Old Annalists as well as to Aeneas Sylvius, and he could not have done this had he not been in command of the New Town forces before.

[12] Březová, p. 350.

[13] Žižka's role is testified by the Old Annalists (p. 31) but not by Březová, who in this connection mentions only Nicholas of Hus. This might indicate that during the battles for the Small Side Nicholas did indeed play the leading role. Pekař (III, 27), on the other hand, concludes that Žižka did not take part in the fight but stayed with the defenders of the Vyšehrad. This would seem strange as the Vyšehrad, at this moment, was not attacked nor in danger of any attack, and as the New Town, in whose service Žižka stood, was the more revolutionary,

For this purpose they had to drive the Royalists from the Small Side, to regain a bridgehead on the left bank of the Vltava and thus to make sure of free passage over the Charles Bridge. They attacked, with great bravery, the strong positions especially at the so-called Saxon House, which guarded the western access to the bridge, the Archiepiscopal Palace, and other strongholds, not heeding the fire from guns which the Royalists had placed in those houses, and others which were aimed at them from the Castle. When night fell the defenders, unable to withstand the fierce onslaught, retired to the safety of the Hradčany, from which the Queen had fled to Kunratice immediately after the outbreak of the fight.

But the Royalists tried to retake the Small Side on the day after, and fierce fights went on for four more days, causing terrible devastation. At the battle's end the Saxon House was still firmly in the hands of the Praguers, and with it the control of both sides of the vital bridge. Žižka, so the Old Annalists say, fought so well that from this time on he was "everywhere in the people's mouth."[14]

Most of the great buildings of the Small Side were destroyed during those fights, indeed the whole borough was a shambles and deserted by the majority of its former (largely German) inhabitants. It had thus been turned, strategically, into a fairly open glacis for the bridgehead held by the troops of Prague. The immediate danger for the city was thus greatly reduced.

Yet this victory was inconclusive. Čeněk of Wartenberg remained in firm control of the Hradčany, from which he summoned reinforcements. On November 6 Prague received a challenge of war from thirty-five barons and about one hundred knights[15] and soon some royal towns, with Kutná Hora at their head, followed suit. In both camps, on the other hand, strong forces worked for agreement: in Prague the moderate elements led by the University; and up on the Hradčany those

---

more active of the Prague cities. Březová, incidentally, does not mention Žižka's part in the storming of the Carthusian monastery either, but in that case Pekař did not draw the same conclusions.

14 "Vzat jest ot lidu na slovo." The phrase, somewhat difficult to translate verbally, has caused some dispute among Czech historians. The Annalists go on to say: "for it was there that he began to wage war." Pekař reasons (see above note 13) that therefore the whole remark should actually refer to Žižka's part in the defenestration. I am inclined to think with F. M. Bartoš, who has devoted a small article to this question (in *Jihočeský Sborník historický*, VI, no. 3) that this is an unnecessary construction. The Annalists' remark about Žižka's beginning to wage war seems quite fitting, as the fight for the Small Side is indeed the real beginning of the Hussite wars if not of the Hussite Revolution. It has, of course, to be admitted that in general the Old Annalists are not as reliable a source as Březová.

15 *Archiv český*, IV, 375ff.

leaders who adhered to the Utraquist creed. They had little difficulty in convincing the Lord High Burgrave that it would, in the interest of Hussitism, be dangerous to weaken too much the power of Prague.

On November 9 a provisional truce was declared, followed four days later by a solemn armistice concluded till April 23, 1420. In this document[16] the Queen and the lords of her party bound themselves to ensure that the freedom of Hussite worship, especially the free Communion in both kinds, not be infringed; while the Prague cities promised that no more attacks should be made upon churches, monasteries, or statues of saints, and that those responsible for such acts, the Taborite pilgrims, should leave the city. This seemed a fair enough agreement, but the Royalists pressed for, and received, one additional concession: the Vyšehrad was to be restored to them.

The surrender, without any fight and without absolute need, of this great castle changed very materially the balance of forces. It reestablished the situation in which the city was exposed to the pressure of the two powerful fortress-districts in the west and in the south. The time was not far off when the folly of this step would be apparent to Prague's citizens, but for the moment the longing for peace prevailed over the warnings of those who could see farther.

Of these, Žižka was the foremost. It was he who had gained the Vyšehrad for the New Town. The surrender of the castle was a personal defeat for him as well as a grave mistake. He was not the man to bear quietly this rebuff. He decided to part ways with Prague.

But the surrender of the castle was not the only reason for Žižka's decision. We hear from a reliable witness that he did not want to underwrite an agreement of peace with people whom he regarded as the enemies of God and His Law.[17] It was, then, not only a question of strategic judgment or personal prestige but also a question of principle that motivated him.[18]

As his new center of action Žižka chose Pilsen, accepting the offer that the Hussite community of that town extended to him through its

16 *Urkundliche Beiträge zur Geschichte des Hussitenkrieges*, ed. F. Palacký, Prague 1873, I, 11. (Quoted hereafter as *Urk. Beiträge.*)

17 ". . . treugas pacis cum eisdem (sc. regalibus) nullomodo tamquam cum dei et sue legis inimicis inire volendo." Březová, p. 356.

18 Pekař (III, 28, 29) tries to confront Žižka, in this situation, with what he thinks was the majority of the Czech nation who wanted peace whereas Žižka supposedly wanted to continue the revolutionary fight at any price and without regard to the national interest. This seems an undue simplification of the situation as well as of Žižka's motives. Any attempt to separate, at this stage, the national from the religious motives must be misleading.

undisputed leader: Wenceslas Koranda. Pilsen, the natural center of western Bohemia, was then also one of the leading centers of Hussitism. Among the five towns which, in the myth of the chiliastic fanatics, would escape destruction, Pilsen—the city of the sun, as it was called—stood first. It was from here that the movement had radiated to other towns especially in the south and southwest of Pilsen, such as Sušice, Klatovy, and Domažlice. Its strategic position, too, was of great importance, as all the important roads entering Bohemia from the west, from Bavaria or Franconia, converged upon the city. Thus it seemed a good place to build what obviously could not now be built in Prague: a strong bulwark of the party that stood for armed resistance to Sigismund.

For these plans Žižka found allies and more than that: the small cadre of a fighting force ready to follow him as a person regardless of the position he held. It was the little troop originally led to Prague by Lord Břeněk of Skála. On their march to Pilsen they were joined by another member of the high nobility, Lord Valkoun of Adlar, as well as by the two knights of Machovice, Chval and Kuneš. It would be wrong to think that the two barons formally acknowledged Žižka as their superior. He had not yet achieved a fame which would make it possible for a member of the high nobility to serve under him without loss of face. But his personality was strong enough to establish his leadership without such formality, and upon his arrival at Pilsen Žižka, supported by Koranda, was appointed as captain of the town's military forces.

Žižka's arrival at Pilsen, after the middle of November, turned the region around this town immediately into one of the theaters of the continuing war, if only on a small scale.[19] He himself avoided any action against those of the royalist party who belonged to the Hussite faith, thus honoring, in spirit, at least that part of the armistice to which, from his religious position, he could agree. Also he could not consider himself strong enough for any major enterprise, whereas the Royalists seemed to increase their strength all the time. Soon they started attacks upon Hussite groups in widely separated parts of the country, feeling that, with the power of Prague neutralized, they could deal now much more easily with the hated heretics.

Most active in these attempts at quick annihilation of Hussitism was the great city of Kutná Hora. In this predominantly German mining

[19] See Březová, p. 357.

community the national and the religious sentiment combined to create a fanatical hatred of the Hussite movement. Persecution of heretics had started early but for a while had been kept in limits by the influence of the royal mint master, Peter Zmrzlík of Svojšín, a patriotic Czech, a friend of John Hus and altogether one of the most attractive, most humane personalities of the time. But after Wenceslas' death Sigismund relieved him from that position. He was replaced by Nicholas of Jemniště, a reliable and even fanatical Anti-Hussite. Under him—whose methods soon earned him the nickname "Divoký" (the Fierce)—the persecution of Hussites immediately took the most atrocious forms. Any adherent of the Chalice who fell into the hands of the Kutnohorians, no matter what age or sex, was killed, and not satisfied with this, the townspeople set a price on the heads of captured Hussites.[20] Czech people who lived in the town's vicinity were terrorized or bribed into betraying anyone suspected of heresy. Without trial these people were executed, and when the town's hangman got too overworked the Hussites were thrown into some of the abandoned mineshafts where, if the fall had not killed them, they were starved to death. Within a relatively short period large numbers of people were murdered in this way—over 1,600 according to one source, over 5,000 according to another. Among them were also the pilgrims from Sezimovo Ústí whom Peter of Sternberg had taken prisoner on November 4. And to add insult to injury the deepest of those mineshafts, containing hundreds of dead bodies, was derisively named Tabor.[21]

The Taborite movement, however, was not easily defeated. An important step toward its consolidation took place just about this time in the lower Lužnice district in south-central Bohemia. The region could boast only few and rather small towns, among them Sezimovo Ústí. This town belonged to the Lords of Ústí and Kamenice, a family that, like many others, was divided over the religious question. During the winter one of the lords, Ulrich, tried to suppress Hussitism in the town by wholesale expulsions and other violent methods, but in February 1420 a large number of Taborites, led by a former sexton, John Hro-

[20] One threescore of groše for laymen, five for priests—rather considerable sums which cannot have failed to lead to widespread denunciation. See the next footnote.

[21] Our most detailed source for these occurrences is a long letter which the city government of Prague, in their attempt to win allies against Sigismund, wrote on July 10, 1420, to the Doge and Council of the Republic of Venice. This letter, interesting for many reasons, stresses particularly the nationalist hatred of the Kutnohorian Germans. See *Urk. Beiträge*, I, 41.

mádka, were able to regain possession of it.[22] They felt, however, that the town, situated rather low in the valley, was difficult to defend. Near the town there was an old fortress, now largely deserted, called Hradiště (bulwark), on a steep hill surrounded on three sides by the waters of the Lužnice River and one of its tributaries. This fortress, too, belonged to one of the Anti-Hussites among the Lords of Ústí who had just begun repairs to make it a stronghold against the Taborites of Sezimovo Ústí. He was too late. With the help of his own brother, a Hussite, his weak resistance was quickly overcome, and virtually all inhabitants of Sezimovo Ústí, together with those who every day came to join the new Taborite community, moved up to the hill of Hradiště. Provisional fortifications and shelter were provided as fast as lumber could be brought up or tents erected. It was fortunate that the winter was unusually mild and by February had turned to spring. To demonstrate their firm resolve never to return, the people of Sezimovo Ústí delivered their town to the flames.

John Hromádka and the priests who had joined him, some already at Sezimovo Ústí, others at Hradiště, felt that this was to be the final center of the Taborite movement. The original name, Hradiště, was still in use for some time, but more and more it was replaced by the name which had identified the movement before. From now on the religious movement and the new settlement remained firmly tied together by the common name: Tabor.

Determined to make their settlement militarily strong, the elders of the new community turned to the man whom the people of Sezimovo Ústí had seen in the foreground of the fight for God's Law during their last, dangerous pilgrimage to the capital early in November. They sent a message to Žižka informing him of the capture and settlement of Hradiště and asking him for help. Žižka responded in a generous way. He ordered his most trusted officer, Chval of Machovice, to proceed from Pilsen to Tabor with a sizable part of the forces at his disposal.

We left Žižka when, soon after his arrival at Pilsen, he was appointed the town's captain. The city itself remained under the domination of Koranda, who now felt strong enough to bring the whole town and district into line with his ideas. In and near Pilsen some monasteries as well as churches built to the honor of saints were destroyed by him and his followers, and the monks as well as other Anti-Hussite in-

[22] The religious family quarrels among the Lords of Ústí are too complicated and too insignificant to be related here in detail.

habitants of the town were expelled. Koranda seems to have acted on his own and without Žižka's cooperation.[23] Žižka could hardly object to these acts as such. He had done much the same, and the time was not far when, learning about the mass murders of Kutná Hora, he would no longer spare the lives of those for whom he entertained a special hatred: the monks. Yet he probably did object to the fact that priests by such acts took charge of warlike enterprises instead of leaving them to the soldier. This may have been one of the reasons for a message which Lord Břeněk and he sent, sometime in February 1420, to the masters of Prague University asking them whether priests, and under what conditions other people, might use the force of arms to defend the faith. The answer,[24] given on February 17, emphatically denied the right of priests to fight or join in battles. But the University admitted in cautious terms that laymen, if there was no other way out, might wage a purely defensive war for the creed. This action, incidentally not the first one of this kind,[25] shows that the leaders of militant Hussitism did not slide into this war without deliberation and moral scruples; it also proves the respect which men like Žižka had for the masters of the University, the men on whom the mantle of Hus had fallen. The incident may well have provided the first cause for the incipient alienation between the two men—Žižka and Koranda—which, however, came into the open only later.

Even before this exchange of messages between Pilsen and Prague the Royalist forces of the Pilsen district, being unable to attack the city itself, had begun a small scale war against the outlying domains of Pilsen. The leader of these troops was Lord Bohuslav of Švamberg (Schwanenberg), member of a powerful Czech-Catholic family who owned the castle of Krasikov, a stronghold about five miles to the northwest of Pilsen. Being in the direct pay of Sigismund he ravaged all Hussite possessions near Pilsen, causing the town considerable material damage and killing many people. We know little about the skirmishes that developed out of these attacks with one exception: sometime in

[23] "Ad induccionem ergo sacerdotum et precipue Wenceslai d. Coranda, qui pro tunc inter ipsos capitalis erat, monasteria civitatis ipsius et ecclesie curieque certe civitati adiacentes destruuntur et diruuntur." (Březová, p. 356.)

[24] Printed in Bartoš, *Do ctyř artykulů* (Prague 1926). See Pekař, I, 98, 99, and also 243, n. 2. Even though Pekař is probably right in thinking that the address of the answer refers to Lord Břeněk this does not exclude the co-authorship of Žižka in the question. See also Jaroslav Prokeš, *Jan Žižka z Trocnova*, Prague 1920, p. 51.

[25] A similar answer had been given before by the two masters, Jacobellus of Stříbro and Christian of Prachatice, to the request of two priests to decide in a dispute between them. Palacký's theory that this first query, too, was made on the request of Žižka and Nicholas of Hus, supposedly in November 1419, is no longer considered valid. See Prokeš, *op.cit.*, p. 47.

December Švamberg, at the head of fairly strong troops, tried to trap Žižka when the latter made a sortie against a Royalist fort called Nekměř, a little to the north of Pilsen. Confident of his strong superiority Švamberg attacked, but was beaten back with heavy losses by Žižka's men who had with them seven wagons "on which there were those snakes (guns) with which they destroy walls."[26] Švamberg's men may not have been used to the thunder of guns, or perhaps they were frightened by the fierce fanaticism of the defenders. The skirmish of Nekměř had, as such, no great significance. But it is the first time that our sources reveal the use made by Žižka of a new weapon: the war wagon.

So far things had not gone badly for Žižka's plan to turn Pilsen into the main bastion of his party. Yet early in 1420 difficulties began to arise. Pilsen, just as Prague, had its group of moderates or conservatives who only grudgingly endured the rule of the fanatic priest Koranda. Many of those who had believed his prophecies that Christ's Kingdom on earth was to come in the middle of February 1420, turned away from him when the date passed eventlessly. The sullen mood of a growing faction in the town turned into open hostility when, by the end of February, the enemy troops outside Pilsen received strong reinforcements, enabling them to block several of the roads connecting the city with the rest of the country.

It was then that Žižka received the request of Tabor for help. He knew that by fulfilling this demand he was weakening his defensive strength. Most likely he knew, even then, that he would not be able to hold Pilsen indefinitely. By strengthening Tabor now he could hope to insure the future of the Taborite movement, securing for it a permanent stronghold. This new bulwark of the faith would not, as Prague and Pilsen, be subject to the changing moods of a citizenry which stood only halfheartedly behind the fight for the Chalice.

Yet, whatever he expected of the future—he was not yet ready to give up Pilsen. He could have little doubt that, by winning this large and geographically so important city, the Royalists would gain a tremendous advantage. Indeed all through the later war Pilsen, in the hands of the Royalists, was to be a thorn in the side of Hussite Bohemia.

Meanwhile the pressure grew. By early March the Royalist army had

[26] Old Annalists, p. 32. The statement, in this chronicle, that Žižka had 300 men and Švamberg 2,000 seems to me open to suspicion, all the more as it happens to be almost exactly the relationship between both sides which is reported, more credibly, of the later battle of Sudoměř. Statements on the numbers of troops in this war have, of course, almost always to be taken with caution.

invested the city, slowly closing the ring around it. Žižka was still in contact with some of his friends in Prague. They advised him to negotiate. The commander of the Royalists was then Lord Wenceslas of Dubá, the man who once had conducted and shielded John Hus on his way to Constance. By now, as Lord Chamberlain, he had become one of Sigismund's trusted followers, but he was not averse to gaining by negotiation what he could otherwise only achieve by heavy sacrifice.

Žižka proffered his conditions: the Communion in the two kinds should be freely allowed in Pilsen to all who wanted to take it, without any pressure or punishment. Those who decided to leave the city, soldiers with their arms, but also other men with their families, should not be molested. It was to be an armistice binding, under the usual guaranties, upon the whole Royalist party.[27]

Dubá accepted. In or about March 20 the agreement was signed. Under the guaranty of free worship the majority of the Hussites in Pilsen preferred to stay. Only a limited number of determined followers decided to accompany Žižka and his small army to the new home, the town built on the salutary mountain, Tabor. Some of them, before departing, burned their valuables on the market place of Pilsen.

It must have been with a heavy heart that Žižka turned his back to the town which he had entered, full of hope, five months before. Again, as once before in Prague, his expectations had been thwarted. But he was not beaten, and he had not lost his firm confidence in the victory of what was, to him, God's own fight. Great tasks, so he knew, awaited him at Tabor. There finally, God would help him to create the power needed to defend His sacred Law.

[27] Březová, p. 359.

# CHAPTER 6

## ŽIŽKA AT TABOR

It was a strange and fateful expedition that set out from Pilsen on March 22 or 23 1420, to reach the safety of Tabor. There were just 400 men, all armed, but some of them only poorly. Since the skirmish of Nekměř, Žižka had added five more to his little train of gun-carrying wagons of which he had now twelve. There were some other wagons with supplies, and on them traveled also the wives and children of soldiers. The leaders were, besides Žižka himself, Lord Břeněk of Skála, Wenceslas Koranda, and another Taborite priest, Markhold of Zbraslavice, a bachelor of Prague University. Only these four and five lesser leaders were mounted.

The calendar showed the beginning of spring, but the season was unusually far advanced, and as they set out through the soft hills of western Bohemia, they saw fruit trees blossom out as if it were May.[1] Those who thought that the time was ripe for extraordinary things to happen were confirmed in their belief by this strange whim of nature. They were not destined to reach their goal without fighting. The solemn armistice concluded at Pilsen was not kept by the Royalists. Messengers had been sent out secretly from Pilsen to inform the King's followers all over the country of the impending march of the little troop which would surely be at the mercy of any strong force sent against them.

Two Royalist groups answered the call. One came from the east, where Kutná Hora raised the strongest contingent, commanded by the town's mint master, Nicholas Divoký. On their westward march they met smaller detachments led by two barons: John Městecký of Opočno and Peter of Sternberg. Anticipating the route which Žižka's little troop was going to travel, the allies forcibly occupied Písek, the city that had first taken its stand with Prague at the outbreak of the revolution.

There the Royalists from the east were joined by three leading Catholic barons of western Bohemia—Bohuslav of Švamberg, the same whom Žižka had fought at Nekměř, Hanuš of Kolovraty of a family which

[1] See R. Hennig, *Katalog bemerkenswerter Witterungsverhältnisse*, Berlin 1904.

played a leading role in western Bohemia for centuries, and Henry of Hradec, grand master of the order of the Knights of St. John at Strakonice.

The Royalist troop altogether numbered some 2,000 men,[2] most of whom, lords, knights, and retainers, were mounted and in heavy armor. The people in the neighborhood called them the "Iron Lords." Against them Žižka's small troop of 400 footsoldiers seemed, indeed, in a hopeless position.

Sometime in the morning of March 25 having marched past Strakonice through the small town of Štěkeň, Žižka crossed the Otava River at a ford near the village of Sudoměř. Soon after, passing through Sudoměř in a southerly direction, he saw the enemy approaching in two columns. His main aim now was to find a position where the terrain would favor his defense. This, however, was not easy, as the Otava valley is, in this region, fairly wide and flat. He could not hope to reach, in time, the wooded hills fringing the valley to the south. There was, however, to the southeast of the village, a number of fishponds which at that time were empty. Žižka decided to use the dam of one of them[3] as a cover for one of his flanks. To his other flank and rear he posted his wagons. Thus he could concentrate his small troop in some depth on a very short front, which gave the enemy no chance fully to employ their superior strength.

The battle began in the mid-afternoon and lasted for several hours. After the first waves of the Royalist assault had been beaten off, the enemy had no alternative but to dismount and try to win the day in a hand-to-hand fight. At one time they nearly succeeded in breaching the line of wagons and damaged two or three of them. But just then it grew dark and in the ensuing melee it became difficult for the attackers to tell friend from foe. The Old Annalist who has left us the most detailed report on the battle[4] says that finally the Royalist lines were hopelessly muddled and that, confounded by the sudden dark in which their weapons met the strong armor of their own fellow-combatants, they exclaimed: "My pike does not pierce, my sword does not cut and my crossbow does not shoot."[5] Thus they finally stopped the assault and retreated, while Žižka, as then was usual for the victor, camped that night on the battlefield.

[2] *Chronicon veteris Collegiati Pragensis*, ed. Höfler, *Geschichtschreiber der husitischen Bewegung*, I, 79, mentions 2,000 horsemen alone.

[3] The Old Annalists (p. 35) mention the name of the pond, Škaredý. It still exists today under the same name.

[4] *op.cit.*, p. 33. [5] *ibid.*

Both sides had fought with grim determination. Accordingly losses were heavy. Among the dead was, on each side, one of the leaders. Žižka's noble friend, Břeněk of Skála, fell during the height of the battle, while of the Royalist lords Henry of Hradec was fatally wounded. Before they had to retire, the Royalists had succeeded in cutting off and surrounding a small body of Žižka's troop, about thirty men, whom Nicholas Divoký ordered to be taken to Kutná Hora. Žižka, on the morning after the battle, proceeded eastward to the town of Týn, crossed the Vltava and then camped in the open, awaiting the arrival of a troop from Tabor which was to escort them to their new haven.

The battle of Sudoměř, though a small affair in the military terms even of that time, was of importance for the development of the Hussite revolution.[6] The Royalist attempt to nip in the bud the rise of a new center of radical Hussitism had been thwarted. Žižka's prestige in Bohemia rose for his success against the determined onslaught by so superior a force. For the first time the use of the war wagons—which, at Nekměř, had just only seemed a helpful expedient in an emergency—appeared as part of a system of tactics by which the long-established superiority of the cavalry over the foot soldier could be challenged. The defense, tactically, became stronger than the attack. Žižka himself fought with supreme bravery, was always in the thick of the fight, and had the gift of inspiring others by his example. But in the eyes of many Hussites it was God's own interference that saved the little army. The sudden fall of dark was a miracle reported in undoubting terms by the Old Annalists.

It was as a leader blessed and helped by God that Žižka was greeted by the Taborite troop that met him in the field near Týn to escort him to safety, and later by the few thousand people who, lining the streets formed by small, primitive wooden houses and huts, greeted the newcomers upon their entry into Hradiště-Tabor. The arrival of newcomers, some of them from rather faraway places, was a normal occurrence during the first months of Tabor's existence. But the arrival of Žižka, the man who had just beaten the "Iron Lords," was an assurance of success bound to open a new chapter in the history of the young community.

We have called the early Tabor a community. This it was, indeed, in the vaguest and most general sense of the word. It was a spiritual

[6] A monograph on the battle of Sudoměř, written by J. V. Šimák, can be found in *Sborník Žižkův*, ed. Urbánek, Prague 1924, pp. 75-81.

movement with strong emotional force but as yet ill-defined aims and organization. Its many meetings had been imposing in the masses of people they attracted and the force of their religious fervor. Most of the speakers were priests and it was they who, quite naturally, exerted their leadership from the beginning. The only layman who at an early stage played a generally acknowledged role in the movement was Nicholas of Hus. But he seems to have had little to do with the original founding of the fortress town of Hradiště-Tabor, and it is doubtful whether he was there at the time of Žižka's arrival.[7] In any case things underwent a rapid change at Tabor as soon as Žižka had made it his headquarters and went to work.

Clear-headed leadership was badly needed. For if the Taborite movement was to be an efficient force in the fight for reform, it could no longer remain an amorphous community. It had to be welded into a functioning organism, with bones and sinews within, and the crust of armored protection without.

Žižka could not expect, nor did he intend, to change the basically theocratic character of the community. That the fight was for the Law of God, that the Law of God should be the Law of the Taborite brethren also in their everyday life, this was as obvious to him as it was to the priests. He did not, therefore, attempt to interfere with the rule of the priests in what could be called the purely civilian administration of the town, including the managing of its financial affairs. The conduct of the war, however, was a different thing. And "the war" was not just military operations, it involved decisions on how many people were to be enlisted, who was to be fought, who to be helped or taken as an ally, with whom and under what conditions an armistice was to be concluded—in short it included all the decisions constituting the foreign policy of the little commonwealth.

To what extent should the priests be allowed to influence this vast field of problems? This question played a considerable role not only at Tabor, but everywhere else in the Hussite camp. From the beginning Žižka's stand was to limit the role of the priests to what was theirs under the Law of God. This, however, was but a principle. In its practical application the line was difficult to draw, and was bound to be an issue of controversies.

[7] After the armistice of November 13 Nicholas too had left Prague. With a small group of his soldiers he occupied the Zelená Hora (green mountain), a hill fortress near Nepomuk to which he gave the Biblical name Mount Olive. There are, however, no reports that he took any part in the fights for and around Pilsen, nor is it known how long he stayed there.

It was on or around April 8 that the community of Tabor was called together to elect four captains "whom they would obey."[8] The number was rather traditional and probably based on the division of the town into four quarters functioning as electoral districts, without, however, limiting the authority of each captain to any one district.[9] Rather did the captains themselves decide in common about the functions each of them had to fulfill. The sequence in which their names appear in the chronicles and documents indicates their difference in rank. From the formula "whom they (the Taborites) would obey," it is obvious, as it is also from the general usage of the word at the time, that the office of captain (capitaneus, in Czech "hejtman") was not purely a military one. Later, through 1422, Žižka is called and calls himself director or regent ("správce") of the Taborite people,[10] indicating even more clearly that his functions were political and administrative as well as military. The expression "Taborite people" has to be understood as including all brethren, that is all the adherents of Tabor, especially all the communities that later acknowledged Tabor's leadership.

The four men elected as Taborite captains early in April 1420 were: Nicholas of Hus, Žižka, Zbyněk of Buchov, and Chval of Machovice, in that order. The election of the first-named (which may even have occurred in his absence) can be understood as the confirmation of his role as the oldest and most widely known lay leader of the movement. Zbyněk of Buchov (often called Buchovec), coming from a family of squires of central Bohemia, was an able officer who had joined the Taborite movement and come to Hradiště some time before the arrival of Žižka. The man nearest to Žižka among his cocaptains was Chval Řepický of Machovice, who had been his faithful follower ever since he had joined him in Prague in the fall of 1419.[11]

During the following period Nicholas of Hus and Žižka generally functioned as the senior officers, the two others as their deputies. On occasion majority decisions were reached.[12] Žižka and Nicholas of Hus divided their functions to some extent so that, during most of the remainder of 1420, Nicholas was considered the main political leader, whereas Žižka was responsible for the military organization and leadership of the Taborite army. In fact it was he who created this force.

[8] Březová (p. 362): "ad quos respectum haberent."

[9] H. Toman, *Husitské válečnictví za doby Žižkovy a Prokopovy* (Hussite warfare in the times of Žižka and Prokop), Prague 1898, pp. 86-88.

[10] See Appendix: *passim*.

[11] See Chapter 5 above.

[12] Toman, *op.cit.*, p. 91.

Strictly speaking, Žižka's military organization and its fighting methods can hardly be said to have developed in any one phase of the war. Some significant features of this work go back to the first period, from the street fighting in Prague to the battle of Sudoměř. Other changes came about much later, especially in 1423 when Žižka felt the need of organizing his military power on a new basis in a different region of Bohemia. Yet it was the phase immediately after his arrival at Tabor that brought about the most important innovations. Thus it seems possible to regard this relatively short period: from March 27, 1420, when Žižka arrived at Tabor, till May 18, when he left the town at the head of a strong army, as the time of the actual birth of this new military power. It therefore may be convenient, at this moment, to describe it briefly, even though a more thorough discussion of some of its aspects and of Žižka's achievements in this field, will have to follow later.[13]

If there was any general principle dominating Žižka's work of creating a new military organization it was this: to disregard the traditions of centuries, and to use to the best advantage whatever manpower and arms were available.

Manpower and its origin was the prime consideration. In every great war which Žižka knew of or had taken part in, the superiority of the mounted and armored knights had been taken for granted. No medieval king could have dared to challenge a strong enemy without an army that contained at least many hundred horse, if possible several thousand. It was obvious that Sigismund, when he tried to establish his right to his kingdom by force, would have more than just a few thousand. And as yet the Royalist party among the Czechs, being led by an important section of the old nobility, was strong in this very way.

Žižka had to recruit his forces from an entirely different background. Of the inhabitants of Tabor who could carry weapons, some were

[13] The short general description which follows here seems necessary for the understanding of the military side of the events to be told, but I have not gone into details as to the technical development of Hussite weapons. The necessary discussion of Žižka as a military organizer and field commander will, of course, follow as events unfold, with some special emphasis upon his offensive use of field artillery in Chapter 18, and the reader will find a summarizing evaluation of Žižka the general in Chapter 29. As to the literature on the subject, the first critical modern treatment, meant to refute some exaggerated claims of older historians, was Max v. Wulf's *Die Hussitische Wagenburg*, Berlin 1889. The only truly thorough treatment of the material, still valuable though obsolete in some special aspects, is Toman's *Husitské válečnictví*, cited above in note 9. (For the issues discussed in this chapter see particularly pp. 150-280). For a somewhat less technical and more historical treatment see O. Frankenberger, *Naše veliká armáda*, Prague 1921, and R. Urbánek, *Žižka a husitské válečnictví*, in *Sborník Žižkův*, Prague 1924. A recent popular treatment, enlivened by excellent illustrations, is contained in E. Wagner, *Jak válčili Husité* (How the Hussites waged war), Prague 1946.

townsmen, little artisans from the burned town of Sezimovo Ústí, and some others who had left their home towns to live on the salutary mountain. Some, perhaps most of these, had traditional arms of the time, pikes, crossbows, and swords. But an even larger part of those whom religious fervor had brought to Tabor were peasants. Most of them, when asked to bring along what weapons they had, would provide clubs or, even more frequently, the flails which they used to thresh their grain. These, in close combat, would provide a formidable weapon when wielded by strong arms. To make them more effective their swipples were studded with iron spikes. As flails were so easily available to a peasant levy, the men thus armed became a regular troop (cepníci), as against those who regularly served as pike or lance bearers (sudličníci).[14] As the war went on battle flails were not only improvised from old threshing flails but also manufactured as war weapons. A third group of soldiers, more likely to be recruited from townsmen or gentry, were the archers with their crossbows.[15]

By making use of all these weapons, Žižka could employ the rather large numbers of men who, in that phase of the war, voluntarily joined his army. But even a large infantry troop could not normally expect to withstand, let alone defeat, any concentration of armed power provided with the usual strength in heavy (armored) and light cavalry. Here again Žižka devised an unorthodox innovation. In Poland he had seen strong, heavily armored cavalry defeated in their attempt to attack or storm a static fortress. And his experience in "guerilla" warfare had taught him the importance of the terrain, the fact that a naturally strong position increases and occasionally multiplies the strength of the defender against an assaulting force. Both advantages were of course limited to static defense. The problem, to Žižka, was to combine the advantages of strong defensive positions with mobility.

The device which Žižka introduced into the development of military art was the war wagon. It was to play a dominant role in many wars all through the fifteenth century and returned to importance in later times whenever conditions were similar, such as in the use of wagons for defense purposes by American pioneers trekking westward, or by the African Dutch in the Boer War.

Was it Žižka who "invented" the war wagon and its employment in the movable "wagon-fortress"? Armies had, of course, made use of wheeled vehicles ever since ancient times for transportation as well as

[14] O. Frankenberger, *op.cit.*, I, 38, 39, 217.

[15] See appendix: Žižka's Battle Song, stanza 4, ll. 1 and 2.

for actual combat (for example in old Persia). But their systematic use as a movable fortress is not clearly documented until the fifteenth century.

The number of wagons used in Žižka's first engagements was small: seven in the first, twelve in the second one. And the wagons themselves were still quite primitive. Like the battle flails, they began as improvisations: regular peasant carts on four wheels, sturdy, made of strong wood and thus giving some protection, but still quite vulnerable. The army which Žižka led north in May had already a large number of wagons though we have no precise knowledge of their number for that campaign. For many ensuing campaigns we have that information and can see very clearly the growing importance of the war wagon until, toward the end of Žižka's life, something like a fixed relationship is reached between the size of an army and the number of its wagons—a relationship which could be considered an optimum and was maintained throughout the later years, long after Žižka's death.[16]

During this time the wagons were improved in various ways. The most important addition was a heavy board suspended from the top on one side of the wagon and giving the people who stood behind it an armor-like additional protection. Other movable boards were used to protect the wheels and to stabilize the wagon in the center between the wheels. Furthermore, when formed into a camp-fortress, the gaps between the wagons were closed by using a special type of heavy shield. The movable fortress that could be put up quickly wherever wanted, mostly on hills, with ditches dug outside the rectangle formed by the wagons much like the Roman legionaries put up their castrum, was practically impregnable. The history of Žižka's later campaigns will show how this basically defensive device did, nevertheless, plays its essential role also in offensive warfare.

The adoption of the war wagon had immediate consequences beyond the technical aspect, by influencing the tactical rules of combat. Medieval war had been largely individual combat, battles essentially tournaments *en masse*, fought with the purpose of killing the foe instead of merely throwing him off saddle. The ideas of battle discipline, of forming tactical bodies and of submitting to the rules of battle organization were alien to the medieval knight who, collecting his retainers under his own banner, would pick his enemy according to his own choice or whim. Battles tended to become melees and there was little opportunity for rational leadership, for superior generalship, to assert itself.

[16] Toman, *op.cit.*, pp. 208ff.

The army which Žižka organized from volunteers of peasant and townsmen background would not, in itself, be inclined to act much differently. A measure of obedience might result from their socially inferior status, as all their leaders were noblemen. But from this social submissiveness to actual military discipline under combat conditions was a wide enough step. The introduction of the war wagon went far in bringing about this change. If those wagons had to be maintained in good fighting condition, had to be quickly put into battle position, had to be defended effectively, then a clear division of function between the members of the crew—up to eighteen in number—became a necessity which would be easily understood. Equally if a Taborite army moved, with the wagons ever ready to be formed into an armed camp, or when it lined up in battle position, the need for adequate defense of each part of the encampment demanded that not only the wagon crews but every other troop play its role according to certain regulations which had to be systematic and rational.[17] Thus the Taborite army, in the way Žižka formed it, acquired a degree of rational subdivision, tactical organization, and actual battle cooperation far beyond anything used before in medieval warfare.[18] Stern punishment was threatened for any breach of this discipline.

By no means the least, and perhaps the most lasting change which Žižka helped to start was the development of field artillery. It was, again, closely connected with the introduction of the war wagon. Of the battle of Nekměř the old chronicler tells us that on his seven wagons Žižka "carried those snakes [an old Czech term for guns] with which they destroy walls." The expression shows that at that time only siege artillery was a weapon familiar to average people. The use of artillery in static warfare had, indeed, been developed to quite some extent in the second half of the fourteenth century, but the weight and clumsiness of these oldest guns severely limited their use for other than static warfare, and wherever they were tried out as a weapon in mobile warfare they had still only played a very modest part, even at Grunwald where both sides employed guns of various types in some numbers. In Žižka's army, guns were used to an increasing extent, on the war wagons, where two or three hand-pieces were carried together with a large number of crossbows, as well as heavier guns on special gun-carriages. At first their effectiveness was, even at this stage, rather a moral

17 See the regulations in Appendix, x.

18 See the discussion of this question by Wulf, *op.cit.*, and Toman's reply, *op.cit.*, pp. 259, 260.

than a material one: the thunderous noise of the exploding powder harmed the enemy's nerves more than the stone balls were apt to harm their bodies or those of their horses. But as early as 1421 we have reports which clearly show the direct influence of artillery in battle and the use Žižka made of it.[19] From those battles only dates the use of field artillery in the full tactical sense.

The period from late March to mid-May 1420, a little over seven weeks, saw just the beginning of this tremendous change. Žižka did not spend all this time within the walls of Tabor. If he wanted his army to be prepared for major tasks at an early date the one and only way was to subject it to a training which was "the real thing." The idea of military education by exercise on training grounds did not exist at the time, and would have seemed ridiculous to his soldiers. Žižka trained them by starting his own little war against Royalist enemies. As early as April 5 he organized a raid against the town of Vožice, some ten miles to the northeast of Tabor. To that little town, which lay under the protection of one of the royal castles, Nicholas Divoký, mint master of Kutná Hora, had retired with his own troops after the battle of Sudoměř. It was in the dark of the early morning that Žižka began the assault. The garrison, taken by surprise, resisted only weakly. The majority with their commander Nicholas Divoký retreated behind the walls of the castle which Žižka had no intention of scaling. Yet the enemy's losses were considerable. They included a fair number of prisoners which Žižka, upon his return to Tabor, offered to exchange for the thirty odd of his own men whom Nicholas had captured at Sudoměř. The exchange was effected and saved the lives of the Taborite soldiers who otherwise would have found a terrible end in the mine shafts of Kutná Hora. No less profitable was the booty which Žižka took: there were arms and, even more important, many riding horses. Upon his return to Tabor Žižka put them to immediate use, training young townsmen, perhaps also some peasants, in the art of mounted fighting and thus adding a small troop of cavalry to his growing force.[29] Armed with crossbows they were to serve as scouts, but in the later development Taborite cavalry, though never given the central role it had in the armies of Žižka's enemies, gained some real importance especially as flank cover for his army on the march and in battle.

A few days later another raid was directed against the little castle of Sedlec, residence of Lord Ulrich of Ústí, the man who had tried so hard

[19] Březová, p. 533. [20] Březová, p. 362, and Aeneas Sylvius, p. 84.

to prevent, by use of force, the town of Sezimovo Ústí from joining the Taborite movement. Žižka's soldiers, many of them former townsmen of Sezimovo Ústí, took bloody vengeance. Lord Ulrich and all his retainers were killed. Six prisoners were told that if one of them was prepared to decapitate his five comrades, his life would be spared. A man named Pinta volunteered to undertake the slaughter, and was actually permitted to join the Taborite army. If our source[21] gives us no reason to think that this was actually on Žižka's order, he certainly did nothing to prevent those cruelties. For the objects of what was, in his eyes, a legitimate and even holy hatred he had no feeling of pity. Yet in remarkable contrast to the foreign fighters against Hussitism he always insisted on sparing the lives of women and children.

Thus when in the same month he conquered the castle of Rabí, one of the strongest fortresses in southwestern Bohemia, about fifty miles from Tabor, the absent owner's two sons, both in their early teens, were put under Žižka's personal protection and later returned to their father, John Krk of Riesenberg, under safe escort. The castle of Rabí itself was burned and then left. It was soon reoccupied and repaired by the Royalists and had to be assaulted by Žižka again at a later stage of the war.

But the same exploit that showed Žižka from his humane side also showed him as the implacable destroyer of those whom he considered as the arch sinners: the monks. Seven of them who had been among the prisoners were burned to death whereas all others were spared.[22] These seven were the first in a long row of victims, no less horrible a custom for the fact that the people on the other side were far less selective in burning their enemies.

In all these conquests of castles and little towns the attitude of Žižka and his soldiers toward the booty is most characteristic for his puritan morals. In every case, especially at Rabí, only arms and horses were kept and taken to Tabor. Everything else, including rich clothing and jewelry, was thrown on a heap outside the castle and burned. No earthly riches should tempt the soldiers of Tabor away from their task: the defense of the Law of God.

Žižka's first raids, those against Vožice and Sedlec, had been directed against enemies who, by breaking the Pilsen armistice, had presented themselves as legitimate objects of attack. Only after the earlier armistice, concluded in November 1419 between the revolutionary party and Queen Sophia, had expired on April 23, did Žižka feel free to conduct a more general offensive against the Royalists. The thrust against

[21] Březová, p. 363. [22] *ibid.*, p. 364.

Rabí formed part of it, but the first and most important enterprise following the end of the armistice was the reconquest of Písek. It was an act of liberation. The Royalist garrison fled and from now on this town, one of the earliest to join the revolution, remained the strongest and most important Taborite community west of the Vltava River.

The last of these limited campaigns, undertaken at the end of April, was directed at Prachatice. The population of this southern town, only twenty miles from both the Bavarian and the Austrian border, consisted largely of Germans who fled before the approach of the Taborites. These, not being able to spare sufficient troops to garrison the town, contented themselves with destroying part of the wall so that the town would not be a bastion for a future enemy.

It is fairly obvious what potential enemy Žižka had in mind: Lord Ulrich of Rosenberg, whose castle and town of Krumlov was only a score of miles to the southeast of Prachatice. Rosenberg, it is true, had on April 20, under the influence of his friend and former guardian Čeněk of Wartenberg, signed a declaration against Sigismund, but in southern Bohemia it can hardly have remained secret that he was still in touch with the King and his allies, the Austrian dukes. Soon afterwards Ulrich openly reverted to the side of the King and remained, though occasionally concluding an armistice with Tabor, one of its bitterest enemies. It was from him that Tabor was in constant danger. For this if for no other reason the town had to be made as strong as possible.

Žižka proved to be an excellent fortress-builder. On his orders Tabor's natural position, a steep hill on a peninsula formed by the Lužnice River and the smaller Tismenice River directly above their juncture, was strengthened by a huge double wall all around.[23] Through the narrow saddle of land separating the two rivers to the east above the town a moat was dug, and here the wall was treble instead of double. The whole fortress, forming a rough hexagon, was strengthened by six mighty tower bastions, one at each of the projecting corners. Originally there was but one gate, leading to the bridge over the Lužnice. These fortifications in their final form were strong enough to make Tabor one of the truly impregnable places of the country. Tabor's defensive strength was considered safe enough when on May 16 an urgent call for help came from Prague. Žižka was well prepared for it. Only two

[23] An impressive report on the fortifications of Tabor is given by Aeneas Sylvius who studied them during his stay at the town. He stresses Žižka's part in their design (Chapter 39, pp. 83, 84).

days later, leaving behind sufficient forces to defend the new fortress, he set out for the capital at the head of an army of several thousand. With this exodus the first phase of Žižka's actions and of the Hussite revolution—that of small scale war on a local level—drew to a close. Events were shaping up toward a decisive fight on the national and international level.

# CHAPTER 7

## SIGISMUND OVERPLAYS HIS HAND

In November 1419 Žižka, the captain of the New Town militia, had resigned and left the city in anger. Now, half a year later, the urgent call went out from Prague to Žižka, the commander of the army of Tabor, and when he arrived he received a joyous welcome from the whole city. This was, indeed, a profound change in the attitude of Prague. To understand it we have to turn back to December 1419, and to examine the policy of the man who more than anyone else held the decision over war and peace in his hands: King Sigismund.

Four months had elapsed since, by the death of his brother, he had inherited the crown of Bohemia. Most of this time he had spent in Hungary but now he finally decided to make an appearance in one of his newly acquired domains. On December 15 he arrived in Brno, in Moravia, and to this city he called for Christmas a diet of the Bohemian estates. Concurrently he informed the German princes, the Prussian Order, and the King of Poland that, early in 1420, he would hold court at Breslau, in Silesia. For a few days he returned to Hungary for a meeting with his wife. Queen Barbara, accused of adultery, had long been separated from her husband, but he had decided to forgive her and to take her back into his good graces.

Back at Brno in time for the diet he found, waiting for him, an illustrious assembly, high clergy, and magnates, headed by the regent, Queen Sophia.[1] She immediately informed Sigismund that she could no longer carry the heavy burden of the office. Sigismund appointed Čeněk of Wartenberg to be regent in her place, quite in accord with his policy of trying to win over the Hussite nobility by a more than friendly treatment. To be on the side of caution he appointed two Catholic barons to the next highest position in the state: Henry of Elsterberg, who, as Lord Chief Steward, took charge of the royal castles, and Wenceslas of Dubá, who, as Lord Chamberlain, was to be in con-

[1] See Březová, pp. 353ff.

trol of the royal towns. In this position, soon afterwards, Dubá took command of the troops investing Pilsen.

If the Czech nobility had expected any clear answers to the questions raised by the diet of September, they were mistaken. The King, especially in the burning religious question, was as evasive as before. He could always claim that this issue was not within his province but was for the Church to decide. Such a decision had already once been taken by the Council of Constance, but the King hinted that a revision might be sought from a future council, and there was no objection from Ferdinand of Lucena,[2] the papal legate present at the diet. Meanwhile, so the King gave to understand, he would not forcibly prevent anyone from taking the Communion in the two kinds.

This prospect, though not held out in any binding form, satisfied the Hussite nobles to the extent that, together with their Catholic peers, they did homage to Sigismund as their rightful ruler. This did not yet make him King of Bohemia. Only the coronation could, according to constitutional usage, elevate him to this position. But the act established the personal relationship of feudal allegiance between the barons and Sigismund. It was a political victory for the King, an important step toward establishing his rule over Bohemia.

The question was now how Sigismund would deal with the royal towns, especially the capital. The representatives of Prague appeared on December 27, and some of Sigismund's retinue found it interesting, if shocking, that they came with their priests and immediately took the Communion in the two kinds. While they were there, the city of Brno had accordingly to be held in a state of excommunication.

The King kept the representatives from Prague waiting for two days. When they were finally admitted to his presence, they were ready to follow the example of the nobility in doing homage to Sigismund. Kneeling before him they asked forgiveness for acts of resistance committed before, and requested a public hearing at which they could defend their faith. If then they should be proved to hold views not in full accordance with the Scripture they would gladly recant them.

The King kept a stern countenance. He first left them in their prostrate position while hurling fierce reproaches against the helpless men. Finally he released them without any promises, but also without expressly refusing their requests. He declared, however, that the people of Prague could not count on his forgiveness until they had removed all

[2] An episcopal seat in southern Spain. Most nineteenth century historians, following the example of Palacký, mistakenly call him Bishop of Lucca. (See Pekař, III, 59.)

rails and chains used to barricade city streets and until they had demolished all newly built fortifications. Further, all discriminations against Catholic clerics had to cease forthwith, and those who had fled should be allowed to return unmolested.[3]

When, on one of the first days of the year 1420, the representatives of Prague returned home with their reports, the councils of the Old and New Town felt that there was nothing to do but to submit. All barricades were removed, and orders were given not to molest, under the penalty of severe punishment, the clerics of the old creed. Many people who had previously left the town—priests and monks as well as German townspeople—returned, many triumphantly announcing that the end of the cursed heretics was near at hand. Hussite Prague, on the other hand, was thrown into a mood of fear and depression.[4]

Sigismund seemed to have achieved a full victory. He tried to consolidate it by an anti-Hussite purge of royal officials, especially among the burgraves of royal castles.

Indeed, if it had not been for the still unorganized, militarily weak Taborite movement, the revolution might have ended then and there. Only two more steps seemed necessary to bring it about: the elimination of the few centers of resistance, especially Pilsen; and Sigismund's entry into Prague, the capital that had promised to open her gates to him.

The siege of Pilsen was, in fact, begun almost immediately, and we know the results. But Sigismund was still not prepared to go to Prague. Was he frightened? Did he feel that he could only enter his new residence at the head of a powerful army? His Czech nobles advised him against it. They feared that the appearance of foreign soldiers would immediately rouse the national sentiment and impair the chances for a religious compromise. But Sigismund would not listen. He was determined to go to Breslau before he went to Prague. At Breslau, surrounded by German princes and the prelates of Rome, he would map out his subsequent steps.

3 Sigismund's reaction in reference to the Praguer's demand for a public hearing is not quite clear. The city of Prague later claimed that Sigismund had granted this demand at Brno, and subsequently had not kept his promise. But it seems more likely that all the King did was not expressly to refuse it, thus evading, as he always tried to do, any formal obligation. See Pekař, III, 40. The report given by *The very pretty chronicle* (see Chapter I above) on the audience of the Prague mission with Sigismund is very inexact. He certainly did not decree that Communion in the two kinds should be reintroduced (with reference to the custom in the original church). This version seems to be an attempt to justify the submission of Prague, an event which the more determined Hussites at a later stage may not have liked to remember.

4 "Quamobrem timor magnus ac pavor veritati adherentes invasit . . ." (Březová, p. 354).

It is difficult to say when Sigismund made up his mind that nothing but a display of great military strength would give him undisputed possession of Bohemia. At Brno it had seemed that peaceful accession to the throne was all he wanted. Yet from the moment he arrived in Breslau—on January 5, 1420—he acted in a very different way. At Brno he had promised that, at least for some time, he would allow Hussite ways of worship, but his orders from Breslau to the royal burgraves and towns showed no trace of such tolerance. Not only did he order his Bohemian subjects to desist from giving any help to the three towns still in active opposition against him—Pilsen, Písek, and Hradec Králové—but he demanded that they should expressly renounce the "Vicklefite" creed, should submit to all orders given by the Roman Church, should prevent any mass gatherings, any spreading of rumors or talks critical of the King's policy, and should deliver any offenders to the higher authorities for prosecution. The order was to be read publicly on the market places of all royal towns.[5]

This policy helps to explain why Sigismund was not willing to go to Prague now, despite the present submissive attitude of the city. For if it was his intention to destroy Hussitism as such, and not just its militant revolutionary representatives, then he had to count upon a much stronger resistance from a much larger part of the nation which he could hardly overcome without the use of strong forces. It seems, then, that the fateful decision to make war upon the majority of the Czech people had been taken even while the King held his amiable conversations with the Hussite nobles at Brno. This was quite in character with the man for whom language was, more often than not, a useful instrument for hiding his thoughts.[6]

First, however, Sigismund had to deal with a question of foreign policy not directly connected with the Bohemian events. He had to arbitrate in the struggle between the Order of the Teutonic Knights and the King of Poland. Representatives of both were already waiting for

[5] See the message to the towns in the district of Žatec, of February 10, in *Urk. Beiträge*, pp. 15, 16, only one of many such messages sent to the royal towns. If we can trust Březová (p. 357), some of these letters must have gone even further in their persecutory intent: he quotes the King as ordering his officials and the towns ". . . quatenus Wikleffistas et Hussitas et calicis practisantes communionem modis omnibus arceant, persequantur et pro posse exterminent."

[6] Pekař, on the other hand, thinks that Sigismund did not make up his mind in these terms before March (III, 41). It is true that only then did the King resort to actions which made his decision for an armed invasion in grand style irrevocable. It is, of course, quite possible that the influences to which Sigismund was exposed at Breslau helped to harden his resolve to use force instead of trying for compromise.

him at Breslau, together with many German princes and bishops and the delegates of thirty-two German towns.

On January 6, having received the homage of the dukes and estates of Silesia, Sigismund held a hearing for both parties and immediately made his award. The main issue was the fate of Samogitia. This Baltic region had long been under the administration of Grand Duke Witold of Lithuania, King Władysław's cousin, vassal, and most influential adviser, who could not be dislodged from there without force. But Sigismund went as far as he could in satisfying the Prussian demands. While Władysław and Witold lived, they should remain in actual occupation of Samogitia, though within a somewhat shrunken area. But they must refrain from strengthening their hold upon this province by the erection of castles or forts, and after their deaths the whole region would revert to the Order. Thus the legal claim of the Order to a territory which they had once taken from Lithuania by force was fully upheld.[7]

The Breslau award of January 1420 had considerable influence upon Bohemia's immediate future. By his decision in favor of the Teutonic Knights Sigismund wanted to strengthen their hand as the need might arise for him to put pressure on Poland again. But the award proved to be a blunder. By bitterly alienating Grand Duke Witold and through him his cousin Władysław, Sigismund forced Poland-Lithuania into the camp of his enemies. Witold especially reacted with white-hot fury when he received the news and resolved to do every conceivable harm to the Roman King. This remained no secret to Sigismund's Bohemian foes.

Most of January and February passed while the King was occupied with routine business of German domestic policy such as enfeoffments and confirmation of privileges. But early in March another matter came up which was implicitly related to the Bohemian question. In July 1418 the guilds of Breslau had revolted against the monopolistic rule of the old patrician families. Some city councilors had been killed and a new council, consisting mostly of members of guilds, was elected. King Wenceslas had condoned the matter. Now Sigismund ordered the arrest of twenty-three men who were considered responsible. A court consisting of patrician councilors from other Silesian towns speedily

[7] The award itself, among other sources, in Windecke, p. 30, and Aschbach, *Geschichte Kaiser Sigismunds*, Hamburg 1841, III, 38-40. For the political significance see also J. Goll, *Čechy a Prusy ve středověku* (Bohemia and Prussia in the Middle Ages), pp. 139-140, and the same author's "König Sigmund und Polen 1419-1436" in *Mitteilungen des Instituts für österreichische Geschichtsforschung* (Innsbruck 1894), XV, 450-451.

condemned all the prisoners to death.[8] The King, confirming the sentence, looked on with his whole retinue when they were decapitated on the market place on March 6. "In this way," so his action seemed to proclaim, "I am going to deal with low-born rebels everywhere!" And soon this intent was confirmed by another act of terror.

A prominent merchant of Prague, John Krása, who had come to Breslau on business, was denounced as having spoken disrespectfully of the Council of Constance and its treatment of Hus and Jerome. He was arrested, taken before a clerical court, and under torture requested to acknowledge that the Council's sentence against Hus was just, that all its rulings had to be obeyed, and that the Communion in the two kinds for laymen was a sinful practice. Krása steadfastly refused to recant, was then dragged by horses, legs first, through the streets of Breslau and finally, still alive and defiant, burned at the stake, a worthy successor to the martyrs of Constance.[9] The whole procedure had been ordered and confirmed by the King.

The news of this outrage quickly reached the victim's home town and caused wild excitement. The treatment of Krása clearly belied all assurances of peaceful intentions given by the King. Obviously it was not only the rebellious Taborites but all Hussites, "all those who took the Communion in the two kinds," against whom he planned to proceed with force.

Two days later the last possible doubts were dispelled when Ferdinand, Bishop of Lucena, the papal legate, solemnly read from the pulpit the papal bull proclaiming a crusade against the heretics of Bohemia: whosoever took arms against them was absolved from all sins.

The bull, dated March 1, had been dispatched from Florence to Prague upon the demand of Sigismund.[10] The King immediately made full use of it. He had not even waited for its proclamation. As early as March 7 orders to mobilize for a campaign in Bohemia had gone out to Silesian and Lusatian towns. On March 15, the same day that Krása had been executed, Sigismund had amplified this order by special regulations: upon entry in Bohemia anyone found practicing heresy and not willing to recant immediately was to be punished by death and

[8] See *Magdeburger Schöppenchronik* (ed. C. Hegel, in *Chroniken deutscher Städte*, VII, 1), p. 349; also Windecke, p. 30, and Aschbach, *op.cit.*, III, 45ff.

[9] Březová, pp. 358, 359. The statement of later historians (as e.g. Aschbach, III, 47) that Krása was a city councilor in the New Town of Prague is not confirmed by contemporary sources.

[10] *Urk. Beiträge*, I, 17, 20.

the loss of all his possessions.[11] Sigismund could have little doubt that his German mercenaries would understand this as a license to kill and rob at will.

The papal bull, preaching the cross against the Hussites, now put this action on a much broader basis. The German princes and bishops assembled at Breslau promised full support and without delay prepared for the assembly of an enormous army. The die had been cast, or so it seemed.

The decision for war, a war of extermination of Hussitism, was so clearly expressed in all those actions of March 1420 that the King would seem to have finally given up his ambiguous game of dealing in different ways with different groups of Hussites. Sigismund, however, still hoped to divide his enemies before conquering them. He was quite aware of the military strength that a united Czech nation might be able to muster. Since the days of his grandfather, King John, the fame of Bohemian arms had echoed throughout Europe. Naturally he thought of this military strength in terms of an armed nobility. If he could persuade the barons, including the Hussite ones, to abstain from action it would be much easier to deal a decisive blow to the townsmen and peasants. Once this was achieved he could deal with the nobles as well.

The greatest of the Hussite grandees, the man whose influence and leadership might sway the majority of the Czech higher nobility, was Čeněk of Wartenberg. To have him under his eyes and under his influence Sigismund had taken him along to Breslau. He kept treating him there with all imaginable honors, hoping to win him over completely. Wartenberg seems to have given the King reason to believe that he had succeeded.[12] This great nobleman, handsome, tremendously wealthy, with manners of convincing and ingratiating sincerity, was one of the worst vacillators ever to hold high office. He would have liked to go along with the King, a policy which would have been in accordance with his upbringing and his social standing. Yet he was not without a true feeling for his nation and for the reformation whose early spread had owed a great deal to his protection.[13] Sigismund's plans

[11] *ibid.*, p. 21, and especially the letter to the town of Bautzen, p. 22.

[12] Windecke, pp. 130, 131, gives a detailed report on the relationship between Sigismund and Wartenberg during the Breslau meetings.

[13] Čeněk of Wartenberg's character has been judged perhaps too severely by many Czech historians while, on the other hand, Pekař, in his interesting character sketch (III, 42-45) shows a strong bias in favor of the man whom he calls "the first gentleman of the Kingdom." For him he is the personification of all that is good and noble in Hussite Bohemia, especially

for annihilating Hussitism filled him with horror, but when he saw that he could not dissuade the King from following this dangerous course he held his tongue. Sigismund, in this case, showed an unusual lack of suspicion. When, on April 10, 1420, the two men parted ways, the King going to Schweidnitz in Lower Silesia, Wartenberg traveling on to Prague, the King had no inkling of Wartenberg's intentions. He would not, otherwise, have allowed him to go on his way, a free man and still regent of Bohemia.

The execution of Krása, followed by the pronouncement of the crusade, forced a drastic change of policy upon Prague. These two events made it clear that submission was not possible except for the price of completely abandoning the Hussite faith. Few even of the most conservative Hussites were prepared to take this step. As the policy of reconciliation had so obviously failed the radicals found their ranks swelled. If, for some time, John Želivský had been forced to keep in the background, he now came to the fore again with a vengeance. His attacks against Sigismund, the apocalyptic dragon with seven heads and seven crowns,[14] helped rallying the people of Prague to renewed activity. Soon the new spirit of resistance pervaded the whole city. As the common danger increased, all Hussites felt the need to forget what difference had arisen between them, and to establish unity of purpose and procedure.[15]

On April 3 a meeting of the councilors and magistrates of the Old and the New Town together with all Hussite priests and the masters of the University took place at the city hall of the Old Town. All present took a solemn oath to stand up for their religion and, if necessary, to fight for it without regard for life and property. The assembly then decided upon a military reorganization. Each town elected four captains who were to be responsible for the keys to the city's gates, and to whom everyone had to pay full obedience. Each of the eight captains was to wield his command with the help of ten subcaptains. To strengthen the city's defenses they ordered, on April 8, a deep moat to be dug south of the New Town, from the Vltava eastward as protection against attacks from the Vyšehrad.

---

as compared with the barbarous fanaticism which to him is represented by the Taborite movement.

[14] Březová, p. 360.

[15] See the reports of Březová who, himself a determined Hussite but a sharp critic of Taboritism and of John Želivský, looked at the new spirit of unified resistance with obvious pleasure (pp. 360-361).

With these acts Prague put herself again at the head of the general movement of resistance, and to make sure of a wide following a message went to all Bohemian towns asking them to send delegates with full power to arrange common actions in defense of the faith. The message contained a fierce and solemn protest against the papal bull, calling it a vile and venomous serpent's egg hatched by the Church, who had long before proved herself not to be a mother but a malicious stepmother to the Czech people. There followed an appeal to the national feeling of the Czechs. The Germans, so they were reminded, had already exterminated the Slavs of eastern Germany. Just such a war of extermination was now planned against the Slav people of Bohemia.[16]

In this tense atmosphere the Germans who had returned at the beginning of the year began again to feel very insecure, and a new wave of emigration began. Some 1,400 families from both towns and a considerable number of Catholic clerics left their homes. Some put themselves under the protection of the Royalist garrisons of the Hradčany and Vyšehrad castles, others went farther so as to be out of the firing line before the capital might be under siege. They were allowed to take their movable goods with them.

It was into this Prague, geared for action and dominated by the spirit of defiance, that Čeněk of Wartenberg returned from Breslau on April 15. He had been in contact with the capital before, and immediately informed the city council that he was going to adhere to the resolutions of April 3. In accordance he took measures which were bound to change the whole political and military situation.

First he made sure of his hold upon the royal castle on the Hradčany. His two lieutenants in charge of the castle administration, John Chudoba of Ralsko and Sigismund of Děčín and Wartenberg, ardent Catholics, were put under arrest, although both were his relatives. Then he posted reliable officers at all important places in the castle and its immediate neighborhood. Next he rounded up all those Catholic priests and Germans who had left Prague during the preceding two weeks, and evicted them from the Hradčany. (Less considerate than the Praguers, he forced them to leave their jewelry and money behind.)

But Wartenberg's most important, most consequential action was to rally a large part of the Hussite nobility against Sigismund in defense

[16] See *Archiv český*, III, 212. Palacký in a footnote to this message (*Geschichte v. Böhmen*, III, 2, 94) draws attention to the remarkable fact that the disappearance of Slav language and civilization in the lands between Elbe and Oder (a process that had largely been concluded by the end of the twelfth century) should be so fully alive in the historical consciousness of the fifteenth century Czechs.

of the Chalice. For his own person he renounced his fealty to the King by a message with which he also returned the precious insignia of the Order of the Dragon. On April 20 he followed this up with a manifesto addressed to all Bohemians and Moravians. The manifesto was published as coming from him and Ulrich of Rosenberg, his former ward and the greatest of Bohemian landowners, possibly without the latter's knowledge.[17] But it speaks in the name of all those who stand "for the freedom of the Law of God" and "for the common welfare of the Czech nation," and its text was certainly set up in close cooperation between Wartenberg and the spokesmen of Prague and its University. It stands at the beginning of a long line of Hussite war documents, and largely served to set the tone of those that followed.

"We ask you all," so the manifesto began, "not to submit to the Roman[18] and Hungarian King Sigismund nor to be subject to him or to obey him as Bohemian King, nor to his officials; for you must know that he has neither been elected as King by the Lords of Bohemia nor has he been crowned, but that he is the great and cruel enemy of the Bohemian Kingdom and Nation." This statement is supported by ten accusations. The most important ones were the insult and dishonor done to the Czechs by the reproach of heresy; Sigismund's part in proclaiming the crusade against all those practicing the Communion in the two kinds; the torture and execution of Krása; Sigismund's guilt in the horrors of Kutná Hora (he is here accused of having ordered the mass murder of Hussites in the mine shafts); and finally Sigismund's responsibility for the death of Hus. "Therefore," so the manifesto goes on to say, "you can understand that King Sigismund means no otherwise but shamefully to destroy and cruelly to exterminate this Kingdom and Crown of Bohemia and especially the Czech Nation. And we hope that, as true Czechs, you will in this hour of need gladly stand by the Crown and Kingdom as you have done before and as your ancestors did. But if, for all our warning, you should ever follow that King or obey him as the King of Bohemia, then you would, under the law, have forfeited your honor, life, and property as men who have not

[17] *Archiv český*, III, 210. In a letter to the town of Kadaň, dated April 19, Sigismund takes notice of the challenge, complains bitterly about it and names Rosenberg as one of its authors (see *Urk. Beiträge*, p. 25), but as early as May begins the regular and intimate correspondence between him and Rosenberg which is largely preserved (published in *Archiv český*) and which shows the Bohemian magnate as Sigismund's close ally and collaborator.

[18] In later documents the reference to Sigismund's Roman title (borne also by his two predecessors, Wenceslas IV and Charles IV) was regularly omitted.

kept faith with their nation and crown; whereas we believe that as wise, faithful, and circumspect men you will never permit such a thing to happen but will show yourselves in all things to be true Czechs.

"Also we want you to know that we stand for nothing else but the following articles: 1) for the common people to take the body and blood of God in both kinds; 2) for the proper and free preaching of the Word of God; 3) for priests to live an exemplary life just as our Lord Christ ordered and as his apostles and after him the Holy Fathers instituted; 4) for the common good of our Czech Kingdom and Nation and for cleansing the name of the Czech Kingdom and Nation from all harmful and slanderous rumors. And if in these articles there should be anything improper, such we would not want nor would we intend to uphold it stubbornly, but in all this we shall willingly be taught by and be obedient to the Holy Scripture."

The manifesto struck home with the force of a thunderbolt. It was as widely broadcast throughout Bohemia and the other countries of the Bohemian Crown as it was technically possible at a time still some decades before the invention of printing. It even penetrated into the neighboring countries. Its electrifying effect was partly due to the very news it conveyed: The leader of Bohemia's high nobility, the regent of the country had allied himself with the great city of Prague against Sigismund. Coming directly from the King's court he now charged him with sinister designs against the very existence of the Czech nation. For all true Hussites, undoubtedly a majority of the nation, the manifesto was a clarion call to active resistance.

It was still more: for the first time since the outbreak of the Hussite revolution a clearly formulated statement of aims was given to all adherents of the new creed. What we find at the end of the manifesto is an early form of the famous Four Articles of Prague, the document which more than anything else was destined to unify all Hussites in their great struggle.

The most important immediate effect of the manifesto of April 20 was the response it evoked from the Hussite nobility. On April 23, the very day on which the armistice concluded in November between Prague and the Royalist forces expired, scores, perhaps hundreds of Hussite noblemen, lords as well as knights, sent their challenge to Sigismund.

It seems that then (and probably even much earlier) a majority of the Czech nobility of Bohemia had accepted the Hussite form of worship and especially the Chalice. Politically, however, they had been less ready to oppose Sigismund's rule than the townspeople, as the feeling of loyalty to their "natural lord" was still quite alive among them. Wartenberg's sharp turn against Sigismund however made it much easier for them to renounce this loyalty, as they would no longer be bound to a man who "unrighteously forceth the faithful Christian to forego the glorious sanctity of the Blood and Body of our Lord, and depriveth them of access to other sacred truths, thereby bringing disgrace upon the Czech nation and ruination upon this country."[19]

The new coalition of Czech towns and nobles, with Wartenberg and Prague at its head, immediately went into action in the two most important fields: the diplomatic and the military.

Diplomatic action was needed because, with the repudiation of Sigismund as a possible ruler, another king had to be found. The Czech patriots' eyes turned to Poland. The common Slav background, the common enmity against German aggressiveness, the memory of a previous time when the two countries had been connected by a personal union,[20] all this played its part in the decision; even more, doubtlessly, the knowledge that the rulers of Poland and Lithuania had felt mortally offended by Sigismund's Breslau award and therefore would be more inclined to support a movement hostile to the King of the Romans than any other European princes.

Wartenberg and his allies in Prague sent a Hussite nobleman, Werner of Rankov, on a mainly exploratory mission to King Władysław.[21] His answer, dilatory but by no means discouraging, did not reach Prague until several weeks later, and by then the whole situation had changed again, as so often in revolutions, in an unexpected way. But the door for negotiations between Bohemia and Poland was opened and remained open.

Less successful were the first military steps undertaken by the Hussite allies. Of the two great royal castles dominating Prague the Hradčany had now, through Wartenberg's action, passed into the hands of

[19] From the text of one of those challenges as quoted by Palacký, *Geschichte von Böhmen*, III, 2, 96.

[20] This was the case from 1291 to 1306, under Wenceslas II and Wenceslas III, the last two kings of the old Czech dynasty of Přemysl.

[21] Our only source for this diplomatic mission and its course is Dlugosz (*op.cit.*, p. 261). Though the basic facts seem to give little reason for doubt, some of the details of his report, especially on Rankov's speech, show factual inconsistencies and cannot be relied upon.

the revolutionaries, but Vyšehrad was still occupied by a strong Royalist garrison. From the day the armistice had ended, a small-scale war began between this castle and the New Town, and though the city itself was protected to some extent by the newly dug moat the Royalists inflicted damage on suburban farms and hamlets. The forces of Prague answered by besieging the Vyšehrad, hoping to conquer the fortress which they had delivered to the Royalists in November as price for the armistice. Considerable efforts were made, but to no avail.

The only military successes of this time were achieved far away from Prague. The people of the Orebite community, in many ways similar to those of Tabor, were able to strengthen their hold upon the town and the region of Hradec Králové in eastern Bohemia. The spiritual leader of this group, the priest Ambrose of Hradec, had mobilized large numbers of people who, toward the end of April, began marching westward under the military command of Lord Hynek Krušina of Lichtenburg. Having conquered on their way one of the strong monastery fortresses of the country, they arrived in Prague on May 2. Krušina (a relation, by the way, of the Lords of Lichtenburg who had backed the band of "Matthew the Leader") was elected captain general of the military forces of Prague, and his own troops were used to reinforce the army besieging the Vyšehrad. Krušina, though not declining the appointment, left Prague soon afterwards for unknown reasons. In consequence the city remained without expert military leadership.

At the same time Žižka had begun his series of small-scale enterprises in southern Bohemia, building up his strength all the time, conquering and burning castles and monasteries. Clearly this campaign was timed so as to strengthen, in cooperation with Prague, the general resistance against Sigismund. Yet this war in the south, though it did more effective damage to the Royalist party than anything else undertaken by Hussite forces at this moment, did not please Čeněk of Wartenberg, and even less Tabor's immediate neighbor, Ulrich of Rosenberg. The two great nobles whose signatures under the manifesto of April 20 had given the resistance movement the character of national unity were loath to find themselves allied with the men of Tabor. Their crude methods of warfare, the destruction of castles and monasteries, caused, so we are told, the Lord High Burgrave to be "gravely dejected."[22] But

[22] Březová, using these terms, links Wartenberg's change of heart directly with the conquest of Rabí castle and the cruelties committed there by Žižka's soldiers (see p. 365). But he also says that Wartenberg was disturbed about the failure of the Praguers to conquer the Vyšehrad. If this was true it would indicate that Wartenberg lost courage in yet another sense: that he became frightened by the difficulties of the military task awaiting the revolutionaries.

this was hardly the whole truth. Though Wartenberg had felt compelled to join the revolutionary side for the sake of his religion, he could not reconcile himself with the realities of a revolutionary movement. The great nobleman and courtier could not overcome the horror of the peasant levies which seemed to threaten the stability of the acknowledged social system. He began to shrink back, with regret, from the results of his own courageous acts. And Sigismund soon got wind of the Lord High Burgrave's change of heart.

The King had left Schweidnitz, in Silesia, at the end of April, having collected a strong army of about 20,000 men, mainly consisting of German troops. At their head and accompanied by the papal legate Ferdinand of Lucena, the King entered Bohemia on May 1 or 2, marching through the county of Glatz. Informed that the Orebite army had left the district of Hradec Králové he decided to take that town, which was the center of Hussitism in eastern Bohemia. No resistance was possible. The gates were opened, and the King found himself received with joy at least by the German minority. He deposed the Czech city council and appointed a new, purely German administration. The papal legate made it known that all those ready to renounce Hussitism and to confess fully would be forgiven.[23]

The King had good reason to show this moderation. The formation of the national front had been a grave shock to him, as he had felt so sure of his success with the Hussite nobility.[24] The policy of dividing his enemies seemed to him as necessary as before. But was it still possible?

The news of Wartenberg's changing attitude reached the King soon after he entered Hradec Králové. This seemed a Godsent chance to destroy Hussite unity. The King approached Wartenberg through two of his most trusted Bohemian counselors, William Zajíc of Hasenburg and Ernest Flaška of Richenburg. They should offer, as a beginning, an armistice for two weeks. But they soon found out that, by secret negotiations, they could obtain much more than that. On the sole condition that Communion in the two kinds be permitted to himself, his family, and the people on his domains, Wartenberg offered to deliver Hradčany castle to the forces of the King whom, only two weeks be-

[23] The best source for Sigismund's moves at this time is the *Magdeburger Schöppenchronik*, based on reports which the captains of the Magdeburg troops in Sigismund's army sent to their city council. (*Chroniken der Deutschen Städte*, VII, 1, pp. 352ff.)

[24] How surprised and shocked the King was is shown very clearly in his letter to Kadaň. (See above, note 17.)

fore, he had denounced as the deadly enemy of the Czech nation.[25] The King, informed of the offer and the condition, quickly accepted both. But the arrangement, or rather the betrayal, was still kept secret. The King's ambassadors, meanwhile, got in touch with the city councils of Prague. At a meeting, on May 6, they assured the city that the King still wanted a peaceful solution of the conflict; that he was prepared to grant the public hearing which the Praguers had demanded at Brno; and that he was ready to receive a delegation from the capital at Kutná Hora whence he intended to go from Hradec Králové.

The city councilors were reluctant, but then Čeněk of Wartenberg rose and warmly recommended the suggestion to send a delegation to the King. Even if no agreement could be reached, at least nothing could be lost by such a step. The city councilors, ignorant of what had been arranged in the secret talks, finally agreed.

The city was dumbfounded when, the day after, they found out what had happened. Early in the morning the Lord High Burgrave had surrendered the castle to three Catholic lords in the King's service: Zajíc of Hasenburg, Wenceslas of Dubá, and his cousin Hynek Hlaváč of Dubá. The gates had been opened for 4,000 Royalist troops, largely Germans. Again both of the great castles dominating the city were in enemy hands, thanks to the treason of the man whom Prague had acknowledged as the leader of the nation.

The people of Prague burst into fierce fury. Their first desire was to punish the traitor. As he was out of their reach they took the Wartenberg banner which, in the regent's honor, had been hoisted on the Old Town city hall, and put it on the pillory of the Old Town. The men of the Prague militia then tried to take the Hradčany by force. But the assault was badly prepared and badly organized. Wartenberg himself left the Hradčany in a hurry as he feared for his life, but the newly strengthened garrison beat the attackers off with heavy losses. Fierce fighting also broke out on the Small Side with the result that whatever had been left standing in that borough after the fighting in November 1419 was now destroyed, so that for long years the whole district lay waste. The Czech inhabitants of the Small Side were transferred to the Old and New Town. But no real advantage was gained for Prague in this battle either. And the city fared even worse in an equally ill-planned assault

[25] Březová, p. 366. Sigismund's biographer Windecke, writing with the knowledge of Wartenberg's later reversals, claimed that his submission was only a trick and that he had locked away all arms hoping that the Prague's subsequent assault against the castle would succeed (p. 131). This is, of course, an impossible construction.

upon the Vyšehrad. This attack was not only repulsed but the defending Royalists answered with a sortie which did great damage to outlying parts of the New Town.

The complete failure of all these haphazardly conducted enterprises had a very discouraging effect. Even after the victories of November, Prague had not dared to keep up its resistance against the Royalists at a time when Sigismund was still far. How could the city hope to challenge him now, with both the great neighboring castles in Royalist hands and the King himself, at the head of a strong army, only some sixty miles away?

A new wave of defeatism took hold of the people of Prague. The more radical group still advocated resistance, but their voice lost much authority when letters of challenge arrived in growing numbers from Catholic lords and knights.[26] Thus submission became once more the policy of the majority.

An emissary sent to the Royalist commanders on the Hradčany found them as ready as before to grant the city an armistice. It was concluded, on or about May 12, for six days during which a delegation of the city, escorted by Lord Wenceslas of Dubá, was to go to Kutná Hora to negotiate with the King.

While his lieutenants concluded the armistice with Prague, King Sigismund arrived at Kutná Hora. He made a triumphal entry into the town. A large procession of the German miners welcomed him outside the gates, promising him through their spokesmen to live and die defending his rule and the old faith. The town itself was crowded with refugees, especially Germans who had fled from Prague, but also priests and monks from some of the destroyed churches and monasteries. The whole mood of the assembly was one of keen expectancy. With the King and his retinue in their midst, with his army camping just outside the walls, how could anyone doubt that the decisive stroke against the Czech heretics was imminent? Hopes ran even higher upon the arrival, a day or two later, of the Prague delegation. To ask for terms of surrender and accept them—this, so it seemed, could be the only purpose of their mission.

Sigismund himself was under the same impression. The audience which he granted to the delegates of the capital was altogether a strange

[26] There were no less than 364 of them. See *Archiv český*, IV, 378. The most detailed treatment of the fighting during the preceding days can be found in Tomek's *Dějepis města Prahy*, IV, 48-52.

repetition of what had occurred, five months before, at Brno. Again the Praguers, six elderly men, among them two unnamed masters of the University, knelt before the King and asked his forgiveness. Again the King scowled at them, and did not give them his terms till he had overwhelmed them with violent and humiliating abuse.

Yet this was more than mere repetition. The Praguers went further than before in their offer of submission. If he but gave them the freedom of the Chalice they would not only open the city's gates but would, if he willed it so, make a breach in the city's wall through which he might, as lord and master, enter the capital.[27]

If Prague's offer went further, so did Sigismund's demands. Without any reference to the religious question he stipulated these conditions for peaceful submission: not only all barricades or fortifications would have to be removed or leveled off, but the citizens of Prague would have to be completely disarmed. All weapons in possession of the Old Town, its inhabitants or its militia were to be collected and delivered to the royal garrison in Hradčany Castle. The weapons in the New Town were to be delivered at the Vyšehrad. Once these conditions were fulfilled the King was ready to repair to Prague, granting the city whatever grace it had deserved by its obedience.

The meaning of all this was unmistakable. Sigismund demanded unconditional surrender. Disarmed, utterly defenseless, the capital would have to bow to any treatment the proud victor might want to inflict upon it. The fate of Krása might well become the fate of all unrepenting adherents of the Chalice.

The conditions, when reported, stunned the assembled city councilors of Prague. But, once having grasped their significance, the men of Prague were free of their dilemma, relieved of the need to choose their future course which had now been mapped out for them by Sigismund himself. With his demand for the city's self-castration the King had overshot his mark. The last great chance of a peaceful solution which, at a late moment, had unexpectedly been offered to him was now irrevocably lost.

[27] *The very pretty chronicle* (see Chapter 1 above) is wrong in assuming that this offer had already been made at Brno. Our sources on the audience at Kutná Hora are Březová, p. 368, the letter of Prague to Venice of July 10, 1420 (*Urk. Beiträge*, I, 39ff. especially p. 42) and Dlugosz (*op.cit.*, pp. 254-255). The latter says that the breaching of the wall was requested by Sigismund who, "Bohemos in eam diem sivi rebelles amplius humiliaturus," made this demand "quatenus ipse cum gente sua non per portarum sed ruinarum loca velut triumphator ingrederetur."

Among the city councilors as among the overwhelming majority of the people of Prague there was hardly a dissenting voice. The meekness of defeatism gave way to the courage of desperation. It united all, moderates and radicals, the masters of the University and the little craftsmen of the New Town. Instead of disarming their militias and dismantling their fortifications as Sigismund had demanded, they set to work to strengthen their defenses in every way. "Wherever there had been one chain before to barricade the streets, they put two, and they locked themselves up against the King."[28]

But they could not and did not rely on their own strength. The enemy's power was too great to take such risk. Some of the moderates may have felt reluctant to renew the alliance with the radicals of Tabor, but if they uttered such qualms they were not heeded. And there was no time to be lost. As soon as the meeting of the councilors was over, Prague's messengers were on their way to all potential allies, especially the Hussite towns in the west and south of the country. They had orders to request help, as strong and as speedy as was humanly possible. None of these requests was answered more promptly than the one received, on May 16, by the community of Tabor.

[28] *The very pretty chronicle*, see Chapter 1 above.

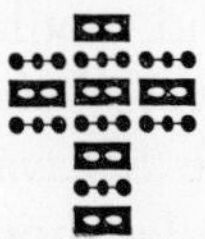

# CHAPTER 8

## THE DEFENSE OF PRAGUE

COMPARED to the troops that Žižka had led, less than two months before, from Pilsen to Tabor, the Taborite host coming to the help of the capital was imposing. It consisted of several thousand fighting men, according to one source[1] no less than 9,000, and with them went the wives of many of them and even children. Their armament consisted of guns and crossbows for the crews of the wagons; lances, maces, and flails for the foot soldiers.[2] Only a few hundred were mounted, but there were many war wagons as well as vehicles for supply.

Prague had asked for speed. The response must have surpassed the highest expectations. Medieval armies were slow, seldom covering more than fifteen to eighteen miles in a day.[3] Only troops consisting entirely of cavalry would normally move faster. But the army of Tabor moved much faster. Of the fifty odd miles separating Tabor from Prague it covered one half in one day, arriving at the towns of Benešov, almost exactly midway, on the forenoon of May 19. Clearly it was Žižka who directed the campaign, though all four of the captains took part in it.[4] Like almost all great generals throughout history, he knew that in war time is precious and speed a prime condition of victory.

Speed was needed especially as the Royalists would not look on quietly while Prague received powerful reinforcements. They tried, indeed, to

[1] *Chronicon veteris Collegiati Pragensis*, in Höfler, *Geschichtschreiber der Husitischen Bewegung*, I, 80. Other chronicles such as Březová (p. 371) only know of "many thousands." It seems likely that the number of 9,000 included the women and children, and that the number of actual combatants was nearer 5,000.

[2] Březová, p. 371.

[3] On the speed of movements during the Hussite wars, see Toman, *Husitské válečnictví*, pp. 234-237.

[4] The *Chronicon veteris Collegiati* (*loc.cit.*) makes Žižka appear as the only one responsible for all decisions on this march. Březová (*loc.cit.*) mentions all four captains, putting Žižka's name last. It appears, however, that he does so for a purely stylistic purpose: having described Nicholas of Hus as "homo magni consilii et providencie," thus praising his political cleverness, he then just adds the names of Buchovec and Chval, ending with the words: "et Johannes Ziska monocolus, supra modum audax et strenuus." Thus Žižka is the only one whose qualities as a military leader are appraised by Březová in this context. The same characterization had been used by Březová before when describing the conquest of Rabí Castle by Žižka.

intercept the Taborite army, and would have had a better chance if they had concentrated their forces before Žižka could cross the one major obstacle on his way: the Sázava River. But when he arrived before Benešov, still some six miles short of the river, only a comparatively weak cavalry troop of 400 horse was there to meet him. Bravely enough they awaited his attack, having been reinforced by some infantry from the town of Benešov, which belonged to the Royalist Lord Peter of Sternberg, Tabor's old enemy of Sudoměř memory.

Žižka sent part of his troops around the enemy to attack the town, which went up in flames. When they saw this happening in their rear the Royalists retired behind the strong walls of the nearby monastery. Žižka tried to take it but gave up immediately when the first assault remained unsuccessful. His task was to lead his army to Prague with as little loss of men and time as possible. He therefore marched on and in the late afternoon reached the Sázava, which he forded near the village of Poříči. He prepared to camp near the river's north shore, but then learned from his scouts that the main Royalist force was approaching in two strong columns from Kutná Hora and from Hradčany, with a third, smaller group nearing from the southwest. Their combined strength was considerably superior to the Taborite army. The troops of the Hradčany were under the command of Wenceslas of Dubá, and among the leaders of the larger army from Kutná Hora we find, for the first time in the Hussite wars, the name of Sigismund's most famous general, a man who had been very successful in some of the King's earlier campaigns, the Florentine Philip Count of Ozora, usually called Pipo Spano. Better than mere numbers his presence indicated that a great effort was made to prevent Žižka's getting through to Prague.[5]

Žižka led his army in the fading light onto a hill overlooking the Sázava valley and the road to Prague. There his troops took up the position which was to become the classical form of Hussite defense: the quadrangle of war wagons, made stronger by a quickly dug moat on the outside. The ensuing battle, fought in the early night, was a victory for Tabor. Though the Royalists' losses were rather light,[6] they

[5] Our source is, beside Březová, the *Chronicon veteris Collegiati* (p. 80). It claims 10,000 horses for Pipo Spano's troops, 1,600 for Dubá's, to which would have to be added at least several hundred men in the third column under Peter of Sternberg, thus adding up to more than 12,000. As in the case of Žižka's 9,000, it seems advisable to think of an army nearer half this strength.

[6] Fifty according to the *Chronicon veteris Collegiati*, only some twenty according to Březová. The lightness of these losses is one more reason to doubt that the size of the forces engaged was as large as claimed by the chronicler.

soon saw that they could never conquer the strong entrenchment and they retired. On the battlefield they left their dead and many standards, showing the red cross of the crusade.

The battle of Poříči seems, in a way, a repetition of Sudoměř. As in that previous fight the Royalists, once their offensive had failed, made no attempt to renew the fight. This decision to give up after a single, not even costly, defeat without considering other possibilities of achieving the strategic objective, shows the fatalistic temper of medieval strategy, here represented by one of the most renowned condottieri of the age. We shall later find Žižka in similar situations and see how very differently he acted. He had at this moment achieved his strategic objective: his army was intact, the way to Prague open. He reached the capital, after another speedy march, in the afternoon of May 20.

The reception which the Taborites received showed the joy and relief of the Prague population. Crowds of people went to meet the allies outside the gates. Once in the town the arrivals were treated to large banquets, and the abundance of food and drinks must have fairly dazzled the rustic guests from the poorer south, as it still lingered in the memory of Prague's sophisticated town secretary many years later.[7] Afterwards the women were lodged in a monastery whereas Žižka led his men to the banks of the Vltava River whence they crossed over to a large island today called "Štvanice." There, protected against sudden attacks, they put up their encampment.

On the following day the Taborite soldiers were permitted to rest and visit the city. Many of them, firmly indoctrinated by Taborite puritanism, were horrified by the luxury they saw. As especially sinful appeared to them the sumptuous fashions of the well-to-do townspeople, the precious gowns, jewelry, and finely woven veils of the women, the carefully cultivated beards and long mustachios of the men. Some Taborites grew so indignant that they tried to cut off those objects of pride, thus causing angry resentment. Complaints were lodged with the Taborite commanders who forbade, under severe penalties, any further molestations of Prague citizens. Other measures, too, were taken to tighten discipline in the Taborite army. From now on daily services were held in which the sermons explained the need to fight for the Law of God and after which the Communion in the two kinds was given. Particular stress was laid upon constant military preparedness.

[7] "Quos Pragenses . . . de victualibus copiosis provident, quorum maxima habundancia profugorum in domibus resperiebatur et precipue in potibus variis ac diversis." Březová, p. 371.

One day of rest was all Žižka granted his men. Already on May 22 he crossed over, with a strong detachment, to the left bank of the Vltava. There, as he had learned, a large convoy with food, arms, and other supplies, escorted by Royalist troops, moved south, destined for the Hradčany. Žižka ambushed them while they were marching through a wood to the northeast of the castle. The escort was put to flight, losing many men, and the raiders returned with prisoners and rich booty, consisting of nineteen heavily loaded wagons. These supplies were most welcome, as the number of people whom the capital had to feed was still growing. On the following day, May 23, troops of three Hussite towns of northwestern Bohemia, Žatec, Louny, and Slaný, arrived in Prague in response to the request sent out a week before.

While the King did not yet feel strong enough for a decisive blow against Prague, he tried a move which would impress the city with his military power, hoping that the advocates of submission might gain the upper hand in the city again. He left Kutná Hora on May 21 or 22. Two days later he camped with his army near the village of Litožnice, less than ten miles east of Prague. There he learned of the loss of supplies for the Hradčany and of the reinforcements which Prague had just received. He did not want to risk an open battle under these conditions. When he heard that Hussite troops were on their way to meet him[8] he retreated to Kutná Hora. This left, for the time being, the military initiative in the hands of Žižka.

At this stage Žižka does not yet seem to have been officially appointed as supreme commander of the military forces defending the capital.[9] But his experience, his renown as a leader "of exceptional bravery and fortitude,"[10] the memory of his recent victories, and his whole strong personality assured him of the determining influence in the councils of war.

His strategic task was essentially defensive. To save Prague was of supreme importance if the cause of the Chalice was to survive. But this did not mean, in Žižka's eyes, a strategy of sitting back and waiting for the enemy attack. He could not then know when exactly the main

[8] Frankenberger (*Naše velká armada*, I, 72) says that Žižka, informed of the arrival of Sigismund's army at Litožnice, immediately decided to throw all Hussite forces against him, seeking to reach a military decision right then and there. This seems a logical conjecture but no specific proof for it can be found in the sources.

[9] But Frankenberger, *op.cit.*, I, 71, assumes such an appointment.

[10] See Březová's characterization quoted above in note 4.

attack would come, but he would use whatever time was left to improve Prague's uncomfortable strategic position. The main disadvantage was, of course, the enemy's possession of the two great castle fortresses dominating the city. As he could not deal with both of them at the same time, he decided to concentrate his strength against the Hradčany, thus reversing the tactics used by the Prague militias during the abortive fights of early May. He could hardly cherish the idea of having to conquer again, under aggravated conditions, the fortress which, in October 1419, he had gained for Prague only to see this success thrown away in the ensuing armistice. He knew that the Vyšehrad was now heavily garrisoned under the able command of the Moravian Lord Všembera of Boskovice. More important: he knew that on the Hradčany provisions were low and that its food situation had become more difficult when the convoy of May 22 had been intercepted by the Taborites. Thus he saw a chance of winning the Hradčany, if not by assault, then by siege.

Žižka's first concern was to neutralize the Vyšehrad. The moat to the south of the New Town had been partly destroyed during the fights early in May. Now Žižka ordered a deeper and wider moat to be dug, somewhat farther north, at a safer distance from the castle hill. He put his Taborite women to work, with them the women of Prague and those who had come with other allied troops, but also boys too young to bear arms, priests, and Jews.[11] On May 30, after five days of hard work, the fortifications were ready to be manned by some Prague militia and the Orebites. All other forces had already begun the siege of the Hradčany on May 28.

With this action Žižka forced the King's hand. For military and political reasons the loss of the great castle would have been a defeat of the first order. Sigismund first tried to relieve the castle by diversionary attacks which would draw away some of Prague's allies. After marching, in a wide semicircle, keeping a safe distance from Prague, toward the northwest he obtained the surrender of Louny with the false claim that Prague had already surrendered. The neighboring town of Slaný had surrendered, on the same basis, to Lord Zajíc of Hasenburg a few days before. A number of the faithful Hussites in this town were

[11] Old Annalists, p. 35. The Jews had taken care to keep out of the religious discussion though some attempts had been made by ardent Hussites to convert them. On the other hand they were prepared to cooperate fully in the defense of the town, and the general distrust against foreigners, especially Germans, which at this time pervaded the city, did not influence their status. See also Ruth Kestenberg, "Hussitentum und Judentum," in *Jahrbuch der Gesellschaft für Geschichte der Juden in der Czechoslovakischen Republik*, Prague 1936, VIII, 12.

burned to death at the order of the papal legate Ferdinand of Lucena.[12]

Painful as the loss of these Hussite strongholds was, militarily it did not have the desired effect. The troops of both towns stayed unwaveringly with Prague. Meanwhile the food shortage on the Hradčany grew more serious, the guns of the Hussite army did considerable damage to the castle and the houses around it; the garrison, reduced to eating horse meat, grew restless, and mounting numbers of Czech soldiers deserted to the Hussite camp. Eventually, after having camped for a while in a well protected position at Zbraslav, to the south of the capital, Sigismund approached the Hradčany with all his troops on June 12, escorting a large convoy with food for the castle. Counting upon Žižka's inclination to fight if offered a chance, he drew up his army in battle position, and while the Hussite troops re-formed to accept the challenge the convoy slipped through. As soon as his purpose was achieved Sigismund ordered quick retreat. Žižka followed him, but the Royalist army escaped at nightfall with only minor losses to its rearguard.[13]

With this clever move Žižka's plan had been thwarted. There was now no more chance of forcing the castle's surrender before the arrival of the main crusading armies. Thus, on June 14, Žižka broke off the siege, and henceforth devoted all his attention to the most urgent task: the further strengthening of the city's defense.

This task demanded, at first, some change in the organization of the city's government, especially as there was never a clear dividing line between military and administrative responsibilities. There was some friction again between Prague's citizens and their allies. Despite the restraining orders of the Taborite commanders the women of Tabor had burnt the monastery of Saint Catherine in the New Town after forcibly evicting the nuns. This had led to renewed protests on the side of the city council. The Taborite leaders, though trying to prevent such acts, were nevertheless in sympathy with the sentiment behind them and dissatisfied with the lack of reformatory zeal shown by the city government. The complaints vented from both sides led to meetings at which representatives of the Prague cities, the University and the allies were present. Under the impact of the growing danger from without, full agreement was reached. New city councils were elected in the Old and New Town, in which the more determined revolutionary elements

[12] Březová, p. 376.
[13] *ibid.*, p. 377.

found stronger representation. One of their first acts was to purge the city from all "enemies of the Law of God." This term referred to those who were not ready to accept the Communion in the two kinds, among them many Germans who, until now, had remained in the town. City officials went from house to house, asking the family heads or, if they were absent, their wives to underwrite a solemn engagement to stand and, if need be, suffer in complete unity with all others for the cause of the Chalice.[14] Those who refused, including wives and children of Germans who had left before, were banished from the city. Their houses were confiscated and some of them given to the Taborites and other allies for use. This measure had more than religious significance. It also made sure that there would be no traitors at work in the city. The term "fifth column" was not yet invented, but the dangers from such a group were real, and the Hussites of Prague did not want to take unnecessary risks.

Another result of the meetings[15] was the agreement reached on the religious aims of the movement. Its basis was the Four Articles which, in the manifesto of May 20, had first become known all through the nation. Its fourth point had then only demanded the cleansing of the good name of the Czech nation from the taint of heresy. Now its emphasis came to rest upon the demand for the punishment of all deadly sins, doubtlessly upon the demand of the Taborite and Orebite representatives. In this new form the Four Articles became the final confession of the Hussite faith, and their preservation and defense the general goal of Hussitism throughout the long war.[16]

It was, of course, to the military needs that Žižka had to devote his personal attention. Upon his demand or advice the system of command was overhauled. Twelve captaincies were created, to be held by four men elected by the Old Town, four by the New Town, and four by Tabor and the other allies. The captains were to be collectively responsible for the keys to the gates and watch towers, and the fortifications were manned by garrisons combining Prague and allied troops. This measure resulted in a closer integration of all troops, without too much regard to their local background, at least as far as the defense of the fortifications was concerned. Only those troops earmarked for mobile operations such as sorties remained in their original frames.

[14] *ibid.*, p. 378 and, for more details, the letter of complaint written to King Sigismund by the Germans exiled from Prague, as quoted by Windecke, *op.cit.*, pp. 149, 150; and Tomek, *Dějepis*, IV, 66, 67.

[15] Especially the one held on June 27. See Březová, p. 374.

[16] A full discussion of the Four Articles follows in Chapter 10.

It is uncertain whether Žižka was one of the twelve captains[17] or whether he now became in form what he had been in fact before: the captain general of the forces of Prague.[18] The latter assumption seems more probable as his next steps were taken in clear view of the general strategy of the city's defense.

Before turning to this new phase of Žižka's activities, however, we have to relate two earlier developments. Though occurring in other parts of the country, both had their bearing upon the general situation which centered on Prague's ability to hold out against the coming storm.

As early as May 31 Sigismund had urged his most powerful supporter in the south, Lord Ulrich of Rosenberg, to undertake a separate campaign against the new fortress town of Tabor, which he rightly regarded as the most dangerous center of resistance next to Prague.[19] He deemed this task so important as to commit to Rosenberg's support some of the Austrian troops at his disposal, under the command of Leopold Krajíř,[20] the royal governor of Budweis. After careful preparation Rosenberg's army began the siege of the fortress[21] while Lord Ulrich, visiting the King, solemnly renounced Hussitism for himself, his vassals, friends, retainers, and subjects.

The Taborite commanders at Prague answered by sending Nicholas of Hus at the head of 350 horsemen to the relief of Tabor. This small troop of cavalry—perhaps all the Taborite army possessed at that moment—was of little use at Prague and could well be spared. Nicholas, on approaching Tabor, managed to get a courier through the enemy lines to inform the defenders that he would attack in the dark during the first hours of June 30, and asked the garrison to sally out at the same time. The plan was fully successful. The besiegers were taken by surprise, and pressed from two sides, suffered heavy losses. The sur-

[17] This is the assumption of Tomek (*Žižka*, p. 48).

[18] This position was held at various times during the earlier phase of the Hussite wars by Krušina of Lichtenburg, Žižka, Hvězda of Vícemilice, and Hašek of Waldstein.

[19] The order to Rosenberg is contained in a letter of May 31 (*Archiv český*, I, 12), the first in a long series of letters exchanged between Sigismund and Rosenberg which were preserved in the archives of the Rosenberg family. It begins with Sigismund's acknowledgment of a message by Rosenberg, thus proving that his cooperation with the King had started already some time earlier. The letter refutes Frankenberger's view (*op.cit.*, p. 75) that the campaign against Tabor, too, was a diversion. On the contrary Sigismund promised Rosenberg to take care that Tabor would receive no help from the Taborite forces then at Prague.

[20] Windecke, who mentions him repeatedly, calls him Kreiher.

[21] According to Březová (p. 380) on June 23, according to the later Rosenberg archivist Březan (*Časopis musea českého*, 1828, IV, 55) about a week earlier.

vivors fled, leaving behind large supplies of food, money and arms, including some heavy siege guns. Tabor was safe.

Rosenberg was fiercely annoyed by this failure. He ordered all Hussite priests whom he could get hold of to be thrown into prison, where several of them were starved to death. The young baron thus began to establish his fame as one of the most dangerous enemies of Hussitism inside Bohemia.

Another grave setback was suffered by the Royalists in eastern Bohemia, the only region where, for a while, all Hussite resistance seemed to have been eliminated. Its center there had been the old city of Hradec Králové[22] which had submitted to Sigismund's army early in May, while its military forces under Lord Hynek Krušina of Lichtenburg had gone to the help of the capital.

When soon afterwards Krušina left Prague, the Orebites in the capital remained under the strong spiritual and political leadership of their most prominent priest: Ambrose of Hradec. He was destined to play an increasingly important role in the history of the Hussite wars and especially of Žižka's life. As now he appeared on the scene for the first time with an important and independent action, it seems useful to look at him and his movement somewhat more closely.[23]

Ambrose, like John Želivský in Prague and Wenceslas Koranda in Pilsen, had taken up the fight against the Roman Church long before the outbreak of the revolution. He was the acknowledged spiritual leader of the reform movement which grew up after the death of Hus in the region of the upper Elbe. Like the other one in the Lužnice region it took the form of assemblies on mountains, mostly on a hill near Třebechovice, a few miles east of Hradec Králové. To it the members of the community gave the name Oreb.[24]

Like Tabor the Orebite movement was puritan and regarded the monastic clergy as their main enemy. Thus, on their way to Prague in May, passing through the region of Mladá Boleslav, the Orebites destroyed the great monastery of Hradiště. Yet there were differences.

[22] The town is situated at the point where the Elbe, after entering the plain of northern Bohemia, becomes navigable for rafts and small river boats. It was traditionally a fief of the Queens of Bohemia. Its German name was Königgrätz, and between it and the village of Sadova the Prussian army achieved, in 1866, its decisive victory over the Austrians.

[23] Ambrose has, to my knowledge, never been given the monographic treatment which he certainly deserves. The nearest approach to it is the well drawn character sketch which Pekař (III, 200ff.) devoted to him and which, despite that historian's bias against the Hussite left, does full justice to Ambrose.

[24] A very militant name, see Isaiah 10:20, 26, and Judges 7:25.

In deviating from the teachings and practices of the Roman Church Oreb did not go as far as Tabor. Nor did the Orebites develop the chiliastic fanaticism that characterized the Taborite radicals. Theirs was a cooler, a more rational mind.

This was largely due to the mind that directed the movement: Ambrose. He was a man of great energy and determination, an excellent organizer, but also a most courageous fighter, cool and undaunted even in desperate situations.

Sometime early in 1419 Queen Sophia suspended Ambrose, because of his vehement attacks against Rome, from his office as priest of the Parish Church of Hradec Králové; but when the revolution broke out in Prague, Hradec Králové was one of the first cities to follow suit, and Ambrose became the undisputed leader of the Hussite people in the town and its surroundings. In November 1419 he was in Prague and took part in the great attack upon the Small Side. Then, if not earlier, he and Žižka must have met. Their acquaintance grew into a close and lifelong friendship.

Better than most Taborite priests Ambrose knew how to get along with people of every station, including those of the high nobility. Thus he was able to win some of the most influential barons and knights of his region for the cause of the reformation, among them Hynek Krušina of Lichtenburg, Aleš Vřešťovský of Riesenburg, and Diviš Bořek of Miletínek, all important figures in Hussite history.

Ambrose was by no means willing to put up with the loss of Hradec Králové. Yet he did not want to weaken the defense of Prague by using the Orebite troops for the reconquest. Confidently leaving them under Žižka's command, he went on his way alone sometime after June 20, succeeded in eluding the Royalist troops and secretly met Lord Aleš of Riesenburg and two squires of his group near Pardubice, where they collected armed men, mostly peasants and charcoal burners from the nearby woods. Reaching Hradec Králové in the early hours of June 25 they assaulted the walls and quickly overwhelmed the surprised German garrison. Under Aleš of Riesenburg's command the town then prepared for Sigismund's countermeasures. The King did, indeed, send a considerable force[25] to retake Hradec Králové. A siege began which, however, made no progress. Early in July the Royalist troops, now needed to invest the capital, were withdrawn. Hradec Králové remained a Hussite town and the center of the Orebite move-

[25] Březová (p. 381) speaks of 10,000 men.

ment. And, under Ambrose's leadership, it remained in permanent contact and close cooperation with Žižka for the rest of his life.

This, then, was the situation in Bohemia at the time when the great armies of the First Anti-Hussite Crusade closed in on the capital: of the provincial centers that had adhered to the reformation two, Louny and Slaný, had been lost in the northwest, but the largest and strongest in that region, Žatec, held out. In the south Tabor and Písek remained unconquered, and in the east Hradec Králové had been regained. The greater part of the country was still dominated by the King's own castles and towns and those of the Royalist nobles. But the threat to Prague that hung over the capital for many months began only now, at the end of June, to take concrete form.

As an unprepared assault on a city as strong as Prague was unlikely, the defenders had to reckon from the beginning with a prolonged siege. For it the enemies had two natural, pivotal points at their disposal: the great castles on the Hradčany and the Vyšehrad. They dominated all exists to the northwest and direct south. From the Hradčany Hill in the northwest a high plateau extends east, forcing the river into an eastward bend and dominating all the northern approaches to the town. Its occupation would easily give the besieging army complete mastery over all the northern parts of the left bank. On that side of the river there was then but one possible avenue of approach and exit: the narrow defile between hill and river to the south of the Small Side. But even that was difficult to use as soon as the besiegers occupied the hills to the south of the Hradčany. Things looked brighter on the right bank, where the Old and New Town lay. True, the south was completely locked off by the Vyšehrad, but between that hill and the place where the New Town Wall reached the river in the north there was a distance of almost three miles uncovered by any fortification outside the city walls. Two natural features dominated it: in the center the softly rising hills later called the "Royal Vineyards," and farther north a long, steep, narrow ridge, running roughly from east to west, parallel to the river. This ridge was called the hill of St. Vitus or, in Czech, Vítkov. The strip of low land, a little under a mile wide, between the hill and the river was called the Hospital Field. Through it ran the main road from Prague to the northeast: to Brandýs, Mladá Boleslav, and Nymburk. Just to the south of the Vítkov Hill ran the main road from Prague to the east, to Český Brod and Kolín. Both roads con-

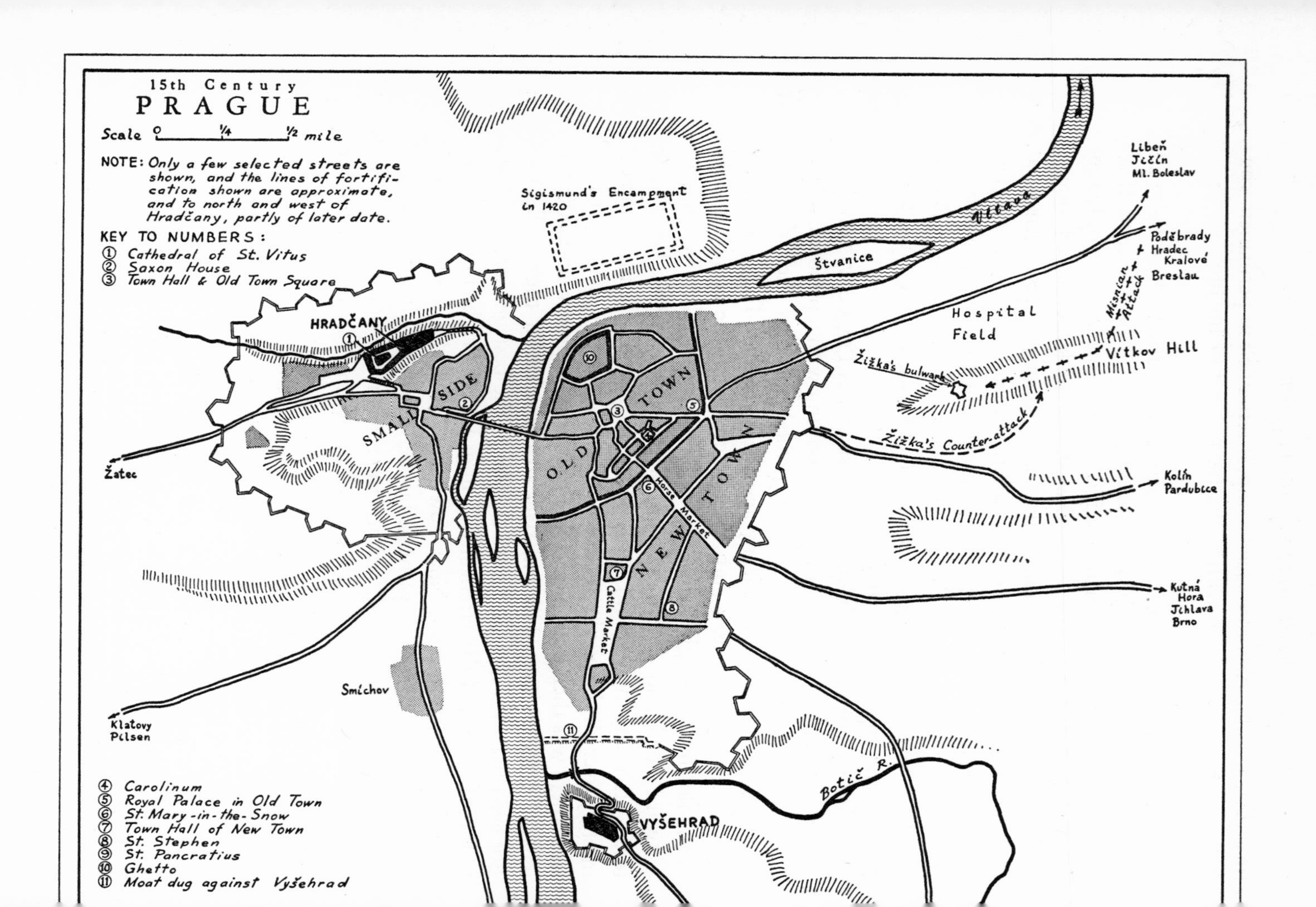
15th Century
PRAGUE
Scale 0 1/4 1/2 mile
NOTE: Only a few selected streets are shown, and the lines of fortification shown are approximate, and to north and west of Hradčany, partly of later date.
KEY TO NUMBERS:
① Cathedral of St. Vitus
② Saxon House
③ Town Hall & Old Town Square
④ Carolinum
⑤ Royal Palace in Old Town
⑥ St. Mary-in-the-Snow
⑦ Town Hall of New Town
⑧ St. Stephen
⑨ St. Pancratius
⑩ Ghetto
⑪ Moat dug against Vyšehrad
Sigismund's Encampment in 1420
Vltava
Štvanice
HRADČANY
SMALL SIDE
OLD TOWN
NEW TOWN
Horse Market
Cattle Market
Hospital Field
Vítkov Hill
Žižka's bulwark
Žižka's Counter-attack
Misnian Attack
Libeň
Jičín
Ml. Boleslav
Poděbrady
Hradec Kralové
Breslau
Kolín
Pardubice
Kutná Hora
Jihlava
Brno
Žatec
Smíchov
Klatovy
Pilsen
Botič R.
VYŠEHRAD

nected the capital with the rich agricultural regions of the Elbe valley from which it received many supplies.

Žižka saw the supreme importance of the Vítkov. If that hill fell into the hands of the enemy, Prague was deprived of all its major supply lines. As long as it could be held two of those lines could be kept open, and the siege would remain ineffective as far as food supplies were concerned.

On the crest of the hill stood an old watchtower, built to protect the vineyards covering the southern slopes of the hill. To the north of it, near the steeper northern slope, Žižka ordered two wooden forts erected.[26] The whole area, combined with the old watchtower, was fortified by a moat and a wall built from earth, solidified with some stones. This bulwark was essentially an improvisation and was not spacious enough to hold more than a small permanent garrison, about thirty men in each of the two forts. But at least Žižka was sure now that the hill would not be occupied by the enemy in a surprise movement. He could rely on his Taborites not to give way without a fight.

With these and some lesser measure (such as cutting down trees and leveling some houses impairing the view from the walls) all had been done that seemed possible in preparation for the great test. Even now the hills to the north, just across the river, grew alive with the teeming masses of foreign troops: one could hear the neighing of their horses across the river, could see the blinking of their armor, their white tents, their standards with the red crosses. Hussite Prague was in a mood of solemn expectancy: grim but far from despondent. God could not abandon those who fought for His Law.

[26] Březová (p. 385) describes this act of Žižka's as a direct anticipation of Sigismund's plans who, so he says: "intenderet montem . . . suis munire gentibus, ut velut tercio castro Pragam sic stringeret, quod nullus civitati Pragensi liber pateret victualium accessus."

# CHAPTER 9

## THE BATTLE OF THE VÍTKOV

JULY 14 is an important day not only in French but also in Czech history. For on this day, 369 years before the storming of the Bastille, Žižka won the Battle of the Vítkov, the only battle fought in the course of the First Crusade against the Hussites. It was the battle that saved Prague.[1]

Sigismund's crusading host was a huge force, quite superior to what ordinarily, at the time, would have been considered a strong army. Its soldiers, so we hear from the most lively and detailed of the various eyewitness reports, the one given by Lawrence of Březová,[2] came "from the different kingdoms, duchies, provinces and districts of the world, intent to conquer the famous and magnificent city of Prague and thus to wipe out and stop forever the Communion with the Chalice. Thus, they hoped, they would obtain indulgence from their guilt and punishment, such as their priests, albeit falsely, had promised them in order to excite them as much as possible to destroy all faithful Czechs of both sexes.

"The size of this army grew till there were more than 150,000 armed men assembled. Among them were archbishops and bishops, the patriarch of Aquileja, several doctors of divinity and other prelates; further, many secular dukes and princes, about forty in number; numerous margraves, counts, barons, and others of noble birth; and so many knights, retainers, townsmen from diverse cities, and peasants, that they covered the whole plain with their encampments, and their tents were drawn up like the houses and streets of three large towns.

"There the people were of many different nations, tribes, and tongues. Besides Bohemians and Moravians there were Hungarians and Croatians, Dalmatians and Bulgarians, Wallachians and Szekelys, Cumans, Tassyans, Ruthenians, Russians, Slavonians, Prutenians, Serbs,

[1] Frankenberger (I, 85) compares the battle in its historic significance to the Battle of Valmy, which halted the Austro-Prussian invasion of France in 1792.

[2] Pp. 383ff.

Thuringians, Styrians, Misnians, Bavarians, Saxons, Austrians, Franconians, Frenchmen, Englishmen, men from Brabant, from Westphalia, Holland and Switzerland, Lusatians, Suabians, Carinthians, Aragonians, Spaniards, Poles, Germans from the Rhine and many others.[3]

"These men stood every day on the fringe of the hill overlooking the river, opposite from the monastery of the Holy Cross and the Church of St. Valentine, and howling like dogs they shouted across the river toward the city: 'Ha, Ha! Hus, Hus! Heretic, Heretic!' And if by any chance a Czech fell into their hands and was not immediately freed by some of the Bohemians belonging to their army, then he was without delay or mercy burned as a heretic, even if he had never taken the communion in the two kinds."[4]

The actual strength of the crusading army was certainly far lower than claimed here, probably nearer 80,000 men—the number estimated by a German chronicler.[5] This would give the besieging army something like a four-to-one, perhaps even five-to-one, superiority over the forces of the defense. Tremendous though it seemed, this was no guaranty of success when the task was as difficult as here: the conquest of one of the largest towns existing in Europe at the time, defended by strong walls, a determined citizenry and a considerable army of even more determined allies.

Therefore Sigismund's plan of action as begun on July 14 was militarily sound: the conquest of the Vítkov, in itself a limited military enterprise, would be the easiest way to insure a complete and effective blockade. Once Prague was cut off from the rest of the country its food supplies were bound to dwindle rapidly, and the relatively large number of defenders, originally an advantage, would turn into a source of calamity. But just because it was sound and rational the plan had been anticipated and acted upon by Žižka.

Březová tells us that the King planned to follow up the conquest of the Vítkov with a threefold attack upon the city itself. This seems likely enough even if it was not meant as an all-out effort. Undertaken right after the conquest of the Vítkov, such an attack might well, in

[3] This list of 33 foreign nations is certainly impressive even though one third of them are German speaking tribes. Of the European nations and nationalities of the time only Scandinavians seem to have been unaffected by the crusading fever, whereas the fact that Italians are not mentioned is due to an erroneous or accidental omission by Březová.

[4] This is fully confirmed by German sources such as *Magdeburger Schöppenchronik*, p. 354. The "shouting across the river" described was quite possible, as the Vltava, though much wider elsewhere in the city, is at this point only about 600 feet wide.

[5] Windecke, p. 110.

Sigismund's view, turn the mood of the citizenry into despair and thus make them give up their resistance. All in all, the King could feel that he laid his plans well. He awaited their development with supreme confidence.

This, then, was the course of the action:[6] the Royalists, a few thousand cavalry, in its majority troops from Meissen and Thuringia with some Silesians and Hungarians, crossed the Vltava soon after noon at its easternmost bend toward the village of Libeň, and from there, turning sharply southward, could make their way without difficulty up to the ridge, as its slopes are much less steep in its northeastern part. Thence they turned westward, attacking the fortifications held by the Taborite outposts in the early afternoon. It seems that the whole maneuver was only observed in Prague when most of the enemy forces were already across the river, perhaps only when the attack had already started. To quote Březová again: ". . . they strongly attacked the forementioned wooden bulwark. They succeeded in crossing the moat, and they took the old watchtower on top of the vineyards. And when they tried to scale the wall erected from earth and stone, two women and one girl[7] together with about 26 men who still held the bulwark defended themselves manfully, hurling stones and lances, for they had neither arrows nor guns. And one of the two women, though she was without armor, surpassed in spirit all men, as she did not want to yield one step. Before Antichrist, so she said, no faithful Christian must ever retreat! And thus, fighting with supreme courage, she was killed and gave up her spirit. Then Žižka sped to their help. But even he might have been slain if his men had not come to his rescue with their battle flails and had freed him from the hands of the enemies." From this as from all other sources it is clear that the attackers were too strong to be withstood for any length of time. They succeeded in scaling two walls and might have overrun both of the wooden bulwarks if the narrowness

[6] Czech sources besides Březová: Old Annalists, p. 37; *Chronicon veteris Collegiati*, p. 81; *Chronicon Treboniense*, Höfler, *Geschichtsschreiber*, I, 51; *Chronicae Boemiae* (Short Chronicles) Höfler, II, 65; *The very pretty chronicle*, see above Chapter I. German and other sources: *Magdeburger Schöppenchronik*, pp. 353f.; a letter of the Margrave of Meissen to the Duke of Bavaria, preserved in French and published by Höfler, *Sitzungsberichte der Akademie der Wissenschaften*, Vienna 1880, vol. 95; Andrew of Ratisbon, Höfler, II, 408. Thomas Ebendorfer of Hasselbach, *Scriptores Rerum Austriacarum*, II, 850ff. Ludolf of Sagan (Tractatus de longevo schismate) ed. Loserth, *Archiv f. öster. Geschichte*, Vienna 1880, vol. 60, p. 476.

[7] Considerable participation of women in the fighting is confirmed by other sources. Thus the above-mentioned letter of the Margrave of Meissen claims the capture of 156 Hussite women, in men's clothes and armed. See also *Magdeburger Schöppenchronik*, p. 356.

of the ridge had not prevented them from making free use of their superiority.

Žižka was still within the walls of Prague when the attack began. But even from the center of the city, he would not have far to go to reach the battlefield. He immediately ordered strong elements of his Taborite forces, together with Prague troops, to proceed to the Vítkov and to attack the enemy from the south. He himself, accompanied by a smaller force comparable to a special crack troop or bodyguard, probably his oldest comrades in arms, hurried to the Vítkov where they arrived some time in advance of the main body. Finding the situation critical, he threw himself into the fight, trying to hold the remaining bulwark with his little troop at all costs and at the risk of his life. From this moment till the arrival of the larger Taborite force there was only a short interval, but this was the military and psychological crisis of the battle when the people of Prague thought "that ruination was imminent and, praying and shedding tears, expected help from heaven alone."[8]

But then the tide turned. On came Žižka's men, climbing the hill through the vineyards on its southern slopes, attacking the left flank of the Germans with indomitable fury. It was the typical deployment of the Taborite troops: in front the priest with the host, then the archers, after them the peasant soldiers with their flails and pikes. And while they approached there were loud shouts on their lips, or more likely, one of the religious battle songs which were to become such an important weapon in their spiritual arsenal.

The shock of this sudden flank attack must have been powerful. But in Březová's account it was largely the sight of the Body of Christ, the sounds of the bells of Prague and of the Hussite battle cries which, in a well-nigh miraculous way, turned the tide. Surely the Germans were struck by a holy terror. They did not believe, as the Czechs did, that God Almighty was entering the battle, but not a few of them who had been told that the Taborites worshiped the Devil[9] may have spotted the Prince of the Underworld in the ranks of the fierce Czech warriors. It was partly this terror which made them—the certain victors of a moment before—turn their backs in unreasoning, irrepressible flight. "Each man," says Březová, "tried to get in front of the other in running away. Many of those who could not resist the onrush of the

[8] Březová, p. 385.

[9] *Magdeburger Schöppenchronik*, p. 353: ". . . de Behmen . . . hadden bi der stad an der Multe (Vltava) einen berch, den heiten se Thabor, dar gingen se up und bededen den duvel an." In the opinion of the men from Magdeburg this fact, that is, the worship of the Devil on Mount Vítkov, was the main reason for the decision to send the Misnians to conquer this hill.

fleeing men, while trying to climb down the steep rock, tumbled and broke their necks, and very many were killed by the pursuers. Thus within one hour about 300 of these enemies were killed, whereas others were fatally wounded and carried away.

"When the King realized what had happened, he returned quietly to his encampment with his whole army, filled with fury, disgust, grief, and bitterness. The soldiers of Prague, however, assembled on the Hospital Field, fell down on their knees and, to render thanks to God, sang with loud voices the Te deum laudamus. For they were conscious that not by their prowess but by a miracle God had given the few of them victory over the enemies. And thus, with hymns and songs on their lips, like dancers, they went back into the city. And there the sounds of lament of the women, virgins, and children, all of whom the enemies of truth had proposed to murder without pity as stubborn heretics and children of heretics, now turned into expressions of exultant joy, and they gave praise to the mercy of God who, almightily, had delivered them from the hands of their cruel enemies."[10]

What were the immediate results of the battle? The Crusader's losses were far from heavy. If we believe one report which says that five hundred had died altogether[11] this was a bad enough loss for the troops of Meissen (who also lost their general, Henry Count of Isenburg). Yet it was a very small proportion of the whole crusading army, in no way sufficient to explain the fact that no further assault was attempted.

It is, of course, fully understandable that the attempt was not renewed on the same day. Every chance of a surprise had now vanished, and there could be no hope to succeed in the face of strong Hussite forces where the initial attack had failed against a mere handful of defenders. Yet the besiegers had not lost all their chances. The attempt to close the iron ring could be repeated, either by employing the available forces in greater distance from the city and in somewhat thinner lines,

[10] Březová ends this paragraph by saying: "On the following day, and ever since, the children of Prague on all the city's streets have sung a new song the author of which is the priest Čapek." Březová then, interrupting his Latin tale, quotes the song, or at least its first part, in the vernacular. Even a somewhat clumsy translation of my own shows, I hope, the immediate impact of the victory on the feelings of the common people of Prague.

Children, let us praise the Lord,
Honor Him in loud accord!
For He frightened and confounded,
Overwhelmed and sternly pounded
All those thousands of Barbarians,
Suabians, Misnians, Hungarians
Who have overrun our land.

With His strong protecting hand
To the winds He has them waved,
And we children are now saved.
Faithful Czechs, let's sing our love
To our Father high above,
With the older folks along
Praising God in joyous song!

[11] Old Annalists, p. 38.

or by renewing, after sufficient preparations and with still stronger forces, the attack upon the Vítkov. It was this latter contingency which was in Žižka's mind when, on the very day after the battle, he ordered the fortifications on the hill to be strengthened. The moat was deepened, the wall, so far mostly earthwork, reconstructed in stone, new bulwarks added to the two older ones. Again the women of Tabor and the other allies, in common with the women of Prague, had to do most of the building. The strengthened fortress was now garrisoned also by stronger troops. From now on the place was called "Žižkov," Žižka's Hill, a name that it has retained to this day, together with the whole borough to its south.[12] Visible from many parts of the city, the Žižkov has become a permanent monument to the man who saved Prague in this fateful hour.

Žižka's expectation that the attack would be renewed remained unfulfilled. It is, of course, one of the purposes of a strong fortress to deter the would-be attacker from even attempting the assault. But when Sigismund decided to desist from all further military operations against Prague it was not only for military but also for political reasons.

The conquest of Prague had been the main goal of the huge military effort that had materialized in the First Crusade against the Hussites. With this in mind the forces had been assembled in so many countries and had been concentrated outside the great city. The supreme command rested, of course, in the hands of Sigismund who, as King of the Romans, was still the temporal head of Christendom and who, by leading the Crusade, also acted as the swordbearer of the Church of Rome. It is difficult to believe that Sigismund had ever contemplated anything less than complete surrender of the rebellious capital. He may have hoped that Prague, having offered surrender twice before, would not now, under such pressure, remain defiant. But when, on July 14, he ordered the attack upon the Vítkov he decided to reach this goal by military means. He must have known that the foreign troops, once the city had surrendered and was occupied by them, would keep killing Czech heretics as they had grown used to doing before. Thus it was certainly not humanitarian consideration that caused him now to make a decision which, at first glance, seems as strange today as it seemed strange

[12] Březová, p. 389, also mentions that many people began to call the hill "the Mountain of the Battle" or "of the Chalice." Actually the name "Žižkov" came almost immediately into general use and can be found in official documents of the city as early as 1427. See Tomek, *Dějepis*, IV, 81, note 45.

and suspicious to the German princes, lords, and bishops in his camp. When, on the day after the defeat of the Vítkov, the commanders of his army ordered the heavy siege guns posted on the heights north of the Vltava to open fire against the Old Town, Sigismund interfered and forbade the bombardment.[13]

If not humanitarian, what was his motive? For one thing Sigismund, little as he cared for the townspeople, still cared for the town. Windecke tells us of the sentimental mood that overcame him when, arriving at the Hradčany, he looked down again upon the beautiful city which he had not seen for many years. "Oh Prague," so he exclaimed, "my own parental heritage, how do I find thee!"[14]

But besides the King's hope to win his capital without having to destroy it first, he had come by now under very strong political pressure. The Czech lords of his entourage, representatives of the Catholic nobility, had all along had strong misgivings about the invasion of Bohemia by a huge army of foreigners. They were prepared to fight the Hussites in a civil war, but it was a different thing to look on or assist while Prague, and with it all Bohemia, perhaps including their own estates, would be occupied and despoiled by foreigners, especially Germans.

But they did not look forward, either, to the possibility that Sigismund might achieve a complete victory in which they, the Catholic nobility of Bohemia, would have so small a part. They still remembered, with uneasy feelings, the relative weakness to which their fathers or grandfathers had temporarily been reduced by Charles IV. The power which they had regained under Wenceslas, they were not willing to lose again to his younger brother. Much as they despised the religious and political revolutionism of the Hussite and especially the Taborite radicals they were not too sorry about the plight of the rich Catholic clergy of Bohemia. They were not averse to seeing it lose much of its worldly possessions—especially while there was a chance that they themselves might eventually be the heirs. For this they could hope only as long as the King remained, to some extent, dependent on their help.

So far they had participated in the Crusade, as this was their only chance to keep matters under control. Now, strange as it may seem, the defeat of the Vítkov played into their hands. After July 14 it was obvious that Prague would never surrender meekly to the army of

[13] *Magdeburger Schöppenchronik*, p. 354. The suspicion that Sigismund may secretly have favored the heretics is also reported by Ludolf of Sagan (*op.cit.*, p. 476) and Thomas Ebendorfer (*op.cit.*, p. 850).

[14] Windecke, p. 132.

foreign enemies. Was there still a chance that she might surrender to the less frightening pressure of Bohemia's Catholic nobility? Doubtful as this seemed, the Catholic lords of Bohemia could, at least, dangle this hope before the eyes of their King. And so they did.

In the days immediately after the battle of the Vítkov "the King held many secret talks with the Bohemian lords, who finally advised the King that he should let the German princes march home with their armies."[15] Windecke gives us what sounds like a fairly authentic record of those secret talks, or at least of their gist. This is what, according to him, the Bohemian lords "with their malicious words" said to Sigismund:[16] "Do not let them conquer the city, oh King! Else the Germans will perceive the power of the Crown of Bohemia, and the Crown will never be safe again from those Germans. Let the armies ride home, Sir, and we, the lords of Bohemia, will give the city of Prague into your power within a month!" Said the King: "How can I believe that? If I let the armies ride home, you will never keep your promise!" Said the Bohemian lords: "Sir, we will lead Your Majesty to the castle of St. Wenceslas and will crown you as a King of Bohemia, and there we will do you homage and swear you loyalty by the Saints, as to our natural lord. Remember: we are the Crown of Bohemia, and not those peasants!"

Proud words indeed. Coupled with the previous promise they were effective. The King, much discouraged by his recent defeat, was eventually convinced that this was the easiest way to achieve his goal, and so he persevered in his resolve not to risk another assault nor to permit the city to be bombarded. And accepting the offer which the Catholic lords of Bohemia had made to him, on July 28 Sigismund had himself crowned as King of Bohemia.

In the royal church built by Charles IV, the beautiful Cathedral of St. Vitus on the Hradčany, in the presence of ten princes and a large crowd of prelates and barons, Conrad, Archbishop of Prague, put the Crown on Sigismund's head, thus giving him, according to Bohemia's time-honored custom, the full legal status as lord of the Kingdom. He became Bohemia's thirteenth king. The solemn act was followed by the oath of allegiance, sworn by all attending lords of the countries of the Bohemian Crown.

True, not nearly all the peers of the realm were present, a fact stressed

[15] *Magdeburger Schöppenchronik*, p. 354.
[16] Windecke, p. 111.

studiously by Sigismund's enemies.[17] More serious was the complete absence of the representatives of the cities, especially those of Prague who, at preceding coronations, had taken an important part in the ceremony. Even so it was difficult to claim that the coronation was legally invalid. There was only one right by which Sigismund's kingship could now still be contested: the right of revolution. It was by this right that Prague, little impressed by what happened on Hradčany Hill, continued the fight.

The military situation had, after the battle of the Vítkov, undergone no palpable change. But in the camp of the besiegers the disappointment of July 14, the frustration of general inactivity, and the growing mutual distrust began to work havoc upon morale, unity of purpose, and the will toward victory. Right after the battle of the Vítkov the crusaders, officers, and soldiers, had voiced their suspicion that some sort of a foul game was being played between the Catholic Bohemians and their heretic compatriots behind the city walls, that the town had been forewarned of the impending assault and the defenders thus put on their guard, and that the King himself was a clandestine heretic. The latter suspicion was strengthened by Sigismund's reluctance to fight and his order not to bombard the city. There was constant friction between the German troops and the Czechs in the King's service, making it necessary for Sigismund to intervene personally so as to forestall bloody clashes.

Even earlier the foreign mercenaries had shown little restraint in killing, preferably burning, Czech people regardless of age, sex, and even creed, and with the increasing frustration this practice became more widespread. For a long time the corpses of more than two hundred "heretics," Czechs who, after capture, had not been burned but simply killed and cut into pieces, lay unburied in the German encampment, rotting under the sun in what was an unusually dry, mercilessly hot summer.[18] The stench rising from those bodies was increased by the evaporations from carcasses of many dead horses and the unremoved garbage and other refuse accruing in the temporary living quarters of some 80,000 people. This decomposing matter attracted swarms of mosquitoes, horseflies, and other insects which made life in the encampment

[17] As shown e.g. by Březová's report (p. 396), who also tells us that in Prague people made fun of the large number of accolades performed by Sigismund at that opportunity, largely honoring men who had done nothing to deserve such promotion. They were, so Březová says, therefore called by the people "painted knights" (milites depicti).

[18] *Magdeburger Schöppenchronik*, p. 354.

more and more unbearable. Soon the troops began to lose more lives from sickness than they ever had lost or were likely to lose from enemy action. In addition a fire broke out which destroyed many tents. Toward the end of July the morale in the army sank to a point where officers and men yearned to get home and be done with the hopeless crusade.

On the side of the besieged there was no corresponding loss of morale. Their grim determination not to surrender was never impaired. The cruel treatment suffered by Czech prisoners at the hands of the Germans was one more reason why not even the thought of surrender could seriously be entertained. All the stronger became the wish of the people to retaliate for the murder of Czech prisoners. The number of Germans which the troops of Prague had taken prisoner was small. During the battle of the Vítkov the Czech soldiers had slain most of those who had not escaped. But in the city hall of the Old Town seventeen Germans were held whose lives the city council intended to save. Enraged by the continued killing of Czech prisoners a crowd of people, Praguers and Taborites, marched to the city hall on July 22 and demanded that the prisoners be delivered to them for retaliation. The councilors, though reluctant, finally felt that they could not resist. One of the prisoners, a priest who promised to give the Communion in the two kinds, was set free, but the other sixteen were conducted to a place where the procedure could be watched by the enemy soldiers from across the river. There, to a man, they were burned. It may have been under this impression that the chronicler from Magdeburg[19] called the Crusade "a truly hateful campaign, for whoever was taken prisoner on either side, for him there was no other outcome but the inhumanly bitter death."

By the time of Sigismund's coronation it was already obvious that the siege would come to an early end. Several German princes and other army chiefs, deeply dissatisfied with the way things were going, had, for some days, impatiently demanded to be allowed to go home. At first Sigismund had hesitated, supposedly because of the impending coronation, in reality because he found himself in great financial difficulties. If Prague had been conquered, the German and Hungarian mercenaries could have been paid off largely from booty made in the city, but now Sigismund did not have the ready cash to fulfill his obligations. He finally solved the problem by confiscating, in the most ruthless manner, all the jewelry and other things made from precious

[19] *ibid.*

metals in the churches and monasteries on the Hradčany. He did, of course, promise to restore all those treasures after the war. But the people of Prague heard of these spoliations with anger, and even those who had seen little merit in the iconoclastic activities of the Taborite priests asked themselves whose sin was graver, that of people who had destroyed, for the sake of a principle, the wooden images or that of the man who, for money's sake, had laid his hands on sacred things of much greater value.[20]

On July 30 the troops were finally paid off, orders were given to break camp, tents and other structures were burned, and the armies that had started so strong and boastfully on their crusading campaign went back to whence they had come, their purpose unachieved. Prague was free. And this was not a fleeting success. Other crusades were to follow but none of the invading armies ever succeeded again in permitting their soldiers to look down upon the roofs and steeples of the great city.

Meanwhile we have, as it were, lost sight of Žižka and his share in the turn of events that was sealed by the withdrawal of the crusading armies. It seems possible that without the interference of the Catholic nobles of Bohemia the battle of the Vítkov would not have remained the only major combat action of this campaign. But whatever could have followed, after July 14 the odds were surely no longer so hopeless for Prague as they may have seemed before.

In another way that battle was, after all, decisive for the outcome of the campaign. Had it been lost, had Sigismund succeeded in taking the Vítkov, then Prague would almost certainly have been doomed to starvation and eventual surrender. Without this victory the political action of the Catholic lords could never have succeeded, could, indeed, never have been started. Without this victory of Žižka's the process of demoralization in the King's camp would never have taken such a swift and paralyzing course.[21] To this extent it was certainly Žižka's genius, his intuitive anticipation of the enemy's most dangerous strategic

[20] Actually the comparison, drawn by Březová (p. 396) sounds somewhat more naïve in his original diction. "Quorum igitur peccatum gravius, eorum scilicet, qui ligneas, aut eorum, qui argenteas ymagines destruxerunt?"

[21] This fact, I believe, is not given sufficient weight in Pekař's careful and interesting analysis of the reasons for Sigismund's failure before Prague (III, 51-58). He is of course quite right in stressing the importance of the political factors, especially of the action of the Catholic lords. This had received too little attention in most earlier treatments of this phase of the war, which used to see in the battle of the Vítkov a military feat of the first order and the sole reason for Sigismund's retreat from Prague. The first one, by the way, to refute this exaggerated view on the basis of military analysis was Frankenberger (*op.cit.*, I, 85).

1. JOHN ŽIŽKA. The "Little Head from Tabor," shortly after 1500. Original in the National Museum in Prague.

2. King Sigismund Directing the Siege of Prague. Illuminated pen drawing fron "Eberhard Windecke: Des Kaisers Sigmunds Buch," manuscript, Hagenau, Diebc Lauber, *ca.* 1440-1450. By permission of H. P. Krauss, New York City.

move and his quick and competent tactical handling of the battle itself, which saved Prague.

And with this stroke, even though measured in the numbers of troops directly involved it was not a "great battle," Žižka achieved more than just the momentary relief of Prague. True, the war was only in its beginnings, potentially the enemy remained overwhelmingly strong, and his will to continue the war was not broken. Yet it was blunted for a considerable period. With the time thus gained, Žižka also gained a chance of strengthening the military power of the Hussite camp, more especially of the Taborite movement, to an extent which was still to surprise all Europe.

CHAPTER 10

# THE FOUR ARTICLES OF PRAGUE

IN MOST WARS throughout history some slender communication between the opposing forces, directly or through the medium of neutrals, was maintained even while the clash of arms was loud and bloody. This was true also during the Hussite wars. But it is most characteristic of these wars that such contacts with the enemy were almost exclusively concerned with religion, and often referred to the Hussite demand for the recognition of the Four Articles of Prague. Indeed it was just during the siege of Prague that this great document received its final shape and was, in this form, presented to the Christian world, including the crusading enemies before the gates.

The history of this charter[1] leads us back to the time before the outbreak of the revolution. A combination of similar demands can be found as early as August 1417, when it figured in the resolutions passed by a synod of the clergy of the University of Prague.[2] Closer to the final form are the first articles of the address directed to Sigismund by the Prague Diet of September 1419.[3] Indeed we find there already, in a

[1] The development of the Four Articles since the beginning of the Hussite wars is, of course, described to some extent in all the more detailed writings on Hussitism. One of the best general treatments is probably contained in Kamil Krofta's beautifully written essay "Husitství po Husovi" (Hussitism after Hus) in his book *Duchovní odkaz Husitství* (The spiritual heritage of Hussitism), a posthumous collection of earlier writings and lectures (Prague 1946). There are several contributions to this question by F. M. Bartoš, especially *Do čtyř artykulů* (Prague 1926) and chapters 2 and 3 of his *Husitství a cizina* (Prague 1931). Pekař treats the history of the Four Articles in relation to the period of the siege of Prague in a special chapter (III, 59-75) and also discusses the general significance of the Articles for Bohemia's history (III, 307-313) and Žižka's understanding of the Articles (II, 170-174). Mathilde Uhlirz's study, "Die Genesis der vier Prager Artikel" (*Sitzungsberichte der K. Akademie der Wissenschaften*, Vienna 1914, 175, 3) is an industrious and in some points valuable comparison of the Four Articles with the writings of Wiclif. In accord with her teacher Loserth the author tries to prove that the main content of the Four Articles can be traced back to Wiclif's teachings. Loserth's whole theory of Hus's slavish dependence on Wiclif has, however, long been proved wrong. Uhlirz's specialized thesis is perhaps partly defensible if its more sweeping claims are reduced to proper measure and limited to the First and Third Articles. I have, unfortunately, not been able to get hold of F. Dvorský's book, *Počátky kalicha a artikule pražké*.

[2] See F. Dvorský as quoted by F. Lützow, *Life and Times of Master John Hus*, pp. 343-344.

[3] See *Archiv český*, III, 206, and above, Chapter 4.

somewhat less striking formulation, all the four demands which appear at the end of Čeněk of Wartenberg's revolutionary manifest of April 20, 1420.[4] After that only the Fourth Article, which then only called for the purging of the good name of Bohemia from slander, underwent an important change, in that its main emphasis came to rest on the additional demand for the punishment and extirpation of mortal sins. While, with the exception of this last demand, the charter as a whole can at least be traced back to 1417, some of its basic ideas are of much older origin. This is especially true of the First Article (in earlier versions it was the second): "*that throughout the Kingdom of Bohemia the Word of God be proclaimed and preached freely by Christian priests.*"[5]

By putting the sermon, preached in the vernacular, in the center of all religious service this demand tended to reduce (and in the puritan worship of the Taborites even to eliminate) much of the traditional ritual with its tinge of magic performance and its inaccessibility to popular understanding. As such the demand reflected a tendency which toward the end of the fourteenth century was rather widespread in Europe and found a particularly impressive advocate in Wiclif.[6] It was, however, fully represented in Bohemia at the same time that Wiclif taught at Oxford, and certainly before his teachings had had time to penetrate into Bohemia, by such predecessors of Hus as the great popular preachers Conrad Waldhauser (d. 1369) and Milič of Kroměříž (d. 1374); others like Matthew of Janov and John Štěkna were slightly younger than Wiclif and may have heard of him, yet they, too, were certainly more indebted to the earlier preachers of reform in Bohemia than to the great Englishman. Hus himself was, of course, in full agreement with Wiclif on this issue, but again it would be wrong to assume that he had to learn from the Oxonian what to himself was so elementary a need. Like his predecessors and followers he practiced what he proclaimed: even at the time of his voluntary exile from Prague, from 1412 to 1414, he never ceased preaching freely, on hills and at crossroads, with the sky as the roof of his church and the Scripture as

[4] *Archiv český*, III, 210, and above, Chapter 7.

[5] For the "official" text of the Articles, that is, the one accepted in July 1420 from which the passages printed in italics are translated, see Březová, pp. 391-395 and *Archiv český*, III, 213ff.

[6] Important contributions in English to the questions of Hus's relation to Wiclif are Otakar Odložilík's "Wycliffe's Influence upon Central and Eastern Europe" (*Slavonic Review*, XXI, 1929), and R. R. Bett's "English and Czech Influences on the Hussite Movement" (*Transactions of the Royal Hist. Soc.*, XXXI, 1939). For a Czech treatment see Bartoš, *Husitství a cizina*, pp. 20-58.

his main guide. It is clearly with this attitude in mind that the first of the Articles of Prague was proclaimed.

It was the Second Article which gave the whole Hussite movement its most popular, its most palpable symbol: the Chalice. For it demands: "*that the Holy Sacrament of the Body and Blood of God, in both kinds, bread and wine, be given freely to all true Christians who are not barred from it by deadly sin; just as our Saviour inaugurated and ordered it.*"

In the long drawn-out theological disputations which arose, on this issue, at the church councils of Constance and Basel and found their echo in countless other oral and written discussions, many highly complex questions were asked and answered. There was, first of all, the problem whether the Church, by abolishing the old practice of giving both bread and wine to the laity, had actually, as the Hussites claimed, divided the sacrament and thereby destroyed its salutary force, or whether, as the Church maintained, each of the two offerings, bread and wine, was transformed by the sacrament into the whole Christ. This discussion was bound to lead to the investigation of the problem of transubstantiation which had already become an issue through Wiclif's theory of remanence and which soon began to plague and to some extent divide Hussitism just as it was to plague and divide, a hundred years later, the Protestant churches at the Conference of Marburg and after.[7] But some of the arguments brought forward in this discussion, especially among those given in defense of the official ruling of the Church of Rome, were on a much more petty level[8] and thus apt to obscure the real significance of the Hussite demand. For the masses of the Hussite people however, people who neither understood nor really cared for the more intricate theological questions, the real significance of the Communion in the two kinds was unmistakable. The Sacrament of the Altar in which Christ, through the real presence of his transformed body and blood, effected the mystic union with the believing Christian—this act was the deepest religious experience, the

[7] Darwell Stone, *History of the Doctrine of the Eucharist*, probably the most detailed study in English, unfortunately treats the contribution of the Czech reformation rather lightly. A very concise review of the history of the Eucharist with special regard to the Chalice is given in H. C. Lea, *History of the Inquisition*, II, 471ff. See further Julius Smend, *Kelchspendung und Kelchversagung in der abendländischen Kirche*, Göttingen 1898.

[8] Thus Ludolf, Abbot of Sagan, one of the most highly regarded learned critics of Hussitism (at the same time an important chronicler), mentions the unsuitability of giving the wine to drunkards or dispensing it during a plague. See *Tractatus de longevo schismate*, ed. J. Loserth, in *Beiträge zur Geschichte der Husitischen Bewegung*, Archiv f. öster. Geschichte, Vienna 1880, vol. 60, pp. 524-526.

holiest of the holies. Why should only part of this experience be granted to the lay folk, why was its entirety reserved to the clergy? Was this not a presumption evincing the same spirit that had created and maintained the political power, worldly riches, and moral corruption of the clergy, all in striking contrast to the ways of Christ and the Apostles? How, furthermore, was it possible to doubt or twist the command of Christ, so clearly expressed in all the four gospels?[9]

More than any other of the Hussite tenets the demand for the Chalice thus expressed the statement—or the discovery—of the idea that before God all men are equal. More than any other, also, the demand for the Chalice could be presented in a simple, visible form. Thus the way the Communion was taken—"sub utraque" or "sub una specie," in both kinds or in one kind, became the distinct borderline between those who were for and those who were against the reformation. The Chalice became the symbol most commonly used as a pictorial expression of the Hussite idea—on the banners of Hussite troops and in the personal seal (and later also in the name) of their greatest leader, Žižka.

Already Matthew of Janov (d. 1394) had recommended the daily Communion, but the later Hussite claim that he had suggested the Chalice for the laity has long been disproved. Hus himself, writing from Constance in January 1415, was still reluctant to commit himself. It was only on June 21, two weeks before his death, that he came out strongly for the Communion in the two kinds. Thereby, consciously defying a decision taken a week earlier by the Council of Constance, he gave the final sanction to the great change in the eyes of his faithful followers.

The man really responsible for the innovation was Jacobellus of Stříbro. It was not his only claim to a role in religious history. He owed his nickname "little Jacob"—in Czech Jakoubek—to his very short stature, but spiritually he was surely a giant of his time and probably the greatest, next to Hus himself, of all Bohemian reformers.[10] A few

[9] The official version refers specifically to the words of Christ at the Last Supper in the Synoptic Gospels, and with special stress to John 6:53-56; further to the very significant explanations of the meaning of the Communion in Chapter 11 of the first letter to the Corinthians; to the canon of Gelasius I (492-496) prohibiting the "division" of the sacrament as a sacrilege; and to a long list of further witnesses from St. Gregory down to Albertus Magnus.

[10] I cannot claim originality in contrasting Jacobellus' small stature and his mental greatness. (See R. W. Seton-Watson, *A History of the Czechs and Slovaks*, London 1943, p. 42.) Of monographs on Jacobellus the most recent one is the book by František Borecký, *Mistr Jakoubek ze Stříbra*, Prague 1945. F. M. Bartoš devoted to him one of his character sketches last published in his *Světci a kacíři* (Witnesses and heretics), Prague 1949, pp. 98ff. In Pekař's *Žižka* the role of Jacobellus in the development of the revolution is treated in the greater parts

years younger than Hus, he was in many ways more radical than the martyr of Constance. In his earlier writings he was not free of chiliastic ideas, and in his "Positio de Antichristo" (1412) he brusquely identified the Pope as Antichrist, as it was he who was foremost among those priests who, in opposition to the example and the teachings of Christ, had been corrupted by temporal riches and pleasure. Jacobellus himself led a life of utter saintliness as acknowledged by all who knew him. In doing so he simply lived as he taught, for he had decidedly puritan views, attacking also the exaggerated and costly beautification of churches and monasteries. There was much in his teaching that Tabor could refer to at a time when the two Hussite parties found themselves disagreeing over questions of ritual. Altogether he can be rated as the foremost figure of the "zealous defenders of the Chalice," but his radicalism was much more exclusively religious than that of the Taborites, and the open revolution of the twenties found in him a somewhat reluctant, worried supporter.

Jacobellus had from the beginning stood foremost in the ranks of those who, with Hus, defended the teachings of Wiclif against the Archbishop of Prague, Zbyněk Zajíc of Hasenburg, who had ordered all of Wiclif's writings to be burned. He stood equally in the front of the fighters against the indulgences sold by Pope John XXIII for his fight against Ladislas of Naples. It seemed natural that, when Hus, on King Wenceslas' demand, retired to Kozí Hrádek in 1412, Jacobellus should at once take over the leadership among the reformers who remained in the capital, and it was but a symbol of this position that Jacobellus' main activity as a preacher was, from then on, connected with John Hus's own temple, the Chapel of Bethlehem. Though he never accepted the position as Rector of the University his prestige remained extraordinary.

Jacobellus seems to have first dispensed the Communion in the two kinds to laymen early in 1414, long before the Council of Constance decided virtually to stigmatize this old Christian custom as heretical.[11] Jacobellus was soon followed by other Hussite clerics, first among them perhaps two priests from Germany who had sought and found refuge in Prague: Nicholas and Peter of Dresden.[12] After the death of Hus the

---

of two chapters (I, 1-31, and 96-113). There is a chapter on Jacobellus in Nejedlý's monumental work on the Hussite song (*Dějiny husitského zpěvu*, Prague 1913, I, 58-105).

11 The claim that in this act, too, Hussitism was following in the footsteps of Wiclif has already been refuted by Smend, *op.cit.*, p. 28.

12 The theory that they (or one of them) were the real originators of the change seems

practice became more and more general in Bohemia, and when, on March 10, 1417, the University of Prague gave its official blessing to the Communion in the two kinds it could only sanction a custom that had spread far and wide through the kingdom.[13]

There can be no doubt that in the negotiations which led up to the acceptance of the Four Articles in 1420 Jacobellus played a dominant role.[14] During the difficult months of spring 1420 no other man could mediate between Prague and Tabor, could bridge the differences that even then had developed between them as could Jacobellus. No one in either party could forget or neglect the fact that the introduction of the Chalice for the laity, the central symbol of the movement had been his work.

Jacobellus, even more than Hus himself, had also directly contributed to the demand which appeared as the third of the Articles of Prague: *"Whereas many priests and monks, by force of temporal law, command great earthly possessions, this being against the orders of Christ, to the detriment of their priestly office, and to the great disadvantage of the lords of the temporal estates; that those priests be deprived of such unlawful power, and that according to the Scriptures they live exemplary lives and be led back to the ways of Christ and the Apostles."*

The attack against the riches and luxury of the Church was, of course, common all through the later Middle Ages. No single man could be made responsible for the demand that the clergy should return to the ways of Christ and the Apostles. Attempts to practice rather than to propagandize such a return or reform can be found in many of the medieval movements of heresy while to some extent the need for reform was recognized and expressed by representatives of the Roman hierarchy as well. The most energetic and impressive criticism of the worldly riches and power of the clergy had come, however, from Wiclif, and Hus and Jacobellus were fully conscious of their debt to the Englishman when they came forward with their plea for a new, clean, and poor priesthood.

---

untenable. It had some significance insofar as the two men from Dresden may have been members of, or at least had connections with, Waldensian groups. There is, however, no proof for the claim that for the Waldensians the Communion in the two kinds had ever been an important issue, and at least in some parts of this large and changing movement transubstantiation had been denied, whereas for Hus and all his direct followers transubstantiation was never in doubt. See especially chapter 4 of Bartoš, *Husitství a cizina*, and Krofta, *Duchovní odkaz husitství*, pp. 66, 67.

13 "The University was led rather than being leader." See Urbánek, *Žižka*, p. 42.

14 See Borecký, *op.cit.*, p. 51, and Bartoš, *Světci a Racíři*, pp. 99, 100.

Of the Four Articles the Third was, in a way, the most political of all, and it had a stronger social effectiveness than the rest. The first two were "democratic" in attacking purely spiritual reservations and monopolies, without any direct implication for the structure of temporal society. The Third Article, however, crossed this border. It attacked what had become, in Bohemia as much as elsewhere, an enormous vested interest. Thereby the Third Article became a powerful weapon in the hands of the reformers. It secured a very wide support for the reform movement from all classes. The masses of little people would feel that, with the temporal riches and the taxing power of the Church abolished, their own burden would be lightened, though the actual outcome of the secularization of Church properties—in Bohemia as in other countries where later the Reformation was successful—hardly ever fulfilled such expectations. Other classes might eventually enjoy the fruits of expropriating Church properties and Church incomes: the nobility as well as the stronger towns. Indeed for some of the lords the expectation of such temporal gains may have provided a stronger enticement to join the reform movement than the more lasting but less palpable gains for the salvation of their souls. It may seem ironical (but is, of course, just as true for the Lutheran Reformation) that such gains from the secularization of Church properties were, in the end, made by the Catholic as well as by the Hussite nobility.[15]

In two of the oil portraits of Žižka, painted in the Protestant Bohemia of the sixteenth century, we find an inscription calling him "superbiae simulet avariciae clericorum severus ultor," the severe avenger of the insolence and avarice of the clergy.[16] By "superbia," of course, is meant the improper claim of the Roman hierarchy to wield temporal power, and the "avaricia" refers to the amassing of earthly possessions of any form. The inscription shows to what extent, in the mind of posterity, Žižka had become identified with the fight for the third of the Four Articles. But the word "ultor," avenger or punisher, points no less to the fourth and last of them: "*That all mortal sins and especially those that are committed publicly, as well as other disorders offending against the Law of God, shall be properly and sensibly prohibited and punished in each estate by those who have the authority to do so; and that*

[15] Windecke, for instance, stresses repeatedly his conviction that Sigismund's Catholic followers among the Bohemian nobility stood by the King mainly in the expectation of being rewarded for these services by being invested with former Church property (see pp. 134, 188).

[16] See the reproductions in K. Guth's article in *Sborník Žižkův*, Prague 1924, pp. 290ff.

*evil and slanderous rumors about this country be cleansed away, thus insuring the general welfare of the Bohemian Kingdom and Nation."*

Whereas the motivation appended to the other three articles mainly explained the need for the demand by quotations from the Scriptures or other religious authorities, the motivation to the Fourth Article goes far beyond such limits. It begins by saying that all those guilty of such sins, and even those who only approve of them, deserve the death penalty. There follows a long list of deadly sins including, for laymen, "adultery, gluttony, thieving, murder, lying, cheating, perjury, conjuring, harmful crafts or such trade that thrives on popular superstition, avarice, usury and similar ills." In addition an even longer list makes it a deadly sin for the clergy to engage in: simony; in the taking of money for priestly functions, all of which are especially named and which include all the sacraments; in the sale of indulgences; in the saying of mass for payment; and in other sins such as "arrogance, avarice, adultery, whoring and other uncleanliness; irascibility, envy, brawling; wrongs done in arbitrary summoning or mistreating people before court, deluding simple folks with hypocritical begging or with false promises so as to obtain their money or other goods for offering or other benefits to the Church." "All these," so the appendix to the article sums up, "each true servant of Christ and true son of the Church should prohibit in himself and in others, and should hate and despise such sins as the devil, so that he remain in everything on the right path and do his duty according to his station and profession."

This long list of deadly sins may sound almost tedious and pedantic to the modern ear. To the contemporaries it rang true and ominous. The sinfulness to which so many servants of the Church—monastic as well as lay priests—had fallen was more than a scandal. It was a terrible danger for the whole of Christianity, even in the eyes of the people to whom this depravity did not necessarily spell the nearness of judgment and the end of the present world. Ever since Konrad Waldhauser and Milič of Kroměříž had hurled their wrathful invectives against clerical corruption, this feeling of a general sickness of society, of the need of a great cleansing, had struck deep roots among the masses of the people. The list of the deadly sins was not a theoretical scheme, a criminal code for the use of judges dealing with possible offenses—it was a picture of things seen daily and a great and solemn warning to Christendom. The danger seemed too great to allow of any further dilatory treatment.

It was Žižka, the "severe avenger," who felt it to be his mission to destroy the evil of deadly sins, especially among the clergy, wherever he could get hold of it. Indeed it seems likely that the Fourth Article in its final, stern wording had been made part of the new charter on the express demand of the Taborites represented at the meeting of June 27, and there can be no doubt that Žižka was one, if not the leading one, of those representatives.[17] But the wording seems to betray that there was some resistance put up by the moderates of the University, for the words: "properly and sensibly prohibited and punished in each estate by those who have the authority[18] to do so," seem to indicate an attempt at limiting the danger of too general and too arbitrary a persecution of sins and sinners. But this caution could not and did not deter Žižka from regarding himself as the legitimate prosecutor, judge, and executor in implementing the Fourth Article. He never had any doubt that this was his office, that he was fully authorized by God and Christ, as was any true Christian with enough power on his hands, to destroy the deadly sins wherever he met them. This view comes out very clearly in his letters, and in the way in which he himself formulated the Fourth Article. He would have had difficulty in understanding how anyone could, in good faith, dispute this authority.[19]

While there were, especially later, considerable differences between the Hussite parties in the understanding of the Four Articles, this was hardly true at the time of their official adoption. In the summer of 1420 they appeared, to all Hussite groups at Prague, as a satisfactory common platform, as an instrument of unity and as a position which could be and had to be defended by all, by arms if need be, and in open discussion if there was an opportunity for it. The feeling that there was a great cause well expressed and well worth fighting and dying for pervades clearly the concluding passage of the document. This is how it reads:

[17] Březová, p. 374.

[18] The Czech term is "úřad," a word possessing almost all the shades of meaning of the English word office.

[19] Žižka's attitude towards the Four Articles, especially towards the Fourth, is carefully elaborated on by Pekař (II, 170-174). I cannot agree with his conclusion that this attitude can only be understood on the basis of chiliasm. There were phases in Žižka's life when he could probably not remain unimpressed by chiliastic arguments brought forward by Taborite priests. Yet there is no trace of chiliastic thought or language in any of his preserved letters and messages, and we know that Žižka's personal relationship to some of the fanatic priests at Tabor who were the main representatives of chiliastic thought, especially Koranda, had cooled off at an early time and later became openly antagonistic. I think that Žižka's special hatred for the monastic clergy whose moral corruption had become one of the main objects of general criticism and detestation can be understood without imputing the chiliastic motive.

"Now if anyone should charge us, in writing or talking, with anything evil, heretical, shameful or unclean, then we ask and beg that such a one should not be believed, as a man speaking slander out of his grudge and hatred, and as a malicious and false witness. For this we boldly confess before the Lord God and before the whole world, that with God's help there is no other intention in our hearts but with all power, strength, and fortitude to serve and dedicate ourselves to the Lord Jesus Christ and to carry through and fulfill His Law and Commands, as it behooves every good Christian. But every evil opponent and everyone who would force and push us away from this good we must resist according to the Law of God and His Truth, and according to our vocation we must, against such violence, defend the Truth and ourselves by the use of worldly arms. And if, through the excess of someone among our people, anything evil should happen, then we declare solemnly that this is not in our intention, for with the help of God we stand against all deadly sins. And if it should seem that someone suffers any harm through us, then it would be either because of the dire necessity or because he is an enemy of God and ourselves, one from whose violence and cruelty we would have to protect the Law of God and ourselves. And above all we solemnly declare that, if we should appear to be doing anything wrong, we are always ready to put it right, and in all things to receive, with an open heart, instruction, and enlightenment from the Holy Scriptures."

Once full agreement had been reached about them, the Four Articles had to be presented to the Czech people and Christendom at large. But the first people to whom they were to be submitted—that is, after the citizens of Prague—were the enemies standing before the gates of the besieged city.

Even while the majority of the population were busy with defense preparations, in the last days of June and early in July, scores of scribes must have been busy writing copy after copy of the manifesto, and hundreds of them were broadcast all over Bohemia and in the neighboring countries. They did not fail to impress people everywhere. Indeed one keeps wondering if, then and there, the Hussite Reformation might not have swept through Europe the way the German-Swiss Reformation did a hundred years later, had it only had at its disposal the tremendous asset of the printed word.

That the leaders of the besieging army received copies of the Four Articles at an early time is known to us from a letter written, probably on one of the first days of July, by the papal legate, Ferdinand Bishop of Lucena, to the city of Prague. From the way the letter numbers the articles we can roughly date it, for it still puts the article on the Chalice first as was done in the draft accepted on June 27, instead of second as in the final version of early July.[20] As the first official answer to the Articles given by one of the highest functionaries of the Church of Rome, the letter is an important and interesting document.

The Bishop begins with bitter complaints. On coming to Bohemia he had seen with his own eyes what otherwise he would have hardly believed: burned monasteries, mutilated images of saints, the expulsion and even the murder of priests and monks—with the result that in many churches divine service had been restricted, in some had totally ceased. Those responsible for such happenings—obviously the Bishop meant the Taborites—are reported to dwell in Prague, and you, the Praguers, hope to defend yourself with their help. "We are amazed that you, who glory in the feeling of being the zealous followers of the Law of God and who are ready to stand with it and, if need be, die for it, have received within your defense the enemies of God, or that you can possibly expect any help from such people. . . ." (This remark shows that the letter was still written before the Battle of the Vítkov.)

The Bishop then turns to the Four Articles, beginning with what then was the Second Article: the demand for the freedom of preaching. What, so he asks, does this imply? "If it means that any person can freely preach, and preach as he pleases, then it is not in order, especially not if the preaching is directed against the doctrines of the Church." The Third Article, demanding the apostolic poverty of the clergy, is, so the Bishop says, not blameworthy as long as it is handled with sensible caution. But, so he continues, "it does not befit you to judge the need of temporal goods for the clerics, nor to expel them from churches or take away their property. For it seems that your desire is rather to acquire their property than to establish the example of a pure life."

The friendliest judgment, somewhat strangely, is given to the first part of the Fourth Article, dealing with the punishment of deadly sins. The Bishop calls it "laudable that you insist on the expurgation of and the desistance from all public mortal peccancies."[21] He reserves his criticism to the far more innocent second part of the article, the cleans-

[20] See *Urk. Beiträge*, I, 34-37.

[21] In an unusual way the Latin of this sentence permits the use of exactly the same words in the translation. This is how it reads in the original: "Quartum laudabile est, cum pro expurgatione et desistentia insistitis omnium publicorum peccatorum mortalium."

ing of the good name of Bohemia from the reproach of heresy. This, the Bishop says, "can only be achieved if those who are infected with errors or who defend heresies denounce them and reconcile themselves to the Church, not, however, if they oppose the Church and even rebel against their king and natural lord, thus adding to the infamy of heresy the crime and infamy of lese majesty."

The article which the Bishop numbers first, on the Chalice for the laity, is the one he answers last, and against this one he summons all his capacity for theological battle. He denies that the Communion in both kinds was the general precept of Christ or has to be considered as an evangelical law which could only be acted against at the price of eternal damnation.

"Even if, as some doctors claim, the Communion in both kinds is perhaps more perfect and meritorious, even then it is preferable to increase the merit by humbly abstaining from the Communion of the Chalice as it is in opposition to the custom of the Universal Church and to the decree of the Council of Constance, than in arrogant presumption to increase the crime and add to the danger. Or, if you still insist in your wish to achieve greater merit through the Communion in both kinds, then you should entreat him who alone has the right to dispense in things spiritual, and not make demands upon His Majesty King Sigismund who administers things temporal."

Finally, after all these theoretical arguments, follows the practical step of diplomacy which the Bishop takes in cooperation with the King: "On this as well as on other questions which you would wish to bring before us we are prepared to listen to you. When you asked the same before from His Majesty the King he would not in this cause, which is a cause of the creed, expose himself to an audience without us. Now we inform you that with our consent His Majesty is prepared to give, if you ask for it, a safe conduct for a sufficient time to those persons whom you want to designate as your spokesmen. And if you want to approach this with good and sober judgment, then there will be room not only for forgiveness but even for grace. But if you should persist in your obstinacy and should not want to go the way of the true salvation, then you will be treated all the more sternly for all the patience and lenience which so far has been shown you."

The generally fairly moderate tone in which the papal legate speaks to the people of Prague may be somewhat surprising. It contrasts oddly with the fierce and uncompromising character of the papal bull of

March 1420, the bull for the enforcement of which the Bishop had joined Sigismund and his crusading army. One might wonder whether there had been any special influence at work which had helped to calm down the desire of the Church to punish and exterminate the heresy and the heretics. If so, then it was almost certainly the influence of the Catholic lords of Bohemia[22] who showed their hand more openly and with a better chance of success later, after the Battle of the Vítkov. Even without such intervention, however, the offer of a hearing at the very time of the siege of Prague was, to the medieval mind and the church practice of the time, less strange than it may seem today. The Church had always regarded herself as the loving mother who, while she had to punish her erring children, still kept her arms wide open to those ready to return to the fold.

The question now was how the men of Prague would react to the message and offer of the legate. The document took some time to reach its destination, for in a long note which the city government of Prague sent to the Doge and Council of Venice, dated July 10, 1420,[23] there is no mention of the offer. On the contrary, the note emphasizes that the hearing for which they had "humbly and modestly begged" had been denied them—a remark clearly alluding to the meeting with the King at Kutná Hora. The note (an important diplomatic document to which we shall have to return later) also shows the degree to which Prague, even before the Battle of the Vítkov, had made up its mind about Sigismund, for the main purpose of this diplomatic démarche was to persuade the government of Venice—a state which had been at war with Sigismund before—to conclude a military alliance with Bohemia against the King and to help her by an invasion of Sigismund's main supporter, the Duke of Austria. Thus the admonitions of the papal legate to the Praguers not to rebel against their "natural lord" were sure to fall on deaf ears. But if Prague was no longer interested, at this stage, in a reconciliation with Sigismund, the same cannot be said about her attitude toward the Church. The Hussites had often requested such a hearing and disputation, and even now, immediately after the victory of the Vítkov, their interest in it was strong enough to overcome all the difficulties which were in the way.

[22] This seems to agree with a remark in a pamphlet sent out by Prague half a year later, on February 8, 1421, which speaks of twenty-four Bohemian lords who had advocated a hearing for the Praguers. (See *Urk. Beiträge*, II, 490.)

[23] *ibid.*, I, 39-43.

These difficulties—this emerges clearly from the somewhat contradictory source reports[24]—were considerable. In the preliminary negotiations, conducted through the good offices of some of the Bohemian Catholic barons, the King's party suggested the conclusion of an armistice. The Praguers answered that they could not enter into such an agreement without full consultation and participation of their allies from the other Bohemian towns. Prague then countered with the request that the hearing should take place in full publicity, at a large assembly to which the army of the crusaders should be admitted. The Praguers should have the permission to read and defend, before this vast audience, the Four Articles in four languages, Czech, Latin, German, and Hungarian. The Catholic party could not possibly accede to this demand: it would have meant exposing thousands of their soldiers to the danger of being proselytized by the very heretics for whose destruction they had been mobilized. The Praguers did not insist though they put forward similar demands on later occasions.

The last difficulty arose over the issue of the safe conduct. The Hussites could never forget the breach of the safe conduct assured to Hus by the same king who now invited them into his camp. To make assurance doubly sure they demanded that for each of the representatives of Prague sent to the hearing one of the imperial dukes or princes in Sigismund's retinue should go to Prague as a hostage. An agreement was finally reached on the basis that the hostages should merely be noblemen.[25] The hearing took place, sometime late in July in the no man's land of the destroyed Small Side, the Hussites having refused to send their delegates up to Hradčany Castle.

Despite all difficulties and elaborate safety precautions, Prague was serious in its attempt to win, by the hearing, recognition for the Hussite view. For the principal spokesman chosen to lead the delegation was the man who was perhaps, of all the masters of Prague University, the least radical or revolutionary, the one most inclined toward a reconciliation with the Church: John Příbram, then dean of the faculty of arts of the University. He was accompanied by some other Hussite

24 The above quoted pamphlet of February 8, 1421, and Březová (pp. 390-391), who in this case, however, shows himself less reliable than usual. See the next note.

25 So far there is no contradiction between the two sources quoted above, but now Březová claims that, despite all the concessions made by Prague, the other side broke off negotiations. For that reason supposedly the masters of Prague decided to let the Four Articles (of whom he now gives the full text) be "addressed" to the crusading army in Latin, Czech and German. That this version is incorrect emerges clearly from the detailed report given in the official pamphlet of Prague of February 1421.

theologians, all, so it seems, masters of the University; by the captains of the town, and by some of the older councilors. There is no mention of the presence of representatives of Tabor or any of the other allied towns; as it was a question of creed the University still claimed the right to speak in the name of all Hussites. The Prague laymen were only present as audience. The same role was played, on the Royalist side, by a number of Catholic lords, most of them Bohemians, whereas the Roman clerics had their spokesmen in Louis, Patriarch of Aquileja, and Simon of Ragusa, Bishop of Trogir.

Master Příbram, for the benefit of the majority of the audience, spoke Czech, and his discourse was immediately translated into Latin by another of the Prague masters. He read, explained, and defended the Four Articles, one by one, and at first the meeting ran, so we are told by the Praguers, in a spirit of harmony beyond all expectations. On the First, Third, and Fourth Articles agreement was reached to the extent that the representatives of the Church of Rome declared them to be worthy of the adherence of every pious Catholic Christian. But on the Second Article the position taken by the two bishops equaled exactly that circumscribed, in his message to Prague, by the papal legate: if it might possibly be considered meritorious the Communion in the two kinds could under no circumstances be regarded as indispensable for salvation.

Here, then, an impasse was reached. Though both sides expressed their will and hope to overcome it, neither would budge from his basic position. The Praguers, always ready to believe in the moral and logical strength of the tenets which to them were so clearly evident, made a last attempt: another disputation should be staged, solely devoted to the remaining point at issue. Both sides should agree in advance that, whichever side should be able to prove its correctness by full use of the Holy Scripture and human reason, should be considered to be on the side of divine truth, and the other should then give way. This, however, the Catholics would not agree to because they had no authority to modify, on their own, tenets or laws sanctified by the authority of the Church and the Council of Constance. Thereupon nothing was left to the representatives of Prague but to return home, and the last attempt at a religious understanding to be undertaken for a long time ended in complete failure.

There is room for doubt whether this report, which was given half a year after the event and which we cannot check by any record from the other side, is wholly correct. The impression, in particular, that nothing stood between Prague and Rome, between Hussitism and the Catholic Church except the narrow question not of the desirability, but of the indispensability of the Chalice—this impression was surely deceptive. In reality the Church was never ready to accept—not only in theory but also in practice—any of the other articles. She was not prepared to admit the principle of the free sermon, was not ready to give up any of her economic and political privileges, and would not have permitted to treat as mortal sins such established practices as the sale of indulgences. The disagreement was even deeper: the very spirit of the last suggestion made by the Hussites—free discussion of the question of the Chalice based purely on the Scriptures and the power of human reasoning—was replete with the spirit of Protestantism, as were, indeed, the Four Articles themselves.[26] Trust in the power of the individual to understand and correctly interpret the will of Christ from the Scriptures was a Protestant idea. If accepted it gave, in its implications, the Christian layman the right to search, more or less free from institutional guidance, for the truth of God in the very sources of Christian religion. The Church of Rome could not concede such liberty, would maintain the claim to be the sole interpreter, the needed intermediary between God and man. No genuine compromise was possible between these two views. It did not prove possible even when many years later, as the result of tremendous military and political pressure, the Council of Basel accepted a somewhat modified and weakened form of the Four Articles, the Basel Compacts: the Holy See, soon after, renounced this acknowledgment, and the struggle went on, in less bloody forms, till and beyond the days of Luther and Calvin.[27]

Thus seen in historical perspective the disputation at the Small Side was not really a failure even though it may have been regarded as such by the contemporaries on both sides. It was not a failure because success, that is a genuine rapprochement and reconciliation, was then no longer a real possibility. In a way the two simultaneous struggles—the spiritual fight for preservation of the Four Articles and the military fight for preservation of Prague—had a very similar outcome: the Hussites had stood their ground in their first, perhaps their greatest crisis.

[26] The degree to which the Four Articles anticipate and contain the basic tenets of later Protestantism is pointed out with great emphasis by L. Krummel, *Utraquisten und Taboriten*, Gotha 1871, pp. 36ff.

[27] These historical facts are strangely neglected by Pekař who in a lengthy passage (III, 69-72) wistfully speculates on the possibilities which the conclusion of peace at that time, instead of sixteen years later, might have opened up for the Czech people and its future.

# CHAPTER 11

## ŽIŽKA'S RETURN TO THE SOUTH

WITH the crusading armies disbanded the first great crisis had passed, but Sigismund was still in the country. He had gone to Kutná Hora where many of his followers among the Bohemian and Moravian lords were with him. He still hoped that, without any further military action, they would succeed in delivering the capital into his hands. But the Catholic lords soon confessed that they could not make good their promise. In the furious commentaries of Sigismund's confidant and biographer Windecke, the King's disappointment and anger is clearly expressed: the lords, so he says, had "contrived a vicious plan." They were all heretics, secretly favoring the "Hussen." There were not four lords in the whole of Bohemia and Moravia who could be trusted.[1]

In reality the lords never had a chance. The King who had come to conquer his capital at the head of an army of foreigners was now utterly unacceptable. The note of July 10, sent to Venice by the government of Prague,[2] leaves no doubt on this. It calls him "our principal foe, our cruel enemy, and the intolerable persecutor of the Bohemian nation," and then gives a long register of the King's crimes, from the murder of Hus and Jerome to that of Krása.

Again the King is charged with the intention of completely exterminating the Hussite population of Prague. There is little new in all these charges—most of them had been hurled against Sigismund before. But the fact that they were made in the framework of a diplomatic démarche, asking the great Italian city republic for an alliance against the common enemy, gave the breach between Prague and Sigismund a still more definite character. The note also shows that by now the city government of Prague regarded itself as the rightful representative of the whole of Bohemia, entitled to undertake, in the name of the Kingdom, important actions of foreign policy.

In this field nothing seemed of greater importance than the quest

[1] Windecke, pp. 133, 134.

[2] *Urk. Beiträge*, I, 39-43.

for another king. Republican ideas, at least on a national level, had hardly developed in Bohemia, except perhaps among the chiliastic fanatics of Tabor, who felt that in the Kingdom of Christ no one but He Himself could presume to rule. For the more realistic foes of Sigismund, among them Žižka, a new king had to be found for two reasons: only a king could effectively unite and defend the realm; and only the firm enthronement of a new, pro-Hussite king could permanently block the way to the throne for Sigismund.

The question who should be Bohemia's new king had occupied the minds of the people of Prague for some time. As early as April a preliminary démarche had been undertaken, as we know, at the court of King Władysław of Poland. The issue had remained a subject of public interest all through the period of the siege.[3] It was officially taken up again at a meeting between the representatives of Prague and her allies in the second half of July. At this meeting Žižka represented the community of Tabor with full power to make binding decisions: as a token of this fact he had been given the great seal of the fortress town. The role of political leadership which he assumed at this stage shows how much his stature had grown by the victory of the Vítkov. Nicholas of Hus—who had once seemed to hope for the crown himself—could no longer be regarded as the first among the leaders of Tabor. Whether, at this time, he had returned from his campaign against Rosenberg or had stayed at Tabor is uncertain. In any case the decision to renew the negotiations with Poland was taken without and, as we can say from our knowledge of later events, against him.

It was resolved at the meeting to send to Poland a more representative mission than before. It was to be headed by Hynek of Kolstein,[4] member of one of the oldest baronial families, a reliable Hussite, a brave officer, and a skilful diplomat. He was to present to King Władysław and his advisers the case against Sigismund, to make them acquainted with the Four Articles of Prague and to request the King to accept the Crown of Bohemia. We have no detailed records of this meeting, except that Žižka, by affixing the seal of Tabor to the credentials issued to Kolstein, expressed his full agreement with the action.[5]

Hynek of Kolstein left Prague on one of the last days of July, travel-

[3] In a song that became popular at this time: "Povstaň, povstaň veliké město Pražské" (Arise, arise, great city of Prague) the demand for the election of a new, Hussite king is voiced clearly.

[4] Hynek took his name from the castle of Kolstein (in German Goldstein or Goldenstein), but belonged to a family more generally known under the name of Waldstein, and was probably a cousin of Lord Hašek of Waldstein, whom we shall meet later in this chapter. On both these barons see Pekař, III, 142-146.

[5] Březová, p. 447.

ing through Silesia to Poland. The councilors of Breslau immediately informed Sigismund, whose answer from Kutná Hora urged them to capture him.[6] They were not successful. Kolstein met Władysław early in August, stayed with him for a short time and returned safely to Prague before the end of September. The moderate success of his mission[7] served, for the moment, to strengthen the hope that the political issues of the revolution would soon be solved and a new, firm government put into power.

This hope, however, was fated to meet many disappointments. One of the reasons was that Hussite unity tended to weaken whenever the pressure from outside relented. Sigismund was still in Bohemia and the two great castles at the city's outskirts were still firmly in the hands of his adherents. Yet, almost as soon as the crusaders had abandoned the siege, frictions and divisions began to show again between the two main Hussite parties: the radicals, under the leadership of the priests of Tabor and of John Želivský, and the moderates, under the influence of the University of Prague. The issue was the same that had led to some irritation almost immediately after the arrival of the Taborite host in Prague two and a half months before. The Taborites, whether priests or peasants, still felt that their puritan principles were not observed sufficiently by the people of the great city; and the citizens, at least the more affluent people of the Old Town as well as the masters of the University, felt that Taborite radicalism went too far both in religious issues and in the changes it tried to impose upon their own urban way of life.

On August 6, a week after the end of the siege, Taborite crowds burned one of the most beautiful monasteries, that of the Knights of the Cross on the Zderaz, in the New Town. This act came, as it were, as a warning in support of a simultaneous démarche which the Taborite priests undertook with the councilors of the Old and the New Town. The document handed to them consisted of twelve points which, so the clergy of Tabor declared, had to be accepted by Prague if the Taborite allies were to stay in the capital.[8] For the most part these Taborite demands sought to apply the principles of the Four Articles in legislative and administrative practice. Thus we find the principle of the Third Article restated in the demand for immediate secularization and na-

[6] *Urk. Beiträge*, I, 45, 46. Sigismund's letter dates from August 11.

[7] See below, Chapter 20.

[8] Březová, pp. 397ff. The date at which this program of twelve points was submitted is August 4.

tionalization of all church estates. In implementation of the Fourth Article the Taborites demanded the closing of all remaining public drinking houses and brothels, prosecution of prostitutes and adulterers, and punishment of merchants or artisans caught cheating. Also the wearing of costly or showy clothes should be prohibited. Some of the well-to-do merchants may have disliked the request that Pagan (read Roman) law and German Law be abolished whenever it collided with the Law of God. The important point 8 requests that the masters of the University should be fully bound by the Law of God and that their preaching and teaching be subject to close supervision. Further, all those who still did not adhere to the Law of God were to be banished.

The most shocking point, put like a sharp exclamation mark at the end of the list, demanded the destruction of all monasteries, of all churches not needed for the service of the faithful, and of all elaborate altars, ornaments, and vessels made out of precious metals. With the rich beauty of Gothic church architecture a great deal of what the people of Prague were proud of would have to be sacrificed.

No wonder that even faithful Hussites trembled at the thought of the barbarous devastation planned by the puritan fanatics. Three more monasteries in the New Town were burned by the Taborites, but when they tried to continue this work in the Old Town which was much richer in religious buildings they met active resistance: hearing that the monastery of St. James was to be burned, the butchers of the Old Town, well organized and conscious of their strength as a guild, formed a living wall in front of the building. The city council of the Old Town then decided to use the monastery—long before deserted by the monks—as a warehouse. In the same way several other religious buildings were preserved by declaring them as necessary for the storage of food or arms. One more church temporarily threatened with destruction, belonging to the nuns of the Holy Ghost, was set aside by the city council for those Germans who had been permitted to remain in Prague.[9] They were allowed to conduct their service in their own language.

In general the zeal of the people of Tabor to do away with "unnecessary" or overly resplendent church buildings can be explained by their genuine aversion to all forms of idolatry. Yet some of their destructive activities seem rather the outgrowth of a general unrest, the cumulative nervousness of people most of whom were uprooted and who had to live far from any home, in unfamiliar and somewhat disquieting

[9] As to the fate of individual churches and monasteries, see Tomek, *Dějepis*, IV, 93-95.

surroundings. It is not to the credit of some of their priestly leaders that, far from curbing those destructive tendencies, they encouraged them.

Thus it was under the leadership of Wenceslas Koranda that, on August 10, a troop of Taborites and of people from the New Town of Prague marched southward to Zbraslav. The great Cistercian monastery in that town was one of the most famous and most beautiful religious buildings of the country. It was also the burial place of kings, among them Wenceslas IV who had been entombed there just a year before. The monastery was undefended and deserted, but its cellars were still full of wine. The soldiers, very much against the Taborite principles of strict self-restraint and sobriety, drank till most of them were completely inebriated. Then they broke into the royal tomb, disinterred the body of Wenceslas and placed him on the altar with a crown of straw on his head. They poured wine on him, shouting: "If thou wert alive, thou wouldst fain drink with us." Eventually they set all the buildings on fire. Still drunk they returned to Prague where, led by some of the Taborite priests, they immediately undertook an improvised attack upon the Vyšehrad. It ended—as was to be expected—in complete failure, and with considerable losses for the attackers.

This whole repulsive episode, especially the violation of King Wenceslas' body, was widely reported and contributed greatly to the feeling, in Prague and elsewhere, that the men of Tabor, including their priestly leaders, were a band of irresponsible, unmanageable terrorists.[10] The question arises how Žižka looked upon these events. It is clear from the sources that he was not present.[11] Possibly he was involved in discussions about the twelve-point program. From his point of view he could not mind the destruction of the great monastery, but excesses committed in a state of wild drunkenness were bound to offend his sense of discipline, all the more as they violated the last of the Four Articles. The arbitrary way in which Koranda assumed the leadership of parts of the Taborite host and the irresponsible adventure against the

[10] See e.g. Březová's angry account, pp. 397ff.

[11] The only chronicle that assumes his presence is, strangely, *The very pretty chronicle* in a passage not quoted in our translation on page 16 of Novotny's edition (Prague 1923). The author obviously takes it for granted that at this time nothing could have been done by Taborite troops without Žižka's presence and leadership. The chronicle continues by devoting much space to the tale of how the King's body was found and hidden by a faithful fisherman. If Žižka had really been there this would have been mentioned by Březová, generally a far more reliable witness, as well as by those sources inimical to Žižka who report the incident, such as Windecke and the *Magdeburger Schöppenchronik*.

Vyšehrad surely contributed to the increasing alienation between the two men.

While Žižka's relationship with some of the Taborite priests began to be strained, he was nevertheless in full agreement with the twelve-point program submitted by the Taborite authorities to the city council of the two towns of Prague. Indeed it would hardly have been transmitted in the form known to us without his assent.[12] But it also bore the stamp of John Želivský, especially in the passage on the supervision of the masters of the University. Thus it was to be expected that the city council of the New Town, which had for a long time been dominated by Želivský, assented to the Taborite program without much discussion. The Old Town was less subservient. There the Taborite program was subjected to a careful scrutiny in which the University was asked to participate. As its representative functioned a remarkable man: Peter Payne,[13] a Wiclifite refugee from Oxford who since 1417 had found a sanctuary and, more than that, a sphere of intense activity in Hussite Prague. He was known there as "Master English" and served his adopted nation not only as a theologian and teacher but also as a gifted and successful diplomat. Payne carefully discussed all twelve points with the councilors. In the outcome the council tried to put off the answer as long as possible, hoping thus to win time either for negotiations or effective counteractions.

The other side, however, soon lost patience. Two weeks after the transmission of the twelve-point program, on August 18, Želivský called an assembly of the people of the Old Town at the city hall. In his address he sharply attacked the city council, claiming that the Taborite allies would not stay in the capital if the present government of the Old Town remained in office. He therefore asked the people to replace them on the spot by a new council, nominating the mayor and the councilors whom he considered fit. The irregular election was held. Intimidated by this show of strength the old city councilors bowed to Želivský's demand to hand him the town seal, which he immediately

[12] For a special discussion of Žižka's position in relation to the 12 points, see Urbánek, *Žižka*, pp. 105-106, 108.

[13] It seems remarkable that twice in the course of history an Englishman by the name of Paine (Payne) was forced to leave his homeland and played an important role, ideologically as well as politically, in a great revolution. The elder Payne whom we shall meet repeatedly in this account later sided with Tabor, survived the revolution and its aftermath and died, an old man, in 1456. There is a short monograph on him by F. M. Bartoš in a collection of essays published under the name *Z Husových a Žižkových času* (From the times of Hus and Žižka), Prague 1925, pp. 100ff. Somewhat outdated, at least as far as Payne's Hussite career is concerned, is J. Baker's book: *A Forgotten Great Englishman: The Life and Work of Peter Payne*, London 1894.

put into the hands of the councilors of his choice. For the moment this step brought him fairly near to effective control over both towns.

The strengthening of Želivský's personal power was probably the main purpose of this whole transaction. The promise that thereby the Taborites would be induced to stay was not fulfilled. Four days later, on August 22, the whole Taborite host with its leaders and priests, its wagons and guns, its women and children left the city, and no official explanation for this step was given or is known to us.

There were, however, some good, strong objective reasons which may have recommended this decision in Žižka's eyes. The special emergency which Tabor's succor had answered had disappeared, at least for the time being. While Žižka wanted the alliance with Prague to be permanent, it was doubtful whether a prolonged stay of his army, with all the frictions liable to arise from it, would not do more harm than good to this alliance. In addition this was harvest time. Many of Žižka's soldiers were not permanent inhabitants of Tabor (it surely had, altogether, not as many citizens as the supposed 9,000 people of the army), but were peasants from regional villages. On their fields the grain was now ripe and waiting to be cut, and horses were needed, too, for the field work. It was important for the survival of Tabor and its nearest allies that food reserves should not dwindle, and later special provisions were made by which the Taborite farms would always retain sufficient manpower to deliver the needed supplies. Even now it was with somewhat smaller forces that, after his uneventful return to Tabor, Žižka started to wage a harrowing war, guerilla warfare almost comparable to the soldiering activities of his youth, against Sigismund's strongest supporter in Bohemia: Ulrich of Rosenberg.

The decision to turn against this baron was, at this stage, quite rational even from the point of view of a general strategy of the revolutionaries. It was their common task to gain, if necessary by force, most of the castles and towns now still in Royalist hands. By neutralizing the forces of Rosenberg and his allies in southern Bohemia this task could be eased while at the same time Žižka's main operational basis at Tabor would become more secure. How much Sigismund counted on Rosenberg's help for his further endeavors to subjugate Bohemia is shown in the lively correspondence between the great baron and his royal master whose letters were carefully kept in the Rosenberg archives. Sigismund constantly urged his vassal to attack the Taborites, and at one stage promised him aid which he never gave.[14] If Rosenberg could

[14] *Archiv český*, I, 12-15.

be eliminated, this would also have an enormous influence upon other members of the Royalist aristocracy. Thus the new phase of Žižka's activity, if less spectacular than the defense of the capital, was nevertheless essential to final victory.

Žižka began his campaign against Rosenberg with his customary speed. Less than a week after his departure from Prague we find him at Písek, reinforcing the small troop he had brought along from Tabor by assembling peasant volunteers from the neighborhood. The people of Vodňany, a royal town just twelve miles to the south, which had for some time been leased to and administered by the Rosenbergs, sent an urgent appeal for help to their lord. The letter[15] tells him that their own soldiers had fled from the town as soon as news had come that Žižka was near: an eloquent testimony to the awe in which the old soldier was held by his enemies. If Rosenberg did not send help immediately the town, so the letter continues, would be lost. Two days later Vodňany was in Žižka's hands. Farther southwest the town of Prachatice submitted to the victor for a second time and promised to adhere to the Four Articles. The new conquests, added to the fact that Písek, Strakonice, and Sušice already belonged to Tabor, gave Žižka a fairly secure domination of most of southwestern Bohemia nearly to the Bavarian border and directly threatened Rosenberg's main city Krumlov, which was hastily reinforced by its owner. But an assault of this place would have been most difficult and costly and Žižka did not attempt it. Instead he returned to Tabor and after a short pause struck again, this time toward the upper reaches of the Lužnice valley. Soběslav was taken without resistance. Farther south Žižka laid siege to the strongly fortified town of Lomnice which surrendered on September 16. Žižka considered it important enough to give it a permanent garrison of Taborite troops, and left them under the captaincy of a young nobleman who had accompanied him from Prague: John Roháč of Dubá. The Lords of Dubá were one of the greatest baronial families of the country. Roháč probably belonged to a branch of less splendor and wealth. He may have been the brother or cousin of Žižka's son-in-law, Henry of Dubá, whom we later also find among the noblemen fighting in Žižka's war. Whereas little is known about Henry we shall hear more about Roháč: he soon became one of Žižka's closest friends and most faithful adherents, and one of the leading figures of the Hussite revolution.

[15] *ibid.*, III, 3.

From Lomnice Žižka went east, conquering the town and castle of Nová Bystřice near the Moravian border. Among the prisoners were the wife and daughter of the town's owner: Lord Leopold Krajíř, once one of the "robber barons" who had fought against the Rosenbergs, now closely allied with them and acting as Sigismund's burgrave and governor at Budweis. No harm was done to the two women, but Žižka ordered the castle to be burned.

Žižka returned to Tabor by a wide detour to the west, which took him into the region of his birth and youth. Just a few miles from Trocnov he conquered the town of Sviny Trhové and left a small garrison at the little fortress or castle guarding the town. It was another outpost in the neighborhood of Rosenberg's residence, Krumlov, which was thus menaced, or at least contained, from both east and west.

The damage done to Rosenberg during this period was, of course, not limited to the conquest of towns and castles. Wherever the Taborite troops could invade his territories they burned or destroyed his fields, drove away cattle, and altogether did whatever would hurt the great baron most. He, on his side, remained almost completely on the defensive. Only once did he achieve a small military victory when he surprised and conquered the castle of Kamenice, belonging to Prokop of Ústí, the Taborite lord who had once helped Hromádka in the conquest of the mountain fortress of Hradiště. And another success, of political rather than military value, was granted to the lord when Wenceslas Koranda, so far the leader of the Taborite clergy, fell into the hands of Rosenberg retainers while traveling from Tabor to Bechyně. This happened in the second half of September, the time when Žižka returned to Tabor from his conquest of Sviny Trhové. The event caused changes of considerable significance on the domestic scene of Tabor.

The question of who should be the acknowledged spiritual leader of the Taborite brethren had been under discussion for a long time, at least since the conference held at Prague on October 1, 1419. Now, one year later, Tabor decided to act, knowing well that Prague was still not ready to follow. Sometime late in September 1420 "the Taborite people in Hradiště, not wanting any longer to be without a spiritual head, concordantly elected Nicholas of Pelhřimov, priest and bachelor of arts, to be their bishop and elder, so that all their priests should respect and obey him, and that nobody should preach the word of God to the people without the bishop's permission."[16] The bishop was even to administer the finances of the community.

[16] Březová, p. 438. The report is contained in only one of the fairly numerous existing

The step taken by the community of Tabor was highly significant and consequential. True, this was not the first time that a heretical movement elected a leader to whom it gave this title—other sects had done it before. But those other sects had worked "underground," whereas the men of Tabor issued, before the eyes of the world, what could be termed an open declaration of independence from the Roman Church. They no longer regarded themselves as subject to the Roman hierarchy, or bound by the sacred tradition of episcopal ordination. The Taborite episcopate, the first of its kind in the history of Protestantism, did not survive, in Bohemia, the man who administered it, as long as Tabor remained an autonomous republic within the Kingdom.[17] But the election of bishops was resumed, soon after Tabor's fall, by its spiritual successor, the Church of the Brethren, and thus the tradition created at Tabor in September 1420 has, in a sense, remained alive to this day.

The new bishop was still a young man, in his middle thirties.[18] He had received his degree of bachelor of arts from the University of Prague about ten years earlier, had in 1415 been ordained as a priest and had identified himself with the reformation at an early date. He also seems to have been one of the first to join the Taborite community at Hradiště, but during the first months of its existence when public attention was largely focused on Koranda, we hear nothing of Nicholas' activities. His intense fervor, his keen knowledge of religious problems, and his gift as a preacher became known when, from May till August, he was not in competition with Koranda's overwhelming personality. And Nicholas' election took place at a moment when Koranda had again disappeared from the scene, this time under circumstances which made it seem quite doubtful whether he would ever return. This helps to explain why not Koranda but Nicholas was chosen.

---

manuscripts of Březová's work (Ms. P.) and thus may not have been contained in the original. Its factual correctness is nevertheless undisputed.

17 There is, however, one case in which a German Hussite, Frederick Reiser, received the consecration as Bishop at Tabor. He was later very active in southern Germany and the Alsace but was finally brought before the Inquisition and burned at the stake in 1458. See Herman Haupt, *Die religiösen Sekten in Franken vor der Reformation*, Würzburg 1882, pp. 44-48, and Bartoš, *Z Husových a Žižkových časů*, p. 122.

18 In the years following his election Nicholas of Pelhřimov is often referred to by contemporary writers as "Biskupec," a sort of diminutive form of the word for bishop (biskup), very much in line with the Czech inclination for nicknames. He later wrote a voluminous work: *Chronica Taboritarum* (Höfler, *Geschichtsschreiber*, vol. 2) of which by far the larger part is not a historical account but a collection of theological treatises and documents in defense of the Taborite point of view. As such it is important, whereas its value as a chronicle is modest. One of its odd features is the fact that he seldom relates names unless they belong to persons of high rank. Thus Žižka is never mentioned by name in this work though he is alluded to a few times as one of the "famous captains" of Tabor. A valuable study on Nicholas' life and work is the chapter by Bartoš in his *Světci a kacíři*, pp. 175-196. See also Pekař, I, 125-138 and II, 87-89.

But why was it that this consequential step was taken just at this time? The answer lies in the last part of the quotation above: nobody should preach the word of God to the people without the bishop's permission. At Tabor men had begun to preach whose ideas and beliefs, whose doubts and disbeliefs, went far beyond what faithful adherents of John Hus could share or even consider. It seemed time to draw the line between the teaching and preaching of the Word of God and the mystical outbursts of some fanatics for whom the Chalice itself had lost its sacred meaning. This, certainly, was the firm conviction of Žižka. His word must, at this moment, have carried all the more weight as the other senior captain, Nicholas of Hus, had left Tabor just a short time before.

It seems likely that Žižka had some part in the election of Nicholas of Pelhřimov, that he at least backed him by his personal influence. In the course of the following year there was the closest cooperation between Žižka and the bishop in their common attempt to deal with the threat of the mysticist fanatics at Tabor. Altogether Nicholas' election helped to safeguard, for the next two years, a workable relationship between Žižka and the clergy of Tabor.

These domestic issues could not detain Žižka very long. The fight against Rosenberg remained his main consideration, and during the first half of October we find him to the west in the upper Otava valley. There he laid siege to the small town and fortress of Bor Panský (today Bor Malý), a place which lay just half way between the two Taborite towns Strakonice and Sušice and at the same time guarded the direct route between the Rosenberg possessions in the south and another important Royalist stronghold: the city and district of Pilsen. The call for help, coming from the defenders of Bor Panský, was answered by both Royalist groups. Ulrich of Rosenberg received strong, mostly German reinforcements from Budweis under the command of Lord Krajíř. From Pilsen there came Bohuslav of Švamberg, Žižka's adversary at the battle of Nekměř, and Henry of Plauen with German mercenaries. When they arrived at Bor Panský on October 12, both town and fortress had already been taken by Žižka. Seeing, however, that Žižka's army was considerably weaker than their own forces they attacked, and there ensued one of the major battles of the war.

From the tactical point of view the battle of Bor Panský is not very interesting,[19] as it was an almost exact replica of the battles of Sudoměř

[19] None of the contemporary chronicles gives a fully adequate account of the battle, and there are no precise data on the numbers of troops employed. Windecke (p. 144) is the only

and Poříči: again Žižka found time to employ his wagon fortress, making use of a hill dominated by the spire of a lonely church. Again the repeated assault of the Royalist cavalry was beaten back with losses so heavy that the enemy finally was forced to retire whereas Žižka, though not without losses to his own troop, maintained his position and could consider himself the victor.

Of greater significance was the strategic aspect of this battle. It prevented the military forces of Rosenberg as well as those of the Pilsen Landfrieden[20] from entering a struggle of far greater importance and one in which they would have been badly needed by Sigismund. It was the fight for the Vyšehrad.

So far the record of events seems to confirm at every step the sober and rationally purposeful way in which—of course always subject to his religious goals—Žižka directed the war effort of Tabor and its allies. It is somewhat difficult to reconcile this general attitude with his actions, or rather his lack of activity, in the following weeks. For almost a month —from October 13 to November 11—there is not a word about him. If he continued his attacks against his neighbor Rosenberg during those four weeks, they must have been on the most insignificant scale and, more important, he missed an excellent opportunity to encounter his main enemy: King Sigismund. The great struggle for the Vyšehrad was fought without Žižka.

The importance of the two great castles outside the city walls of Prague, the Hradčany and the Vyšehrad, has been stressed before in this account. The Vyšehrad had been the first of the royal castles ever to fall to the revolutionaries, thanks to Žižka's resolute and well-timed action in October 1419. Its abandonment, soon after, by Prague had been one if not the main reason compelling Žižka to resign from the captaincy of the New Town's military forces, and it seems that the bitterness which he had felt at the time kept smouldering in his mind for a long time. He had never denied his help to Prague before when the capital was in need of it, especially when she was threatened by

one to give details on the losses: he claims that on each side 800 men were killed. One cannot put much reliance on these figures, and it seems unlikely that Žižka's losses equaled those of his enemies. For a modern treatment, see Frankenberger, I, 91.

[20] The German word "landfrieden" (peace of the land) signified alliances, mostly concluded between one or more towns and nobles of one particular region, against outsiders or enemies. In Bohemia there developed, at the time, two permanent organizations of this kind, both standing against Prague and Hussitism: the powerful Landfrieden of Pilsen and the less important one of Loket (or Ellbogen) near the present-day Karlovy Vary (Karlsbad).

Sigismund. He would come to her help again as we shall soon have occasion to report. But at this stage, even though Tabor's help as well as that of the other allies was again requested by Prague, Žižka's answer was grudging. Help was not denied outright but limited to a mere "token participation." Forty horses was all that Tabor sent on October 4, more than two weeks after the first request for help had been received. The little troop was under the command of Nicholas of Hus who thus found himself in a rather insignificant position among the military leaders in charge of the operations against the Vyšehrad. True, at that moment the war against Ulrich of Rosenberg was still conducted with much vigor, and the battle of Bor Panský had not yet been won. But a week later, after this battle had weakened Tabor's nearest enemies, it should have been possible for Žižka to reinforce the Taborite troop at Prague with strong forces under his own command. Reinforcements, indeed, were sent, but again only in very small numbers, and Žižka himself stayed away. The contrast between the succor granted by the other allies and the meager participation of Tabor was noticed and commented on in Prague.[21] Žižka, so it seemed, found it difficult to bury the old grudge. Somehow his role at this moment recalls Achilles sulking in his tent while the Achaeans were embattled before the walls of Troy.

With Žižka out of sight, the first place among the military leaders of the Hussites naturally fell to one of the barons. Hynek Krušina of Lichtenburg, the man who had first led the Orebite troops to Prague and had right then been appointed captain general of the Prague forces, was now given the top command of the Hussite army starting to besiege the Vyšehrad. Under Krušina served his brother John as well as another Orebite nobleman, Diviš Bořek of Miletínek. The most important among the other leaders were Hynek of Kolstein who by this time had returned from his first mission to Poland, and Victorin Boček of Poděbrady, prominent member of the Kunštat family, who was to become one of the greatest of Hussite war leaders and one of Žižka's closest, most faithful personal friends. Together with auxiliaries from Žatec and Louny the whole Hussite siege army may have amounted to some 12,000 men. Their main encampment, blocking access to the fortress from the southeast, was built in the neighborhood of the Church of St. Pancratius. The siege had begun in the middle of September and seems to have been effective from the beginning even

[21] Březová, pp. 432, 434.

though the full force of the Hussite army was not assembled till early in October.

Just as the siege of the Hradčany in May 1420 so the siege of the Vyšehrad forced Sigismund's hand. The King had spent most of the summer and early fall at Kutná Hora, having with him still a fair-sized army of some 16,000 men. As a first answer to the siege he tried a number of diversionary threats such as moving against the town of Žatec, circling the capital from the west, and all the way burning those of his subjects who took the Communion in the two kinds. This, however, proved of little avail and the call for help from the Vyšehrad became more urgent, protesting that for some weeks the garrison had eaten nothing but horse flesh and that even this last resort was about to fail. A clever scheme to move boats overland to the Berounka River, a tributary which joins the Vltava just south of Prague, and thence to supply the Vyšehrad by water was thwarted through precautions taken against just this contingency.

Time now was running short. Supplies had dwindled to a minimum when Lord Všembera of Boskovice, the able and respected commander of the Vyšehrad, and Lord Krušina of Lichtenburg met under a flag of truce on October 28. They concluded the following agreement: if by nightfall on October 31 no effective help had arrived, then at nine on the following morning the castle with all heavy arms would be surrendered honorably, the defenders being allowed to withdraw freely with their hand weapons.

In concluding this agreement Všembera still hoped for Sigismund's help to arrive in time. The King, after a short stay on the Hradčany, now moved his army to the south of Prague, then turned around northward in the direction of St. Pancratius. But he still hesitated as usual, waiting for the arrival of the Moravians, two thousand men under the command of Lord Henry of Plumlov. They did not join him till late in the evening of October 31 when there was no time left to organize and begin the assault. Thus by waiting the King lost much more than he gained, for the Moravians could only strengthen the frontal attack, while the garrison of the Vyšehrad, once the day had passed, were bound by their recent pledge not to participate in the impending battle. Could the besiegers have been attacked from the rear as well as from the front the outcome might have been different. But Všembera was an honest man and, to the great disappointment of Sigismund, kept his word of honor.

When the Royalist generals, especially the Moravians under the leadership of Henry of Plumlov, realized the difficulty of a frontal attack they warned the King not to attempt it. But Sigismund could be as headstrong at times as he was hesitant and irresolute at others. Accusing the Moravians of cowardice he ordered them to attack where they were most exposed to the fire of the entrenched Hussites, giving a less dangerous task to his Hungarian and German troops.[22]

The result was as Sigismund's general had feared. The frontal assault was repulsed. A Hussite counterattack threw the Royalists into confusion in which they suffered heavy losses, some five hundred in dead and fatally wounded alone, among them the flower of Moravia's nobility, with their leader Henry of Plumlov at their head. The Hussites took many prisoners, and their losses were light.

Among the Royalist Bohemians who fell was Lord Peter of Sternberg, the man whose attack against the pilgrims of Sezimovo Ústí had started open warfare in November 1419. (His death made it possible for his widow Perchta, long a secret believer in the Hussite faith, to declare her adherence to the Four Articles and to conclude an alliance with Prague. This step added the great castles of Sternberg and Konopiště as well as the important town of Benešov to the Hussite part of Bohemia.) The list of those who died for Sigismund also included a Russian prince: George, Duke of Smolensk, who had made common cause with the King hoping that through his help he would regain his lost heritage. But all he gained was a grave in far Bohemia.

As soon as the battle was over the Vyšehrad surrendered, as arranged before, to the Hussite commanders. Many Czech soldiers joined the revolutionary party. The others, including the German mercenaries, marched off without being molested. The Praguers, to make sure that the Vyšehrad could no more be used as a stronghold against them, immediately destroyed the strong northern walls of the fortress. It was the beginning of a successive if sometimes interrupted process of destruction which went on through the following centuries until, to the

22 The battle of the Vyšehrad is one of the best documented events of the Hussite wars. The Old Annalists treat it in great detail (pp. 38-42), Březová (pp. 438-442) reports the battle carefully. If he did not witness it directly he must have visited the battlefield immediately afterwards. His account, with its deeply felt lament over the slain sons of the nobility of Bohemia and Moravia is, in its way, a classic and has been recognized as such by almost every historian concerned with that period. The most important account of the battle from the Royalist side is given by Windecke (pp. 134-136). He claims that the battle was lost by the King because during the height of the battle Nicholas of Jemniště, the mint master of Kutná Hora, turned to flight with a troop of 1,500 horse. A very exact modern treatment is given by Frankenberger, *op.cit.*, I, 102-108.

3. HUSSITE WAGON FORTRESS. Pen drawing, Vienna, *ca.* 1450, reproduced from Toman, *Husitské válečnictví*, Prague 1898.

Czaslaw.

deep regret of later Czech generations, little was left of Prague's second great castle, its royal palace, its churches and other great buildings, except the foundations—a field of study for modern archaeologists.

Though in the Battle of the Vyšehrad stronger forces were engaged in open combat than on the Vítkov it can hardly be said that the engagement was of quite as great political importance. This time it was not a question of saving but rather of strengthening Prague and the revolution. Sigismund, of course, was further than ever from his goal. In his angry search for scapegoats he heaped reproaches upon his Bohemian vassals, in an outbreak of fury which almost led to bloodshed between the Czechs and Hungarians at his court.[23] During the following weeks Sigismund again held court at Kutná Hora and Čáslav as he had done in summer, still trying to keep as many as possible of his Bohemian nobility from deserting to the revolution.

For the citizens of Prague the victory was a triumph of the first order. Not only were they freed from the threat of a Royalist stronghold in their immediate neighborhood, they also had proved to be a strong and efficient military power. Whereas on the Vítkov the part of the allies, especially Tabor, had been decisive, it was the Praguers this time who withstood the main assault of the Royalist forces and who formed the main element of the counterattack.

Prague had claimed the leadership of the nation before. It could do so now with even more justification, with even stronger confidence. This feeling is clearly expressed in a message sent out four days after the battle on November 5, by the capital and the lords fighting with it, to all Bohemians.[24] It is, in the main, an attempt to pry loose from Sigismund all those Czech elements which, for reasons of dynastic loyalty or out of religious conservatism, still felt it necessary to obey the King. Among the arguments used for this purpose those of a nationalist character are by far the most important. The King is made responsible for the indiscriminate slaughter or burning of Czech people, including women and children. He has brought terrible shame upon the Czech nation by charging it, undeservedly, with the crime of heresy. He has consistently tried to make the foreigners great in this country and to make them settle down in the towns from which he wants to expel the Czech people. At the Battle of the Vyšehrad he has sacrificed the lives of noblemen of the Czech nation before those of any others.

[23] Windecke, p. 135.

[24] *Archiv český*, III, 217.

"The Germans and Hungarians, the most cruel enemies of our nation, he pities and gives them preference before the Czechs. He has always acted with the purpose of making the Czechs of both parties (meaning Hussite and Catholic) murder one another and thus to weaken the nation so much that he then can exterminate them with the help of his Germans and Hungarians." Sigismund is finally charged with having openly said that he would give away all Hungary if in return he could make sure that no Czechs were left in the Czech country. The message then appeals to all Czechs of all parties to unite in the fight against the King, and declares that those who continue to stand by him would themselves have to be considered as enemies of the Czech nation and be treated as such. There could be no more eloquent testimony for the strength of nationalist feeling among the Hussite revolutionaries than this document.

The message, supported by the solid facts of a more hopeful military situation, proved to be effective. The number of Czech noblemen who joined the revolution increased considerably during the late fall of 1420, and some of those who did not join it outright began, at least, to waver in their support of Sigismund.

This seems to have been true, too, in the case of the young baron whom the King rightly considered as his strongest and most important Bohemian vassal, Ulrich of Rosenberg. The once so lively correspondence between the two men grew rather listless during this period. Sometime in October Rosenberg complained that Sigismund had left him under the constant attack of Tabor and had never sent him the promised help. Sigismund's answer, dated November 4 from Kutná Hora,[25] is couched in terms of almost humble apology. He cannot now send his friend any help, owing to the loss of so many good and brave men at the Vyšehrad. Rosenberg should not take this amiss, he should not waver in his loyalty, nor should he cease to inflict as much damage as possible upon the common enemy, and he, Sigismund, will surely give him whatever advice and help he can afford.

After this letter there is silence between the two men for a considerable time, and when Sigismund wrote him again it was in Latin, not in the familiar Czech which the polyglot King had mastered fully. Rosenberg for the moment was still undecided what to do. His hatred for the revolutionaries, especially for his Taborite neighbors, was genuine enough, and cannot but have increased for all the damage they

[25] *ibid.*, I, 15.

had done him. But if the King could not help him to safeguard his domains he had to think of other means.

It was Žižka who, by the resumption of full-scale war against the great lord, helped him to make up his mind. During the first days of November he still marked time, perhaps just to see how the political situation after the Battle of the Vyšehrad would develop in Bohemia. But soon afterwards we find him in full action.

The first object of Žižka's November campaign was Prachatice. This town had been conquered and its walls partly demolished during Žižka's first operations from Tabor in early spring. In September the town, its walls rebuilt, had submitted again to Tabor and promised full freedom of worship to the adherents of the Four Articles. But the promise was not kept. Relying upon the protection of Rosenberg the men of Prachatice decided to take their stand against Tabor after all, and had begun to purge their town from those who took the Chalice, driving out a few, imprisoning others, and even burning some who resisted forcible reconversion.

Žižka found the town in a state of full preparedness, all gates locked and the walls fully manned. He asked the defenders to open the gates and permit the Taborites to enter, led by their priests with the Body of Christ. If they complied, so he pledged his word, no harm would be done to their lives or possessions.[26] But the people of Prachatice answered scornfully: they had the Body of Christ, and they had all the priests they needed. They had no use for those who had come with the Taborite army. This answer was to cost them dearly. In a thunderous outbreak of wrath Žižka swore that he would not spare a soul once the town was conquered. He ordered the walls to be scaled at many places while a rain of missiles drove the defenders from the ramparts. The first Taborites to get across the walls opened the gates, and in a short time the little town was subdued. Of the male adults 135 fell during the fight at the walls and in the streets, another 92 were captured and brought before Žižka. Of those only seven—all of them adherents of the Chalice—were freed. All others the enraged conqueror ordered, true to his word, to be killed. They were herded into the parish vestry and the building set on fire. As always Žižka made sure that no harm was done to women and children, but they had to leave the town. Immediately afterwards Taborite peasants were settled in the town which from

[26] Žižka's action against Prachatice is told by Březová, obviously after reports received from eye-witnesses, in great detail, Žižka's utterances being quoted in direct speech (pp. 443-445).

now on remained an important stronghold of the expanding dominion of Tabor as well as an ever effective threat to Lord Ulrich of Rosenberg.

Almost at the same time the Royalist magnate suffered another grave setback by losing one of his strongest castles, Přibenice, a place which had been doubly valuable to him since it lay in the Lužnice valley only a few miles below Tabor and had been used as a base against this city, threatening the route leading from Tabor southwest to the Vltava valley. It was at Přibenice that Wenceslas Koranda, after having been captured by Rosenberg forces in September, had been held as prisoner and hostage, together with some other Taborites who had accompanied him on his trip to Bechyně. In the early hours of November 13 he succeeded, with the help of his fellow prisoners, in overcoming the guards in the tower where he was held. He sent word to Zbyněk of Buchov, the captain who at the moment was in charge at Tabor. Zbyněk sped to Přibenice, and before the burgrave and his men had time to recover from their surprise the cooperation between Koranda with his helpers up in the tower and the Taborite troop outside the walls led to the conquest of the castle which had been considered impregnable. With it also fell the smaller fortress of Přibeničky, on the opposite side of the river. A troop of mercenaries which Rosenberg sent to defend the castle came too late. They were routed in a skirmish with Zbyněk's soldiers.

This whole episode was a tribute to the energy, resourcefulness, and presence of mind of one man: Koranda. Events which immediately followed throw some more light on the character of this remarkable priest. Among the people taken prisoner when Přibenice was conquered was a prelate of the Roman Church, Herman, titular bishop of Nicopolis. Long before the revolution, especially in 1417, under the protection of Čeněk of Wartenberg—this man had ordained a number of Hussite clergymen. Later he had returned to Catholic orthodoxy and had expressed his regret at having "ordained all those rascals." Koranda had his revenge, and the bishop, "a good man" as the old chronicle[27] assures us, was drowned in the Lužnice River despite all his entreaties and promises that he would rejoin the Hussites and again ordain the Taborite priests. Koranda obviously did not mind sending a man to his death as long as he himself was not physically involved in this act. He had, however, during the fights for the castle, thrown stones from the watchtower which, as he thought, had killed a man. Consequently he vowed that from now on he would never hold mass again as, having broken the fifth commandment, his hands were no longer clean. It is

[27] Old Annalists, pp. 42, 43.

difficult not to think of this double ethics as hypocritical, though we have to beware of modern value judgments and have to acknowledge that at the time it seemed more natural to obey a religious law in as literal a way as possible.

With the threefold loss of these days, Ulrich of Rosenberg finally felt that he had had enough. The long sustained guerilla warfare against his possessions—his towns and villages, his fields and herds, his orchards and fishponds—had been a terrible drain on his resources. His influence upon his peers, which had increased at the time of Čeněk of Wartenberg's defection, was now waning, especially after Sigismund's recent defeat. Rosenberg did not like fighting a losing battle without respite. At least he needed a truce. This suggestion was passed on to the Taborite leaders, and was accepted.

The advantages gained by this agreement for the Hussite cause were considerable. For the next few months Tabor was free to move in other regions of Bohemia without having to guard anxiously its southern borders. In the eyes of the people of Bohemia Rosenberg's step would look like a declaration of doubt in Sigismund's chances. But the main reason why Žižka agreed to the armistice must have been the religious clause stipulated in the agreement.

Of the documents exchanged on November 18, 1420, the one made out by Tabor has survived in the original, thanks to the care with which the Rosenberg family kept their archives at Třeboň. It is commonly considered as the first of the few preserved letters and other personal messages of Žižka.[28] In it, besides the high indemnities pledged by both parties in case the armistice were broken, we find Rosenberg's main concession: he will permit and keep, on all his domains and manors, the Four Articles of Prague. Thus at least for the duration of the armistice—till February 4, 1421—the freedom of Hussite worship is gained for most of southern Bohemia.[29] This success was of greater weight in Žižka's mind than any purely military or political triumph. He was God's soldier. If God granted the victory of His Law without further effort of arms—who was he, Žižka, to reject such a gift?

There is one more point of interest in the text of that old parchment. It is the last time that, just as in the documents of his youth, he names himself: "Jan, called Žižka, of Trocnov." His name leads the list of

[28] See Appendix: I, and *Archiv český*, III, 280.

[29] This freedom was actually granted on those of Rosenberg's possessions where the population was wholly or partly Czech. Rosenberg later excused himself that the measure could not be enforced in places with only German inhabitants.

the four Taborite captains, one Pavlík of Mutice signing last in place of the absent Nicholas of Hus. It is taken for granted that the four speak in the name of the whole Taborite community. As a fifth signatory appears the city of Písek, the place where, obviously, the negotiations were conducted and concluded.

Žižka styled himself somewhat differently in another letter, dated only four days later, November 22, from Prachatice where he had returned, perhaps to supervise the reconstruction of the town's fortifications. This one, preserved in German in Windecke's chronicle,[30] names him, together with Chval of Machovice, as captain general (oberst houptman) of Tabor, and is signed in addition by the newly appointed captain of Prachatice, Jeník of Meckov. The letter, addressed "to the brethren and neighbors," might in Windecke's text be a translation from the Czech, but it seems more likely that it was German in the original. In the neighborhood of Prachatice few if any Czech towns and villages were left that had not joined the revolution. Those remaining aloof were mostly German, and if Žižka wanted to address them he may well have done so in their own language.

The gist of the letter is an attempt to reassure the neighboring communities, to counteract the widespread fear that he and his Taborites are their enemies, intent on destroying them all. He tries to blame this reputation on the propaganda directed against Tabor "by the lords," doubtlessly meaning Rosenberg and his people, but it seems likely that the fate of Prachatice was more effective in spreading anxiety among the neighbors than any propaganda could have done. Nor could the remainder of the letter be very reassuring to those people who were not ready to join the Hussite creed. There Žižka explains that his enemies are only "all evil priests and laymen who write and stand against the holy evangel," all those, in other words, who do not agree with the Four Articles which he quotes immediately, stressing especially the need to abolish the rule of the priests, "from the Pope to the lowest." And the letter ends with a request which almost sounds like an ultimatum: Žižka expects a written answer, obviously one expressing agreement. Where such an answer fails to arrive it can only be concluded that the addressees "want to be the enemies of God and of all Taborite Brethren."

We can hardly claim that this letter is a masterpiece of diplomacy. Žižka shows himself, without any disguise, as the man he was: forth-

[30] Appendix, II, and Windecke, p. 148.

right, obsessed by his religious devotion and by the deep conviction that no good Christian can fail to agree with him, always ready to accept as friends those who themselves accept the Four Articles, but just as ready to fight to the bitter end the "enemies of God and the Taborite Brethren." There were times and situations later when he would show his ability to compromise for the sake of Hussite unity. But just as Ulrich of Rosenberg had been able to obtain his armistice only at the price of acknowledging the Four Articles, so Žižka would not compromise with anyone not ready to accept "the Law of God."

But now, in November 1420, he could look back for the first time upon his fight with a sense of great achievement. Under his leadership Tabor had, in less than eight months, become a great power in the country, supreme in the south, the region from which he had come himself, respected and feared in the rest of Bohemia. True there had been setbacks, had been the shadows of dissent between him and some of the priests of Tabor, and of dissent between Tabor and Prague. But there was no reason to consider those difficulties as unsurmountable. Žižka himself could contribute to their solution with the great authority which he now enjoyed. We shall soon find him engaged in just this endeavor.

CHAPTER 12

# NICHOLAS OF HUS AND THE CONFLICT WITH PRAGUE

THE people of Prague were, as we know, divided according to their more conservative or more radical leanings, with the latter groups being under the influence of John Želivský. His power had greatly increased in the course of the spring and summer of 1420, and after the forced municipal elections of August 18 he seemed to wield nearly as strong an influence in the Old Town as he had, now almost traditionally, in the New Town.

The fight for the Vyšehrad, however, changed this situation. That great battle was fought with only limited help from the more radical allies. It was won by Prague under the leadership of some great noblemen none of whom was in favor of the Taborites and their religious and political radicalism. The man who at this time represented the community of Tabor at Prague, Nicholas of Hus, commanded a small troop which would not impress the population as Žižka's army had done in the spring. Nevertheless he acted in a haughty, commanding, uncompromising way, always trying to press his views upon the majority of other leaders.

Nicholas began to show himself as a difficult ally even before the Battle of the Vyšehrad. When the negotiations with Všembera of Boskovice got under way, Krušina of Lichtenburg, the Hussite commander in chief, consulted all the leaders of Prague and allied troops as to the terms for the Royalist garrison. All agreed except Nicholas of Hus who considered those terms as too generous. Though completely outvoted he held to his opinion, and to confirm his protest he withdrew his troops from the island off the Vyšehrad which he had occupied[1] and marched to Prague. Only after considerable efforts on the side of the other commanders was he finally prevailed upon to sign the armistice agreement, and then joined the Prague army at St. Pancratius.[2]

[1] He had taken over this task to prevent supplies from being shipped to the garrison on the Vltava River (See Březová, p. 434.)

[2] Březová, pp. 437, 438.

After the capitulation of the Vyšehrad Nicholas remained in Prague, participating in some minor military enterprises. But the presence of Taborite troops in Prague led again to frictions. The Taborites were especially incensed by the fact that the Utraquist priests of Prague still ministered to their congregations in the same vestments that were worn by the Catholic clergy, and this "struggle over the ornates" caused much ill feeling on both sides. Of much greater real significance, however, was the question of how to find a new king. This, then, was made the main point of discussion for a meeting which was called on November 14 by the city councils of both towns.

In the debate most of the participants—Praguers as well as allied barons—argued in favor of repeating the offer to the ruling princes of Poland-Lithuania, but in a more solemn form, through a larger and more representative delegation. The only dissenting voice came from Nicholas of Hus. He claimed that it had never been considered admissible by Tabor to elect as King of Bohemia anyone but a born Czech. It was easy for Hynek of Kolstein to prove him wrong. He produced the credentials given to him early in August for his mission to Poland, which, as everyone could see, had among the seals affixed to it that of the community of Tabor. Nicholas could not openly disavow the absent Žižka. But he was by no means reconciled with the decision, grumbling under his breath as Březová observed.[3] Possibly he felt thwarted not only in his principles but also in his personal ambitions which, as once King Wenceslas had feared, did not stop short of the crown itself.

After the decision in favor of a more representative embassy to Poland had been accepted by a large majority, issues of religious ritual came up for discussion.

It turned into an open attack upon Tabor and its practices. A resolution was submitted containing two main points: nobody should be allowed to spread new religious teachings in the city unless he could prove them to be well founded in the Scriptures or to be evident on the basis of infallible reasoning. Even then he must not publish them before they were approved by a committee of four masters of the University to be elected by the community of Prague for this special task. Furthermore all clerics of Prague should, especially when celebrating mass, use the traditional vestments, omitting only superfluous pomp or splendor. This resolution, too, was passed against the dissent and vigorous protest of Nicholas of Hus.

3 "Tacens remurmuravit." Březová, p. 447.

The results of this meeting were not only a setback for Tabor, but also for John Želivský. We have no reason to think that the issue of the vestments ever played an important role in his policy, but the negotiations with the dynasty of Poland were not to his liking. As the leader of what Palacký somewhat anachronistically called the "democratic party" Želivský could see hardly any great advantages in the election of a foreign king who in all likelihood would have to cooperate closely with Bohemia's high nobility. He hardly could dream of a republic as a permanent form of government for Bohemia. But if, eventually, the country had to be turned back into the hands of a king, then he would prefer someone as independent as possible from the lords, a man who would recognize and cooperate with the new social forces that had begun to rise in Prague and in the country at large. It would, therefore, first be necessary to strengthen those forces, to consolidate their rule over the country by close cooperation between the Prague "left" and the Taborite elements, before the question of who should become king could be tackled profitably.[4]

The decision of November 14 was thus taken over Želivský's head. And his position was even more clearly affected by the ban on "new teachings" not approved by the University. For if the sermons of the Taborite priests contained "novel" teachings of which the more conservative masters disapproved, so did his own. There was almost constant friction between him and the University and lately even the more vigorous reformers of the great school, especially Jacobellus of Stříbro, had begun to look askance at his violent and persuasive plea for a changed society.

But at the moment there was little he could do about it. The aristocratic leaders of the armed forces who had been the victors of the Vyšehrad, in coalition with the University and the patricians of the Old Town, were too strong for him. He had to swallow an even more awkward rebuff to his influence. Things having gone so far, the conserva-

[4] The role of few of the Hussite leaders is so strongly disputed as that of John Želivský in whom modern historians, according to their personal views, saw an evil demagogue or a far-seeing statesman. As we have no means of quoting him on his stand to the "Royal question" we have to depend on conclusions drawn from his actions. It cannot have been a matter of chance that Hynek of Kolstein's second embassy, sent to Poland at a time when Želivský's power was at its weakest, contained a strong and representative delegation of the Prague city governments whereas a later diplomatic mission, dispatched at the time of his return to power, did not include any official representatives of the city. The question is discussed by Goll (*K. Sigmund und Polen*, pp. 466-467), who thinks that Želivský's would have accepted a Hussite king, and by Pekař (III, 113, 114) who regards him, probably rightly, as strongly opposed to the Polish-Lithuanian candidature.

tive elements in Prague did not see why they should put up any longer with city councils which had been elected to please the Taborites and to give John Želivský the directing voice in the affairs of the capital. On November 19 the citizens of the Old Town held new elections in which Želivský's friends were replaced by people more in line with the wishes of the patrician element. Even in the New Town, Želivský's old domain, elections brought a more conservative group into power. The office of mayor fell to a former high official at the court of King Wenceslas whose name, Nicholas Kozíhlava (Goat's Head), again shows us the Czech love for nicknames and may have reflected the looks of the man.[5]

John Želivský had the keen judgment but also the patience of the statesman-politician. He knew his time would come again. Nicholas of Hus, on the other hand, lacked patience and felt unable to concede even a temporary defeat. He realized, however, that mere protests would get him nowhere. Taborite influence on Prague had been greatest whenever Tabor's military strength had been needed and had shown its effectiveness. Nicholas therefore tried to use this lever before renewing his demands. Even in the Prague region the Royalists were still in possession of some castles and towns from which they could harass the communications between Prague and the provinces. One of these was the castle and town of Říčany, only some fourteen miles southeast of Prague, owned by the Royalist Lord Diviš of Říčany.

Against this place Nicholas of Hus moved sometime in the second half of November. But even with the reinforcements he had received from Tabor his forces were rather weak. Therefore he asked Prague for help. As success would benefit the Praguers much more than Tabor, they could hardly refuse. Their commander however, Hynek Krušina, shunned any participation in this enterprise. Declaring that he had to look after his own domains, which were threatened by Sigismund, he resigned from his post and left Prague. Though his fears were certainly not unfounded—the King had lately taken his revenge by doing much damage to the possessions of some Hussite lords[6]—it was generally presumed in Prague that he was unwilling to cooperate closely with Nicholas, to whose overbearing manners and methods he had taken a hearty dislike.[7]

Soon afterwards, on November 24, a fairly strong force of Prague

[5] See Tomek, *Dějepis*, IV, p. 115.
[6] See Březová, p. 443.
[7] *ibid.*, p. 449.

troops joined those of Tabor in the siege of Říčany, accompanied as usual by some priests. As soon as they began to celebrate mass in their ornate vestments in full view of the Taborites, trouble broke out. Taborite soldiers tried to prevent them from proceeding. A violent conflict seemed imminent, but the leaders intervened. They agreed that each army would celebrate mass in its own way during the siege. The issue should be submitted to new discussions when the campaign was over.

Nicholas of Hus, however, was too impatient to wait for the end of the siege. He went back to Prague in a renewed attempt to reestablish Taborite influence there. Appearing before the new council he demanded that the agreement concluded last May, concerning Taborite participation in the city's defense, should be kept or renewed. That agreement had given the allies joint responsibility with the Prague forces for guarding the walls, gates, towers, and even city halls. But the Prague authorities answered that those measures had been taken in view of the danger then threatening the capital. As there was no such danger now there was no reason to renew the emergency measures. Having achieved nothing but another rebuff Nicholas angrily returned to the siege of Říčany.

This was the situation in which Žižka decided to go to Prague. There is no doubt that he looked at the widening rift between Tabor and Prague as unfortunate. It would be wrong to think of him as one standing "above the parties." He was one of the men of Tabor and felt as such. Yet it would be equally wrong to assume that he shared every view voiced and approved of every step taken by the more radical leaders. His position clearly differed from that of the other senior captain as far as the offer of the crown to the rulers of Poland-Lithuania was concerned. And all later evidence shows that in the question of the vestments he held with the masters of the University rather than with Koranda and Nicholas of Hus.

There is one other indication that in going to Prague Žižka meant to mediate rather than merely to defend Nicholas of Hus and his party friends. It is the company in which he traveled. With him were four Hussite noblemen: the brothers Peter and Purkhart of Janovice, Peter Zmrzlík of Svojšín, and Ulrich Vavák. The two last named were especially close friends of the Taborite leader. Vavák was a fairly young man, the only one of the powerful lords of Jindřichův Hradec who had joined the revolution. He had been so impressed by Žižka that he decided to serve with him. He had already accompanied the old soldier on his summer campaign to Lomnice, Nová Bystřice, and Sviny Trhové. Peter Zmrzlík was an older man, renowned throughout Bohemia as one of the closest, most highly trusted friends of John Hus. He had long been mint master of Kutná Hora, a position as influential politically as it was financially profitable to the holder. It had been one of Sigismund's first acts after the death of his brother to get rid of Zmrzlík and to put the brutal Nicholas of Jemniště in his place. The common hatred of the "Hungarian King" was only one of the bonds that united Žižka and Zmrzlík.[8]

Though personal friends of Žižka, the four barons were by no means Taborites (in the sense in which this was true of a very few other barons such as Prokop of Ústí or Roháč of Dubá). They were zealous Hussites, stout adherents of the revolution against Sigismund, and for just this reason would try to heal the rift between Tabor and Prague. They traveled with Žižka and his troops until they reached the neighborhood of Říčany. There Žižka joined, for the time being, the forces engaged in the siege whereas the four lords went on to Prague with the direct purpose of clearing up the misunderstandings that had arisen.

On December 4 Diviš of Říčany surrendered town and castle according to an agreement which allowed the lord, his family, his retainers, and all others to save their lives and all those possessions which they could carry with them. This agreement, however, was not kept by the Taborites, to the consternation of many contemporaries. When the women of Říčany left their homes the Taborite women, who often showed even less restraint than the men, threw themselves upon them and took from them all those possessions, clothes as well as jewelry, which they had been allowed to take along. A very much worse fate overtook seven priests who had been among the besieged. They were separated from all others on the express order of Žižka and burned to death.[9]

On December 6 the troops of Prague and Tabor returned to the capital. Two days later the political meeting which meanwhile had been prepared by the four lords was held in the Monastery of St. Ambrose, officially called by the councils of the Old and the New Town and the captains of Tabor. The organizers feared that popular demonstrations

[8] On Zmrzlík see Bartoš, *Čechy v době Husově*, p. 220.

[9] See Old Annalists, p. 43. For Tomek's view (*Žižka*, p. 74) that this was a punishment for special crimes there is no confirmation in the sources.

might disturb the proceedings. Therefore strict rulings were provided, which among other things, excluded all women and all priests from the meeting. It took its course in full order. At the end of the meeting, only one major point of disagreement seemed to remain: that of the vestments. As this was a question of ritual it was determined that this point should be submitted to a thorough public discussion between the clerics of Tabor and those of Prague. Lord Ulrich Vavák, as the nobleman of the highest standing among the mediators, was requested to arrange the matter.

Vavák ruled that the disputation should take place in the afternoon of December 10, in the main hall of the Charles College (Carolinum) of the University. As a gesture of good will the city council of the Old Town invited the leaders of all groups, including the lords and the Taborite captains, to a banquet to be held at the city hall before the disputation. Žižka and his friends accepted the invitation, but Nicholas of Hus, still upset about the series of defeats he had suffered, declined with an excuse as strange as it was impolite: the banquet might give his enemies an opportunity to murder him. Instead he decided to leave Prague at once, vowing that as long as he lived he would not return to this rotten city. Fate, however, willed it otherwise. Accompanied by some of his closest friends among the Taborite officers, he rode south, but hardly had he passed through the city gates when his horse stumbled and fell, throwing the rider off in so unfortunate a way that Nicholas suffered a broken leg and severe concussions in his chest. Despite his protests his friends carried him back into Prague where, in the large house previously belonging to Ulrich of Rosenberg,[10] he was given over to the care of physicians.

At about the same time the banquet at the city hall was held in what seems to have been a friendly and promising atmosphere. Yet difficulties developed even before the public discussion got under way. The clerics of Tabor suddenly objected to the place chosen by Lord Vavák, the Carolinum, as being part of the University against whom they were supposed to argue. Vavák got in touch with the masters and with Žižka, and it was agreed to hold the disputation at the large house owned in the Old Town by Peter Zmrzlík.

Participants and audience filled the house to overflowing. All the well-known masters of the University were present, with the rector, Prokop of Pilsen, at their head. The spokesmen of the Taborite clergy

[10] Nicholas had, in some unexplained way, taken possession of this house after the conquest of the castle of Přibenice by Tabor. See Tomek, *Dějepis*, IV, 122.

were led by their bishop, Nicholas of Pelhřimov. Besides the mediating lords—Vavák again acting as chairman—the main lay leaders were the city councilors of Prague and, on the Taborite side, Žižka, Chval of Machovice, and Lord Roháč of Dubá. The latter, though not yet officially one of the captains of Tabor, had already become fully identified with the Taborite cause.

The Taborite clergymen had expected that the disputation would immediately turn to the question of the vestments. But Prokop of Pilsen, the rector, declared in his opening speech that this question could be discussed only as part of the whole structure of Taborite teachings, much of which was a danger to Christianity and to the Czech people. He therefore ordered Master Peter of Mladeňovice to read, in Latin and Czech, a long list of alleged erroneous, damaging, and even outright heretical beliefs held by Tabor and its clergy. There were seventy-two of those supposed to be held by all Tabor, with a score of additional ones held by "some" Taborites.[11]

We have earlier[12] tried to give the gist of the Taborite teachings as represented by the accusations of the University. There were the chiliastic beliefs, prophecies and demands based on the conviction that Christ would appear shortly to establish His Kingdom—a set of tenets which were now losing strength as the date for the event had passed almost a year before. There were the theses banning anything outside the Scriptures as a source of religious truth. There were the tenets directed against the worship of Saints, the iconoclastic principles directed against their pictures and statues, the demand for the destruction of "unnecessary" churches and chapels, finally even doubts in transubstantiation—all these and many other theses were there read for everyone to hear. Also the specific role of the clergy at Tabor was mentioned in an accusing way: the election of a bishop, the admission and ordination of laymen as priests, the undignified way of ministering in ordinary clothes, the fact that some Taborite priests had married, and finally the contradiction between the Hussite teachings against the worldly domination of priests and the dominating role actually played by the priests in all Taborite communities.

Peter of Mladeňovice ended by declaring that the masters of the University did not intend to indict or inculpate anybody present. Their aim was to establish the erroneous and partly even heretical character

[11] The list fills fourteen pages in Goll's edition of Březová's chronicle (pp. 452-465).
[12] See Chapter 5 above.

of those teachings and to warn the whole Czech nation not to be misled by them or for those men whom they heard teaching them.

While the articles were being read the men of Tabor grew restless and excited. When Peter of Mladeňovice had finished, Chval of Machovice jumped up and angrily protested the way in which Tabor's creed was attacked by the masters. Chval was a good soldier but hardly able to judge the theological implications (and actual contradictions) of the seventy-two articles. In his blind zeal to defend his sect he claimed: "I firmly believe in every one of the articles you have read." Roháč of Dubá complained that the masters of the University were acting worse than the Roman clergy at Constance. There the Czech Hussites were charged only with forty erroneous articles, here Tabor is accused of more than seventy.

The first among the Taborite priests to answer was Martin Houska, often called Loquis because of his oratorial gifts. He stood up for the theses with which Tabor was charged. Less naïve, however, than Chval of Machovice he declared that in various cases the Taborite tenets had been distorted or misrepresented and could be judged fairly only after these distortions had been removed. In a similar sense spoke Bishop Nicholas of Pelhřimov and Priest Markold of Zbraslavice.

The masters of the University answered that they were willing to prove publicly, from the Scriptures and other sources, the erroneous or heretical character of each of the articles. When Houska demanded that the articles should be presented to the Taborites in written form he was told that anyone ready to defend the articles was welcome to study them in the form they had been read.

At this point the discussion seemed to have reached an impasse. But now Nicholas of Pelhřimov rose, attempting at this late stage to direct the disputation to the original issue: the question of the vestments. He spoke at some length about this, going back to Christ and the Apostles who had taken the Last Supper in their workaday clothes. Jacobellus of Stříbro answered that the church ritual contained two elements: those based on the Will of God as revealed in the Scriptures which are unalterable; others which developed as human institutions and could be altered. The vestments, he said, belonged to the latter ones, but since their use was neither contrary to the Law of God nor harmful there was no need to suppress them. Jacobellus ended by handing a written declaration to the chairman and suggesting that an equally clear statement to this question should, within a certain time, be handed in also by the Taborite clergy. The study of both would then make it easier to arrive at the truth.

Jacobellus' statement seems to have been made with the purpose of ending the proceedings in a somewhat more conciliatory spirit, and thus they were understood, too, by the Taborite side. It was finally resolved that both parties should, within one month, deliver their written statements to the mayor of the Old Town as well as to some other persons to be named by both contending sides. Then the meeting was adjourned.

The official Taborite statement on the vestments was soon afterwards prepared by the clergy of Tabor[13] and was taken to Prague by Wenceslas Koranda. His attempt, however, to gain acceptance for it by another public disputation remained unsuccessful. With another lengthy reply from the University[14] the matter came, for the time being, to an inconclusive end.

The disputation in Zmrzlík's house helps us toward a better understanding of the rift that had developed between Prague and Tabor as religious centers—a rift that had been inherent in the initial conceptions of both sides. But it also informs us on the stand that some of the main actors had taken at this time.

Among the Utraquist or Calixtine doctors and masters of the University there was, by this time, a strong tendency toward orthodoxy, toward a more and more strictly defined set of creeds and rituals deviating as little as possible from that of Rome. The emergence of what Palacký has called the Hussite or Utraquist High Church can be fully discerned. It could surprise no one that this tendency was strongly favored by the more conservative masters—men like John Příbram, Christian of Prachatice, or the present rector Prokop of Pilsen. It was more significant that the greatest of Hus's co-reformers, the man who had done more than anyone else to develop a new Hussite theology and whose teachings had had much influence also upon Tabor—that Jacobellus of Stříbro should have taken such a strong stand against Tabor, contending with all his theological scholarship even the side issue of the vestments. His move to the right closed the ranks of the leading theologians of Prague, and left only one man of real stature to represent the more radical tendencies in the capital. John Želivský

[13] The Taborite statement on the vestments is the only contribution of some value which, to this phase of events, can be found in Nicholas of Pelhřimov's *Chronicon Taboritarum*. See Höfler, II, 488.

[14] *ibid.*, II, 501.

did not even take part in the meeting, knowing well that his presence or activity would, at this stage, do little good to his friends of Tabor or to his own followers in Prague. He would have to bide his time.

Just as important as for Prague was the disputation of December 10 for Tabor and the development of its religious forces and groupings. Having to defend themselves against the attacks of the University the priests of Tabor seemed to present a united front at the disputation. Yet we know that prior to these events trouble had developed among the Taborite clergy on the grounds of dissenting religious teachings. It had been for this reason that in September Nicholas of Pelhřimov, a man less identified than Koranda with chiliastic ideas, had been elected bishop. The discussion of the seventy-two articles was bound to bring some of these conflicts into the open. There were not a few among those articles which were entirely acceptable to Martin Houska—and perhaps even to Koranda who happened to be in Tabor at the time—but which appeared highly doubtful if not outright heretical to Nicholas of Pelhřimov and many others of the Taborite clergy. This was true of some of the mystic or pantheistic beliefs, and most of all of the doubts in transubstantiation.

We have, I believe, to look for reservations of the same character if we want to appraise the attitude which Žižka took at the meeting in the house of his friend Zmrzlík. From the chronicle we gain only one piece of information: he was silent. But his silence at this moment when his people were under attack and when not only its priests but his comrades in arms, Chval and Roháč, stood up in valiant defense of Tabor—this silence surely was more eloquent than many words could have been. Was it only that, having come to Prague to mediate, he did not now want to relinquish his role as mediator?[15] This would hardly have been in character with the man. Had he believed that the articles read against Tabor contained unfair and slanderous distortions of what was really preached and taught at home—he could not have stood there in grim silence all through the long discussion. Nor would he have hesitated to come out in favor of the articles if he had, like Chval, thought of them as the true faith. His silence could only have one meaning: he knew that most of the articles read were a correct rendering of tenets that had been taught at Tabor. And he was strongly critical of many of them—so critical that, if he did not want to join Tabor's accusers, all he could do was to remain silent.

[15] This is Tomek's theory. See his *Žižka,* p. 75.

Žižka had been middle-aged when he had undergone the deep experience of Hus's preaching and teaching. Now he was too old to remain open-minded in his judgment on questions of the creed. He was now as intolerant as were his enemies. Those that stood against the Law of God—and most especially priests—were in his eyes heretics, seducers, instruments of the most terrible corruption of the human soul, people who had to be exterminated in order to save all others from the snares of Satan and Anti-Christ. The discovery that such heresy could exist not only among the Roman clergy but also among the priests of Tabor must have startled and frightened him, and the stand taken by Jacobellus of Stříbro may have sharpened the suspicions which he had harbored before. He could hardly forget that it was Jacobellus of Stříbro who was mainly responsible for the Four Articles of Prague, and even though he tended to interpret them in his own way he never doubted that this great charter was the guiding light for all faithful Czechs.

The Žižka who left the great meeting of December 10 must have been a thoughtful and worried man. He would have to keep a strict watch, back at Tabor, to make sure that heresy did not raise its dangerous head too high. He would have to expect considerable resistance from some of the Taborite priests, and he could not be sure that, in the long run, his influence would prevail over theirs. Yet just now an event was to occur which would make him the undisputed head among the temporal leaders of the Taborite community.

In the town palace of the Rosenbergs at Prague lay Nicholas of Hus, the senior captain of Tabor,[16] nursing the injuries which his strong body had received in his recent accident. His remark that the Praguers might seek his life was certainly ill-founded: the city's foremost physicians did their best for him. They skillfully mended his broken leg, but they were unable to restore his crushed chest. He struggled along for two weeks, finding it increasingly difficult and painful to breathe. On Christmas Eve, 1420, he died.

The news spread quickly through the city which was preparing to celebrate the birth of the Lord. Some people, especially in the New Town, mourned him, thinking his death a grave loss to the cause of

[16] In an agreement, as such without importance, concluded on December 23 between Tabor and some of Ulrich of Rosenberg's burgraves the captains of Tabor are still named in their old order with the dying Nicholas of Hus named first and Žižka (who also may have been absent at the conclusion of the agreement) second. See *Archiv český*, III, 494.

the new creed, whereas the majority of the citizens seemed to feel relief rather than regret. "They thanked God," so Březová tells us, "that in His Grace he had delivered them from a cunning man who had used his knowledge to further not peace and love but disunity and hatred between the parties."[17]

Today, with centuries gone, how should we evaluate the man who ranked with Žižka during the first year and a half of the Hussite revolution? He proved to be a good soldier when in June 1420 before the gates of Tabor, he routed the considerable army of Ulrich of Rosenberg and Leopold Krajíř. No one, on the other hand, ever compared him to Žižka in this regard. It is as a politician and party leader that Nicholas' role was disputed. Palacký, among others, considered him a statesman of stature while he was reluctant to concede the same to Žižka.

But a closer scrutiny of his achievements hardly seems to warrant such praise. It is true that he knew how to organize people, how to handle mass meetings; that he quickly appraised his friends and foes and their role in a given situation; and that driven hard by his boundless ambition, he would be ready for action while others, including Žižka, might still ponder the consequences. Yet he went strangely wrong in judging his chances and was apt to underrate his enemies. Especially those hasty actions by which he alienated a growing number of people outside the Taborite camp make it doubtful whether he could ever have become a national leader in the true sense.

It was probably just incidental that the great embassy to Poland which had been decided upon on November 14 and which Nicholas of Hus had so vigorously opposed did not get under way while he was alive. But hardly had he died—and with him the dream of kingship for a Bohemian knight—when Hynek of Kolstein with his large retinue of noblemen and representatives of Prague[18] began his travels, leaving the city at the hour when Christmas Day, 1420, had ended. About the same time Žižka, too, left Prague with his troops, and returned to Tabor.

[17] Březová, p. 451.

[18] *ibid.*, p. 465. On the composition and character of that mission, see below Chapter 17.

# CHAPTER 13

## CONQUERORS EAST AND WEST

The beginning of the new year saw Žižka return from his excursion into politics to his own sphere: the waging of the war. It was one of the unusual features of this new campaign that he began it when the worst of the winter was still imminent. But his peasants were hardy men and by attacking at such time he was most likely to surprise his enemies.

With Chval of Machovice and his friend Peter Zmrzlík as lieutenants, Žižka set out on a long march which took him into the region dominated by the Landfrieden of Pilsen. This powerful alliance of Royalist lords, squires, and towns was the strongest force inside Bohemia with which now, after the armistice with Rosenberg, the country's Hussite forces were still in open warfare.

Žižka attacked the Pilsen region not in its eastern part where his enemies would be most likely to expect him but in the west where he could threaten its connections with Germany.[1] The first gains of the campaign were the fortified monastery and small town of Chotěšov, some twelve miles southwest of the city of Pilsen which he had quietly by-passed on his way. Farther northwest he then took the monastery of Kladruby. Both monasteries had been abandoned in time by their monastic inhabitants. Kladruby was a strong fortress and was now used as such by the Taborite army. As commander of the new garrison Žižka left his friend Zmrzlík. He then tried to go one step further in cutting the main lines of communication between Pilsen and the Empire by investing Stříbro, a town of considerable size and strength, on the main route from Pilsen to Cheb and to German Franconia. At the same time a harrowing war was waged against the outlying possessions of the city of Pilsen.

The people of Pilsen, in a somewhat hypocritical fashion, lodged a written complaint about this treatment. Žižka answered in a letter

[1] Main sources for this campaign: Březová, p. 469, Old Annalists, p. 44, *Chronicon veteris Collegiati*, Höfler, I, 82.

addressed to the Landfrieden of Pilsen (but omitting expressly the barons belonging to it).[2] In this he explained, as a judge would explain his sentence to the criminal, why he felt it necessary to burn their houses and destroy their land. Had they not defied every one of the Four Articles of Prague though they had been among the first to be preached the true Law of God? Especially, had they not supported those guilty of deadly sins, "first among them the heretical King, that violator of virgins and women, that murderer and incendiary who seeks to destroy the Czech nation"? After this outbreak of truly Žižkaesque wrath the writer warns the estates of the Pilsen region—from the knights downwards—not to let themselves be seduced any longer by the great lords allied with the King: they only want to make them lose their souls as well as their earthly possessions. He chides them for having broken the promises given in March 1420, but he is not astounded, for "whoever keepeth not faith with God will not keep faith with man either." But he still hopes that God will grant them to escape from the snares of His enemies and to find the way back to Him.

The letter, written obviously under strong emotion and without too much forethought, reveals much of Žižka's personality. It shows his thoughts still dominated by the Four Articles. It shows his furious hatred of the "heretical King," a hatred which never abated as long as he lived. It shows, in the same sentence, his national feeling. And finally it shows that, at least at times, Žižka harbored a special distrust of the great lords whom he thought more liable to be corrupted by the King than the lower estates—this notwithstanding the fact that he found among those lords a small but steadily growing number of close friends. We shall hear immediately how he acquired one of them: by making a friend out of a foe whom he had just denounced in the letter to the Pilsen Landfrieden as one of the evil lords allied with Sigismund.

Žižka had hardly begun the siege of Stříbro when a piece of intelligence made him change his mind. He heard that Bohuslav of Švamberg, with a not very strong troop, had just gone to his great castle of Krasikov, only a few miles to the north of Stříbro, presumably to prepare countermeasures against Žižka's offensive.

We have met the lord of Švamberg before. A hardy, vigorous man in his thirties, he had been Žižka's adversary at Nekměř, at Sudoměř, and at Bor Panský, in other words whenever the Landfrieden of Pilsen

[2] The "Knights and squires, the townsmen and farmers of the Landfrieden of Pilsen." See Appendix, III.

had been in the forefront of the fight, and he had more or less acted as the Landfrieden's commander in chief. If it was possible to deprive that strong organization of its most active and intrepid fighter—surely this was a greater blow to Sigismund than the conquest of a town. Thus Žižka, leaving Stříbro for later, turned against the castle. When on the second day the tower dominating the drawbridge was taken, Švamberg informed Žižka that he was willing to surrender—not, however, to the Taborite troops but to Zmrzlík who, as he knew, was in command near Kladruby. Žižka had no objections, and so Zmrzlík was called and arranged for the surrender: Švamberg's retainers would be allowed to go free under bail to make sure they would not fight the Hussites again. Lord Bohuslav, however, would remain a captive in his own castle. Žižka saw to it that the conditions of the surrender were strictly fulfilled, quenching without much difficulty the grumbling of some of his soldiers who felt that Švamberg did not deserve so mild a treatment.

The story, however, had an unusual sequel. Žižka was interested in this prisoner who had been such a valiant foe. After some months he was removed from Krasikov to the castle of Přibenice, in Tabor's immediate neighborhood where Žižka could visit him occasionally. By October 1421 Bohuslav of Švamberg was a free man again, fighting vigorously in the war—but this time on the side of Tabor, the side of Žižka, against Sigismund.

What had happened? Of the several sources which mention his capture and his conversion, only one[3] gives us a convincing explanation: it was Žižka who "enticed him to join his heresy." Still a few months later, in February 1422, he sent a letter of challenge to his relative, Ulrich of Rosenberg, telling him that he would fight for the Law of God to his dying day. He proved as good as his word.

The swift conquest of some important fortified places west of Pilsen, followed by the capture of Švamberg and his retainers, was bound to arouse the anxiety not only of the people of Pilsen but also of Sigismund. The King had spent Christmas at Litoměřice. The call for help

[3] Aeneas Sylvius (pp. 88, 89): "Zisca . . . Booslaum . . . in haeresim suam pellexit." He should have known, as one of his first-hand sources for this part of his book was Ulrich of Rosenberg who was, of course, well informed on all the details of Švamberg's actions. Švamberg's surrender is reported in great detail by Březová (p. 469). As for the date of Švamberg's leaving Krasikov for Přibenice see *Chronicon veteris Collegiati*, Höfler, I, 84, 85. The Old Analists (p. 53) see his conversion simply as a result of his anger about Sigismund's indifference to his fate, but this is a wrong and unfair imputation, especially when his very strong and sincere letter to Sigismund (*Archiv český*, III, 369) and his later actions are taken into account. As for the dating of these events see, among others, Bezold, *K. Sigismund und die Reichskriege gegen die Hussiten*, Excurs, pp. 136ff.

from the Landfrieden induced him to go to Pilsen some time before the middle of January. As usual he did not feel strong enough with the troops he had. But this time his clamor for military help quickly found favorable answers. Žižka's offensive so near the border of Bavaria and the Upper Palatinate had been observed with consternation in those countries. What if the terrible heretics spread the war beyond the limits of Bohemia? January 1421 produced the first of those almost hysterical flurries of excitement which took hold of the German duchies in Bavaria, Franconia, and Meissen whenever the Hussite wars approached their borders. Yet it was not until many years later that, exasperated by the long and bloody sequence of crusades, the Hussites finally carried the war into enemy territory.

Žižka's next objective: the town of Tachov, due west of Krasikov, was only about seven miles from one of the passes leading into Germany, and was inhabited mostly by Germans. Their frantic call for help, supported by the urgent bids of the King, resulted in the mobilization of strong German forces, put up by Nürnberg and other cities as well as by the Bavarian Dukes John and Otto and Duke Henry of Landshut. The last named received a highly confident letter from Sigismund. "We intend," so he says, "to save the town Tachov by our personal effort, and with the help of God, of yourself, and of our followers. We expect, this time, to put an end to this heresy altogether and thereby amply to bestead Christendom and the Christian faith."[4] There follow orders where the German forces are to meet those of the King. He seemed to feel pretty sure that Žižka, by venturing so far west, had run into a trap which had only to be closed by sufficient forces—and the revolution would lose its crack troops and with them its chances.

Žižka never underrated an enemy. If there was need he would fight much superior forces, but he disliked taking unnecessary risks. His troops available for battle had been weakened by the garrisons he had left at Chotěšov, Kladruby, and Krasikov. He did not consider giving up these valuable fortresses. To engage the King and his allies with the small army left to him would have been foolhardy. He raised the siege of Tachov, considerably reinforced the garrisons at those three places, and with the remainder of his troops returned to Tabor to assemble new, stronger forces. At the same time, about January 17, he asked Prague to help him to drive the King out of western Bohemia.

Sigismund, finding that there was no Taborite field army left which he could trap, decided to attack the largest of the three Taborite gar-

[4] *Urk. Beiträge*, pp. 57, 58.

risons, the one at Kladruby. When Lord Zmrzlík had gone to Krasikov, Žižkov had put Chval of Machovice in command at Kladruby. Even with the reinforcements left by Žižka he had probably less than a thousand men to defend the place. Sigismund's siege army, on the other hand, grew considerably by the arrival of the German auxiliaries. In a German intelligence report its strength is given as 12,000 men.[5]

Despite this enormous superiority the siege turned into a long sustained affair, lasting through the second half of January and the first week of February. Sigismund's siege guns did less damage to the besieged than these did, with their own artillery and their frequent sorties, to the besiegers. Fire weapons had, of course, a very short range and the besiegers had to be so near the walls of the fortress that they could hear the shouts of the garrison. The Taborite soldiers indulged in the Homeric custom of heckling the enemy. "Where," so they would call, "is the heretic King, the Antichrist? Tell him to come here and start his assault if he wants to conquer the place!"[6] Sigismund did not follow the advice but kept behind the safe walls of Stříbro.

Žižka's request for help was met promptly by the Praguers. They put up an army of 7,000 men, with 320 wagons. Among its leaders was William Kostka of Postupice, known to us from his participation in the Polish-Prussian War. Together with the troops which Žižka mobilized at Tabor the Hussites were now no longer much inferior to the King. On February 6 their forces met at Dobříš, twenty-five miles southwest of Prague, and from there marched due west in the direction of Pilsen. When they arrived before Rokycany, the town willingly opened its gates. It belonged to the Archbishop of Prague, who seems at this time to have entered already into negotiations with the capital. For the Taborite soldiers to march peaceably through a town ruled by a prince of the Roman Church was a strange experience. Some of them could not bear so much self-denial. They forced their way into the Monastery of St. Augustine where they wrought considerable destruction, and an unhappy cleric who may have been incautious enough to argue with them was killed.[7]

From Rokycany the allied armies struck south toward Kladruby, thus by-passing Pilsen. Soon the stage seemed set for a decisive battle. But Sigismund, for all his recent boasts, lost heart as soon as he saw that in strength his own forces and those of his enemies were fairly evenly matched. On February 8, just a day before the two armies would

[5] A letter from Nürnberg to Ulm, *ibid.*, p. 63. [6] Březová, p. 471.
[7] *ibid.*, p. 472.

have clashed, he raised the siege of Kladruby, sent his German auxiliaries back west and himself repaired with haste to Litoměřice. Even there he did not stay long. Before February was out he went to Kutná Hora, and early in March left Bohemia altogether, traveling by slow stages through Moravia back to Hungary. The hope "to put an end to this heresy" had been disappointed again, and what is more, he now seems to have gained a very much clearer perception of his Taborite foe. In a letter to Ulrich of Rosenberg, still from Kladruby, we find for the first time Žižka's name mentioned by the King. He calls him "the special promoter and director of the Wiklefite heresy,"[8] and urges Rosenberg in strong language not to conclude another armistice with him but to fight him to the limit of his capacity. The letter, in official Latin, was the first which he wrote to Rosenberg after a long period of silence. It is clear enough that he strongly resented the armistice concluded between Rosenberg and Žižka in November. This armistice had just expired (on February 4). We have no record indicating its renewal, but neither did Rosenberg obey the King's orders to attack. For the next months southern Bohemia enjoyed a period of uneasy peace, and the correspondence between Sigismund and Rosenberg shows an even longer gap than the one before.[9]

The King's retreat and Rosenberg's inactivity made it easy for the combined might of Tabor and Prague to concentrate against the place which had been the eventual objective of Žižka's campaign at the start: the great city of Pilsen, strongest single partner of the alliance called the Pilsen Landfrieden. For the second time within one year Pilsen was completely besieged. But now the tables were turned, and the defenders of 1420 had become the attackers of 1421.

The siege—always very difficult when a large town was the objective—was carried on with great vigor by the Hussites. Soon all suburbs, together with the town mills, were in Hussite hands. The town walls were under bombardment and had constantly to be repaired by the defenders. Still they fought on with a courage which even their Hussite enemies admired. Only when in the fourth week several outer bulwarks began to crumble and no relief was in sight, did they try to negotiate their way out of this situation which militarily had become hopeless.

It seems strange that, at this very promising moment, the Hussite

[8] *Urk. Beiträge*, pp. 63, 64.

[9] An exchange of letters between Rosenberg and the King seems to have taken place in April 1421 (see *Archiv český*, III, 225) but no letters are preserved until a written invitation to Rosenberg of July 14, 1422, shows that the baron is once again persona grata with the King.

leaders were prepared to consider anything but surrender. In retrospect we can say that this was one of the gravest mistakes made by them during the early years of the Hussite wars. If, after surrender, Pilsen had been forced to receive a Hussite garrison within its walls, it could not so easily have become the festering boil in the flesh of Hussite Bohemia during the years to follow. Compared with the treatment that other towns received—even those that surrendered freely and were spared any punishment—the concessions made to Pilsen show an unrealistic softness.

The men who negotiated for Pilsen knew well how to exploit the "weak spots" in the Hussite mentality. The hope which they dangled before the eyes of the leaders of Prague and Tabor was that Pilsen could achieve for them the full freedom of the Four Articles throughout Bohemia. They offered to send an embassy to Sigismund (who by this time had arrived at Brno in Moravia) with the task solemnly to entreat the King: to accede to the Four Articles of Prague; not to impede their practical implementation; and specifically to permit the people of the Pilsen Landfrieden to accede to them. Anticipating or answering the objection that the King would refuse so far-reaching concessions the Pilseners further offered that in any case, even if they should not be successful with the King, they would, within the space of one month, give full freedom to the preaching of the Four Articles in all the cities, towns, and villages of the Landfrieden, so that Hussite priests could freely move in that region to spread their gospel and dispense the Communion in the two kinds.

In this form[10] the offer was accepted by the Hussites and an armistice concluded till January 1, 1422. On the Hussite side it was signed by the Praguers, Taborites, and allied barons; on the side of the Landfrieden by the city of Pilsen, the barons of the region, and the towns of Stříbro, Tachov, and Domažlice. Of these towns only the last named, thirty miles southwest of Pilsen near the Bavarian border, was permanently won for Hussitism. Some weeks later a fight broke out between the Catholic and the Hussite people in the town. The latter remained victorious, and Domažlice joined the Taborite federation.[11]

It still seems strange that Žižka signed this armistice. Perhaps he did not want new trouble to arise out of this issue between Tabor and Prague. He may also, in accordance with the conciliatory phrase in his letter of January, have felt that he should not deny the people of

[10] See Březová, pp. 472, 473.
[11] See Žižka's two letters to the people of Domažlice, Appendix, IV, VI.

Pilsen another chance to redeem themselves before the eyes of God. He might have acted differently if he had then already been aware of events which had taken place, only a short time before, in eastern Bohemia.

Late in January a Taborite troop, consisting of approximately 1,000 men, tried to establish some bases for their community in the upper Elbe valley. They were led by Hromádka of Jistebnice, the man who had first organized the Taborite community in Sezimovo Ústí and Hradiště. He divided his little army in two groups of which the smaller one occupied the town of Přelouč, on the Elbe between Kolín and Pardubice, the larger one Chotěboř, twenty-five miles farther south near Německý Brod. Soon afterwards a Kutnohorian army under their infamous mint master, Nicholas "the Fierce," helped by Lord John Městecký of Opočno, one of Sigismund's most devoted supporters, reconquered Přelouč, killing many Taborites on the spot and leading one hundred and twenty-five men away to Kutná Hora. Early in February the same Royalists, joined by some other lords among whom was one of Sigismund's personal courtiers, Půta of Častolovice, laid siege to Chotěboř where Hromádka himself was in command. His garrison had been weakened as he had sent several troops out for provisioning. After a few days of resistance he asked for terms. John Městecký agreed that, if the Taborites surrendered the town, the lords would be bound in honor not to harm them. But the lords' honor was not involved, so they believed, as they were only dealing with heretics. Thus three hundred of the Taborite men were burned on the spot while their women were forced to watch the spectacle. (One of them, so the old chronicler tells us,[12] ran into the flames to burn with her husband.) The others were herded together and marched off to Kutná Hora. The long march must have been much like the awful treks of political prisoners under the totalitarian regimes of our century. People too weak to walk were clubbed down and left dying. On the top of a hill a fire was lit which burned another forty men. Those arriving alive at Kutná Hora were thrown into the mine-shafts. More than 700 of Hromádka's men were the helpless victims of this mass murder, and Hromádka himself was taken to Chrudím and publicly burned in the town square.

The mass murder of Chotěboř did more than any other single act to

[12] Old Annalists, p. 43. The report given there is fully confirmed, with some additional details, by the *Chronicon veteris Collegiati*. (Höfler, I, 82, 83.) According to Březová (p. 470) the number of victims amounted to over 1,000. As to the notion that there is no need to keep faith with heretics see Březová, p. 429.

fan the hatred of Hussite Bohemia against her enemies and to arouse the thirst for bloody vengeance. The first to feel it were the people of Chomútov against whom the combined Hussite armies turned after leaving the Pilsen region. The siege began on March 14. One day later the defenders, reinforced by squires of the neighborhood, defeated a strong Hussite assault. In fact they felt so sure of themselves that they poured derision on the attackers. On the third day, however, another assault broke the defense, and the Hussite soldiers, penetrating into the town from two sides, mercilessly killed all male inhabitants, even those ready to accept the Hussite creed. The Hussite commanders tried to make one exception: they offered complete immunity to the Jews in case they let themselves be converted. But, so we hear, they chose to burn rather than to abandon the faith of their fathers.[13]

As in every case when an enemy town was conquered by Hussite troops, orders had been given to spare the lives of women and children. But this time the leaders could not fully control the dammed-up fury, especially of the Taborite women. Some of the women of Chomútov were led out of the town by them and there stripped and killed. Others were luckier and escaped with their children, but the only men left alive were a group of thirty who were pardoned to bury the dead. "According to hearsay" between 2,200 and 2,400 people lost their lives.[14] Even a smaller and probably more accurate estimate, 1,360 people, represents an enormous number for a medieval town. The Taborite victims at Chotěboř had been revenged doubly or threefold.

The fate of Chomútov struck terror into the hearts of the enemies of Hussitism. The news spread quickly through Germany and was widely and fearfully commented on.[15] Even more frightened were those Bohemian towns which so far had stayed with Sigismund, especially those whose inhabitants were mostly German.

After a short rest in friendly Žatec the allied armies turned back toward Prague. Their way led them through the towns of Louny and

[13] *Chronicon veteris Collegiati*, Höfler, I, 83.

[14] This is the way the Old Annalists (p. 44) put it in their report. Březová (p. 477) is especially horrified because even pregnant women were killed by the Taborite amazons.

[15] See the letter of the Nürnberg city council to Cheb, in *Urk. Beiträge*, I, 68. The *Magdeburger Schöppenchronik* which, after reporting the battle of the Vyšehrad, had hardly carried any news on Bohemia, gives a long and excited account of the conquest of Chomútov, adding some doubtful atrocity stories to the harsh enough truth (p. 356). According to this source the fate of Chomútov was shared by the town of Kadaň where, supposedly, "heretics of Prague . . . slew all the Germans they could find in the town." Of other sources the above-mentioned letter of Nürnberg says that "the Wiklefites are planning to march toward Kadaň." From Czech sources we know only that the town, either then or somewhat later, submitted to the suzerainty of Prague.

Slaný. They had joined the revolution in its beginnings but had been taken and garrisoned by Sigismund in May 1420. Now the Royalist garrisons had fled and both towns, welcoming the victors, returned to the Hussite fold.

On March 22 the armies of Prague and Tabor, and with them Žižka, entered the capital. Especially for the Taborite army this had been a long sustained campaign, lasting for almost three months and involving a great deal of fighting. But it had been worth-while. The main parts of western and northwestern Bohemia had been gained or regained for the Chalice. A large number of castles had been taken (among them many not mentioned in this account), and most of the important lines of communication were now free of enemy interference. The next—and as it seemed last—large region of Bohemia to be liberated from the King's power was eastern Bohemia, and Žižka's stay in Prague in those days of late March were used to work out plans for the common campaign in this direction. There remained only two important places in the region of Prague which still adhered to the King: Beroun, about 20 miles southwest of Prague, and Mělník, equally far to the north at the confluence of the Elbe and Vltava rivers, both still functioning as awkward road blocks. In Beroun especially, several anti-Hussites from Prague, including three masters of the University, had found a refuge and center of activity. The town was strongly garrisoned and commanded by one of Sigismund's Italian condottieri, Rodolfo Bece, who had served the King before in his wars against Venice.

Žižka personally undertook, with his Taborites and some Prague troops, to reduce the place. It was conquered after a siege of six days. Bece and many others fell in the fight. Thirty-seven persons, among them the three masters, were burned to death.[16]

The Mělníkers did not wait for Hussite troops to arrive before their gates. They sent an embassy to Prague fully acknowledging the capital as their suzerain. They would keep and defend the Four Articles to the limit of their strength. They would not accept Sigismund as King, nor permit Queen Sophia to enter the town without Prague's permission. They would obey the authorities of Prague as their own. This treaty of submission served as a model for many later treaties of a similar character[17] which all helped to increase and stabilize the power and authority of Prague within the Kingdom.

[16] Březová, p. 478.

[17] See the texts of two of those treaties in *Archiv český*, I, 201, and 204, some more in VI, and *Urk. Beiträge*, I, 99 and 123.

The siege of Beroun lasted from March 26 till April 1, and immediately after its fall Žižka returned to Tabor, though the military plans worked out between him and Prague meant leading the allied armies toward the east. The main reason for this trip south was that the trouble brewing at Tabor had grown increasingly menacing in his eyes and in those of his friends. Things had come to a head by an event immediately preceding the conquest of Beroun. At that time Priest Antoch, one of the radicals of the Taborite clergy, preached in the Old Town Square of Prague to the Taborite soldiers. In his sermon he compared the capital with the "beast with two horns" from the Revelation of St. John. One horn represented the councilors of the Old Town, the other the masters of the University who had heretically insisted on the vestments. Antoch exhorted his listeners not to stay in Prague nor give any help to the Praguers. This was a call to mutiny as the Taborite soldiers had received orders that very day for a campaign which would help the Praguers. A group of Taborite soldiers followed the seditious call and set out for Tabor, led by Antoch and one or two other priests. As soon as Žižka heard what was happening he hurried after them, and when the priests refused to stop he flew into a rage and beat them with his bare fists. This drastic action seems to have quelled the mutiny, for, as the chronicler[18] tells us, "on the same day he rode with the Praguers to Beroun."

Yet the episode must have been a grave shock to him. It was the first time that Taborite soldiers had shown themselves capable of disobeying their old commander. It was also the first open clash between Tabor's general and part of its clergy, prejudging a matter which he had always considered within his own province: the military alliance with Prague. And as he could easily conclude, this affront against him was based on the same religious radicalism which had caused so much trouble before between Prague and Tabor. It was, indeed, high time for him to go home and face those seditious elements among the Taborite priesthood.

We have mentioned before the existence of parties and groupings among the people of Tabor and especially among their monastic leaders. The election of Nicholas of Pelhřimov by the moderate majority had been an attempt to control the more radical elements. The tendency that disturbed the moderates at this time was not, or no longer, an emanation of the original chiliasm, but rather the movement known to the contemporaries as Pikhartism or Picardism. This term derives

[18] Březová, p. 477.

from the name "Beghard," covering a variety of religious (but not always heretical) movements and trends which flourished in Flanders, western France, and part of the Rhineland from the thirteenth through the fifteenth century. Among them were mystics whose teachings went clearly against the established doctrines of the Church especially in the sect known as "the Brethren and Sisters of the Free Spirit." There was a strong pantheist trend in their belief. They thought that God was everywhere, in everything, especially in themselves; they denied the existence of the Devil and the original sin, and in some instances this belief in the goodness of everything that is in man, including all his impulses, tempted them to indulge in sexual excesses, though it would be a grave wrong to charge the whole movement with immorality. The almost complete identity of what was taught by the Pikharts of Tabor with the tenets of the older, western sect (together with the use of the name) leaves little doubt in the foreign origin of this movement,[19] which is also confirmed by contemporary[20] reports. Pikhart heretics were later persecuted in Prague as well as at Tabor. The name Pikhart finally had a highly derogatory connotation and was used to voice the suspicion of heresy against anybody whom moderate Hussites suspected of over-radical leanings.[21]

It was the priest Martin Houska who became, in the fall and winter of 1420, the leading spokesman of the Pikhart teachings at Tabor. Březová calls him "the principal disseminator of all Taborite errors."[22]

[19] The question of the origin of the radical trends at Tabor has been a subject of extended controversies among Czech historians. They centered upon the problem whether and to what extent Waldensian influence can be discerned or proved in the Taborite movement. It is too intricate and specialized a question to be entered here in detail, especially as so much of it, for lack of documentary proof, is based on more or less subtle conjectures. Among the twentieth century authors Pekař considers Waldensian influence to be very strong whereas Bartoš denies it, especially in his book *Husitství a cizina* (Hussitism and the foreign world), pointing, among other things, to the fact that Waldensianism was accepted in Bohemia mostly by people of German origin. For a treatment of this special question in English see H. C. Lea, *A History of the Inquisition*, II, 427-437. It is surprising that the much more obvious influence of the "Brethren of the Free Spirit" upon the Taborite Pikharts has found little consideration among modern Czech historians though the connection was pointed out, a century ago, by Palacký. On the Brethren of the Free Spirit, their beliefs and their fate see Lea, *op.cit.*, II, 350-377, further A. G. Seesholtz, *Friends of God, Practical Mysteries of the Fourteenth Century*, New York 1934, pp. 20-23, 103-104, 182-183, and R. M. Jones, *The Flowering of Mysticism*, New York 1939, pp. 51-60. The basic work on the Beghards is still J. L. Mosheim's Latin tractate *De Beghardis et Beguinabus*, Leipzig 1720.

[20] Březová, p. 431, says that in 1418 fifteen "Picardi" arrived in Prague with their families, claiming that they had been expelled from their homeland because they had been adherents of the Law of God.

[21] This tendency appears quite patently in Březová's chronicle, *passim*.

[22] p. 470.

Early in December his position among the Taborite clergy was still so strong that he was one of the priests presenting the Taborite point of view at the great disputation in the house of Zmrzlík. Only seven weeks later, on January 29, Houska was a prisoner under the grave charge of heresy. The man who arrested him was Lord Ulrich Vavák, Žižka's close friend, and one of the leaders in the mediation between Prague and Tabor. The assumption that Žižka stood behind Vavák's move, if he had not actually requested it, is strengthened by the reason given for the arrest: Houska had just begun teaching and practicing a new heresy: the priest was no longer to put the holy wafer into the mouth of the communicant, speaking the words which turned the bread into the Body of Christ. He should give the bread to the whole congregation, asking them to break and divide it among themselves. For, so Houska argued, had not Christ himself done this at the Last Supper?

Houska's act had, of course, a profound significance. Through it he denied the reality of transubstantiation and replaced it by something similar to what later became known as the commemorative understanding of the Eucharist. But for the overwhelming majority of Hussites, and probably even for most Taborites, the transubstantiation and the real presence of Christ at the Communion was a dogma which to doubt was a revolting act of disbelief. The Hussites had demanded the Communion in the two kinds because it was, as they felt, more in accordance with the teachings of the original church, and because they were not willing to forego even a part of "this goodness" as Žižka put it in his letter to the Pilsen Landfrieden. What were they fighting and dying for if the Communion was not an effective act in the process of saving the soul of the Christian?

We know some of Houska's arguments from a polemic tractate written against him and his followers by Master John Příbram, the leader of the conservative Utraquists.[23] From these arguments Houska appears as a strongly rationalistic thinker—a trait by no means contradictory to his mystic leanings, and certainly equally unbearable to his more scholastically inclined adversaries. As Christ's Body, having been resurrected, was now in heaven it could not be simultaneously present in the host. For the priests to claim that by saying a few words and making the sign of the cross over the bread they were turning it into the Body of Christ was nothing better than conjuring and cheating the people.

[23] *Contra articulos Picardorum.* The tractate has never been fully published. See *Urk. Beiträge*, III, 204-208, further Krofta in *Časopis musea českého*, 1899, pp. 209ff. and 1903, pp. 425ff., and Pekař, *Žižka*, I, 139ff. and notes on p. 257.

One can feel, even through Příbram's accusations, that the young priest was an extraordinary and extraordinarily attractive person. Born in Moravia probably less than thirty years before, he had made his way to the top in the indistinct and inofficial Taborite hierarchy mainly through his overwhelming eloquence which had procured him the name Loquis and other epithets such as "the New Prophet Daniel" or "the Angel of the Hosts of God." In his personal preachings and in some tractates which he wrote to the Taborite community of Písek he showed the clarity and wit of his thinking, his freedom from all dogmatic prejudice, and his complete fearlessness. He never hesitated to attack what he thought was wrong and did not even spare the memory of the venerated Master Matthew of Janov, the man who had urged the frequent taking of the Holy Communion and who, as Houska dared to say, was mainly responsible for all this idolatrous "kneeling before that bread."

Houska's courage did not leave him when he was put behind prison bars. In a letter to his friends at Tabor he confidently defended his beliefs. He was, so he said, not afraid to die for them, but he asked to be heard before he was judged. The Taborite clergy interceded with Vavák who thereupon released him, probably stipulating that his errors be dealt with properly by the Taborite priests themselves. This was done, and considerable pressure put on the young preacher. Houska eventually revoked in public his special heresy.

How serious an error it was even in the eyes of the moderate Taborites is shown in a letter written on February 28 by Bishop Nicholas of Pelhřimov and another prominent Taborite cleric, Master John of Jičín, to Jacobellus of Stříbro and John Příbram.[24] It is a solemn warning to the University and community of Prague, describing in detail the teachings and nefarious practices of the Pikharts. ("Like the heathens or the most perfidious among the Jews they throw the sacrament of the Body of Christ out of the monstrances and tread on it.") Prague should watch carefully that its people were not infected. Upon this warning the clergy of Prague was ordered to preach about the dangers of Pikhartism from all pulpits. All house owners were ordered to refuse lodging to anyone infected by Pikhartism and immediately to inform the city authorities against such people. Soon afterwards a Prague artisan who proved to be a confirmed Pikhart was publicly burned.

The Taborite clergy dealt mildly with Houska whose eloquence and sincerity had gained him friends and sympathizers even among those

[24] Březová, p. 474.

who did not share all his views. They could hardly treat with equal leniency a group of people who had gone much further in their pantheistic beliefs than Houska, showing more clearly the influence of the "Brethren of the Free Spirit." Their leader, originally a friend of Houska's was a priest called Peter Kániš. All human impulses, so they pronounced, came from God and were manifestations of God. There was no original sin, and they themselves were as innocent as Adam and Eve in Paradise. It was wrong to curb in any way the sexual desire. Those licentious ideas were hateful in the extreme to the puritan minds of all true Taborites, and the priests of Tabor decided that the town had to be cleansed from their presence and influence. About three hundred of them, including Kániš, were banned from the town and isolated in the fortress of Přibenice.

It was there that they met their fate in the person of Žižka, on his return from Prague to Tabor. He thought it necessary to go himself to Přibenice and to find out more about the strange fanatics who had been isolated there. He led the whole group under escort to Klokoty, a village near Tabor, where he attempted to do what the moderate priests at Tabor had not succeeded in doing: to convince them by all the arguments at his disposal that they had fallen into the snares of the Devil, and that their only salvation lay in a return to the Law of God.[25] But fifty of these people, including Peter Kániš, steadfastly refused to listen and did not flinch when finally Žižka ordered them to be burned, because they had lost their souls forever.[26] The victims, on the other hand, were very confident for their souls. Smiling, they mounted the stake and exclaimed that this very day they would rule with Christ in Heaven.

The movement, however, was not stamped out by this auto-da-fé. Many people who had been held at Přibenice had escaped and were now at large, hiding in the woods. At Tabor itself the poison was still circulating, and hardly had Žižka left the town later in April when another twenty-five were burned at the order of the Taborite clergy. Žižka had not finished yet with the man whom he considered the main culprit, the "principal disseminator" of the Pikhart errors, Martin Houska.

Meanwhile, on April 13, a strong army of Prague troops left the

25 Březová, p. 475. Another important source is a largely rhymed chronicle published in Appendix 3 of the Old Annalists, pp. 476ff.

26 The strength of this consideration in Žižka's mind emerges very clearly from his letter to Pilsen. See Appendix, III.

capital to start what was to become one of the most successful Hussite offensives inside the Kingdom. At the time it began, Prague had not officially appointed a captain general, but from all accounts it is clear that the actual leader of her armies was John Želivský. It remains something of a riddle how, after the political defeats he had suffered at the end of 1420, he recaptured so much power. In any case his command lasted throughout the campaign, even though the troops of the capital were soon reinforced by some great noblemen with their retainers. The first to join them were the Orebites with their old leaders Krušina of Lichtenburg and Diviš Bořek of Miletínek, followed by the brothers Victorin and Hynek of Kunštat. On April 16 the Hussite army arrived before Český Brod, a strongly fortified town defended by several hundred German mercenaries. The town was assaulted and stormed the day after. Most of the defenders were killed fighting. Several houses where Sigismund's soldiers tried to hide were burned. Eighteen priests who clung to the Communion in one kind received no more mercy from the Praguers than they would have from the Taborites.

This swift and bloody conquest, added to the memory of what had happened at Chomútov and Beroun, had a tremendous psychological effect. One after the other of the towns in the wide, fertile Elbe valley surrendered and concluded treaties of alliance with and submission to Prague before the Hussite army even had reached them: Kouřim and Nymburk and Kolín, together with many smaller towns, castles, and monasteries. An embassy promising submission and support also came from farther south: from the royal town of Čáslav where the Chalice had always had many adherents among the citizens. All the last-named towns were predominantly Czech in character, and none of them ever abandoned the Chalice in the later development of the war.

With Kolín and Čáslav in Hussite hands the city of Kutná Hora, lying just in between those two towns, was now dangerously threatened. Yet the Kutnohorians, always the most active enemies of Hussitism, decided to offer resistance. Mobilizing their considerable forces they marched on April 23 toward Kolín where the bulk of the Hussite army was stationed on that day. But when the men in their vanguard realized the strength of the Hussites they lost heart and the Kutnohorian force speedily retreated behind the walls of their city. On the day after, they sent emissaries to Kolín, who put up a very effective plea for their city. They reminded the Praguers of the wealth and beauty of their famed town and of the great income which the whole kingdom used to receive from its silver mines. It would be a great pity if Prague was to destroy this "precious jewel of the kingdom." Kutná Hora would acknowledge the suzerainty of the capital and adhere to the Four Articles if those who felt unable to conform were permitted to leave the town with their movable belongings. The Hussite leaders accepted, stipulating only that the Kutnohorians were to do public repentance for their crimes. Perhaps there was some doubt whether the silver mines, which from now on would prove a great economic asset to Hussite Bohemia (and a corresponding loss to Sigismund) could be worked competently by men who lacked the knowledge of the experienced German miners. Even so the lenient treatment of Kutná Hora clearly showed the realism and the statesmanlike moderation of which John Želivský was capable.

Želivský represented the Hussite community at the great ceremony of public repentance which took place on April 25. The whole population of Kutná Hora, men, women, and children, led by priests carrying the host, went out toward the monastery of Sedlec, and when they got within sight of the assembled soldiers of Prague, they all fell on their knees and in unison asked forgiveness for their crimes from the Praguers. John Želivský then preached to them, reminding them of every one of their numerous misdeeds, and exhorted them not to repeat them, which they promised with tears in their eyes. Želivský thereupon pronounced the mercy bestowed on the repentant town "by God and the Praguers." "And after ample tears had flowed on both sides, soon the voices rose to heaven singing alternately the Te Deum laudamus, one verse being sung by the Praguers, the other by the Kutnohorians."[27] Eventually the Kutnohorians returned to the city, accompanied by a limited number of Prague emissaries who should help to establish the new order of things.

Perhaps this scene can teach us more about the spirit of the time and the mind of the Hussite people than a learned discourse. Surely even Želivský, for all his sophistication, was perfectly sincere when he spoke those words of reproach, warning, and final absolution. Those thousands of other people involved in this solemn ceremony cried because they were witnessing a great act of salvation. A whole town full of Sauls were turned into Pauls by it, and they, the adherents of the Law of God, had made that possible, to the rejoicing of the angels in heaven. These people from Prague, captains and councilors, merchants and craftsmen, workers, peasants and mercenary soldiers, were in their

[27] Březová, p. 480.

majority no fanatics comparable to the chiliastic crowds of early Tabor. Yet their faith in God and themselves, deeply humble and highly self-confident at the same time, made them trust firmly that God would forgive where they had forgiven. It is perhaps only on that basis that we can understand the quick change of temper in the treatment of different towns: the uninhibited, merciless slaughter of Sigismund's mercenaries at Český Brod—men who, after all, had done nothing but their duty as soldiers—and the more than clement treatment granted to the Kutnohorians despite the appalling register of their atrocities.

From Kutná Hora the army of Prague marched via Čáslav eastward toward Chrudim, and it was before the walls of that strongly fortified town that they were joined, on April 26, by the Taborite army under Žižka. The Hussite forces were now stronger than at any time before, and the people of Chrudim would have preferred to submit without fight, but their captain and governor, Lord John Městecký of Opočno, would have none of it. He had always hated the Hussites, and in addition, remembering Chotěboř, he probably thought that the Hussites would act toward him as he had toward Hromádka's men. Only two days later when all outer fortifications had already been stormed, he understood that military resistance had become hopeless, and therefore declared himself ready to surrender the town, to ask for forgiveness, and to adhere himself to the Four Articles. The allies took him at his word though they had every reason to suspect that he never meant what he said.

Having garrisoned Chrudim the Hussite armies marched eastward toward Vysoké Mýto, and from there Žižka with his Taborites went on toward the south, taking—or rather freeing—the town of Polička. The allies joined forces again before Litomyšl, seat of the easternmost bishopric of Bohemia. The bishop had fled to Moravia and this town, too, surrendered without a fight. The allies had now reached the border of Moravia. On one of the first days of May they crossed it, leaving some troops in the town of Svitavy which had asked for their protection against Sigismund. They did, however, not feel ready to penetrate deeper into Moravia at this stage. Also the men from Hradec Králové pleaded for a march northward into the region of the upper Elbe. There they had old enemies: the German inhabitants of the town Jaroměř, captained by one of Sigismund's staunch adherents, Lord Hynek Červenohorský. Having sent desperate pleas for help to Silesia,[28]

[28] See the letter in *Urk. Beiträge*, I, 86, where the fate of the other cities of eastern Bohemia is quoted and Silesia warned that she will be the next to be invaded by the Hussites.

Jaroměř kept up a stiff fight for several days before surrendering. This time the petition for mercy found less receptive ears. The besiegers' only concession was to let the townspeople keep their naked lives. The stipulation was literally enforced, men and women having to leave the town stripped to their shirts. Twenty-four priests were given the choice to accept the Four Articles or die. Remarkably no less than twenty-one preferred death to conversion. Červenohorský was taken to Prague as a prisoner.

Nevertheless the field before Jaroměř, too, became the scene of a great act of forgiveness. Ever since his treasonable surrender of the Hradčany, Čeněk of Wartenberg, once regent of the Kingdom and acknowledged leader of Hussite Bohemia, had lived a precarious life of retirement from public affairs, still taking the Communion in the two kinds but otherwise on friendly terms with the Royalists. But the Hussite offensive into eastern and northeastern Bohemia—the region where he had his richest possessions—frightened him, and after the conquest of Český Brod he repeatedly approached the Praguers with a view toward reconciliation. The essential condition, he was told, was a complete break with Sigismund. Eventually he found himself ready to change color for the third (but by no means last) time of his life. Confronting his accusers, notably John Želivský, as a repentant sinner he "totally reconciled himself with the community of Prague,"[29] and his tattered banner was removed from the pillory of Prague where it had been exhibited, a mark of his shame, for a whole turbulent year.

Having fulfilled the plea of their Orebite allies to eliminate Jaroměř, the Praguers considered the purpose of their campaign satisfactorily achieved. Indeed almost all of eastern Bohemia, with the rich plains on both sides of the Elbe, were now conquered, all the important towns securely in their hands and under their administration.[30] Consequently their army returned from Jaroměř to Prague where they arrived in the middle of May.

Žižka, however, was not yet ready to call off his campaign. He had taken the field almost two weeks later than the Praguers. In carrying on now he found the full support of the Orebites, whose spiritual director was his old friend Ambrose of Hradec. With the forces of both sects Žižka struck farther north along the upper Elbe in the di-

[29] Březová, p. 483.

[30] In some if not in all cases the Praguers, so as to prevent any possible act of insubordination, insisted on breaking down one part of the wall. See Březová, p. 480.

rection of Silesia. The town of Dvůr Králové, the first of importance on his way, surrendered without fight, but Trutnov, only seven miles from the border, and with German inhabitants, had to be taken by force and was largely burned down.

Žižka did not cross the border as the Silesians had feared. Instead he turned west. After a long march of between ninety and one hundred miles, during which he also received the surrender of Mladá Boleslav, he moved against the city of Litoměřice, at the time the most important of northern Bohemia. In Litoměřice Hussitism had been harshly persecuted. Many people had been drowned in the wide and deep waters of the Elbe. The townspeople, sufficiently frightened by the results of the recent campaign, wanted to surrender, but were terrified by the idea that Žižka and his grim warriors might not spare them even then. Thus at the mere approach of his army they sent emissaries to Prague offering full submission on the terms agreed with the towns of the east. The Praguers accepted and sent messengers to Žižka asking him to acknowledge this agreement. This procedure of acting over his head seems to have annoyed him greatly, and instead of complying he began to assault the town. But this move does not seem to have been meant very seriously, for as soon as the attack had been repulsed he ordered the siege to be raised. If he had really intended in defiance of Prague to take the town he would hardly have been discouraged by a single failure.[31] Later Prague appointed Hynek of Kolstein, at the moment still ambassador to Poland, as governor of Litoměřice.

One of the last days of May saw the Taborites on their way southward. The archiepiscopal town of Roudnice opened its gates to them. Like Rokycany, it did not entirely escape the puritan zeal with which the Taborite soldiers viewed the rich architecture of some ecclesiastical buildings, but at least none of the people were harmed. Upon arrival in Prague Žižka separated from his army, which he sent back to Tabor. He with some of his co-captains seems to have stayed in the capital for a few days. Early in June we find him again in the east, at Čáslav, but this time in a political rather than a military capacity.

One more event has to be added to the list of Žižka's actions in May 1421. While the main part of his army was engaged in the siege of Litoměřice, he himself conquered, with a small troop, a wooden fort standing on a hill near the village of Třebusín, just a few miles to the east of Litoměřice. The bulwark had been built by and probably still

[31] This argument is also offered by Tomek, *Žižka* (p. 94). No specific motivation is recorded in any of the chronicles.

belonged to the Order of the Teutonic Knights, his first enemies in a great war. This fort he appropriated to himself, had it rebuilt in stone and permanently occupied. He gave this little castle of his the name "Kalich" (Chalice). It is after this castle that he now named himself. The "Jan Žižka z Trocnova" was replaced by the signature "Jan Žižka z Kalicha." Also his brother, Jaroslav, who had probably served with him throughout most of his campaigns, was now titled "of the Chalice."

We can, from these facts, learn a good deal about Žižka. By taking the name of a castle, he rose out of the ranks of the squires into that of the knights. He seems to have received his knighthood before, after the conquest of Krasikov early in 1421.[32] That he was conscious of these differences in rank is quite obvious, especially from the so-called "Military Ordinance," dating from July 1423.[33]

The geographical choice of the castle seems not quite without significance. It was far from his original home, far also from Tabor, in the far north of Bohemia where the enemies of the Chalice, barons and towns, were still fairly strong.

No doubt the size of the castle was characteristic of the man who owned it. He who could have acquired one of the greatest castles of the kingdom was satisfied with a place which could only be called "castle" because it had towers and walls, a place which would always be a fort rather than a dwelling. Wealth, indeed, meant nothing to him. At Tabor he had, so it seems, not even a house that he could call his own.

But by far the greatest significance lies, of course, in the choice of the name.[34] Even earlier he had changed his coat of arms. That of his family had been a crab, perhaps alluding to the sign of the Cancer. In the document fixing the armistice with Rosenberg, Žižka's seal already showed the Chalice. Now, through both his castle and his name, he identified himself completely with the symbol which stood, in the eyes of all Hussites, for the new creed, for the Four Articles of Prague and for the Communion in the two kinds. I find it difficult to discover, anywhere in history, a case of a great man able to express so simply and so strikingly his personal identification with an idea which was also the dominant idea of his nation and his time. John Žižka of the Chalice—it was a name of utter devotion, as it was a name of the highest pride. It was, in the last instance, a name of faith.

[32] See Old Annalists, p. 50. Palacký as editor put the date, probably mistakenly, to January 1422.

[33] See Appendix, x, and the detailed treatment of the Ordinance in Chapter 23.

[34] See, in this connection also, the passages in Pekař (II, 195, 196).

## CHAPTER 14

# THE NATIONAL ASSEMBLY OF ČÁSLAV

THE WEEKS following the victorious spring campaign of 1421 witnessed an unbroken sequence of Hussite successes. Even before the army of the Praguers had returned from the east the capital began a siege of Hradčany castle—the last great Royalist bulwark in the immediate neighborhood of the capital. On May 25 an armistice was signed, and according to its main clause the castle was surrendered two weeks later, no effective help having arrived meanwhile for the garrison. This success was important from the military point of view, but far more so politically. Prague had regained what had been the hereditary seat of Bohemia's kings through centuries, and with it the great church of St. Vitus, the cathedral of the archdiocese of Prague.

An even greater political success was achieved when the lord of the cathedral, the Archbishop of Prague, was won over himself to the Hussite cause. Konrad of Vechta, a born German hailing from Westphalia, had spent the last months in some isolation in his fortified town of Roudnice. He had shared, during the first phases of the war, in the effort to stem the rising tide of Hussitism and had put the crown of St. Wenceslas on the head of King Sigismund. Yet his relative mildness and caution in dealing with the heretics soon made him suspect in the eyes of the Royalists. Early in 1421 King Sigismund complained to the Holy See about the Archbishop's lukewarm attitude. When in February the Hussite armies passed unopposed through the Archbishop's town of Rokycany, the Royalists answered with open hostility. Soon afterwards Lord Hanuš of Kolovrat, one of the leaders of the Pilsen Landfrieden, raided the archiepiscopal town of Příbram. This act only helped Conrad to make up his mind. On April 21, after prolonged negotiations, a solemn contract was signed between him and the city councils of both towns.[1] Thereby this great prince of the Roman church publicly undertook to adhere to and defend the Four Articles of Prague, to renounce his allegiance to Sigismund and not to acknowledge

[1] See *Urk. Beiträge*, I, 78ff.

him at any time without the consent of the city of Prague, the lords, squires, armies, and communities adhering to the Four Articles. In return both towns of Prague declared that they would never desert the Archbishop but support him in all difficulties that might result from his present action. The prelate immediately implemented this agreement by a corresponding letter to the King.[2]

The Archbishop's conversion to the Four Articles was an event of sensational importance in the eyes of both friend and foe. To prevent the Romanist clergy of Bohemia from following the footsteps of their superior, who had already called a general synod to Roudnice,[3] the Archbishop was declared unfit to administer the archdiocese, and John, Bishop of Olomouc, was appointed as its administrator.

King Sigismund, however, felt that this was not enough. He had to take the wind out of the sails of his opponents without, on the other hand, making any permanent commitments. He authorized Ulrich of Rosenberg to declare that the King, up to the time of a public discussion, would permit the practice of the Four Articles, and that he, Rosenberg, would follow his example.[4] This declaration, however, was soon retracted and had hardly any influence upon the course of events.

The accession of the Archbishop was viewed as a doubtful gain by the radicals of Tabor. They rightly expected that this act would tend to strengthen the conservative trend within the clergy of Prague where the old hopes of a reconciliation with Rome were bound to be revived. But for those conservatives themselves, and beyond that for all the center elements, the event was highly gratifying. Apart from the moral strengthening of their cause it brought a respectable number of towns such as Roudnice, Rokycany, Příbram, and Rožmitál into the Hussite orbit without a struggle. It could now be said, for the first time, that by far the largest part of the nation had taken its stand behind the Chalice. This at least was true as far as Bohemia herself was concerned.

It was just because the revolution had been so successful in the heart-

[2] *ibid.*, I, 82.

[3] For the details see Tomek, *Dějepis*, IV, 149-154.

[4] *Archiv český*, III, 225. The date of the letter (April 25, only four days after the Archbishop's official declaration) makes it seem unlikely that the news of it had traveled from Prague to the King (who was then in or near Olomouc in Moravia) and back to Rosenberg's residence at Krumlov. But before the news of the conversion to the Four Articles was officially released, Conrad had spent something like a week negotiating in the capital, a fact on which Sigismund was doubtlessly well informed and which was quite sufficient for him to draw his conclusions. Chronologically as well as on the basis of political logics this explanation of Sigismund's and Rosenberg's action seems more convincing than Pekař's suggestion (III, 90) that it was due to the intercession of the Landfrieden of Pilsen as promised in the armistice of March 11, 1420.

land of the Bohemian empire that its leaders could now afford to look beyond its narrower limits to the dependencies of the Crown of St. Wenceslas. The two northern crownlands, Silesia and Lusatia, where the Slavic population was only a minority, had from the beginning rejected the Hussite movement. The dukes and cities of Silesia as well as the so-called Six-towns, the dominating league of cities in Lusatia, had acknowledged Sigismund as their lord and sovereign—a gesture which in their eyes fulfilled, in the spirit as well as the letter, their feudal duties toward the Crown of Bohemia. The Hussites on the other hand felt that this duty was not to the King but to the Kingdom of which they considered themselves, the Estates of Bohemia, as the only legitimate representatives. But they knew quite well that it would be difficult if not impossible to enforce this point of view without a war of conquest, an undertaking which so far was certainly beyond their power.

The situation was very different in regard to the eastern crownland, the Margravate of Moravia. It had been closely tied up with Bohemia for many centuries. The bulk of its population was Czech and so was its nobility, which could hardly be distinguished from that of Bohemia. Only in the cities was German influence still strong. There had been no barriers of language or political institutions which could have stemmed the influx of Hussite ideas into the Margravate. By and large the religious and political conditions in Moravia therefore tended to follow those of its greater neighbor to the west. Especially in the south, centered in a region at the lower Morava River, there was even a Taborite movement, which just at this time—early in 1421—had begun to be active enough to attract considerable attention.[5] It had proved strong enough to resist and bloodily defeat first the combined assault of troops sent by the dukes of Austria and the Bishop of Olomouc, and a later attack attempted by Hungarian troops dispatched by Sigismund.

Yet up to the spring of 1421 the nobility of Moravia had been reluctant in declaring for the Chalice. Sigismund's Hungary was too near for comfort. It was easy for the King to send sizable forces into the Margravate at short notice. Furthermore the Moravian primate, Bishop John "the Iron" of Olomouc, had proved a most efficient and energetic defender of the Catholic Church. He had fought the reform movement fiercely from its beginnings and was therefore feared by many who

[5] The date of the establishment of the Moravian "New Tabor," near the town of Strážnice, is given in Březová's Chornicle (p. 473) as February 1421. The question of the religious struggle in Moravia at that time has received a most thorough treatment by Otakar Odložilík in his book *Z počátků husitství na Moravě* (first published in *Časopis matice moravské*, 1925).

might otherwise have shown more openly their inclination to the Chalice.

This state of things could not last when, by the spring offensive of the allies, all of eastern Bohemia came under Hussite domination and even one Moravian town, Svitavy, was taken under Prague's protection. Some light is thrown upon the situation as it had then developed by a letter[6] written by a Moravian baron, who had joined the reform movement and lived in Bohemia, to some friends among his Moravian peers. He warns them that plans are afoot for the Hussites to enter the Margravate in two columns, one led by Žižka, the other by the Praguers and lords. The Moravian estates, lords, knights, and squires, should not hesitate to declare their adherence to the Four Articles of Prague, nor should they consider themselves any longer as the subjects of Sigismund since the Hussites did not recognize his kingship.

The advice was followed, and two Moravian lords known as adherents of the Chalice, Peter of Strážnice and John of Lomnice, were dispatched to meet the Hussite allies before they would, as it was feared, cross in force the Moravian border. When they met the Hussite leaders in the field in eastern Bohemia, they promised that the Moravian estates would accept the Four Articles and confirm once more their loyalty to the Kingdom of Bohemia. The Hussites suggested that this step be taken in a solemn, legally binding form. The estates of both countries should meet in a common diet. Thus arose the plan to call, for the first time since the outbreak of the Hussite wars, a great assembly of the estates of the Bohemian Crown.

As soon as the idea was conceived it became obvious that a general diet would have far greater significance than just to reintegrate Moravia into the body politic of the Kingdom. What would have seemed impossible even a few months earlier seemed quite feasible now. Hussite Bohemia had, through the conquests and gains made in the preceding winter and spring, become so strong that it could, as victor, invite the Royalist side to a common meeting. The task of the diet, under these circumstances, would be to gain general acceptance for the basic principles of the Hussite Reformation and revolution; to create conditions which put an end to the fratricidal strife between Czech and Czech; to find a permanent solution for the question of who should be Bohemia's king; and finally to create a provisional government with an

[6] *Archiv český*, III, 300. Palacký thinks that the writer is Hašek of Waldstein, but it seems difficult to prove his identity.

executive strong enough to pacify and rule the country until the new king would take over.

It was with these goals in mind that on May 18 the city governments of Prague's Old and New Town sent out their invitation—in their own name as well as that of Archbishop Conrad and the Hussite lords. The diet was to take place at Čáslav, beginning on June 1. This town lay conveniently on one of the main roads connecting central Bohemia with Moravia, and the Hussite party could feel sure about the political and religious sympathies of the townspeople. The invitation was directed to the estates of all the four countries of the Bohemian Crown, but it seems doubtful that a favorable answer was ever expected from Silesia or Lusatia. Their inclusion, however, tended to state the principle that the Kingdom of Bohemia was and remained their suzerain and that nobody who did not enjoy the full recognition of the Bohemian estates could claim their allegiance. Also, by stressing the need for a pacification of the whole realm, the two northern countries were warned to abstain from further acts of aggression against Bohemia. The invitation guaranteed full immunity from attack for all those traveling to Čáslav to take part in the diet, a clause meant as a general safe-conduct for the Romanist and Royalist participants. It was meticulously observed.

The Diet of Čáslav began two days later than originally planned, on June 3 and finished its business within five days. The important documents of the assembly bear the date of June 7. There are four of those and from them, aided by the report of Březová,[7] we derive most of our knowledge on the assembly. One of them is a message sent to Sigismund in answer to a communication received from the King, and in the main it contains a series of accusations. Two are messages to the estates of Silesia and Lusatia who had not followed the invitation and were now reprimanded and threatened for their faithless and traitorous behavior.[8]

But by far the most important document is a general manifesto issued by the diet and signed by all participants. It served, at the same time, as a list of presence, a record of proceedings, a statement of principles and resolutions, and an act of legislature. It is a document of

[7] Pp. 485-491. The rest of this chapter is essentially a shorter version of this writer's article "The National Assembly of Čáslav," published in *Medievalia et Humanistica*, VIII, Boulder 1954, pp. 32-55, and containing additional documentation.

[8] *Urk. Beiträge*, pp. 116-117; Ludolf of Sagan, *Tractatus de longevo schismate*, pp. 501, 502; Cochlaeus, *Historia Hussitarum*, Mainz 1549, pp. 201ff.

some 1,500 words, written in the forceful, rather laconic, and concentrated Czech of the time. It deserves a rather careful analysis.[9]

The list of presence—and it seems safe to assume that at least all those mentioned by name were really there—is in itself of high interest. It is, simultaneously, an indication of rank. It had been so much a matter of course for the barons to hold the first rank in a general diet that even Březová, talking of the diet, often uses the term "barones" for the whole body of members. The list, however, presents the names in the following order:

1. The Burgomasters and Councilors of the Great (read Old) and New Town of Prague;
2. Conrad, by the Grace of God Archbishop of the Cathedral of Prague and Legate of the Papal See;
3. The Lords of the Kingdom;
4. The Regents of the people and towns of Tabor;
5. The Mint Master of Kutná Hora;
6. The Knights and Squires of the Kingdom;
7. Other towns and communities (no longer mentioned by the names of their representatives).

The city of Prague, as the "head of the Kingdom" (caput regni), had been responsible for the calling of the assembly. Thus it may not be too surprising to see the "glorious city," as it is expressly called at another place in the document, named before everyone else. Yet the fact that at this stage the nobles had to put up with a place after the capital is highly significant for the change which had occurred in so short a time. Prague's rank was now based on her quality as the capital and the seat of the University, but even more on her military strength and the commanding position of power which she had acquired in the Hussite camp, especially in the course of the last year. Even so the recognition of the leading city as superior to the nobility remains an extraordinary fact, hardly duplicated in European history until much later.

The Archbishop, of course, had to come next after Prague. He is the only member of the clergy mentioned by name as present. He may

[9] The manifesto is preserved in two versions, one as quoted by Březová (pp. 486-488), the other, doubtlessly the original and authentic one, in a manuscript kept in the archives of the Princes of Lobkovice and published in *Archiv český*, III, 226-230. Březová's version clearly shows the traces of later editing by the Prague authorities, in eliminations (e.g., the omission of the name of Želivský who, by the time Březová wrote his chronicle, had been executed) as well as in additions (especially the adding of the Margravate of Moravia every time the Kingdom of Bohemia is mentioned, though the Moravian estates acceded to the resolutions of Čáslav only six weeks after the end of the diet).

have functioned as a sort of honorary chairman, yet we hear little of his activities, and it seems that he behaved with great reserve.

The list of the lords includes altogether 22 names. Only 20, however, officially represented the baronial estate. One, Peter Zmrzlík of Svojšín, appeared as mint master of Kutná Hora, a position to which he had recently been reappointed at the request of the Kutnohorians and with the full consent of the Praguers and doubtlessly also of his friend Žižka. The other one, John Roháč of Dubá, appears last among the four "regents of Tabor." In all likelihood he had acquired this position, either through election or appointment by Žižka, soon after the death of Nicholas of Hus in December 1420.

Six of the barons listed by name had, until now or recently, been adherents of the King and the Church of Rome. First in rank among them was Ulrich of Rosenberg. Yet his presence at Čáslav after his recent, somewhat equivocal actions was perhaps less surprising than that of some older die-hards such as the brothers of Dubá. They came, making use of the safe-conduct, and it seems most remarkable that none of them refused to sign the manifesto with all that it implied. The only regional group of the Czech nobility not represented at all were the lords (and knights) of the Landfrieden of Pilsen—a bad omen for their future relations to Hussite Bohemia.

Nearest to the Romanist lords in their views and political attitudes, and forming, so to speak, the farthest right among the adherents of the Chalice, was Čeněk of Wartenberg who appeared with four or five of his relatives and personal friends.[10] Of the twelve barons who had been more constant supporters of the Chalice, five belonged to what we might term the Hussite center. Their leader, in rank as well as in political and military prestige, was Hynek Krušina of Lichtenburg.[11] The remaining seven were all men of the left: either personal friends of Žižka (Ulrich Vavák, the brothers Victorin and Hynek of Podě-

[10] For Pekař's thesis (III, 99ff.) that Wartenberg was, beyond his role as a suitable mediator, in every way the guiding spirit of the diet, I cannot find any trace of evidence, nor can I consider it as especially likely. After his recent thorough humiliation before John Želivský and the armies of Prague and Tabor he can no longer have impressed even the lords of the Hussite center, let alone the more radical groups, as a man of exceptional strength. See the discussion of the "Anti-Taborite" tendencies of the diet as alleged by Pekař in notes 12 and 15 below.

[11] In this group we should also have to include Hynek of Kolstein whom Březová, in the introductory part of his account (p. 485), mistakenly lists as present. Actually, on June 7, he was still on his way back from Poland to Prague where he arrived on June 10. (He probably signed the manifesto immediately upon his arrival.) Also to this group belonged Vaněk of Jenstein who was to head the next embassy to Poland-Lithuania.

brady, Peter Zmrzlík, and the faithful Roháč), or at least, like the two lords of Borotín, closely allied with the Taborite party.

The Taborite community was as fully represented as possible, with Žižka leading the list, followed by Zbyněk of Buchov, Chval of Machovice, and Roháč of Dubá.[12] Of the twenty-five knights and squires listed (not counting the three older captains of Tabor), none played any important role in the further course of events. With the unnamed representatives of the towns and the many retainers, without whom none of the noble lords would travel, the total number of Bohemian representatives was considerable. The Moravians had sent word that they would arrive two days later. Thus the Bohemians started the proceedings by themselves, beginning, as usual, with a solemn service in the great Church of SS. Peter and Paul. It also served as the place of convention as no other building would have been large enough to hold so many people.

The Moravians who arrived on June 5 were led by the Margravate's highest official, William of Pernstein,[13] together with the two men who had conducted the preliminary negotiations for Moravia: Peter Kravařský of Strážnice and John of Lomnice. Březová tells us that many other nobles appeared from Moravia, but no mention is made of the towns, and indeed it seems likely that the majority of them, dominated by Catholic Germans, were not willing to take part in an assembly called by heretics.

The assembly cannot have been idle even during the first two days,

12 Pekař (III, 103, 104) submits the theory that at the Čáslav Diet Žižka was not present at all. If this were true it would afford some (though not sufficient) support to his thesis that the diet, largely directed by Čeněk of Wartenberg, tried to organize the country against Žižka and Tabor. The only basis for his assumption is a letter of the town of Tachov, dated June 7, asking for help against the "Husses" besieging nearby Rabí Castle. Žižka, the letter says, is with them. (See Siegel, "Briefe und Urkunden zur Geschichte des Hussitenkrieges," in *Zeitschrift des Vereins f. d. Geschichte Mährens und Schlesiens*, XXII, 1918.) Against this testimony stands Žižka's name on the list of presence, further his election into the regency council into which no one else was elected who was not also mentioned as present (except the townsmen who do not figure in the list of presence), furthermore the diet's letter to Upper Lusatia as quoted by Cochlaeus, *Bellum Hussitarum*, p. 201, and the Moravian message appearing in *Archiv český*, VI, 398. Pekař does, indeed, admit that a possible mistake in the dating of the letter may invalidate his conclusions. There seems to be an even easier explanation: the claim of the people of Tachov that immediate danger threatened from Žižka himself made their plea for help appear far more urgent. The country was rife with fast-traveling rumors, and the Taborite troops may have boasted that they would soon be joined by their invincible chief. Žižka was, indeed, with them before June was over, and it was at this siege that he received the injury to his one remaining eye which eventually led to his complete blindness. Another of Pekař's arguments for Zižka's absence is that he is not especially mentioned by Březová. But Březová mentions by name only nine of the leading barons whom he remembers (one of them wrongly), and ignores all the rest.

13 He was "zemský hejtman," a title having the approximate meaning of governor.

as the drafting of the messages and resolutions, especially of the manifesto, must have taken many days of work. Some of it may have been done in Prague before the assembly convened, but the manifesto shows clearly the result of careful, often laborious compromise which must have taken place in what we would call caucus meetings.

The task of formulating the general goals of the diet was performed in what became the preamble of the manifesto, preceded by the list of presence and followed by the official version of the Four Articles.[14] This preamble reflects the determination, but also the skill with which the victorious Hussites tried to establish a platform on which a truly representative assembly of all Bohemia and Moravia could agree. It is clear that in the eyes of all Hussites the "troubles, tumults, ruinations" mentioned in the preamble were, overwhelmingly, the guilt of the King and the Royalist party,[15] and in the message sent to Sigismund by the assembly the King was unsparingly charged with this very guilt. But the majority at Čáslav was careful not to hurt the feelings of the Royalist minority, whom only thus they could hope to win over to their own side. Those disorders, therefore, are only described as having "broken out," due to existing disunity, which to heal was now the first and most important task. This attempt to forget what divided them and stress what could unite them, implying a strong appeal to patriotism, proved more successful than, under the circumstances, it might have seemed possible to expect. Only a very weak "unless" remained as a limitation to the general acceptance of the Four Articles: they had to be kept and defended by all signatories unless they could be proved wrong from the Scriptures. This limitation was usual in those theological statements, it occurred similarly in the concluding motivation of the

[14] There is only one minor modification in Article 2: the Eucharist is to be given in both kinds to all true Christians, "old and young." This was a victory for those who, very much against the views of the Roman hierarchy, considered children as in need of, and able to receive, the Holy Communion.

[15] One of the strangest arguments proffered by Pekař in support of his understanding of the political situation at Čáslav (see above, note 12) is the claim that this whole passage, with its complaint about the general disorder in the country, is a veiled attack of the lords against Žižka and his methods of warfare. This argument completely neglects the dominant feeling of hostility against Sigismund among the Hussite majority as well as the considerable number of Žižka's personal friends among the barons present. In addition Pekař himself admits (III, 92) that at this time (i.e. the conquest of Český Brod) the methods of Prague in making war did not differ at all from those of Tabor. But Pekař does not claim that the sentence in the preamble refers to Prague. Pekař's thesis could not even be considered unless he were right in his conjecture that Žižka did not take part in the diet as otherwise Žižka would be supposed to have approved and signed a document directed against himself. Even then (that is if his name had been added to the list of signatories without his presence and knowledge) he would probably have protested and we would know about it.

Four Articles, and it was limited itself by the clause that the error had to be proved irrefutably to the masters and priests.

The Moravian lords agreed at once to this first part of the manifesto. This had been expected, as it had been promised during the preliminary negotiations. That the Royalists of Bohemia also agreed was a moral victory of the first order for the Hussites. There is no reason to believe that any pressure was brought to bear upon them except the force of persuasion. The safe-conduct would have protected them even if they had refused to accede.

Stronger resistance on the side of the Royalist lords was to be expected as soon as the issue of Sigismund's position came to the fore. Yet, for more than one reason, it had to be faced. For the great majority of the Hussites this question had long been decided. They could and would not forgive him the attempt to conquer the land of his birth with the help of foreign armies. Some of them would rather compromise in the religious field than in this purely political question. In regard to this issue, at least, the nationalist feeling had grown stronger and more effective than all other considerations.

Besides, the leading groups of Hussite Bohemia had gone too far in their search for a new king to retract their steps at this stage. Three embassies had now been sent to Poland and Lithuania in pursuit of this goal, and only a few weeks earlier a message had reached the capital from Cracow, saying that Bohemia's ambassador Hynek of Kolstein, now on his way home, had met with considerable success at the court of Grand Duke Witold of Lithuania.[16] To bring those negotiations to a successful conclusion it was obviously of the greatest importance to have a united Bohemia standing behind the impending election of a new king, united in the solemn form which only the diet of the Kingdom could provide. All these reasons would have made a solution of the "royal question" unavoidable in any case. But in addition Sigismund himself helped to bring it about.

Since the middle of May the King had dwelt in Hungary, holding court at the town of Trenčín in modern Slovakia. He found himself beset with difficulties from all sides. The Turks seriously threatened Transylvania. The Republic of Venice had resumed her military activities in Dalmatia, perhaps encouraged by the diplomatic *démarche* through which Prague in July 1420 had offered an alliance to the Adriatic power. Sigismund was aware of the progress which the Hussite

[16] *Urk. Beiträge*, I, 93.

embassies had made in Poland and Lithuania, and had reason to fear that the elector of Brandenburg, Frederick of Hohenzollern, might ally himself through dynastic bonds with the Polish crown.[17] In Rome as well as in the Empire dissatisfaction was growing with the way in which Sigismund had handled the Czech heresy.

From his point of view Sigismund could hardly expect anything good to come out of the Čáslav diet. But he was shrewd enough not to underrate its importance. He sent two of his Bohemian courtiers, Aleš Holický of Sternberg and Půta of Častolovice, to Čáslav. They carried a letter of the King which they were supposed to read and, if necessary, explain to the assembly. The King's delegates presented their credentials, probably on June 5, after the arrival of the Moravians. The question whether they should be received at all was discussed at some length. The majority finally decided to give them a hearing, which would in itself not constitute any obligation on the side of the assembly.

In his letter[18] Sigismund shows himself the clever diplomat we know him to be. Its dominating note is in full accord with the original, basic purpose of the assembly: pacification and reorganization of the Kingdom. He does not demand, he rather entreats and implores them in his softest tones to end the armed resistance against their lawful king for which, so he says, there is no sensible justification. As far as the Four Articles and especially the demand for Communion in the two kinds is concerned, he claims never to have taken a definite stand against it but to have repeatedly expressed his willingness to arrange another public discussion for his Bohemian subjects. (That hundreds—and, with the victims of the First Crusade—thousands of men and women had lost their lives on his bidding, for nothing worse than taking the Communion in both kinds, is here conveniently forgotten by Sigismund.) And, so he continues in almost abject terms, "should anybody consider that we be the cause for certain disturbances in this Kingdom, then we shall willingly amend that, and shall take advice to set it right, so that we could not be to blame for any disorder." So as, however, to balance this sweet cajolery with the proper threat, he adds that if the estates persevered in their stubbornness and in their endeavor to "press him out of his Kingdom of Bohemia" he, the King, is left with no other alternative but the use of force, an obvious reference to the current preparations for a second crusade.

The diet decided to answer the King in written form. This message

[17] See Sigismund's warning letter to Frederick, *ibid.*, I, 64.
[18] Dated from Trenčín, May 27. See *Archiv český*, III, 225, 226.

refers in its introductory sentence to Sigismund's offer to make amends for any wrongs which should have come about through his fault. "Here," so the message says drily, "follows the list of those wrongs and outrages."

The list contains fourteen points. The first two concern the burning of John Hus and Jerome, the third Sigismund's part in the unjust reproach of heresy hurled against the Czechs at Constance. The fourth, fifth, and sixth accuse the King of having permitted and encouraged the preaching of the crusade at Breslau, of having personally organized and led that crusade into Bohemia, and of being responsible for all the atrocities committed by the crusading armies inside Bohemia. "Those princes and foreigners, led by Your Highness, have burned, devastated and looted this country of Bohemia, have burned faithful Czechs, priests, and laymen, men, women and children, and have done violence to virgins and women."[19] Points 7 and 8 charge him with having murdered at Breslau the Prague citizen Krása, and of having ordered the execution of Breslau citizens for offenses already forgiven by King Wenceslas. Point 9 refers to the cession, without permission of the Bohemian estates, of Brandenburg to Frederick of Hohenzollern; points 10 to 12 to the illegal seizure of the golden crowns of Bohemia and the Empire and of the Bohemian crown jewels; point 13 to the theft, as it is put, of the Bohemian "land tables," that is the registers of landed property, as well as of the special treasury providing for needy widows and orphans of the nobility. The last point finally charges the King generally with oppression of the old freedoms and rights of the estates of Bohemia and Moravia.

The fourteen points of accusation are followed by four positive demands. They are: 1) The King should stop the slanderous and insulting incriminations of the two Czech countries. 2) He should restore Brandenburg to the Bohemian Crown. 3) He should return the crowns, jewelry, land tables and other documents which he has taken away illegally. 4) He should restrain the neighboring countries, especially those belonging to the Bohemian Crown, from further invading and devastating the soil of Bohemia and Moravia and from further shedding the blood of true Christians. In conclusion the letter quotes and stresses the Four Articles of Prague "for which we have all chosen to stand to the end," and declares that the estates will insist upon the old orders, rights, and freedoms granted to them by the King's predecessors.

[19] See above, note 15. The similarity of expressions shows clearly who is meant as the object of the more general complaints in the preamble of the manifesto: Sigismund, not Žižka and Tabor.

To some extent this message seems strange: its two parts do not seem to fit together. The list of accusations does not seem to admit of any other conclusion but the declaration: "you are no longer fit to rule over us." This, indeed, was the conclusion drawn in the manifesto, but the message ends instead with concrete demands for amends. This, so it seems, was done upon the request of the former Royalists among the members who wanted to leave a door open for the King as well as for themselves. The majority probably agreed to it because, on the one hand, there is not even a hint in the letter that the fulfillment of those demands would bring about the acceptance of Sigismund as king, and as, on the other hand, the chances for Sigismund's accepting those demands were practically nil. He could, for example, not now take away Brandenburg from Frederick of Hohenzollern, could not even be expected to stop the preparations for a second crusade which would renew the horrors committed during the first.

The declaration, then, which contained the solemn deposition of Sigismund, was to be part of the general manifesto and there we find it, right after the acceptance of the Four Articles of Prague, as point 5. But as was to be expected the decision was not reached without controversy. The Moravians were the first to make reservations: they were ready to sign the whole manifesto, but as far as point 5 (the King's deposition) was concerned they wanted a delay of six weeks so as to be able to give fair notice to the King and thus safeguard their honor. Probably they wanted the delay also to see how the war situation would develop. Their demand was granted, and they signed a declaration of their own in which they promised after the six weeks fully to accede to point 5, whereas the rest of the declaration is identical with that of the Bohemian estates.[20] Disagreements of a more substantial nature appeared among the Bohemians. Here it was the question of how absolute and irrevocable the act of deposition should be made. The former Royalists wanted a loophole for possible negotiations. The Hussite majority, however, insisted on a strong and definite wording. In particular it should not prejudice the negotiations with Poland and Lithuania,[21] whose princes obviously would not be interested in a throne which was only half vacant.

The spirit of unity and compromise, here as all through the course of the assembly, remained victorious, but it was a somewhat curious,

[20] The Moravian declaration is undated but was obviously passed simultaneously with the manifesto, i.e. on June 7. See *Archiv český*, VI, 398-400.

[21] See Březová, p. 486.

almost naïve compromise that was achieved, in that somehow each party had its own way. The manifesto does contain the most solemn declaration abrogating Sigismund's kingship. Yet, in one dependent clause, a reservation is added which, in guarded terms, admits the possibility that this decision could be revised.

"The Hungarian King Sigismund," so the manifesto says in point 5, "through whose injustice and cruelty the whole Bohemian Kingdom underwent great harm, we have never accepted as king, nor as lord of the hereditary Crown of Bohemia, which he has, by his own unworthiness, made himself unfit to bear; nor will we accept him, as long as our own and his life will last, save for the will of the Lord God, and the will and vote of the glorious city of Prague, the Lords of Bohemia, the community of Tabor, the knights and squires, towns and other communities of Bohemia that have acceded or will still accede to the truth of the aforementioned articles. For this king is a notorious despiser of those sacred truths which are clearly proven from the Holy Scriptures, and the deadly enemy of the honor and the people of the Czech nation." The following sentence threatens to punish anyone who helps, with advice or action, the deposed King.

Some details are notable in this wording. The reservation is put not at the end, but in the middle of the declaration which thus ends on the severely hostile note, describing the King as the enemy of the nation.[22] The reference, in the reservation, to the will of God as a circumstance which might result in a change of attitude is fairly common in medieval pronouncements that are in any way comparable. The fact, on the other hand, that any change is made dependent on the consent of all the groups represented at Čáslav gives, as it were, each of them singly the right to veto any later revision of the present act of deposition. The Hussite majority could thus feel fairly secure in their chance to deny the throne to Sigismund, all the more as they counted on having the throne occupied, before long, by a king of their own choice.

Sigismund was deeply shocked by the defection of some of his trusted adherents among the Bohemian nobility,[23] but in his public utterances he chose to ignore it. He sent a final reply to the Bohemian estates which made no mention of the manifesto but took up a number of

[22] The word here used, "vrah," has a much more disparaging connotation than just enemy, being also the word for murderer.

[23] Windecke, always our best source on the King's reflections and moods, does not mention the diet, but he seldom talks of Rosenberg without some disparaging characterizations such as "ein halber Husse" (p. 144) and even Aleš Holický of Sternberg who acted at Čáslav as the King's ambassador and advocate is in Windecke's eyes one of those who ruin the King (p. 133).

points in the message sent him by the diet.[24] He denies being guilty of the death of Hus and Jerome, on the contrary claims that his attitude at Constance had brought him into trouble with the Church. He claims that he has taken the crowns, jewels, and documents only to save them from destruction. His letter shows that it is the unity achieved and expressed at Čáslav that disturbs him most of all. He therefore tries to appeal to those whom he expects to be critical of the Taborites ("those who have destroyed the monasteries and churches erected to the honor of God"). It is they, he says, "who have the princes, near and far, nay the whole of Christendom incited against this Kingdom, not we; . . . With the agreements you have concluded among yourselves . . . you harmed yourselves and your rights and liberties." It was a tactical device which Sigismund was going to operate repeatedly in the future.

The task of the great assembly at Čáslav, as is often the case with comparable endeavors, became more difficult the more it progressed. The most difficult task—because here the assembly found itself on foreign and untried ground—was the practical organization of a national government which, as long as there was as yet no new king, would implement the general principles accepted by the diet. There was nothing new in the control and limitation of the king's power by a parliamentary body operating on the basis of majority decisions. But all this left the job of practical policy or, as we would say, the executive branch of government, in the hands of one man, the king, or in case of his absence, a regent. Here, now, the attempt was made to replace the one-man rule of the regent with the cooperative rule of a larger regency council. In it all religious and political factions would find a place and frame within which to vent and thrash out their differences and yet arrive at a functioning policy. It was an early attempt at executive government by consent. The diet elected twenty "wise, steadfast, and faithful men" to be the Kingdom's "officers, directors, and regents."

The composition of this regency council is highly revealing. Only five of its members were barons. Prague was represented by four members, the community of Tabor by its two senior captains, Žižka and Zbyněk of Buchov. Four other towns had one member each; the remaining five seats were occupied by squires. Among the barons two, Rosenberg and Henry of Dubá, had until recently opposed the Chalice. Three, Čeněk of Wartenberg, Hynek Krušina of Lichtenburg, and Ulrich Vavák of Hradec belonged to the older Utraquists, representing the

24 Březová, pp. 492, 493, and *Archiv český*, III, pp. 232, 233.

Hussite right, center, and left within the higher nobility. Two of the cities, Žatec and Hradec Králové, were royal towns which had stood on the side of the revolution from the beginning. Kouřim, also a royal town, had only recently joined the Hussite camp and had acknowledged the suzerainty of Prague, thus practically adding a fifth seat on the council to those held by the capital. Rožmitál, the fourth town, owed allegiance to Archbishop Conrad, a choice which may have been intended to give that prelate some voice in the council in acknowledgment of his conversion to the Four Articles.

In terms of social standing, the cities and the lesser gentry (if we include the captains of Tabor) were strongest. Yet no single group in the whole body had a clearly predominant position, and even a "coalition" of two groups such as Prague and the lords would not have yielded an absolute majority. This, indeed, seems to have been the intention, as it should have tended to strengthen, in the council, the same spirit of unity and compromise which dominated the assembly.

The powers of the regency council were clearly defined, which seems to prove that it was not intended to give it exactly the same position as that enjoyed by the king.[25] Nevertheless they were wide enough. They are given "by the force of this writing the full power and right to govern, so as to pacify and in every way establish order in the country of Bohemia, to suppress all quarrels and conflicts and stop all disorders whatever which have broken out or may break out between communities or persons in the Kingdom of Bohemia." The following clause establishes the duty of all and every one to obey all orders of the council, whether they be arrived at by unanimous vote or by majority decision. The council is even empowered to use force so as to make everybody in the Kingdom adhere to the resolutions laid down in the manifesto, and the signatories commit themselves to regard all those who refuse to adhere as their enemies.

The general principle of popular duties toward the self-elected national government is especially stressed in regard to service in arms. The new dangers threatening the Kingdom from outside made it necessary to give the regents sufficient military authority. Special stress was therefore laid in the manifesto on the duty of all the people to follow, in the protection of the homeland, any call to arms by the council, and to go without questioning wherever the council might

[25] On those qualifications see Tomek, *Žižka*, pp. 98, 99. Březová, on the other hand, formulates (p. 486): XX eliguntur . . . qui sede vacante regni regia negocia prout rex potestatem habeant pertractare.

send them. In cases of insubordination the council was empowered to use force.

Here again the manifesto shows features unusual for the time and heralding a modern development. The diet did not appeal to any feudal duties for its call to arms; nor did it give any special reasons why people should follow the call, except just the need to defend the nation. The principle of this general duty was probably never stated in medieval Europe before in equally compelling terms.

It is fully understandable that the men of Čáslav felt considerable uncertainty about the experiment of government upon which they were embarking. Nevertheless it seems strange that they should have put limitations in their way which were bound to hamper this enterprise from the very beginning. Thus they gave the communities represented in the council the right to recall their representatives and elect different persons in their place—a measure which, though in principle very democratic, tended to weaken the effectiveness of the provisional government.[26] This clause seems even stranger if considered in connection with the short life which the assembly granted the council. For that body was only to hold power till the day of St. Wenceslas, September 28, barely four months. No provisions were made to prolong its life if such should prove necessary, only one change being considered possible: the council should hand over its power if and when, prior to the end of its mandate, a new king should have been installed. Perhaps the assembly would not have imposed those narrow limitations upon the council had they not been somewhat overconfident about the speedy success of the negotiations with Poland and Lithuania.

The last part of the manifesto returns to the religious issues, but this time in a practical way. Whenever the regents are faced with religious problems which they feel unable to solve they shall refer to two clerics for advice: John of Příbram and John Želivský. This measure, again, shows the tendency prevailing at Čáslav: to achieve compromise at almost any cost, and not always with due regard to the question whether such a compromise would work. For these two men were adversaries: Příbram one of the most conservative among the

[26] It does not seem impossible that the passing of this clause foreshadowed the political development in Prague, that is the fall, three weeks later, of the city government of which the four representatives of Prague in the regency council were members, and its replacement by followers of John Želivský. If there were a connection between the two events it would prove that even behind the scenes of the Čáslav diet Želivský exerted considerable influence, possibly through his Taborite friends and one or the other of the leftist barons.

masters of the University, Želivský the leader of the Prague radicals. It could hardly be expected that they would now cooperate in amity or agree in their advice. Apart from this temporary measure the diet resolved that a general synod of the whole Bohemian clergy should convene under the presidency of the Archbishop, so as to establish a permanent religious order based on the Four Articles of Prague.

In its last phase the diet of Čáslav was still required to deal with an actual emergency. It received the news that the Dukes of Silesia had begun an invasion of Bohemia, following a summons which they, as well as the Lusatians, had received from Sigismund nearly three weeks before,[27] with the order to "exterminate the heretics." The German mercenaries from Silesia did as they were told. Crossing the border in force near Náchod, they began a fearful slaughter of the Czech people in the district. Among other cruelties we hear that about forty young boys were mutilated so that either their right hand and left foot, or their left hand and right foot, were cut off.[28] The men at Čáslav must have heard the news with a heavy heart. It was clear that the Silesians were but harbingers of a much more powerful invasion which was being prepared against their country. It seemed unwise to concentrate too many of the nation's available forces against them, but the order was given that the lords of the northeastern region, as well as the Orebite community with the city of Hradec Králové, should immediately mobilize all their forces and put them in the field at Náchod within a week.

After this action, in a serious and solemn mood, the participants held a last service, concluding with the Te Deum, and adjourned.

The diet of Čáslav was only one of a number of official conventions of the Bohemian estates which took place in the course of the Hussite wars. Again and again the attempt was made to transform, by common agreement, "those disorders into order, and those tumults into peace and concord," repeating on those occasions the very wording of the preamble of Čáslav. None of them achieved this goal, just as the diet of Čáslav could not achieve it. The conflict was too deep, too basic, to be resolved by the good will of some individual men. Yet it would be wrong to see, in this meeting of the estates of Bohemia and Moravia, only an episode. While none of its immediate achievements survived

[27] See the King's letter of May 18 to the Six-Towns, *Urk. Beiträge*, I, 95.
[28] Březová, p. 491, and Old Annalists, p. 46.

long, none of its greater ambitions, ideas, and experiments was permanently lost. It is the first great representative gathering on the continent of Europe which may be called a "national assembly," in the sense that its members, albeit not always very clearly, sensed the need for a national organization of their community as distinct from a merely feudal order of their kingdom. In the act of deposing Sigismund as having shown himself, by his own unworthiness, unfit to rule, memories may have been involved of the old medieval right of resistance to the king, but besides continuing an old tradition the event began, or created, a new one: the modern one of national freedom against tyranny, as claimed by the Dutch against Philip, the English against Charles, the Americans against George, and the French against Louis.

Finally we observe at Čáslav, more distinctly than before or after during this revolution, an extraordinary effort at party cooperation and party compromise resulting in executive government by consent. It did not work, but this cannot surprise us nor detract from the merit which we usually attribute to pioneer work. More than two centuries later the English Commonwealth, as an attempt at government without king and by consent, did not work well though it was based on a much more highly developed society. The Hussite experiment could not work simply because, under the feudalist conditions of the time, the existing parties could not develop those valid sets of rules under which they operate in modern democratic societies. That the attempt was made at all seems worth remembering.

There were, nevertheless, some direct results of importance. The unity displayed at the assembly helped materially in the subsequent, if temporary, cooperation with Poland-Lithuania, which was a factor of weight in the Hussite survival. Internally, too, the diet helped toward temporary consolidation. Though it did not prevent "disorder," it did prevent, for the next sixteen months, which was a highly critical period, the outbreak of open conflict among the leading Hussite power groups: Prague, the Hussite lords, and Tabor. It is this period which likewise saw the greatest military triumphs to be achieved by Žižka in his fight against Sigismund.

Žižka's personal role at Čáslav has been under dispute.[29] There is no

[29] Tomek (*Žižka*, p. 98) says: "The resolutions of the Čáslav diet were, without doubt, generally in accord with Žižka's wishes. Without his consent they could not even have been passed." Similarly judges Urbánek (*Žižka*, pp. 147ff.). Prokeš (*Jan Žižka z Trocnova*, pp. 81ff.) claims that Žižka together with the Praguers had called the diet—a claim for which I cannot

firm documentary basis on which to judge this issue. Yet we know enough about the man to be able, without too much guesswork, to understand his position within the assembly.

The general acceptance of the Four Articles, the guiding principles of his life and work, cannot but have filled him with the highest satisfaction. And the accession, to this charter, of a man like Ulrich of Rosenberg may well have appeared to him as the completion of a salutary process which he, Žižka, had helped to start when he made freedom for the Four Articles on Rosenberg's possessions the condition for the armistice of November 1420. All the more furious grew his hatred of the faithless baron when this man reverted, a few months later, to the support of Sigismund and orthodox Catholicism.

In the discussion of the King's deposition Žižka naturally stood in the forefront of those who insisted on a radical solution. His willingness to serve as one of the twenty regents, his indorsement, in particular, of the military clauses in the manifesto shows that, far from being just a rabid partisan of Taborite extremism, he was well able to think in wider terms, to compromise with dissenting groups and to subordinate his narrower interests to those of the nation. We can feel sure that he meant it when he signed the clause which required all military forces of the nation, including those of Tabor, to go without questioning wherever the regency council would send them. There was no power in the Kingdom strong enough to force such a policy on him against his free will.

To this extent, then, Žižka's role at Čáslav was as considerable as it was constructive. Yet I do not believe that we should envisage him as the leading spirit of the assembly. Though feeling far from inferior to the great lords of the Kingdom, though on terms of real friendship with some of them, he hardly felt fully at home where they had gathered as a caste. He was no diplomat, no political busybody, and though he could talk well and impressively to his peasant soldiers on the need to fight for the Law of God, he was neither quick-witted nor polished

---

find any proof. Furthest in his claims for Žižka's leadership goes Bartoš who treats the question in *Z Husových a Žižkových časů*, p. 83, *Světci a kacíři*, p. 111, and *Jan Žižka z Kalicha* (*Žižková doba*, VIII, 21). "The famous diet of Čáslav," so he says in the last-named publication, "is truly one of the greatest successes achieved by Žižka through his generalship and statesmanship." I feel that he decidedly goes too far in giving Žižka virtually all the credit for the work of the diet. The other extreme is represented by Pekař whose whole chapter on Čáslav (III, 98-104) is a polemic against the above quoted sentences of Tomek's and who devotes great effort to the attempt to prove that, if Žižka was at Čáslav at all, he suffered there a political defeat at the hands of Čeněk of Wartenberg and his friends. I have dealt with his most obviously forced arguments above (notes 10, 12, 15, 19).

enough to enjoy making speeches before a great political assembly. Very different from his attitude in the field, in council he probably left the initiative, the suggestions, and ideas, to other men, then thought things through quietly and carefully, and finally gave his vote and said his word when it was needed. He was no less respected for this by the assembly who knew from experience, whether friend or foe, his hard, unbreakable spirit and his hard, unbreakable sword.

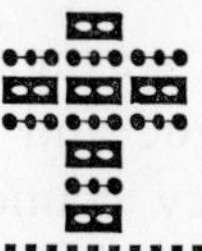

# CHAPTER 15

## GOD AND THE PRAGUERS

THREE WEEKS after the end of the Čáslav diet the political situation in Prague was changed once more by one of Želivský's sudden and dramatic actions. The occasion for it was created, indirectly, by the invasion from Silesia.

By the middle of June very considerable Hussite forces had been concentrated, as ordered by the diet of Čáslav, in the region of Náchod not far from the Silesian border. They included the retainers and soldiers of Čeněk of Wartenberg and of some of his relatives, also the Orebite army which was led, as it had often been before, by Hynek Krušina of Lichtenburg, and with them the town militia of Hradec Králové. The latter forces were accompanied, as usual, by Orebite priests, first among them Ambrose of Hradec who had never ceased to dominate the spiritual and political life of the city throughout those twelve months since he had regained it, almost single-handed, from Sigismund's mercenaries. It seemed natural that Wartenberg, as the highest in rank and as one of the foremost members of the regency council, was in overall command.

As soon as the Silesians learned about the strength of the Bohemian armies they hastily retired into Silesia. When the Bohemian army followed them toward the border the Silesians sent an embassy to Čeněk of Wartenberg, asking him for an armistice with the promise not to molest Bohemia any longer. Wartenberg immediately agreed and forbade not only his own forces but also his allies from Hradec Králové to cross the border into Silesia.

This order of Wartenberg's caused great alarm among some of the Orebite leaders, and Ambrose of Hradec became their spokesman. He charged Wartenberg in public with treasonable intentions, claiming that he did not really intend to fight the King and the enemies of the Chalice. The Orebite peasant soldiers grew so excited that they threatened to kill the great baron with their battle flails and could only be restrained with some difficulty. Eventually the whole army was paid off and sent home.

Ambrose of Hradec, however, was not willing to let the matter rest. On June 23 he arrived in Prague and protested to the city and the Prague members of the regency council against Wartenberg's supposedly treasonable conduct. The whole of Silesia, so he argued, could by now be in Hussite hands and all danger of future invasions from the north removed if Wartenberg had given permission to pursue the invaders across the border.

Wartenberg found a spirited defender in Krušina of Lichtenburg. Březová, who in this issue takes sides strongly for the barons, claims that Krušina "satisfactorily explained the innocence of Lord Čeněk and the other barons," yet he admits that the population of Prague was split over the issue, with a large part siding with Ambrose.[1]

The merits of the issue are not easy to decide. Ambrose had already made up his mind on a question on which others were still very reluctant to commit themselves. Should the foreign invasions be answered in kind? Would this not constitute a breach of the law, laid down solemnly by the University upon the request of Tabor,[2] that only a strictly defensive war for the Law of God was permissible? True, Ambrose could argue that Silesia was not really a foreign country, that she owed allegiance to the Bohemian Crown and that her aggression did not have to be judged any differently than, say, that of the Pilsen Landfrieden. But the great majority of Hussite leaders judged otherwise. In the outcome there was to be no invasion of any of the neighboring countries until 1426. Even Žižka, who could certainly not be accused of lack of courage, never made use of the many opportunities he had to strike in hot pursuit of invading forces across the borders of the Kingdom[3]—with the exception, of course, of Moravia which was much closer to Bohemia and where the Chalice, once it had gained official recognition, had to be defended against its enemies.

Ambrose's reactions, nevertheless, remain understandable. The Silesian forces had wrought terrible destruction, and the agreement with Wartenberg let them go scot-free. Wartenberg's policy in the past easily supported the suspicion that he was playing a double game. Ambrose's opinion was shared by John Želivský, but apart from the merits of the case he saw a good chance for political action. On June 30, before

[1] Březová, pp. 491, 492.

[2] See above, Chapter 5, notes 24, 25.

[3] Žižka's supposed campaign into Hungary (in fall 1423) is a legend, as convincingly proved by Pekař. See later, Chapter 24. The consistency which Žižka showed in this regard confirms me in the belief that he had considerable respect for the principles laid down by the masters of the University, especially by Jacobellus, and in my interpretation of his attitude at the December meeting in the house of Zmrzlík.

the general excitement throughout the city had died down, the bells of Želivský's church, St. Mary in the Snow, rang the alarm. It was a signal for large crowds from the New Town to march toward the Old Town city hall where they frightened the councilors into delivering the seals. The election of a new council followed two days later, but this time Želivský also obtained an important change in the structure of the city government. The old division—Old Town, New Town, and Small Side—was to disappear. The Small Side had already ceased to exist as a functioning community following the fierce and destructive battles fought over it. Now all Prague was to be one community, and whereas previously the Old Town had had eighteen councilors and the New Town twelve, both parts together should now elect thirty, fifteen from each part, but all of them together administering the whole city.[4] John Želivský could expect his power to be more solidly entrenched by the strengthening of the New Town elements within the council. The change also entailed a replacement of Prague's representatives in the regency council, who from now on would be faithful followers of Želivský.

His position was now such that no political decisions could be made without or against him. He had most of the "substantial" citizens of the Old Town intimidated to the extent that they would be wary of opposing him. The only remaining stronghold of resistance was the University. It was from this side that the damaging reproach of Pikhartism was thrown against him as well as against some of the New Town councilors of his choice. Želivský knew well that counterattack was the best defense. He was going to prove that the real offenders against the true faith were in the camp of the masters. As the first victim of his attack he selected Christian of Prachatice, priest at the Church of St. Michael in the Old Town. Christian had been one of Hus's old friends, but apart from giving the Communion in the two kinds he had gone back all the way to the ritual of the Roman Church. He celebrated mass with all the special pomp which even the Hussite High Church had ordered to be dropped, used only Latin in his services and refused to give the Communion to anyone under age, in defiance of the text of the Four Articles as approved by the diet of Čáslav.

By public attacks against Christian and his Romanist leanings Želivský managed to get the masses of his followers so excited against the master that he might have succeeded in driving him out of his office and the city if the University had not found an opportunity, just at this moment,

[4] Březová, pp. 496. For more details see Tomek, *Dějepis*, IV, 181ff.

to submit the case to a higher authority. On July 4 there convened in Prague the general synod of the clergy of Bohemia, the calling of which had been ordered by the diet of Čáslav. Archbishop Conrad should have presided, but as the councilors with whom he had concluded his agreements in April had by now lost their positions he did not feel too secure in the capital. Excusing himself because of sickness, he empowered two of the masters, Prokop of Pilsen and John of Příbram, to act as his vicars and to co-opt two others whom they thought fit for this office. They appointed Jacobellus of Stříbro and, as the fourth, John Želivský, expecting that he would be less dangerous as a member of the presidium of the synod than outside of it.

The great synod of July 4 was supposed to bring together all priests of the Kingdom, but few of those priests who, after the Archbishop's conversion to the Chalice, had still clung to the orthodox Roman creed, made use of the safe-conduct offered to them. Thus the synod was, in reality, the first official congregation of the Hussite clergy from all parts of the Kingdom. It was decided to organize this large body into four regional groups: that of Prague, which included most of central Bohemia, Žatec for the west and northwest, Hradec Králové for the east, and Tabor for the south. It is obvious that this was more than a purely regional division, for the priests of the south were, in their overwhelming majority, adherents of the Taborite sect, whereas in the east the Orebites were predominant. Each of the four groups was, during the first days, to sit as a separate committee and was given a certain number of articles on which to deliberate and report. The results of these deliberations, put together in the form of twenty-three resolutions,[5] were read in a plenary session of the synod by Master John of Příbram, in the presence of a large number of laymen, among them Ulrich of Rosenberg who probably represented the regency council, Žižka's friend Victorin Boček of Poděbrady, several representatives of the city council of Prague, and many knights and squires.

The twenty-three articles read show to some extent in the special field of religious beliefs, of church ritual, and church administration, the spirit of compromise at work which had dominated the Čáslav diet. Yet they also reflect the self-assurance and authority of the masters of the University to a degree which allowed only limited concessions to the Taborite group. As such can be listed the emphasis on the poverty of clergymen and the ban on accepting any monetary rewards for religious func-

[5] *Urk. Beiträge,* pp. 128ff.

tions, the repeated stress that all mortal sins have to be extirpated, and to some extent the last of the articles, which says that for such rituals which have been dispensed with, new ones, more rational and useful, may be introduced and kept. The rule, also included in the articles, that no priest should wield power in secular affairs, must have evoked a smile on the face of John Želivský, who was, however, too shrewd a politician to oppose it.

The inveterate struggle over vestments was decided against Tabor. Mass should be celebrated in vestments but without any unnecessary pomp. Yet it is wrong to deduce from this decision—as has often been done[6]—that the general tendency of the synod was wholly anti-Taborite. The real danger against which the synod tried to defend the Hussite Reformation was Pikhartism, and though it had flourished first at Tabor the official leaders of the Taborite clergy had also been the first to act against it and to warn Prague against its heretical excesses. Nicholas of Pelhřimov and his friends (including the absent Žižka) were at that time in full agreement with those articles which said that priests must not teach or preach any novel interpretations of the Eucharist. In particular they shall hold that "in the bread and wine the whole Jesus, God and Man, with his true body and blood really present" is given to the communicant. The emphasis in another article on frequent Communion and on the need to give the Eucharist whenever any other sacrament is given may also have been meant as a retort to Houska who had so often ridiculed the kneeling before the host.

The last group of articles are mostly concerned with priestly discipline. They threaten punishment to any clergyman who breaks the vow of chastity, who gets himself drunk, who behaves in an undignified way or uses profane language, all measures in agreement with Taborite puritanism.[7] But they also oblige priests to hold the canonical hours, to receive auricular confession when requested, and to have holy water and oil for unctions ready in their churches.

The last-mentioned regulations together with the article on the vestments were more strongly opposed by Tabor than the clauses concerned with dogma. Each article was subjected to a vote of the four regional groups. Whereas the clergies of Prague, Žatec, and Hradec

[6] For once we find even Tomek (who treats the matter in *Žižka*, pp. 112, 113, and in *Dějepis*, IV, 184-188) and Pekař (*Žižka*, III, 106, 107) in general agreement. See against their view Goll, *Čechy a Prusy*, p. 147, n. 25.

[7] Priest marriages (which would, of course, fall under the general prohibition for priests to have any sexual intercourse) are not reported from Tabor until some later time, and the sexual license of the Adamites was frowned at by official Tabor just as much as by the Prague masters. See Chapter 16.

Králové accepted them as a whole, the Taborites divided their votes, agreeing to some of them, opposing others.

It was fairly obvious that this disagreement was final and would not be revoked under pressure. The shock about the Pikhart heresies had drawn the two main groups of the Hussite clergy nearer to each other for a while, at least in the field of dogma, but even the moderate Taborites would not be compelled to return to all those rituals which for them were symbols of Romanist hypocrisy and idolatry.

There was a clause in the resolutions of Čáslav which threatened in advance all priests not conforming to the findings of the synod with disciplinary punishment by the archiepiscopal administration. It was clear that this clause could not be enforced against Tabor, even if the new central authority of the Hussite Church created by the synod in the third of the articles wanted to do so.

This, however, was not to be expected. For the four men whom the synod elected as "supreme governors, directors, and administrators" to rule the Church of Bohemia with the consent of the Archbishop were the same men who had functioned as the presidium of the synod, though in slightly different order: Jacobellus of Stříbro as the most universally respected among the masters was the first, followed by John of Příbram, and Prokop of Pilsen. The last was John Želivský who was too powerful to be omitted from this body. He could be relied upon to veto any punitive proceedings against Tabor which would destroy the existing measure of unity and cooperation between Prague and its strongest ally.

Like the Čáslav diet, the Prague synod of July 1421 did not achieve a permanent solution of the problems submitted to it, and the organization created to administer the Hussite Church never functioned for the whole of Hussite Bohemia. But at least a beginning had been made in the creation of a central authority for the reformed church, and if new, grave internal troubles were bound to reappear they were at least postponed to a time when they could no longer prove fatal.

Minor troubles, indeed, were not slow in arising. The Taborite priests who had come to Prague for the synod tried to promulgate their views before the street crowds and in some cases attacked publicly those of the Prague clergy whom they considered too "Romanist." Two Taborite priests, Prokop the Bald (who was to achieve more fame later as a Taborite war leader than as a cleric) and one Philip, were actually installed as priests at one of the churches in the New Town after the former Utraquist priests had been driven out by the crowd. Attempts were made again to replace Christian of Prachatice by a priest named William, one of John Želivský's closest friends and most devoted followers who had, however, become suspected of Pikhartism.[8] The more conservative citizens of the town grew alarmed at the situation. Some of them would see little difference anyhow between Taborite and Pikhart teachings.

It was, strangely enough for the fifteenth century, not the men but the women of this class who were courageous enough to stem the tide of religious radicalism. It seems rather likely that they followed suggestions given to them by one or the other of the masters of the University, but once undertaken their action was carried through bravely. A large number of them marched to the Old Town city hall, now the seat of the government for all of Prague. They obtained an audience from the councilors before whom one of them read a resolution signed by all. This document[9] is an impressive testimony for the alertness, maturity, and political common sense of those Czech middle class women of Prague. In the beginning they pay their compliments to the great services done to the capital by the community of Tabor. "Their help has been highly beneficent for us, and for this we are grateful and trust that there are many of them who fear God and are good people. But some of them, priests and other members of the community of both sexes, have fallen into errors regarding the Holy Sacrament of the Body of God and the Blood of God and in some other points. And these errors have been proclaimed almost everywhere in Christendom and most of all in this city of Prague." The petition then alludes to the expulsion of good priests and the installation, in their place, of Taborite priests infected by errors, and demands that the councilors take energetic measures against any further progress of Pikhartism in the capital.

The councilors, probably more in fear of John Želivský than of the Taborites, tried to evade an answer and asked the women to disperse and go home. But they remained steadfast and the councilors, rather helpless in the face of this unusual demonstration, had the whole crowd locked up in the great hall where they had assembled. Two hours later they reopened the parley and promised to submit the issue to a full assembly of the citizenry.

At this assembly, a few days afterwards, the petition of the women was read again and made so strong an impression upon the population

[8] This suspicion was almost certainly unfounded. See Chapter 19.

[9] Březová, pp. 595-597.

that it resulted in a considerable change in Prague's policy toward the Taborite elements. Several priests, among them Prokop the Bald, were arrested under the charge of Pikhartism, though after some time they were found not guilty and released. In a second general assembly, on July 21, resolutions were passed which gave the masters of the University (though officially in the form of the four regents of the Church) firm control over all clerics in Prague. Without their express permission no one was to hold services in any of the Prague churches, and no preaching was allowed outside the churches. Priests disregarding these orders faced the death penalty. A religious police of fifty men was created to investigate and to prosecute persons suspected of Pikhartism, if found guilty. But the Prague conservatives, much to their credit, realized and tried to prevent the danger which a general wave of denunciation would have brought about. They decreed that if anyone was denounced of Pikhart errors he was to be confronted with the informer. If he was found innocent, the informer was to suffer the penalty which the accused would have suffered if he had been guilty. This measure proved a healthy deterrent against unscrupulous people who might otherwise have vented their hatred on people with whom they had personal quarrels.

This change in the religious and political atmosphere of the capital was certainly not to the liking of John Želivský, and he might have prevented it if he had been present. But, believing perhaps that after the end of the general synod things were well enough under the control of his followers, he had left Prague almost immediately afterwards. The rule, accepted by the synod, that no priest should wield secular power, did not deter him from exercising again the functions of a military leader.

The campaign which he began was in perfect agreement with the resolutions of the Čáslav diet. Several of the lords and towns in the northernmost region of Bohemia, near the border of Meissen, had not only failed to adhere to the Čáslav protocol but had, on the contrary, kept waging a small-scale war, especially against Žatec and Louny. These two Hussite cities asked for help. Accordingly, Prague sent her troops to finish the job in the north which had been done so efficiently in the east. Around July 10 the forces of the three cities met in the region of Roudnice and after having conquered the town and castle of Bílina, not without considerable shedding of blood, they moved toward Most (in German, Brüx). Learning that the margraves of Meissen had collected a considerable force to support the German Catholics in northern Bohemia, John Želivský requested reinforcements from Prague, which arrived on July 22. The army then began to invest the city and the strong castle dominating it.

The Hussite siege guns succeeded in destroying part of the fortifications. The defenders therefore offered to surrender if only allowed to retain their naked lives. The noblemen serving with the Hussite armies —their names are unknown—recommended acceptance, but John Želivský refused, arguing that if he let those people escape he would have to fight them again on another day and at another place.

Želivský's attitude, in this case, contrasts strangely with the caution and moderation he had shown repeatedly during the campaign in eastern Bohemia. Perhaps this was a reflection of his nationalism: Most and the country around it was predominantly German whereas eastern Bohemia, except for the German element in some towns, was wholly Czech. It seems also that the success of the eastern campaign had gone to his head. He did not realize how different a task he had to face now. In eastern Bohemia the Hussites had never been opposed by a large field army, and his present army, even with the reinforcements received recently, was much weaker than the Hussite allies had been in the eastern campaign. Also in his present army the proportion of mercenary soldiers seems to have been stronger than in previous campaigns.[10] Yet no army was ever surer of its invincibility or more contemptuous of the enemy.

There was probably even more wrong with John Želivský's leadership than with the troops themselves. Having experienced his magic power over the masses of the little people of Prague, he was so sure of his way that he no longer felt any need for advice. (To his very end he flattered himself on being a highly competent strategist.) But his lack of actual experience, the only school in the art of war existing at the time, shows badly in the whole conduct of this campaign. It was clearly a mistake even in purely military terms that, flouting the advice of his lieutenants, he refused to accept Most's offer of surrender while the Meissen army was speeding toward him. Had he been in the possession of city and castle when the enemy arrived, they might never have sought

[10] Frankenberger, in his careful and interesting analysis of this campaign (I, 128-135), claims on p. 131 that the troops of Prague were by far the worst, and especially the least disciplined, of all Hussite troops. I think this is a doubtful generalization. In the battle of the Vyšehrad, under the energetic and experienced leadership of Krušina of Lichtenburg, the Prague troops had given an excellent account of themselves, and they were to fight well in the coming winter campaign under the overall command of Žižka.

a battle or, if they had, they would have had to fight it under disadvantageous circumstances.

The enemy army which reached the region north of Most on August 5 was under the command of one of the Margraves of Meissen, and with him were three of the Catholic lords of northern Bohemia. The troops of Meissen may not have been much stronger than those of Prague, but contained a far larger proportion of heavy cavalry. John Želivský could have made up for this disadvantage by the use of his battle wagons. By this time, a year and a half after their first introduction by Žižka, they formed part of all Hussite armies. The battle wagons of Prague had been drawn up on a hill southwest of the castle, together with siege guns and other heavy equipment. Here, then, the Praguers could have awaited the attack of the enemy.

But John Želivský's foremost thought was to prevent the Misnians from raising the siege of Most.[11] He moved his army to the north of the town, astride the road on which the enemy were nearing. Thereby he placed his troops in the wide plain of the Bílina valley where they had no natural protection and where the enemy cavalry had full freedom of movement. The battle wagons, meanwhile, were left on the hill near the castle, guarded only by some small detachments.

The battle which thus developed, on August 5, to the north of Most[12] began with a head-on collision of the two armies in which the heavily armored horse of the Misnians were naturally superior to the Hussite infantry. The van of the Hussites was quickly overrun by the Misnians and the Hussite army soon retreated toward their camp. They had suffered heavy losses which amounted, in dead alone, to some four hundred men.[13] The Misnians pursued the beaten Hussites but did not get very far as the bulk of the Prague soldiers managed to collect in the camp on the hill where the enemy's advance was easily brought to a halt. They even suffered considerable losses themselves as soon as they got within range of the Hussite guns.

So far the results of the battle, though bitter enough for the Hussite army, were far from disastrous. True, there was no longer any hope for

[11] Frankenberger (*ibid.*) thinks that Želivský tried to repeat the Hussite tactics of the battle of the Vyšehrad.

[12] For sources on the battle see especially *Chronicon veteris Collegiati*, Höfler, I, 84. Březová's story (pp. 507f.) is important rather in its psychological implications than in its factual account. The reflection of the Meissen victory in German circles is best revealed by Ludolf of Sagan (p. 532) who claims triumphantly and with enormous exaggeration that Hussite losses amounted to several thousand men. On other sources, especially the later city chronicler of Most, Leonis, see Toman, *Husitské válečnictví*, pp. 325ff.

[13] Thus the *Chronicon veteris Collegiati*. According to Březová about 1,000 men were killed on both sides.

a speedy conquest of the town and castle of Most, whose defenders had by now joined hands with the Misnians. But the last phase of the battle had confirmed the experience that even an inferior Hussite force, weakened by battle losses, could repulse the assault of a strong enemy as long as it made full use of its movable fortress. In the hands of a vigorous commander in whom his soldiers trusted the troops of Prague might have stayed put and fought again.

But John Želivský, once his decision had led to a painful defeat, was not able to regain his grip on his men. The morale in the Hussite army tumbled from the height of overconfidence to the depth of despair, and nothing was done to restore it. In the middle of the night after the battle, without any palpable reason, a panic broke out in the Hussite camp. People told one another that all was lost, that they were surrounded, that there was nothing they could do but run for their lives. There began a stampede, wild, unreasoning, and irresistible. All wagons, all guns, all heavy equipment which might have slowed the flight were left behind and the soldiers fled, trying to gain the safety of the walled towns to the south of Most, such as Chomutov, Žatec, or Louny. Only when they had reached those places could they be collected, but they ceased to be an army. The Misnians did not even think of pursuit but were satisfied with reaping the rich booty.

The battle of Most was probably the worst of the few defeats suffered by Hussite troops in their long war with foreign invaders. It was certainly by far the worst suffered up to this time. And again, as before in the battle of the Vítkov and in some other instances, we are faced with the enormous power of purely psychological factors which outweigh, or rather multiply in their effect, the objective, measurable military facts. Only this time those factors worked against the Hussites. They had been defeated in battle—and the truth of this fact was so terrible not because the town of Most had failed to be conquered, not because some hundreds of Czech soldiers had died, but because God, who so far had fought for them as they had fought for him, had suddenly turned against them. It was before this decision of God himself that the Hussite army turned into a desperate rabble running for their lives.

And thus, too, the defeat of Most was understood by the people of Prague. God had ceased to be their ally. It was in those terms that the priests of Prague preached from all pulpits on the following Sunday. "As long," so they said, "as we fought for His most holy truth in the spirit of compassion and humility, all our enterprises prospered. But now since our brethren have fallen into evil ways, fighting not for the truth of God but for spoils, pitilessly robbing even the poor and killing fellow-humans more cruelly than heathens, our Lord has become angry and has permitted this plague to hit us. Therefore let us turn away from those evil ways, let us humbly submit to God's just will, and pray to Him that he deign to let his anger subside and his grace return to us."[14] These sermons, reported in what is probably a fairly accurate digest by the town secretary of Prague, were self-accusations explaining the defeat which, by any other reason, would have seemed inexplicable. But they were not only self-accusations—there was one who stood accused more than all others. John Želivský was, quite obviously, the main object of popular anger—not so much because he had proved himself an incompetent general but because, as the military and spiritual leader of the Prague armies for the last four months, he had committed or permitted deeds offensive in the eyes of the Lord. It seems likely that the reproach of "killing fellow-humans more cruelly than heathens" contains a reference to the treatment of the people of Bílina and Želivský's refusal to let the people of Most surrender and spare their lives.

From the moment that Želivský returned to Prague his political leadership, too, stood under a cloud. He could not now, as he had done before, try to recede into the background and expect time to work for him. He now had too many enemies, among the lords as well as the conservative citizens and the masters of the University, who would use such a phase of retirement to undo all he had done. At first he still tried to be careful in his political tactics. He did not even attempt to have the strict religious legislation of July 21 revised, though it was probably due to him that some of the Taborite priests arrested on the suspicion of Pikhartism were released. But on the whole his political methods became less subtle, more dictatorial, the more he felt the opposition against him growing and his popularity endangered.

It was clear that Prague had to do more than to pray and repent if she wanted to uphold her position as the strongest military and political power in Hussite Bohemia. Soon after the remnants of the beaten army had returned, a general levy of three quarters of the city's militia was ordered, and around the middle of August the new army took the field and marched northward to drive the Misnians out of Bohemia.

[14] Březová, p. 508.

The Margrave of Meissen and his soldiers should have been fairly confident after the victory they had just won. Yet, hearing whom they were supposed to fight, they did not dare to meet this foe but retreated across the border as soon as the army of Prague had got as far as Louny. The Misnians were really fleeing before a name. For the man whom they feared so much that they could not face him was, at this moment, only the shadow of himself. He was sick, and the horse he rode had to be led by the reins. He was totally blind. This man was John Žižka of the Chalice.

# CHAPTER 16

## THE BLIND LEADER AND HIS VICTIMS

A CLAUSE passed by the diet of Čáslav authorized the use of force by the regency council so as to induce all Czechs to accept the Four Articles. Probably it had been accepted upon the demand of Žižka.[1] He had acted according to this principle even before, but now, being himself one of the regents, he could feel that this was his duty to the solemn obligations contracted at Čáslav no less than his duty to God. It seemed natural enough for him to direct his attention first to southern Bohemia. There was peace now between Tabor and Ulrich of Rosenberg who had solemnly adhered to the Four Articles and had become a member of the regency council. There was still armistice with the people of the Pilsen Landfrieden, though their attitude was disquieting. They had not sent any representatives to Čáslav, and Hussite priests who, following the armistice agreement, had tried to enter the town to preach there had found the gates closed against them.[2]

Expecting support from the Pilsen Landfrieden the great Lords of Riesenberg,[3] Sigismund's adherents from the beginning, reoccupied and rebuilt two castles near the Taborite town of Horažd'ovice: Bor and Rabí. Both castles had been conquered by Žižka in April 1420 but for lack of manpower had only been partly destroyed and left unoccupied. In Royalist hands they were a threat to Horažd'ovice, and if a letter written from Tachov is dated correctly,[4] Taborite troops already began to move against them while the diet of Čáslav was still in session, probably upon a written order from Žižka.

Soon after the end of the diet, by the middle of June, Žižka was again with his Taborites, directing first the operations against Bor. With the fortress there fell into his hands a noble prisoner: Meinhard of Jin-

[1] Pekař (III, 101) considers the clause the only one in the Čáslav manifesto which "sounds Taborite."

[2] Březová, p. 473.

[3] No relatives of the Lords of Riesenburg. The original owner of Rabí, Krk of Riesenberg, was the father of the two boys whom Žižka took under his personal protection when he first conquered the castle.

[4] See above, Chapter 14, note 12.

dřichův Hradec, a cousin of Žižka's friend Ulrich Vavák. Upon Žižka's orders he was interned at Přibenice. There he joined, for a short while, another great lord who had suffered the same fate earlier in the year: Bohuslav of Švamberg.

From Bor Žižka moved on to Rabí, again personally directing the assault against the strong castle. This brought him within shooting range of the archers defending the castle. Whether by accident or the good marksmanship of one of those archers—an arrow hit him in his right eye, the one not already blind.

Žižka's injury must have been severe. He was taken without delay to Prague by an old comrade in arms who had fought at his side in the battle of the Vítkov: Matthew Lauda of Chlumčany, later known as captain of Písek.[5] Maybe a splinter remained in Žižka's eye or on the long way to Prague suppuration set in, but in any case the Prague physicians found him in a most critical condition. He "barely survived," says one of our sources.[6] The fact that Žižka, a man of such inexhaustible energy and enterprise, submitted to the doctors' order and remained under their supervision for two long months, is sufficient proof for it. Eventually it was rather his iron nature than their art of healing which made him rally again. For some time he still hoped to regain the sight of his eye. By the middle of August, however, the doctors had told him that there was no hope.[7] That was the time of the disaster of Most. Žižka's presence in Prague, despite his illness, seemed a godsend. His name, at least, would strike terror in the hearts of the German invaders. So he got up from his sickbed and went along in what might have become a long and difficult campaign. The enemy, as we know, did not wait to see the man who could not have seen them if they had met.

How did Žižka take this blow? What did it mean to him? How did it influence or change him? As so often we are faced here with the lack of "human interest" which the medieval world showed toward the fate of the individual. Žižka's blindness was taken notice of by most contemporary and near-contemporary chroniclers of Bohemia, indeed no event in his life seems more safely confirmed than this,[8] but it is reported as an event of some importance for the course of the war rather than as a personal misfortune which had happened to a man. Even

[5] See on him Tomek, *Žižka*, 107.

[6] *The very pretty chronicle*, Chapter 1 above, and p. 17 in Novotny's edition.

[7] Březová, p. 509.

[8] Apart from the sources quoted above (Březová and *The very pretty chronicle*) see Old Annalists, p. 46, *Chronicon veteris Collegiati*, p. 84.

Březová who knew Žižka well, who admired him and who seems to have been well informed about the physicians' judgment on this case, reports the fact of his blindness in a dependent clause, not at the time he was blinded but in connection with his first reappearance as a soldier in the campaign against the Misnians.[9] There is one exception, and characteristically it is the writer who, of all the near-contemporary authors on the Hussite war, had traveled farthest away from the purely medieval mentality: Aeneas Sylvius. Being, however, also a great Roman prelate, his human interest in Žižka was partly propagandist, partly just literary, and we cannot expect sympathy from him. Storming the castle of Rabí, so he tells us,[10] "he lost the one eye which still saw the light of the skies, as it was pierced by an arrow. Carried thence to Prague and treated by physicians he was cured of his wound so that he retained his life, but the light of his eye he never regained. Yet even so he did not relinquish his labor as a conqueror of castles or his conduct of the affairs military. The blind people were well pleased to follow a blind leader. Future generations will be astonished by this story rather than believe it."

The sentence on the blind people—it sounds much better in his concise Latin: "Coeco populo coecus placuit ductor"—was clearly one of which its author was proud.[11] In his concluding prophecy he was not too far off the truth either. The story of a general who continued his career after having completely lost his eyesight was indeed well-nigh unbelievable, and it certainly needs to be explained.

It seems especially strange that Žižka's greatest victories were won not before but after he lost the sight of both eyes. It therefore is understandable that two modern historians have seriously questioned the fact as such. One of them, devoting a lengthy monograph to the question, came to the definite conclusion that Žižka could not have been fully blinded, in other words that he regained his eyesight soon after his injury.[12] This theory, however, can only be considered if our most im-

[9] *Loc.cit.* From now on Březová, whenever he mentions Žižka in connection with his military enterprises, says "frater Ziska, quamvis utroque oculo coecus. . . ."

[10] Chapter 44, p. 89.

[11] Poland's Dlugosz liked it so well that he copied it verbally. See *Opera omnia*, VIII, 269.

[12] This suggestion was first offered tentatively by Pekař (III, 114-118), but eventually discarded in favor of the theory that Žižka's later battles were won largely through the participation of his experienced lieutenants, in particular of Hvězda of Vícemilice. In his recent study "Byl Žižka slepý" (Was Žižka blind?) V. Chaloupecký has renewed and defended Pekař's earlier suggestions, reviewing in considerable detail much of Žižka's military career with special reference to the question of his eyesight. (*Věstník české akademie* R.LX, 1951, No. 6, pp. 145-169.) He operates from the beginning on the basis of the following categorical statement: either Žižka was blind—then he himself cannot have won those victories. Or he did win those vic-

portant sources are discarded, that is, if their authors are believed to have consciously deviated from the truth. This, so it seems to me, is in this case a doubtful and even dangerous assumption.[13] We may also point at the fact that the earliest pictorial representations of Žižka show him as a completely blind man.[14]

There is, on the other hand, an explanation which still seems the best possible: that Žižka made his decisions on the basis of very exact descriptions of the terrain and the military situation given to him by his subordinates.[15] This would, of course, presuppose an extraordinary ability on the part of the old general to ask all the pertinent questions and to translate the answers immediately into a clear, composite picture. It must, however, not be forgotten that the scenes of the great battles to follow were limited in extension, and were therefore rather easily described in relatively simple terms. Also some of these places where fighting occurred in the following years were already familiar to Žižka from the time before his blindness.

There is, on the other hand, no reason and not even a serious chance for assuming that Žižka's main military decisions, after his blindness, ceased to be his own, that he began to share his command with his foremost lieutenants. From all we know he never relied, as does a modern commander-in-chief, on a "chief of staff." All the real decisions were and remained his own.

There is no indication that his prestige, his authority, or the loyalty of his friends and followers toward him, suffered any setback owing to the loss of his eyesight. We have heard that the Praguers asked him for his help even while he was still recovering, and the number of barons and other noblemen who would ally themselves with him and

---

tories—then he cannot have been blind. Then he goes on to prove, with perfectly valid arguments, that those victories were indeed won by Žižka and not by his lieutenants. But his premise does not seem sufficiently convincing.

13 Chaloupecký suggests that all those chroniclers who know of Žižka's blindness as a continuing condition rely upon Březová as the prime source. (This, in itself, is a doubtful proposition, especially in regard to the *Chronicon veteris Collegiati.*) He then argues that Březová tended to attribute all Hussite victories to the miraculous interference of God and that Žižka's supposed blindness fitted in especially well with this tendency. It is, indeed, true that Březová shows this tendency, for instance in his report on the battle of the Vítkov. Nowhere, on the other hand, does it appear that this tendency has led him to outright falsification of facts. If Žižka regained his sight Březová was bound to know it, and his frequently repeated assertions that he was "utroque oculo coecus" would be so many conscious lies. This seems strongly contradicted by our general impression of Březová as one of the more careful and reliable chroniclers of his time.

14 E.g. in the Jena Manuscript, showing Žižka in heaven, holding a flag with the Chalice in one hand and a key in the other, or in the Göttingen Manuscript, showing him riding at the head of his army. Both date from the fifteenth century.

15 This explanation has been fairly generally accepted since Palacký's time.

fight under his command increased rather than diminished after his loss of sight. Clearly the forces emanating from his personality, his impact upon people, remained unimpaired.

There is still the question how Žižka's feelings, how his state of mind were affected by the permanent night that had descended upon him. But all we can say is that he acted as sure of himself, of his tasks, and his powers as ever before. It has been asked[16] whether he, the man who saw in every event the hand of God, would not have regarded this blow as a punishment inflicted upon him by the Lord. Again the only possible answer can be derived from his actions. From now on he showed even less patience than before with people who seemed to offend his creed. His first known deeds after he had lost his sight show him from his most intolerant side, and so we can presume that, if he probed himself and his past performance and found it wanting in the eyes of God, it was that he had not been hard and persistent enough in the persecution of those guilty of mortal sin, especially heresy. Those who were heretics in his views had reason to fear the blind Žižka even more than the seeing.

The first victim of Žižka's increasing zeal against evil teachers was Martin Houska. We have heard of him last when in February, on the intercession of his Taborite friends, he had been released from his imprisonment by Lord Ulrich Vavák, and had publicly revoked his teachings on the Eucharist.

Throughout the time when Žižka was absent from Tabor, about seven consecutive weeks, the young priest, still a free man, went on with his work, but it seems that he could not restrain himself to the extent which caution should have imposed on him. During the days of the Čáslav diet, knowing that the old general would soon return to Tabor, Houska grew frightened and left the town, together with another Pikhart priest, Prokop the One-eyed,[17] hoping to reach safety in his birthland Moravia. There he may have intended to join the very radical "Taborite" movement in the region of Strážnice. When he entered Chrudim on his way east his presence became known to Diviš Bořek of Miletínek, the Orebite nobleman who had been made captain governor of the town after its conquest by Žižka and the Praguers. Diviš had him

[16] By Pekař (*loc.cit.*). His answer generally agrees with the one given by the author.

[17] There were, at this time, no less than four Hussite priests by the name of Prokop: Prokop the One-eyed, Houska's friend; the Prague master Prokop of Pilsen; further, Prokop the Bald, later also called the Great, who at this time was in Prague and suspected of Pikhart leanings; and finally the Orebite priest who was usually called Prokůpek (Prokop the Little).

arrested and began to question him personally on his views about the Eucharist. By now Houska had recovered the courage to stand for his convictions. He declared that the body of Christ was in heaven though his spirit was with the communicant at the ceremony of the Eucharist. Incensed by this relapse into heresy Diviš was about to have him burned to death. By chance, however, Ambrose of Hradec, the leading Orebite priest and Žižka's close friend, passed Chrudim on his way to Hradec Králové. He approached Diviš with the request to deliver Houska into his hands. He might still convince him of his errors and thus save his life and his soul.

Ambrose's action, a testimony to his humane intentions, proved unavailing. Taking Houska to Hradec Králové he spent two weeks trying to reconvert him, but the prisoner remained stubborn. At the time hopes ran high for a unification of Hussite dogma and ritual under the authority of Archbishop Conrad, and the great synod of Prague was being prepared. Ambrose thus felt it his duty to yield the prisoner to the archiepiscopal authorities, and sometime around June 20 he was taken to the Archbishop's residence at Roudnice where he spent many weeks in a dark prison. No one but the priests of the archiepiscopal chapter was allowed to see him so he would not again infect others with his heresy. Many attempts were made to reconvert him, but he stuck to what he believed, "not a spark" of the recognition of the truth could be discovered in his answers.

It was at this stage that Žižka took a hand in the proceedings, immediately upon his return from the short campaign which frightened the Misnians out of Bohemia.[18] Throughout his long illness he had followed closely the development in the field of religious unification, and the fight of the Prague Masters and the great majority of the synod against Pikhartism had his full approval. He felt that, by himself and by others, more patience had been shown to Houska than his stubborn insistence merited. He therefore called on the heads of the city government to take the prisoner out of the spiritual authorities at Roudnice, to have him conveyed to Prague and burned there publicly on the Old Town Square, as an effective deterrent to all Pikhart sinners still rampant in the city.

The Prague authorities agreed that it was time for the secular arm to intervene, but they did not dare to take Houska to Prague for his execution, fearing that his followers in the capital might revolt. Instead they

[18] Březová tells the story of Houska's persecution in great detail (pp. 493-495). According to him Houska's imprisonment at Roudnice lasted exactly two months, from June 22 to August 21. Žižka's *démarche* to the Prague city council may have taken place about a week before Houska's execution.

sent one of the councilors, accompanied by the city's executioner, to Roudnice. Houska and his fellow-sufferer Prokop were now subjected to the most painful torture to make them confess which were the sources of their heresy and what accomplices they had in the capital. Houska remained silent. When asked a last time to recant and return to the true belief he answered: "Not we are in error, but you who kneel before the bread." On September 21, in the presence of a large number of spectators, the two men were led to the stake. When his executioners asked them whether they would not beg those people to pray for their souls Houska answered: "We do not need their prayers. Ask them to pray for those who really need them." Then, firmly and without any signs of fear, like Hus and Jerome before them, the two men mounted the stake. "Praised be God our Lord," so concludes Březová's account, "who drove away and destroyed the wolves that wanted to invade His flock!"

The number of people who, during those years of war and persecution, had to die for their faith cannot be counted, nor can their suffering be measured. Most of them were little people whose names were never remembered, people who did not ask for it but were caught and crushed between the millstones of history. Some others, on both sides, Hussite and Catholic, were heroes, men and women who could have saved themselves by denying what they believed but who preferred death to such enforced conversion or lie. Martin Houska was one of these. His understanding of the Eucharist contained no elements of skepticism. On the contrary he was a mystic thinker, and though his insistence on the "kneeling before that bread" as a special, an idolatrous sin may seem rather narrow, his ideas in general were neither narrow nor overly fixed upon symbols. "Christ," so he says in one of his writings quoted by John of Příbram,[19] "is that sacred Spirit of whom the Scriptures say: 'and I shall send you another one to comfort you,' meaning Himself, but different and turned Spirit. And thus Christ has become Spirit and as such will be with us to the end of the world. Thus, too, He is in the bread and wine of the Holy Eucharist which is highly effective if taken in the way in which Christ gave it Himself. . . . If only those liars . . . could understand that Christ, sitting with His body at the right of God, is present everywhere with His Spirit. . . . Nothing that was created should be so exalted that we are tempted to see God in it. Therefore whoever seeks the Son elsewhere but in the Father, and the Father elsewhere but in the Son, and who wants to

[19] See above, Chapter 13, note 26.

pray to and worship either of them as being somewhere else, is an idolater."

These teachings, indeed, went far beyond what the majority of the Bohemian Church reformers allowed themselves to believe. After his death, almost imperceptibly, the theological development at Tabor inclined more and more toward his ideas. But as long as he lived his teachings on the Eucharist, so much the center of Hussite thought, were bound to evoke the most violent resistance. Militant Hussitism with Žižka in the lead did not yet know any other way of dealing with such deviations than those used against itself by the Church of Rome.

It seems strange and rather unfair that Martin Houska, this ecstatic but clean and subtle thinker and martyr, should have been connected with, and indeed should even have been made responsible for, the crude and repulsive movement of religious anarchism best known to history under the name of the Adamites.[20] As human phenomena Houska's Pikhartism, devoutly Christian and stressing purely spiritual values, and the vulgar indulgence of the Adamites in the uninhibited satisfaction of all natural impulses, are surely worlds apart, and Houska would have been as appalled by their excesses as were all other parts of Bohemian society. Yet the existence of a common source for both cannot be denied. Both elements are present already in the mystical movement from which they stem: the Brethren of the Free Spirit.

The Adamites, a few hundred people who had escaped from the persecution visited upon them by Tabor and Žižka early in the year, had drifted southward from the region of Tabor and Přibenice, hiding in the woods during the day, getting their food at night time by pillaging. Finally they had somehow settled down in the wooded valley of the

[20] By the contemporaries this connection was taken for granted. See Březová's report on the Adamites (pp. 517-520) as well as the chapter "On the Nudists" (O naháčích) contained in the rhymed chronicle published by Palacký as appendix 3 to the Old Annalists (*Scripta Rerum Bohemicarum*, III, 476-478). The *Chronicon veteris Collegiati*, in its report on Žižka's action against them, also calls the Adamites "Pikharts" (Höfler I, 85). The extraordinary interest which this movement evoked at the time as well as later finds a telling testimony in its treatment by Aeneas Sylvius. He devotes a whole chapter (41, pp. 84, 85) to their movement on which he gives us some additional information, especially on the attitude of the Adamite women. As his source he names Ulrich of Rosenberg whom he personally questioned about those people. He takes some trouble to explain why Žižka, though a heretical criminal himself, got incensed about the Adamite criminals and destroyed them. Similarly the Catholic Cochlaeus in his *Historia Hussitarum* (Mainz 1548, p. 218) calls the expedition against the Adamites "unum Ziskae bellum laudabile." Windecke, on the other hand, introduces his report on the Adamites (p. 129) with the words: "At that time the Husses accepted a heresy, that part of them went around naked both men and women . . . ," a rather nasty way of making the reader believe that the Adamite customs were more or less accepted by the Hussite community at large.

Nežárka River, not far from the towns of Jindřichův Hradec and Stráž, where a large island served as their retreat and headquarters. Their anarchism did not tolerate any authority, neither captains nor priests, but a peasant by the name of Nicholas functioned for a while as their leader. Though he himself soon took the name of Moses the whole group were occasionally called Nicolaites after him.

The first and basic belief of the Adamites was that they had regained fully the state of innocence which Adam and Eve had enjoyed in Paradise. Therefore they discarded all clothing, and "not minding heat or cold, went naked at all times." They further held that God was only in themselves, just as there was no devil except in humans. Christ, so they said, was their brother, but a rather untrustworthy one as he had died. They, or at least some of them, believed themselves to be immortal.

All impulses were considered good, even divine. The sexual desire was not to be inhibited in the least. Whenever and wherever one of them felt attracted by another one of the group he would ask her (or she him) to cohabit, and it was sin for the desired partner to refuse. All men had all women in common, marriage was prohibited, and they liked to engage in group dances which would end as group orgies.

They gave a free rein not only to the impulses provided by nature to create life, but also to those aggressive wishes tending to cause death. Considering themselves the only humans living the real, immortal life, and all others not worth living, they went out at night, surprising the villages in the neighborhood, taking the food and pitilessly killing all inhabitants, men, women, children, even the babies in their cradles.

There are many reports on the Adamites, but the most authentic source on their beliefs and behavior is a report sent by Žižka to the city council of Prague.[21] It seems based on careful questioning, and as it fully agrees with all other sources we have no reason to doubt its factual truth.

Žižka had long been determined to put an end to the Adamite menace, but the timing of his action was due, at least partly, to a request he received in October from the Lords of Stráž and of Jindřichův Hradec—the latter being relatives of his friend Ulrich Vavák—whose domains were suffering badly under the depredations of the sectarians.

21 This report (Březová, pp. 517, 518) belongs to the small number of Žižka's letters and messages which, by some happy accident, have been preserved. Yet as it is only a piece of intelligence, containing not a word of personal information (except, of course, the fact that Žižka considered all these goings-on as criminal), the report has never been included in any of the several existing publications of Žižka's letters. For the same reason it is not included in the appendix to this book.

Two small towns and a number of villages had already been ravaged by their bands and many lives lost to them. Žižka was, of course, more than willing to help his friends. But for once he seems to have underrated an enemy: he first sent one of his captains, Bořek Klatovský, with a troop of four hundred men, believing this force ample to finish off that unorganized rabble. He was wrong. The fanatic sectarians, men and women, made good use of their natural island fortress and fought with reckless bravery, believing in the claim of their leaders that anyone trying to attack them would immediately turn blind and could not possibly harm them. It is somewhat ironical that they were, in the end, overwhelmed by the troops of a blind man. But before he succeeded Žižka had lost a good many of his men among whom was their captain Klatovský, and had to move in reinforcements. Most of the Adamites fell in the fierce battle, only forty were taken prisoners. All but one of them were burned to death. The one whose life was spared was questioned by the general personally, his answers figuring in Žižka's report to Prague.

The strong impression which the Adamites made upon the contemporaries seems to be somewhat out of proportion to their actual role. The deep shock which they caused can only be understood against the background of Hussite, and especially Taborite, puritanism. We have pointed out earlier how much the general reproach of unchastity contributed to the popular hatred for the mendicant orders. We have seen that the closing and physical destruction of houses of ill fame was one of the first acts of the revolution. The Taborites were often reproached for the brutality of their warfare, but never for any sexual excesses, in glaring contrast to the foreign invaders, the Germans, but even more Sigismund's Hungarian mercenaries.[22] The worst that Žižka personally had to say about his archenemy, King Sigismund, was to call him "the violator of women and virgins."[23] The Hussite majority—and in this case it was an overwhelming majority—could only see with horror the uninhibited display of impulses which the morals of their society had forced them to restrain with such strictness in themselves. They could not permit their own self-esteem to be dimmed by the existence of this strange and terrible sect.

[22] Some examples of these can be found in the *Chronicon veteris Collegiati*, p. 85, *The very pretty chronicle* (Chapter I above, and p. 19 in Novotný's edition), Březová, p. 513 and the Old Annalists, p. 49. The last-named report mentions the feeling among the Hussite soldiers that those vile deeds must be avenged at all costs.

[23] In his letter to the Pilsen Landfrieden, see Appendix, III.

Even though the main group of the Adamites was completely annihilated in the battle—or rather the massacre—at the Nežárka River, the life of the sect was not yet extinguished. Adherents of their creed, in very small groups, lived on in some parts of southern Bohemia, and traces of them can be found much later, even in the eighteenth century. But they had become harmless eccentrics, secretly nursing their pantheist ideas.[24] As a movement of some consequence they had ceased to exist after Žižka had dealt with them. In the opinion of his contemporaries as well as his own he had acted like a surgeon who, by cutting out a dangerous tumor, had saved the health of the community which he served.

[24] See the monograph on this subject titled: "Adamiten und Deisten in Böhmen" in Josef Svátek's *Culturhistorische Bilder aus Böhmen*, Vienna 1879, incidentally a rather superficial and highly biased presentation.

# CHAPTER 17

## THE TIME OF THE SECOND CRUSADE

Martin Houska's execution, the result of Žižka's intervention, took place on August 21, the slaughter of the Adamites on October 21, 1421.[1] Two months separate these dates, and the events that filled them were of an importance which, from the national point of view, completely overshadowed Žižka's struggle with those radical sectarians. It was the time of the Second Crusade.

The preparations for this vast enterprise had been going on for many months, pushed ahead with untiring energy by the new papal legate to the Empire, Cardinal Branda. The imperial diet which met at Nürnberg in April, and in more concrete forms the meeting of the princes at Wesel in late May had worked out the plans for a huge mobilization of forces, and further meetings (at Görlitz and Mainz in June, and at Boppard on the Rhine in July) fixed in detail the duties of each prince or town and the dates at which they were to take the field. At Mainz, on June 29, Sigismund's chancellor George Bishop of Passau appeared as the King's representative, giving the princes full power to do everything they deemed necessary for the full success of the campaign, and promising that Sigismund himself with his Hungarians would be in time to help in the undertaking. The date set for crossing the border near Cheb was August 24, and to make sure that the Bohemians would not receive any help from outside a message was sent by the princes to King Władysław of Poland, threatening to wage an imperial war against him if he should give any support to the heretics. Sigismund also tried to inveigle the Prussian Order to attack Poland.

The renewed seriousness of the situation had already been called to the attention of the defenders of the Chalice by the two smaller invasions from the north: from Silesia in June, and from Meissen in July. The Hussites, very much in the manner of the time, reacted slowly.

[1] According to the *Chronicon veteris Collegiati* (p. 85) the destruction of the Adamites took place on August 27, but Březová twice mentions the date of what he considers a highly memorable event as October 21 (pp. 517-520).

Only at the very end of July, when the state and scope of the German preparations must have been well known throughout Bohemia, did the regency council show any signs of awakening to the danger. Its two ranking members, Ulrich of Rosenberg and Čeněk of Wartenberg, called a new diet to Český Brod for August 17. This was still six weeks before the power of the council was supposed to lapse, but probably the regents felt that the responsibility for the steps to be taken was too grave to be borne by any less representative authority.

Prague received the invitation at the time when John Želivský was still with his army in the field—it was about a week before the disaster of Most—and the city council immediately accepted it, informing Želivský by messenger. Želivský protested even before his return, and as soon as he was back from his inglorious campaign he took steps to prevent the capital from participating in the diet. He was keenly aware that since the days of Čáslav the trend in the religious as well as the political development had gone against him. He could foresee that a new diet, called by Rosenberg and Wartenberg, even if they acted within their rights as the first members of the regency council, would try to fortify still further the position of the barons as against the coalition of Prague and Tabor. Weakened as he was by his defeat at Most, he was not willing to confront the power of the lords and to risk another loss of face and influence. In addition he had to expect that a majority of the diet would favor electing Grand Duke Witold of Lithuania as king, without insisting on the guaranties originally demanded for the protection of the Four Articles.[2]

The issue was hotly debated in Prague and opinions clashed whether Prague's promise to take part in the diet should be kept or retracted. Eventually a compromise was reached: Prague suggested that Kutná Hora instead of Český Brod should be the meeting place. Four delegates of Prague would attend but only as observers, without power to accept decisions which would bind the city. They should have their quarters in the neighboring town of Kolín.

On August 17 or 18 the majority of those invited actually met at Kutná Hora, but were annoyed to find that the capital was not properly represented and that therefore the validity of their decisions would be dubious. Consequently they sent two of the lords to Prague to press for a delegation with full power. Both men had the reputation of being zealous defenders of the Chalice: Ulrich Vavák and John Sádlo of

[2] In the opinion of Goll (*Čechy a Prusy*, p. 148) this lack of religious guaranties was the main reason why Želivský would not support the election of Witold.

Smilkov. Sádlo had been a friend of John Hus, had served Wenceslas IV as private secretary, and had later been burgrave of Karlstein Castle. He had lost that important position in December 1419 when Sigismund had purged all great royal offices from the adherents of the Chalice, and thus could not be suspected of being the King's friend any more than Vavák.

The two lords did their best to convince the councilors that, in the face of the great issues to be discussed, Prague's full participation was indispensable. The discussion led to sharp personal clashes between John Želivský and the two lords, who scolded him for his meddling in political affairs and reminded him that he himself, as one of the four directors of the Hussite Church, had subscribed to the order forbidding priests to assume any temporal rule. They finally obtained what they had sought: a delegation with full power which, besides some of the councilors, also contained the masters John Příbram and Prokop of Pilsen, who should advise the diet in religious matters. John Želikovský could only register this decision as another defeat. It confirmed him in his conviction that the lords, whatever the shade of their religious and political color, were his enemies and would finally have to be deprived of much of their power if Prague's hegemony was to be preserved and the goals of the revolution realized.[3]

The diet of Kutná Hora, after all those contretemps, finally got under way on August 21. No list of presence, no record of proceedings is preserved. Thus we have no fully conclusive proof that Žižka was present, though one of our sources[4] mentions him as responsible for an important decision made by the diet. It is, of course, altogether likely that he was there. He was one of the members of the regency council upon whose authority the diet was called. As it was some time (per-

[3] Březová (p. 525) says in this connection that Želivský tried to undermine the trust of the Praguers in the lords and wanted to have them excluded from their previous functions as generals of the capital.

[4] The Old Annalists (p. 47) say that the embassy which the diet sent to Poland to inform Witold of his election (see later in this chapter) was sent by "the Praguers and Žižka." Though this description cannot be considered as fully correct—the limitations of Prague's participation in this embassy will be discussed later in this chapter—the mention of Žižka cannot simply be put aside as untrustworthy (as implicitly done by Pekař, III, 114). The fact, in particular, that Tabor was not officially represented in that embassy has no significance except that Žižka, quite generally, thought it unnecessary to insist on Taborite representatives in those embassies led by religiously reliable Hussite noblemen. Hynek of Kolstein's first embassy to Poland, whose credentials are known to have carried Žižka's and Tabor's seals, nevertheless, did not contain any Taborite representatives. Novotný's argument in *Sborník Žižkův*, p. 122, against accepting the version of the Old Annalists does not seem fully convincing either.

haps as much as ten days) after his return from the short campaign against the Misnians, the state of his health can no longer have been a hindrance. And one of the diet's first decisions reflects his policy if it was not actually suggested by him.

This decision concerned the position of the mint master of Kutná Hora. Peter Zmrzlík, who had been the city's chief magistrate for many years under King Wenceslas, had been reappointed to that position after Kutná Hora had submitted to the capital early in May. But in August he had fallen ill, and having gone to Prague for treatment he had died there on August 16. The death of one of the most gifted, most unselfishly devoted fighters for the Chalice among the Czech nobility was as grave a loss for the Hussite cause as for Žižka personally to whom he had proved a true friend.

Zmrzlík had been one of the representatives of the "left wing" of the nobility, the one that favored cooperation with Tabor. It was in Žižka's interest that his successor should belong to the same group. Thus, from his point of view, the diet could not make a better choice than to elect Ulrich Vavák to this office. Simultaneously it was decided that the income from the silver mines, which for a few months had gone directly to the capital, should again be used for the benefit of the whole Kingdom.[5] Unfortunately Vavák, too, was not fated to enjoy his office for long. On September 22 he died, victim of a plague epidemic which made its first appearance at Kutná Hora before the diet adjourned.[6] Thus Žižka lost two of his best friends within less than six weeks.

The appointment of a mint master was, of course, only a minor matter compared to such issues as the defense against the new crusade and the election of a new king. There was also considerable uncertainty about Bohemia's national government during the coming months. Five weeks from now the rule of the regency council was supposed to end. It could not be expected that, within so short a time, the new king would take over even if he were elected and invited immediately. It seems that the majority of the diet would do nothing that might embarrass or deter the prospective ruler. Therefore the whole issue re-

[5] One of the reasons for this decision was the fact that Prague, early in 1421, had established its own mint, using for metal largely the gold, silver, and copper confiscated in the monasteries and in those churches where services had been discontinued. See Tomek, *Dějepis*, IV, 174, 197.

[6] After Vavák's death the full income of the mint was, till the conquest of the town by Žižka in July 1424, again monopolized by Prague, and the capital nominated one Nicholas, otherwise unknown, as mint master. See Palacký, *Urk. Beiträge*, I, 124, and Tomek, *Dějepis*, IV, 199.

mained open to the end of the session. On September 4, resolutions were accepted concerning the two other main issues, but nothing was done to replace the old regency council nor, as far as can be ascertained, was its life span prolonged beyond the original date, September 28.

By far the most important political decision taken by the diet of Kutná Hora was the solemn declaration, equaling an election, that the estates of Bohemia "postulated" Grand Duke Witold of Lithuania as their king. This, surely, was an act of such consequence that the regency council could not have taken it with any degree of legal authority. The Grand Duke himself would not have considered the offer as sufficiently supported if it had not been made by a national diet. The election closed, as it were, the first chapter in this long and highly complicated diplomatic game. It seems time to look at it somewhat more closely.[7]

Of the two princes to whom Hussite Bohemia offered her crown one, King Władysław Jagiello, never considered accepting it. He had friendly enough feelings for the Czech nation and had, especially after the Breslau Award, reason to dislike Sigismund, but his ambitions—at 72 years—were rather to see his dynasty firmly established in Poland by the birth of a male heir than to add new crowns to the one he bore. In addition, having to live down the fact that he was born a heathen, he was careful to obey the rulings of the Council of Constance and would therefore not connect his name too closely with a movement accused of heresy. Later he began to persecute its adherents in Poland with increasing severity.[8]

Less inhibited by his own religious conscience as well as by his political considerations was his cousin Witold. He had changed his religion three times, first accepting the Roman Creed, then was rebaptized by the Eastern Orthodox Church, but eventually returned to the Western faith. During his years with the Greek Church he had, of course, been a "Utraquist," that is, he had received the Communion in both kinds. In 1417 he had refused the demand of the Bishop of Dorpat (Tartu) to arrest or punish a Bohemian nobleman who had publicly defended

[7] See for the background of the following development V. Novotný, *Několik příspěvků*, in *Sborník Žižkův*, Prague 1924; J. Goll, *K. Sigmund und Polen*, in *Mitteilungen d. Inst. f. öster. Geschichtsforschung*, 1894, 1895; and Olgerd P. Sherbowitz-Wetzor, "The Polish Foreign Policy under King Władysław Jagiello in relation with the Hussite movement in Bohemia," unpublished Harvard dissertation, 1933, valuable as a summary of Polish political trends though thin and sometimes incorrect in the treatment of the Bohemian side of the picture.

[8] The development of Hussitism within Poland is treated with great sympathy, though probably exaggerating its strength, by Count Krasiński in his *Historical Sketch of the Reformation in Poland*, London 1838, I, 57-91.

Hussitism before all his courtiers. Finally the fate of Samogitia—the issue which had led to the enmity against Sigismund—was much more important to Witold as ruler of Lithuania than to his cousin in Poland. These facts make it understandable that the Czechs soon set more hope in Witold than in Władysław.

Yet even Witold was not willing to break, without highly compelling reasons, with the Holy See. Had he done so he would have given the Prussian order a new lease on life for its claims that it had to fight Lithuania for the sake of Western Christianity and therefore deserved the support of Pope and Empire. There were times when Witold was highly interested in the Bohemian offer, not only because he wanted to punish or blackmail Sigismund but also because he was too ambitious a man not to long for the title of king, a craving which never left him to his dying day.[9] Yet he could seriously consider acceptance only under one of two conditions: if there was still a possibility of reconciling the Czech heretics with the Church; or, if the Czech nation should prove so strong, so definitely invincible, that no possible European coalition would be able to threaten effectively the huge Slavic federation which would result from a personal union between Bohemia and Poland-Lithuania. Of these two possibilities only the first one would have been approved by Władysław. Witold, on the other hand, also played with the second idea. Therefore his willingness to accept the Bohemian crown increased with every great success of the Bohemian arms, and began to wilt whenever they seemed in danger of being overwhelmed or when disunity threatened the Hussite ranks. But as he still had to put up with Władysław's feelings he was forced to act as if he firmly believed in the first chance: to lead the Hussites back into the arms of the Church. This, of course, was also the way in which he would have to explain his actions to the Pope.

On his first trip, Hynek of Kolstein saw Władysław at Wolborz early in August 1420 and submitted to the Polish ruler the text of the Four Articles.[10] Władysław was very cautious in his answer, excusing

[9] On Witold's interest in the royal title see among others K. Lohmeyer, *Witowd, Grossfürst v. Littauen*, in *Zur altpreussischen Geschichte*, Gotha 1907, p. 280.

[10] The most important source for these diplomatic talks is Dlugosz who reports on Kolstein's first trip in *Opera omnia*, IX, 266ff. Unfortunately he is an utterly unreliable witness. He gives all the speeches made by both the Czech ambassadors and the King in extenso, but they are all later reconstructions (Dlugosz writes more than 40 years after the event) and the list of ambassadors which he gives really belongs to the second, not the first embassy. His main purpose is to show that neither Władysław nor Witold ever considered helping the heretics, except toward a reconciliation with the Church. How he distorts the truth to make

himself with the need to consult with his "most beloved brother, Alexander Witold, Duke of Lithuania." Kolstein seems to have seen Witold somewhat later and even then have formed his opinion that the Lithuanian Grand Duke was more interested in the offer and was, despite his advanced years, more youthful and energetic than his cousin.

Kolstein's second embassy started on its way on Christmas Day, 1420. To it belonged also the Orebite Lord Aleš of Riesenburg, a man who was on good terms with Žižka, probably through their common friendship with Ambrose of Hradec. The University of Prague was represented by two of its masters, John of Reinstein, called "Cardinal," and the Englishman Peter Payne. There were further several knights and a very complete representation of the city councils of both Prague towns.[11] Their first impression was somewhat awkward: wherever they set foot the Church imposed an interdict. But Władysław received them not without friendliness. His polite refusal to accept the crown was expected, indeed the renewal of the offer was hardly more than a formality, but the Bohemians had to have his good will and permission before proceeding on their way to Witold. Their reception there was, in their impression, highly encouraging. Witold, after hesitating for some weeks, seemed willing to go far in fulfilling their wishes. He was cautious enough not to grant, before witnesses, those guaranties for the full acceptance and protection of the Four Articles which the Hussite ambassadors demanded as their only condition for making Witold their king. But he left them under the impression that eventually he would accept this obligation.[12] He told them that for a while he would have to be represented in Bohemia by one of the princes of his house. And he had the Czech embassy accompanied, on their way back to Bohemia,

---

his point can be seen from his claim that Hynek's first embassy went to Poland against the protest of Žižka, whereas the opposite is true. But even this rather loose association with the chief of heretics—that he was one of those responsible for the offer of the crown—was more than Jagiellone court historiography was ready to admit.

[11] On the personalities of the ambassadors, especially the city representatives, see Tomek, *Dějepis*, IV, 126. The instructions given to them are published by Novotný in *Několik příspěvků . . . , Sborník Žižkův.*

[12] See the letter from a Polish nobleman to Prague, *Urk. Beiträge*, I, 92, and especially the enthusiastic response of Prague to Hynek's report in the city's letter of acknowledgment to Witold, *ibid.*, I. 121. Pekař's assumption that Hynek could never have seriously believed in the possibility of winning Witold for the defense of the Four Articles (I, 112) is certainly mistaken, as proved convincingly by the official letter sent by Prague sometime in the middle of June. If the men of the Hussite delegation had had no hope of finding in Witold a protector of their creed, they would have warned the people at home and Witold would never have been elected. This obvious conclusion also disposes of the inventions of Dlugosz, who (IX, 271) makes Witold tell his visitors that he favors acceptance of their offer just to spite Sigismund (!), but only if they return to the Church of Rome and renounce the Four Articles.

by Wyszek Raczyński, a Polish nobleman of his entourage who proved to be very friendly toward the Hussite creed[13] and went a good deal further in his assurances than his royal master. The confidence which took hold of the Hussites is shown by a letter of humble gratitude in which the city council of Prague, still before John Želivský's purge of late June, acknowledged the Grand Duke's readiness to become their king.

We can be sure that John Želivský had nothing to do with the wording of this letter.[14] Indeed he seems to have been the only one who distrusted the foreign prince, feeling that Witold was giving assurances without real guaranties, and that, as a supporter of the reformation, he could not be relied upon.

The diet of Kutná Hora did not follow Želivský. It followed the advice given with great emphasis by Hynek of Kolstein. For the great majority of the diet, Witold's election meant completing the work done at Čáslav. There the old king had solemnly been deposed—here a new king was called to take his place on the throne of Bohemia, and only this act seemed to make Sigismund's deposition final and irrevocable.[15]

Which, then, was Žižka's attitude? Did he share the distrust of John Želivský? Or was he not, rather, led in his consideration by his hatred of Sigismund and his determination to bar the return of this "heretic king" to the throne? From all we know about him only the second answer can be correct. It is also supported by the one source nearest to the event which tells us of his attitude at this moment.[16] From it we have to conclude that the new mission to Witold, informing him of his election and asking him to come and mount the throne of Bohemia, was dispatched with Žižka's full support.[17]

Lord Hynek of Kolstein did not lead the new embassy. Prague had rewarded him, after his return in June, with the governorship of Li-

[13] Raczyński became a fervent Hussite, joined the Taborite community and eventually died for his beliefs in the last fight with Sigismund in 1437.

[14] Novotný (*loc.cit.*) thinks that Želivský, at this stage, did not yet strongly object.

[15] See Březová, p. 570.

[16] Old Annalists, p. 47. (See above, note 4.) The report is contained in Text D, one of the older manuscripts dating from the first half of the fifteenth century.

[17] There is, however, a later note which contradicts our assumption. Aeneas Sylvius, talking of the legations sent to Witold (but without clear reference to any one of them) adds (p. 92): "with Žižka and his faction opposing, who held that free men need no king." But the very argument proffered for Žižka's opposition makes Sylvius' remark suspect, as it is amply clear that, up to a short time before, Žižka was far from holding such republican views, and as there is no proof whatsoever that he embraced them at any later date. Yet Sylvius' story is given much credit by Pekař (II, 123; III, 114) who completely identifies Žižka's policy in this question with that of Želivský.

tomĕřice. In his place went Vaněk of Jenstein, one of the lords who had formed the Hussite center at the diet of Čáslav. With him went William Kostka of Postupice, well known in Poland as leader of Czech auxiliaries during the Prussian Wars of 1410 and 1414. Like him the other two delegates, Hlas of Kamenice and Vaněk Pivo, were knights who for some time had stood in the service of the capital. This time, however, none of the town councilors went along. Prague was thus represented only in an indirect way, obviously an expression of the misgivings with which the capital's real master, John Želivský, saw the embassy start.[18]

The further fate of this embassy—it was intercepted on the way to Poland by one of the Silesian dukes[19]—was out of the hands of the diet and belongs to a later phase of the development. But the diet had still one more task: it had to organize the defense of the realm against the Second Crusade. The assembly resolved that all their members with all their available forces should meet, on September 18, at Český Brod. The fact that a town to the east, not to the west of Prague was chosen as the rallying place shows that the Hussite leaders still reckoned at that moment with an attack from two sides. This worst expectation luckily failed to materialize. The threat from the west was soon the only acute one.

It was a formidable threat indeed. The new crusading army was even larger than the one which had besieged Prague fifteen months earlier. Several sources, Hussite and German, estimated its strength as above 200,000, in one case even at 230,000.[20] More creditable though probably still exaggerating is the number of 125,000 given by less boastful German sources. Among their leaders were the archbishop-electors of Cologne and Treves and the archbishop of Magdeburg who had joined Cardinal Branda as princes of the Church, further Louis Count Palatine, Erich Duke of Saxony, one of the sons of the elector of Brandenburg and many other imperial princes, counts, and barons.

18 This interpretation of the embassy's composition, given by Pekař (III, 113), seems fully convincing. Novotný's claim (*op.cit.*, 121), that the embassy consisted entirely of knights, and the conclusions he draws from it are manifestly wrong. Vaněk of Jenstein appears as one of the lords in both the Čáslav manifesto and the letter of the estates of Bohemia to those of Lusatia (Cochlaeus, *Historia Hussitarum*, 201ff). According to Tomek (*Dějepis*, IV, 198) he was a nephew of the former Archbishop of Prague, John of Jenstein.

19 See below, Chapter 20.

20 The larger numbers are given among others by Březová, the *Chronicon veteris Collegiati*, and Thomas Ebendorfer of Hasselbach, the smaller by Andreas of Ratisbon. Windecke who, knowing the costs of the undertaking, is generally best informed on numbers, only speaks of "much more than 100,000."

The army got on its way from Cheb on August 28. They found little resistance, yet they killed, upon express order,[21] all Czechs who fell into their hands except small children. In a few days they got to Mašt'ov, twelve miles short of Žatec. At the same time the Misnians attacked again with strong forces from the north, conquered Kadaň and occupied Chomútov whose Hussite garrison had evacuted the city before. Then they began to invest Bílina, while one of their Bohemian allies, Lord Sigismund of Wartenberg, began to assault Žižka's new Castle of the Chalice near Litoměřice. Both these enterprises came to nothing. On September 13 a Prague army moved north. Hearing of this both the troops from Meissen and Wartenberg retreated and joined the main army of the crusaders before Žatec.

The total force defending Žatec which, besides the town's militia, also included the former garrison of Chomútov, numbered 6,000 men. Even a fraction of the crusading army should have sufficed to overcome the town's resistance which alone, at this moment, seemed to bar the further advance on Prague. Less than a week after the siege had begun, on September 19, the crusaders made six assaults upon the city, but each of them was repulsed, and the besiegers did not even succeed in conquering some of the suburbs outside the wall.

The defeat marked the beginning of a psychological process similar to that which had undermined the morale of Sigismund's army after the Battle of the Vítkov. There was keen disappointment over Sigismund's absence. As it became clear that it would take weeks before the King would move, rumors spread that he did not really want the heretics suppressed. The German leaders started quarreling and accusing each other for their lack of success.

Still the siege went on. The besiegers attempted to send out birds with flaming material tied to their feet, hoping that they could thus set the town on fire, but the birds did not seem to fly in the right direction, and the scheme proved another failure.

On September 30 the defenders, well aware of this development, made a very successful sortie which caused considerable losses in dead, wounded, and prisoners to the crusaders. Even so they might have continued in the hope that hunger would eventually force the town to surrender. But on October 2 they were informed that a great Hussite army, containing forces of Prague and her allies, was approaching from Slaný. The German princes had not the courage to face them, and it seems that Žižka's name as one of the leaders helped to make the threat seem

21 See the letter from Nürnberg to Ulm of September 1, in *Urk. Beiträge*, I, 144.

even more formidable. On the same day they broke camp in great haste, but found themselves hampered in this effort by a great fire which had broken out in their tents. The men of Žatec, seeing the enemy in this disorganized retreat, sallied out from their town and caused the fleeing Germans great losses though their forces were not sufficient for a regular pursuit. Altogether the siege, from its beginning to the most inglorious end, seems to have cost the crusading army about 2,000 dead. The crusaders immediately left Bohemia, having suffered what was indeed, as all our chroniclers stress, a most shameful defeat. Their efforts had come to naught, due to the spirited resistance of a single town of no great size or manpower, and they had never even met the main body of the Hussite forces.

The outcome of the Second Crusade was as disastrous for the enemies of Bohemia as the first. Yet the feeling of victorious deliverance could not be quite as overwhelming as it had been in the previous year. First of all the danger had not yet passed: the attack from the east was still to come, even though its bad timing made it somewhat less dangerous. Also the main forces of the Hussites had moved rather slowly, and there was little evidence of energetic leadership or advance planning. On the date set by the diet of Kutná Hora, September 18, not all the lords present at the diet had come to Český Brod with their retainers. The date was late anyhow; the crusaders stood deep in northwestern Bohemia and the siege of Žatec had already begun. Prague had acted before on its own account and had sent calls for help to its allies including Žižka.

Of Žižka's doings in this phase we would know next to nothing if we did not have his own testimony. From Kutná Hora he went to Tabor to mobilize troops, and on September 12 we find him about twenty-five miles west of the town, on the castle of Orlík which belonged to the young Lords of Svojšín, Peter and John, the sons of his close friend Zmrzlík who had died four weeks before. The visit, so soon after the father's death, must have been a gesture of friendship, reassuring the two young men, both zealous Hussites, that he would stand by them as he had stood by their father. But the letter to Domažlice from which we derive the knowledge of his sojourn at Orlík[22] shows very clearly that the national defense was, at this moment, foremost in his mind.

[22] The letter to Domažlice is not preserved in the original. The first source in which it appears in its Czech version is a short book by the Prague minister Havel Žalanský, printed in 1619. About the same time a German translation appeared in Theobald's *Hussiten-Krieg*. Like most of Žižka's letters it was dated only as to the day in the Saints' calendar, without

Domažlice was the only one of the towns originally belonging to the Pilsen Landfrieden which had gone over entirely to the Hussite side soon after the armistice of March. There had been a fight within the town in which the adherents of the Chalice prevailed against strong and, as it seems, well armed resistance. Now one group of the German crusading army, striking south after the conquest of Kynžvart, had begun to devastate the Czech settlements in the region between Tachov and Domažlice. The people of this town therefore appealed for help to the chief of the Taborite community to which they belonged. Žižka, in what is rightly considered the most forceful and impressive of all his letters, admonished them to remain steadfast. He reminded them of the struggles of old times in which their Czech ancestors bravely withstood the onslaught of German invaders. He reminded them also of their own brave fight of recent memory. "As yet," so he told them, "the arm of God has not grown shorter."

In addition the letter gives them fairly precise orders how to mobilize their resources. And it gives them—and us—the news that Žižka is "drafting men from all sides against such enemies and destroyers of the Czech land." He expects to be with them soon.

The letter is a very telling testimony to Žižka's strong national feeling and to his consciousness of a national tradition. But no less important is the information which it contains. He is engaged in mobilizing forces "from all sides." Žižka had ceased to limit his recruiting activities to the geographic area of Tabor and southern Bohemia. He had built his own castle far in the north, but he was even more strongly interested in another area: the reaches of the upper Elbe, region of the Orebite brethren, the land between Hradec Králové and Čáslav.

Soon after, perhaps even during his stay at Orlík castle, Žižka must have received Prague's call for help. There is no doubt that he answered

naming the year. Later historians, beginning with the Jesuit Balbin in the seventeenth century, believed it to belong to 1422 (September 11), and this opinion was also held by Pekař in 1928, in the second volume of his *Žižka* (p. 270). In vol. III (p. 119), which appeared two years later, he made a strong case for placing the letter in 1421 (September 12). I think his arguments are fully convincing, but would add one more. The letter undoubtedly deals with the impact of a German invasion which has already begun. The Third Crusade, however, did not get under way until the middle of October 1422, and Tomek has to assume a premature crossing of the border from Bavaria to make the letter understandable (*Žižka*, p. 147). There is, however, not the slightest trace in the sources for such an invasion. By assuming 1421 as the correct date such constructions become superfluous, and the letter fits far better into the general picture of Žižka's movements and of his political position at the time. The stress especially that now is the time to deal with foreign enemies seems more appropriate now than a year later when the "domestic enemies" were again very much in the foreground of Žižka's thoughts. For the text in English see Appendix, IV.

it with whatever troops he had available, and took part in the march to Slaný. From there the combined Hussite army had just begun to move on to relieve Žatec when it received the news of the German retreat. Without any further action the Hussite army, and with them presumably Žižka, returned to Prague where they arrived on October 4.

As the danger from the west receded, the threat from the east—from Sigismund's Hungary—began to loom larger. Soon those men among the Czech nobility who in their hearts had never been with the Hussite revolution began to waver again. Some of them only waited for the moment when Sigismund's appearance at the head of a great army would help them to resume their normal station: at the side of their liege lord, delivered from the unnatural alliance with the town mobs of Prague and the peasants of Tabor and Oreb.

This was also true of Ulrich of Rosenberg. For a short while he had played his role as one of the leaders of the Hussite commonwealth and as the highest in social rank among the members of the regency council. He had also time to repair, but hardly to forget, many of the damages done to him by Tabor in the previous year. The invasion from Germany had already led Rosenberg's neighbor to the northwest, the Pilsen Landfrieden, to break, without any apparent excuse, the armistice with the Hussites which should have lasted till the end of the year. On one of the last days of July, they had surprised and occupied the archiepiscopal town of Rokycany. The next to move in Rosenberg's immediate neighborhood was the town of Budweis, after Pilsen the strongest remaining bulwark of Royalist power in the country, commanded by Leopold Krajíř, one of Sigismund's ablest officers. Early in October he received a message from the King[23] that all was ready in Hungary for his great campaign and that the troops of Budweis should start operating against Tabor. The letter was written in Bratislava, on October 2, the very day the crusaders began to pull out from Žatec, but when he wrote it Sigismund still hoped they would stay long enough for an effective two-front attack.

Rosenberg, too, was under this impression. His personal correspondence with Sigismund had ceased during the preceding months but he had never been quite out of touch with the King. If Krajíř now moved, soon after receiving the royal message, against the Taborite town of Lomnice he could do so with much more confidence if things had been straightened out beforehand between him and the Lord of Rosenberg.

[23] *Urk. Beiträge*, I, 155.

The doubtful attitude of some of the lords had not remained unobserved in Prague. John Želivský, always apprehensive about their motives, found his suspicions confirmed. His error of judgment was that he did not discriminate. He thought of the barons in general as a caste which, bound by their traditions and interests, all tended to disrupt or destroy the work done by the revolution. Only if they could be reduced to a secondary role, if the leadership of the more radical groups in Prague and Tabor could be firmly established all through the nation, only then would, in his eyes, the cause of the Chalice be safe. Driven by these motives he engineered another political coup on October 19th, which, for all practical purposes, made him the dictator of Prague.

On that day he called a meeting of the citizenry of the whole town at the Church of St. Stephen. In one of his eloquent speeches he attacked the lords in general as traitors to the Hussite cause and as men who could never be relied upon to serve faithfully as the city's military leaders. The people of Prague, so he declared, could easily dispense with their services if they elected, out of their own ranks, a captain general with sufficient power, a man possessed of the true military virtues as well of the true, unwavering faith in the Law of God.[24]

When he had finished several of his adherents shouted that the right man was at hand: John Hvězda of Vícemilice,[25] a young officer hailing from the lower nobility who had served at various times with the Taborite forces as well as with the town militia of Prague and had shown considerable bravery and military talent. John Želivský knew him as an enthusiastic admirer of his as well as of Žižka's. The powerful priest felt that in Hvězda he had found the right instrument through which he could wield the unlimited power he desired.

The majority of the assembly, that is Želivský's adherents, strongly applauded this nomination. Hvězda was thereupon declared elected by acclamation and in addition was given extraordinary powers. He could demand full obedience not only from his military subordinates but also from the civilian population. He could subject, without process of law, anyone offending against his authority to punishments ranging from imprisonment and exile to loss of life. He could even remove councilors

[24] Březová, p. 514.

[25] The young squire of Vícemilice bore a very proud name: Hvězda means "star." He may, indeed, have felt and behaved like a star, finding himself suddenly and without much warning in such an exalted position. But the popular wit of the Prague population had another name in store for him, rather apt to damp any conceit on his side: they called him "Bzdinka" which means "little fart." Yet so commonplace were nicknames, even derisive ones, to the Czech people that he himself does not seem to have resented it much, and that many Czech historians, without any thought of malice, continuously refer to the Hussite general under the nickname.

whom he considered unfit for office, and could, without elections, replace them with men of his own choice. In addition measures were passed for the tightening of military discipline, setting the death penalty for the avoidance of military service as well as for desertion. The general was to administer his office with the help of four captains who were also elected at the same session. It is more than obvious that the real dictator was not, and was not meant to be, the young captain general. He would in all questions of political importance defer to John Želivský.

Since the outbreak of the revolution, and with the disappearance of the royal control which had been exerted through the chamberlain or subchamberlain of the Kingdom, Prague had been not only a republic but, to a very considerable extent, a democracy. It was by the use of the methods of direct democracy, by the influence wielded through popular assemblies or town meetings, that Želivský had acquired his power. But so far he had held it by the same methods. He had needed majorities to rule, and had seldom failed to find them. Now, with one stroke, he had abolished this primitive but fairly effective democratic system, and had forced a military dictatorship upon the city. It was surely a symptom of weakness, of somewhat shaken self-confidence rather than of strength that Želivský took this step.

On the very day after the coup d'état, he used his new strength in an act of terror, directed against a member of the hated high nobility. Among those lords who had failed to appear on August 18 at Český Brod was also Sádlo of Smilkov, the former burgrave of Karlstein. He was therefore accused, by Želivský and his friends, of treasonable intentions. On October 20 he arrived in Prague to justify himself, having been told before that he had nothing to fear. But on Želivský's orders he was immediately arrested, summarily sentenced to death without having been heard, and executed the following night.

The people of Prague could not help feeling that John Želivský, with this bloody act, was venting a personal grudge against his victim. After all it was Sádlo who, together with Vavák, had publicly attacked Želivský as a priest illicitly mingling in worldly affairs, and who had thereby defeated him on the issue of Prague's participation in the diet of Kutná Hora. When, on the following day, Sádlo's execution became known a large part of the citizenry voiced their disapproval, but Želivský, once on the path of terrorist oppression, answered with more of it. Many people were arrested. Five city councilors who had previously opposed the killing of Sádlo or had otherwise shown any lack of subservience to Želivský's wishes were, according to the measures passed two days earlier, unseated and replaced by more obsequious men.

I have mentioned earlier the apparent lack of organization, sense of purpose, and leadership which characterizes the Hussite efforts in answer to the Second Crusade. This also reflects upon Žižka. In so many cases, before and after, it was just his energy and initiative which provided the necessary leadership. But here, for once, he seems to have lagged in what he himself considered his principal mission. Perhaps he needed some months before he overcame the frightful handicap of his blindness to the extent that he was fully his old self again. But there may also have been another reason. It was a period in which his relationship to the clerical leadership of Tabor underwent a change for the worse.

In April he could still count on the support of Tabor's clergy, especially of the bishop, in his efforts to suppress the Pikhart movement. But returning to Tabor from the diet of Kutná Hora early in September after an absence of many months,[26] he found the spiritual climate changed. Not a few of the priests were "radicals" and had been close to Houska even without openly favoring Pikhartism. There was more than one area of disagreement between those men and the general. Žižka had failed to give them support in the great disputation in Zmrzlík's house; he was at best lukewarm, if not opposed to them, on the issue of the vestments, and his fierce persecution of Houska and the Pikharts filled them with fear. Sometime later we hear that Wenceslas Koranda, the leader of the more radical faction among the Taborite priests, was careful to keep clear of Žižka at all times because of his fear of him.[27]

The growing estrangement between Žižka and the Taborite clergy—in the end even his relationship to Nicholas of Pelhřimov seems to have cooled off—created serious difficulties for the general. Žižka had always wanted to exclude the priests from those functions which he considered belonged in the province of the captains. But there was one area in which he needed them and was quite dependent on their cooperation. It was the question of recruitment.

Manpower, of course, was always an important consideration, but during the first months of the revolution not much effort was needed

[26] He had probably been at Tabor, for a very short stay, between his return from the diet of Čáslav and his campaign against Bor and Rabí. Even that would mean that he had been absent for three months. Otherwise it would have been four and a half months: the whole period since the beginning of his campaign to eastern Bohemia.

[27] Tomek, *Žižka*, p. 150.

to procure it. Attracted by the unusual hopes and promises emanating from the chiliastic prophecies the peasants flocked to the armies of Tabor, expecting to acquire eternal salvation as well as riddance from worldly burdens. In the meantime a process of considerable sobering had set in, especially as Tabor had soon begun to reimpose on the peasants all tax burdens originally owed to the landlords. Recruitment was no longer so easy and successful. It could not be tackled without the help of those who had the strongest, most continuous influence upon the minds of the rural masses: the priests. How much Žižka took it for granted that recruiting was the proper job of the priests is very clearly expressed in his letter to Domažlice of September 12.

For priests who were no longer in agreement with Žižka's policy it would not be difficult to sabotage his work, or at least put up a sort of passive resistance, by simply being lax in their recruiting efforts. The troops therefore which he had at his disposal when joining the army of Prague at Slaný in September would be somewhat less than impressive, and this, indeed, would explain well enough his lack of strong leadership during this phase.

But it would explain even more than that. If Žižka had found that the region of Tabor no longer gave him the manpower he needed, then he had to get it elsewhere, preferably where he could rely on the full support of the local clergy. There was only one such region: the upper Elbe valley, the land between Hradec Králové and Čáslav, the spiritual dominion of the man who was his most devoted friend among the Hussite clergy: Ambrose of Hradec. The need for recruitment, thus, explains well the fact that, sometime during the second week of October, we find Žižka in the region of Čáslav.

It is not quite impossible that Žižka had also gone to Čáslav to forestall an expected movement of Royalist troops in this region.[28] But it does not seem likely. For Žižka's next move took him in a direction opposite to the one from which Sigismund's main invasion was to be expected. He marched, with all the troops he had, straight to the southernmost corner of Bohemia.

The call which Žižka followed came from the Taborite captain who was nearest to Žižka throughout his life: Lord Roháč of Dubá. Roháč had taken over the command of the town and fortress of Lomnice when Žižka had conquered that place just a year before. It had become the

[28] This second assumption is made by Tomek, *op.cit.*, p. 114. For Žižka's stay in the region of Čáslav, see Březová, p. 518: "de confinio Czaslaviensi, ubi pro tunc fuerat. . . ."

most powerful stronghold of Tabor in the immediate neighborhood of Budweis. Thus it was a natural objective for the Royalists when, upon Sigismund's command, the forces of Budweis, helped by those of Ulrich of Rosenberg, took the offensive early in October. Their commander Leopold Krajíř began to besiege Lomnice.

Sometime around the tenth of that month Žižka with his troops sped down from eastern Bohemia to relieve Lomnice. Krajíř retreated before Žižka had reached the town, but Žižka was now back in his old, familiar country and fighting an old, familiar war: he had to punish the traitor Ulrich of Rosenberg.

Crossing over to the left bank of the Vltava River he first attacked Rosenberg's castle Poděhúsy, near the town of Netolice. Having conquered and burned it he returned, soon after the middle of October, to the eastern region of Rosenberg's dominion, where his town and castle of Soběslav formed a worthwhile military goal. There, during the months of the armistice, the Taborites had been able to move and preach freely, but now Rosenberg had them thrown out. Žižka was again successful, the castle was destroyed and part of the town walls leveled.

It was after the conquest of Soběslav that Žižka decided to use his presence in this region for a very special task which had lingered in his mind for a long time: the destruction of the Adamites. What this meant for him and how he did it has been told before.

Žižka's forces, at the time, were far from sufficient to attack the two major enemy strongholds in the south: Rosenberg's town of Krumlov whose enormous fortifications look imposing even today, or the great city of Budweis. Yet he might have continued in his harrowing war against both these enemies if a new call for help had not come to him, this time against an even stronger power, the Pilsen Landfrieden.

We have seen that this federation of Catholic towns and nobles had broken the pledges given in the armistice of March and re-entered the war as early as July 1421. They had assisted the Germans during the time of the Second Crusade, but had been rather quiet for the first few weeks after. On October 26 however they attacked and took the small fortress of Štěnovice, south of Pilsen, which had been held by Taborite forces since the beginning of the armistice. After killing all the people they found there, about sixty men, they went west and laid siege to the strong fortress of Krasikov, which Žižka had conquered in January. With the Pilseners was the man who claimed the castle's ownership,

Krušina of Švamberg, younger brother of Lord Bohuslav. The two brothers now stood in opposite camps, and it was with Bohuslav of Švamberg at his side that Žižka went on his long march—about 120 miles as the crow flies—from the southeast to the west of Bohemia.

That Žižka went this long way to save Krasikov was well justified from the military point of view, for if the Pilseners had succeeded in conquering the Taborite castles in the far west, Krasikov and Kladruby, they would have their backs free and would be much better able to move, in support of Sigismund, against the center of Hussite Bohemia. Nevertheless personal motives played a role, too, just as they had when Žižka came to relieve Roháč at Lomnice. Žižka, always as faithful to his friends as he was hard and without mercy to an unrepenting enemy, could also be generous and grateful to an enemy who had turned into a friend. Even if its military significance had been less impressive he would have gone to great length to save the castle for its rightful owner who was now one of God's soldiers.

It took Žižka and Švamberg several days to reach the region northwest of Pilsen. It was early November when he stood before Krasikov. He attacked the besiegers and drove them off. Then he saw to it that the place received sufficient provisions in case the enemy attempted to renew the siege. His own army was not strong enough to leave any of his troops with the garrison. At the same time the enemy received strong reinforcements, mainly from Henry of Plauen, one of the greatest and richest lords of the Pilsen Landfrieden. Žižka could not risk so unequal a struggle and retired southward as far as Klatovy, the Taborite town where he could hope to get some additional troops. Of his movements at this moment we are informed mainly by a letter of the Pilseners to the town of Cheb,[29] dated November 12. Švamberg and Žižka, so we hear, are "with all their power at Nepomuk [fifteen miles northeast of Klatovy], intending to lay waste and burn our town and our whole district." Therefore Pilsen asks, for God's and Christendom's sake, that the people of Cheb send whatever horse and infantry they have available, to meet their own forces at Stříbo within four days.

Whether Žižka's intentions at this time were really to wage a general offensive against Pilsen may be doubtful. As his forces remained rela-

29 Published, from the town archives of Cheb, by Bezold, *K. Sigmund u. d. Reichskriege g. d. Hussiten*, Excurse A, I, 136. Also printed by Palacký in *Urk. Beiträge*, I, 271, where the letter is erroneously placed in 1422. The letter gives only "next Sunday" (bis zuntag) as the proposed date of the meeting at Stříbro. Why Pekař (III, 122) concludes that this means November 22 (which was ten days later and a Saturday) is difficult to understand.

tively weak—he had less than 2,000 men[30]—it seems more likely that he wanted to forestall or oppose a new move of the Landfrieden against one of the Taborite castles in the far west. There were renewed fights, probably near Krasikov,[31] in the days right after the middle of November. We have no details except that the enemy forces continued growing (Cheb was probably not the only town to send troops), and that by mid-November Henry of Plauen commanded an army vastly superior to that of his foe. Žižka therefore decided to retreat, not south toward one of the Taborite towns where the enemy had too many strongholds, but northeast in the direction of Žatec. Henry of Plauen, confident that he could easily beat the Taborites, followed him and as he was especially strong in cavalry, steadily gained in his pursuit. There were skirmishes between the enemy's van and Žižka's rearguard, but after retreating for a whole day the Taborite commander resolved to make a stand. As his inferiority was more marked than ever before, he needed a very strong natural position to defend himself. He found it near the town of Žlutice, on a mountain called Vladař.[32]

The Vladař is a solitary hill, rising about eight hundred feet above the surrounding valleys. As its name (it means ruler) indicates, it completely dominates the region. Its slopes are steep, except for the northwest where a small village, called Zahoří, leans against its softer flank. It must have been a hard job for Žižka's men to get the wagons and guns up to the bare, fairly level summit, but once up there they held an unusually strong position.

Henry of Plauen nevertheless would have had a good chance against the Taborites if he had just occupied the village of Zahoří. Žižka's troops, to leave their mountain stronghold, were forced to pass through this place. But Henry of Plauen was not satisfied with a siege. He sent assault after assault against the Taborite entrenchment, making no inroads but suffering heavy losses in the process. The Taborite troops hardly lost a man, but after three days on the mountain the cold began to trouble them and their provisions were nearly exhausted. Therefore Žižka, counting that the enemy had by now been weakened sufficiently, resolved to use the following night to strike. The daring enterprise was altogether successful. Attacking at the darkest hour he took the Roy-

30 See Rynešova, *Listař Oldřicha z Rožmberka*, p. 43 (as quoted by Chaloupecký, *op.cit.*, p. 155).

31 This, at least, can be concluded from the general direction of his later movements as reported by Březová, pp. 524f.

32 The main source for the battle of the Vladař is Březová, p. 525. An exact description of the terrain and the possibilities offered to both attack and defense is given by Frankenberger, I, 159ff.

alist troops by surprise. Men, horse, and wagons had beaten their way through their lines before the enemy had rallied to offer effective resistance. Nor was he able to renew the pursuit. Unmolested Žižka's troops marched toward Žatec and were met, even before they reached the city, by a contingent of troops from that friendly town.

Of the fair number of tactically defensive battles which Žižka fought and won, the battle of the Vladař (fought just before November 20) is one of the more impressive ones. The general plan, of course, follows the familiar pattern, seen before at Sudoměř, Poříćí, and Bor Panský. But more distinctly than ever before the terrain had to provide the balance of strength. And whereas in the previous battles the enemy had grown tired after some hours of fighting and had retreated, Henry of Plauen was not so easily discouraged. Žižka had thus been forced to go over from the defensive to an offensive tactic to extricate his troops from this dangerous situation. Again he put nature to his service, using the dark of the night to balance the unequal strength.

The victory of the Vladař gave a new impetus to the national prestige of the blind general. Březová who since the middle of August had taken little notice of him (with the exception of his report on the Adamites and their end) devotes a chapter[33] full of admiration to his last march from the region of Krasikov to Žatec and to the manner in which he managed to beat his way through Henry of Plauen's great army. And the people of Žatec received him with the honors due to a victor. It was a fitting prelude to a far greater, far more important triumph.

[33] *Loc.cit.*

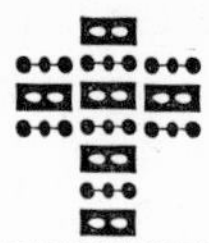

CHAPTER 18

## SIGISMUND'S GRAVEST DEFEAT

DISAPPOINTED at Sigismund's failure to support the Second Crusade at the promised time, some of the German princes had accused the King of unwillingness to suppress the heresy. But they were wrong. The King was as determined as ever to reconquer Bohemia for himself and the Church of Rome. He had some rather valid excuses for being late on the scene and could not anticipate the undignified haste with which the crusaders pulled out of Bohemia at the beginning of October. Once he knew that the time for a simultaneous attack had passed and that the Hussites could fight him with their backs free he might have done better to postpone his offensive to the following spring or summer. But when after long hesitation he had made up his mind to go ahead, he was not to be discouraged. All through the fall of 1421 he prepared his invasion with great care and little hurry. His one dominating consideration was, as always, to be strong numerically, and this desire was now strengthened by the fact that he could no longer count upon the German crusaders. The bulk of his troops were men from all regions of Hungary, including large groups of southern and eastern Slavs and Rumanians. This army, especially strong in cavalry, was put under the command of his Italian field marshal Philip de Scolari, Count of Ozora, usually called Pipo Spano. Pipo moved into Moravia in the first half of October, going as far north as Olomouc where he was reinforced by the troops of the Bishop of Olomouc and a little later was joined by Silesian and Lusatian forces, led by the Bishop of Breslau and some of the Silesian dukes. Sigismund himself crossed the Hungarian border into Moravia on October 16 but stayed at Brumov (only five miles from the border north of the Slovakian town of Trenčín) for eleven days, again waiting for more troops.[1] Only then he moved

[1] See the King's letter to Cheb, written from Brumov on October 18 in which he expresses his disappointment at the retreat of the German crusaders, explains that he has now a very strong army amply able to deal with the Bohemians and will no longer wait for anyone. At the same time he says that he expects reinforcements from Hungary "today or tomorrow," Yet he stayed at Brumov for eight more days. (*Urk. Beiträge*, I, 162.)

on westward to Brno where he now assembled all the forces he could muster at that moment: Hungarians, Silesians, and Lusatians, the archiepiscopal forces of Olomouc, and some troops brought along by Duke Albert of Austria.

With the forces now at his disposal—they are estimated by contemporary chroniclers[2] at about 60,000 men but were probably about 40,000—Sigismund had still an excellent opportunity to strike at the heart of the Hussite commonwealth. Its forces were badly divided. Žižka, with his army of Taborite and probably some Orebite trops, was engaged in a difficult struggle with the Pilsen Landfrieden from which, if only the King acted with dispatch and energy, he might not be able to extricate himself in time to help the capital.

The forces of Prague, too, were ill prepared for a great struggle. Their command was now in the hands of John Hvězda, but the young officer had no experience in handling a large body of men. He moved somewhat aimlessly in the region between Kouřim and Čáslav through which the King's army could be expected to advance toward Prague, and at Kutná Hora his troops showed their lack of discipline by plundering the houses of Jews as well as of Christians although they had been ordered not to enter the town.

Sigismund, however, was not ready to make use of this still favorable situation. As so often he wanted to combine political and psychological pressure with military force. He called a diet of the estates of the Margravate to which a majority of the Moravian barons appeared, even of those who only in June had declared their loyalty to the Hussite cause and had abrogated Sigismund's kingship. They now renounced all those acts and acknowledged the King as their rightful ruler.[3] In addition Sigismund demanded and obtained from all present a solemn oath condemning the Four Articles as heresy and swearing never to adhere to them again. Only half a year earlier he had permitted Ulrich of Rosenberg to pronounce that he would not object to the practice of the Four Articles until another public hearing of the issue could be arranged. Now he went back on his word and showed once more to all Hussites who might have considered compromise with him that he could not possibly be trusted.

This fact, of course, did not deter those Bohemian lords who had only

[2] Březová (p. 529) says over 60,000, the Old Annalists (p. 49) about 50,000. Aeneas Sylvius (p. 90) says that Pipo's Hungarian cavalry alone numbered 15,000. Ludolf of Sagan only stresses the fact that in the battles before Kutná Hora Sigismund's army was at least three or four times as strong as that of the heretics (p. 543).

[3] The declaration is printed in *Urk. Beiträge*, I, 166-171.

waited for the opportunity to rejoin the Royalist part. Ulrich of Rosenberg had deserted the revolution some weeks earlier and was on his way to Moravia where he joined the King's troops at Jihlava. So did John Městecký who forgot all his solemn oaths and the more than lenient treatment he had received at the hands of the Hussites. Among those who joined the King was also Čeněk of Wartenberg with some of his relatives, thereby confirming all the suspicions which Ambrose of Hradec and John Želivský had voiced. No doubt Želivský's new terrorist methods, especially the killing of Sádlo, had widened the gap between the conservative groups of the nobility and the radicals of Prague and Tabor. Yet not one of those barons who before this had proved to be loyal supporters of the Chalice went over to the King.

By the great and solemn act he put on at Brno Sigismund did not gain much that he could not have gained better if he had concentrated on his main task: the conquest of Bohemia. Indeed his political strategy was as faulty as his military. His insistence on the complete outlawing of the Four Articles would politically unite all Hussites, while the time he spent in Brno—from November 1 to November 17—destroyed his chances of finding them militarily divided and weak. During this period Hvězda became more active: on November 14 he laid siege to the castle and town of Malešov, south of Kutná Hora, which surrendered five days later. More important, the following days were those of the Vladař. When Sigismund finally moved on, still not into Bohemia but to Jihlava in western Moravia, Žižka was about to enter Žatec at the head of his unbeaten and unweakened army.

For ten more days Sigismund tarried at Jihlava with his main force. Now even his Hungarians grew impatient. Their general Pipo told Sigismund that there was no need to wait for more reinforcements, especially for Germans whom he seems to have disliked heartily.[4] Sigismund now permitted him with his Hungarian cavalry to make a limited thrust into eastern Bohemia. About November 22 he conquered the little town of Polička, which in spring had surrendered to Žižka and had then acknowledged Prague as its suzerain. The inhabitants of the town were slaughtered. If the report[5] is true that 1,300 were killed, few can have been spared.

Pipo's troops did not follow up this success but turned back into

[4] Windecke, p. 120: "This Pipo . . . is said to have asked the King why he wanted any more of the Germans, those sons of bitches (hundeskinder). He was strong enough anyhow." Ludolf of Sagan (p. 543) also reports that the King was urged on by his generals to be more enterprising.

[5] Březová, p. 528.

Moravia to join the main army at Jihlava. Nevertheless, the attack alarmed the Hussites. Hvězda whose troops were the only sizable force covering the capital saw that his strength was far from sufficient to challenge that of the King. He therefore returned to Prague where he arrived on November 25. On the same day an emergency meeting was called and the city council sent express couriers "to Žižka and his Taborite brethren and to all other adherents of the truth, nobles as well as cities and rural communities, asking them speedily to convene at Prague so as to oppose the heretical King, for the sake of their faith and honor and the freedom of the Law of God."[6] The request probably reached Žižka at Tabor on the day after.[7] It electrified the old soldier. If his blindness had handicapped him at any time, he was now as alert, as conscious of all needs, as ready for command and action as ever before. This new urgency overcame all laxness or hidden opposition inside Tabor. Three days later Žižka was able to depart at the head of an army which was better equipped if not stronger than any he had led before.

The moment when he arrived at Prague is described by Březová in the following words: "On the first day of December brother Žižka, though blind in both eyes, entered the city of Prague with his brethren and sisters, with his troops of horse and his battle wagons, with his priests who as usual carried before themselves the venerable sacrament of the Body of Christ while all great bells were rung in the towers of the town hall and the churches. From all over the town the priests and the people of both sexes thronged by, likewise carrying the venerable sacrament of the altar, and thus he was received by all the people with such honors as if he were the prince of the land, and he was fêted with ample food, so he would faithfully stand by the Praguers and drive the inhuman King out of the country. . . ."[8] It was an unusual demonstration of devotion and hope pinned to the grim figure of the old man.

Žižka immediately started discussing the plans for the campaign with the Prague authorities. His leadership from this moment on was a foregone conclusion. It was, as Březová put it,[9] "Žižka with the Taborites

[6] *ibid.*, p. 529.

[7] Tomek (*Žižka*, p. 122) as well as Frankenberger (I, 166) thought that after the battle of the Vladař Žižka remained at Žatec and that it was there that Prague's request for help reached him. This, however, is unlikely. Between November 20, the approximate date of his arrival at Žatec, and November 25 or 26 he had ample time to lead his army back to Tabor. Březová's report as quoted above seems to make it rather clear that the message reached him at Tabor, and the army he led to Prague appears to have been considerably stronger than the troops used for the preceding campaign against the Pilsen Landfrieden. See also Pekař, IV, 89.

[8] Březová, p. 529.

[9] *ibid.*, p. 532.

and Praguers." In the contemporary reports on the great battles of winter 1421-1422 Hvězda's name is not mentioned again though we know that he kept his position as captain general of Prague and took part in the operations. Only during the first phase—the move to Kutná Hora—Taborites and Praguers marched separately.

In going to Kutná Hora Žižka again anticipated Sigismund's intentions, but this time it was easy. Sigismund had finally, on one of the first days of December, crossed the Bohemian border north of Jihlava and had marched to Humpolec, intending to strike at Kutná Hora by going north via Ledeč. The choice of Kutná Hora as his first objective made good enough sense. Once he could conquer and hold it, the whole of eastern Bohemia became well-nigh untenable for Prague. He knew that part of the population, especially of the German miners, were ready to welcome him, as through his agents he was in constant touch with some of their leaders. In addition not a few Kutnohorians who had (under the generous agreement granted to them by Prague) left the town because they did not want to adhere to the Four Articles had joined Sigismund's army and were held in readiness as a special troop. Kutná Hora held, of course, a very particular attraction for Sigismund: its rich silver mines would help to solve a good deal of his perennial pecuniary troubles.

When, on December 9, Žižka approached the city with the Taborite troops a large delegation of the citizenry rode out on horseback to meet him, pretending, as Březová puts it, that they were glad about his arrival but really loathing it in their hearts as they were frightened of the ferocity of the Taborite soldiers. Their fears were unfounded. Žižka's troops showed better discipline than had Hvězda's Praguers a few weeks earlier. The bulk of his army camped outside the walls and Žižka's order not to enter the city was obeyed. Only some of the leaders with small detachments as well as the Taborite priests went in, and the latter celebrated mass in the Church of St. John, permitting townspeople to take part or look on. Their informal, puritan way, especially the fact that the priests wore no ornate vestments, shocked the Kutnohorian Germans so that they were now quite convinced that those Czechs were the "worst heretics, deserving to be persecuted by all true Christians." From now on, so we hear, those Germans waited with even greater impatience for Sigismund's arrival.[10]

They had still to wait, Sigismund's movements remained puzzlingly

[10] P. 530. Březová gives here a rather exact description of the way in which mass was celebrated by the Taborite clergy.

slow. He spent considerable time in the small town of Ledeč, and altogether consumed twenty days covering the fifty miles from Jihlava to Kutná Hora. All the time his Hungarians destroyed Czech villages, burned the men, mutilated the boys, raped the women and girls. The behavior of his troops was so atrocious that not one of the Czech chronicles which describe his invasion omits reference to it, and Lawrence of Březová adds to his own record a bitter invocation, a sort of ex post facto prophecy of the punishment which this army would receive for its misdeeds.[11]

On the side of the Hussites Žižka used the time to inspect and, where necessary, strengthen the fortifications at Kutná Hora and the neighboring town of Čáslav. There he also received reinforcements. He himself directed the recruitment of soldiers in the town and its surroundings,[12] but even more valuable was the arrival of three great barons with their retainers and soldiers. Two of them were Moravians who had defied Sigismund's bid: Lord Hašek of Waldstein, a relative of Hynek of Kolstein, and Wenceslas of Kravař, son of Lord Peter of Strážnice, one of the leaders of the Moravian Hussites at the diet of Čáslav. The third to arrive was Victorin of Poděbrady whose close friendship with Žižka probably dated from their cooperation during the spring campaign in eastern Bohemia. From there, with his allies and troops, Žižka returned to Kutná Hora in time to make all final preparations.

On Sunday, December 21, early in the morning Žižka's scouts brought the news of the approach of Sigismund's army. After divine services had been held, criers went through all streets to tell the people of Kutná Hora to be ready to defend the city according to their oaths, and not to be frightened by the King's power as Žižka, the Praguers, and the lords would not desert them. Then, with bells ringing, the troops that had camped in the town were assembled and in their majority, together with some Kutnohorian militia, left the town through the Kouřim Gate in the west. A small detachment of Hussite troops was thought sufficient, together with the greater part of the town militia, to defend the walls in case of an attempted assault. They were put under the command of the mint master, a Prague citizen named Nicholas who had succeeded in this office after Ulrich Vavák's death. Clearly Žižka was not aware of the acute threat of treason lurking in the city.

[11] *ibid.*, pp. 531f. See also Old Annalists, p. 49.

[12] See the reference to his previous recruiting activities around Čáslav in Březová, p. 518.

Sigismund's army was nearing from the west. He had made a detour, to avoid being held up by the fortress of Malešov, which had been conquered by Hvězda a few weeks earlier. Žižka thus had to defend the western approaches to the city. He marched out on the road to Kouřim, but after less than half a mile's march turned off to the right and took up a position on a wide elevation from which he could hope to keep two roads under observation and to some extent under fire: the road to Kouřim on his left wing and the road to Kolín on his right. He had just time to put up his wagon fortress when the King's army came into view, marching through the village of Přitoky.

The operations now undertaken by the Royalists show considerable skill, clearly reflecting the experience and shrewdness for which Pipo of Ozora was noted. He began by fanning out with his troops toward the northeast from the road on which the Royalist army had come. As he had at least 30,000 men to Žižka's 10,000 to 12,000 and as the strong proportion of cavalry in his army made him highly mobile, he had no difficulty in extending his left wing to stand north of the Hussite right, near or at the road to Kolín. To make this array of strength look especially formidable the Royalists filled some gaps in their widely spread-out front with cattle, hoping to deceive the Hussites into mistaking them for horses.

From this extended position the Hungarian cavalry now was ordered to undertake sustained frontal attacks against the Hussite positions. They continued throughout the morning and early afternoon, but each time the enemy came within shooting distance of Žižka's artillery they were repulsed. Březová claims that in the process they suffered heavy losses, but from his own, unusually detailed report of the battle[13] it becomes clear enough that Pipo never meant to force the issue by these frontal attacks but that his main aim was to keep the Hussites fully occupied and to detract their attention from what he was going to do later. As long as daylight lasted the Hussites could believe that they were the victors. They stood their ground well enough, including even those Kutnohorian detachments which fought on their side and probably consisted mainly of Czech citizens of the town. The growing effectiveness of Hussite artillery may have been a surprise to the Hungarians and a source of pride to Žižka's troops. Yet the day was to end with a resounding success for Sigismund.

As soon as the early dusk of the year's shortest day sufficiently reduced visibility, Pipo sent elements of his left wing, led on by a detach-

[13] Pp. 532ff.

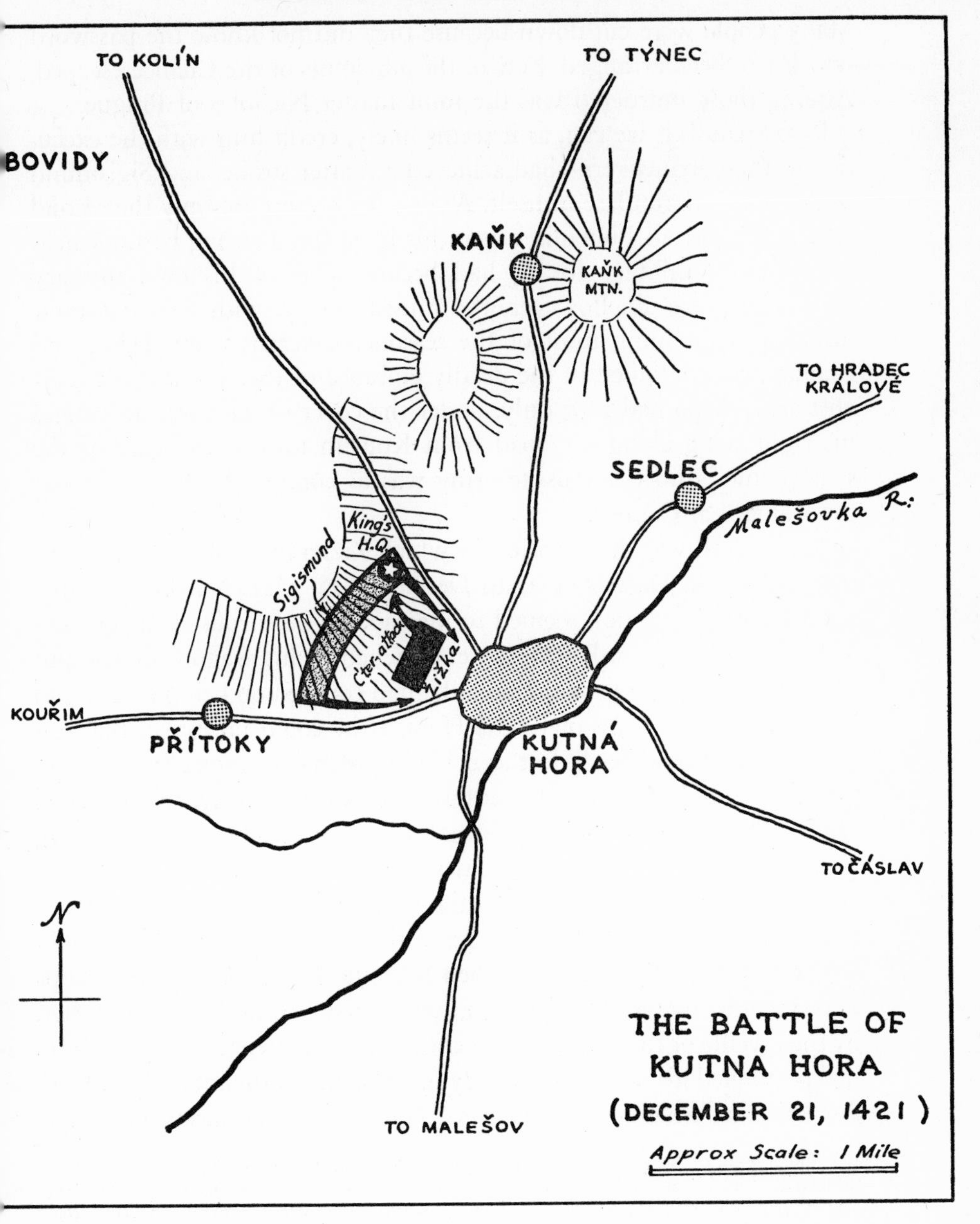


ment formed by Kutnohorian Germans, around Žižka's right flank to the Kolín Gate. Special signs had been arranged by the King's agents, and the troop of militia supposed to defend the gate opened it to the Royalists. Immediately the Germans in the town who were accomplices of this conspiracy began a fierce slaughter of all Hussites in the town.

Many people were cut down because they did not know the password which had been arranged. Few of the adherents of the Chalice escaped. Among those murdered was the mint master Nicholas of Prague.

Pipo Spano—if we can, as it seems likely, credit him with the execution of these maneuvers—had achieved a master stroke, and Sigismund could well congratulate himself. At one fell swoop not only the second richest prize of all Bohemia was in his hand but a strong bastion, held by fair-sized military forces, had become part of his own military strength. Above all, however, the Hussite army, with Žižka at their head and containing most of the seasoned veterans from Tabor and Prague, was contained in the deadly embrace of the city and the Royalist army. Pipo had now only, under the cover of darkness, to extend his right wing along the road from Kouřim toward the gate of the same name[14] and the Hussite army was as completely surrounded as the Romans at Cannae.

This indeed was the situation in which Žižka found himself early in the night from December 21 to December 22, 1421. Not even on the Vladař had his position seemed so inescapably disastrous as at this moment. True he was still strongly entrenched in his wagon fortress but his army was poorly provisioned as he had counted on being able to fall back on the rich stores of Kutná Hora. If he could not break the iron ring he was as hopelessly lost as if his impregnable wagon fortress had never existed. And he had to act fast. The Royalist army, strengthened already by the addition of the Kutnohorians, was, as he probably knew, about to receive further reinforcements from Hungary.

Žižka had to force a breach in the enemy lines, and the only choice open to him was the exact timing and the exact place where he would attack. He chose the moment when he could expect the enemy troops to be satisfied that all was quiet and when they had not yet been alerted by the reveille of the morning. He chose the place where the King, who had postponed his triumphant entry into the city to the following morning, had established his headquarters.[15] He knew that Sigismund, where-

[14] This closing of the gap, not especially mentioned in any of the chronicles (which nevertheless agree on the fact of Žižka's being completely surrounded) is probably the real substance behind Březová's remark that after the fighting which lasted into the night "exercitus regis non longe a Pragensium exercitu se collocavit, ut de Montibus (Latin for Hora) sibi victualia darentur." See also *The very pretty chronicle*, Chapter 1 above and p. 19 in Novotný's edition.

[15] This, at least, is the way in which I think Březová's words "surgentes ad locum, quem rex cum gente sua occupaverat" should be understood, as the whole vast area occupied by the Royalist army could hardly be properly called "locus." Also the "surgentes" seems to describe an uphill move which would apply only to a very limited part of the terrain where the Royalists had taken up positions, that is only to their left or northern wing.

ever possible, avoided getting involved in battle actions, and he could hope that the King with his whole following would tend to give way rather than to endanger his precious person.

The last words which Březová writes about this night battle—and they are, unfortunately, the last words of his whole invaluable chronicle[16]—give us at least a general idea of how Žižka managed to breach the circle drawn around his troops. "They marched forward," so he says, "and by shooting at the enemy with their guns they drove the King with his whole army from the positions they had held. And when morning came. . . ."

We shall soon consider how Březová's unfinished sentence has to be completed. The one before seems, to the modern reader, very simple and unsensational. Of course, so we might think, having artillery Žižka would use it to open the way through the enemy ranks. But this was far from a matter of course. On the contrary we have, in these few words, the first clear proof of the tactical use of field artillery: the use of fire weapons for a tactically offensive operation. Possibly this was not really the first such case: maybe Žižka himself had used them in a similar way when he rushed down from the Vladař and burst through the sleeping troops of Henry of Plauen. But of that we have no certain knowledge. And otherwise artillery had, up to this time, always been used in a purely static way: in besieging towns, in defending them and in defending entrenchments in the field as at Grunwald in 1410. Even the use of artillery in the wagon fortress was still stationary in a tactical sense, though assembling the fortress may have formed a link in a chain of strategically offensive moves.

Here, however, the guns shooting from Žižka's wagons, which stopped rolling only to fire, as well as the howitzers, which began to form part of his equipment, were given the specific task and had the specific effect which field artillery was to have in battles for centuries to come: not just to block or discourage an enemy approach but to destroy the enemy's chance or will to stay where he was; to dislodge him, to drive him back, to open a way for one's own troops. The field artillery of our motorized present, including tanks and self-propelled guns, can have no other basic

[16] The abrupt end of Březová's chronicle at one of the most dramatic moments in the history of the Hussite war is generally considered to be due to his death which probably occurred in 1436. He had been working at his great book for a considerable time, basing his tale on careful notes or diaries he had taken while the events occurred, and on the many documents to which, as secretary of the New Town of Prague, he had access. See Goll's introduction to his edition of Březová's chronicle, Lützow, *Lectures on the Historians of Bohemia*, London 1905, pp. 35ff., and J. B. Čapek's introduction to Březová's great victory poem (*Piseň o vítězství u Domažlic*, Prague 1951, Orbis).

task. And though we can assume that in the night battle of Kutná Hora the psychological effect was still at least as great and important as the real destructive power of the missiles released by those primitive guns,[17] they fulfilled this basic task even if fear of destruction partly acted in place of destruction itself.

The history of the second phase of the battle of Kutná Hora is, in this sense, the history of another revolution in the art of war brought about by Žižka, a tactical discovery or invention more permanent than the introduction of the battle wagon.[18]

Březová's short and undramatic report squares well with the reports given by the other chronicles. It only seems to contain one exaggeration: the claim that the Hussites drove "the King with his whole army" from their positions. This was neither necessary nor possible. Žižka's aim, at this stage, was to break out of the encirclement, to regain his freedom of movement and eventually to lead his army to a place where it could be reprovisioned. He could not possibly seek a military decision until he had at least his rear free or covered. That this was his plan and that he acted accordingly "when morning came," emerges clearly from the other chronicles." He fought," so *The very pretty chronicle* reports, "his way straight through [the King's] army, for there was no other way he could go with his troops. And so he marched less than a quarter mile [about a mile and a half in modern terms] till day came, and again he ordered his war wagons to be put in defense position. But the King did not move to fight him, but waited for reinforcements, for he knew that they were near. And so Žižka gave orders for a march to Kolín."[19] Roughly the same version is given by the Old Annalists,[20] with the difference that they describe the place where Žižka's army was encircled as "below the Kaňk mountain." The Kaňk is a hill about two and a half miles to the north of Kutná Hora, the highest elevation in the immediate neighborhood of the town, dominating its northern approaches. The chronicler (who wrote several decades after the event)[21] may only

[17] A detailed description of Hussite field guns and their workings is given in Toman, *Husitské válečnictví*, pp. 157-169.

[18] Yet the significance of this step has so far hardly been noticed by modern historians. Thus Toman, though he quotes Březová's passage twice (pp. 180 and 272) does not see that it strongly supports his own contention that Žižka was able to use his wagons with their guns for offensive operations.

[19] See Chapter I above, and pp. 18 and 19 in Novotný's edition.

[20] P. 49. The complete encirclement is also strongly stressed by Dlugosz (XIII, 280) who, however, knows nothing of the fight which breached the Royalist ring.

[21] The report is contained in texts L and M which both belong to the second half of the fifteenth century. It thus is much later than either Březová or *The very pretty chronicle*.

have meant to indicate that Žižka's position before his breakthrough was somewhere north of the Kouřim Gate, or he may have mixed up his position during the night with the one he took up on the following day, waiting in vain for Sigismund to attack. In any case those three words "below the Kaňk" led whole generations of historians to a complete misinterpretation of the course of events.[22] Žižka, so they surmised, broke through the enemy at Kutná Hora, marched on to the Kaňk, was pursued by the King's army and again completely surrounded, and in the following night, from December 22 to 23, he broke through the King's forces for a second time. Only recently has this strange version been repudiated.[23] There is no indication that the King ever tried to pursue the Hussite army, on the contrary German sources[24] prove rather conclusively that once he was in the possession of Kutná Hora he felt no need for further military action. Far from understanding that Žižka's escape undid most of the success achieved on December 21, he considered himself as the victor to the extent that he hoped again for a voluntary submission of the capital. This hope, further his wish to crown his victory by a triumphant entry into Kutná Hora, and probably also his hope to see the promised reinforcements from Hungary arrive, combined in countering the advice surely given to him by his field commanders that Žižka's army should be pursued and destroyed. Žižka himself had clearly expected such a pursuit. He knew that the light cavalry of the Hungarians was fully able to catch up with him. It was for this reason that, after daybreak on December 22, he formed another wagon fortress, very likely on the southern or western slope of the Kaňk Hill, just off the road to Kolín. Only when he had convinced himself that he was not pursued by the enemy did he march on, reaching Kolín on the same day.

For our understanding of the further development it is important to

[22] This misinterpretation first occurs in the Epitome of Balbin, the seventeenth century Jesuit historian of Bohemia, and then persists through all following presentations, including as careful a study of the military history of the Hussite wars as Frankenberger's. In consequence Frankenberger's chapter on the battle of Kutná Hora (I, 169-175) is, except for the description of the terrain and the initial deployment of forces, of little value, as is the account by Toman (*Husitské válečnictví*, pp. 271-273).

[23] The merit belongs to Pekař who studied the sources with more critical care and better understanding than his predecessors. (See his *Žižka*, III, 130-137, and in more detail the corresponding notes in vol. IV, especially 94ff.) But while he was completely right in rejecting the version of Žižka's repeated encirclement—first before Kutná Hora and then on the Kaňk—and was the first to recognize that all reports on the encirclement refer to one and the same set of facts, he did not see anything remarkable (or, as he put it, anything dramatic) in the way in which Žižka extricated himself from this fatal position.

[24] Ludolf of Sagan, pp. 542, 543, and Andreas of Ratisbon, *Chronica Husitarum*, p. 373.

keep the season clearly in mind. Winter had by now descended on the Bohemian land, an early and severe winter. Around Christmas rivers and streams were covered with a crust of ice. The King's troops were bound to suffer badly under the cold. They would be quite unwilling to camp in the open, but as the King himself would not put up with discomfort for his own person and his retinue or irritate his adherents in Kutná Hora, he did not billet many troops in the city. Instead he allowed a large part of his army to disperse in the neighboring villages, especially in the region between Kutná Hora and Čáslav where they would also serve to contain the Hussite garrison of the latter town. As the only precaution against a surprise from the north a fairly strong body of Hungarian troops was posted in and around Nebovidy, a large village about three miles northwest of Kutná Hora, halfway between that city and Kolín.

Having thus disposed of his forces and trusting that the Hussite army, having made good its escape, would likewise go into winter quarters the King thought the time ripe for another diplomatic attempt to convince Prague of the futility of resistance. The emissary whom he sent to the capital[25] was a Polish nobleman, Zawisza Czarny of Garbów, who had served as a go-between in the difficult negotiations between Sigismund and Władysław. He had joined the court of Sigismund some time before with the task of trying for a reconciliation between the two kings, and Sigismund had treated him with the utmost courtesy and distinction. By sending him now to Prague the King obviously hoped to impress upon the capital the fact that he was in close touch with Władysław and that the Praguers should not expect any help from Poland. But this diplomatic interlude turned out a complete failure. Zawisza rejoined the King's court at Kutná Hora soon after Christmas.

It seems strange that the King's agents told him so little about what was going on meanwhile in the camp of his enemies. Žižka was far from regarding the campaign as finished. For him it had just begun. But to complete it he needed a stronger army. The two weeks following the retreat to Kolín, including the Christmas days, were occupied with recruiting new forces and putting them into shape. He got his men "from the land around Jičín and all the districts in the neighborhood."[26] Jičín as the central point indicates rather clearly the region from which

[25] Tomek who treats this episode in some detail (*Žižka*, pp. 127, 128) thinks the negotiations took place in Kolín, but this I regard as unlikely as no decision could have been taken except in Prague itself. The main source in this case are the court records of Rosenberg.

[26] Old Annalists, p. 49.

Žižka received his additional manpower: the area within the large bend of the upper Elbe, square in form and bordered by the towns of Dvůr Králové, Hradec Králové, Pardubice, Kolín, Nymburk, and Mladá Boleslav. It was the natural region for recruitment: near enough and yet, for the moment, out of Sigismund's reach. And in its eastern part Žižka could feel sure of the full support of the local clergy, the Orebite priests under the leadership of his friend Ambrose of Hradec. Some Orebite elements seem to have been in Žižka's army before, especially in the autumn of 1421. Now they grew much stronger. Even so his army was still inferior to Sigismund's. What made up for the difference was that Žižka had his troops together, whereas Sigismund's forces were widely dispersed. Also Žižka now held the initiative and could spring a surprise on his foe.

In the early morning of January 6 Žižka struck. He turned against the largest body of Royalists which he would meet on his way from Kolín to Kutná Hora: the troops in and near Nebovidy. They were quite unprepared when they saw the nearing Hussite columns and heard them shout their battle songs. The Royalist officers tried quickly to form battle lines, but before they had fully succeeded the Hussites were on them. In some places resistance was stiff, but under the circumstances it could not last long. The Hussites killed many enemies and made a number of prisoners, and before an hour had passed the bulk of the Royalists, especially those who had horses to ride, were in headlong flight toward Kutná Hora.[27]

When the news of the defeat of Nebovidy reached Kutná Hora, Sigismund immediately called a war council. If the King himself did not full realize the seriousness of the situation, Pipo and his other generals must have told him the bitter truth. With the position of Nebovidy overrun, the strongest force which had been immediately available was weakened and in flight. True they were only a few thousand men, but the bulk of his army was so dispersed that it could not be concentrated at a moment's notice. Kutná Hora was a strong enough fortress, but if it was to be defended all troops in the immediate surroundings had to be thrown into the city and even then there was no guaranty that it could hold out against growing Hussite pressure. The King was soon convinced that he could not personally risk remaining

[27] The only chronicler giving details on the battle of Nebovidy is Dlugosz. He is of some value as a source also for the rest of this campaign, owing to the fact that he made extensive use of a personal report which Zawisza of Garbów rendered to King Władysław after his return to Poland. (See *Opera omnia*, XIII, 280ff.)

in a town threatened by his enemies. He asked the Bohemian and Moravian barons in his retinue to defend the city on their own, supported only by the Kutnohorian militia. But they showed no inclination to undertake so hopeless and thankless a task.

Sigismund now decided that Kutná Hora was to be evacuated by all his forces, that his army should retreat and in the process reform, and that somewhere farther south a stand was to be made. But Sigismund wanted to make sure that the "jewel of the Kingdom" should not again fall into the hands of the revolutionaries. The city was to be completely destroyed. Most of the German inhabitants were anyhow eager to escape, but the order to evacuate was given without regard to the readiness of individuals and some older people were simply forced to go along. As soon as the greater part of the population had left, the Hungarian troops who had stayed longest set fire to the town just as the King had ordered, but they did not do their job very thoroughly as they could not resist the temptation to plunder the rich houses of the German patricians. In the end they did not get far with their loot which only proved a burden in the fast retreat.[28]

After the victory of Nebovidy, Žižka had ordered immediate pursuit of the enemy fleeing toward Kutná Hora. His cavalry reached the town late in the evening, not too long after the Hungarians had pulled out. Whether on their own accord or on Žižka's orders, the first thing they did was to quench the flames which had not spread yet beyond individual buildings. Thus the major part of the city was saved. Žižka, so it seems, spent the night in the city—all these events occurred on this one day, January 6—but early on the following day the pursuit was resumed.

On Sigismund's side the great retreat went on, first in a hurried and badly organized way, along the main road from Kutná Hora southeast toward Německý Brod and the Moravian border, though a detour had to be made to avoid Čáslav. Slowly, in the course of the two following days, some order was reestablished, soldiers found again the troops they belonged to, and after having covered over twenty miles the King

[28] The story of Sigismund's retreat and Žižka's pursuit from Kutná Hora to Německý Brod is told by a large number of chroniclers from both sides in a generally identical way. We shall, in the following notes, only point out those sources that are most specific on any given phase. The story of the evacuation and the burning of Kutná Hora is told best by Windecke (p. 120) and in a letter of the city council of Nürnberg to the city of Frankfurt (*Urk. Beiträge*, I, 175). Both these sources also stress the fact that the Hungarians were unwilling to fight, Windecke telling this as hearsay and giving himself, as the main reason for the defeat, treason on the side of the Moravians and Bohemians fighting for Sigismund. As there were few, especially of the latter, in Sigismund's army this is a rather farfetched explanation for the catastrophe.

felt that things were now well enough under control to attempt a stand. Apparently it was at this moment that Pipo and the Hungarian officers advised the King against it, pointing out to him that the morale of the troops was still too shaky to send them against the victorious and terrible Hussites. The King, however, overrode them, and the army, or at least that large part of it which by this time had been concentrated, took its position, sometime in the late morning of January 8, on a hill near the little town of Habry, about fourteen miles north of Německý Brod.

"The King's army puts up its troops in battle line. They plant their standards. Then there sounds a tremendous blast of trumpets, and manfully the Czechs run to attack them. The Hungarians turn their backs. But what profit could the King's power achieve when God Himself sent this powerful terror into their souls? They desert their standards, they press their spurs into the flanks of their horses, and they flee like people to whom no other salvation is left but flight. Those however who cannot flee fast enough yield their bodies to Death." This description by one of the contemporary chronicles[29] gives us most of what we know on the decisive battle in one of the most decisive campaigns of the war. There may, indeed, not have been much more to it: a frontal attack which, in the first onrush, broke the enemy's lines and completely shattered his morale. We can only add from other sources[30] that from this moment on the Royalist's retreat turned into a wild, disorderly rout in which they left most of their heavy weapons as well as all of their supply train on the road and continuously suffered heavy losses in men. The Hussites kept on their heels all the time.

When, by nightfall, the King and his retinue had reached the neighborhood of Německý Brod, he ordered this town to be defended so as to cover his own retreat in which he continued throughout the night. Thus some of the Royalist troops that were still able to put up a fight tried for a last time to offer resistance outside the walls, and many were killed in this attempt. Under the cover of these brave men and of the descending night a considerable part of the army escaped into the town and thence over the bridge which crossed the Sázava River into safety. But as crowds of soldiers jammed up in front of the narrow bridge orders were given for the cavalry to pass the river at other points by simply riding across the ice. For a while this worked, but when their ranks widened and began to include large numbers of heavy cavalry

29 *Chronicon veteris Collegiati*, p. 85.

30 Especially Old Annalists, p. 49, and shorter *The very pretty chronicle*, the *Chronicon veteris Collegiati*, Dlugosz and Windecke, *loc.cit.*

the ice gave under the heavy load. Soon a long stretch of the river was alive with hundreds of men and horses desperately trying to work their way out of the freezing water, being crushed by the ice floes or pulled down by the weight of their armor. In the dark of the night it was difficult to give any help. In the following days 548 heavily armored bodies were dragged from the river.[31]

Further pursuit of Sigismund—who in the early morning of January 9 reached the comparative safety of Jihlava—was hardly considered by Žižka. He had reached his prime objective: the King and the greater part of his Hungarian troops had been driven out of Bohemia. His troops, a large part of them on foot, had covered forty miles in three days of grim winter weather since leaving Kolín, and they had fought three battles in the process. They were tired, and as they had to stick to their heavy battle wagons and howitzers they could not expect to catch up with those enemy troops who had abandoned all heavy equipment and now were traveling light and fast.

Žižka therefore decided in favor of the task that lay right before him: the conquest of Německý Brod. It was the only town of significance in eastern Bohemia which, being rather out of the way, had been left unconquered by the Hussite allies during their great campaign in spring 1421. As its name (it means "German ford") indicates, it was mostly inhabited by Germans who were as opposed to Hussitism as the Germans of Kutná Hora. Besides the town's militia its defenders now included a considerable troop of Royalist soldiers, most of them Hungarians but also Moravians and some Poles who were the retainers of the Polish noblemen in the King's following, first among them Zawisza of Garbów. This baron, a strict adherent of the knightly codes of earlier times, regarded it as his duty of honor to stay with those men who covered the King's retreat with their bodies.[32] As he had by far the greatest prestige among the persons of rank present, the command of the town naturally fell to him.

On the morning of January 9 the Hussites opened heavy fire with their siege guns upon the walls. Zawisza answered with whatever guns and other weapons were at hand, and he managed to beat off an assault attempted by the Czechs. But the Hussite gunfire, continuing all day

[31] Old Annalists, p. 50.

[32] Dlugosz (XIII, 281) makes a special point of the fact that Zawisza could easily have escaped together with the greater part of Sigismund's followers. Zawisza's knightly virtues are praised in the most glowing terms by the same chronicler in a long poem when he relates the man's death—again in Sigismund's service—in a war against the Turks in 1428 (XIII, 356ff.)

and into the night, heavily damaged the town's fortifications. Therefore on the following morning, knowing that the town could not hold out for long, Zawisza let Žižka know that he was prepared to discuss the town's surrender. Negotiations had actually got under way when a troop of Hussite soldiers, acting without Žižka's knowledge, discovered some breach or weakened part in the wall and using it, penetrated into the town. Believing themselves betrayed the defenders again manned the walls and opened fire upon the besiegers, but now it was too late and within a short time great numbers of Hussite soldiers had entered and began a fierce slaughter of the men in the town, Hungarians and Germans alike. Žižka's men who up to this moment, especially in their behavior at Kutná Hora, had shown remarkable discipline, now really got out of hand, and the killing was accompanied by a great deal of burning and looting. Žižka was greatly annoyed by the fact that he had lost control over his men and had not been able, at this stage, to prevent their excesses.[33] The fate from which Kutná Hora had been saved now overtook Německý Brod: it was almost completely destroyed, and stood in ruins for months. "Wolves and dogs," so one of the chroniclers[34] puts it, "ate the corpses on the town's square." Even in this orgy of desperate killing, however, Žižka's old principle of sparing women and children was maintained.[35] The Royalist leaders, among them Lord Zawisza, were taken prisoner and conducted to Prague. After some months the Polish noblemen were released and returned to their homeland with reports on what they had seen and experienced.

What were the results of this memorable campaign? We have no certain data on the King's losses in manpower. The cost in lives at the battle of Nebovidy may not have been heavy. The number of dead at Německý Brod, including the German defenders, is recorded by two independent sources[36] as 1,500, not counting the hundreds drowned in the Sázava. But the greatest losses were, of course, sustained by the Royalists in the battle of Habry and the following pursuit. For this phase of the campaign we have two very different figures, one saying that 2,000,

[33] See Žižka's letter to the people of Skalice and Náchod of April, 1423 (Appendix, IX).

[34] The late texts L and M of the Old Annalists, p. 50. Their claim that the town remained deserted for seven years is of course a tremendous exaggeration. Already early in 1423 it was chosen by Žižka as meeting place for an important conference.

[35] Windecke (p. 120) relates: "they won the town and burned it and slew the men, young and old." A later copyist, not satisfied with this version, added after the word men the words "children and women."

[36] *Chronicon veteris Collegiati*, p. 85, and Old Annalists, p. 48.

and the other that 12,000 men were lost by the King.[37] The truth may lie somewhere in between, but even if the lowest number is accepted it still adds up, with the losses suffered at Německý Brod, to over 4,000—eight times as many as in the battle of the Vítkov and in itself, under medieval conditions, the equivalent of a sizable army. No less astounding must have been the losses in material which were largely turned into gains for the victors. Apart from the abandoned war material and horses, more than 500 wagons with provisions were collected in the field before Německý Brod, and the list of contents[38] covers food, ready cash, clothing, jewelry, and books, some of which, strangely enough, were in Hebrew. Clearly the King had prepared himself for a long and comfortable stay in Bohemia.

Sigismund was, during his long kingship of half a century, notoriously unlucky in the field, but not since 1396 when the Turks had mauled his army at Nicopolis had he suffered so disastrous a defeat. Whipped out of the country of his birth by his own compatriots, he must for once really have felt the pain of humiliation. How discouraged he was can be seen from his subsequent actions: he left Jihlava after a short rest, going first to Brno, where a greater distance separated him from his Hussite enemies. In March he went on farther east to Kroměříž and then, after attending his daughter's wedding to Duke Albert of Austria, returned to Hungary. For a great number of years he did not dare to get even near the borders of Bohemia, giving up all plans to direct military actions against the Hussites and leaving the task of fighting them to the German princes. This spelled the end of all attempts at a coordinated two-front war against Bohemia which was by far the greatest military danger to Hussitism. In this sense, then, the short campaign of January 1422 was and remained decisive for the survival of the Hussite movement.

By the same token Žižka, who had already saved the movement in its initial phases through his victory on the Vítkov, had now laid a fairly firm basis for its continued existence as far as this could be done by military means. Perhaps his genius shone strongest when, in the desperate night battle of Kutná Hora on December 21, he measured his own ingenuity against that of Pipo of Ozora and prevailed, overcoming the handicaps of inferior numbers and unexpected treason. From then on the King, by his blunders in carelessly dispersing his troops and by his neglect of better advice, had played into his hands.

[37] The 12,000 are given by the slightly older text L, 2,000 by text M of the Old Annalists, p. 50.

[38] *ibid.*, p. 49.

In the battles fought between Kolín and Německý Brod success mainly depended on relentless energy and stamina. Yet these battles, too, show the imprint of the unusual: it was fairly common for medieval generals to pursue an enemy, that is to march after him in the attempt to join battle. But to follow up a victory by a continued pursuit over scores of miles, to press on after a beaten enemy so as to achieve his complete destruction—this was by no means usual or "normal." It was "normal" only for Žižka who always acted according to the military needs of the situation as his unfettered mind saw them.

On January 11, the day after the conquest of Německý Brod, a victory celebration took place in the Hussite camp outside the town. The troops displayed the captured enemy banners and a number of their leaders were dubbed knights. According to one version[39] Žižka was among them, but it seems more likely that this is an error in the date, and that he had received that honor a year earlier. There was a number of men who had distinguished themselves in the campaign—among them, as it seems, especially Lord Hašek of Waldstein[40]—but Žižka's leadership was clearly the decisive factor.

This was recognized by all groups of Hussites at least by the title which he could now assume. In a letter sent from Německý Brod on the very day after the conquest he signs himself: "Director of all communities of the land of Bohemia which adhere to and fulfill the Law of God"—in other words: commander in chief of all Hussite forces in Bohemia.[41] Žižka was highly meticulous in the way he used his titles.[42] Thus there is little doubt that the overall leadership which had

[39] The creation of many knights is recorded in the texts L and M of Old Annalists. Palacký as editor inserted, at the same place, a short sentence from text B which originally referred to the same day in 1421, thinking this dating a mistake and feeling that Žižka deserved the honor better after his decisive victories over Sigismund. I agree with Pekař who thinks (III, 141; IV, 100) that the original date is correct. It would put the knighting right after the conquest of Krasikov, and the man who dubbed him may well have been his friend Zmrzlík.

[40] Pekař strongly stresses Waldstein's role during this campaign, contending that Žižka has been given too much credit for it. He identifies, for this purpose, Waldstein with a fabulous "Lord Phenko" who occurs in the role of a prominent enemy of Sigismund in the Chronicle of the Roman Kings of Thomas Ebendorfer of Hasselbach. Actually the only basis for attributing to Waldstein an important role during the campaign is his subsequent position in Bohemian politics as captain of Prague and the mention of his name in a contemporary folk song (reconstructed from a verbal Polish translation) celebrating the victory over Sigismund. See Diels, "Ein Hussitenlied auf K. Siegmund," *Archiv für slawische Philologie*, 1928, pp. 97-108. Even there, however, Žižka's name appears much more prominently than that of Hašek of Waldstein.

[41] See the letter to Třeboň in Appendix, V. The same phrase, only somewhat more detailed as to the different estates, as "adhering to the Law of God" also occurs at other opportunities where it denotes the whole of Hussite Bohemia. See e.g. the preamble to the instructions given to Hynek of Kolstein in December 1420, published by Novotný in *Sborník Žižkův*, p. 131.

[42] See e.g. Žižka's later letters when, finding his relationship to Prague and Tabor difficult to define, he used no title at all (Appendix, VIII and IX).

fallen to him after his arrival in Prague in December 1421 had received formal recognition, in the course of his victorious campaign, from all Hussite groups: the capital, the forces of Tabor and Oreb, and the Hussite lords. The extraordinary prestige which he now enjoyed emerges just as clearly from contemporary German sources.[43]

Soon after the great victory celebration, camp was broken and the Hussite army returned to Prague where it arrived two days later, received with jubilation by the people. Březová, had he lived a little longer, might have presented us with a colorful description of the way in which the victor of Kutná Hora, Nebovidy, Habry and Německý Brod, the deliverer "from the inhuman King," was greeted by the population of the capital. He had amply justified all their hopes and prayers. But now he was inevitably drawn back into the problems and conflicts of Bohemia's political organization which assumed a new and acute aspect as always when the grave military danger and with it the urgent need for unity had vanished.

[43] Thus Windecke (pp. 144, 197, 198) calls him "der Hussen und Ketzer houptman." Ludolf of Sagan, discussing this phase, stresses the fact that not only the Taborites were under his command but "quem et Pragenses pro capitaneo habuerunt," and Andrew of Ratisbon (*Chronica Hussitarum*, ed. Leidinger, p. 349) also calls him the captain of the Praguers, probably using the latter word as a synonym for all "heretics."

# CHAPTER 19

## THE END OF JOHN ŽELIVSKÝ

THE YEAR 1421 had seen John Želivský and his party gain a firmly predominant position by the unification of the city governments of both towns and especially by the dictatorship imposed on the city in October. The exigencies of the war, however, operated against Želivský. Through most of November and December his captain general Hvězda had to stay away from Prague, trying to counter Sigismund's moves. Absent with him were strong parts of the Prague militia who could have been expected to stand by the present regime. Thus the conservative groups began to recover their self-confidence again. Their resistance stiffened, and they found a leader who in strength and determination was Želivský's equal, in national prestige his superior: Jacobellus of Stříbro. The struggle for the religious and political leadership in the capital began to take the form of a duel between these two priests at the very time when the fate of the nation was to be decided on the battlefields of eastern Bohemia.

Why did Jacobellus, once the most radical reformer among the masters of the University, now turn against John Želivský? Quite soon after the outbreak of the revolution Jacobellus' attitude toward the Hussite left had cooled off, but for a long time there had been no direct, open conflict between him and Želivský. The Synod of Prague of July 1421 had elected both men, together with Prokop of Pilsen and John Příbram, as directors of the Hussite Church. It seems that at first Jacobellus tried to mediate between Želivský and the other two masters. As time went on this became ever more difficult. Želivský was especially annoyed when in August 1421 Příbram and Prokop of Pilsen were invited by the lords to serve as religious advisers to the diet of Kutná Hora, the diet in which Prague was represented against Želivský's wishes. From then on, both those conservative masters were, in the eyes of Želivský and his party, nothing but the henchmen of "the lords,"[1] doubly compromised as

[1] See Březová, p. 510, and Novotný, "Několik příspěkvů," in *Sborník Žižkův*, p. 121.

the two main initiators of that diet, Rosenberg and Wartenberg, deserted the Hussite camp so soon afterwards.

Jacobellus, on the other hand, had serious and increasing misgivings about Želivský's policy. As the first priest to dispense the Communion in the two kinds he naturally despised all Pikhart leanings and all doubts in the real presence of Christ in the Eucharist. Želivský's much more tolerant attitude toward this heresy, if nothing worse, seemed a neglect of duty. Finally Jacobellus, who took the Third Article of Prague as seriously as the Second, could not look with any favor upon the strong worldly rule wielded by Želivský over the capital or upon the specific class character of this rule. He could not share Želivský's social and political attitudes, his enmity against the lords, the patricians, and the University. Thus he moved ever closer to the conservative masters, and finally even took the lead in the great struggle against Želivský.

John Želivský was not willing to let himself be pushed into the defensive. Early in November 1421, he renewed the attack against the most unpopular of the Calixtine masters: Christian of Prachatice. To some extent Christian had laid himself open to this attack by lodging complaints against Želivský with the city councilors. On November 9, Želivský's followers crowded together before Christian's church, St. Michael, threatening to drown Christian, and he could only save himself by accepting, as copreacher in his church, Želivský's most active and devoted follower, Priest William.

The masters of the University, with Jacobellus in the lead, felt that Želivský's one-sided actions, conducted through the medium of the easily aroused masses of the New Town, had to be stopped. The opportunity presented itself on November 12 at a general meeting of the Prague clergy—the masters as well as the other priests—which had been called for a double purpose: to attempt a new stabilization of conditions in the religious life of the city, and to answer an important message just received from Grand Duke Witold of Lithuania. We shall leave this second issue aside for the moment, but we know that Želivský was not in favor of Witold's candidature, and this fact contributed to the general tension between him and the majority of the clergy of Prague.[2]

The main attention was focused upon a writ formulated and pre-

[2] The meeting of November 12 and the resolutions adopted there for the reorganization of the Church is reported in great detail by Březová (pp. 521ff.), but he does not mention at all the other issue: the answer to Witold. See below Chapter 20.

sented by Jacobellus of Stříbro and Peter Payne. The Oxonian had only in October returned from the mission to Poland-Lithuania where, together with John "Cardinal" of Reinstein, he had represented the University of Prague. He had been absent from Prague for ten months, having departed with Hynek of Kolstein's second embassy in December 1420. As far as we know, there had never been any rift between John Želivský and the Englishman, whose general views were much less conservative than those of Příbram and Prokop of Pilsen. It may well have been for just this reason that Jacobellus, in a last attempt to overcome the conflict by a compromise, had asked Payne to assist him in his task.

The writ submitted by Jacobellus and Payne was, in the main, a confirmation of all the general rules accepted by the Synod of Prague in July 1421. In particular it tried to strengthen the authority of the four directors elected to head the Hussite Church, especially in regard to "novel teaching" and the old customs of the Church which were not to be discontinued without express permission. A final paragraph, clearly referring to the way in which Priest William had been installed as preacher at St. Michael, made the appointment of new preachers dependent on a strict examination by the directors of their morals, their attitude toward the dogma, and their ability. Indeed John Želivský smilingly commented: "These proposals are directed against me and William." But he could not prevent the great majority of the clerics from accepting the proposals which were now to be put before the whole community.

At a town meeting held two days later Želivský led the counterattack against the present composition of the church directory. His adherents assaulted with special vehemence Prokop of Pilsen and John Příbram. Many people demanded that Želivský should be sole director of the Hussite Church. But Želivský refused in an elegant way. He was neither worthy nor able, so he said, to rule over such a great organization. He suggested the election of Jacobellus and Payne. He would be glad to function as their assistant and to carry as much of the burden of the work as he could.

After a stormy discussion the majority elected Želivský as the only director with the provision that he might co-opt other clerics to help him. The election should be submitted for approval, however, to the members of the Prague militia which stood, at that time, in the field near Čáslav. Democratic feeling was clearly alive among the people of Prague.

Those men who risked their lives defending the city and the Law of God were not to be deprived of their vote.

The people of the army did, indeed, freely discuss the issue. There was strong opposition against a one-man rule of the Church. Instead they demanded that again a four-man committee should take over, consisting of Želivský, Jacobellus, Peter Payne, and John of Reinstein. This solution was finally accepted.

On the surface the change in the administration of the Hussite Church looks like another victory, though an incomplete one, for John Želivský. He had got rid of the two masters to whom, because of their subservience to the lords, he had raised the most serious objections. His refusal to take over the administration singlehanded was not, as some of his adversaries thought,[3] merely a political maneuver. He had the poorer elements of the city still solidly behind him, but he could not neglect and challenge all other groups or, by taking over the sole responsibility, make himself too easy a target for their accusations. Thus the new composition of the directory seemed the best that he could expect under the circumstances.

But Želivský's success, if such it can be termed, was hollow. With the elimination of the two conservatives, the role of Jacobellus in the church directory became different. Where before he had occupied something of a middle position he was now, before his own conscience and that of the other masters, the only one strong enough to stop what he considered the religiously and politically subversive activities of Želivský. The mild mediator turned into a watchful and even wrathful adversary.

During the following weeks the tension between the two groups rose slowly but steadily. Jacobellus even adopted Želivský's own methods by leading a procession of people to the Old Town city hall, unsuccessfully trying to force the abdication of the city council, which consisted entirely of Želivský's followers.[4] The situation came to a head, however, only after the Hussite armies had returned to Prague from Německý Brod.

The presence of these large military forces with their victorious leaders changed the political climate. Those men had saved the nation, had thrown the "inhuman King" out of the country. Among them were several barons with their retainers. Želivský's policy to restrict or suppress their influence could hardly prevail against these powerful facts.

[3] For example, Březová, *loc.cit.*

[4] See Priest William's accusation, in *Archiv český*, III, 237.

There were many discussions between the leaders of the armies and those of both parties. The decision finally came at a meeting held on February 5 in which only those men took part who had held important commands during the last phase of the war. They acted as arbitrators, and their ruling was acknowledged in advance by the parties of Prague.

There were nineteen men present at the meeting. Žižka had with him his two Taborite captains Zbyněk of Buchov and Roháč of Dubá, but among the people who had fought under his direct command were also four Orebite captains, two of whom, Bernhard of Valečov and Beneš of Mokrovousy, later belonged to his innermost circle of followers. As captains of Prague's own army we find four men, among them Hvězda of Vícemilice, but also the Orebite nobleman Diviš Bořek of Miletínek. Among the seven independent barons present were Hynek of Kolstein, who had not taken part in the campaign of Kutná Hora but had, early in January, beaten back a Royalist attack against Litoměřice; further, his cousin Hašek of Waldstein, the Lords Victorin and John Puška of Kunštat and Lord Valkoun of Adlary, who in 1419 had accompanied Žižka to Pilsen and had been close to Tabor ever since.

These men who now held the political fate of Prague in their hands were of very different backgrounds and held different views. They were all determined Hussites and enemies of Sigismund. Some of the lords, among them certainly Hašek of Waldstein but probably also Hynek of Kolstein, looked with disfavor upon all forms of radicalism. But these men were in a minority. They could not have forced their opinion on the combined strength of the Taborite and Orebite captains, the captains of Prague and those lords who had consistently and closely cooperated with Žižka. Yet the decision of the arbitrators turned out to be all against John Želivský and opened the way for a radical change on the political scene of Prague.

This decision[5] ordered the immediate re-election of the city councils of both towns. None of the burgomasters or councilors put into office by one of the last three elections (beginning with that of August 18, 1420) were allowed to be candidates now. For one year no changes whatever in the composition of the council should be permitted. Severe punishment, including death were threatened against persons disturbing the internal peace or teaching heretical (read Pikhart) tenets. If one of the parties should not accept or keep this ruling the arbitrators

[5] *Archiv český*, I, 209-212.

obliged themselves to consider that party as having acted against honor and trust, and to help the other party with all their means (read the troops under their command). In all things religious the last word was to remain with the directory such as it had lately been established: Jacobellus, Payne, Reinstein—and John Želivský. It was the only foothold left to this man or his party in the public life of the city, and it would be a precarious foothold indeed.

The immediate consequences of this ruling, as they emerged in the general elections held four days later, on February 9, were obvious. Whereas previously the conservative minority had been kept out of office and influence, the same happened now to the popular majority. It seems surprising that Žižka, his Taborite captains, his Orebite friends, and even the captains of Prague should have accepted this one-sided solution. That they did not resist it, that at least a very strong majority of the arbitrators were resolved to destroy Želivský's influence seems beyond question.

How can we explain this attitude especially on the side of Žižka? There is only one convincing explanation for the fact that he and those who followed his policy decided not for their old ally Želivský, not for a compromise solution limiting his power, but for an all-out policy against him. This is the influence of Jacobellus of Stříbro.

We have to remember that the religious motives overshadowed all others in Žižka's mind. As long as there had been no religious conflict between Jacobellus and Želivský there was no reason for Žižka to withdraw his support from Želivský, whose general policy, that of unrelenting fight against Sigismund and of a permanent alliance between Prague and Tabor, was also Žižka's policy. But the suspicions of Pikhart leanings that had fallen on Želivský and some of his adherents, as well as Želivský's political and military ambitions, that is the worldly rule of a priest, must have clouded their relationship. Most likely it was the determined stand taken by Jacobellus, the originator of the Communion in the two kinds and main author of the Four Articles, which clinched the issue in Žižka's mind. The Law of God had to be defended in all its purity, with no shadow of a heretical deviation compromising the cause. As to this issue he could still look upon Jacobellus, in many ways the successor of Hus, as the foremost judge. Even if he could have foreseen more clearly how this decision would endanger the alliance between Prague and Tabor and thus upset the political balance in the Hussite camp—and he seems to have been rather slow in seeing this clearly enough—his decision might not have been any different.

One of the arbitrators at least should have seen the handwriting on the wall: John Hvězda. He probably tried to oppose the decision of the majority, but his voice carried little weight. On the day when the new city government took over he was dismissed, and rather curtly, without any thanks. In his place the city government appointed Lord Hašek of Waldstein as captain general. The dictatorial powers which had been voted to his predecessor and of which young Hvězda himself had made little use were not renewed, but Hašek was a strong man and had strong backers among the new councilors as well as among his peers outside the city. More clearly than any other factor his nomination and his activities during the following weeks showed from where the wind was blowing.

It seems that Žižka left Prague for Tabor soon after the arbitrators had given their ruling, certainly not later than the middle of February. There were military tasks requiring his attention—the war against Rosenberg as well as renewed attacks of the Pilsen Landfrieden, who prepared again to invest Krasikov. But he was probably just as much concerned with the religious development inside the Taborite community. Later in the month a general synod of the Taborite clergy took place at Písek, and it is likely that Žižka was present.

The new regime of the conservative party in Prague set out immediately to fortify its own position and to destroy as much as possible of the remaining political and economic power of its adversaries. They went about this task with a good deal of vindictiveness.[6] People of this party whom the city, at the time of Želivský's power, had rewarded for their services by giving them houses or vineyards were now without notice deprived of those holdings, and later in February a number of Želivský's active adherents in the New Town were arrested under the accusation of Pikhart deviations. After a few weeks they had to be released as none of these charges could be proved.

John Želivský found himself in a position in which a weaker man might have lost heart. Nothing was left of his political power in Prague, and beyond that his alliance with the Taborite and Orebite groups had not stood the test of a real crisis. He must have felt betrayed by them, especially by Žižka. But he was far from ready to give in. He was still very conscious of his personal strength: the extraordinary appeal he had

[6] See Priest William's report on the murder of Želivský as quoted later in note 8.

for the masses of the little people in the New Town. He could not be prevented from propounding his religious and political views, before crowds of excited listeners, from the pulpit of St. Mary in the Snow, and there were other men among the clergy of the New Town who would follow his example. With greater severity and bitterness than ever before, he attacked the "faithless lords" and the masters of the University who complied with all their wishes. He also spoke up at the meetings of the church directory, the only body of influence where he was still represented. In the weeks following the elections of February 9 those meetings turned more and more into personal duels between him and Jacobellus. It seems that the famous master, perhaps somewhat self-conscious because of his short stature, lost his self-control much faster than Želivský. During one of those heated controversies Jacobellus was so carried away by his anger that he hurled fierce reproaches at Želivský: "You are the man," so he cried, "who is responsible for all these uproars and all this shedding of blood. It is you who has led astray the people of Bohemia and Moravia."[7]

Jacobellus went even further in his attempts to stop Želivský. On March 7 he visited the city councilors and launched a solemn complaint with them over Želivský's continued subversive activities. They had, so he told them, shown too much patience; it was time to proceed against him with more energy.

Jacobellus would have regretted his step had he realized its full impact. For it confirmed them in following through with a plan which they had just devised. Its main author was the new captain general, Hašek of Waldstein.

Waldstein's hatred for Želivský may have had more than one cause. He was ambitious and surely liked his new, influential position. As long as Želivský was there he could never feel quite sure that it would last. He was class- and rank-conscious enough to dislike the very idea of a society in which the role of the nobility would be limited. And he may have felt that the death of John Sádlo, the execution of a high nobleman on the order of a popular priest, had to be revenged. In any case he found willing conspirators among the new city councilors, and he assured them that he would take all military precautions necessary to prevent any serious trouble.

The city council, on March 8, sent messengers to John Želivský and eleven of his most prominent friends or followers in the New Town, inviting these men to appear at the city hall of the Old Town on the

[7] *Archiv český*, III, 237.

following morning. Želivský and all but two of the other men followed the request. On the events that took place at the city hall and afterwards we have an unusually detailed, lively report from an eye witness who was Želivský's close friend. Though his authorship is not announced there can be no doubt that the writer was Priest William.[8]

Upon Želivský's arrival, so we learn from it, the city councilors pretended that the purpose for this conference was to have Želivský's advice on military affairs. Should the armed forces of Prague be sent into Moravia or should they help the Taborites in the relief of Krasikov? Želivský suggested the castle of Křivoklát, nearer Prague, as the best immediate objective, as the Taborites could for the moment rely on the help of their confederate cities. The councilors prolonged this discussion, supposedly so as to give the captain general, Hašek of Waldstein, the benefit of Želivský's advice, but in reality because they still hoped to round up some of Želivský's close political friends. Eventually all those that had arrived were arrested and shackled. Only Želivský himself was permitted to go freely to his execution. All the men arrested swore to Priest William that they were firm believers in transubstantiation and quite innocent of any Pikhart leanings of which some of them had been accused. Besides John Želivský himself, nine of his leading adherents were beheaded without any pretense at proper legal procedure.

The city government tried to keep the executions secret, at least for a while, but the knowledge of them spread quickly throughout the city and caused an outbreak of fierce popular fury.

The security measures taken by the captain general proved utterly inadequate. The guards placed at the city hall and in some of the main roads leading from the Old Town Square to the New Town were overrun in no time by the excited people who had armed themselves for the onrush toward the Old Town city hall. Hašek of Waldstein fled from the city to save his life, caring little for the fate of his accomplices among the city councilors. Some of them were arrested immediately, others who tried to hide were found after a house-to-house search. Seven of them, together with the judge and two other men involved, were executed. Many of the masters of the University were arrested. In some of their houses as well as in college buildings the infuriated mob destroyed furniture, books, and other valuables. For the first time,

[8] Published by Palacký as appendix 4 to his editions of the Old Annalists, pp. 480-485. William's authorship is assumed by all modern historians, the script represents his point of view exactly as expressed in his public accusations as quoted above in note 4.

too, the Jews of Prague had to suffer. Their quarter, not far from the center of the Old Town, was invaded by a crowd from the New Town and considerable damage done to their property, though none of them seems to have suffered any bodily harm.[9]

Immediately after Želivský's solemn burial new elections were held —only a month after the ruling of the arbitrators had banned any elections for a full year—and they resulted in a city government of the party of Želivský. Leading among the new councilors were one Jerome Šrol[10] who had, as William's report shows, narrowly escaped the fate of Želivský, and the two brothers Charvát, one of whom had been a member of the regency council elected at Čáslav.

On March 15 a town meeting at the Old Town city hall decided the fate of the arrested masters of the University. Priest William acted as accuser. He directed his reproaches mainly against Jacobellus, but implicated eight other masters as well.[11] He did not claim that they had directly conspired with Lord Hašek and the city council for the murder of Želivský but made them morally responsible for the deed, as they had consistently agitated against him and had tried to slander his adherents with the calumnous charge of Pikhartism. He asked for a judgment which would make them realize their guilt. The community, after a lengthy discussion, decided to banish them from Prague. They were to be taken to Hradec Králové where, under the supervision of Priest Ambrose, they should repent their sins.

Prague was now again ruled by the party of John Želivský, but it was a party without a leader. With him the Hussite movement lost one of its greatest, most dynamic personalities.[12]

Želivský's attraction for the masses of the little people especially in the New Town could not have found a more eloquent testimony than their collective, spontaneous uprising after his death. But his influence

[9] Old Annalists, pp. 51, 52. See also O. Schürer, *Prag* (Munich 1930), p. 107.

[10] Šrol was, already in his student days, a fervent follower of Hus and later one of the most influential representatives of Želivský's party among the citizens of the Old Town. See Tomek, *Dějepis*, IV, 233.

[11] *Archiv český*, III, 237.

[12] Few of the great personalities of the period have been treated in as utterly partisan a way even by modern historians as has Želivský. For both Tomek (e.g. in *Žižka*, p. 132) and Pekař (III, 11ff.) Želivský is only a fanatic demagogue. Palacký treated him more fairly, and so did Novotný (*Sborník Žižkův*, p. 129). Nejedlý (*Dějiny husitského zpěvu*, II, 299ff.) admires him, and the Marxian historians of present-day Czechoslovakia have elevated him to an especially high rank in their scale of historical values. See e.g. the chapter on him in F. Graus, *Městká chudina v době předhusitské*, Prague 1949, or J. Macek, *Husitské revoluční hnutí*, Prague 1952, 101ff. I have, unfortunately, not been able to get hold of the monograph of B. Auštecká, *Jan Želivský jako politik*, Prague 1925.

was never limited to the lowest strata. For two years he managed to strengthen his position, generally by the democratic technique of winning votes through public persuasion but also by the use of patronage, and he could not have succeeded, had not a substantial proportion of the middle class elements of Prague been swayed at times toward his policy. In the early summer of 1421 he had reached the zenith of his strength by these means, but then he made the two great mistakes of his life: his assumption of the military command in what turned out to be a very unlucky campaign, and his tepid attitude towards Pikhartism. There may have been real tolerance behind his religious policy, but if this attitude would recommend him in the eyes of our time it was a dark spot in the eyes of his more rigid contemporaries and in the end deprived him of the support of groups inside Prague and of allies as important as Žižka. Only when this weakness threatened his position and with it his goals did he abandon his previous democratic methods for the cruder ways of a military dictatorship "by proxy." This, however, only hastened his downfall.

It can hardly be denied that he was ambitious, that he sought power, that he clung to it and enjoyed using it. But he did not seek power only for its own sake. Nor would it be fair to see in him, as one of his modern critics has done,[13] a professional revolutionary who wished the revolution to remain in permanence. Perhaps none of his contemporaries had as clear and as comprehensive a view of what the goals of this revolution should be as had Želivský. His basic consideration, as that of all true Hussites, was the freedom of their faith. Unlike his great adversary Jacobellus he realized that, in the world in which he lived, this could only be accomplished by giving the nation which had rallied behind the Chalice sufficient military strength. He also realized, in complete agreement with Žižka, that this strength could not be obtained by merely relying on the voluntary services of the nobility, but that the lower strata of both the urban and the rural population had to be mobilized as well. He regarded, not without good reason, the city of Prague as the natural center of such a movement of mass resistance. Here he found not only a cadre of trusting and trusted followers but also, especially among the guilds-people, a tradition of strength and leadership which could not have been found elsewhere. In close cooperation with the Taborite and Orebite movements and towns, Prague, as head of the Kingdom, could organize the strength of the nation. The way in which, during the great spring campaign of 1421,

[13] Pekař, III, 105ff.

Prague carried through this program is a testimony to the forceful and constructive statesmanship of which, at his best, John Želivský was capable. Unfortunately this series of combined military and political successes induced him to trust, quite unrealistically, his own ability and strength as military leader.

It was unavoidable that this whole policy should bring him into conflict with parts of the high nobility whose role, in his conception, was at best a modest one. Yet the intense individualism of these men would have made it possible to cooperate with some of them—perhaps many of them—just as Žižka did. John Želivský, however, looked on those men not as individuals but as a class or a caste. In the long run, this generalizing judgment proved to be right but it was not, or not yet, fully justified at this time, and was tragically dangerous in its results. For by generalizing, by directing his attack against the whole class where he might have limited it to individuals, he caused his enemies to close their ranks and caused some of his friends to desert him when he needed them most. And when, in his zeal to destroy potential traitors, he burdened himself with the responsibility for the death of Sádlo, he even gave his enemies something like an excuse for the bloody purge of March 1422.

From the moment, however, when he disappeared from the scene, the cooperation between Prague and the communities of Tabor and Oreb became more difficult, less firm, less reliable. The next phase of Hussite history is still dominated by repeated attempts at domestic consolidation, but frequently accompanied by the tendency to exclude, or at least reduce, the role of the masses of the New Town and of the two great sectarian communities. Želivský's own center of power, the political organization of the "poor people" of the New Town, nevertheless remained in existence for many years. When it succumbed in 1434 not much of the strength of Tabor was able to survive this blow. It was essentially the end of the revolution, though not of the reformation. Only after his body had lain in the grave for twelve years, only then could his bold, militant spirit be buried as well.

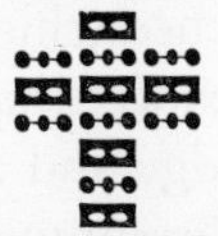

## CHAPTER 20

# THE PRINCE FROM LITHUANIA

THE diet of Kutná Hora had appointed an embassy to inform Grand Duke Witold of his election as King of Bohemia and to secure the speedy assumption of his rule. The men of the diet were not yet aware, then, of a highly unfavorable turn in Poland's attitude. King Władysław and his advisers had carefully observed the development of the war. They were well informed about the plans for a two-front campaign against Hussite Bohemia which, at that moment, made the chances for a success of the revolution look dim.[1] Władysław's support for Witold's Bohemian policy had always been based on the hope that the pressure exerted upon Sigismund might lead to a revision of the Breslau Award. The Prussian Order would, of course, oppose such a revision, but it was held in check through the influence of elector Frederick of Brandenburg whose friendship with Poland had grown into an actual alliance.

In this situation Władysław tried for a direct understanding with Sigismund. His offer went far: if the King of the Romans agreed to a revision of the Breslau Award, Poland would not only withdraw any support for the Czechs but if necessary would even help Sigismund to regain possession of Bohemia. It seems doubtful whether this policy had the full support of Witold, but he did not openly oppose it. Władysław sent two influential counselors, Duke John of Tarnów and his personal secretary Zbigniew Oleśnicki, later bishop of Cracow, to Hungary to confer with Sigismund.[2] The negotiations were prolonged and although they were supposed to be secret, they became known in Bohemia. They could not fail to cause consternation and distrust especially among those who had supported the Lithuanian candidacy primarily as a political weapon against Sigismund. The knowledge of these negotiations also helps to explain the coolness which, from now on, characterizes Žižka's attitude toward Witold. He knew, from his personal

[1] Sigismund himself had seen to this by asking the papal legate Cardinal Branda to inform and influence the King of Poland. See his letter to Branda in *Urk. Beiträge*, I, 136ff.

[2] See about this mission Goll, *Čechy a Prusy*, p. 158.

stay in Poland, the strong influence which the Grand Duke had on his cousin, and could thus hardly expect that those negotiations were conducted without his full knowledge and approval.[3]

The Polish offer presented Sigismund with a splendid opportunity to isolate the Czech rebels diplomatically before the intended great double offensive against them got under way. Fortunately for the Czechs he would not pay the price which Władysław demanded. He was reluctant to abandon the Prussian Order which he considered too valuable an ally in case he should again have any trouble with Poland, and he knew about the hopes, entertained in some Polish quarters, for the return of Silesia to Polish suzerainty.[4] It was an event occurring in Silesia that now abruptly shattered Władysław's hopes for an understanding with Sigismund.

The Czech embassy, led by Lord Vaněk of Jenstein, left Bohemia about September 10, equipped with credentials not only from Bohemia but also from Witold's representative Raczyński.[5] When the four ambassadors with their retinue of thirty-six men passed through Ratibor in Upper Silesia they were arrested by Duke John of Ratibor and Opava. He sent the news of his catch and a request for instructions to Sigismund. For Sigismund the very fact that this embassy had got under way was proof of the insincerity of Władysław's offer, and he asked for the captives to be delivered into his hands. In Poland and Lithuania, on the other hand, the arrest caused fierce resentment. Władysław, trying to avoid a complete break, merely sent one of his leading diplomats, Nicholas Siestrzeniec, to Ratibor to warn the Duke that his act might have serious repercussions.[6] But Witold's letter to the Duke was an ultimatum, threatening him with military measures in case the captives were not released immediately. For the moment a feeling of solidarity

[3] Novotný ("Několik příspěvků . . . ," in *Sborník Žižkův*), and with him Pekař put Žižka's turn against the Lithuanian candidature at a much earlier date, and in Pekař's case Žižka's well-documented support of Kolstein's first embassy to Poland appears just as a short, passing mood of cooperation. Yet none of the contemporary sources give the slightest indication for such an early change of heart. Žižka's attitude at the time of the diet of Kutná Hora has been discussed before, as have the contradicting versions of Aeneas Sylvius and the Old Annalists. That later in 1422 Žižka had become rather cool to Witold's candidature can be deduced, to some extent, from his actions as we shall see later, but the one early source which can be quoted in confirmation, Windecke (pp. 114-115), clearly speaks, in this connection, of the Taborite leader's attitude in 1422, not of any previous phase. See Pekař, III, 179.

[4] The fear for Silesia as a basic motive in Sigismund's policy toward Poland is specially stressed, and treated in detail, by A. Lewicki, "Ein Blick in die Politik Sigmunds," *Archiv für öster. Geschichte*, vol. 68.

[5] This, at least, must be concluded from Witold's letter to John of Ratibor, *Urk. Beiträge*, I, 153.

[6] See Duke John's letter to Přemek, Duke of Opava, *ibid.*, I, 146.

with the Czechs captured the imagination of a considerable part of the Polish people, and Witold and his party made full use of it.[7]

Among the men who voiced their resentment was Prince Sigismund Korybut, one of King Władysław's nephews, who declared that neither the King nor the Grand Duke would abandon the Czechs.[8] He had a strong personal interest in the matter: it was he whom Witold had proposed to send to Bohemia as his viceroy. Soon afterwards the Grand Duke sent messengers to Prague to suggest a common punitive expedition of Polish-Lithuanian troops under Korybut's command and of the Czech troops against the Silesian duke. When Witold's emissaries arrived—on October 23—it had already become too late to save the Czech embassy which John of Opava had extradited to Sigismund. The King had them taken to the Spielberg, the ill-famed prison fortress at Brno, and there all the retainers were executed, while the four ambassadors themselves were sent on to Trenčín in Hungary. The punitive expedition, now more than ever, might have appealed to the sentiment of the Czechs, but the reconquest of Moravia and the imminent invasion of Bohemia by Sigismund made it impossible to spare the military forces for such an undertaking.

Despite his annoyance King Władysław did not yet resign himself to a break with Sigismund. In particular he was still interested in the possibility of a dynastic liaison with Sigismund's family. To discuss this possibility he sent Zawisza of Garbow to Sigismund's court. (His mission ended, as we know, with his capture by the Czech army under Žižka after the conquest of Německý Brod. Władysław soon gave in to the urging of Witold to marry his young niece Sophia, Princess of Olszany, who eventually fulfilled the King's hopes for heirs to his throne.)

Witold meanwhile kept pursuing his goal: to become King of Bohemia if this could be done without too much risk. As long as the outcome of the impending campaign was doubtful he could protract his decisions by debating with the Hussites the question of their reconciliation to the Church. He used for his purpose the two masters who had come to him with Hynek of Kolstein but had stayed longer in his

[7] See note 4 above. That Witold's energetic policy was about to prevail in Poland is shown in a letter which Duke John received from a well-meaning Polish adviser, Abraham Niger (*Urk. Beiträge*, I, 153). He tells the Duke not to let himself be influenced by Sigismund's demands, for "loquitur vulgus, velit rex vel nolit, nisi eos liberos dimittat ab eadem captivitate, volumus eos ulcisci usque largifluam sanguinis effusionem, qui ille . . . inter nos et fratres nostros Boemos jam factam vult infringere unionem. . . ." To judge from this letter the intended help for and cooperation with Bohemia was really popular in Poland at this time.

[8] *ibid.*, I, 148.

entourage: Peter Payne and John of Reinstein. Payne also took a prominent part in that meeting of the masters and priests of Prague which, on November 12, drafted an answer to Witold. It was the same meeting which tried, in the direct outcome unsuccessfully, to limit the power of John Želivský.[9]

The message to Witold still insisted on his acceptance of the Four Articles, but conceded that this should take place after a public disputation to be held in Bohemia, Poland, or Lithuania. Only if the Four Articles should be proved to be in disagreement with the Scriptures, a case really thought impossible, would the Hussites consider themselves in the wrong. If they were in agreement with the Scriptures and the usage of the early Church, the Grand Duke should acknowledge and defend them.[10] This answer, tactically, was a slight retreat, but no basic principle had been sacrificed.

No theological arguments could speak as convincingly as the stark facts of war. Žižka's great victories of January 1422 finally satisfied Witold that the time for action was at hand. Sometime earlier Sigismund had written to the Prussian Order and the Silesian towns, commanding them to attack Poland-Lithuania should the two royal cousins give any support to the Hussites.[11] Now, with Sigismund's defeat before their eyes, Witold could trust that they would think twice before obeying this command and that thus, in military terms at least, he had little to risk. It still took him some time to obtain Władysław's permission,[12] but on March 5 the Grand Duke announced, in a letter to Pope Martin V, that he was going to send his nephew Sigismund Korybut to Bohemia as his personal representative.[13]

In this message the Lithuanian ruler reminded the Pope of the terrible wars which had cost so much Christian blood. Yet all those invasions had not led the people of Bohemia back to religious obedience. On the contrary, their victories and the unfortunate shedding of the blood of true Christians on both sides had only strengthened their pertinacity. They had, however, by repeated embassies urged him to deign to accept them, and had promised through letters and legations

[9] See above Chapter 19, n. 2.

[10] The letter is published by Caro in *Liber Canc. Stanislai Ciolek*, II, *Archiv für öster. Geschichte*, vol. 52, 1874, no. 54. See Goll, *Čechy a Prusy*, 149, and Novotný, *Sborník Žižkův*, p. 129.

[11] *Urk. Beiträge*, I, 156, 157.

[12] Cf. a letter by the commander of the Prussian Order at Daugavpils (Dünaburg), quoted by Goll, *op.cit.*, p. 162, n. 54.

[13] *Urk. Beiträge*, I, 186ff. See also Goll, *op.cit.*, pp. 163ff.

that, if thus received, they would return to the lap of the Universal Church and to obedience to the Holy See.

Therefore, to protect them under his own power, he had ordered his nephew, the Prince Sigismund, to proceed to Bohemia and there to work faithfully and with all his strength for the reconciliation of those schismatics with the Church and for the sending of a free and secure embassy from them to the Pope. In return the Pope is asked to suspend for some time the process against them.

The letter, as this short paraphrase shows, is guarded in all directions. Witold does not say that he has accepted the Bohemian crown, only that he has taken the Czechs under his protection. He tries to ward off, as well as he can, the likely reproach that he is aiding a heretical movement. The Hussites, though schismatic (a very much weaker accusation than heresy), are true Christians, and the blood shed on their side is to be regretted as much as that of the Catholic fighters. The final implication is that what Sigismund's brutal methods could and would never achieve might well be achieved by the methods of careful and well-meaning guidance. Thus the Pope might eventually relinquish his support of Sigismund and give some chance to a ruler less handicapped by the hatred of a majority of the Czech nation.

Obviously the Pope would be reluctant to make such a move. Sigismund's position in the Empire had not weakened to an extent that would have made it easy for the Curia to drop him in favor of a convert like Witold. If such a policy was to have any attraction at all, it had to promise considerable rewards. Thus Witold went far in holding out, before the Pope, the prospect of Hussite submission which, as the letter suggests, the Czechs had promised almost unconditionally.

Here the Grand Duke permitted himself not only a dangerous inaccuracy, but also laid down a mental reservation. If, at any time, he felt that his Bohemian venture became too dangerous or too costly, he could use the failure of the reconciliation to shake off his protégés, at least as long as he had not taken the final, irrevocable step of having himself crowned. The wish to avoid, or postpone as long as possible, such a binding decision explains his reluctance to go to Bohemia more convincingly than the urgent tasks of government which supposedly kept him still in his homeland. Meanwhile his nephew, Sigismund Korybut, would effectively represent him in his new realm.

What sort of man was this Prince to whom Witold committed so delicate and difficult a task? His father Dimitri Korybut,[14] one of Władysław Jagiello's younger brothers, had died early, in 1399. The Prince, then a boy in his early teens, had been brought up under the close supervision of the King who may, for a while, have considered him as a possible heir. He was given a very careful and complete education which made him as proficient in the use of the pen as in the arts of war. He took an active part in the two campaigns against the Prussian Order in 1410 and 1414, where he met some of the Czech noblemen who led the auxiliary troops from Bohemia. The younger Korybut had a winning, ingratiating way in dealing with people though he could be hard and tough if he considered this necessary to achieve his aims.

For the Prince, now a man in his early thirties, Witold's offer to go to Bohemia as his governor or viceroy must have seemed as an extraordinary and wonderful opportunity. His sentiments had from the first been with the Czechs in their undaunted struggle against the Germans, the old enemies of both Poland and Lithuania. Also his ambition was aroused. There was now no longer any question of his ever succeeding Władysław, and Witold had nearer relatives with better claims to succeed him in Lithuania. But if he represented the childless Grand Duke in Bohemia, was not there a real opportunity for him? Could he not hope, one day, to put the ancient and glorious crown of St. Wenceslas on his head?

Even if such thought may not yet have occupied too prominent a place in his mind, the task of ruling this strong and virile nation, of gaining their confidence, uniting them under a firm leadership—and finally directing them out of the impasse in which they found themselves, must have attracted this self-confident and strong-willed young man. And he prepared himself carefully for his task, which he knew to be difficult.

Half of April had passed before Korybut could leave Cracow at the head of a rather small army, mostly Polish and Ruthenian, the main cadre of which consisted of 2,500 horse.[15] Soon afterwards he received

[14] To denote the fact that the name Korybut was first borne by Prince Sigismund's father, some Czech historians such as Tomek and Novotný have called him Sigismund Korybutovič. Actually the name Korybut was never used in official documents, where the Prince always appears as "Sigismundus Dux," but Dlugosz, who should have known, always uses the name Korybut, and so did Palacký, Goll, Pekař, and others. I think this is more correct, as the "Korybut" was really used by father and son as cognomen. If the relation to the father were to be expressed in Russian form, he should be called after the father's first name: Sigismund Dimitrievič Korybut.

[15] See the letter from the Dean of the Chapter of Liegnitz to the Grand Master of the Prus-

reinforcements from Poland-Lithuania which increased his strength to about twice that size. Marching through the Silesian duchy of Těšín—whose duke did not dare to offer any resistance—he entered Moravia and turned first against Olomouc, strongest Catholic and Royalist center in the Margravate. If he had gained this important place, he would have come to Bohemia with vastly increased prestige. But the city was too strong, and after having suffered some losses he abandoned the attempt and attacked the less formidable town of Uničov. It was captured and became, for some time, Korybut's headquarters.

The Prince now lost no time in working for his primary goal: to establish an effective control over the Kingdom. Before long this task would make the calling of another national diet necessary. But Korybut was too shrewd and cautious to call such a diet before he had made himself more fully acquainted with the conditions in the country and had gained a wide enough following.[16] First of all he took a step apt to increase the confidence of all Hussite groups. At the earliest opportunity and in full view of his Polish and Czech retinue he took the Communion in both kinds.[17] Thereby he boldly stepped across the line which divided the two great camps of Hussite and Anti-Hussite, and professed his adherence to the great reform and its basic symbols. It took some real courage to do this, as it was a challenge to the Church of Rome and as Korybut could never expect his uncle, King Władysław, to approve of it.

Next the Prince tried to establish personal contact with the leading men of Hussite Bohemia by inviting them to personal meetings. He could make contact easily with the people of the Hussite center who had mainly been responsible for Witold's election and could count on playing a major role under Korybut's regency. Some of them, probably including such men as Hynek Krušina of Lichtenburg, Hynek of Kolstein, and Hašek of Waldstein, joined the Prince at Uničov, and it is natural that they informed him on the political structure of Bohemia in the light of their own convictions. They were, of course, op-

---

sian Order, dated April 25 (*Urk. Beiträge*, I, 190ff.) which is an important source on the situation in that it not only describes precisely Korybut's movements at the time but also the attitudes of Poland, of Sigismund, and even the fight between the Pilsen Landfrieden and Žižka.

16 From here on, the sequence of events till June 11, as told in this book, differs from that which has up to now generally been taken for granted, namely that, before going to Prague, Korybut called the Bohemian estates for a general diet. The reasons why I consider this assumption as mistaken are given later in this chapter, mainly under notes 33 and 39.

17 The report about this, given by the Old Annalists (p. 52), expresses the deep satisfaction that the Prince fulfilled in this way what he had promised before to the Czech ambassadors.

posed to their Romanist peers, but also to Tabor and its ways of waging war. It was under their influence that Korybut now approached the leading figure of the Taborite movement: Žižka.

Soon after his participation in the meeting of the arbitrators which had deprived John Želivský of his power, Žižka had left the capital and in the following weeks had devoted his attention largely to the war against the Landfrieden of Pilsen. The Pilseners tried again to rid themselves of the powerful threat which the Taborite castle of Krasikov presented to their connections with Germany, and again Žižka was determined not to let go of this strategically important position in the rear of his enemies.[18] He asked for help from Prague, but the political disturbances culminating in the execution of Želivský prevented such help from materializing. At one stage the Pilseners thought they had Žižka surrounded and at bay, and looked forward with gusto to the moment when, "as good, pious people, they would burn to death the evil heretic and his helpers."[19] Yet Žižka, far from letting himself be caught, was soon afterwards, on April 12, able to conquer one of the towns of the Landfrieden, Žlutice, as well as some other fortified places.[20] Among the latter was the castle of Gutstein near Teplá. From a letter written soon afterwards by Žižka to the people of Domažlice[21] it appears that the owner of the castle fell in that fight and that his widow put herself under Žižka's protection. The letter is a testimony to the human kindness which Žižka could show toward people whom he did not consider as God's enemies, and especially toward women and children.

Soon afterwards we find Žižka farther south, besieging the town of Horšův Týn, very near the German border, which caused considerable commotion in the Upper Palatinate. On the outcome of this last attempt our sources contradict one another,[22] but it seems that before

[18] Main sources are *The very pretty chronicle*, p. 19 in Novotný's edition (the passage is, as relatively unimportant, left out in the translation in Chapter I of this book), and the letter of the Dean of Liegnitz quoted above in note 18.

[19] ". . . und thuen alz gute vrome lewte und hoffen, sy werden den bozen ketzer Syska und seyn helfer do gewynnen und vorbornen." Thus in the letter quoted above.

[20] According to the Old Annalists (p. 52) Žlutice was conquered by the Praguers, but the more detailed report by *The very pretty chronicle* (*loc.cit.*), which gives us the precise date, as well as the fact that Žlutice is only about a day's march from Gutstein and that we have no other news of a campaign of the Praguers at that date, makes this version seem unlikely.

[21] See Appendix, VI.

[22] *The very pretty chronicle* (*loc.cit.*) says that Žižka conquers Horšův Týn and that "they killed, in storming it, many brave people." (Thus Pekař's remark, III, 171, that Žižka's presence at Horšův Týn is not mentioned in the sources, is a mistake.) There is, on the other hand, a

the end of April Žižka had returned to Tabor and there received his first message from Prince Korybut.

Neither this letter nor Žižka's answer are preserved in their full text,[23] but we know that the Prince asked Žižka to stop "laying waste the land of Bohemia." From a later, somewhat parallel message[24] we can conclude that he presented himself to the addressee as having been "appointed by the most illustrious Prince and Lord, Alexander alias Witold, by the grace of God Grand Duke of Lithuania, postulated King of Bohemia, to defend and liberate the Law of God and to pacify and govern the Land of Bohemia." And from the same indirect source we can infer, with considerable certainty, that he concluded by inviting Žižka to a personal meeting.

Korybut's letter, or at least the reference to Žižka's "laying waste the land of Bohemia," made the old soldier burn with anger. His war against the Pilsen Landfrieden and the Lord of Rosenberg was, in his conviction, a holy war against the enemies of God, a punishment of deadly sinners as commanded by the last of the Four Articles. To refer to this war as if it were a predatory struggle for selfish ends was an insult which he was not going to stand from anyone. Therefore he answered the Prince "as rudely as he possibly could." He gave him "what was on his mind, calling him therefore a damned murderous and incendiary prince."

Korybut, as we can imagine of a prince bred in the atmosphere of the royal court of Poland, "was greatly astonished, but learning that Žižka was a man victorious in fighting, favored by battle luck and invincible in wars, the Prince put up with it. And then the two men met, and they felt friendship for one another, and the Prince called Žižka father, and Žižka called the Prince son."[25]

The naïve and brisk way in which the old chronicle reports the main

---

letter from Nürnberg to Ulm claiming to have heard from Duke John of Bavaria that, after having besieged Horšův Týn, "die Hussen dadannen etwas hinter sich gerukt seyn, und doch noch besammt ligen." See *Urk. Beiträge*, I, 199.

[23] The history of this exchange of messages as well as of the following development in the relationship between Korybut and Žižka is told, with fair precision, by the Old Annalists, *loc.cit.*

[24] Korybut's letter to Ulrich of Rosenberg, written on May 21, 1422, in *Archiv český*, III, 239.

[25] In the Czech original of the Old Annalists Žižka calls the Prince "pane synu" which may be translated "my lord son," though it does not sound nearly as stiffly formal. It does however indicate that Žižka respected, even in so intimate an expression of friendship, the existing difference of rank. This intimacy must have struck contemporaries as rather astonishing, as it is also reported by *The very pretty chronicle* which otherwise, as the reader finds in Chapter I of this book, treats the relationship between Žižka and Korybut in a rather perfunctory way.

events in the early relationship between these two men obviously omits some relevant stages. Korybut must have realized that his purpose of internal pacification could not be served well by a continued feud with the great soldier. He may also have received advice from people less biased against Tabor than Waldstein and his friends, most likely from the two lords of Poděbrady who could indeed give the Prince a more balanced judgment on Žižka's character and policy, on his military genius and his religious ideas. Through a personal mediator such as Victorin of Poděbrady,[26] Korybut seems to have repeated his invitation. And his emissary would have stressed, in talking to Žižka, the step which could not fail to impress the Knight of the Chalice and of which he might not yet have been aware when receiving Korybut's first communication: that in challenge to Rome the Prince had taken the Communion in both kinds.[27] The knowledge of this profession to the Chalice could well induce Žižka to accept Korybut's invitation.

By the beginning of May the Prince had left Uničov,[28] traveling in easy stages westward toward Prague, on a way which would lead him through Vysoké Mýto, Chrudim, Čáslav, and Kutná Hora. Surely he met more people and made more friends as he went along, and at any one of the places mentioned he may have had the friendly encounter with Žižka of which the chronicle tells us.

Korybut now attempted to gain Žižka's active support for his general policy of internal pacification and for a stronger, more effective government. The following development makes it sure that Žižka promised this support, though, as it seems, not without presenting his conditions. First among them would be the vigorous prosecution of the war in defense of the Chalice, that is, against Sigismund and his direct allies. In particular Žižka seems to have demanded a free hand in his fight against Ulrich of Rosenberg. In this case, however, the Prince's answer cannot, or not yet, have been an unqualified yes, as he still hoped to gain the great lord's submission by diplomatic means.

It was most important for Korybut to have gained the good will and the friendship of Žižka in addition to that of the Hussite lords

[26] This convincing hypothesis was first offered by Pekař, III, 162.

[27] This point is rightly stressed by Novotný, *Sborník Žižkův*, p. 131, even though on the basis of the usual, incorrect dating of the diet called by Korybut he speaks in this connection of the Four Articles in general, not only of Article Two which refers to the Chalice.

[28] For Pekař's claim (III, 153) that before the end of April Korybut had entered Bohemia there is no proof in the sources. It is probably based on the assumption that, between Korybut's crossing over to Bohemia and his arrival in Prague on May 16, Korybut called and took part in a general diet.

and knights. Now he could face the crucial task of establishing his position in the capital. The city council, though dominated by the spirit of John Želivský, could hardly dare to refuse entry to the Prince and his army once he could show himself supported not only by most of the lords but also by the great leader of Tabor. Thus when the Prince from Lithuania arrived before the gates of the capital on May 16, they were not closed against him.[29] The Prince's reception by the city councilors was, however, very cool. They feared, so we hear, for the continuance of their office and showed little readiness to acknowledge him as their lord.

On the following day, a Sunday, Korybut rode with his retinue into the New Town.[30] There he experienced a pleasant surprise. Large crowds greeted him with enthusiasm. There is no need to think, for this reason, of those little people as especially fickle. The excitement over the murder of Želivský had died down, and apart from the understandable curiosity that the appearance of the Prince aroused they knew that he took the Communion in the two kinds. Surely he had done so this very morning and thus could be considered a true Christian, obeying the Law of God.

The Prince showed the greatest friendliness and affability toward the people who crowded around him. Soon their enthusiasm grew so that it needed an outlet. They wanted to see their new idol in the full possession of power. Leading his horse by the reins back into the Old Town and to the city hall they demanded that keys and seals be handed over to him. The city councilors, "seeing that the community was very excited," quickly put those symbols of their power at the disposal of the Prince. Korybut accepted their resignation and called new elections for the following day. "And thus did the rule of Šrol and Charvát take its end."[31]

The city council elected on May 18 brought, of course, a victory of the more conservative groups. It began its rule by paying homage to Prince Korybut as regent of the Kingdom. With this act added to the support

[29] The dating of this event is not absolutely certain, as the texts of the Old Annalists (p. 52) differ on the date of the arrival. The most likely version (text L) gives the 16th, a Saturday, as the date, text M the 17th, whereas Bartošek of Drahonice (*Fontes Rerum Bohemicarum*, v) gives (p. 592) an earlier date: "circa festum s. Stanislai," that is, about May 8.

[30] The Old Annalists, *loc.cit.*, say that on the Sunday afterwards he visited the New Town. Tomek (*Dějepis*, iv, 244) concludes that the visit took place on May 24 but it seems unlikely that Korybut should have waited for so long before taking the measures which legalized his role in the capital, and I think that the earlier date which is more generally accepted is the correct one.

[31] Old Annalists, p. 53.

promised to him by most of the Hussite lords as well as by the head of Tabor, Korybut could now feel far enough advanced on the way to universal recognition to address even people whose resistance might be more stubborn. First among them was Ulrich of Rosenberg. Writing him[32] on May 21, three days after his official recognition by Prague, he could, with but little exaggeration, claim to have been "accepted in full accord by the lords of the land, the lords of Prague, the knights, squires, towns, and all communities adhering to the Law of God."[33] He warned the lord that "he should no longer oppose the Law of God as clearly proved by the Holy Scripture, nor impair those truths." Then follows the demand, familiar from Korybut's early letter to Žižka, that the lord should "cease to lay waste the land of our lord and uncle, the Grand Duke." Rosenberg is finally ordered to appear personally or represented by a plenipotentiary, in Prague or wherever the Prince may dwell at the time, on Whitsunday (May 31). If he fails to do so he will be considered a willful and obstinate destroyer of the country and oppressor of the freedom of God's Law, and forceful measures will be taken against him.

Identical or similar letters, it seems, were sent to other Royalist lords such as Čeněk of Wartenberg or John Městecký of Opočno, but in all cases without the desired success. The last named baron was, indeed, the object of a punitive campaign led by Korybut some time later in the year, whereas Rosenberg and his possessions were now left to the increasingly effective punishment which the forces of Tabor inflicted upon their neighbor to the south.[34] The available forces of Prague as well as some of the Polish and Ruthenian troops were meantime committed to another ambitious undertaking: the conquest of the castle of Karlstein, last remaining Royalist stronghold in the region around Prague and perhaps the strongest fortress in all Bohemia.

The Prince himself spent only little time with his troops in the field

[32] *Archiv český*, III, 239.

[33] It is this sentence which caused Palacký to assume that the diet called by Korybut to Čáslav (for the date of which he had no other clue) had already taken place before the Prince reached Prague. This assumption was then accepted, without any further examination, by all later historians. As however the "lords of Prague" did not accept Korybut till May 18, the letter can really not be understood as a reference to an earlier diet but only to the successive acts of recognition of which the homage done by the new city council of Prague was, at that date, the last and most important.

[34] The Taborites never seem to have fully stopped the guerilla fights against the Rosenberg possessions, but these assaults were intensified at the end of May 1422 as testified by the Rosenberg court records, ed. Mareš, p. 47. (See also Tomek, *Žižka*, p. 142.) There is no mention of Žižka himself directing those operations which may indicate that, at least for some time in late May and early June, he was absent from the Tabor region. Very likely it was the time spent in Korybut's entourage.

before Karlstein. The political task of unification demanded his continued presence in Prague. On May 28 the new city council called a town meeting. A decree was read which the council had passed after careful consultation with the Prince.[35] Though legislated by the commune it nevertheless expressly implemented Korybut's policy. It began with the pronouncement of a "year of grace," that is, an amnesty, especially for previous political offenses. "His Highness Prince Sigismund," so it continued, "with the whole community, poor and rich alike, have resolved that all the discords should be ended which have arisen between the brethren because of the death of the Priest John, of honored memory, and of other men who were slain at that time; and that all masters, lords, squires, and townsmen who for that reason and fearing for their lives left the city should return, and that those guilty should submit humbly and apologize to the Prince and the community; and that all thus stand in concord and unity by the Truths of God and help one another; and that they bear not grudges but graciously, like loving brethren, forgive one another."

This appeal is followed by sharp measures intended to prevent the outbreak of troubles not only between the citizens themselves but also between them and the Polish soldiers quartered in the town. In particular all gambling, all duelling, and all sexual excesses were to be punished with heavy penalties, including death, and confiscation of property was threatened to people who refused to take money coined by the Prague mint.[36] Also the community, upon the request of the Prince, "granted and ordered" the release from prison of Zawisza of Garbów, King Władysław's former ambassador to King Sigismund who had been captured at Německý Brod, and finally put the castle on the Hradčany at the disposal of Korybut.

With this decree Korybut made a strong effort to overcome the internal tensions and dissensions in Prague. The amnesty, of course, worked in favor of the conservatives. The masters of the University could now return from Hradec Králové—indeed they were sent for in a hurry as a new synod of all Hussite priests was called to take place

[35] *Archiv český*, I, 213-215.

[36] These short items give us some insight into the economic situation prevailing at the time. The long war had considerably diminished the production as well as the importation of goods, the latter more especially because of the trade embargo which Sigismund had imposed upon Bohemia even though he could never fully enforce it. (See e.g. *Urk. Beiträge*, I, 189, 344.) On the other hand, the coining of money had had to be stepped up, not only in Kutná Hora but also in Prague, and at times even at other places, so as to pay the troops. Often the metal used had not the full standard. Thus an inflation resulted and some of the money not coined at Kutná Hora was considered as under value and its acceptance refused.

in Prague, under the presidency of Archbishop Conrad, as early as May 31. Among the lords who had left the town "in fear" and who now were assured forgiveness was Hašek of Waldstein, and the recall of the "treacherous lord" alienated many of those who had first received Korybut with enthusiasm. That opposition in the New Town quickly began to raise its head is shown by another decree issued only two days later: among other things it threatens punishment for anyone insulting or slandering His Highness Prince Sigismund. The opposition, however, was not yet serious. Korybut had the situation well in hand and was determined to keep it so, "being affable and friendly to the noble ones and those who wanted to live quietly, but to the seditious and criminal ones a very harsh punisher."[37]

Korybut's method of proceeding step by step in his campaign for general support and recognition had worked well. Now was the time to consolidate those gains, to give them the necessary legal form: he had to be solemnly recognized as regent of the Kingdom by a diet of the estates of Bohemia and Moravia. It seems that he valued the force of tradition. It had been in the early days of June 1421 that, at Čáslav, the Hussite Commonwealth of Bohemia and Moravia had achieved the strongest expression of national unity. It was to the same place, to Čáslav, that Korybut now called his first diet, and the date on which it was to convene was the very day on which, a year before, the manifesto of the national assembly had been passed and signed: June 7. Again, as then, the diet was called for both Bohemia and Moravia.[38]

Unfortunately none of the official documents of the diet have been preserved. Up to the present even the date has seemed in doubt. Only from a letter, written by a Moravian town in response to Korybut's invitation, do we know this date and can we reconstruct in part the text of the invitations sent out by the Prince late in May; only from a declaration signed by Žižka and from a much later communication by

[37] Thus Aeneas Sylvius (chapter 44, p. 92), and with the same words Dlugosz (who could know and might have changed the diction if he had not thought it fitting), *Opera omnia*, XIII, 290.

[38] To what extent the Moravian estates took part in the diet is a difficult question to answer. Yet it seems that the participation was far from insignificant. It was indeed strong enough to shock some of the Catholic observers. Thus both Ludolf of Sagan (*Tractatus* . . . , p. 542) and Andrew of Ratisbon (in Leidinger's edition, p. 373) complain bitterly about those Moravians (Ludolf says "aliqui," Andrew "plurimi") who, after swearing off Hussitism to Sigismund at the diet at Brno in November 1421, soon relapsed into heresy ("velut canes ad vomitum redierunt," as Andrew puts it drastically). Those remarks can hardly refer to a much later date as Ludolf's chronicle does not go beyond the late summer of 1422.

Grand Duke Witold do we derive some limited knowledge of what really occurred at the diet.[39]

The invitations asked the prospective participants to appear at the diet or send representatives with full power to act for them, on the Sunday of the Holy Trinity. As his objective the Prince declared that he wanted "with the council of the lords of the land, those of Prague, the knights, squires, towns, and other communities adhering to the Truth and the Law of God to deliberate on the ways how those be

[39] For Palacký and the Czech historians of the nineteenth century the only source which told them about the diet was a phrase in a letter written to the Hussites in March 1423 and published by Palacký in *Urk. Beiträge*, I, 286ff. It says: "Insuper scribitis, quomodo praetactus Dux Sigismundus in Czaslaviensi conventione manifeste promisset omnibus, velle eosdem articulos [the Four Articles of Prague] effectualiter tenere et complere." This, of course, gave no clue at all as to the date of the diet, and Palacký, as mentioned before, took Korybut's letter to Rosenberg as an indication that the diet had already taken place before that letter had been written—which would make the time before Korybut's arrival in Prague the only possible date. The reasons against accepting this early date as correct have been given above in note 33. A notice pointing to a much later date is contained in an Austrian source (the Chronicle of Klosterneuburg, in *Archiv für Kunde österreich. Geschichtsquellen*, 1853, VII, 247) saying that "deselben iars [1422] haben die Hussen herczog Sigmunden aufgeworffen zu einem Khuenik umb s. Catharin tag in der stat Phaesslaech, ain meill von dem Perg" (Berg, short for Kuttenberg, German for Kutná Hora). This date (November 25) is, of course, equally impossible and only indicates that the news of the diet, in a fairly distorted form which mixes up regency and kingship, reached the Austrian chronicler several months after the event. The right date could only be established through the discovery of a letter written by the town of Znojmo in Moravia to Korybut, dated June 2, 1422, and referring to the Prince's invitation for June 7. It was published by Augustin Neumann in his book *Nové prameny k dějinám husitství na Moravě* (New sources to the history of Hussitism in Moravia), Olomouc 1930, p. 55. Neumann made no use of this important find, the significance of which he did not recognize, nor did Pekař who mentioned the letter (*Žižka*, IV). Yet it is this letter which, by giving us the right date and by quoting the terms of Korybut's invitation, makes all other known facts fall into place. Only now does Korybut's policy assume a logical and consistent pattern. The relationship between him and Žižka in particular appears now in a new perspective: Žižka's famous declaration in Korybut's support, given just four days after the beginning of the diet (that is probably signed on the closing day simultaneously with the other resolutions of the diet which unfortunately are not preserved) can now be correctly placed and understood and becomes itself a source for the history of the diet. (See later in the text.) The relevant passages in the letter of Znojmo, a town very near the Austrian border and with a strongly German population, read as follows: "Als uns ewr gnad geschriben und auch an uns begeret hat ettleich auch uns mit vollem gewalt zu ew zuschicken auf den suntag der heiligen drivaltikeit nechst koement, das haben wir wol verstanden . . . (There follows the excuse that the town had done homage first to Sigismund and then to Duke Albert of Austria whom the king had enfeoffed with the town, and that it could not now transfer its loyalty to the prince). . . . Ob wir auf den vorbenannten tag mit vollem gewalt zu ew nicht schickten, so wesset ir wol, daz wir unseren will wollten haben, und daz uns die verderbnusse der land Behem and Merhern laid wer (Neumann's text reads, surely mistakenly, "lieb wer") und daz wir zu dheim geleichen nicht meinten zu treten, und *ir wolt mit rate der lantherren, der von Prag, rittern, knechten, steten und anderen gemainen, die zu der andacht und dem gepot Gots genaigt sind darczu gedenken, daz das understanden und die andacht und das gepot gots nicht undergedrungen wurde.* Lassen wir ew wissen, daz wir *der land zu Behem und Merhern ere und nucz* gern sehen und ist uns zu mal laid, daz die in soelich abnemen und verderben, darinne sy yecz steent, komen sind." The letter ends with the repeated declaration that the town wants to remain true to the old faith. (Italics are mine.)

fully upheld and the Truth and the Law of God be secured against subversion . . . for the honor and the welfare of the countries of Bohemia and Moravia." It is a language familiar to us from the manifesto accepted a year before at Čáslav. And just as on that first great assembly, so now again the Four Articles of Prague served as the assembly's unifying symbol; Prince Sigismund Korybut, as the representative of the "Postulated King," Alexander Witold, promised the members of the diet that he would "hold and effectively fulfill" the articles of the Hussite charter.[40] Thus the Prince took upon himself the solemn obligation which the Hussite ambassadors had always asked for, yet had never received in written and binding form in their long sustained negotiations with Grand Duke Witold.

In return this official gathering now did what Korybut, with clever inaccuracy, had already anticipated in his letter to Ulrich of Rosenberg; they acknowledged and accepted him, pending the arrival and coronation of Grand Duke Witold, as the regent of the Kingdom of Bohemia and the Margravate of Moravia whom they would obey as their lord.[41] Thus for the first time since the death of King Wenceslas IV almost three years before the Kingdom was again under the effective control of a monarchical ruler acknowledged as rightful by the great majority of the nation.

We have said that none of the documents of the diet has survived, but there is one exception. In one of the official journals of the city of Prague we find an entry containing the copy of a declaration signed by Žižka.[42] From its date, June 11, which probably was the concluding day of the diet, as well as from its content there seems little doubt that it was the outcome of discussions held at the diet between Korybut and Žižka. Its language largely reflects Korybut's thought and policy as laid down in the decree published by the community of Prague on May 28: all the stress is laid upon mutual forgiveness and general reconciliation between the two main Hussite parties.[43] But it also re-

40 See Witold's letter quoted at the beginning of note 39.

41 An additional proof for the fact that the official recognition of Korybut as regent did not take place earlier can be derived from the wording of the various pronouncements and decrees of the city government of Prague issued around this time and published in *Archiv český*, I, 213-215, and VI, 406, 408-409. Whereas up to the end of May these pronouncements call the Prince only His Highness Prince Sigismund, he is later, that is, after the diet, called fairly regularly "zprávce království českého a markrabství moravského" (regent of the Bohemian Kingdom and the Moravian Margravate).

42 See Appendix, VII.

43 This fact is strongly stressed by Pekař in his elaborate commentary to Žižka's declaration (III, 158-163). It is actually overstressed. According to him the Prince has induced Žižka to sign a declaration set up by the princely chancery which is essentially foreign to Žižka's basic attitude and policy.

flects the main events which had taken place in the course of the diet: the acknowledgment of Korybut as the country's regent, and a resolution obviously accepted by all members of the diet, very similar to one of the resolutions of the first Čáslav diet,[44] saying that the assembled representatives of the estates of the Kingdom would punish severely all attempts at uprising or the renewal of internal fights. Žižka's message lists all those whom he promised to support in those measures of national discipline: His Highness the Prince, the lords councilors (of Prague), the lords, knights, squires, and all communities of the faithful (i.e. those adhering to the Law of God), in other words the estates as represented at the diet. It is worth noticing that in his list the representatives of Prague kept their place before the barons of the realm just as in the official documents of the earlier diet of Čáslav.

Žižka's declaration lists the towns which, with him, recognized the Prince as Bohemia's regent. It includes all the important Taborite places in two groups: the royal towns first, the subject towns afterwards. But only two of the Taborite captains besides Žižka are mentioned: Chval of Machovice and Zbyněk of Buchov. This fact does not necessarily show a split in the rank of the Taborite leaders: it only indicates that those three men represented the Taborite brotherhood at the diet of June 1422. Roháč of Dubá, who had been the fourth Taborite representative a year before, may have been too involved, as commander of Lomnice, in the continuing fight against Ulrich of Rosenberg to leave his post. But there was at least one man whose absence in Žižka's declaration of loyalty can hardly have been incidental: Bohuslav of Švamberg, in social rank most prominent among the military leaders of the brotherhood. Korybut would hardly have omitted to invite him personally. By his nonattendance he demonstrated against the Prince and his policy of national reconciliation.[45] We do, indeed, find him soon afterwards as the protagonist of that radical Hussite group to whom any thought of compromise was unbearable.

It was, of course, just the existence of this radical group which explains the need for Žižka's declaration. Otherwise it should have been enough for Žižka and his friends just to sign the general agreements arrived at by the diet. But Korybut, so it seems, felt the need for a spe-

[44] It is the passage saying that those not adhering to the agreements of the diet and the Four Articles shall be regarded and treated as enemies by all signatories.

[45] Palacký has already (III, 2,304) pointed out that Švamberg's absence, to which he associates that of Hvězda, must have had political significance. The same conclusions were drawn by later historians (e.g. Tomek, *Žižka*, p. 149) whereas Pekař (III, 160) sees no symptoms for any split within the Taborite movement at this time.

cial action with regard to those Hussite elements which were least willing to follow him, people who still suspected that the Prince, under orders from his uncles, intended to lead Bohemia back to the Catholic fold. If they could not be placated by the Prince's solemn acceptance of the Four Articles, then perhaps a strong word from the greatest military leader of the revolution would achieve this end.

Thus there is no doubt that the initiative for this step was taken by Korybut, and that Žižka complied with his wish. He could do so as he fully agreed with the immediate goal of Korybut's policy: the establishment of a strong, united front of all Hussite Czechs without difference of rank or station against all who did not adhere to the Truth of God. Žižka had shown more than once that this was his policy: in supporting the Polish-Lithuanian candidacy from the beginning; in trying to mediate the internal conflicts of Prague in the winter of 1420-1421; in supporting the principles and the government established at the first diet of Čáslav; in participating in the arbitration action of February 1422. Now again he was found ready to support a move toward national unification, especially after Korybut had solemnly obliged himself to fulfill and protect the Four Articles. In this spirit Žižka now "accepted His Highness the Prince as our helper and as the supreme regent of this land," and declared that he would "gladly obey his Highness, support him and give him our counsel in all rightful things faithfully, so help us God." Though accepting many of the expressions used by the Prince himself in the admonitions toward a policy of internal peace and mutual forgiveness, the declaration nevertheless shows the self-confidence and dignity of a man conscious of his own great role in the life of the nation. And, indeed, only in this way could the declaration be of real use to Korybut. Only thus could the former adherents of John Želivský in Prague be expected to listen to it and be impressed by it.

Žižka's declaration of loyalty contains, however, one remarkable omission: in accepting Korybut as regent, the Taborite leader does not mention with one word the sovereign in whose name Korybut was to rule: Grand Duke Witold. Was this an incident without any meaning?[46] It seems unlikely. In the later official references to Korybut's role, such as the documents of Prague, Witold's name as that of the "Postulated King" is nearly always inserted. Žižka was meticulous in his observance

[46] This is Pekař's theory (III, 159). But already Goll (*Čechy a Prusy*, p. 170) had pointed out the strangeness of this failure to mention Witold, and Novotný (*Žižkův Sborník*, p. 131) used this fact to corroborate his previous statements on Žižka's opposition to Witold.

of formalities, and Korybut himself might well have asked for the declaration to include the name of his uncle. It would seem that Žižka, though by now he trusted Korybut, was not quite ready to extend this trust to Witold whom, with Władysław, he held responsible for the recent negotiations with Sigismund. Korybut may have felt that it was better to obtain from Žižka a declaration of support limited to his person than to receive none at all. But perhaps he was quite satisfied with a success which was due to his personal policy rather than to his position as Witold's viceroy. He may well have doubted, by this time, whether the old Grand Duke would ever set foot on Bohemian soil, and his hope of eventually gaining the crown of Bohemia may have been swelled on the day when the estates of Bohemia and Moravia did homage to him, Sigismund Korybut.

There is no certain knowledge about Žižka's moves after the diet of June 1422. Not till late in July can we locate him with some certainty: engaged again in the old, grim war against Ulrich of Rosenberg. That war had not stopped during the time of the diet, and it seems likely that at its end Žižka immediately returned to the region of Tabor to take over again the direction of this perennial fight.[47] Korybut, too, left Čáslav to devote his attention to a military task: the siege of the Karlstein. This looks like a reasonable division of labor, each of the two great military powers of Bohemia concentrating against the enemy that was nearest and whose conquest seemed within the power of each partner. This, indeed, must have been the original understanding. Korybut supervised the organization of the siege, though he never seems to have spent more than a few consecutive days in the camp before the fortress, feeling that political tasks still forced him to spend much of his time in the capital. After some weeks it became clear that the siege, though undertaken with considerable forces and supported by four of the heaviest siege guns then available, made little headway, owing not only to the strength of the castle but also to the spirited defense put up by its garrison under the able burgrave Tluksa of Buřenice.[48] In this situation the Prince might well have asked for help from the forces of Tabor and from Žižka whose experience in the conquest of fortresses would have been most valuable. But it seems that

[47] See the entries in the Rosenberg court books, ed. Mareš, *op.cit.*, pp. 47ff., and Březan's reports in *Časopis musea českého*, 1828, IV, 57.

[48] On the men engaged in this defense see Tomek, *Dějepis*, IV, 250; on the technical side of the siege Toman, *Husitské válečnictví*, pp. 302ff.

Korybut never made such a request, presumably because he did not want to become too dependent, militarily, on the power of Tabor.[49]

How much Korybut was still in need of that support from the left which Žižka's proclamation was meant to give him soon became apparent in Prague. Opposition against his government grew as soon as the honeymoon of the early days of princely rule were over. The masses, especially in the New Town, came to realize that the restoration of the monarchy tended to deprive them of their unusual and historically premature freedom. Their increasingly loud grumbling and agitating caused Korybut and the city council to pass new restrictive measures. Meetings not officially licensed or held in secret were forbidden. Landlords and hostelries were made responsible for those sheltered by them. The guilds had to oblige themselves to observe and protect the order and quiet in the town, and four masters in each guild were nominated to supervise the members and be responsible for their behavior.[50]

The Prince took other measures to strengthen his hold, economically as well as politically. The mint of Prague was put at his disposal. And the more important mint of Kutná Hora, administered by appointees of Prague since the death of Lord Vavák of Hradec, was also taken over by the regent. He gave the lucrative, but also politically important position of mint master to Lord Hašek of Waldstein. Other sources of economic strength were the confiscated clerical holdings all over the country, most of which Prague had administered since the original owners had been driven out. The man now to take over their administration was the newly appointed royal subchamberlain: William Kostka of Postupice. Kostka had served with the embassy which the diet of Kutná Hora had sent to Witold in September 1421. He was thus one of the men captured by the Duke of Ratibor and extradited to Sigismund. Whereas all the retainers of that embassy had been killed on Sigismund's orders, Kostka as well as the other noblemen were now exchanged against some noble prisoners in the hands of Prague, among them Lord Hynek Červenohorský who had been captured by the Praguers at Jaroměř. Kostka was given considerable landed property as compensation for his sufferings in captivity. He became one of Korybut's most influential supporters and advisers.

When Korybut entered into the position of the sovereign it was but logical that the royal prerogative of supervising the cities should revert

[49] Pekař (III, 164), though not claiming that Žižka directly refused any help in the siege, nevertheless takes Tabor's nonparticipation in the siege as a proof for his contention that Žižka's declaration on June 11 does not express his real policy toward Korybut.

[50] See Tomek, *Dějepis*, IV, 255.

to him, and accordingly the various captain governors of those towns, all of them appointed by Prague, now did homage to the Prince Regent. But this increase of power for the Regent spelled a corresponding loss of power for the capital and, in the last instance, for the burgher class of Prague. Even though, immediately after the change of the city government, two councilors and two other citizens of Prague were appointed as members of Korybut's council of advisers, the influence of the higher nobility, largely restricted in the time of Prague's hegemony, was now again much more in evidence. John Želivský's apprehensions thus were partly vindicated.

Not all royal towns could so smoothly be taken over by Korybut's administration. Some of them, though adhering to the Hussite cause, had never submitted to Prague. There were, in the first place, the former royal towns now belonging to the Taborite brotherhood, which claimed the rights of an autonomous federation. A similar autonomy had been enjoyed by the city of Žatec. It had managed to keep, throughout these years, in most friendly relations with Prague and Tabor alike, and its glorious defense during the Second Crusade had given it a high standing among Hussite cities. Korybut does not seem to have felt any need to reinforce his authority there.

But things were different in the case of another autonomous city: the Orebite center of Hradec Králové. At the time when he entered Bohemia, Korybut was as little welcome to Ambrose and the city council which he dominated as to Želivský's party then ruling in Prague. Early in August Korybut decided to reduce Hradec Králové to the same status which by then obtained in most other royal towns. He went there at the head of some troops and demanded admission. There was no resistance. The Prince had the city councilors arrested and taken to the neighboring castle of Třebechovice, to be replaced, as before in Prague, by people more in agreement with the new state of things.[51] The combined office of captain and burgrave was given to Diviš Bořek of Miletínek, one of the leading noblemen of the Orebite camp. Diviš had played a prominent role in the revolution from the beginning, had helped Hynek Krušina of Lichtenburg in leading the first contingent of the Orebite soldiers to Prague, had taken part in the battle of the Vyšehrad and had fought, in close cooperation with Žižka, in the later phases of the great spring campaign of 1421. Since then he had served as Prague's captain-governor at Chrudim. He and Ambrose had until now been friends, but it seems that Diviš's appoint-

[51] See Old Annalists, p. 53. The time is shortly before August 10, the date of the attack upon Opočno.

ment resulted in marring this relationship. The conjecture of a modern historian that Ambrose complained about the whole procedure to his friend Žižka[52] seems well within the realm of possibilities.

At the time, this episode seemed of only limited interest. From Hradec Králové Korybut went on to the castle of Opočno, residence of Lord John Městecký, surely one of the worst enemies of the Hussite cause, but the assault against his castle failed, and Korybut soon gave up and returned to the more important siege of Karlstein.

The real significance of this campaign lay in the tensions it created within the Orebite camp. They had grave implications for a later phase of the revolution and of Žižka's life. Indeed the question arises whether, right then, Korybut's action at Hradec Králové did not throw a shadow upon the relations between Žižka's Tabor and Korybut's national government. Žižka had long been deeply interested in the Orebite movement, which seemed especially close to his own religious ideas. He was equally interested in the geographic region where it flourished and where, among the clergy and nobility, he had found some of his most devoted followers. For Tabor the enforced change at Hradec Králové could, indeed, have an ominous meaning. If Korybut had not respected the autonomy which the town in the east had been able to preserve for almost three years, would he not be tempted, as soon as he felt strong enough, equally to reduce the autonomous positions of the royal towns adhering to the Taborite brotherhood? Was the personal friendship and cooperation between Korybut and Žižka breaking down, less than four months after they had met and demonstrated their friendship, barely two months after Žižka's declaration of loyalty?

As far as Žižka is concerned the answer emerges from his subsequent actions. We know, first of all, something about his personal relationship to the new burgrave of Hradec Králové. There is, for a long time, no trace of a friction between Diviš Bořek of Miletínek and Žižka—on the contrary we find the Orebite nobleman, some months later, supporting Žižka in a fight in which other Hussite groups stood aloof, if not yet against him. But we have a more precise evidence against the theory[53] of an early break between Žižka and Korybut. Several weeks after the seizure of Hradec Králové the two men undertook a common political action. Both (and, as we hear, "many other," obviously Bohemian noblemen) simultaneously wrote letters to the Margraves of Meissen who, in support of a new crusade, were about to invade Bohemia. These

[52] Pekař, III, 175.

[53] As presented by Pekař, *loc.cit.*

letters threatened the German princes with severe countermeasures in case they renewed their injurious activity on Bohemian soil. Though clearly writing upon Korybut's suggestion, Žižka in his letter (of which, unfortunately, only a few fragmentary lines have been preserved) indulged in his own vigorous style, using terms like "obstinate heretics" and "lawless, blood-thirsty murderers."

Our only witness, the learned Abbot Ludolf of Sagan,[54] was deeply shocked at this disrespectful or, as he calls it, "contumelious way of addressing those magnificent, illustrious and venerable princes because they, fighting for the true faith, wanted to destroy, in a most just war, those Hussites, Taborites, and Wyclefites and thus to consecrate their hands in the blood of those heretics." In expressing his annoyance that the prospective victims dared insult their prospective butchers, the old abbot has given us an unusually fine example of that self-righteousness of which, not without justification, he himself accused Žižka. In any case his report helps us to understand Žižka's relationship to Korybut in the late summer or early fall of 1422.

In this letter Žižka still called himself captain of the people of Tabor. But for all we know it may have been the last time that he used this title. And when we conclude from his writing that as late as September 1422 Žižka felt still bound by his declaration of loyalty to Korybut, the same cannot be said of the whole of Tabor. On the contrary, right then forces were at work in the Taborite community which planned to overthrow the princely government at Prague. Indeed we shall soon find that Žižka was about to lose his firm hold on parts of the fraternity of Tabor, and his continued loyalty to the Prince Regent may have been one of the reasons. This development was surely ominous, all the more as it came to a head at the very time when, as the letters to Meissen show, the enemies were again preparing to storm the ramparts of Hussite Bohemia. It was fortunate that their strength, this time, was less threatening than their intentions.

[54] *Tractatus de longevo schismate*, pp. 532-534. This source, however, presents us with a problem. According to a report of a Breslau prelate visiting Sagan, the Abbot Ludolf had died as early as August 22, 1422. (See Loserth's introduction in *Arch. für öster. Geschichte*, vol. 60, p. 370). There is no proper chronological order in the later chapters of his "tractate," Korybut being referred to as early as chapter 61 and then again under 83, but it seems impossible that all the facts referred to after chapter 61 should have occurred before the date mentioned above. In particular the concluding report on Korybut's defeat before the Karlstein, though containing mistakes, clearly points to the events which occurred on October 22, two months after the supposed date of Ludolf's death. It seems quite possible that this date is wrong, and equally possible that the one existing copy (found by Palacký in the Library of St. Mark at Venice), a rather corrupt manuscript dating from 1466, contains a text which had already been tampered with and added to by the monks of Sagan or other copyists after the abbot's death. On Ludolf as a source for the Taborite movement, see also Pekař, I, 63-70.

## CHAPTER 21

# A PERIOD OF DISAPPOINTMENTS

THE political consolidation which Bohemia reached under Korybut's leadership in the spring and summer of 1422 was bound to have a notable impact upon the general situation in central Europe. What had been, only a couple of years before, a fanatical but loosely coordinated rebel movement had now grown into a well organized ruling party, headed by a widely recognized central authority, and the close alliance, if not yet personal union, with the greatest power of eastern Europe made it appear unassailable.

For Sigismund and the princes of the Empire this turn of events was upsetting to the highest degree. Sigismund knew, of course, that Witold had kept the Holy See informed about his intentions, and understood well enough the political motives behind the policy of the Grand Duke. He bitterly complained to the Pope,[1] especially about the papal legate in Poland, Zeno, who had encouraged Witold's Bohemian policy and had generally worked for the revision of the Breslau Award.[2] Sigismund also pointed out that Korybut's attempt to reconcile the "rebels" with the Church was only a pretense meant to deprive him of his Bohemian heritage. On May 21 Martin V answered Sigismund,[3] energetically denying that he had advised or permitted Witold to give his protection to the heretics. On the same day he wrote to both Władysław and Witold, demanding they should stop giving any support to Hussite Bohemia.[4]

The papal action would, in due course, have its influence, especially on Władysław, who was far from happy about Korybut's religious policy in Bohemia. But its immediate effect was blunted by Sigismund himself. For he was, eventually, successful in his repeated attempt to goad the Prussian Order into war against Poland. It began on July 14.[5]

[1] See the correspondence in *Urk. Beiträge*, I, 199ff.

[2] *ibid.*, I, 211, 214.

[3] *ibid.*, I, 212.

[4] See Caro, *Liber cancellarii Stanislai Ciolek, Archiv für österreichische Geschichte*, LII, 179-182.

[5] See Goll, *Čechy a Prusy*, pp. 167, 172.

If Sigismund had hoped that in this way he could punish his Polish-Lithuanian enemies or at least put strong pressure on them, he overrated the military strength of the Knights. A short summer campaign proved to the Order how hopeless was their resistance against the combined Polish-Lithuanian power. Promises of help given to them by Sigismund and the princes of the Empire came too late.

The Peace of Lake Mielno,[6] signed on September 27, treated the Order leniently, leaving it with the Province of Pomorze which still barred Poland's exit to the Baltic Sea. Yet the victors got what they considered their immediate goal. The Prussian Order agreed (not without mental reservations) to the complete annulment of the Breslau Award. Some border districts were ceded to Poland and, more important, Lithuania was to have and retain Samogitia for all time. One of Witold's long cherished dreams was fulfilled, if this agreement could be made to last.

How would Sigismund take this blow? The King had, on July 30, joined the German princes at the Reichstag of Nürnberg. It was supposed to organize and finance a Third Crusade against Bohemia. On receiving the news of the Prussian defeat some of the princes were inclined to leave Bohemia alone and concentrate all forces against Poland.[7] Sigismund might not have objected to such a policy. But there were men at Nürnberg influential enough to prevent this move which indeed might have cemented rather than shaken the union between Poland-Lithuania and Hussite Bohemia. Foremost among them was the Elector of Brandenburg, Frederick I. Though he could not directly help his Polish allies he was not willing to see his policy of friendship with the Polish court destroyed by an imperial war against Władysław. He was strongly supported by the papal legate, Cardinal Branda, who never ceased urging the assembly to concentrate all efforts against the Bohemian menace. Thus all that happened in regard to Poland was a message of friendly admonition sent by the German Electors to King Władysław,[8] explaining to him how meritorious it would be if, instead of attacking the Christian Knights of the Teutonic Order, he would join in the effort to suppress the Bohemian heresy which the presence of his nephew in Bohemia did so much to encourage.

The Reichstag's session proved disappointing for the advocates of a strong Third Crusade. The plan to raise a universal imperial tax of one

[6] For the text see *Codex Diplomaticus Lithuaniae*, ed. Raczyński, Breslau 1845, pp. 285-292.
[7] *Deutsche Reichstagsakten*, Munich 1867ff., VIII, 151.
[8] *Codex Diplomaticus Lithuaniae*, pp. 292-295.

per cent with which to pay a huge number of professional soldiers fell through owing to the opposition of the imperial cities. They were unwilling thus to lay their wealth open to public scrutiny. Instead the diet fell back on the way of charging every unit of the Empire, princes as cities, with duties to provide a certain number of horse and infantry, basing these levies on the so-called Imperial Matrix. Very soon, however, it became clear that each was eager to keep his obligations as low as possible. Besides mobilizing for the crusade the Reichstag resolved to put up smaller forces for a long period, for the so-called "daily war" which should harrow the Hussites permanently and help their enemies inside Bohemia.[9]

On September 4, in Nürnberg's Sebaldus Church, Cardinal Branda solemnly handed the banner blessed by the Pope to King Sigismund. Sigismund appointed Frederick, the Elector of Brandenburg, as supreme commander of the imperial forces.[10] Ostensibly this was a high honor, but Sigismund did not really expect Frederick to do well against the terrible Bohemians. He would have been happy to see the Elector compromised in the eyes of the Germans. Frederick, on the other hand, could not well refuse to accept the dubious honor without laying himself open to the reproach of aiding the heretics.

The Elector of Brandenburg decided to make the best of an unpromising task. On the day of St. Michael, September 29, the troops from the west were instructed to meet near the Franconian border town of Tirschenreuth before crossing over into Bohemia. At the same time a Misnian force including over 4,000 men had assembled north of the Erzgebirge, ready for the invasion but expecting reinforcements from Silesia and Lusatia, many of which never arrived.[11] In the further development the army from Meissen, organized mainly by Margrave William, turned out to be the strongest single force sent by any one of the German princes. It was probably just for this reason that the Margraves of Meissen were singled out by Korybut, Žižka, and other Hussite leaders for the angry challenge discussed in the previous chapter.

Those letters seemed to indicate a vigorous closing of Hussite ranks. Yet at this very moment national unity was split by a militant partisan action which brought the Hussite community to the brink of civil war. This action tried to re-establish, by a surprise coup, a government of

9 *Deutsche Reichstagsakten*, VIII, 156, and Palacký, *Urk. Beiträge*, I, 232ff.

10 *Urk. Beiträge*, I, 236.

11 See the letters of Margrave William of Meissen to Frederick of Brandenburg, *ibid.*, I, 239ff., and especially 244.

the radicals in Prague, and its authors and leaders were Lord Bohuslav of Švamberg and a man who had only recently become one of Tabor's captains: John Hvězda of Vícemilice.[12] They had established secret contact with some of Hvězda's friends among the Želivist party in the New Town. On September 30 the two men, at the head of a Taborite troop ("secretly assembled," as our chronicler emphasizes) approached the capital, knowing that Prince Korybut was at the time in the camp before Karlstein. When they reached Krč, a village only a few miles to the south, William Kostka, together with Prague's new captain Wenceslas Carda of Petrovice,[13] met them at the head of some troops and asked about the purpose of this whole undertaking. They answered that they had been invited to come. Kostka, who behaved all through this critical phase with great circumspection, thought it unwise at this stage to stop them by force. He even saw to it that the Taborites, when they had arrived in the New Town, were given food and fodder.

On the following day the Taborite leaders went to the city hall of the Old Town and demanded that a general town meeting be called. The councilors declined, but offered to pass on to the community any message the Taborite leaders might have. These however declared: "If you do not call the community, we shall call them ourselves." Švamberg and Hvězda then arranged a march of their troops through the main streets, hoping that they would thus encourage large masses of people to rally to them. The success of this parade was modest. The Taborites occupied several houses, but before they could establish themselves in a strong enough position some Prague and Polish troops under Carda's command systematically closed up the main thoroughfares of the Old Town and slowly pushed the Taborites back into the New Town. Some Taborite soldiers were captured, the bulk of the invaders however rallied on the large horse market, later called Wenceslas Square. The outbreak of large scale fighting was prevented in the last moment when William Kostka, reminding Bohuslav of Švamberg of their old personal friendship, obtained the Taborite leader's agreement to an armistice for the rest of the day.

So far everything had gone wrong with the ill-advised expedition, and the two leaders decided to cut their losses and quit the attempt. They left the city before sunset, "very shamefully" as the chronicler

[12] Most of our knowledge on the attempted coup of St. Michael's 1422 stems from a long and rather precise account in some early texts of the Old Annalists (pp. 54-56). See also Tomek, *Dějepis*, IV, 254-258.

[13] Carda seems to have been appointed captain general of Prague by Korybut. He played an important role especially in later years (e.g. 1428). See Tomek, *Dějepis*, IV, 156, 403ff.

adds. A number of Prague citizens who had been in secret agreement with them also left as they feared the retribution which was sure to come.

It did come promptly. Prince Korybut hurried from the encampment before the Karlstein[14] to Prague where he arrived on the day after the Taborite retreat. At a town meeting called right upon his arrival new measures were passed to prevent any recurrence of the event.[15] They mainly concerned ways in which to effect a fast mobilization of the militia whenever, as a sign of imminent danger, the bells of the two city halls should ring alarm. The previous ban on secret meetings was renewed, the property of all who had left with the Taborites confiscated. Distrust against the Želivist elements in the New Town is expressed in an order to repair and maintain the old wall, long considered obsolete, which separated the two sister-towns. Finally strict punishment threatened anyone teaching heretical views on the Holy Eucharist, a measure which showed to what extent Taboritism and Želivism in Prague was still—or again—identified with Pikhartism.

This Želivist movement, even though its participation had disappointed the Taborite leaders, was indeed far from dead, and it seems that the new suppressive measures, as sometimes before, served to revive rather than to destroy it. When, some days later, another town meeting was called, a crowd of people opened the gates of the prison next to the Old Town City Hall and liberated the Taborites who had been taken prisoner on the day of the coup. This rebellious act so infuriated Prince Korybut that he ordered all those caught taking part in it to be beheaded.[16] The city councilors tried in vain to intervene after the executions had gone on for some time. Only when Kostka, again evincing his good judgment and sense of moderation, showed his anger toward the Prince Regent in no uncertain terms, did Korybut order the slaughter to be stopped.[17]

The attempted coup of St. Michael's Day hurt the Hussite cause badly. We cannot be sure whether Bohuslav of Švamberg or Hvězda of Vícemilice was primarily responsible for it. Hvězda's motives are easy to understand. He still resented the way in which, just half a year earlier,

[14] The Old Annalists (*loc.cit.*) say that because Korybut left the camp at the Karlstein at this moment the fortress remained unconquered. Actually the siege continued, but it is likely, of course, that the coup, by leading Korybut to weaken the besieging forces, strengthened the determination of the defenders to hold out.

[15] See *Archiv český*, I, 216.

[16] Old Annalists, p. 55.

[17] *ibid.*, p. 56.

he had been dismissed by the Praguers from his position as captain general[18] and he trusted that he had still a strong enough following in the capital to make the venture worth trying. Švamberg, on the other hand, would hardly have staked his reputation on this undertaking if he had not really wished for the overthrow of Korybut's government.

The consequences, of course, were the opposite of what the Taborite leaders had hoped. Instead of strengthening the more radical element in Prague the attempted coup actually weakened its chances, at least in the Old Town. The general feeling between the ruling circles of Prague and the sectarian communities in the country was poisoned to the extent that the old chronicler, at the end of his account, could say without much exaggeration: "And from this time the Praguers and the Taborites began fighting one another."[19]

There remains a great question mark. What about Žižka? Was he absent from Tabor? Was he there but ignorant of the secret preparations? Did he know of them but was unable to interfere? Or was he, after all, in agreement with its authors?

The last conjecture can definitely be excluded. The action taken by Korybut and Žižka in sending their letters of challenge to the Margraves of Meissen can only have taken place, measuring in days, not in weeks, a very short time before the attempted coup of September 30, as only then the news of the Misnian preparations can have reached the Hussites. Žižka could not well cooperate with the Prince Regent in a matter of national importance and simultaneously support an enterprise directed against Korybut's national leadership. There is, indeed, a much later report which tells us that Žižka wrote a letter of apology to the Praguers, strongly disapproving of the coup of his two junior captains, and that the city council, in an answer, expressed their gratification about the content of this message.[20]

Korybut and his political friends in Prague may have found some comfort in Žižka's personal disapproval, but this could not repair the damage done. The situation was tense enough, with German troops

[18] Pekař assumes (III, 148) that after the execution of Želivský and the ensuing overthrow of the city council, Hvězda again took the place of Hašek of Waldstein as captain general of Prague. He would then have lost his position for a second time with the appointment of Carda by Korybut. This would, of course, provide an even stronger motive for his action in September.

[19] Old Annalists, *loc.cit.*

[20] Theobald, *Hussiten Krieg*, p. 301. This report is probably based on older sources, since lost. It also says that Žižka refused to recognize Korybut "as King." This might just express his determination not to relinquish Tabor's autonomous status.

ready to strike from Meissen and Franconia while the Karlstein was still unconquered.[21] Korybut could not feel sure that the military effort of the crusaders, after the solemn proceedings of Nürnberg, would remain so far below that of previous years. He felt compelled to draw on some of the troops engaged in besieging the Karlstein. Consequently this army shrank to rather small dimensions.

It was from the north, from Meissen, that the danger threatened first and strongest. On October 7 Margrave William crossed the mountains with his troops,[22] operating first from the region of Most against Chomútov. This town he conquered without meeting much resistance. A few days later Frederick himself began to move his troops, containing mainly his own contingents from Brandenburg and those of the Bishops of Würzburg and Bamberg, from Tirschenreuth across the border to Tachov. There he joined up with forces dispatched by the Pilsen Landfrieden and the town of Cheb (Eger). He expected to be further reinforced by troops from the German cities, some of which had reached Cheb in small numbers, and by the armies of the electors of the Palatinate and of Cologne. These had been sent—too late to be of any use—to Prussia to help the Order against Poland and were now supposed to take part in the Crusade. All those troops were to join up with the Misnian, Silesian, and Lusatian forces in the region of Rakovník, some twenty-five miles south of Louny, from where they were to move first to relieve the besieged Karlstein. In these hopeful terms Frederick sent a message of encouragement on October 15 to the captains of the Karlstein's garrison.[23]

In reality things looked far less promising for the crusaders. The rich surviving correspondence[24] between the generalissimo and the many princes, spiritual and temporal, who were expected to follow his banner, shows little of the crusading spirit. Frederick, in his letters, desperately tries to hold them to their duty, to goad them into fulfilling their obligations, to bolster their morale. They, on the other hand, keep accusing each other and third parties for the lack of cooperation, for the lack of manpower, of arms, of horses, of money. Among the ecclesias-

21 The account of the Third Crusade given in the following pages leaves out many details which are known but in terms of the general development seem rather insignificant. The Third Crusade is probably the best documented of all the great campaigns against Hussite Bohemia, especially from the German side. Accordingly it has also been treated in great detail by modern historians. See e.g. the excellent account given by Bezold, *K. Sigmund*, . . . who devoted 40 pages (I, 90-130) to this event including its preparatory stages.

22 *Urk. Beiträge*, I, 244.

23 *ibid.*, I, 251.

24 It contains twenty-seven letters, beginning at the end of September and going through November. See *Urk. Beiträge*, I, 238-256, 260-267, and II, 499ff.

tical lords John, Bishop of Würzburg, had put the strongest contingent in the field—he himself lists 600 battle horses and 500 draft horses—but he was reluctant from the beginning to commit himself to what he considered an entirely inauspicious campaign. He advises the generalissimo to give up in time rather than expend his efforts senselessly.[25] The shadow of the inglorious crusades of 1420 and 1421 was not so easily dispelled. The Bishop's letter shows, furthermore, that King Sigismund himself had done little to support this enterprise. He had accepted offers from several imperial cities to substitute money payments to him personally for the levies imposed upon them by the Reichstag, although he said himself that the imperial army was not strong enough for its task.

No wonder that this general mood led to defections all along the line. Duke Henry Rampold of Glogau who had assembled and was supposed to command the Silesian forces for which Frederick and the Misnians were waiting released his troops even before they had crossed the border,[26] and when Korybut with Czech and Polish troops marched to Louny the Misnians retreated and were about to abandon their task altogether. Frederick hurried to Most, met Duke William and persuaded him to stick it through a little longer and to reenter the campaign fully if the Lusatians and Silesians could be induced to do likewise. With this hope—which again was never fulfilled—Frederick went to rejoin his forces in the west, but before he could reach Tachov the Bishops of Würzburg and Bamberg whose forces comprised a considerable part of the crusading army had left with their troops, and this encouraged the captains of Cheb to ask for permission to go home as well. Frederick refused, he still did not want to give up. There should be no shadow of a doubt in the minds of the German princes that he was resolved to see the matter through.

The relief of the Karlstein had figured in the original plans of the campaign. Now, with his forces so badly depleted, it became the one and only goal for Frederick. He hoped, in this endeavor, for considerable support from the Pilsen Landfrieden. The chances for success seemed to improve by a turn of fortune at this particular theater of war. On October 22 the combined Czech-Polish forces, though reduced in strength since Korybut had left for northern Bohemia, attempted a general assault. Four times on that day the besiegers stormed, only to be thrown back every time with heavy losses. Later that day the garri-

[25] *ibid.*, pp. 240, 241.

[26] *ibid.*, p. 256.

son answered with a sortie in force, hitting the exhausted besiegers hard and killing many of them.

These events marked the end of any hope to conquer the mighty fortress. Especially the Polish soldiers grew restless and demanded to be relieved. Inside the fortress, on the other hand, optimism grew. A messenger who got through to Tachov told Elector Frederick on October 25, two days after the latter's return from Most, that if he could only help them with a troop of 400 horse, they would finish off the besiegers.[27] Frederick's first reaction was to order the Royalist lords of the Landfrieden to send the required forces, but as he could get no fast action he decided to lead the relief army himself. Before he had gone far he was overtaken by a messenger informing him of a Hussite offer of armistice talks to be held at Kadaň. He returned to Tachov and after some discussions with his Bohemian advisers resolved to accept the invitation. He left Lord Henry of Plauen in charge of all troops remaining at Tachov, amounting at this time to about 3,500 horse and some infantry, with the order to dispatch, as soon as possible the expedition for the relief of the Karlstein.

The peace move which thus interrupted Frederick's offensive had started about a week before the elector was informed about it, and the initiative had been taken by Korybut himself. The Prince Regent had, as mentioned earlier, led a combined Czech-Polish army northward to meet the threat from Meissen, and his appearance at Louny had been sufficient to deter the Misnians from all further adventures. Indeed the whole military situation began, by October 20, to look much more favorable for Hussite Bohemia, owing to the defections in the German ranks and the reluctance of the remaining German leaders to get involved in any serious fighting. From the military point of view Korybut would have had the choice of returning to the Karlstein—in which case the defeat of October 22 might never have occurred—or of directly attacking the crusaders in the region of Tachov. His forces can hardly have been inferior to Frederick's shrunken army, even supposing that such an offensive in the west would have stirred the Pilsen Landfrieden to stronger efforts.

Why, then, did Korybut neglect both possibilities and instead try his hand in a diplomatic *démarche* for peace? The official proposal made by

[27] A main source for the following development (including the story of the armistice negotiations) is a long report written by Frederick of Brandenburg to the Dukes John and Otto of Bavaria, published first by Bezold (*K. Sigmund*, I, 150ff.). See also *Urk. Beiträge*, II, 499ff.

the Czechs—it was submitted to the retreating Misnians, probably because they were the nearest—suggested a long truce which would make it possible to arrange for a public hearing, that old Hussite demand which had never been given up even after the failure of the disputation held amidst the ruins of the Small Side in July 1420. This offer was meant seriously, even though, after the failure of the negotiations, Elector Frederick considered it merely as a cunning maneuver of the Czechs intended to prevent him from relieving the Karlstein.[28] His suspicion was strengthened by the overcautious way in which Korybut proceeded. The Prince dispatched a rather solemn embassy, led by Archbishop Conrad of Prague and including such important noblemen as Hašek of Waldstein and John Puška of Kunstat. But he sent them to Žatec, not to Kadaň. Frederick's offer of a safe conduct to Kadaň was never used, nor were the Royalists given a chance to go to Žatec. Instead the negotiations were conducted by the exchange of written messages between the two towns, which are fifteen miles apart. There were differences over the duration of the armistice and over the inclusion of the Royalist garrison on the Karlstein—the Czechs wanted to separate this issue and deal with the Karlstein directly. But on both points agreement seemed possible. Then, after the discussions had gone on for over a week, they collapsed over a final point: the Czechs, ready to conclude the armistice with all German princes as well as with the Catholic barons of Bohemia, were not prepared to include King Sigismund and the dukes and towns of the two northern countries of the Bohemian crown, Silesia and Lusatia. As Frederick put it, very disappointedly, "they did not want at all to have our gracious Lord, the King, for their Lord." And this limitation gives us perhaps a better chance to understand the political background of Korybut's action.

The Prince cannot have been unaware, by this time, of the increasing pressure brought to bear by the Pope on both his uncles. It was an aggravating situation that the Czechs, led by a prince of the royal house of Poland, were now fighting the crusaders led by the one German prince who had been a consistent friend of Poland. It is possible that Korybut's peace move was made upon direct suggestion from the Polish or Lithuanian court, but even if this was not the case the Prince Regent was sufficiently alert to the needs of keeping some avenues of international contact open. The general directive given to him by Witold—to work for a reconciliation between the Hussites and the Church—was still valid and suggested that any road toward peace, if

[28] *ibid.*

it might bring an open hearing for the Hussites, should be fully explored.

In Bohemia Korybut could get support for such a move for reconciliation with the Church, which was very different from unconditional submission to the Church. But no such support would have been forthcoming for an attempt to reconcile the nation with King Sigismund. Obviously the Prince never considered such an attempt. He was the representative of a man whom the majority of the Czechs still called their "postulated" king. While it seemed doubtful whether Witold would ever redeem his promise there was still the hope that he, Korybut, would himself eventually become King of Bohemia. Thus his own policy was exactly the same as that of the majority of the Hussite leaders: peace with the Church of Rome? Yes, if it could be achieved without abandoning the Four Articles. Peace with Sigismund? No, certainly not on the terms of recognizing him as King of Bohemia. On this basis alone could the Hussites at this stage offer a long term agreement to Frederick of Hohenzollern. And just on these terms the Elector could not accept it.

Frederick's disappointment—and his belief that he had been the victim of an insincere maneuver—was strengthened when he learned upon his return to Tachov that an armistice had meantime (on November 8) been signed between the Hussites and the Karlstein.[29] It was concluded for a full year on the basis of the status quo, with no changes to be made in the castle's defense works, or in the earthworks and towers erected by the besiegers. The remainder of the besieging army left immediately to join Korybut's troops in northern Bohemia. In Frederick's opinion this was a success for the Hussites. Seen against the extraordinary effort made by Korybut—the siege had lasted over five months—it must really be considered as a success for the brave defenders. But it did, for the moment, free Czech and Polish troops for action against the crusaders.

Once more the lords of the Pilsen Landfrieden—especially the brothers Frederick and Hanuš of Kolovraty—attempted to arrange a conference at the castle of Žebrák which might lead to an armistice, and again the Elector of Brandenburg gave them a free hand.[30] But these negotiations, too, remained without result. As November was nearing its end the two armies had not yet been in contact. Some little fighting seems to have taken place in connection with the "daily war" planned by the Empire, but the forces which had arrived from Germany for this purpose

[29] *Archiv český*, VI, 407. [30] *Urk. Beiträge*, I, 267, 272.

counted only in the hundreds.[31] Mars, so it seemed, had fallen asleep again before he was fully awake. Before the end of the year all the crusading forces had left Bohemia. For the third time a crusade had ended in failure. But for the first (and last) time the crusaders had stood on Bohemia's soil without suffering a crushing defeat. The lack of results could certainly not be ascribed to mistakes made by Frederick of Brandenburg, and his prestige did not, as Sigismund had hoped, suffer any damage. For Hussite Bohemia the end of the Third Crusade signified the beginning of a new long spell of rest. As so often before, this lack of pressure from outside only served to revitalize the tensions at home.

After the Taborite raid of late September those tensions never fully subsided. If there had been any cooperation between Korybut's Prague and Tabor at that time, surely we would hear something about Tabor's participation in the defense against the common enemy.[32] There are indeed indications that the guerilla war against Rosenberg continued as it had done for a long time, and it could be argued that by his activity, at least, Tabor kept Lord Ulrich from giving any support to the crusaders.[33] But it is more than doubtful whether this was the purpose. By the middle of November, far from thinking of mutual support against the German invaders, both Hussite sides were actually preparing to fight each other. Prague, so Elector Frederick heard soon after the armistice with the Karlstein,[34] tried to hire troops where she could get them, even from the Bohemian Royalists. The Elector, for a while, hoped to make use of this deep rift inside the Hussite camp, but on November 26 he learned that negotiations had begun between Prague and Tabor and that both expected an early agreement.

A sort of peace indeed was restored between the two Hussite groups before any bloodshed had occurred. But it was an uneasy peace, lasting in this form only for about five months.[35]

[31] Frederick in his letter quoted above, *Urk. Beiträge*, II, 499, talks of 800 horse.

[32] Tomek however (*Dějepis*, IV, 266, and *Žižka*, p. 154) lets Žižka take the field with his Taborites before November 18 to attack the Pilsen Landfrieden. His sources are a letter from Pilsen which Palacký (*Urk. Beiträge*, I, 51) correctly dated 1420, and another one (*ibid.*, I, 271) which he mistakenly dated 1422. In reality the last mentioned letter belongs to 1421. (See above Chapter 17, note 32.) Tomek puts both into 1422, with little justification. See his footnote 81 in *Dějepis*, IV, and compare Pekař, III, 176, and corresponding notes in IV.

[33] On November 6 Ulrich of Rosenberg, from Krumlov, wrote to Elector Frederick, asking him to be informed on the state of the negotiations with the Hussites, and expressing the hope that he would not be forgotten but included in any armistice agreement (*Urk. Beiträge*, I, 266). It is not clear whether he believed that Tabor would take part in such a settlement. In reality Tabor is nowhere mentioned as an actual or possible participant.

[34] In the above-mentioned letter of November 26, *Urk. Beiträge*, II, 499.

[35] In April 1423 Prague began the siege of the Taborite fortress of Křiženec. See Chapter 22.

The rift, as we know, was old and largely ideological. The question arises why it was now so much more difficult to bridge. Perhaps the adventure of Švamberg and Hvězda still rankled in the minds of Korybut and his friends. Also those conservatives who hoped that Korybut might achieve a reconciliation with the Church of Rome were bound to regard the radicals in the south as an unwelcome liability. In this connection it is significant that lately the power and influence of Hašek of Waldstein had grown steadily. In addition to his strong power as mint master of Kutná Hora, he was employed by Korybut for such important services as the negotiations with Frederick of Brandenburg; and the conclusion of the armistice with the Karlstein seems, in the main, to have been his work. His political views are known to us: he hated the radicals of the Želivist party of Prague whom he had deprived of their great leader. He was just as opposed to Tabor.

But Taborite resentment against Prague and Korybut was equally strong. Again the reasons are plain. Korybut's somewhat highhanded way of reducing Hradec Králové had caused uneasiness, if not outright suspicion, which was reawakened by the negotiations with the German crusaders, even though Sigismund was excluded as a possible partner. Finally the special role played by Hašek of Waldstein may have increased the resentment at Tabor and strengthened the suspicion that a deal with Sigismund was not entirely out of the question.[36]

In discussing this period of increasing tension we have hardly mentioned Žižka's name. One of his modern biographers[37] has suggested that in the negotiations between Prague and Tabor, late in November, Žižka worked most strongly for reconciliation. This assumption, based on his previous record, would seem acceptable if we could be sure that he was still considered, or considered himself, as the military and political leader of Tabor. This, however, is quite doubtful. During the winter 1422-1423 Žižka disappears completely from all contemporary records—it is the longest phase of his life during the revolution in which our sources dry up to such an extent. When he finally re-emerges, in March 1423, he has left Tabor, never to return there again. Sometime before this date there was a grave crisis in his relationship with the Taborite community which ended in the parting of ways; this much is sure. There are good reasons to assume that his move had occurred long before March. And if we permit ourselves to conjecture on the basis of what

[36] In February 1425 Hašek actually went over to Sigismund. See *Urk. Beiträge*, I, 325, 338.
[37] Tomek, in *Dějepis*, IV, 268.

we know of Žižka's policy and of his previous attitudes, then, it seems to me, the complete lack of any Taborite participation in the defense against the Third Crusade makes it likely that the break between the Taborite community and its old general had already occurred many weeks before the end of 1422.

The precise date of the break, presumably, will remain unknown. Not so the reasons for it. They are clearly based on the increasing hostility which a growing part of the Taborite clergy showed toward the general. To some extent these conflicts go back to the old struggle over transubstantiation. His merciless persecution of all forms of Pikhartism had never found the full support of all Taborite priests. We know who among them was most strongly opposed to Žižka's policy: Wenceslas Koranda, the fighting priest whose whole temper was not too far from the mystical fervor of Houska and his friends. This affinity is confirmed by the reports of one of Pikhartism's most determined enemies, John of Příbram.[38]

Žižka's position, nevertheless, was and remained strong enough as long as he had the full backing of the moderate clerics, in particular of Bishop Nicholas. But in February 1422, a synod of Tabor's priests took place at Písek. This assembly served to strengthen the solidarity of the Taborite clergy. In particular it appears that at this time Nicholas of Pelhřimov began to approach the views of the group around Koranda. It is from the Bishop that we know of this synod,[39] but unfortunately he reports the resolutions taken at this and two later synods (of 1424) without making it clear which of them belong to 1422. In any case we find him later in full agreement with Koranda and much nearer to some Pikhart views, though he himself had indicted them, in the strongest possible terms, in his letter to the University of February 1421.

It seems clear that Bishop Nicholas had succumbed to the pressure from a stronger personality. And Koranda's powerful influence thus deprived Žižka of the main support he had had among the Taborite clerics. But Pikhartism was not the only controversial issue. There was the quarrel over the vestments which arose again and again between Tabor and Prague, much to Žižka's annoyance whose less radical attitude in this question is emphasized especially by the author of *The very pretty chronicle.*[40]

[38] See Pekař, I, 147, 148.
[39] In his Taborite chronicle, see Höfler, II, 484ff.
[40] Pekař (III, 257) doubts the reliability of this report, arguing that Žižka could not have been Tabor's leader for three years and yet disagree with its priests on questions of ritual. A strange argument in view of the known conflicts between Žižka and the priests.

All this does not yet explain why a man of Žižka's national stature could not impose his will on the priests and people of Tabor. To understand this we have to remember the special character of the Taborite community. This federation of cities, now dominating a considerable territory with some subject towns and many rural settlements, was a theocratic commonwealth. It was governed by a clergy which had taken over all the functions of lordship previously belonging to the king as sovereign of the larger towns or to the barons from whom the small towns and rural communities had been wrested. At Tabor-Hradiště itself no city government other than that of the priests existed. A civil town constitution was only introduced many years later. As yet the power of the clergy was growing rather than diminishing, and the time was not too far off when even the conduct of the war was to pass into the hands of a strong priestly leader.

The influence of Žižka and his co-captains upon the Taborite people had also been limited by the short periods of time they had been present. Žižka in particular had spent many months in the field, and only short weeks in between at Tabor. The priests on the other hand were always present, always active, not just Sunday preachers whose words might be forgotten. Their attitudes, ideas, and prejudices were bound to shape the minds of the whole community.

This all-pervading priestly influence must have been a difficult adversary to fight, especially after the Synod of Písek had done away with some of the internal dissensions within the Taborite clergy. Žižka could not well lead his Taborite soldiers against the men who, in their eyes, had long become the true preachers of the Law of God. It was, after all, through their recruiting fervor that he had been able to build up his army. He could only fight this struggle by arguing. This he did, and it seems that especially in disputes with Koranda he grew so fiercely angry that the priest no longer dared to face him. Yet a struggle of words surely was the one war which Žižka was not likely to win, especially against men who had learned better than he to express their views on questions of theology.

Thus, in the end, it was Žižka who had to give way. And rather than sacrifice his convictions he sacrificed the advantages which his position as captain general of the Taborite community had given him, and the command of the army which he himself had created. He does not seem to have thought of this step as a definite break, and when, soon afterwards, a reconciliation between him and the leaders of Tabor took place he wrote to his friends about this in terms of the deepest satisfaction.[41] One other factor made his fateful and difficult decision easier: he knew where to go. There was a community where he would be more than welcome and where his leadership had long been acknowledged by laymen and priests alike. It was the Orebite brotherhood.

Starting with and profiting from Žižka's triumphant victories over Sigismund, the year 1422 had raised Hussite Bohemia to a climax of military and political strength, only to end in disappointments. By the beginning of 1423 Prague and Tabor looked at each other with hardly concealed hostility, and another conflict, inside Tabor, had led to Žižka's separation from his old comrades in arms. As if this were not enough, the Hussite commonwealth was to lose, soon afterwards, the support which Poland-Lithuania had given her in 1422.

The strong pressure to which the Church of Rome subjected King Władysław and Grand Duke Witold had not relented throughout the fall of 1422. Władysław indeed was more than ready to call off all support given to Bohemia, provided only that Sigismund would acknowledge the peace of Lake Mielno and thereby agree to the revision of the Breslau Award. This was what Zawisza of Garbów, again the King's ambassador to Sigismund, told the latter when he visited him in Hungary.[42] There followed an exchange of views between some of the leading Hungarian and Polish grandees. Actual negotiations started early in December,[43] and the Polish-Lithuanian rulers were confident enough to order Prince Korybut to leave Prague, though not yet Bohemia. This tactical move probably shows Witold's hand. The Grand Duke would not dispense yet with the strong political weapon that the Prince's presence in Bohemia had proved to be, but in ordering Korybut out of Prague he could claim to have given a proof of his good will.

Korybut did, indeed, leave Prague on Christmas Eve. It must have been as grave a disappointment to him as to his Czech followers. He took up residence somewhere in eastern Bohemia[44] without, so far, officially resigning his office as regent. There seemed still a chance that the negotiations would come to naught, especially when Sigismund made a last attempt to solve the problem by creating a grand alliance against Poland. It was to include the Kingdom of Hungary, the Bishop of

[41] In his letter to the two brothers of Valečov, see Appendix, VIII.

[42] See the letter of Ludwig of Lans to the Grand Master of the Prussian Order in Grünhagen, *Geschichtsquellen*, p. 23.

[43] See Goll, *Čechy a Prusy*, p. 174, and Caro, *op.cit.*, LII, 193ff.

[44] Tomek (*Žižka*, p. 156) thinks it most likely that he took up residence at Hradec Králové. Pekař (IV, 118) opposes this view.

Breslau, all Silesian dukes and cities, the Lusatian Six-towns, and last but not least the Prussian Order.

The message in which Sigismund developed this plan[45] is an interesting document. In it we find, for the first time in history, the suggestion that Poland should be partitioned "as soon as, with the help of God, the Kingdom . . . will be gained by conquest." Much of the territory that Sigismund hoped to gain for Hungary—Galicia and Podolia, together with Moldavia—was what another ruler of Hungary, Queen Maria Theresa, actually obtained three and a half centuries later through the First Partition of Poland. As yet the time was not ripe for this noble enterprise. The planned alliance was, in reality, not so grand. The Prussia of 1422 was only a shadow of what the state of the Teutonic Knights had been till the middle of the fourteenth century, and nobody could then foresee the much greater Prussia of Frederick's descendant and namesake. Nor was there as yet a strong Russia to back this coalition, as most of its west and south was at the command of Witold.

It was the realism of his Hungarian magnates which forced the King back into the realm of possibilities. Those lords declared "they had no intention to die or be ruined for the benefit of the Prussians,"[46] and Sigismund's Bohemian advisers for whom he sent early in March concurred in this opinion. Finally the negotiation gained speed. On March 13 King Sigismund, now holding court in the Zips (or Spíš), near the Polish border and with the snow-covered peaks of the High Tatra in the background, sent the Polish ambassador to Cracow with a personal invitation to Władysław and Witold. Both princes hurried to the meeting, and after a few days of additional negotiation a full agreement was signed in the town of Kežmarok (Käsmark).[47] In it Sigismund solemnly relinquished the Breslau Award and acknowledged the Peace of Lake Mielno, thus underwriting Samogitia's status as an integral part of the Lithuanian Empire. Władysław and Witold could feel that their aggressive Bohemian policy had paid a handsome dividend.

To liquidate this policy once it had served its purpose—this, of course, was the price they had promised to pay. And now they would prove impressively to all Christendom that they had never dreamed of aiding a heretic cause. Prince Korybut was ordered immediately to return to Poland with his troops. More than that: if the heretics refused to submit to the Church, a strong Polish-Lithuanian army, with one of the

[45] *Urk. Beiträge*, I, 275, 276. [46] *ibid.*, I, 285.
[47] Text in *Codex Diplomaticus Lithuaniae*, 300ff.

royal cousins at their head, was going to join the grand alliance against the Hussites which Sigismund now triumphantly announced for the coming summer.[48] While the Poles would strike from the north, Hungary would invade from the east, Austria, under Sigismund's son-in-law Albert, from the south, the Dukes of Silesia, the Margraves of Meissen, the Elector of Saxony and many other German princes from the northwest and west. The date set for all of them to take the field was July 24.[49]

Even before this final turn of events the Praguers had sent a message to Grand Duke Witold, asking him to delay no longer the fulfillment of his promise: to come to Bohemia, to let himself be crowned and assume the responsibilities of government. Witold's answer[50] was only given on one of the last days of March, after the agreement of Kežmarok had been signed. In this letter Witold now consumes, not without relish, the fruits of his shrewd caution. Its dominating theme is: "I deny everything you claim, and you cannot prove me wrong as you have never received anything in writing." Never had he formally accepted the Bohemian crown, never had he promised to protect, or ordered Prince Korybut to protect, the heretical Four Articles. If, as the Praguers claimed, Prince Korybut had really publicly obliged himself at the diet of Čáslav to hold and effectively implement the Four Articles, then he had done this without the Grand Duke's knowledge and permission and would have to answer for it. The letter also anticipates the reproach that he had deceived the Bohemians. Not he but they have acted deceitfully. He had sent Korybut only because, relying on the Bohemians' promises, he had firmly counted on their willingness to return to obedience toward the Church of Rome. This hope had proved a delusion. Therefore "we have concluded a solemn agreement with the illustrious prince and lord, the King of the Romans, of Hungary and Bohemia [*sic!*], our dearest brother and friend, and have made peace with him for all times." He, Witold, will stand with the Roman Church, with King Sigismund, with the other Catholic princes and with the whole of Christendom, and will help them in the fight

[48] See Sigismund's letters, *Urk. Beiträge*, I, 288, as well as in Caro, *op.cit.*, XLV, 524ff. and the Pope's letter, *ibid.*, LII, 207.

[49] But a little later, in Sigismund's letter to the Bishop of Ratisbon of April 22 (*Urk. Beiträge*, I, 295) the date had already been postponed by about a month.

[50] The message from Prague is not preserved but its main points can easily be reconstructed from Witold's answer. See the letter in *Urk. Beiträge*, I, 286-288. I am giving its content without closely following the sequence of its arguments.

against the Bohemians. He has therefore ordered Korybut presently to leave the lands of the Bohemian Crown. If, however, they want to abandon their errors he, together with King Władysław, is still willing to mediate between them and the Church.

This offer to mediate is all that is left of the policy of protection which, just over a year ago, Witold had challengingly announced to the world. It can hardly have given much comfort to those Hussites who had diligently worked for Witold's Bohemian kingship ever since spring 1420. All the hopes pinned to this solution were now dashed. Hussite Bohemia relapsed into complete isolation.

For Prince Korybut there was little left but to obey the orders he had received from his uncles. He could not defy them without, so it seemed, losing all support at home. He may have hoped that this would not be the end of his connection with Bohemia, and some of the men who had come with him decided to stay and keep fighting on the side of their Czech brethren.

King Sigismund had given a safe-conduct to Korybut and his troops for their march across Moravia. A day or two before March 26 they crossed the soft wooded hills which divide eastern Bohemia from Moravia, and soon afterwards the little army, veterans of a year of war for the Chalice, dispersed in the wide plains of Poland.

## CHAPTER 22

# THE SECOND TABOR

At the moment when Prince Korybut disappeared from the foreground of the Bohemian scene, Žižka reappeared. Indeed it is Žižka to whom we owe the knowledge of the approximate date of Korybut's departure. In a letter written on March 26 he says: "Besides I want to give you the news that the Prince has left the country."

The letter was dispatched from Vilémov, a small place near Čáslav. It is one of a number of messages which Žižka, as he tells us himself, sent to all his adherents in eastern Bohemia, some to noblemen who had fought with or under Žižka, others to the towns of the region. The letters were largely identical, with variations in the text if needed. These facts emerge clearly from the two messages that have been preserved.[1]

Their purpose was to invite those noblemen and towns of the Orebite region to a meeting, to be held at Německý Brod soon afterwards, at Easter time, on April 7. "There," so the messages say, "at the very place where we have sinned, we will do penance. . . . Furthermore we will then and at the same place, under the guidance of the Lord God and His Sacred Law, consult and resolve with all who are faithful to him, with the council of the poor and the rich, and stay united as one man against all faithless deceivers at home and abroad."

From the letter to the towns—the one preserved is addressed to the neighboring towns of Česká Skalice and Náchod—we hear why to Žižka such penance seems needed. He reminds his friends of the great victory over Sigismund achieved in January 1422. Then, Žižka says, God himself deigned to fight for us. But we, instead of being truly grateful, "indulged in greed, pillage, wanton pride and betrayal, and thus we made our Lord God angry, and ever since there has not been much good that we have achieved. And the Lord God rightly punishes us for our sins."

Žižka, we thus learn, was deeply dissatisfied with the way things had been going lately, and well he might be. But for him there was only

[1] See the two letters from Vilémov, Appendix, VIII, IX.

one explanation: a religious one. God was annoyed about the behavior of the Hussite troops at the conquest of Německý Brod.[2] "Our sins," says Žižka, thus taking full responsibility for acts which he had not been able to prevent.

But once His wrath was placated, God would again help His servants in the liberation of His Sacred Truth and in the destruction of the "evil and faithless heretics." There was, thus, a new need to organize the forces of the faithful, those who would follow Žižka in his good fight. They were the Orebites of eastern Bohemia. This brotherhood was going to replace for Žižka the old Tabor which had not fully kept faith with him. Tabor, however, was not just a geographic or political term —it was an idea which was bound to go with Žižka wherever he went. Thus, in one of these letters, he called the new community the "Lesser Tabor," lesser surely only in terms of outward appearance, somehow in the sense of the Latin "secundus." The letter seems to indicate that the expression had been coined earlier, even though it is the only place where we find it used.

While still the lesser one in the area it dominated, the Orebite community, too, had spread out strongly since its beginnings. At the outbreak of the revolution it had, in the main, been limited to Hradec Králové and the rural areas near it. But the conditions for its expansion improved when, in spring 1421, the Hussite armies conquered or received the submission of all major cities and towns in eastern Bohemia. True, all of them, with the exception of Hradec Králové itself, acknowledged the suzerainty of Prague. This, however, did not prevent them from accepting the Orebite form of Hussitism which in any case deviated much less from the teachings of the Prague masters than that of Tabor. Prague on her side acknowledged some form of regional autonomy for the Orebite community in the religious field, as shown by the organization of the great synod of Prague in July 1421. By 1423 the area where the Orebite brotherhood was strong seems to have reached roughly from a line connecting Mnichovo Hradiště, Dvůr Králové, and Náchod in the north to the Sázava River in the south.[3] As yet this Orebite region had not developed a political coherence and

[2] This is the interpretation given to this passage by every Czech historian with the single exception of Pekař. I cannot see how any other understanding is possible, especially in view of the emphatic passage in paragraph 2 of the letter to Skalice and Náchod (See Appendix, IX). Nor does Pekař (II, 183) give any clear alternative interpretation.

[3] The western boundary of this roughly triangular sphere of Orebite influence seems to have run from Mnichovo Hradiště (where the brothers of Valečov, soon to be mentioned, had their holdings) to Čáslav. Čáslav itself belonged to it; not, however, Kutná Hora and Kolín.

strength comparable to the Taborite federation in the south. The region still contained some towns and districts not linked up with the Orebite brotherhood. And as long as Korybut maintained his position as regent and with it a fairly strong central power there could be no question of political autonomy for the Orebite region. But Korybut's departure from Prague and his recall to Poland changed the situation.

The submission of all those towns to Prague in 1421 had been based on individual treaties between them and the capital.[4] These treaties had lapsed when the towns did homage to Korybut as the bearer of royal power. With Korybut gone—what was their status now? Did the city government of Prague automatically recover the rights it had ceded to the Prince Regent in 1422? This, certainly, was the view taken by Prague and by such men as Hašek of Waldstein and William Kostka.[5] But it was not necessarily the view of the former royal towns of eastern Bohemia or of their Orebite population. It was a difficult question, liable to arouse serious disagreement, even open conflict.

Did Žižka, by calling the Easter meeting of Německý Brod, try to challenge Prague on this issue? His letters in themselves show no such intention. Nor does it seem that Prague understood this meeting as an act threatening her prerogatives in the region. Otherwise she would have tried to prevent a man like Diviš Bořek of Miletínek, still her captain governor at Chrudim and in addition governor of Hradec Králové, from cooperating with Žižka's efforts at organizing the "Lesser Tabor." This cooperation, as we shall presently see, was quite close at the time.

Yet it can hardly be denied that Žižka's action portended the danger of such conflicts for the future. Originally his relationship to the towns and the nobles of the Orebite region was a purely personal one. It was based on the experiences of the common campaigns of April and May 1421 and January 1422 in which Žižka's leadership had been acknowledged, first de facto and later also officially. His personal friendship with Ambrose of Hradec and some of the leading nobles of the communities gave this relationship increased strength and stability. The messages for the Easter meeting as well as the following events show to what extent Žižka's leadership was accepted by them. Even so a situation might develop in which Žižka would feel the need for a tighter organization, for a commonwealth as coherent and as fully autonomous

[4] See above, Chapter 13, note 17.

[5] Kostka's position as subchamberlain, though derived from Korybut's nomination, gave him on the basis of old constitutional tradition special influence upon the administration of the royal towns.

as Tabor had been. This would necessarily collide with Prague's claim of being the suzerain power over the towns of eastern Bohemia.

Prague's inactivity in the face of this new development in the east may be explained by the fact that as yet her attention was focused on the old Tabor rather than on the new. In any case it gave Žižka time for what must have been a fairly systematic buildup of his Orebite forces, and the meeting at Německý Brod was one of the main steps in a process of military organization comparable to his work at Tabor early in 1420, but conducted with the increased authority and the added experience of the last three years.

We shall not attempt to construct a list of all the towns and nobles present at the meeting, but some conclusions can be drawn from what evidence we have. Thus the invitation that went out to the subject towns of Náchod and Skalice makes it obvious that their lords, the brothers of Kunštat-Poděbrady, were not left uninformed or uninvited; both had been close friends of Žižka's for some time. Of the other Orebite barons one, Hynek Krušina of Lichtenburg, had long ceased to cooperate with this group. His friends were men like Hašek of Waldstein, and he wanted no part of any Tabor, old or new. There was, however, another baron of at least equal standing upon whom Ambrose —and with him Žižka—could count as a firm supporter.[6] Aleš Vřešťovský of Riesenburg had helped Ambrose in June 1420 in the reconquest of Hradec Králové and had been its governor afterwards. In the following period he had spent many months as a member of Hynek of Kolstein's great embassy in Poland and Lithuania. But early in 1423 he had resumed his role as one of the leaders of the Orebite community.

There were a number of knights and squires who, under Žižka's command, had led Orebite troops in the two campaigns in eastern Bohemia and especially during the offensive of January 1422. Two of them had taken part, soon afterwards, in the meeting of the arbitrators in Prague, and both, Beneš of Mokrovousy and Bernhard of Valečov, were to play an important role in the new "Lesser Tabor." It was Bernhard of Valečov, together with his brother Bartoš, to whom one of the two preserved messages was addressed.

Of knightly origin was also Diviš Bořek of Miletínek, but like some other knights (such as William Kostka) he had grown so much in stature, political influence, and wealth that he had become rather an

[6] Březová calls him (on p. 381): "veritatis et legis Christi non modicus zelator."

equal to the lords.[7] Whether or not he was present at Německý Brod, his actions soon afterwards manifest the cooperation which the meeting was meant to bring about.

The main objectives of the meeting were, as we learn from both of the preserved messages, the common penance and the holding of a common "council of the poor and the rich"[8] on how to fight for the Law of God. But Žižka's letter to the knights of Valečov also gives us information on the political and military situation of the time. Negotiations had taken place between Žižka and the "Old" Tabor which had led to complete agreement. The Taborites, so Žižka says, have "declared of their own free will that they will follow my orders as at any time before." He has consequently asked them to mobilize for a new campaign. It seems that Žižka, at this time, planned a strong action against the remaining German and Catholic towns and nobles of the north, in the region bordering Lusatia. The Orebite community, however, or at least several of its leading nobles such as the brothers of Valečov, were at this time already involved in an important regional fight.

The enemy they had taken on was Lord Čeněk of Wartenberg who, ever since the autumn of 1421, had supported Sigismund. He was to the Orebite community very much like what Ulrich of Rosenberg was to Tabor. His domains cut into the Orebite region in an awkward way. His town of Bydžov was, for instance, only seventeen miles west of Hradec Králové.[9] From Žižka's letter—he asked his friends not to conclude an armistice with Wartenberg—it appears that this war, conducted largely in the guerilla fashion familiar to us from the struggle between Tabor and Rosenberg, had gone on for a considerable time, and that Žižka had had some part in directing it.

Žižka's demand that no armistice be concluded with Wartenberg was followed. Actually the war against him was much intensified. The basis for Žižka's campaign, which had obviously been discussed and decided upon at Německý Brod, was Hradec Králové. Its captain governor Diviš Bořek took a prominent part in this campaign as Žižka's principal

[7] See about this Pekař, IV, 139, n. 3. But several contemporary sources, among them the *Chronicon veteris Collegiati*, whose author seems to have been closely attached to Diviš, call him "dominus." (See e.g. Höfler, I, 86, 87.)

[8] Meaning everybody, from every station.

[9] The other important center of Wartenberg's possessions was the town of Jičín. It seems that in Wartenberg's possessions Hussite worship had been tolerated even after the lord's last break with the Hussite side, as we find Žižka recruiting in the area of Jičín as late as January 1422. See Chapter 18.

lieutenant, helped by another Orebite knight from the Čáslav region, Hertvik of Rušinov.[10]

Wartenberg had, for more than a year, played a rather inconspicuous role in the political affairs of the country. So far he had escaped any punishment for his repeated treason. It would seem that Korybut during his regency avoided putting any severe pressure on him. There was no punitive expedition against him like the one attempted against Lord John Městecký of Opočno. There is, on the other hand, no trace of any rapprochement between Wartenberg and Korybut[11] though the Prince may have hoped for it. On the contrary we find the lord sometime afterwards officially listed in the ranks of the Catholic lords[12] which might indicate that this time he had gone the whole length of the way in repudiating the Chalice. This, of course, would justify the attack against him in the eyes of all Hussites.

The invasion of his domains now forced Wartenberg into action. He had no difficulty in finding allies among his numerous friends and relatives in northern Bohemia. Only two of them are mentioned in our sources:[13] Ernest Flaška of Pardubice, a zealous supporter of King Sigismund who had taken part, two years earlier, in the callous slaughter of the Taborites at Chotěboř; and Henry Berka of Dubá, one of five brothers in this powerful clan and a participant, with Wartenberg, in the first diet of Čáslav. The army of the lords, a few thousand strong, consisted largely of cavalry, but was reinforced by battle wagons and guns, while Žižka had under him "only two rows of wagons," that is altogether 120 wagons which indicates a total strength of between 2,400 and and 3,000 men.

Žižka's army had operated in the vicinity of Jičín. When the Royalists approached, he retreated in the direction of Hradec Králové. Near the town of Hořice he found a suitable place to establish his wagon fortress. There was a hill on which a small church, devoted to St. Gotthard, provided a landmark as well as a good observation point.

The battle of Hořice, fought on April 20, 1423, follows in all essentials the well established pattern of Žižka's defensive-offensive tactics.

[10] The *Chronicon veteris Collegiati*, the source nearest to the event, puts it (p. 86): "Zizka cum domino Divissio de Miletnik et cum Hertwikone et cum Grecensibus" (the troops of Hradec Králové).

[11] Pekař's suggestion (III, 156) that Wartenberg probably took part in the second diet of Čáslav is based on wrong premises and would anyhow seem unlikely in view of the following development in Wartenberg's policy.

[12] At the St. Gallus diet in Prague. See Chapter 24.

[13] Old Annalists, p. 56; *Chronicon veteris Collegiati*, p. 86, further text Sa of Old Annalists as quoted by Pekař, III, 205.

As at Sudoměř, at Bor Panský, or on the Vladař, he gave the enemy a chance to attack only under conditions strongly favoring the defense. In this case, so our most detailed report[14] says, the lords were forced to dismount as the slopes were too steep for mounted charge, and were repeatedly repelled by the fire from the wagon fortress. Only when the attacks had lasted a considerable time did Žižka order his untired men to counterattack in full strength. The Royalists were put to flight, losing all their wagons and guns and many horses. Lord Čeněk, so we hear, "escaped with a small part of his people" which would indicate that his loss in men, too, was grave.

Žižka's victory at Hořice—it was his most important action since the battle of Německý Brod, fifteen months earlier—gave the Orebite forces the chance to roam at will in the region so far dominated by Wartenberg, and enabled them to participate freely and without concern for their own communities in Žižka's future campaigns. Žižka followed up his victory by an attack on the castle of Kozojedy which seems to have belonged to Wartenberg.[15] "And they conquered it, and burned sixty." With these laconic words closes the account on the April campaign in the region of the upper Elbe.

In May the center of Hussite military activities shifted toward the lower course of the river, the region northeast of Litoměřice. It was the campaign for which Žižka had planned some time in March when he had asked for the mobilization of the forces of Old Tabor. But before the Taborites were free to move north, grave trouble developed within the Hussite ranks. For the first time in the history of the revolution it took the form of an armed struggle.

It was Prague which began the hostilities. A fairly strong body of her forces, cavalry and infantry, moved against the Taborite fortress Křížencc and began to besiege the place. Křížencc lay in the neighborhood of the town of Načeradec, some eighteen miles northeast of Tabor. It was important in that it covered the approaches to Tabor from Čáslav, that is, from the Orebite region, but also from Kutná Hora where Lord Hašek of Waldstein was mint master and governor. He, so it seems, led the Prague forces, and under his command were also troops that had fought for and been paid by King Sigismund—most probably noblemen and retainers from the Karlstein with whom Hašek had con-

[14] Old Annalists, *loc.cit.*

[15] Old Annalists, *loc.cit.* As to the ownership of the castle see Tomek, *Žižka*, p. 160, n. 100.

cluded the recent armistice.[16] It was, indeed, an ominous step: the men from Prague, adherents of the Chalice, fighting side by side with some of their old Royalist enemies against the Taborite community.

What were the reasons for this sudden attack? Tabor's Bishop Nicholas[17] tells us that the Praguers acted on the instigation of some of their priests who were incensed about the Taborite ways of worshiping, especially about their serving the Holy Mass without using the traditional vestments. This explanation for a military expedition of some size is not as strange as it would appear to the modern mind. The question of the vestments had long divided the clerics of the two Hussite camps in a bitter controversy. Tabor was and remained, in the eyes of the Prague masters, under the shadow of a cloud. Was not the deviation of those who served the Holy Mass without vestments indicative of a deeper, truly heretical deviation—the doubt in the real presence of Christ and in the fullness of transubstantiation?

That the issue of the vestments had a good deal to do with the military expedition against Kříž접enec is, indeed, obvious from the rather strange outcome of this struggle: it ended in a public disputation concerning the vestments. Yet the explanation given by Bishop Nicholas seems unsatisfactory or incomplete, as an expedition against a small fortress would hardly have frightened the Taborite clergy into submission to Prague in a question of ritual. More likely the priestly anger was used by people to whom the religious issues were of minor importance compared to the very real struggle for power between Prague and Tabor. In the eyes of a man like Hašek of Waldstein, Křížzenec castle had solid significance. It was a potential link between the two great sectarian communities in the south and in the east of which the latter, by Žižka's move, had become so threatening. By taking Křížzenec he would perhaps weaken both Tabor and Oreb. In the background of such thoughts was the hope of destroying eventually the dangerous autonomy of the Taborite federation and its cities, which at best regarded themselves as allies, never as subjects of Prague.

The siege of Křížzenec lasted well into May. Tabor does not seem to have been worried too much about it, as a few weeks were allowed to pass until a Taborite army, under the command of Lord Bohuslav of Švamberg, came to the relief of the fortress. As the Taborite troops

[16] Tomek (*Žižka*, p. 159) also suggests troops from the Pilsen Landfrieden, but this seems less likely as this federation rarely sent its troops to fight outside its own region. (For example, cf. its attitude during the Third Crusade as told previously.)

[17] See his "Chronicle" (Höfler, II, 574, 575), which is our main source on the events of Křížzenec and Konopiště as told in the following paragraphs.

were superior in numbers the Praguers did not dare to accept battle, but raised the siege. A truce was concluded according to which both armies should meet again a few days later at the castle of Konopiště, quite near Benešov. The castle belonged to Perchta of Sternberg, the Hussite dowager who, after her Royalist husband's death, had publicly declared and maintained her friendship with Prague as well as Tabor. On this neutral ground there met, about the middle of May 1423, the two armies with their men and horses, their wagons and guns. The mood, so we hear, was not very peaceful on either side, and a bloody battle might have broken out right then if some of the leaders on both sides had not interfered, urging that the issue of the vestments should be submitted to a peaceable discussion. It was agreed that a final settlement of the question should be sought by a meeting of priests and lay leaders of both parties to be held, again at Konopiště, on June 26. And to take the bitterness out of the discussion the Taborites suggested that for once priests of both sides should celebrate the mass in the reverse way: the Taborites in full vestments, the Praguers without them. Indeed one of the Taborite priests, Prokop the Bald, immediately celebrated the mass in vestments. The priests of Prague, however, though officiating without their full ornate vestments, could not be persuaded to dispense with their white surplices.

The fact that peace was restored before the armed struggle between Prague and Tabor had assumed any major proportions was also due to the appearance of a rather unexpected visitor in the camp before Konopiště. It was a Polish nobleman, Nicholas Siestrzeniec, Burgrave of Bedzin. He brought a message from King Władysław of Poland to the Estates of Bohemia.[18] It renewed the offer of mediation made in Witold's harsh message of March, but in a much more friendly and conciliatory form, strongly appealing to the common Slavic heritage of both nations and arguing that a full return to the Church of Rome would alone prevent a continuation of the heinous destruction of the land and the people of Bohemia. Although Sigismund had not objected to Władysław's mediation,[19] the Polish action seems to indicate an interesting reversal of political trends in Poland and Lithuania. Witold, having achieved his goals in regard to Samogitia, had dropped his Czech "protégés" permanently, and forthwith ceased to give them any support whatever. In Poland, on the other hand, the party which

[18] See Goll, *Čechy a Prusy*, pp. 179ff.; and Pekař, who (III, 189, 190) quotes and discusses the letter in detail.

[19] Pekař (*loc.cit.*) even thinks that the step was taken entirely on the basis of the understanding achieved at Kežmarok.

had supported the Bohemian alliance now became much more active. This group of men, led by the powerful Chancellor Szafraniec, felt that there was still a good deal to be gained by continuing some support for Hussite Bohemia. The agreement of Kežmarok, though beneficial to Lithuania, had not yielded enough for Poland, and continued pressure on both Sigismund and the Prussian Order might still produce considerable rewards.[20] It was this political group with which Korybut, on his return to Poland, began to cooperate very closely.

To them, too, belonged Siestrzeniec. From Konopiště he went on to Prague, accompanied by some of the leaders of both Hussite parties, and from his own report[21] we learn that he went even further than Władysław in his urgings for a peaceful solution of the great struggle with the Church of Rome. Following, however, the advice of some Hussite noblemen he carefully refrained from even mentioning King Sigismund or from disputing the evangelical truth of the Four Articles. The answer to Władysław—the Masters of Prague dispatched it only on June 6[22]—expressed readiness to negotiate on the basis of a general hearing, but also the determination to stand by the sacred truth till death.

Siestrzeniec's mission, though unable to achieve any real rapprochement between the Hussites and Rome, had nevertheless two important results. It led to the resumption of friendly relations between Prague and at least one powerful fraction of the Polish ruling class; and it helped the Czech parties at Konopiště to overcome the hard feelings they had against each other and to establish, for the purpose of negotiations with the Polish mediator, some measure of unity.[23]

This more peaceable spirit between Prague and Tabor was maintained also at the negotiations which about a month later took place, again at Konopiště, between all the prominent representatives of the clergy of both camps, with some of the lay leaders present as "auditors."[24] Little agreement was reached on the question of the vestments, and a renewed discussion of the role of Purgatory in the Christian faith left unbridged gaps of understanding. But at least the issue of transubstantiation was resolved, for the time being, in the way which Prague

[20] See Sherbowitz-Wetzor, *The Polish Foreign Policy . . .*, pp. 170ff.

[21] See *Codex Witoldi*, p. 600.

[22] *ibid.*, p. 594.

[23] This connection was first seen and discussed by Pekař, III, 189ff.

[24] They included, on the side of Prague, one nobleman (Smil Holický of Sternberg) and one townsman (Simon of the White Lion); on the side of Tabor Chval of Machovice and Matěj Lauda of Chlumčany, the latter Žižka's host during his sickness in 1421. See Tomek, *Dějepis*, IV, 280.

demanded. Tabor, in other words, still tried to steer clear of Pikhart deviations.

The agreement of Konopiště reopened the way for concerted action. Indeed the following campaign in northern Bohemia—it lasted through June and part of July—seems to reflect a Hussite movement more united than it had been for a long time. We hear of an assembly of Hussite troops in this region as early as May, when a squadron of four hundred horse with some infantry and wagons moved north from Mělník.[25] We cannot be sure to which Hussite group these forces belonged. Mělník's captain, appointed by Prague, was John Smiřický. This nobleman seems to have stood fairly close to Žižka at an early time. He took part in the spring campaign of 1421 on Žižka's side, even after the Praguers had concluded their offensive. He also was among Žižka's lieutenants during the great battles from Kutná Hora to Německý Brod. If he now took the field—we find him soon afterwards operating with the two knights of Valečov—he might conceivably have acted on his own and without special order from Prague. The same, however, can hardly have been true in the case of another captain of Prague: Hynek of Kolstein, governor of Litoměřice, whom we also find at Žižka's side early in June. He was, as we know, one of the leading lords of the Hussite center which, by the desertion of Wartenberg and his friends, had now become the Hussite "Right." Hynek surely acted on orders from the capital. The old alliance seemed fully reestablished, especially as, about the same time, Bohulav of Švamberg with his Taborite army arrived, obviously coming directly from Konopiště.[26]

Our main source on the movements of the allies are the reports, written in a highly alarmed mood, which Hynek Berka of Dubá, brother of that Henry who had just fought against Žižka in the battle of Hořice, wrote to the Lusatian Six-towns and to Duke Henry Rumpold of Glogau, and some other letters dispatched by the town of Zittau and clearly based on Dubá's reports.[27] The lords of Dubá, the greatest landowners in the region directly south of the border, badly wanted the help of their northern neighbors, and to make the need appear as

[25] See the letter of John of Michalovice from Bezděz to Česká Lipa in *Urk. Beiträge*, I, 297.

[26] In Dubá's letter (*Urk. Beiträge*, I, 101) the name is written Ewanberg. It is clearly a slip of the pen: the scribe intended to write Swanberg according to the German spelling of the time. Švamberg's presence is confirmed by a later report. See below, note 31.

[27] *ibid.*, I, 101, 102, 103, 119. It is a series of messages all of which, with the exception of the one quoted in note 26, Palacký wrongly dated 1421. About this and some more details of the military movements, cf. Tomek, *Dějepis*, IV, 275, 276, and n. 88.

urgent as possible they told them that "Žižka with the Praguers" or "Žižka with his helpers" was about to invade Lusatia. In reality this never was the intention of Žižka or any of his "helpers." The purpose of the campaign was quite clearly to do away with those strong Royalist positions which still gave the German enemies of Hussite Bohemia a permanent "bridgehead" inside the country. Apart from conquering some small places, considerable time was spent in the siege of one of the strongest castles of the region. It was the "New Castle," also called Panna, meaning "Virgin." Its lord, Sigismund of Wartenberg, greatest of Čeněk's relatives of the same name, seems to have given to his castle this devoutly Catholic name only recently, that is after Žižka had erected his own castle of the Chalice in the neighborhood.[28] In September 1421, at the time of the Second Crusade, Sigismund of Wartenberg had unsuccessfully tried to conquer Žižka's castle. Now it was Žižka's turn. The siege of Panna Castle lasted a few weeks, but the outcome is unknown.

Now, for the first time in this war, we find Žižka using his own castle as the base of his operations. For a short while the castle of the Chalice seems to have served as the rallying point for most of the military leaders of Hussite Bohemia, and it is likely that within its walls discussions began about a more ambitious enterprise, an offensive of grand scale for the conquest of Moravia.

An expedition into Moravia had been considered in Prague early in 1422.[29] Prince Korybut, even before entering Bohemia, had made an attempt at gaining part of the Margravate, but only one city, Uničov, was won permanently. The Margravate had meantime been given by Sigismund as a fief to his son-in-law, Albert of Austria. Albert in the south, and Bishop John "the Iron" of Olomouc in the north, were doing all in their power to stifle or destroy the strong Hussite movement which despite all the persecution had remained alive in the country. It was thus time, from the Hussite point of view, for an effective and permanent liberation of the sister country.

Preparations must have gone on for some time before, toward the end of June, the expedition got under way. When the army started on its way to the southeast, it had among its leaders not only the captains of Prague—Hašek of Waldstein and Hynek of Kolstein—but also some of the most important Orebite leaders: Diviš Bořek of Miletínek, Žižka's

[28] See Pekař, III, 206.

[29] E.g. the discussion between the Prague councilors and John Želivský immediately before the latter's execution, mentioned above in Chapter 19.

associate at Hořice and captain governor of Hradec Králové, and the brothers Hynek and Victorin of Poděbrady, both among Žižka's closest friends.

The great invasion of Moravia started—and ended—without Žižka. But the names of those people show clearly that the campaign was not undertaken without Žižka's blessing. I believe it even possible to assert that he fully intended to take part in it. This, of course, cannot be proven, but the fact that he took an early opportunity to lead his troops into Moravia, where we find him fighting less than three months later,[30] makes this assumption probable. It would seem that he promised his friends to follow them into the Margravate as soon as possible, just as, in spring 1421, he had joined the army of Prague with his Taborites a few weeks after the campaign had started.

But if this conjecture is accepted, why did he not set out with all others? It seems that the castle of Panna was still unconquered, and perhaps he wanted to see this matter through even if it meant that others—the troops of Prague and part of the Orebites—would march into Moravia in advance of himself. In fact not only some of the Orebite contingents but also the Taborite forces under Bohuslav of Švamberg,[31] stayed with him for some time in the neighborhood of Litoměřice, surely not without a military purpose.

This, I think, could be fairly sufficient explanation. But there was still another reason for delay, perhaps just additional, perhaps the one that really mattered to Žižka. For while the campaign in Moravia was already under way he assembled, probably at his castle of the Chalice, another gathering of friends and followers, all of them leaders of soldiers, similar to the one that he had called to Německý Brod three months earlier.[32] It was a meeting that produced the most important document of Žižka's career and profoundly changed the political situation in Bohemia.

[30] See Chapter 24 of this book.

[31] On July 27, "at a time when great hailstones fell," Švamberg went away from Panna Castle, going south, but avoiding Prague. See Old Annalists, p. 56.

[32] For the dating of this meeting, see next chapter.

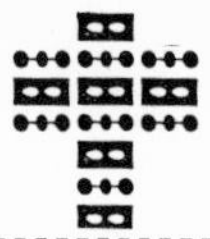

# CHAPTER 23

## THE LAW OF GOD AND THE LAW OF WAR

THE great document which was the product of the second meeting of Žižka's new military brotherhood has gone into history as "Žižka's Military Ordinance."[1] It is by far the longest and in many ways the most revealing document of which Žižka was the principal author. And its main significance was that it gave the Second or Lesser Tabor a new, stricter military and political constitution.

As a historical document the Military Ordinance has to be understood and evaluated on its own, with only limited help to be gained from background information. To begin with, the date of both the meeting and the document can be derived only from internal evidence, more precisely from the list of its signatories. This list and the list of those men (among them some of Žižka's best friends) who took part in the Moravian campaign are mutually exclusive. A close look at these names shows that this cannot have been so by mere accident. The proper date, therefore, is sometime in July, while the Moravian campaign was already under way.[2]

[1] Žižkův vojenský řád. See Appendix, x. The document and its history and meaning has had, of course, much attention from Czech historians. See Pekař, II, 174-179, and III, 222-228; Tomek, *Žižka*, pp. 168-173; and Toman, *Husitské Válečnictví*, pp. 13-32. The latter devotes much space to comparisons of Žižka's Military Ordinance with similar contemporary or near-contemporary documents, Czech as well as German. In particular he has succeeded in proving that the military statutes connected with the name of John Hájek of Hodětín, long believed to be earlier than Žižka's ordinance and one of the sources for its statutes, is actually a considerably later document.

[2] This is the second important instance (after that of the Čáslav diet of 1422) where I disagree with the dates accepted so far and where I believe that my revised date contributes to a better understanding of the sequence of events. In this case, however, the date has always been under dispute. Tomek (*Žižka*, p. 169) and Pekař (III, 223), for once in general agreement, have assumed that the date was the early fall of 1423. Others such as Bartoš (e.g. in *Žižkova doba*, VIII, 28) or Urbánek (*Lipany a konec polních vojsk*, Prague 1934, p. 59) believe that the Ordinance had its origin in the meeting at Německý Brod in April. But if this were true, then we should find among the signatories the two Lords of Poděbrady, men much nearer to Žižka than their cousin Sezema. We should also (as Pekař correctly points out) expect to find Diviš of Miletínek. If, on the other hand, the date were early fall, then, of course, we should no longer expect to find Diviš on the list, but the Lords of Poděbrady would still be-

But why was that action taken just at this time—at a moment when it meant delaying Žižka's participation in the Moravian campaign? The text gives us only limited clues. In support of the need for a tighter discipline, it says that through disobedience "we have undergone great losses both in the lives of brethren and in our possessions." The passage seems to refer to recent reverses suffered during the spring campaign in northern Bohemia, events which never caught the attention of the chroniclers. At least it is difficult to think of any other campaign in which these "great losses" among the fighters of the brotherhoods could have occurred.[3]

This leads us to the conclusion that things had not gone too well during the campaign in June and July 1423. But whatever reverses took place—they cannot have taken the form of a lost battle. Such an event would not have remained unnoticed, especially not in the German camp. More likely it was improvised or badly coordinated assaults upon one of the Royalist strongholds of the region such as Panna Castle which resulted in those losses. This becomes even more likely when connected with another piece of information. On July 27 Bohuslav of Švamberg with his Taborites left the region of Litoměřice and returned to Tabor.[4] He did this, says one of the Czech historians,[5] "doubtlessly upon his [Žižka's] order." But the opposite is much more likely. Panna, as far as we know, was still unconquered. Therefore the sudden departure of the Taborites cannot have been welcome to Žižka. It would rather seem to have been caused by disagreement. Indeed July 1423 had marked the last instance for a long time of a full military cooperation between the two Tabors. It was followed by a new and prolonged alienation between them, that is between Žižka and Bohuslav of Švamberg.[6] There was no other opportunity for the renewed break between them to occur but those days when both men stood near or before the castle of Panna in July 1423. In Žižka's eyes any lack of subordination on Švamberg's part must have appeared as a breach of that promise to "obey his commands as at any time before" which he had quoted in

long there, as would Hvězda who meanwhile had left the Old Tabor and joined Žižka's brotherhood. In both cases the additional question would arise why not one of the signatories of the Ordinance took part in the Moravian campaign. This would be especially true in the case of Sezema of Kunštat who clearly was more directly interested in the Margravate than his cousins.

[3] Theoretically it could be argued that Žižka wanted to refer to the defeat of Most, but this seems unlikely as this event occurred two years earlier, and as none of the brotherhoods nor any of Žižka's personal friends was involved in this debacle.

[4] Old Annalists, p. 56.

[5] Tomek, *Dějepis*, IV, 281.

[6] About the relationship between Tabor and Žižka's brotherhood, see the last additions at the end of Pekař's *Žižka*, IV.

his letter of March 26. It looks as if this break was an additional reason, though hardly the only one, why Žižka felt the urgent need at this time to call the meeting which was to become a sort of "constitutional assembly" for the Orebite brotherhood in arms.

The number of people who took part in it and set their signatures to the great document was not very large. If we leave aside the burgomasters and councilors of the Orebite towns of Hradec Králové, Čáslav, Jaroměř and Dvůr Králové—they signed, as usual, only with their titles, not their names—we find forty-six persons on the list of presence: four lords, twelve knights in addition to Žižka himself, and twenty-nine others of lower standing, several of them squires, others townsmen, a few perhaps even peasants by origin.[7] Some of these belonged to Žižka's old bodyguard, men who had followed him through all his battles and had become trusted subaltern officers; they had now, with their old chief, left Tabor and joined the eastern brotherhood. Others were Orebite leaders of long standing (two of them even called themselves "the Orebite" instead of giving the name of their origin). With them was also a Polish officer, a man who presumably had come with Korybut and had stayed with Žižka.

This list of signatories, very carefully graded according to rank,[8] shows that Žižka by no means neglected the traditional social order. Yet he upset it in a sovereign way by putting himself at the head of all signatories, thus indicating that his was the highest place in the community. And he upset it again when he placed, first among the lords, his old comrade in arms John Roháč of Dubá, the only one of the Taborite generals who had left Tabor together with Žižka. As an owner of land and castles Roháč was hardly an equal to any one of the other barons, but by advancing him to the first place Žižka appointed him, as it were, as his deputy, perhaps even as his possible successor.[9]

[7] In a couple of cases it may seem somewhat doubtful where, among the list of the low-born men, names begin and end. This, of course, determines the total number. I am here following Pekař's suggestion for the correct division of names (II, 277, n. 3). See also his commentaries on the signatories, III, 224-226.

[8] It is peculiar that even the towns, though all of them royal towns, are carefully graded. Hradec Králové and Čáslav are named right after the lords and the most prominent knights. Then, after some more knights and squires, follows Jaroměř. The last town to be named, after some more squires and townsmen, is Dvůr Králové. At the end follows the list of Žižka's Taborite and Orebite subalterns, with the last seven possibly of peasant origin.

[9] During the rest of Žižka's life Roháč had to contend for the position as second in command with John Hvězda, but later (in 1427) he was captain governor of Čáslav which was something like the second capital of the Orebite (then called Orphan) brotherhood, and after the battle of Lipany in 1434 he was for a while captain general of what was left of the forces of Tabor. See Tomek, *Dějepis*, IV, 315, 369, 666.

Altogether the later fate of those four barons who follow Žižka as signatories of the Ordinance is revealing not only for their own persons but also for Žižka's choice and for the influence he had upon them. With three of them it lasted for a long time after Žižka's death. Sezema Boček was one of the Moravian Kunštats, resident at Jevišovice, probably the son of an early companion of Žižka, and one of the relatively small number of Moravian barons who had stood against Sigismund from the beginning. His firmness remained unbroken even by the long time spent as a prisoner in Royalist hands. He may have joined Žižka through the mediation of his cousin Victorin of Poděbrady. Eleven years later he fought at Lipany with Tabor against the coalition of his peers. He survived the great defeat by again being taken prisoner.

This fate was shared by Roháč of Dubá.[10] But Roháč, standing for Žižka's ideas with more stubborn determination than anyone else, was soon afterwards again at the head of Tabor's weakened forces. He did not relent for a moment in his fight against the "heretical King," but was eventually, after the long and heroic defense of his castle Zion, captured and hanged. The third of the three, John of Potstein and Žampach, did not live long enough to be faced with the grim decision of Lipany. Yet he, too, was to be found on the side of Tabor as late as 1428.[11]

But the career of the man who, after Roháč, led the list of the lords was very different. It was Aleš of Riesenburg, one of Bohemia's leading magnates whose adherence must have shed considerable luster upon the new fighting brotherhood. His role in Hussite history might be compared to that of General Monk in the Puritan revolution. Riesenburg remained long connected with the Orebite movement, but in a much less exposed way than the other three lords. He also kept friendly relations with the more conservative groups. Ten years later he was elected regent of Bohemia, and in this function he helped to smooth the way for the compromise with Church and Emperor which found its expression in the Basel Compacts and in the eventual recognition of Sigismund as King of Bohemia.[12]

[10] See Urbánek, *Lipany a konec polních vojsk*, pp. 148, 157.

[11] The John of Potstein and Žampach whom we meet in the list of signatories is not identical with that John Kolda of Žampach who fought at Lipany and was to play a considerable role later. See Pekař, III, 224 and Sedláček, *Hrady, zámky a tvrze království českého*, II, 126, 127. John of Potstein was married to the widow of Žižka's old friend Ulrich Vavák, and it was perhaps through her that he became one of Žižka's followers.

[12] See Chapter 30, and Tomek, *Dějepis*, pp. 607, 664ff., 714.

Among the knights and squires, too, we find some familiar names: Žižka's Orebite friends, the knights of Valečov, as well a Beneš of Mokrovousy[13] who like them had fought at Německý Brod and had served with the Prague arbitrators in February 1422. Among them also appears the name of Žižka's brother, Jaroslav of the Chalice, who had followed his older brother through his campaigns and had stuck to him when he left the Old Tabor for the "lesser" one.

The list of presence, here as in the other great documents of the time,[14] does not stand at the beginning. It follows after a preamble which defines in general terms the aims of the military brotherhood. And this would not be Žižka's brotherhood if its aims were not defined in religious terms. The signatories feel enlightened by the faith in and knowledge of the "certain, enduring, revealed and proved Truth and Law of God." And again this would not be Žižka's voice if those words were not followed up by the Four Articles of Prague. It is for the fourth time that we find the Hussite Charter quoted by him, but whereas in his earlier communications the Articles were usually summed up in a condensed way[15] they are, this time, quoted at some length and with short commentaries which give them the peculiarly Žižkaesque flavor and meaning. The freedom of the Word of God shall not only be ensured by having it preached everywhere, "no one place excepted," but all those who hear it and receive it in their hearts shall lead and teach others toward it. The brotherhood of laymen receives, in this version, a position which may be called Protestant or perhaps even Presbyterian in its significance. The article on the Eucharist stresses the need to give the bread and wine to the children from the earliest times, and demands that it be taken at least every Sunday. The article on the life of the clergy is somewhat less outspoken in its condemnation of the earthly rule of priests than the wording used in Žižka's letter from Prachatice of November 1420, and the main emphasis is laid on apostolic poverty and the suppression of simony. But the Fourth Article —the one on the eradication of sin—shows again Žižka's impassioned and imperious conviction that he is fully entitled and called upon to cleanse this world from all sins.[16] And for the first time we are given to

[13] Pekař (III, 225) gives his interesting life story in some detail.

[14] See, for instance, the great manifesto of the first diet of Čáslav in Chapter 14.

[15] See the armistice agreement with Rosenberg and the letters to the neighbors from Prachatice and to the Landfrieden of Pilsen, in Appendix, I, II, III.

[16] Compare his version: "that *we* stop, suppress and destroy all sins . . ." with the official Prague version of 1420: "that all mortal sins . . . be properly and sensibly prohibited and

understand that this task will not be limited, in the long run, to one country or nation. For these sins, the mortal and even the venial ones, shall be suppressed "in the kings" as well as the members of all other estates, thus at least tentatively establishing an international demand, valid throughout Christendom. In the first place, of course, this great self-purge is up to the Czechs, the people chosen by God to fight for Him at this time. Thus anyone who does not want to adhere to and fight for the Four Articles cannot be tolerated in Žižka's army, nor anywhere else in the country. There shall be no refuge for such unbelievers anywhere, in any of all possible settlements or dwellings which are carefully enumerated, "no place excepted or exempted." And the preamble or first part of the document ends with the mutual assurance of the signatories that they will, with God's help, exert all their power to convert ("admonish, advise, push and urge") everyone "toward this goodness." Tolerance, certainly, had no place in this program.

The second part of the document is introduced by a sentence intended to show the specific spirit and mood in which all signatories demand and accept the statutes of the military ordinance. They act in the knowledge that all earthly things pass away but the Truth of God endures through the ages. Perhaps it characterizes Žižka's position in history that this expression of an essentially medieval mood serves to introduce a very hard, realistic, and in its goals rather modern set of military laws.

Then there follows the list of the names, with "Brother" Žižka (he is the only one here called by this title) at the head. "We all," so continues the text, "command all of you that there be orderly obedience." And this demand is motivated by the reference to the losses suffered through disobedience and lack of discipline. Such happenings shall be prevented by enforcing the set of military rules laid down in twelve points.

The order in which those statutes are presented reflects the movement of the army from the moment the camp is broken. Great emphasis is placed on the need for proper marching order: people must stick to the troop they are assigned to, troops must maintain whichever place was assigned to them in the whole army column, they must keep apart and never get in one another's way, nor lose contact with one another. Van, rear, and flanks are to be properly guarded. There are strict rules

punished by those who have the authority to do so. . . ." The following clause, on the cleansing of Bohemia from all slanderous rumors, is entirely missing in Žižka's version. See also Pekař, II, 170ff., and my commentary to the Fourth Article in Chapter 10 of this book.

for billeting, encamping and the lighting of fires. And before each undertaking people have to kneel down and to pray for God's help. Careless captains whose neglect of proper conduct and circumspection results in losses to the army are subject to the severest punishment. A rather long paragraph deals with the fair distribution of booty among the various "communities."

The last five paragraphs contain only measures which have the character of a penal code. Offenses to be punished are brawls, armed quarrels, desertion, and all imaginable forms of sin and moral turpitude. The punishment threatened to all those offenders is of the utmost severity. In one or two cases banishment or flogging are allowed, but for most of the crimes loss of life and property is considered the only fitting punishment, and the "elders," that is the commanding officers, are then only given the choice of the specific death penalty they want to inflict, such as clubbing, decapitation, hanging, drowning, and burning.

This military code is followed by a third and last part which, like the first one, returns to the religious principles, demands, and goals of the brotherhood. God is sure to help a fighting community that keeps the Four Articles. To be a worthy member of this community you have to live a good, devout, and clean Christian life. But these generalities lead on to a powerful appeal for general support, directed to the communities of all estates. And again this appeal goes beyond the boundaries of the Kingdom. It includes "all regions," as well as the community of "the princes" at the head of all others, a reference which would not make sense if limited to Bohemia. Only in the following words some special emphasis is put on "all faithful Czechs." And the same order is repeated in a sentence assuring help to "all the faithful everywhere in the Holy Church, and especially in the Czech and Slav nation." This appeal and promise seems to reflect the knowledge that Hussitism had, at this time, gained adherents outside the land of its origin.[17] The document ends with a solemn and forceful invocation of God and the Holy Trinity.

Apart from the religious content and the purely military rules laid down in the Ordinance of July 1423 it gives us some revealing information on the social order existing in Žižka's new military commonwealth. We pointed earlier to the careful way in which the signatories, indi-

[17] See e.g. King Władysław's letter to Witold on the measures taken against Hussitism in Poland, *Urk. Beiträge*, I, 305.

viduals as well as towns, were listed according to rank. The same careful listing of the various estates in their order of rank occurs with some regularity in the following text, in the statutes of war as well as in the final appeal to the faithful. The list of signatories itself ends with the words ". . . and all the communities, those of the lords, of the knights, the squires, and the townsmen, no one being excepted or exempted." Later the handling and distribution of the booty of war is put in the hands of elders especially elected for this job "from all communities, those of the lords, the knights, the townsmen, and the peasants."

This division of a large group of people into separate "communities" according to the estate to which they belonged is not, in itself, unusual or surprising. We would expect it in connection with any political structure or organization, but hardly in a document to provide rules for an army.[18]

Their existence in Žižka's brotherhood shows that it was divided in two different and independent ways: vertically, that is in military units of which the "rota," a troop normally of one hundred men,[19] is the one mentioned regularly in the ordinance; and horizontally, that is in the various communities which clearly form as many political organisms, each or most of them being represented in each military unit. And whereas the actual military orders were transmitted from the top commanders down through the subordinate captains to the various military units, the horizontal communities through their elected representatives or elders had some say in religious, political, or other questions not directly connected with the military conduct of the war. The lowest of them, the community of the peasants, was not considered quite worthy to be listed among the groups signing the new covenant, even though some of their members signed personally and though they were entitled to send their elected elders to take part in the less solemn yet important business of distributing the booty.[20] A passage in Žižka's declaration of loyalty for Korybut indicates that such "communities" of the various estates had already existed among the Taborite brotherhood.[21] Žižka thus organized his new brotherhood in its political structure largely after the model of the older one. And just as the older one had not only been an army but also a state so the new, the lesser Tabor quite clearly was, to all intents and purposes, a state. But it dif-

18 Compare e.g. the various German military statutes printed in the last chapter of Toman's *Husitské válečnictví* (especially those on pp. 396-420).

19 *ibid.*, p. 212.

20 See point 7 of the statutes in the Military Ordinance.

21 See Appendix, VII.

fered from Tabor-Hradiště in two regards of consequence: the army was to be held together by a tighter system of subordination and discipline which would prevent some of the troubles that Žižka had encountered at the other Tabor. In fact it now fully developed into a standing army, the "field-army," an organization with its own laws, its own government and its own, largely conscriptive and eventually quite predatory war economy. (It was a direction in which the Older Tabor soon followed suit.)[22] In addition the role of the clergy, in the younger community, was to be limited to what Žižka had always considered its proper domain: the spiritual direction of the struggle for God's Law. It is characteristic that the document mentions the clergy only at the very end in an almost casual way. The Lesser Tabor, too, was to be a theocracy. But it was to be ruled by God himself whose Law was unmistakable—not by priests.

It may seem odd that just the Military Ordinance with its emphasis on the scale of social rank has been quoted by Czech historians—beginning with Palacký—as proving the "democratic" principles of Žižka. Yet this suggestion is not as implausible as a cursory glance would make it appear. For more often than not, this list of ranks is mentioned just for the purpose of stressing that a man, convicted of having violated this military code, should be punished, no matter which estate or "community" he belonged to, and that this rank or person should not exempt him from either his duties or the penalties due to him. No less than six times this principle is stated with the greatest emphasis.

Clearly nothing was further from Žižka's mind than to abolish the differences of rank or station which characterized the structure of society at his time. Surely he believed that their existence was willed by God, just as Luther believed a century later. Only because God called him to liberate His truth and His law did he himself assume a role unheard of for a man of his station. But he had no delusions of greatness beyond this very specific role, as proved by his whole style of life and, in the Military Ordinance, by the fact that his own brother was given precisely the place to which his station entitled him. And yet, while he took the feudal order very much for granted, his actions constitute a significant step toward its destruction. In his army the lords and knights might be given prominent command position as was proper and customary. Even the adherence of princes was considered a possibility, of men who could not be expected to serve in any but the

[22] About the development of the Hussite field army (polní vojsko) in this phase, see Urbánek, *Lipany*, pp. 59ff.

highest positions.[23] Yet the Law of the new commonwealth, the Law of War which was based on the Law of God, would see no difference between the highest and the lowest. Not only before God but even before the Law of His War all men were equal. John Želivský had once assumed the right of the city judges of Prague to judge and execute a noble lord. Now Žižka, with the solemn approval of some of the leading noblemen of the realm, assumed on principle a similar right in the name of the reconstituted Orebite brotherhood. In the end no caste system can last if there is equal justice, and if the laws of the community are for (or against) everyone alike, "no one being excepted or exempted."

The creation of the new organization, somewhat comparable to the organization of the New Model by Cromwell with its sharply increased discipline, marked the beginning of a new phase in the history of the Hussite war. For the first time Žižka had both an army and a political organization which was entirely his own. He could organize his community as he and his closest friends saw fit, could give the leading positions to people whom he trusted completely and could thus establish his position as military and political head of the Orebite communities without any competing claims from either clerical or lay elements. And by doing this he established, for all practical purposes, a claim to autonomy if not even sovereignty.

In this new situation it would have been almost a miracle if an open clash with the claims of Prague could have been avoided. The clash occurred very quickly and at the place which would have to form the capital of the new commonwealth: at Hradec Králové.

This city had been the center of the Orebite movement from its prerevolutionary beginnings, due mainly to the strong leadership of Priest Ambrose. He had, almost singlehanded, liberated the town from its Royalist occupation in spring 1420. After that Hradec Králové, just like Žatec and the Taborite cities, had been an independent ally of Prague. Only in August 1422 had Prince Korybut occupied the city, and put Diviš Bořek of Miletínek as his governor over it. Diviš now ruled the town as the representative of Prague, but this had not prevented him from closely cooperating with Žižka when the old general transferred his activity from Tabor to the Orebite region. He had fought under Žižka in the battle of Hořice, and their friendship seems to have been undisturbed up to the time when Diviš left for Moravia. But this friendship was turned into open hostility by a development which the old chronicle[24]

[23] See Pekař, II, 189, and p. 276, n. 1.

[24] Old Annalists, p. 57.

tells us in the following words: "Lord Diviš governed over Hradec, and [when he left for Moravia] he set his brother, Lord Jetřich, over the town. And they [the people of Hradec Králové] sent a message to Brother Žižka, and he marched from Litoměřice to Hradec, and the community opened the gates to him. And they drove Lord Jetřich out of Hradec, and they destroyed the castle."

No event in Žižka's life has perplexed his biographers and the historians of Hussitism as much as this sudden and apparently unmotivated turn against a man who shortly before had been his friend and ally. Do we have to think of Žižka's action as a treacherous conspiracy between him and Ambrose of Hradec? Or was it perhaps Žižka's answer to a treasonous move on the part of Diviš Bořek?[25] In reality no such assumption seems necessary for the understanding of the events that occurred at Hradec Králové at the very end of July 1423.

[25] Tomek's rather weak "excuse" for Žižka's action (*Žižka*, p. 165) claims that Diviš had, in the Moravian campaign, allied himself too closely with Prague. Pekař, on the other hand, uses Žižka's seizure of Hradec Králové as a cornerstone in his construction of Žižka's character and politics (III, 203, 208-210). Under the influence of Ambrose, so reads his version, Žižka decided to take the city out of Diviš' hands and secure it for the radical party. But as Diviš was a strong man with powerful support, Žižka had to go about this with great caution. Diviš must not have the slightest inkling of what was afoot. So Žižka lies low until Diviš, together with other leading fighters for the national cause, have gone on the Moravian campaign, which is so important for Hussite Bohemia. Then only he goes ahead, with no regard whatever for the fact that he thereby strikes his friends and allies in the back while they are engaged in this patriotic task, or that he thereby destroys the peace which had been concluded at Konopiště. Thus the incident, according to Pekař, proves how utterly mistaken Tomek is in thinking that internal peace and order and national solidarity was one of Žižka's main goals and considerations. Even if we admit that Tomek's conception of Žižka errs by emasculating the revolutionary in Žižka, Pekař, it seems to me, errs by falling into the opposite extreme. All of Žižka's constructive acts (enumerated in Chapter 20 of this book in connection with his declaration of loyalty for Korybut) are either neglected or understood as fleeting moods of reasonableness in a man whose true mind was that of an unremitting and irresponsible rebel. The most elaborate attempt to refute his theory in regard to the seizure of Hradec Králové has been made by F. M. Bartoš in an article in *Jihočeský sborník historický*, VI, 3 (*Sborník Žižkův*), pp. 96-108. He points out that, at this time, Sigismund tried to win support in Bohemia through Polish channels, and that Diviš Bořek, in 1427, was engaged in treasonable negotiations with the King's party. (See also Tomek, *Dějepis*, IV, 379.) Žižka, so Bartoš argues, may have had some advance knowledge of these treasonous plans. This somewhat farfetched explanation, however, entirely overlooks or neglects the fact that in fall 1424, after the peace of Libeň and long before those supposed treasonous plans got anywhere, Žižka and Diviš again marched as allies (though surely no longer as friends) in a common campaign toward Moravia. To some extent the unsatisfactory character of both versions, the accusing as well as the apologizing one, can be attributed to the fact that their authors were mistaken about the date of the meeting which accepted the Military Ordinance (see above, notes 2 through 5). Thus the direct connection between both events (the change in the structure of the Orebite community and the seizure of Hradec Králové) escaped their attention and the whole development with its wide political and social implications was wrongly reduced to a question of political ethics on a mainly personal level.

It would, of course, be helpful if we had more information, if for instance we knew what exactly was in the message sent by the city council of Hradec Králové to Žižka. So much, however, appears sure: there had been trouble between Jetřich of Miletínek and the city before Žižka's arrival, and this was the reason for the urgent message which caused Žižka to hurry to the Orebite capital. Its source, too, is clearly implied in the new situation. For by signing the Military Ordinance, the four Orebite cities led by Hradec Králové had actually committed an act of rebellion against Prague which still claimed suzerainty over these formerly royal towns.[26] By pledging unqualified obedience to the captains and elders of the new military commonwealth, that is, to Žižka, they implicitly renounced all allegiance to the "Lords of Prague."

It is doubtful whether Žižka himself saw things quite in this light. His assumption of the leadership of the Orebite communities had been an almost gradual process until, probably motivated by his difficulties with Bohuslav of Švamberg, he had felt it necessary to create a more rigid framework for his Lesser Tabor. He would not necessarily have to anticipate, on the basis of previous experience, any resistance to this step on the side of Diviš Bořek of Miletínek. Diviš had, after all, gone along with Žižka completely, supporting his leadership and fighting at his side. It is, of course, impossible to say how Diviš would have reacted if he had been present at the time when the Orebite community was given its new constitution. But he was far away, his brother Jetřich acting as his deputy in the cities where he was governor—not only at Hradec Králové but also, as it seems, at Jaroměř and Dvůr Králové.[27] It would naturally appear more difficult for the deputy to take a stand in a situation like this. If Jetřich tolerated what was going on—was he doing right by his brother, or could he be reproached with neglect of his duty? And in addition there is the possibility that by this time the political leaders of Prague had really grown alarmed about what went on in the east, and had warned or instructed Jetřich accordingly.

Whatever our guesses may be about those details—and unfortunately they can be nothing better than guesses—we are on much safer ground with the more general assumption that the conflict between Hradec Králové and Jetřich had its roots in the competing claims of Žižka and Prague for the suzerainty over the Orebite towns. Žižka, at this stage,

[26] In discussing the date of the Military Ordinance (III, 222) Pekař acknowledges the fact that if it had been passed in April (at the meeting of Německý Brod) the signature of the cities would have implied a rebellion against Prague. This is, of course, just as true when we presume, for the reasons given above, July as the right date.

[27] See *Chronicon veteris Collegiati*, p. 86; Pekař, III, 196; and Urbánek, *Lipany*, p. 58.

could not possibly tolerate an attempt by Prague, or by Jetřich of Miletínek as Prague's representative, to question or attack his rights as head of the new commonwealth. Thus he took a determined action, undoubtedly in complete agreement with Ambrose of Hradec. The result was Jetřich's removal and, in the further and unforeseen course of events, the riot at Hradec Králové where the excited people stormed and destroyed the old castle of the queens of Bohemia, symbol of a dependence which they felt they had shaken off when they joined Žižka's new brotherhood.

But now that things had taken this violent turn at Hradec Králové, all chances were lost that Diviš Bořek might still go along with Žižka. He, indeed, could hardly see anything but treachery in the way his brother had been expelled from the city which had been under his, Diviš' command for almost a year. In the same way Žižka probably saw nothing but the treachery of Prague in the attack that was now loosened upon him. As clearly as at any time in history we can see here how the logic of circumstances rather than the ill will of the leading actors produced a conflict of the gravest consequences. The bloody struggle that broke out over these issues would dominate the Bohemian scene for a long time and would not end until most of Žižka's life span had run out.

# CHAPTER 24

## "ARK AGAINST ARK"

In March 1423 King Sigismund in Hungary and Pope Martin V in Rome had felt sure that this year would see an unsurpassed effort of Christian kings and princes everywhere, in the north, south, and west, to exterminate the Bohemian heresy. But when spring turned into summer all these hopes wilted. Of the many European princes who had promised armed aid only one was as good as his word: King Eric, the powerful ruler of the three Scandinavian kingdoms, landed an army in Germany, but on hearing that no one else had made any preparations he re-embarked his troops and angrily returned to Copenhagen.[1] The German princes had waited for Sigismund to take some initiative but none was forthcoming. In Poland King Władysław's attempt to recruit troops for a campaign against the Hussites met with considerable resistance,[2] and as he, too, saw that Sigismund made none of the moves envisaged at Kežmarok he resigned himself to this situation.

As the danger of a crusade had vanished the Hussites could, in July 1423,[3] devote their attention to the sister country of Moravia. Sigismund had given it as a fief to his son-in-law Albert of Austria, never asking the Bohemian estates for their permission.[4]

We have earlier mentioned the strong participation of Orebite noblemen in this campaign:[5] Diviš Bořek of Miletínek, who seems to have been in overall command, the brothers of Podebřady and their uncle

[1] See the Pope's letter to Witold of February 14, 1424, in *Urk. Beiträge*, I, 321.

[2] See King Władysław's letter to his "Russian" subjects (in the region of Lwów), *ibid.*, I, 303.

[3] Pekař (III, 207) thinks the campaign began in the middle of June. But the only basis for this guess is the fact that Hynek of Kolstein was, on June 11, still in the neighborhood of Litoměřice. As the Hussite army returned from Moravia at the beginning of August I think that early July is a more likely date.

[4] Pekař (IV, 138, and III, 232, n. 2) thinks there was little protest or resentment. But the repeated campaigns in Moravia testify differently, and the reaction of the Bohemian estates to such procedure cannot possibly have been any weaker in the case of Moravia than it was in the case of Brandenburg. (See above the list of grievances in the letter sent by the first diet of Čáslav to Sigismund, Chapter 14.)

[5] See *Chronicon veteris Collegiati* (whose author may have taken part in this campaign as one of Diviš' friends and followers—he certainly took part in the ensuing battle of Strachův Dvůr against Žižka), p. 86, and Old Annalists, p. 56.

John Puška. In addition there were Hašek of Waldstein, Hynek of Kolstein, and Hynek Krušina of Lichtenburg.[6] The considerable number of prominent barons present indicates that this was a formidable army. The Hussites struck right into the south of the Margravate,[7] where they may have hoped to surprise Archduke Albert's main forces. One of their early gains was the town of Slavkov southeast of Brno, better known by its German name Austerlitz as the place of one of Napoleon's greatest victories. From there they turned east reaching the valley of the Morava River at the town of Kvasice which they also conquered. From here on they worked their way back in a northerly direction. This took them first to Kroměříž (in German Kremsier), an important city on the Morava River. Here, finally, they met an enemy army, led by John Bishop of Olomouc and Přemek Duke of Opava. The long and bitter battle, fought out before the walls of Kroměříž, ended in a complete victory of the Hussites. The Royalists fled. Kroměříž surrendered two days later. The prisoners included several leading Moravian barons of the King's party. Soon afterwards the Hussites took Vyškov, due west of Kroměříž, and the larger town of Přerov east of the Morava River.

The northward move which the campaign had taken in its later phases suggests that the next goal was Olomouc. Its conquest would have established a firm Hussite rule over northern Moravia. The chances might not have been bad if Žižka with his troops could have joined the lords and Praguers in the assault. Something like this, I presume, had been envisaged when the whole enterprise was planned by the Hussite leaders.[8] We can understand the fierce resentment of Diviš Bořek when, at the end of July, he received news of Žižka's latest move. The old general was not on his way to Moravia but had just helped to drive his brother and deputy Jetřich out of Hradec Králové.

Diviš immediately cut his campaign short and marched northwest with his allies. Those who followed him were Hašek of Waldstein, Hynek Krušina of Lichtenburg, and the older Kunštat, John Puška. His two nephews, Victorin and Hynek of Poděbrady, would never have

[6] John Puška of Kunštat and Hynek Krušina of Lichtenburg are not mentioned in the early part of the account on the Moravian campaign (*Chronicon veteris Collegiati*, *loc.cit.*) but both took part in the later offensive against Žižka. As it seems that Diviš with the Prague and allied troops turned against Žižka directly upon returning from Moravia (see the following narrative) we can assume that the two noblemen were with the expedition from the beginning.

[7] The following account is in general agreement with the one given by Pekař (III, 207, 208) which makes better use of the sources than others such as e.g. Tomek's (*Dějepis*, IV, 279).

[8] See the reasons for this conjecture in the last three paragraphs of Chapter 22.

considered taking Diviš' side, and it seems that they never quite forgave their uncle for fighting against Žižka.[9] It is interesting that Hynek of Kolstein, too, absented himself even though his general policy was nearer to that of Prague than of Tabor or Oreb.

What now happened is told by one of the chroniclers[10] in the following words: "Lord Diviš thereupon, returning from Moravia and taking the Praguers along with him, wanted to take revenge over the people of Hradec because they had driven out his brother. And together with the Praguers he marched toward Hradec. And Brother Žižka with the men of Hradec marched out of the town to meet them. And a battle was joined at the Strachův Dvůr[11] between the two sides. And there went Ark against Ark.[12] And the Praguers fled, having been beaten by Žižka on that field. And there they killed many people, and about two hundred they made prisoners. And Diviš escaped with his retainers to the hill.[13] And that priest who had carried the Ark on the side of the Praguers, him Žižka killed with his battle club. And this came to pass on the Wednesday before St. Lawrence" (August 4). Essentially the same story is told by an eye-witness[14] who concludes with the words: "Ego vix effugi" (I barely escaped).

He, too, reports the slaying of the priest, a detail that impressed him more than all other details of the battle. It is, indeed, a strange happening, all the more as it could hardly have occurred in the heat of battle.[15] We can only assume that after the battle the blind old warrior ordered the priest to be brought before him as one whom he considered especially responsible—how could a priest dare to lead his troops, under the sacred symbol of the Body of Christ, against him, Žižka, the selected instrument of God's Will and the true servant of His Law? In his

[9] See Tomek, *Dějepis*, IV, 351, n. 59, and Old Annalists, p. 66, no. 157.

[10] Old Annalists, p. 56.

[11] Strachův (or Strauchův) Dvůr was a farm or small hamlet quite near Hradec Králové, probably southwest of the city.

[12] "Ark" is the expression used for the vessel which contained the sacred host and which, fixed to a pole, was carried high and visible to all in front of Hussite armies by priests. See above e.g. Březová's description of the approaching Taborites in the battle of the Vítkov, in Chapter 9.

[13] "Hora," here surely meaning Kunětická Hora, a hill not too far from the battlefield, where Diviš had a castle. Tomek (*Žižka*, p. 167) mistakenly thinks of Kutná Hora.

[14] *Chronicon veteris Collegiati*, p. 87. He reports the total number of losses suffered by the lords and Praguers, that is, dead and prisoners, as 300.

[15] Pekař however (III, 115, 116, 211) understands the account as describing Žižka in battle action—and therefore doubts his complete blindness. This argument is then used in more detail by Chaloupecký in his article in *Věstník české akademie*, 1951, LX, 167. See above, Chapter 16.

flaming indignation then he let his battle club fall on the man's skull.[16] The episode shows us Žižka the man in his uninhibited fanaticism and his fierce self-righteousness, doubly blind when a sudden rage darkened his mind.

Yet in at least one regard he had proved the strength of his vision as impressively as ever. In this battle, for the first time, his enemies were Hussite soldiers, many of whom had fought under him before, as had their leader. Diviš was, in addition, himself a strong and imaginative military leader as he was to prove most impressively later in the great battle of Lipany in 1434. Against Žižka, however, all this seemed of no avail. His fame of invincibility received new support.

But this victory was far from decisive. The military potential of Prague and her allies was still great, not too much of it had been committed and destroyed at Strachův Dvůr. Žižka had to count with renewed attempts of the Praguers to enforce by armed intervention their claims of suzerainty over the Orebite cities. Hradec Králové, the strongest and most populous of them, could most easily take care of itself. Žižka left it under the command of Matthew Lupák, a man who, it seems, had been captain of its militia for some time.[17] Žižka himself went, with the main part of his field troops, to Čáslav, the second truly important city of his brotherhood, to strengthen its defense. He did not come too soon. Sometime in the middle of August a considerable army of Praguers and lords, led, as it seems, by Hašek of Waldstein, began to invest the city. The siege lasted some time, but whatever assaults were attempted remained ineffective.[18] Žižka's associates nevertheless began to fear for him. Matthew Lupák mobilized units of the town militias of Hradec Králové and Jaroměř and marched south to relieve his besieged chief. Hašek of Waldstein decided to intercept him. He marched to Kolín from where he could pounce upon Lupák's troops before they had crossed the Elbe. The Orebites reached the northern bank of the river near Týnec, eight miles upstream from Kolín, and in the immediate neighborhood of that town Hašek surprised and de-

[16] Hajek of Libočany, the mid-sixteenth century historian, in a clearly spurious story, makes Žižka say: "I had to ordain this priest of the Praguers." On this elaboration see Tomek, *Žižka*, p. 167, n. 3.

[17] Tomek (*Dějepis*, IV, 46) on the basis of a passage in the Old Annalists, p. 37, where Lupák is mentioned together with Ambrose of Hradec, suggests that he, too, may have been a priest. Pekař (III, 211) follows this suggestion. I would be reluctant to accept it on evidence as weak as this, all the more as it contradicts Žižka's general policy of keeping priests from wielding any military power. See e.g. the fact that as close a friend as Ambrose was not invited or allowed by Žižka to sign the Military Ordinance.

[18] Old Annalists, p. 56, no. 133, and *Chronicon veteris Collegiati*, p. 87.

feated them on August 22. The Orebites lost about three hundred men, but among them was their commander Lupák.[19] He was slain by one of Hašek's lieutenants, John Černín of Mlazovice, a knight from the region of Jičín. The loss of this battle—one of the few notable reverses suffered by his brotherhood though not by himself—could not leave Žižka unconcerned, but it seems that he was even more incensed by the death of Lupák. He would not forget it till—in almost Homeric fashion—the dead friend was avenged.

The defeat of the Orebite forces at Týnec should have made Žižka's position at Čáslav more difficult. Instead we hear that soon afterwards the siege was raised, that the lords and troops of Prague pulled off quietly and put a strong garrison into nearby Kutná Hora whose defense they considered as more important than the conquest of Čáslav. Žižka's adversaries, so it seems, had been frightened by a sortie in force which took Žižka and his men into the immediate neighborhood of Kutná Hora while all or part of the Kutnohorian militia was engaged farther north under Hašek's command. Prague, for military as well as for financial reasons, could ill afford to lose Kutná Hora.

With the end of the siege Žižka had regained his freedom of movement. The military position, and with it the political independence, of his Orebite federation of towns had been successfully defended and was intact. In terms of battles lost and won, on the other hand, this first phase of the civil war had ended in something like a draw. This situation, it seems, was officially sanctioned by the conclusion of an armistice.[20] But the fight between the Orebites and the Catholic lords went on, and late in August or early in September Sigismund's most rabid supporters, John Městecký of Opočno and Půta of Častolovice, staged a raid against one of the outer suburbs of Hradec Králové, killing some people and burning some buildings.[21] But for a long period—almost exactly six months, till early March 1424—no trace of any battle between the two Hussite parties can be found in the sources. The armistice, thus, was probably concluded just for these six months.

The use which Žižka made of this breathing space testifies to his basic imperturbability and steadiness of purpose. The enemy, in the

[19] According to the *Chronicon Treboniense* (Höfler, I, 53), Lupák's defeat preceded the siege of Čáslav, but this makes little sense and is clearly contradicted by the two sources quoted in note 18.

[20] It was Tomek (*Žižka*, p. 168) who first pointed out that Žižka could hardly have started his September campaign to Moravia if he had not been able, on the basis of an armistice, to leave the Orebite region without worrying for its safety.

[21] *Chronicon veteris Collegiati*, *loc.cit.*, and Old Annalists, p. 57, no. 134.

first place, was Sigismund with his followers. It had been resolved to fight him (and his son-in-law) by a campaign in Moravia. Žižka's own part in this undertaking had not yet been played. The strife between the Hussites had merely postponed this duty. Now, as it were, he resumed the task where the others had left off some weeks earlier. But while the army of the lords had struck into the south central region of the Margravate Žižka selected the west, the region nearest to southern Bohemia and especially familiar to him.

Sometime in the first half of September, he approached the Moravian border coming from the direction of Německý Brod. He intended to bypass Jihlava[22] but its garrison, probably militia reinforced by Austrian mercenaries, marched out to meet him. In the ensuing battle the Royalists were thoroughly beaten. They fled, and Žižka pursued them right to the walls of the town. Žižka now began to besiege Jihlava, but it proved too strong for him, and after some time he gave up.[23] From Jihlava he marched straight south, twenty miles farther in the direction of the Austrian border. And on September 19 he attacked and conquered the less formidable town of Telč.[24]

In this connection we learn that among Žižka's lieutenants on this campaign was John Hvězda of Vícemilice. He seems to have joined Žižka in August, taking with him some more troops from the Old Tabor. From now on we find him permanently in Žižka's camp, either fighting at his side or serving at his order as one of his captain governors. Yet by joining Žižka he had not quite broken with Tabor-Hradiště. He rather seems to have functioned as a sort of representative of the old Tabor to the new one.[25] In this way, then, some contact between the two groups was maintained, though for a while it ceased to be close.

After the conquest of Telč the history of Žižka's first and only cam-

22 Old Annalists, p. 57, no. 133.

23 Windecke, p. 201, no. 239. The report fits the campaign of 1423 better than the only other campaign which could be considered: Korybut's offensive of October 1425. (See Tomek, IV, 329.) The fact that the name of the Hussite leader is not mentioned proves, of course, nothing, as Windecke does not even mention Žižka's name in his account of Sigismund's defeat at Německý Brod (p. 120). Windecke claims that the "Hussen" had killed two thousand people in the course of this fight—a figure which does not only refer to the battle of Jihlava but to the whole campaign.

24 Höfler, II, 63.

25 Pekař (III, 238) thinks that Hvězda left Tabor together with Žižka and Roháč of Dubá. The fact that his name does not appear in the list of the signatories of the Military Ordinance does not seem to him to have any significance. But this is a somewhat lighthearted way of disposing of what must be regarded an important piece of evidence. That Hvězda had not cut all links with the old Tabor is evinced by later developments. Almost immediately after Žižka's death he returned to the service of the older brotherhood. See also Pekař, III, 275-277.

paign outside the Kingdom of Bohemia proper becomes quite obscure. There are two reports, both written long after the event and both implying that Žižka went much farther, that he actually left Moravia and entered foreign soil. One of them tells us of a great invasion of Hungary, the other of a march into Austria. Both, so we know today, are mistaken in that neither country was ever invaded by Žižka.

The story of the invasion of Hungary—in the original text[26] it was told as having happened in 1422—says that Žižka led his troops into the very heart of the country, to a place near Esztergom which is less than thirty miles from Sigismund's capital Buda, today's Budapest. It goes on to tell that the Hungarians concentrated great masses of cavalry against him. The main part of this lengthy report treats the way in which Žižka extricated himself from this difficult situation, making extensive use of the cover which the terrain and his battle wagons could provide for his troops. In the end the Hungarians, finding themselves thwarted in every attempt to get at Žižka's troops, exclaimed in exasperation: this is no man, this is the devil himself. And, so concludes the writer, this was the most difficult task which Žižka ever had to perform.

This Hungarian "anabasis" has long occupied a special niche in all historical writings concerned with Žižka and the Hussite wars, including even monographs on the subject.[27] There seemed some special satisfaction in finding Bohemia's greatest military hero for once switching from the role of merely defending the Law of God at home to attacking the ever aggressive enemy on his own ground. Besides it seemed possible to draw some important general conclusions on the organization of Žižka's army on the move and his defensive tactics.[28]

Even this, however, is of doubtful value. One of Žižka's latest biographers, Josef Pekař,[29] has proved convincingly that there was no in-

[26] Old Annalists, pp. 58-61.

[27] On the bibliography to the supposed Hungarian campaign see Pekař, III, 216, and corresponding notes in vol. IV.

[28] See especially Toman, *Husitské válečnictví*, pp. 329-335.

[29] Pekař devoted to this task a whole chapter in III, 212-221. His main arguments are: the only source (text M of the Old Annalists) is very late, presumably sixteenth century. It also contains a great many quite unbelievable details about Žižka murdering tens of thousands of people, in Moravia, Bohemia, Hungary, and Silesia, which Palacký omitted. This makes the source highly suspect. In addition there is not a trace of this seemingly so important event in any of the contemporary sources, Czech, German, or Hungarian. Nor is there any indication that Sigismund, who at the time dwelt at Buda, reacted in any way to an offensive stroke which would have taken his most dangerous enemy so near to his residence. The report of the Old Annalist does not give any reason why Žižka should have undertaken so daring and, at the same time, so futile an expedition which would have made little sense in the frame of the general war situation. Finally, the similarity between the campaign described here and that of 1431 is such that it can hardly be accidental. The whole account then, according to Pekař,

vasion of Hungary in either 1422 or 1423. He has shown that the whole episode, as described in the chronicle, really reflects events of a much later time, i.e. the campaign conducted by the Orebite (then called Orphan) army in November 1431, seven years after Žižka's death.[30] As a consequence Žižka's march into Hungary has now generally been written off as unhistorical even though some Czech historians were very reluctant to give their assent.[31]

Much less attention has been paid to the other variant,[32] understandably so as it focuses on a rather trivial detail: on the way Žižka, having invaded Austria, managed to seize a herd of cattle from across the Danube. Nevertheless the story may contain a grain of truth. If, from Telč, Žižka marched southeast toward the Austrian border, he would soon reach a river which at some points forms the borderline. (Its name—Dyje—could to a foreign ear easily sound like Dunaj, the Czech name for Danube.) Such a march would point to Znojmo as his goal. And an attack upon this stubbornly anti-Hussite city[33] would tend to give this whole campaign the degree of purpose which generally characterized Žižka's strategy.[34]

Žižka, so it seems, did not return from Moravia until early in October. In that month events occurred which would have called him back whatever the (largely unknown) outcome of his campaign had been. For the first time in the history of the revolution we find the conservative Hussites openly allying themselves with the Catholic element of the Bohemian nobility.

---

indicates the tendency of later writers to attribute great military achievements of the time to Žižka even when Žižka was already dead. (A glaring example of this tendency is Aeneas Sylvius' report on the battle of Ústí [chapter 44] which lets Žižka appear as the victor though this battle was fought long after his death.)

30 Tomek, *Dějepis*, IV, 498-500.

31 E.g. Urbánek, *Lipany*, pp. 63 and 192, and Chaloupecký, *op.cit.*, p. 147.

32 Aeneas Sylvius, chapter 44. Arriving at the banks of the Danube, so he says, Žižka found a deserted village, with most cattle transported to an island in the river. Žižka ordered some cows on his side of the river to be beaten. Their mooing attracted the cattle on the island which swam back, thus falling prey to Žižka's soldiers. The story is supposed to show Žižka's resourcefulness.

33 See Znojmo's letter to Korybut in A. Neumann, *Nové prameny k dějinám husitství na Moravě*, p. 55.

34 In some sixteenth century histories such as Hajek's, Žižka's Moravian campaign is claimed to have ended by a march into the Morava Valley, where he conquered Kvasice, fought before the walls of Kroměříž, etc. Pekař has already pointed out that this is a mistake based on confusing Žižka's campaign with that of Diviš of Miletínek earlier in the year. (See Pekař, III, 213.) Kroměříž, it might be added, was in spring 1424 still securely in the hands of the same Hussite forces which had taken over the government of the town after its conquest by Diviš in summer 1423. See Palacký, *Urk. Beiträge*, I, 324, no. 286.

Even earlier, in September, the two men who since Korybut's departure had virtually ruled Prague, Hašek of Waldstein and William Kostka of Postupice, called a conference of representatives of all the royal towns which still recognized Prague's suzerainty.[35] They met at Nymburk, a city on the Elbe rather near the western fringe of the Orebite commonwealth and standing under the captaincy of Lord John Puška, the only one of the Kunštats who had sided against Žižka. The invitation emphasizes that the country is rife with tumults, violence, and lawlessness, and that there is need for counsel on how to re-establish order and peace. The conference resulted in a step of the greatest consequence: representatives of Hussite lords and towns would meet with their Catholic peers at another place in the same region: at Kolín.[36] The Catholic lords were agreeable if they could get permission from King Sigismund.[37] To explore the King's mind John Městecký of Opočno and Půta of Častolovice visited him at Buda. As a result the meeting was actually called for early October.

The delegates at Kolín set themselves the difficult task to overcome, first of all, their religious quarrels. As always when the question of an understanding with Rome arose, the Hussites put forward the demand for a public hearing on the Four Articles. They were confident enough of the strength of their position to accept Brno, Moravia's capital which was now in the hands of Duke Albert of Austria, as the place for such a disputation. As in previous suggestions of the same type[38] the final judgment was to rest with an audience of laymen, "lords, townsmen, knights, and squires," who would have to decide whether the Hussite Charter was in agreement with the Scriptures.

The date envisaged for this public hearing was the beginning of 1424, and originally it was intended to leave all political questions to be tackled afterwards. Then however this order was reversed, and a great diet was called to convene at the capital for a very early date: October 16. It has become known, in Czech annals, as the St. Gall's diet.

The unexpectedly early calling of the diet was probably due to Žižka's reappearance on the Bohemian scene. It was well known that the

[35] *Archiv. český*, VI, 410.

[36] On this meeting as well as on the following diet of Prague see *Archiv český*, III, 240ff.

[37] It seems doubtful whether, at this stage, the question of a safe conduct from Sigismund for the Hussite delegates was already mentioned. (See Pekař, III, 231.) This first mission of the two lords seems reflected in the beginning of paragraph no. 197, on p. 172, of Windecke's *Denkwürdigkeiten*.

[38] See the disputation on the Small Side, as reported above in Chapter 10, and the suggestions for a public hearing made by the Hussites in connection with Korybut's peace offer to Frederick of Brandenburg, Chapter 21.

policy pursued at Nymburk and Kolín was opposed by him, as it implied another questioning of the Four Articles and as he feared and detested any compromise with Sigismund. But in the eyes of the Hussite conservatives Žižka was more than a barrier on the way to conciliation with Rome. He had failed to submit, with his communities, to the suzerainty of the capital. His standing field army was a political danger and, as it lived off the land of its enemies, a terrible nuisance. Yet it had grown so strong that it seemed doubtful whether Prague and her allies could reduce the Lesser Tabor to the subject status where it would cease to be a danger. The alliance with the Royalists of Bohemia thus would have seemed a military necessity to many of the Hussite conservatives even if this act could not have been made to look proper and justifiable as offering a way toward public disputation and possible peace with Rome.

The St. Gall diet lasted for two weeks, till November 1. Its resolutions are laid down in a document comparable in form to that of the first diet of Čáslav.[39] The preamble, indeed, is almost identical. But this time the representatives of Prague are listed after Archbishop Conrad and the lords, not, as at Čáslav, at the head of the list of presence. And while, at Čáslav, the initial complaint about "the many, diverse and great troubles, tumults, ruinations . . ." had clearly been directed against Sigismund's followers, the same words this time were directed against a different target: Žižka. While, at Čáslav, the community of Tabor had been represented very fully, the two Tabors of 1423 were not represented at all.[40]

The resolutions of the diet are laid down in six main points. The first one confirms the plans for a public hearing to be held at Brno at the beginning of 1424, with safe conduct guaranteed to the Hussites. Both sides will submit to the findings of the audience which are to be derived, clearly and lastingly, from the Scriptures.

Point three had already figured in the resolutions of both diets of Čáslav: all people of the Kingdom shall adhere, or be forced to adhere, to the resolutions here accepted. But again this measure, once directed against Royalist groups like the Pilsen Landfrieden, was now directed against Žižka and the Orebite community.

Point four establishes an armistice till the Day of St. Martin in 1424, that is, for a whole year. All conquered estates shall be returned to

39 *Archiv český*, III, 240.

40 For modern treatments of the diet, see Tomek, *Dějepis*, IV, 286-293, and Pekař, III, 229-235.

their original owners, but destroyed fortifications shall not be rebuilt. If, by the end of the armistice, no permanent understanding has been achieved, then those estates have to go back into the hands of their conquerors. The people banished from Prague in 1420, most of them Germans, are not included in this restitution settlement.

Points five and six are concerned with economic problems. The roads of the Kingdom shall be kept open for the movement of merchants and their goods. The coining of money outside the mint of Kutná Hora is prohibited under the threat of severe punishment. Special offices shall be established for the examination of current money. The measure shows the extent of illegal coining and inflation that had resulted from steadily diminished production and increasing cash expenses on the side of the lords, the cities, and the autonomous communities, especially in payment for the troops, their equipment, and their provisions.

By far the most important of the six points, however, was the second. It created a new regency council, superficially similar to the one established by the first diet of Čáslav. Yet nothing shows more clearly the change in the political situation than a comparison of these two governmental bodies.

The diet of Čáslav had elected a regency council of twenty men, representing all Hussite groups and all estates. They all had accepted the Four Articles before being elected. This time the number was restricted to twelve regents, six of them Hussites and six "barones sub una," that is, Catholics. Among the latter we find Čeněk of Wartenberg, Ulrich of Rosenberg (who was elected even though he was not present), and a leading representative of the Pilsen Landfrieden: Frederick of Kolovraty. There were two other barons from the north, one from central Bohemia.[41]

On the Hussite side we find the leaders of the conservative nobility: Hašek of Waldstein, Hynek of Kolstein, and Hynek Krušina of Lichtenburg; one of the lords who had generally belonged to the left: Herman of Borotín;[42] and two knights: Diviš Bořek of Miletínek and John Smiřický, Prague's captain governor at Mělník. If it had

[41] The last mentioned is Aleš Holický of Sternberg, known to us as one of Sigismund's ambassadors at the first diet of Čáslav. Some months later he went over to the Hussite side.

[42] Herman of Borotín, a baron whose estates lay in the region of Tabor, had since 1420 taken the side of the southern community and remained allied to it till his death in 1425. It seems likely that this election was intended to neutralize the Old Tabor in the impending fight between the conservative nobility of both creeds against Žižka and the Orebites. On the other hand it seems hardly possible to consider Borotín (as Pekař does, with some reservation, in III, 233) as the official representative of Tabor at the diet. Nothing in the records justifies such an assumption. See also below, the beginning of Chapter 25.

not been for the two last-named men the new regency council would have consisted entirely of barons. But as both Miletínek and Smiřický, in terms of wealth and social standing, belonged to the very highest group of their estate, they hardly impaired the homogeneity of this body. There were no squires among the members, no townsmen, not even any "lords of Prague," that is, city councilors.

With the regency council of the St. Gall diet the high nobility of Bohemia tried to take over again the government of the Kingdom. The class character of this new ruling body as a baronical oligarchy excluded all other potential centers of power. Prague, once so strong, seemed at the mercy of the magnates, notwithstanding the clause which obliges all signatories "to defend, if necessary, with all their force the capital city of Prague against all who might plot against her safety, so that this city be preserved in its power and sustained in its order." This passage may indicate that even then there was some apprehension lest Žižka should attempt to conquer Prague.[43]

King Sigismund's name is not mentioned in these records. Nevertheless the Royalists hoped that the program of internal appeasement approved by the diet would eventually lead to the recognition of his kingship. Sigismund himself was kept informed by Ulrich of Rosenberg who had been elected into the council of regents although he had not been present at the diet. On November 24 Sigismund wrote to Rosenberg, warning him not to adhere to the agreements of the St. Gall diet until he fully knew the King's intentions.[44] Soon afterwards, the King received a more detailed report on the St. Gall diet, again through John Městecký and Půta of Častolovice.[45] On this basis he agreed to grant safe conducts to the Hussites for their travel to Brno. In the question, however, of a lay jury to decide about the Four Articles he withheld his agreement, having been warned off by the papal legate Cardinal Branda.[46] Thereby, however, the whole scheme fell through. The Hussites would not submit the decision to any authority which they would have had to consider as biased. The idea of a public hearing remained in

[43] But Tomek, *Dějepis*, IV, 288, thinks that the passage is put in because of Švamberg's and Hvězda's raid a year earlier.

[44] *Urk. Beiträge*, I, 308.

[45] Windecke (p. 172) tells us that the two lords arrived at Stuhlweissenburg in Hungary on the day of St. Elizabeth (November 19). He must have erred by about a week as the King's letter to Rosenberg of November 24 (see note 48) clearly was written before their arrival.

[46] See Sigismund's letter to Rosenberg of November 30 in *Archiv český*, I, 17.

abeyance, to be taken up in the following spring, this time in negotiations with King Władysław of Poland.

There is another version of the reasons why no agreement was reached on the public hearing between Sigismund and the Hussite nobility. "The Husses and Heretics of Prague had come to an understanding with Žižka . . . and thus they were and remained rascal Husses and Heretics as before."[47] This version, coming from a source very near Sigismund, shows that in the King's entourage Žižka was rightly considered the most consistent enemy of any compromise, any attempt at an understanding between the adherents of the Chalice and King Sigismund. The failure of this latest diplomatic interlude was therefore laid at his door.

The explanation itself, of course, was wrong. There was, as yet, so soon after the St. Gall diet, no understanding between Žižka and the Hussite conservatives. It is true that there was no fight of "Ark against Ark" until March 1424. But this can be explained by the armistice concluded between both Hussite parties in September, as Žižka scrupulously stuck to those agreements that he had signed.

There had been no armistice between him and the Royalists. They were still legitimate objects of his holy war. He could not possibly feel bound by the general armistice concluded at the St. Gall diet—agreements in which he and his communities had had no part, which had been concluded not with but against him. Thus we cannot be surprised to find him embattled again in the Orebite region at the very beginning of the year 1424, once more in the depth of the winter. And his foes, this time, were truly "natural": the lords of Opočno and Častolovice, old arch-enemies of Tabor, responsible for the slaughter of Chotěboř, who had attacked Hradec Králové a short time before they went on their repeated mission to their liege Lord Sigismund. And as if all this had not been enough, Žižka had just been informed about a plot on the side of these men aimed at his personal destruction.

On November 22 a letter was dispatched to Žižka from Hradec Králové.[48] The author was Priest Ambrose who wrote it with his own hand. As cosigners appear John Hvězda who, as we have to conclude from this source, had meantime been appointed by Žižka as captain of Hradec Králové's forces, as well as the burgomaster and the councilors of that city. The document is the only preserved piece of his correspondence in which Žižka is the addressee, not the writer.

[47] Windecke, *loc.cit.*
[48] *Archiv český*, III, 302.

The letter is the outcome of a hurried meeting which the men in authority at the Orebite center had called upon discovering the shocking news of a plot to assassinate their beloved chief. It had been betrayed by a man of the "party of those of Opočno" who had been taken prisoner. (The war between those lords and Hradec Králové had gone on without interruption throughout the fall of 1423.) The prisoner had informed them that the prospective murderer dwelt already among Žižka's soldiers. He had been given ten three-scores of groše and was to receive another thirty three-scores in cash upon the fulfillment of his mission—a handsome reward indeed amounting in buying power to a few thousand dollars. Luckily the man was known to one of the soldiers of Hradec Králové, "Paul with the black curly head," and therefore this Paul is sent as the messenger with this letter and with the task of identifying the hired murderer and informing the general on all details of the plot. Žižka is asked to trust him and to believe all he is going to hear from him. And the letter ends with the words: "May the Almighty Lord protect thee, for His own praise and for the well-being of the communities of the faithful."

The man whom Lord John Městecký of Opočno, perhaps in agreement with other men of his party, had hired for the murder of Žižka never had a chance to claim the outstanding seventy-five percent of the blood money. Sometime before the end of the year Žižka moved from Čáslav up to Hradec Králové. From there he marched north with his troops early in January to punish the men whom he had reason to hate and despise more than any other enemies. John Městecký and Půta of Častolovice—the two lords had become inseparable friends—had received succor from two other Royalist barons of the region: Ernest of Černčice and Hynek Červenohorský, the latter known to us as Royalist captain of Jaroměř before May 1421.[49] It was very near Jaroměř, at the little town of Skalice, that the two armies met. Žižka thoroughly defeated the Royalists who suffered great losses in dead and prisoners.[50]

After the battle of Skalice nearly two months passed without any major action. Early in March, Žižka fought against a Hussite lord, John Krušina of Lichtenburg, brother of Hynek, the former Orebite leader. It was probably the date when the armistice of September had expired, but even this does not explain why Žižka selected Krušina's castle Hos-

[49] In the report on this battle by the Old Annalists the baron is called *John* Červenohorský which, however, can only be an error as there was no member of this family bearing this Christian name at the time. See Tomek, *Žižka*, p. 185, n. 14.

[50] Old Annalists, p. 62 and *Chronicon veteris Collegiati*, p. 87.

tinné as the target for an attack which, according to the chronicler[51] remained unsuccessful. Had Krušina, following the orders of the St. Gall diet, given support to one of the Catholic lords attacked by the Orebites? It is the only plausible explanation offered so far for Žižka's action.[52]

Much clearer are the motives for his next move: it was directed against the castle and small town of Mlazovice,[53] property and residence of John Černín, who had been Hašek of Waldstein's lieutenant in the battle of Týnec in August 1423 and had personally killed Lupák, the captain of Hradec Králové. Now Žižka settled the account. Mlazovice was destroyed, Černín himself was killed. The episode shows the intensely personal element which was still present in Žižka's warfare, however rational it appears in its tactical and technical aspects when compared with the ways of his contemporaries.

But was it really so rational, even in those relative terms? What we know of his warfare in the early spring of 1424 seems to reflect little of his clearness of purpose in military or political terms. We read of some other knights or squires, followers of Čeněk of Wartenberg, attacked and of some more villages or little towns taken and burned.[54] It was a war of pitiless and thorough destruction, refuting the romantic idea that "total war" is an invention of our modern, technological, and God-forsaken age. But what was the plan behind all these raids? Had Žižka's holy war degenerated into mere revolutionary banditry?

Palacký has said that Žižka's last year, 1424, was also his bloodiest year. Maybe so. But we would be greatly mistaken if we concluded, from our fragmentary knowledge of this guerilla war of March and April 1424, that the grand conception of Žižka's theocratic Bohemian commonwealth, and of the strategy to attain it, had been lost. On the contrary, at no other time was his policy, political and military, as clearly outlined as during the later spring and summer of that year, and at no time did it get as near to realization as then. But not until May 1424 can we see these plans unfold.

[51] Old Annalists, *loc.cit.*

[52] The explanation is Tomek's. See his *Žižka*, p. 186.

[53] Old Annalists, *loc.cit.*

[54] *ibid.* See also Pekař, III, 238, 239.

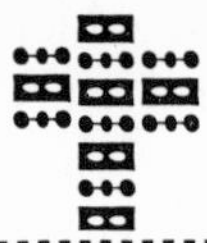

# CHAPTER 25

## THE ROAD TO MALEŠOV

IN JULY 1423 Lord Bohuslav of Švamberg had separated himself from Žižka and had led his army back south. For the remainder of 1423 we are without news of Tabor. Only one occurrence can be understood as reflecting Tabor's position at that time: The election of Lord Herman of Borotín to the regency council in November 1423. Even though this baron was not one of Tabor's permanent military leaders, as was for example Bohuslav of Švamberg, his connection with the brotherhood —before as well as after the St. Gall diet—was so close that his presence at the diet and in the regency council cannot be considered as a mere incident. Obviously the lords of both creeds had felt it important to eliminate Old Tabor as a possible enemy at a moment when they tried to join all available forces against Žižka. Borotín's signature under the armistice agreement of November and his presence in the regency council did not bind the Taborite community, but he would hardly have taken those steps if Tabor had strongly opposed them. Clearly Tabor was quite willing to stay neutral in the struggle between Žižka and the broad coalition of his enemies.

Why this should have been so remains somewhat difficult to understand. We can only refer, as an explanation, to the reasons for the break between Žižka and Tabor discussed previously,[1] especially the likelihood of personal conflicts between Žižka and Bohuslav of Švamberg.

The policy of neutrality conducted by Tabor in the winter 1423-1424 is not a matter of conjecture. We have documentary proof for it, though from a somewhat later date. On February 10, 1424, the Taborite communities, together with some of the lords allied with it, concluded an

[1] See above, Chapter 21. Pekař, toward the end of vol. III, devotes a chapter to this question (pp. 253-260) which, however, does not give any clearcut answers either. He stresses, however, much more than I have done the possibility that Tabor, or at least its clergy, was dissatisfied with the rough and pitiless character of Žižka's warfare. I don't believe that this could have been the main reason for the break, as otherwise it would be quite inexplicable why, soon after Žižka's death, Tabor elected Žižka's disciple Hvězda as captain general, a man who, as Pekař himself admits, was and remained just as reckless in his methods of warfare as Žižka had been.

armistice with the Pilsen Landfrieden.[2] Besides Tabor-Hradiště it included the towns of Písek, Klatovy, Prachatice, and Sušice—in other words, the more important towns of the old Taborite brotherhood with the exception of Domažlice. This city, as we know, had always had especially close ties with Žižka[3] and therefore seems to have temporarily relinquished her bonds with the Taborite federation. Žižka's party, incidentally, had one more foothold left in the south: the town and castle of Lomnice, still held by Roháč of Dubá.

For Žižka this armistice was a painful setback. If in March 1423 he had still counted on the Taborite communities as a reliable following, if in June and July they had at least functioned as his allies, they had now taken a stand which left his enemies free to concentrate all their forces against him. The Pilsen Landfrieden in particular had never dared to interfere up to now in any battles in central or eastern Bohemia. Now, with Tabor out of the way, they could enter the fight against Žižka without fear.

It took Žižka some time to react to this situation. In April he was still engaged in the guerilla warfare in the Orebite region. Only in the beginning of May was he ready to take a decisive action. There is nothing strange about this. Only when faced with a clear emergency would Žižka act with the swiftness which alone could save the day. In other contingencies he usually counted the odds carefully and took his time. Once he had clarified the issues in his mind his decision would show that combination of great daring and apparent simplicity of design which throughout history has been one of the marks of true generalship.

The military potential of the Lesser Tabor was as yet limited, and in view of the strong alliance of his enemies Žižka could not denude his Orebite cities of their militia forces. For any major offensive move he had to rely on his standing army. With it he decided to attack the Pilsen Landfrieden, some 150 miles from his present bases and separated from them by the now hostile region of Prague and her subject towns. For the first time during the later phase of Žižka's leadership we have, from a generally reliable and competent source,[4] a precise information

2 From the Archives at Cheb published by K. Siegel in *Zeitschrift d. Ver. f. Geschichte Mährens und Schlesiens*, XXII, 1918, p. 48. See also Pekař, IV, 155.

3 Two of his preserved letters were addressed to that town, apparently only a fragment of a much richer correspondence between Žižka and Domažlice. See M. Millauer, *Diplomatisch-historische Aufsätze über J. Žižka*, Prague 1824, p. 8.

4 Bartošek of Drahonice (or Drahenice). He was a squire from southern Bohemia, serving

on the strength of his forces. He had with him 500 horse and 7,000 other troops with 300 wagons, a strong but far from overwhelming body of troops.

The Pilsen Landfrieden, if attacked in their own region, could collect forces stronger than that. Žižka could hardly expect, with his present army, to conquer the great city of Pilsen. He could, however, harrow and harm the forces of the Landfrieden so that in the future they would still be wary of adventures in distant theaters of war. He could, furthermore, hope to pick up at least some troops of the old Taborite federation if he showed himself in their immediate vicinity.

This, indeed, would have a significance far beyond the numerical increase of his army. If he induced one or the other of the older Taborite towns to join him, and renounce the recent armistice with Pilsen, then the Landfrieden could no longer feel safe and free to act. And if he regained control of a significant part of Old Tabor, then this would be the only strong answer to the challenge offered by the united front of Hussite and Catholic barons. It would be a great step forward on the way to mobilizing as many as possible of the Hussite towns against the power of the high nobility.

Žižka, as we know, had been reluctant to accept John Želivský's generalizing views on the high nobility as a treacherous, religiously and politically untrustworthy class of people. He had never excluded from his friendship those barons who truly stood by what he considered the demands of God's Law. Nor was he to do so at any later time.

But the closing of ranks among the conservative barons of both creeds could not remain without influence upon his actions. For all the support he had received from his baronial friends the mainstay of his political and military strength had still come from the Hussite towns. A federation of Bohemian towns far beyond the geographic limits of the Orebite region would therefore be the most effective instrument for the reestablishment of a strong, united Hussite commonwealth, fully devoted to the victory and the fulfillment of the Law of God. It was to the creation of such a strong coalition of towns—if possible voluntary, if need be by force—that Žižka devoted himself in this spring and summer of 1424.[5]

---

during the Hussite wars with the Royalists, at times with the Karlstein garrison. See on him Pekař, II, 104-105. His chronicle is edited by Goll in *Fontes rerum Bohemicarum*, v, 591ff. The quoted figures appear on p. 592.

[5] In most previous historical accounts it appears almost as a matter of chance that Žižka, standing before Prague in the late summer of 1424, had as his allies a majority of the most important cities of the Kingdom. Yet at least in Pekař's account (III, 244, 254) it becomes clear

Exactly when Žižka started on his great march westward is unknown, but by the middle of May he had already been in the region of Pilsen for some time, and his attacks upon the possessions of the Landfrieden had been vigorous and successful enough to induce that federation to send out calls for help. On May 17 the Royalist garrison on the Karlstein sent them a small squadron of cavalry under the leadership of two lords,[6] and help was sought and received also from other Royalist centers.[7] Apart from these and its own town militias (Pilsen, Stříbro, Tachov, and some smaller communities) the Landfrieden was joined by the forces of at least five regional lords, among them Hanuš of Kolovraty and Krušina of Švamberg, Bohuslav's younger brother.

Žižka, with Hvězda and Roháč as his lieutenants,[8] began his attacks in the southern part of the Pilsen region, that is between Klatovy and the city of Pilsen. There "he burned many towns and villages." But he also received the help and adherence of two Taborite towns: of Klatovy and the neighboring Sušice.[9] Klatovy in particular put 300 men of her town militia under his command.

In the second phase of this campaign, Žižka shifted his attacks farther to the north, the region between Pilsen and Královice. In that neighborhood the newly reinforced army of the Landfrieden eventually sought to challenge him, but Žižka did not accept battle. Instead he continued his march northward.[10] The army of the Landfrieden did not pursue Žižka's army for any distance but turned back south before even reaching Královice.[11]

It seems that Žižka did not want to risk a decision at a moment when

---

that this was the result of a very systematic policy on the part of Žižka, even though Pekař, with his usual bias, treats this policy only as a testimony for Žižka's regrettable recklessness.

[6] Our main source on this campaign is Bartošek of Drahonice (*loc.cit*). But Bartošek wrongly puts it into June. Tomek (*Dějepis*, IV, 297, n. 1) discovered an expense account of the Karlstein garrison which permitted the exact dating of this and some following events in which the Karlstein forces were involved. He did, however, believe that Žižka had campaigned twice in the Pilsen region during the spring of 1424, even though he (as before him Palacký) recognized (*ibid.*, p. 301, n. 5) that Bartošek's dates were impossible. Only Pekař (III, 243) saw the right solution: there was only one campaign to the Pilsen region. The notices in the Karlstein account and Bartošek's reports cover one and the same sequence of events.

[7] Bartošek (p. 592) mentions troops from the Podbrdy (that is the region around Příbram) besides those from the Karlstein.

[8] Bartošek (*loc.cit.*) mentions only Hvězda, but from other sources we know that, in the later stages of the campaign, Roháč too was present, very likely from the beginning.

[9] Both towns are named as part of Žižka's federation in the armistice concluded with Rosenberg in September 1424. (See Chapter 27 below.) Klatovy's help to Žižka is expressly mentioned in Bartošek's chronicle, p. 593.

[10] Bartošek, with some exaggeration, describes this retreat as flight.

[11] Instead they turned on Klatovy, burning an outer bulwark, "suburbium in Glatovia satis bonum et firmum." See appendix to Bartošek's chronicle, p. 626.

he had hope of strengthening, without any risks, his federation of towns and thereby broadening the basis for all later enterprises. From Královice one day's march would take him to Žatec. That town's adherence would weigh more heavily in his favor than almost any other gain that would presently seem within his reach. The city had proved its strength especially during the Second Crusade. After having regained, with Klatovy, Sušice and probably also Domažlice, control at least over some part of the southwest, the conclusion of a firm alliance with Žatec would assure him a strong position in the northwest as well. This, indeed, was to be the result of Žižka's appearance. Žatec had always been on friendly terms with the old knight of the Chalice. Agreements were now concluded which gave Žižka the certainty that in the case of an all-out struggle Žatec would be on his side. And when, after a stay of some days, Žižka marched on eastward to Louny he achieved there the same result.[12]

It is at this point that Prague reentered the scene as an active participant. After the defeat of Strachův Dvůr nothing much had been heard of her for a long time. At the St. Gall diet, though it took place in Prague, the elected government of the city stood largely in the shadow of the great lords. By and large Prague's policy was still made, or at least greatly influenced, by the two men who had played a dominant role there ever since Prince Korybut had ruled over the Kingdom and its capital: Lord Hašek of Waldstein and William Kostka of Postupice. Their main interest as well as that of the University was still focused in the early spring of 1424 upon attempts at reconciliation with the Church, conducted through the mediation of the royal court of Poland.[13] Thus the capital does not seem to have taken any notice when, at the beginning of May, Žižka and his army by-passed Prague on their long march from the Orebite region to Klatovy. Nor do we hear of any help given to the Pilsen Landfrieden when that federation was attacked by Žižka, though on the basis of the obligations entered into at the St. Gall diet Prague should have had the duty to render such assistance. This inactivity may reflect the feeling of the city's population that as long as Žižka only attacked the Pilsen Landfrieden he was not doing anything very wrong, no matter what the agreements of the St. Gall diet might say about such a contingency.

But things were different in regard to Žatec and Louny. Žatec, to be

[12] This can only be concluded from the later actions of the Launyans. See Pekař, III, 244.

[13] About this and the general policy of Prague early in 1424, see the beginning of Chapter 26.

sure, had throughout maintained its autonomy, but early in 1424 the city was still regarded as a reliable ally by Prague.[14] It must have been a shock for the lords of the capital to see this strong city now firmly ally itself with Žižka. And the adherence of Louny to Žižka's federation was, in a way, even more upsetting. For ever since spring 1421, Louny had acknowledged the suzerainty of Prague. Her joining up with Žižka was, from the point of view of Prague, another rebellion quite like the one by which the Orebite cities had shaken off Prague's supremacy. And Louny—barely thirty-five miles distant from Prague—was too near for comfort. It must have been at the time when Žižka entered Louny, that is about May 25 or 26,[15] that the leaders of Prague decided it was time to stop the steady growth of his forces. They not only mobilized their own troops but also asked for speedy help from other sides, including the garrison of the Karlstein and the Landfrieden of Pilsen.[16] Thus the coalition of Hussite Conservatives and Catholic Royalists, clearly foreshadowed by the agreements of the St. Gall diet, finally materialized in the form of a powerful army, numerically much superior to Žižka's forces.

Žižka meantime marched eastward toward the valley of the Elbe. According to a late source[17] he reached the river at Roudnice and thence followed its course upstream, always keeping on its left bank. In this way he got ever nearer to Prague. He must have crossed the Vltava a short distance before its junction with the Elbe at Mělník. Even then he was only about twenty miles from the capital and was still getting nearer.

It seems impossible that Žižka, at this stage, should have intended to attack Prague. His forces were quite insufficient for this purpose. Of course he knew at this time of the preparations made in the capital, and his plan, under these conditions, almost certainly was to return, without unnecessary delay, to one of the two cities which had become the almost equally ranking capitals of his brotherhood: Hradec Krá-

[14] See the mention of Žatec in the agreement concluded early in 1424 between Prague and Lord Aleš Holický of Sternberg, *Archiv český*, I, 151.

[15] It is at this date that, according to the Karlstein expense account (Tomek, *loc.cit.*), the forces sent to help the Pilsen Landfrieden returned.

[16] See the phrase in the *Chronicon Treboniense* (Höfler, I, 53) "Pragensibus cum lantfridone." Tomek (*Dějepis*, IV, 297, n. 2) believes that this refers to the alliance of lords and towns concluded at the St. Gall diet. I think (in agreement with Pekař, III, 244) that it is really the Pilsen Landfrieden that is meant, as the term, at least in Bohemia (not in Germany), had at this time assumed this special connotation.

[17] Hajek of Libočany. See Toman, *Hus. Valečnictví*, p. 336, n. 3.

lové or Čáslav. At either place he could easily defend himself, and to either of them he could summon reinforcements. The actual direction of his march points to Čáslav. In Prague, on the other hand, it is just possible that Žižka's homeward march which took him so near the great city was thought to be directed against the capital.

The great attack against Žižka began at the moment when he was about to reach the small town of Kostelec, only fifteen miles northeast of Prague. He had just time to put his wagon fortress in defense position, making use of a slight elevation in the immediate neighborhood of the little town.[18] This area, including the town, lies within a rather narrow bend of the river, open to the south. That exit was completely blocked by the enemy army. Once more, as on the Vladař and before Kutná Hora, Žižka seemed in the deadly embrace of a superior army, and once more hopes ran high among his enemies that this time, after all, he was truly caught. The complete confidence with which the leaders of the army of Prague, probably with Čeněk of Wartenberg and Hašek of Waldstein at the head,[19] looked forward to the moment of victory becomes clear from the messages they sent out. One of them reached the Bohemian Royalist barons who happened to dwell at the court of King Sigismund in Hungary. Among them was Ulrich of Rosenberg. The scene which took place at the arrival of this message is preserved by an eye-witness.[20] This is what he tells us:

"On the same day there came the message that the Praguers in Bohemia had invested Zissko, the captain of the Husses and Heretics, and that he would not get out of this. And there spoke some of the barons, especially the Lord of Rosenberg: 'Our Lord King, that man Zissko is being besieged so he cannot get away.' Said the King: 'He will get away.' Said the Lord of Rosenberg: 'Sire, he will not get away.' Said the King: 'He will get away.' Said the Bohemian lords as with one voice: 'He will not get away.' Thus the King acted to sting those barons because they had not done their best as they should properly have done but suffered such a base fellow of knavish birth to rule over Bohemia though they might quite well have prevented it. Then the Bohemian lords spoke up and said: 'Gracious Sire, would you bet a palfrey horse on our word that Zissko will not get away?' Then Sigemont the Roman King said: 'Yea I know, you ask me to bet so I shall lose!' All this the King did to ridicule those lords, as he knew well that they did not mean

[18] For details on the topography of Kostelec, see Toman, *loc.cit.*

[19] See the Neuberg manuscript (Old Annalists Text Sa) quoted by Toman, *op.cit.*, p. 337.

[20] Windecke, p. 197.

to keep faith with him, and he had always paid them back with benefactions. And then, soon afterwards, there came the message that Zissko had got away!"

Thus far our chronicler. He fails to describe the faces of the noble lords at the moment the second message arrived. Their consternation about the elusiveness of that base fellow was surely matched by the amazed anger of the leaders of the Prague army.

But this time Žižka did not battle his way through the ranks of his besiegers as he had done so often. Instead he managed to pass on the news of his adversity to his friends of Kunštat, Victorin and Hynek, who were at their castle Poděbrady, some twenty-five miles farther up the river. "And Lord Hynek Boček of Poděbrady came to his help, and led Žižka with his people away from there."[21] How did he do it? Did he, or did his guides know of a seldom used ford in this neighborhood? Or did he bring boats and rafts in which, during the dead of night,[22] Žižka's army was ferried across the river? Perhaps both techniques were combined. In any case the Praguers, when morning came, found empty camping grounds where a strong wagon fortress had stood the evening before. Žižka was safely on the north bank of the Elbe. It all had happened in the night of June 4, after a siege lasting six or seven days.[23]

Žižka immediately resumed his eastward march whereas the Praguers, first separated from him by the river, followed him upstream. At the first opportunity—probably at Brandýs—they too crossed over to the north bank. Žižka had to go around Nymburk and there the Praguers regained some of the time lost previously. At Poděbrady they almost caught up with him, but Žižka had already recrossed to the south bank, covered by the forces of the lords of Kunštat. At this moment, so we hear,[24] some parleying took place between both sides in which Hynek of Poděbrady played a prominent role. Perhaps he tried to mediate, but unsuccessfully, and in the course of those talks the Praguers arrested him. He was, for some time, kept as a prisoner, first at Nymburk and later at Mělník.

[21] Old Annalists, p. 62. Similarly text Sa, but with the claim that it was Victorin.

[22] The belief that this operation took place at night is not supported by documentary evidence, but it seems almost certain as Žižka had begun all similar movements at night time and as, if undertaken by day, it would have been discovered and perhaps prevented by the Praguers. See also Toman, *loc.cit.*, and Pekař, III, 239.

[23] By June 2 the Karlstein garrison, according to its expense account book (Tomek, *loc.cit.*) knew of the siege of Kostelec and sent troops to help. Thus the siege must have started at the latest on May 31, perhaps earlier. Žižka, according to Text Sa of Old Annalists (Toman, *op.cit.*, p. 337), escaped from Kostelec three days before the battle of Malešov, fought on June 7.

[24] Old Annalists, p. 62.

Hynek's brother Victorin, however, now joined Žižka's army with his retainers, and the march in the direction of Čáslav was resumed. To reach this city Žižka had to avoid Kolín and Kutná Hora. He was closely followed by the pursuing army, occasionally having to fight minor rearguard actions. Soon after bypassing Kutná Hora, Žižka decided to make a stand. He had, once more, found the place where he could trust his arms and his art of war.

Žižka was now near the little fortress of Malešov, once (in November 1421) conquered by the troops of Prague which then stood under the command of John Hvězda of Vícemilice. Hvězda was with Žižka now, together with Roháč, Victorin of Kunštat, and the brothers of Valečov,[25] and he probably knew the terrain especially well. But this whole region was, of course, most familiar to Žižka too. It was less than five miles from Kutná Hora, less than ten from Čáslav, and quite near his old road of victory between Kolín and Německý Brod. There was something familiar even about the date on which Žižka "turned around against the Praguers." It was June 7, the day on which, in 1421, the first diet of Čáslav had ended with a wide agreement between all national parties—the day also when, in 1422, the second diet of Čáslav had opened with Prince Korybut's declaration for the Four Articles of Prague.

The greatness of this battle, and the deep impression it made upon the contemporaries, is evinced by the chroniclers. Whereas some of the previous encounters are often registered only in one or two of the chronicles of the time, the Battle of Malešov is recorded, more or less extensively, in no less than seven contemporary or near-contemporary chronicles.[26] There is, however, one report which goes into great detail. It is part of a text which, in general, is rather late, but the account itself makes an authentic impression, and its first editor, Palacký, may well have been right in thinking that it was written by, or based on the report of, one of Žižka's soldiers.[27]

[25] *Chronicon veteris Collegiati*, p. 87.

[26] Old Annalists, *loc.cit.; Chronicon veteris Collegiati, loc.cit.; Chronicon Treboniense*, p. 53; Bartošek of Drahonice, p. 592; *The very pretty chronicle* (ed. Novotný), p. 20; Windecke, p. 197; Aeneas Sylvius, Chapter 44, p. 95. If text Sa of the Old Annalists is counted separately, the number is increased to eight.

[27] Old Annalists, pp. 62, 63. The detailed report belongs to texts L and M. The latter is the same which (on pp. 58 to 61 in Palacký's edition) contains the spurious tale about Žižka's campaign in Hungary, a fact which Pekař (III, 240) uses as an argument against the trustworthiness also of this report on the battle of Malešov. But though this text is contained in one manuscript, it would be wrong to assume that all of it is the work of one chronicler. I have

Žižka, according to this report, "marched rapidly before his pursuers so he would somewhere find a place favorable to put up his forces in battle order. And he got clear with his wagons, moving them up to a hill, and there he put up his wagon fort and waited for the Praguers. Those were chasing him, believing that he was already in full flight before them. And their detachments did not even properly wait for those in their rear. And thus they marched across the valley where Žižka was already waiting for them.

"And Žižka, in his preparation for the battle, arranged his forces in the following way: He put up his battle wagons wheels to wheel, and organized his detachments, first the cavalry, after that the infantry. Then he ordered some of the supply wagons taken out of the column and to be filled with rocks. And he put those wagons in the centre of his battle line between the cavalry detachments. . . .

"And when half of the enemy had crossed the bottom of the valley he ordered his cavalry to move, and the foot-soldiers in between the cavalry had to roll those wagons forward. And when the enemy troops approached and it seemed as if the two armies were about to clash, he ordered those wagons to be launched so they rolled down upon them from the hill. And thus he disrupted their formations with all those wagons. After that he ordered the guns to fire, and then he ordered his troops to charge. And thus it came that the enemy could not employ their battle order or make proper use of their troops, and they turned to flight. And when they began to flee they dragged along those who had marched behind them, so that in the end all were on the run.

"And thus Žižka obtained victory, and he captured their guns, their wagons and their other arms, blind as he was on both eyes. There were killed large numbers of citizens of the great city of Prague, and many people of knightly rank. And people agree that fourteen hundred people were slain on that day."

For a better understanding of this report a short description of the topography of the battlefield seems necessary. Careful studies made in the neighborhood of Malešov seem to have established, to a satisfactory degree, the actual place where the great clash occurred.[28] The dominating feature of this region is a large, fairly flat-topped elevation called Štimberky. It is surrounded on three sides—south, west, and

---

not been able to discover any essential contradictions between this text and the other sources which Pekař claims to have found.

[28] See Toman, *op.cit.*, pp. 339ff.

north—by the valley of a small river, the Malešovka, which, coming from the southeast, describes a horseshoe bend or loop. The Štimberky hill is highest in its northern part, slopes down rather steeply in the west, but forms a lower step or terrace in the south. The river valley, still wide in the east, narrows down in its western course. At the

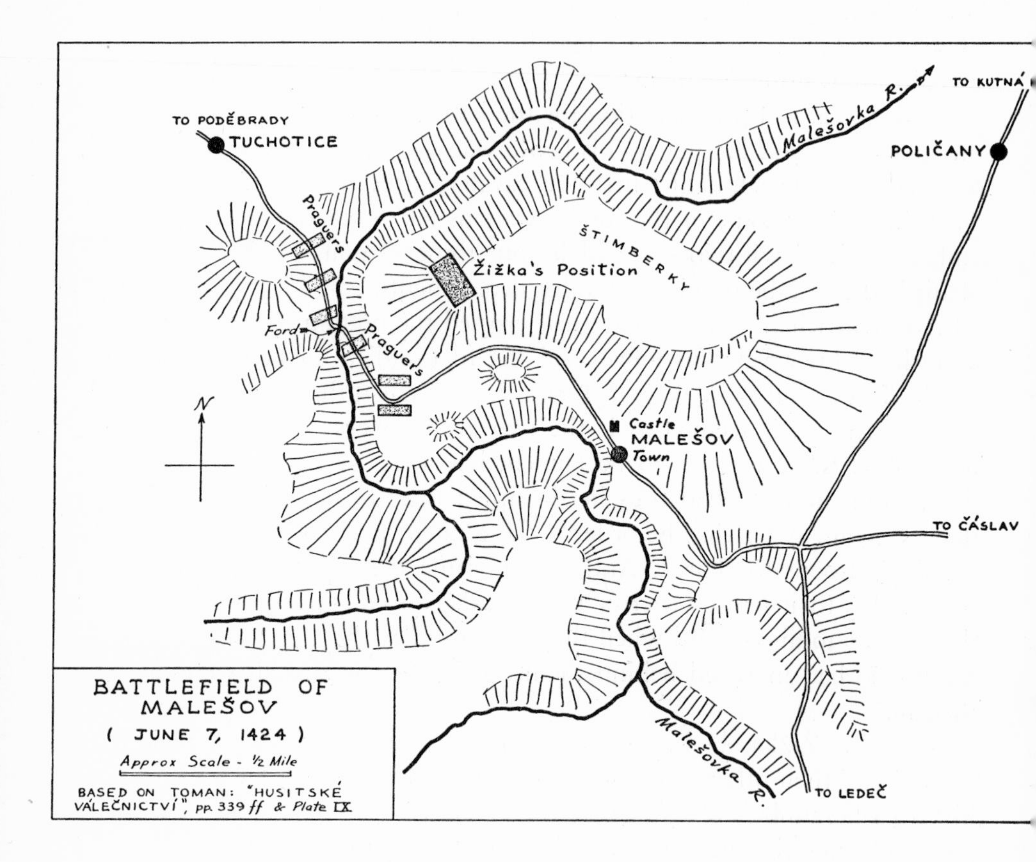


entrance to this narrow valley lies Malešov. Half a mile farther west the river turns sharply from its western to a northern direction, then later turns back more softly toward the northeast.

The road taken by Žižka and in his pursuit by the Praguers enters the Malešovka valley from the northwest, from the village of Tuchotice. The modern road crosses the river by means of a high bridge, but in the old times it led right to the bottom of the valley, forded the river in an oblique, southeasterly direction and then rose fairly steeply to gain the height of the terrace mentioned before. Turning from the southeasterly into an easterly direction it continued for a stretch on this terrace above the river, finally again descending to the bottom of the valley at Malešov and continuing east toward Čáslav.

Žižka then, after having entered and crossed the Malešovka valley and having reached the height of the terrace, left the road soon after it turned east and gained a higher position north of this turn. There he established his wagon fortress. His encampment overlooked the place where, just to the west of his position, the road crossed the river, and dominated the whole stretch of the road where it worked itself up from the bottom of the valley toward the terrace.

The choice of this position shows that Žižka, here as always, knew how to use the terrain, but this time in a more interesting and more subtle way than ever before. Our reports point clearly to what must be considered the most essential feature of Žižka's battle plan: he began his attack at the moment when only half of the enemy army, strung out along the narrow road, had crossed the valley bottom. Thus, when the fight began, a large portion of the Prague army was quite unable to take any part in it. The van and the other forward elements of the Praguers, however, were exposed to Žižka's flank attack. Compared to this general plan of attack it would seem that the trick of the stone-filled wagons, striking though it has seemed to some of Žižka's modern biographers or historians,[29] played only a secondary role. There is no reason to doubt that the old general, resourceful as he was, improvised those self-propelled juggernauts which, when they had a chance to gain sufficient speed on the slope, may have terrified the Prague troops, and if they turned over before reaching the marching line of the enemy, may still have spilled an uncomfortable avalanche of heavy rocks upon them.[30] But even discounting this clever device with its mainly psychological impact, Žižka had virtually won the battle at the moment that the army of Prague, by its unprotected march across the valley and up to the terrace, had exposed itself to the concentrated impact of Žižka's forces against its left flank. Once its forward elements had succumbed to it, the center would try to fall back across the river, thereby affecting all the rest including the rear. The vigorous pursuit which would be the conclusion to a battle won by Žižka probably brought the number of dead up to those 1,400 which we find as the most frequently mentioned figure of Prague's casualties in the chronicles.[31] Among them

[29] E.g. Tomek, *Žižka*, p. 193. Toman (*op.cit.*, p. 344) thinks of the use of those wagons as a diversionary move.

[30] Toman (*op.cit.*, p. 341) has found traces of old stone quarries on the hill.

[31] Old Annalists (*loc.cit.*), *Chronicon Treboniense* (p. 53) and Bartošek of Drahonice (p. 592) agree in this figure, the latter, however, differing from the others in the claim that this figure

the sources mention two lords and three of the prominent knights in the service of the capital. One of the former was Henry of Dubá, Žižka's son-in-law. Whether he had fought with or against his father-in-law has never been established beyond dispute.[32]

The battle of Malešov was one of the greatest of the Hussite wars not only in terms of forces engaged and losses suffered. It largely determined the course of Bohemia's domestic history for the next decade. Not till the battle of Lipany, fought on May 30, 1434, did the coalition of lords and Praguers achieve what it had set out to do ten years earlier: the destruction of the field armies created by Žižka. But by then these same field armies, under other leaders, had demonstrated the invincibility, the indestructibility of the Hussite movement so convincingly to the rest of Europe and to the Church of Rome that the attempt to suppress it by force of arms from outside had been given up. In this sense Žižka, at Malešov, saved the Hussite movement and insured its survival for the third time.

But the immediate impact of the battle was no less striking. At one fell swoop most of the cities of eastern Bohemia which so far had still been ruled over by Prague were now lost by the capital and gained by Žižka. The first step in this direction was taken on the very evening after the battle of Malešov. Having completed his pursuit Žižka marched to Kutná Hora where the frightened inhabitants dared to put up hardly any resistance.

Yet the city was not treated leniently. The Kutnohorian militia had taken part in the battle against Žižka,[33] and besides he could hardly have forgotten what had happened there in the days before Christmas 1421. When Žižka's army entered the city many people were killed and even a church where some of them had taken refuge was set on fire. Many houses, once saved by Žižka's troops from the fire laid by Sigismund's Hungarians, were now burned down.[34] Yet Žižka and

contains the losses of both sides. As the *Chronicon veteris Collegiati* gives 1,200 as the loss of the Praguers there is the possibility that Bartošek is right, i.e. that 200 men were lost on Žižka's side. (See also Tomek, *Dějepis*, IV, 299, n. 4.) The figures of 3,000 dead given by Aeneas Sylvius and 4,000 given by text Sa of the Old Annalists are unlikely. *The very pretty chronicle* (p. 20) only says that, "because of this battle, there were many widows and orphans in Prague and elsewhere in the land."

[32] See Tomek, *loc.cit.*, and Pekař, II, 17 and 18. In one of the texts of the Old Annalists Dubá's first name is given as Andrew.

[33] Text Sa of Old Annalists as quoted by Toman, *loc.cit.*

[34] Old Annalists (p. 63), say that "Žižka burned what remained." Text Sa of the Annalists (*loc.cit.*) goes even further and claims that for a quarter of a year no living soul was left in Kutná Hora (which, of course, is a very obvious exaggeration and is contradicted even by Windecke, p. 198).

his party had a strong interest in Kutná Hora's continued functioning as the great mining and minting center for Bohemia's silver supply. This, indeed, was the main gain for Žižka and the main loss for Prague in this action.

Žižka did not appoint a successor to Lord Hašek as mint master but turned the administration of the mines and the mint over to some experienced foremen of the mining community.[35] To a large extent the originally purely German mining population, especially after the conquest by Žižka, was replaced by Czechs, many of them veterans of Žižka's army. A few years later the city and its mines came to be governed by two captains, one nominated by the Orebites (then called Orphans), the other by the Taborite community.[36]

Having firmly established his rule at Kutná Hora Žižka turned back west, to Kouřim. The town was still under the captaincy of Diviš Bořek of Miletínek, but he did not try to organize any resistance. Kouřim submitted to Žižka much as it had submitted to Prague in April 1421. In the same way Žižka received, during the remainder of June,[37] the surrender or adherence of Český Brod and Nymburk. With Nymburk gained, all the great Elbe towns except Kolín were now under Žižka's rule. And the inclusion of Český Brod pushed the Orebite dominion to within twenty miles from the capital. There is no mention of any resistance on the part of Prague—its military power had simply collapsed as a result of Malešov. Altogether the June campaign put the whole vast region of eastern Bohemia, which, with Žižka's strong support, had been subjected to Prague in 1421, now under Žižka's domination.

Only some scattered fragments of information on Žižka's activities are preserved for the next two months. Sometime in July—probably after having spent some time in one of the Orebite centers, Čáslav or Hradec Králové—he went to the northeastern corner of this region, to the town of Turnov, common property of two royalist lords: Henry of Wartenberg, one of Čenék's numerous cousins, and John of Michalovice, who was a member of the regency council elected by the St. Gall diet. The town was conquered, and among the victims were the monks

35 See Tomek, *Žižka*, p. 194.

36 *Archiv český*, VI, 420. About the settling of Taborite and Orebite soldiers in Kutná Hora see J. Šimek, *Kutná Hora v XV a XVI století*, Kutná Hora 1907, Chapter I.

37 Owing to the wrong dating of the campaign in the Pilsen region by Bartošek of Drahonice (see above, n. 6) modern historians have assumed that all this was the work of a couple of days (e.g. Tomek, *Žižka*, p. 194). Pekař's correction has invalidated this unlikely assumption.

of a Dominican monastery which was burned down with its inhabitants.[38] Altogether Žižka seems, at this time, to have wrought much destruction wherever he went, and to have indulged in his old, cruel ways as "severe avenger of the sins of the clergy." Sometime later we hear that he burned four monks at Libochovice, a town between Litoměřice and Louny, this time however with the specific claim that these clerics had done violence to women.[39]

This event took place on September 1. From it we also learn that, in the meantime, Žižka had gone from Turnov to the region of Litoměřice where he may have spent some time—the last time—at his own castle of the Chalice, planning for the next great move. That this would be directed at no less a goal than Prague herself could perhaps be concluded even earlier. For in the middle of July he had sent Hvězda with some troops south to conquer and garrison the castle of Ostromeč, near Živohoust' at the Vltava, some twenty-five miles south of the capital,[40] a move probably intended to block or hamper an important river-crossing as well as the southward communications of Prague.

But before Žižka made his final move in the great game he had to mobilize his forces as fully as possible. He could, of course, rely on his own field army, surely with a generous succor from the militias of the Orebite cities. But he also wanted to make good use of the forces of his western allies, cities like Žatec, Louny, Klatovy, and it seems that he completed the business of collecting his forces in the city or region of Žatec. From there, from the west, he approached the capital, and by September 8 or 9[41] he encamped with his army near the village of Libeň, within view of the famous Vítkov hill, or rather the Žižkov as it was now called in memory of his own glorious defense of the capital four years before. Now he stood on the other side of the walls of Prague.

But inside those walls a great change had occurred during the few months that had elapsed since the battle of Malešov. The capital had again become the residence of a monarchical ruler, a man to whom Žižka, two years earlier, had promised loyalty and obedience. Žižka must have been aware of this fact for many weeks. As yet, however, this knowledge had not changed his plans.

38 Old Annalists, p. 63, no. 139, and identical *Chronicon Treboniense*, p. 54.

39 Veleslavin's Historical Calendar as quoted by Tomek, *Dějepis*, IV, 305, n. 8.

40 Bartošek of Drahonice, p. 593.

41 On September 10 the Karlstein garrison had news about Žižka's move against Prague. See the quotation from the garrison's expense account, Tomek, IV, 305, n. 9.

# CHAPTER 26

## KORYBUT RETURNS, AND ŽIŽKA THREATENS PRAGUE

DURING the first years of the revolution even most of the conservative Hussites, people who kept alive their ardent hope for a reconciliation with the Church of Rome, had never seriously considered acknowledging Sigismund's claims to the kingship. At the end of 1423, however, as a result especially of the St. Gall diet, this constancy seemed to weaken for the first time. We have mentioned earlier the negotiations conducted with Sigismund through John Městecký and Půta of Častolovice. True, their object was to arrange a public hearing on the Four Articles. Yet Sigismund would hardly have involved himself in lengthy discussions about the safe-conduct to be given to the Hussite representatives if he had not seen in those preliminary contacts a bridge across which he might eventually proceed toward the possession of his dynastic heritage. He was quite eager to continue these discussions.[1] It was the Hussites who broke them off rather abruptly. Sigismund, in his disappointment, eventually came forward with new but rather vague plans for a fourth crusade[2] and with very strict orders reinforcing the embargo on exports from the Empire into Bohemia.[3]

More than any other Hussite group,[4] the city of Prague was responsible for the sudden collapse of the negotiations with Sigismund. The majority of its people had not overcome their old hatred for the King. For a long time, their voice had not carried too much weight. A city council much like the one elected in May 1422, soon after Korybut's arrival, seems still to have held office. It had been able to maintain a stability in rather striking contrast to the frequent changes which had characterized Prague's city government during the early years of the revolution. The man most responsible for this remarkable normalcy was

[1] See Sigismund's letter to Ulrich of Rosenberg, *Urk. Beiträge*, I, 321.

[2] *ibid.*, I, 333, 342.

[3] *ibid.*, I, 339, 340, 344.

[4] That there was also at this time a reaction against Sigismund within the high nobility is shown by the defection of Aleš Holický of Sternberg. See *Archiv český*, I, 151.

William Kostka. Still functioning as subchamberlain, the official responsible for supervising the government of the royal towns, he proved himself a strong and competent administrator. Having belonged to the Hussite center he held in general with the more conservative elements, but he knew when to relent and show moderation as he had proved after the Taborite raid of September 1422.[5] Under his supervision the Želivist elements in the New Town had not much chance of actively influencing the city's policy, yet he would avoid antagonizing them unnecessarily, and clearly nothing would irritate them as much as any deal with Sigismund.

But there was probably another reason why Kostka did not like the political trend that had developed at the St. Gall diet.[6] A deal with Sigismund would obviously dim the hopes for a reestablishment of monarchical rule with Prince Korybut as the ruler. This hope had never completely vanished, either among Korybut's adherents in Bohemia or among the pro-Bohemian party in Poland. Least of all had it been given up by Korybut himself. The Prince was surely still communicating with his friends in Prague, especially Kostka, whose Polish contacts ever since 1410 had been closer and stronger than those of any other Hussite leader, with the possible exception of Hynek of Kolstein.

In the first half of March, then, those contacts were reactivated by sending a diplomatic mission from Prague to Poland, followed by another one in April.[7] That the extreme right wing of the Hussites had ceased to wield the paramount influence at the capital is shown by the character and political color of the men leading those missions. The first embassy was entrusted to one of the least conservative masters of the University: the Englishman Peter Payne who already in 1421 had taken part in Hynek of Kolstein's second embassy. The second mission was led by Valkoun of Adlary, one of Žižka's earliest supporters among the high nobility who had accompanied him from Prague to Pilsen in November 1419, had gone on with him to Tabor five months later and

[5] See above, Chapter 21. Kostka is one of the most interesting and even most attractive figures of the Hussite revolution, though a great deal of his life as a national leader fills the story of later years which go beyond the frame of this book, especially his role in 1427 when he thwarted a baronial conspiracy to play Prague into the hands of the Royalists, and his diplomatic activity in connection with the Council of Basel. Much more than Čeněk of Wartenberg, whom Pekař wrongly singles out for such praise, he deserves to be considered as the model of the temperate and circumspect Hussite leader for whom the interest of his nation is paramount. It is regrettable that, as far as I am aware, no monograph on him has ever been written.

[6] It seems quite possible that he showed disagreement with the trend prevailing at the diet as he was not elected into the regency council, though he should have had at least as much claim to this position as Diviš of Miletínek or John Smiřický, both knights by origin.

[7] Dlugosz, *Opera omnia*, XIII, 323ff. See below n. 9.

was still to be found fighting at the side of Tabor as late as 1427.[8] The choice of these men might well reflect a temporary change in the feeling of Prague toward Žižka, which was only reversed again in May after Žatec and Louny had deserted Prague and allied themselves with the Orebite federation.

Payne's embassy[9] arrived in Poland almost in the footsteps of King Sigismund who, to prove his friendship for his "brother Władysław," had taken part at Cracow in the coronation festivities for the young Queen Sophia. The Praguers saw the Polish King at Wislica on March 25 and immediately renewed their demand for a hearing on the Four Articles, this time, however, not in Brno but in one of Moravia's Hussite towns, in Uničov or Kroměříž. The suggestion, immediately passed on to Sigismund, was declined. From Wislica the delegation went on to Lithuania and on April 25 met Grand Duke Witold at Przelom near Grodno. There the Czechs put forward an entirely new, surprising political demand. If, so they declared, you do not want to fulfill your previous promise to become our king, then at least permit your nephew, Prince Korybut, to mount the Bohemian throne. We would like to have him for our king, indeed we have already elected him.

Witold's answer was a sharp refusal. If Prince Korybut were to go to Bohemia he would regard and treat him as an enemy. A similar, though less harshly worded answer was given to Lord Valkoun when this second ambassador, at about the same time, asked Władysław for his agreement to Korybut's candidature.

But Władysław was remarkably ill-informed about what was going on between some of his powerful advisers and the Czechs. There is no doubt that Valkoun of Adlary saw Korybut before he returned to Prague sometime in May. And these negotiations were secretly supported by the men of the pro-Bohemian party, especially the Lord Chancellor of Poland, John Szafraniec.[10] Władysław only perceived an early result of this procedure: the Bohemian interest in an early hearing about the Four Articles seemed to have vanished. Deeply annoyed by what he believed to be a long-planned maneuver he began to mobilize some troops in the south around Cracow and then on June 17 wrote a letter to the Bohemians in which he repeated his intention, al-

[8] Tomek, *Dějepis*, IV, 360.

[9] For the best treatment of this phase of relations between Hussite Bohemia and Poland see Goll, "K. Sigmund und Polen," *Mitteilungen des Instituts für öster. Geschichte*, XVI, 233ff., also Pekař, III, 249ff.

[10] See A. Prochaska, "W Kwestyi Polsko Hussickiej," *Przewodnik Naukowy i literacki*, VIII, 1880, pp. 85-90; and O. P. Sherbowitz-Wetzor, *The Polish Foreign Policy . . .*, 195ff.

ready expressed a year ago, to fight them in alliance with King Sigismund.[11] A day or two later the incredible happened, incredible at least and utterly exasperating to the unsuspecting King: his own nephew, defying his strict orders, collected a small troop of half a thousand horse[12] and with them marched south, through Silesia where no one opposed him, and via Osoblaha reached Moravia.

It was perhaps only then that he learned of the newest turn of events in Bohemia, of Prague's defeat at the hand of Žižka or at least of the dreadful extent and effect of this defeat. But if Korybut regretted his daring step, now it was too late to reverse it. On June 29 he arrived in Prague.

Back in Poland King Władysław burned with anger and shame. He was very much afraid that he, too, would be suspected. Soon letter after letter left his chancery,[13] protesting his ignorance and innocence, accusing and cursing his disobedient nephew whom he disowned and whose estate he confiscated. He wrote to the German electors, singly and collectively, wrote to Sigismund, wrote to the Pope.

Even so he did not succeed in fully convincing Sigismund and his son-in-law Albert of Austria. For when, later in July, a Polish army of 5,000 men really entered Moravia and marched toward Olomouc in order to join Albert's forces against the Hussites, the gates of the city, on Albert's orders, were closed against the Poles. After two weeks of futile waiting they went home, surely to the intense satisfaction of Chancellor Szafraniec. There was, after all, to be no war between Poland and Hussite Bohemia.

For the people of Prague Korybut's arrival was a welcome event. And if Korybut himself should have felt discouraged by the weakened state in which he found Prague and its forces he did not show it in his first action of importance. He wrote a letter of challenge, or we might call it a declaration of war, to King Sigismund and to his son-in-law Albert of Austria, in which he called himself "postulated and elected King of Bohemia and Moravia."[14] He accused Sigismund of having oppressed the Truth of God, especially the Four Articles and the Communion in

[11] Dlugosz, *loc.cit.*, and *Urk. Beiträge*, I, 348.

[12] Dlugosz (p. 328) speaks of numerous troops, Bartošek of Drahonice (p. 592) of only 400 horse.

[13] *Urk. Beiträge*, pp. 348, 352, 354, and *Liber cancellarii Stanislai Ciolek*, *Archiv f. öster. Geschichte*, XLV, 350, 359, 361, 363, 364.

[14] The letter, undated, appears in Windecke, p. 168. Its approximate date is supplied by a reference to it in Sigismund's letter to Frederick of Brandenburg of July 14, *Deutsche Reichstagsakten*, VIII, 365.

the two kinds, and of having refused a free hearing to the Hussites. He ended with the assurance that he would fight for this truth to the limit of his strength.

It is the first and last time that the Prince used the title "king" in what is preserved of his correspondence. He was never to achieve the universal recognition which would have led to his coronation. At this moment the strongly worded letter almost gives the impression that he was whistling in the dark. Yet it was probably also good politics. If, disowned as he was by his uncles, he yet wanted to establish for himself a leading position in Bohemia which could eventually lead to the fulfillment of his dream of kingship, then he would have to try for a reconciliation between Prague and Žižka. And the one bond that could reunite them was their common antagonism against Sigismund.

But the Prince would still have to establish more firmly his rule over Prague and that part of Bohemia subject to it. He demanded and obtained from the city a renewal of the powers and privileges which he had enjoyed during his previous regency, including especially the administration of the royal towns still under Prague's domination.[15]

The number of these towns, however, had greatly decreased since Korybut had first held the regency. Of eighteen royal towns then under his direct rule only nine had remained, and four of those, precariously isolated in the easternmost part of the country,[16] could hardly be expected to be of any help to the capital in its hour of greatest danger. Nearer Prague there were still Kolín in the east, Mělník and Litoměřice in the north, Slaný and Beroun in the west, but no succor was forthcoming from them either.

Thus Prince Korybut, hardly more than two months after his return to the Bohemian capital, found himself in perilous isolation. The people of Prague knew Žižka well, but only as an ally and friend who had saved them twice. Now he stood before the gates, a threatening enemy. Those days in early September 1424 must have been a time of terrible, anguished tension in the old capital city of Bohemia.

What were Žižka's intentions at this moment? In turning his sword against the "mother of cities"[17]—how far would he want to go? Did he

[15] See the release of Litoměřice from its obligations to Prague in favor of Korybut, dated July 19, in *Archiv český*, I, 219.

[16] They were Chrudim, Vysoké Mýto, Litomyšl, and Polička. The nine cities lost were Hradec Králové, Dvůr Králové, Jaroměř, Čáslav, Kutná Hora, Kouřim, Nymburk, Český Brod, and Německý Brod. On the fate of the royal cities in 1424 and 1425, see Tomek, *Dějepis*, IV, 318, 319, 333.

[17] "Matka měst"—one of the epithets often used in relation to Prague.

want to destroy "the great whore Babylon" as some of the early Taborite fanatics would have liked to do? Hardly. His relation to the capital had been too long, too intimate for such a thought to persist in his mind, even if he had felt hatred against the city at certain moments, such as when he slew the priest at the battle of Strachův Dvůr. Besides there were thousands of people in the city who looked up to him and were ready to follow him in his religious as well as political ways. To add this reservoir of human strength to the mighty forces of townsmen and peasants which he had assembled and steadily increased since his separation from Tabor-Hradiště—this hope surely must have been foremost in his mind. By gaining the capital he would achieve a measure of strength which could no longer be challenged by anyone. He would then be able to cleanse Bohemia from all enemies of God and give freedom to His Truth and His Law.

This was a goal worth the heavy risk of an attack upon the great city, and its direct results would depend on what the city would do. There was a good chance that it would not fight him to the last—that it would surrender before it was too late.

It was an unusual and climactic situation for Žižka as well as all other protagonists in this great drama. Yet all we know about it from contemporary sources is the surprising fact that, before any serious attack was undertaken, on September 14, 1424, peace was concluded between Žižka and Prague. Only some thirty years after the event Aeneas Sylvius wrote a lively and detailed account on the tense hours before the intended attack.[18] Unfortunately we can never be quite sure how much of what he writes is fiction.

Some skirmishes, so Sylvius tells us, had already begun before the gates of the city. But in both camps many people thought ill of this whole fight, and on both sides some made Žižka, some the Praguers responsible for it. In Žižka's encampment there was some angry and excited talk. It was very wrong, so those soldiers said, to bear down with arms upon this city which was the head of the Kingdom and with whom there was no disagreement on religion. Bohemia's power could not last if her people fought one another instead of concentrating all strength against the Roman Emperor.[19] Therefore Žižka, so the Roman prelate continues, called his army together and addressed them in the following speech:

[18] Last part of chapter 44, pp. 96 and 97.

[19] Aeneas Sylvius always calls Sigismund Emperor although he was, at the time, just Roman King and was crowned as Emperor only in 1433.

"Brethren, do not be bitter against me, and do not accuse the man who has spent his life for your welfare. Still fresh are the laurels of the victories which you have gained under my command. Never yet have I led you to any place whence you have not returned victoriously. It is you who, thereby, have become famous and wealthy. I, on my part, have lost the light of my eyes for your cause, and already I walk in perpetual darkness. From all those wars, conducted so successfully, nothing remains to me but an empty name. For you I have struggled, for you I have conquered. I do not regret those labors, nor has my blindness been too hard to bear as long as I could work, first and foremost, in the furtherance of your cause.

"I do not persecute the Praguers for my own ends, and they are thirsting for your blood, not mine. Little would it avail them to destroy me, who am an old man already, and blind in both eyes. It is your strong arms they fear, and your spirit so undaunted in danger. Surely either you or they have to perish, and while they lay their ambush for me it is your souls they expect to fall prey to them. The armed enemies inside our country are more dangerous than our foreign enemies. Therefore it is necessary to crush the rebellion at home. Unless we conquer Prague, that rebellion will be free to destroy our people even before the news of our division reaches Sigismund. With fewer people, all spurred by the same spirit, we can expect the Emperor's attack with more assurance than if the Praguers, people whom we cannot trust, fight in our ranks.

"To make sure, however, that you can accuse me no longer, I shall give you the power to decide yourself in free council. If it pleases you to grant peace to the Praguers I shall not refuse, nor shall there be any subterfuge in my doing so. If, on the other hand, you decide for war, I shall be ready to serve you. Whatever decision you arrive at, Žižka will help you to carry out your resolve."

Žižka's speech, so Aeneas Sylvius relates, changed the mind of his soldiers. "They voted for war, multitudes of them hurried to get hold of their weapons, they rushed toward the walls of the city to challenge the enemy, to begin the battle for the gates, to drive back the defenders into the city. Žižka himself prepared everything for the city's conquest." With these words, still maintaining the tension of his exciting story, the Italian historian concludes one of the longest and richest chapters of his once famous book.

The beginning of his report on Žižka before the gates of Prague seems pretty near the truth. The large army which Žižka had assembled would contain many elements who had not yet been under his permanent influence long enough to follow him unquestioningly on whatever road he wanted to lead them,[20] and no task could raise their scruples as strongly as the attack on Prague.

Žižka's elaborate speech, however, is a different matter. Should we really believe that Žižka, when addressing his soldiers, would talk about himself in phrases constantly appealing to their sympathy as a poor, blind old man, and at the same time flattering them by his reference to their valor? Can we imagine Žižka making a speech of the highest importance without referring with one word to God, to His Law, to the Four Articles? The simple device of comparing this speech with any one of his letters and messages proves convincingly that much of it is not Žižka's voice that we hear but that of Aeneas Sylvius.

Are we, then, to conclude that the whole speech is spurious, that it was wholly invented by the prelate? Surely he would have had no qualms in doing just that, in the interest of effective storytelling. Yet there are elements in the speech which sound rather authentic. We know for instance that Žižka was inclined to compare the importance of the fight against domestic foes with the need to struggle against foreign enemies.[21] It also seems in accordance with Žižka's peculiar self-righteousness that he should regard not his own actions but those of his Hussite adversaries as a "rebellion"—as an unlawful and sinful revolt against the brotherhood of the God-fearing, God-inspired Czechs. There is finally his assurance that it is better to fight with a smaller troop of concordantly inspired men than with a larger army containing untrustworthy elements. This, too, seems a truly Žižkaesque thought, quite in character with the man who taught his people never to mind the enemies' great numbers.[22]

On the grounds of these elements—all contained in the second half of the speech—it seems permissible to assume that Žižka did, indeed, address his troops when he perceived the dissatisfaction in their ranks, using some of the arguments just noted, and that Aeneas Sylvius, through the very good contacts at his disposal, was informed about them. The rest of the speech—especially its first part—was then made up by him according to what he felt Žižka should have said. Even this, however, is not entirely without value to us as it contributes to our

20 This point is made convincingly by Pekař, III, 262.

21 For Žižka's letter of encouragement to Domažlice, see Appendix, IV.

22 For "Žižka's battle song," see Appendix, XI. There is no disagreement among Czech historians that it was written under the direct influence of Žižka's ideas and expresses them perfectly.

knowledge of the impression which Žižka had made upon his contemporaries and especially his enemies. Impossible as it seems that Žižka should himself have emphasized his unselfish devotion to his cause and his indifference to fame or worldly riches, this emphasis was high praise coming from the pen of a leading Roman prelate. Aeneas Sylvius had, indeed, gone rather far in what might almost be called the glorification of one of the most dangerous heretics of all times,[23] and, as we shall see, he would feel obliged to make up for it.[24]

All preparations, we have heard, had been made for a grand assault upon the city, and yet it did not get under way. How was Žižka's firm resolve thwarted at this last moment?

The initiative for concluding a peace agreement came from Prince Korybut who sent an envoy to Žižka with an offer of peace and renewed cooperation. From his point of view, indeed, everything was at stake at this instance. If there was to be any future for him and his policy, peace had to be concluded with Žižka at almost any price.

Korybut's position, politically and legally, was precarious. Prague had recognized him again as head of the state, but geographically speaking this left him with very limited power. His position had not again been confirmed by a national diet, even though the Hussite elements in Bohemia's nobility had long ceased to pay any attention to the regency council elected at the St. Gall diet and were willing again to recognize the Prince at least as regent. But Žižka's actions during the last few weeks made it amply clear that in his opinion his previous declaration of loyalty had been invalidated by Korybut's return to Poland. Korybut could perhaps hope to reawaken some of the old friendship once personal contact was established again. But for this to happen, a more powerful agent had to be introduced than the memory of an old act of homage. It would have to come from the one sphere which had overwhelming importance in Žižka's mind: the religious.

Žižka—as has been discussed earlier—had never wavered in his basic religious beliefs, had never deviated from the Truth of God as, to his mind, it had been revealed by the teachings of Master John Hus. He had, in particular, adhered firmly to the teachings about the special significance of the Eucharist as expressed by the frequent giving of both the bread and wine to laymen of all ages. He had thereby followed the teaching and the ritual practices of Jacobellus of Stříbro.

[23] See about this Pekař's treatment of Aeneas Sylvius as a source on Žižka, in *Český časopis historický*, 1924, pp. 423ff. and in his *Žižka*, II, 119-129, and especially 127.

[24] See below, Chapter 27.

Jacobellus, indeed, hated bloodshed, and can no longer have looked with favor upon Žižka's bloody career. Yet he as well as the other conservative masters of Prague were aware of Žižka's deep devotion to the basic religious principles established by him. It was probably on the basis of this knowledge that the leaders of Prague—Prince Korybut surely would consult about this with the masters of the University—selected the envoy to be sent to Žižka. It was not incidental that they chose a cleric who was personally and ideologically especially near to Jacobellus of Stříbro: John Rokycana.[25]

A history of the Hussite movement throughout the fifteenth century would require many pages to introduce the man who for nearly two scores of years, till his death in 1471, had headed the Utraquist Church, most of this time as its elected Archbishop, and had defended its principles and its character as a national church with unusual force and skill. (The Pope, incidentally, against whom he had to struggle hardest was none other than Pius II, the former bishop and author Aeneas Sylvius.)

In Žižka's life Rokycana appeared only late and episodically, yet at this special conjuncture his role was important enough. The young preacher had not yet received his master's diploma at this time, but Aeneas Sylvius was right in stressing that at the time of Žižka's siege he had already achieved a good name and considerable authority in the councils of the city.[26] But what we learn from him on the actual negotiations is scanty: "He departed with the consent of the citizens, repaired to the encampment and reconciled Žižka with the city." Only the result appears in our Czech sources:[27] "On Wednesday, the day of the Holy Cross [September 14], a concordance and reconciliation was achieved between Prince Sigismund Korybut and the Praguers on one side, and Žižka on the other side. . . . And they confirmed this peace to one another by a security of 14,000 threescores of good Bohemian groše [an enormous sum at the time]. And on the Hospital Field[28] they carried together and piled up a huge heap of stones as a sign for the prementioned compact, so that, if any of the two parties should ever infringe upon it, the guilty ones should be buried beneath those stones." One of our sources,[29] however, inserts the sentence: "But Žižka said

[25] Aeneas Sylvius, chapter 45, p. 97.

[26] *ibid.*: "Etiam nomine et authoritate valebat, quum Zisca Pragam obsideret."

[27] The reports in the *Chronicon veteris Collegiati* (p. 87), the *Chronicon Treboniense* (p. 54) and the Old Annalists (p. 63) are almost identically worded.

[28] The Old Annalists (*loc.cit.*) say St. Ambrose in the New Town.

[29] *ibid.*

at the peace-making: this peace will last as long as it did after the compact of Konopiště."

We may feel cheated for being so sparsely informed. The meeting between Rokycana and Žižka surely was of the highest interest, personally and historically. It has tempted writers and artists to try their hands in filling the gap. Short of such fictional treatment we can feel secure at least in believing that Rokycana appealed to Žižka's religious loyalties and to his patriotism. It also seems that he could, in Korybut's name, make a substantial offer. If peace could be concluded, then Korybut and the Praguers, together with their allies among the nobility, would concentrate all their forces for a grand action against the foreign enemies, against Sigismund and his son-in-law Albert who was about to fortify his rule over Moravia. A great all-Hussite campaign could be conducted for the liberation of Moravia, under the supreme command of Žižka. These steps, indeed, were taken almost immediately afterwards, and if they were suggested by Rokycana during those negotiations then we can understand even better why Žižka should have agreed to the solemn compact of September 14.

But his skeptical remark—this peace would last no longer than the one concluded at Konopiště—shows that Žižka was not free of misgivings. (The remark seems too realistic and precise not to be regarded as historical.) In a question of extraordinary consequence, Žižka had changed his mind. Would it be to the good? Not even today, from the hindsight of our historical knowledge, can we answer this question with an unqualified yes. To be sure much bloodshed, much destruction was avoided, and for many Czech patriots it may be "pleasing to think that the great Bohemian warrior at the moment of his death was again on terms of friendship with his countrymen."[30] But it could also be argued that, by agreeing to the peace of Libeň, Žižka left his lifework, his work as the principal leader of the Hussite revolution, unfinished.

Like so many other revolutions, the Hussite movement led, at an early stage, to a division of sovereignty, to a precarious balance of powers inside Hussite Bohemia which was bound to erupt, again and again, into open civil war. Žižka had been rather slow to see this truth, largely because he thought always first and foremost in religious, not in political or social terms. Only after his separation from Tabor-Hradiště—after he was no longer preoccupied with questions of religious orthodoxy and heterodoxy within his own camp—had he fully awakened to the

[30] Lützow, *Bohemia, An Historical Sketch*, London 1939, p. 141.

need to organize his party in terms of strong mass support, not only from the rural districts but also from as many cities as possible. In the space of one year he had made extraordinary progress in this direction, and the adherence of Žatec, Louny, and three of the older Taborite towns had given his federation an increasingly national, all-Bohemian character. If he could now have established himself in Prague, then the gigantic job was done: the eight or nine remaining royal towns could no longer have stood apart. For the Hussite nobility, too, only one alternative would be left—to join up with Žižka or to seek the doubtful protection of Sigismund.[31] Thus the divided sovereignty inside the Hussite camp might have been overcome in favor of a new, all-national, all-Hussite brotherhood which, according to the Military Ordinance, would have left room for the "communities" of all social classes as long as they followed the Law of God.

The peace of Libeň meant that this work of unification remained unfinished. Instead of creating an incontestable authority, a single sovereignty, it reaffirmed the old unsatisfactory cooperation of the main centers of power in terms of an alliance, and thus perpetuated the dual sovereignty. True it gave Žižka some safeguards—clearly Korybut had to recognize the autonomous status of Žižka's federation and to renounce all claims to those many cities now belonging to it.[32] But this only meant that the other possibility of a unified sovereignty—the reestablishment of full royal power—was equally thwarted. This dual sovereignty was to last for another decade. Never had its abolition looked so near as in the days before the reconciliation between Žižka and Korybut, and never, in the decade after this, were the chances as good again. This split was only overcome—but by the other side—in 1434, when the battle of Lipany finally wiped out the results of the battle of Malešov.

For the moment, however, internal peace had returned to the Hussite commonwealth after thirteen months of civil war, and Žižka entered Prague[33] not as conqueror but again as friend and ally. And it

[31] An example for the second move is given by Hašek of Waldstein. His negotiations with Sigismund and Albert of Austria began late in 1424 and the deal was concluded early in the following year. See the letters of Olomouc in *Urk. Beiträge*, I, especially nos. 325 and 338.

[32] The wording of the treaty is not preserved, but there can be no doubt that this recognition was either expressed or implied. See also Pekař, III, 263.

[33] Tomek (*Žižka*, p. 20) refers to a passage in Windecke (p. 198, no. 235 in Altmann's edition) as proof for Žižka's stay in Prague after the Peace of Libeň. But this statement ". . . daz der Zisko . . . bi den Pragern were gewest . . ." is hardly needed in this case. Hajek of

seems that, once the ice was broken between Korybut and Žižka, true cooperation was reestablished between them. But there was little time left for this healed friendship to bear any fruit for Hussite Bohemia.

---

Libočany (edition of 1541, p. 207) even knows of a solemn reception which Žižka was given in Prague.

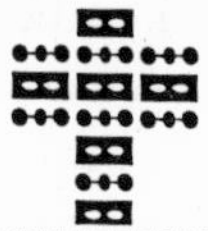

## CHAPTER 27

# PEACE TO ALL CZECHS, WAR TO SIGISMUND

On September 10, while Žižka still stood unreconciled before the gates of Prague, a document was signed in the south reflecting one of the strangest of the many strange turns to be observed in this long and often puzzling struggle. It was an agreement between the Taborite federation and its baronial allies on the one side, Lord Ulrich of Rosenberg and some of his friends on the other.[1] The two parties concluded an armistice to last for five weeks—one of the few indications of the fact that there had still been, even late in 1424, some fighting between Tabor and Rosenberg.[2] The document contains more than one surprise, but by far the greatest is its main purpose: an agreement with King Sigismund for a hearing to be conducted with his permission. Those five weeks should enable Lord Ulrich of Rosenberg to conduct the preliminary negotiations with Sigismund for the Taborite community, and the Four Articles which were to form the subject of the hearing should remain free, in the meantime, to be practiced without any interference on the side of Rosenberg and his friends. With Rosenberg signed three other barons of his region and four of his burgraves. Tabor is represented by its two older captains Chval of Machovice and Zbyněk of Buchov, further by a number of noblemen, first among them, of course, Bohuslav of Švamberg, after him Herman of Borotín, Peter Zmrzlík the Younger, and Nicholas Sokol of Lamberg, the two last-named both the sons of the late friends of Žižka's. Of the cities of the Taborite federation only Písek and Prachatice are named besides Tabor-Hradiště, as the other ones had gone over to Žižka by that time.

That Tabor should have been ready at this time to approach the

[1] *Archiv český*, III, 245. See also the very detailed résumé in Tomek, *Žižka*, pp. 198, 199, and Pekař's commentary, III, 255, 256.

[2] Another indication can be found in Sigismund's letter to Ulrich of Rosenberg in which he expresses his sympathy for the latter's bad luck in the war and invites him to Buda where, soon afterwards, we found him in Windecke's story quoted verbatim in Chapter 25. See *Urk. Beiträge*, I, 333.

"heretical king"—or to be approached by his followers—with a view to a hearing under his sponsorship, this surely is surprising and difficult to understand. There was nothing—except perhaps for the earlier armistice with Pilsen and the general inactivity of Old Tabor—that would have prepared us for such a move.[3] Nor does it, as we know from the later development, indicate any permanent change of direction on the side of Tabor. For only a few weeks later the Taborites appointed Hvězda as their captain general, and in the following year we find him as well as Bohuslav of Švamberg, at the head of Taborite troops, fighting against Sigismund as fiercely as ever before. So far no satisfactory explanation has been given. We might venture the guess that Tabor, at a moment when it was drastically weakened by the defection of several of its towns, tried to refortify its position by an altogether new and unexpected move, and thus hoped to demonstrate that it was still a power to be reckoned with. We may add to this our knowledge that among the Taborite clergy around this time the feeling began to grow that the war, especially in the cruel and destructive way it was conducted, was not in accord with Christian principles.[4] All this, however, seems an incomplete and somewhat unsatisfactory explanation.

It would appear natural that Tabor's move for a hearing sponsored by Sigismund was sharply resented by Žižka, perhaps that it alienated him still further from his old comrades in arms at Tabor. But here again we are due for a surprise. For the armistice expressly includes Žižka and his adherents in southern Bohemia, the towns of Klatovy, Sušice, and Lomnice[5] and some of his friends among the regional nobility. This, indeed, makes a strange thing appear even stranger. Does it really mean that Žižka approved of this move which went so strikingly against all he had stood for?

It has to be well understood that neither Žižka nor any one of his present associates actually signed the armistice, but that he was included in it by a common agreement of the contracting parties. We probably have to interpret this clause as an undertaking of Tabor, answering a demand of Rosenberg, by which the brotherhood vouched that the

[3] A letter of Sigismund to Rosenberg of October 10 (*Archiv český*, I, 18) might almost be understood as if this demand for such a hearing had been prepared by some earlier soundings on the side of Tabor. It can, however, just as well be understood as referring to the negotiations of late 1423, and this seems the more likely interpretation.

[4] See the meeting of the Taborite clergy held at Klatovy in November. (Nicholas of Pelhřimov's Taborite Chronicle, Höfler, II, 482.)

[5] Domažlice is not named, probably because it was geographically too far removed from Rosenberg's domains and thus in no danger of direct conflict with him.

baron's holdings, for those five weeks, would be safe also from attacks on the part of the towns now adhering to Žižka's brotherhood.[6] The Taborites could give this guaranty without too much risk as they knew that those towns had already sent their available troops northward to help Žižka in his campaign against Prague.

There is, then, the possibility that the Taborites gave their guaranty of nonaggression on the part of Žižka without the latter's knowledge. Or, perhaps even more likely, Žižka was just informed of the intention of Tabor to conclude a short armistice with its neighbor—an action which in itself would not have appeared as particularly significant or dangerous. But in either case we can, with great certainty, exclude the possibility that Žižka approved of the purpose of the agreement. Though we have not his word for it, his actions in the following weeks speak an unmistakable language.

There was one place where the situation, especially in regard to Žižka, was rather badly misjudged. This place was the court of Sigismund at Buda. The King's reaction to Rosenberg's news about the Taborite request[7] shows a good deal of rather unrealistic optimism. The bitter contempt with which he had usually spoken about the Taborites and their peasant armies has vanished, and it seems that it would have given him special pleasure to show his always demanding Bohemian vassals that he could achieve by diplomacy what they had never achieved by force of arms: the taming of those fierce sectarians. His answer to Rosenberg does not mention Žižka, but from another source we learn that he had not forgotten him and was conscious enough of the fact that an understanding with Tabor-Hradiště alone would not be enough. This source is, once more, Aeneas Sylvius.[8]

Sigismund, so he says, perceiving that all things always turned out in favor of Žižka and that he was already the only one on whom the state of affairs in Bohemia depended, made an attempt to achieve a secret agreement with him. He offered to bestow upon him the government of the whole Kingdom, the command of all its armies and large yearly payments in gold, provided only he proclaimed Sigismund as king and administered the cities of Bohemia in Sigismund's name.

[6] This interpretation—I believe it to be the only correct one—is given by Pekař, III, 256. Tomek had earlier proffered the suggestion that Žižka agreed to the armistice because this would make it easier for the Taborite federation to send him help in his fight with Prague (*Žižka*, p. 199). But the only Taborite towns which gave such help were the ones that had left the old federation and gone over to Žižka.

[7] See the letter mentioned above, note 3.

[8] Chapter 46, p. 98.

Sylvius continues with a fierce blast of indignation at Sigismund, "son of an emperor and himself an emperor and king of many countries whose name was venerated all over Europe and feared by the barbarian nations." How shameful for all Christianity to see him offer wealth and the highest honors to a man born from parents hardly to be called noble, an old, blind but daringly sacrilegious heretic, just so this man might deign to adhere to the King's party. And, so Sylvius claims to know, Žižka actually accepted the offer, and the disgraceful deal would have been consummated if Divine Charity had not intervened in time.

It is less difficult here than in many other cases to separate fact from fiction. Sigismund knew, of course, of Žižka's inclusion in the armistice of September 10, and we can hardly blame him if he concluded from this fact that the Orebite general might, after all, be approached with a view to arriving at some understanding. Sigismund was a cynic who surely thought, long before Walpole, that every man had his price. He had followed with amazement and something like grudging admiration the way in which "that base man of knavish origin" had safely emerged from every jeopardy and had lately been able to add strength to strength. He also had to consider Korybut's claims to the throne of Bohemia. A deal with Žižka, even if it was expensive, would effectively counteract this danger.[9] We have to think of the time immediately before the Peace of Libeň, or at least before the news of this agreement between Žižka and Korybut had reached the King.

In this situation, then, Sigismund considered an offer to Žižka which would at least assure to the Hussite leader the undisturbed rule over the cities which he had been able to organize in his federation. He must, at least, have discussed this possibility with some of his advisers, and in this way the story eventually reached the Italian prelate. But whether the offer was ever dispatched to Žižka seems more than doubtful, and the rest—the assertion of Žižka's acceptance—is of course a calumnious invention which gave Sylvius the chance to demonstrate in an effective way the workings of Divine Charity, of the *deus ex machina* operating world history. No modern historian has ever mistaken it for the truth.[10]

If there was any question on which there existed complete and indubitable agreement between Žižka and Korybut it was their antago-

[9] See Tomek, *Žižka*, p. 197, and (for the connection between Sylvius's story and the armistice Pilsen-Rosenberg) Urbánek, *Žižka*, pp. 273, 274.

[10] See e.g. Pekař, III, 269.

nism to Sigismund. It was surely on the basis of this common antagonism that Korybut now managed to obtain Žižka's agreement for a new action of internal pacification—very much on the line of his old policy of 1422—which should include, as far as possible, also the Catholic elements of the nation. These, indeed, were bound to be deeply impressed by the sudden change of the political situation: the reconciliation and cooperation of Prague and Žižka's now immensely strong brotherhood. It was a front which could not be beaten and against which even defensive resistance seemed to offer little chance, at least as long as no help could be expected from outside Bohemia. And at this moment it was clear enough that no such help would be forthcoming before the spring or summer of 1425.

Under this impression the Catholic lords and the Pilsen Landfrieden agreed, very soon after the Peace of Libeň, to take part in a meeting designed to find a basis for agreement. Representatives of both sides were sent to west central Bohemia, with the Hussites staying at Beroun, a royal town now subject to Korybut, the Catholics at Žebrák, a large castle some eleven miles farther southeast owned by the Lords of Kolovraty. After some exchange of opinions by message both parties finally got together at a "common diet" at the town of Zdice, halfway between the two places named and almost exactly halfway between Prague and Pilsen. The proceedings began around September 23 and were concluded on or near October 1.[11]

There are some parallels between this meeting and the one held the year before at Kolín. Again the assembly was supposed to prepare a great all-national diet, and again the Four Articles should be submitted to a hearing before a great jury of laymen, both at the same place in March 1425.

But there the similarity ends, for there was no question of the hearing being sponsored by Sigismund, nor by Władysław of Poland. Though the two parties were not limited in the choice of the "doctors," the theologians who were to do the pleading and arguing, the jury was to be strictly national. It was to consist of a hundred men chosen by each side from the ranks of the lords, of the knights and squires, and of the towns and the "communities," the latter expression referring to the two brotherhoods of the Old and the New Tabor. Issues on which no complete agreement was reached by the whole body were to be

[11] For the (undated) resolutions of the diet see *Archiv český*, III, 248. The dates are derived from entries into the expense account of the Karlstein garrison whose burgrave, Tluksa of Buřenice, went to Žebrák as representative of the great castle. See Tomek, *Dějepis*, IV, 309, n. 16.

submitted to a smaller committee. The decision then arrived at was to be binding for both sides.

The idea of a religious agreement to be reached on a purely national basis essentially implied a return to the first diet of Čáslav rather than to the St. Gall diet. And the spirit of Čáslav was alive also in the main political clauses accepted at Zdice. There was to be an armistice till March, but it was expressly limited to the Bohemian parties, while foreigners, that is Sigismund and his allies, were excluded from it.[12] The Catholic lords even agreed that if any of their number wanted to help the Hussites in their continued war against Sigismund, they would not object nor try to prevent him. We can imagine Sigismund's fierce anger at this agreement which indeed he drastically expressed in two letters to Ulrich of Rosenberg.[13]

There was further, as at Čáslav and at the St. Gall diet, the clause that Bohemians not prepared to accede within four weeks should be induced by force—but as at Čáslav this clause could now only refer to recalcitrant nobles or towns of the Catholic camp. (The participating members of the Catholic party obligated themselves to put up, if needed, a troop of 2,000 men for the enforcement of this clause.)

The resolutions, finally, contain a clause which signifies an early, somewhat groping, and surely premature expression of the spirit of tolerance, thereby anticipating a much later, even then still pioneering development of the Bohemian Reformation.[14] For the duration of the armistice everyone should be free to worship, and listen to sermons, anywhere he pleased. In other words the coercion which the various religious communities so far exerted upon the individuals belonging to them was to be suspended.

The measure was, of course, limited to this short period of barely six months, with the view that once the truth had been fully established, enforcement would follow again. It may also be doubted whether even this temporary freedom of choice for the individual was ever fully practiced. Yet the fact remains that, only nine years after the burning of Hus, only five after the outbreak of this fierce war (and 174 years

[12] A somewhat strange paragraph permits the Margraves of Meissen, of all foreign sovereigns, to adhere to the agreement. They made no use of this permission.

[13] *Archiv český*, I, 19, 21.

[14] See e.g. the statutes passed by the diet of Kutná Hora in 1485, under the rule of Vladislav II, in which Utraquists and Catholics guaranteed each other not only the freedom of worship according to their religion but also freed subject individuals from the need to worship according to the religion of their lords. In comparison with this agreement the Peace of Augsburg, concluded 80 years later, and even the famed Edict of Nantes, issued 113 years later, appear as steps backward rather than forward. See also Chapter 30 below.

before the Edict of Nantes) the attempt was made, perhaps half consciously, to work for tolerance rather than to incite religious hatred.

We hardly need to emphasize that this clause did not correspond to Žižka's ideas and that it was accepted not because he liked it but, at best, because he did not oppose it. We have seen before that once he had committed himself to a general line of policy, he would not be too grudgingly anxious about concessions in detail, and in the case of this clause he may, indeed, have overlooked its full significance, being already engrossed in his plans for the next phase of action, the coming campaign against Sigismund and Albert.

The accord of Zdice, in the form in which it came to us,[15] does not show the names of any signatories. Thus we have no knowledge whether Žižka actually took part in the proceedings or only kept himself informed on its course and gave his final sanction at the end. But that the agreement as a whole was concluded with his consent and that of his party, this we do not have to deduce from our knowledge of the general balance of power existing at the moment. There is a better proof: the place where the great national diet and the public hearing of March 1425 was to be held was Kouřim, a city which had belonged to the Orebite brotherhood since Žižka's victory at Malešov. The great decisions which were expected from this assembly were, in other words, to be taken under Žižka's eyes, and he and the brethren of his field army would be able to safeguard the Law of God. Thus he could go about his new task without remorse or worry.

[15] A copy of the resolutions made for the Catholic side. See above, note 11.

# CHAPTER 28

## DEATH DEFEATS THE UNDEFEATED

THE diet of Zdice ended on October 1 at the latest. In the days immediately following the last preparations were made for one of the greatest campaigns ever undertaken by the Hussite armies. Its purpose was to rescue Moravia from the domination by Sigismund's son-in-law, Duke Albert of Austria. Neither of the two campaigns conducted the year before had been able to achieve this to any extent. All but five or six of the towns and most of the castles of the Margravate were under Albert's power and it was obvious that only a major effort could oust the Austrian from his firm position in the Margravate.

But the campaign also had something like a symbolic significance. Each of the two Hussite parties, first the Praguers with their baronial allies, then Žižka with his Orebites, had made isolated thrusts into Moravia, only to turn their swords against one another between and after these campaigns. Now the rift was overcome and the hope could prevail that no more would "ark stand against ark." What could express the fraternal unity better than the common effort to liberate the sister country to the east?

The Hussite troops which had been mobilized for this campaign are said to have numbered at least 20,000 men,[1] and this estimate was probably not much exaggerated. The Czech army contained strong forces of Prague and its allied cities, Žižka's field army and troops from the cities of his brotherhood, finally also some contingents of Old Tabor[2] who now, for the first time since spring 1423, went to fight again under their old chief. With them, perhaps as their commander, came one of the lords adhering to the brotherhood of Tabor-Hradiště: Nicholas Sokol of Lamberg.

Žižka held the supreme command[3] and among his lieutenants in

[1] Windecke, p. 169.

[2] Tabor's presence at the preceding discussions at Zdice is an indication for it, and the participation of Sokol makes it appear certain. See also Pekař, III, 268.

[3] This is to be concluded from the way in which the *Chronicon veteris Collegiati* (p. 87) words the beginning of its report on the campaign.

charge of the Orebite and Taborite troops we find John Hvězda of Vícemilice and another knight who had earlier fought with Tabor, Kuneš of Bělovice. Kuneš had gone over to Žižka with Hvězda[4] and had probably distinguished himself at Malešov, for now he appears already as a soldier of rank and soon he was to acquire a leading position in the Orebite brotherhood.[5] Of Žižka's baronial friends only one is mentioned as present: Victorin of Poděbrady, who also had stood at his side at Malešov.

The troops of Prague were, of course, led by Korybut, but the Prince had with him two of the most experienced military leaders among the older allies and captains of the capital: Hynek of Kolstein and Diviš Bořek of Miletínek. It would be interesting to know whether there had been anything like a personal reconciliation between Diviš and Žižka, but it seems clear that on the march from Prague to Moravia the two generals had little opportunity of seeing one another. Diviš led the van with some of the troops of the capital and crossed the Moravian border ahead of the main body of the army.[6]

The march must have begun on October 3 or 4[7] and for a last time Žižka followed, or at least touched, his old road of victory by leading his troops through Německý Brod. From there they continued westward toward Moravia in the general direction of Brno but stopped about two marching hours short of the border, laying siege to the great castle of Přibyslav.

This move seems somewhat puzzling. The castle belonged to a prominent Royalist, Lord Čeněk of Ronov, and he was one of the men whom the people of Tabor had reason to hate: he, together with John Městecký and Půta of Častolovice, had taken part in the infamous mass murder of Hromadka and his Taborites after the surrender of Chotěboř. But under the armistice of Zdice he should have been safe from attack.[8] The most likely explanation is that the defenders of the castle, perhaps in a fit of foolhardy loyalty toward Sigismund, tried to stem the invasion of this great army into Moravia where, incidentally, the family of Ronov had other possessions. The castle of Přibyslav was not strong enough to hold the Hussites for more than a few days. But this was time enough to prevent Žižka from ever leaving again the land of his birth.

[4] See Tomek, *Dějepis*, IV, 256.

[5] He was, after the return to Bohemia, elected captain of the Orphans (Orebites). See *Chronicon veteris Collegiati, loc.cit.*

[6] *ibid.*

[7] According to Balbín (*Epitome*, p. 455), who probably used earlier sources, the Hussite army arrived before Přibyslav on October 6. See also Tomek, *Žižka*, p. 203.

[8] Attention was drawn to this particular question by Pekař, III, 270.

The old general soon fell sick in the encampment before Přibyslav. Whether the disease that struck him was really the bubonic plague—which, of course, was endemic in the Europe of the fifteenth century—or some other sickness[9] is difficult to judge from our sparse reports.[10] All we have to go by is the account by one of the Old Annalists, the most detailed of the versions given in contemporary or near-contemporary chronicles.[11] This is what we learn from it:

"There [before the castle of Přibyslav] Brother John Žižka fell sick with a mortal sickness from the plague. And in making his bequest he told his dear, faithful brethren and Czechs, the Lord Victorin, Lord John Bzdinka (Hvězda) and Kuneš, that they should go on fighting for the love of God, and should steadfastly and faithfully defend the Truth of God for eternal reward. And then already Brother Žižka recommended his soul to the dear God, and thus he died and ended his life on that Wednesday before St. Gall (October 11, 1424). And there his people took for themselves the name Orphans, as if they had lost their father. And they conquered the castle of Přibyslav, and they burned the people who fought back at them in the castle, about sixty men in arms, and the castle they also burned and demolished. And after this the priest Prokůpek (Prokop the Lesser) and the priest Ambrose conducted him, when he was already dead, to Hradec Králové, and there they buried him in the Church of the Holy Ghost by the main altar. But later he was conveyed to Čáslav and there buried in the Church [of SS. Peter and Paul]."

This report leaves little to be added. It is in its main features, including Žižka's last orders, confirmed by a later account perhaps based on early sources.[12] It could be expected that men like Victorin of Poděbrady and Hvězda would be present in the dying hour of their friend, and we may only wonder why Roháč was not there. But as he is not mentioned at all in connection with the Moravian campaign of 1424 it may be assumed that, for reasons unknown to us, he did not take part in this enterprise. According to a much later account based on personal

[9] I see little point in quoting the rather feebly founded attempts at a medical discussion of Žižka's illness.

[10] Old Annalists, p. 64; *Chronicon veteris Collegiati*, p. 87; *Chronicon Treboniense*, p. 54; *The very pretty chronicle* (Novotný's ed.), p. 21.

[11] Old Annalists, *loc.cit.*

[12] Hájek of Libočany, p. 207. After this, however, Hájek reverts to Aeneas Sylvius' account, soon to be discussed. See also Pekař, III, 272, 273.

memories Žižka died on the lap of one of his personal secretaries and assistants Michael Koudela of Žitenice, a devoted and mourning servant who also helped in conducting the body to burial.[13]

But Žižka was not mourned only by a few friends. The whole army, says Aeneas Sylvius,[14] was overcome by immense sadness and lament, "and they accused the fate which destined their leader, never defeated in battle, to be finally defeated by Death." The soldiers of his Orebite field army, as we have heard just before, henceforth called themselves Orphans, "as if they had lost their father." And, so adds the author of *The very pretty chronicle* at the end of the Hussite wars,[15] "thus they have been called ever since." Orphans (in Czech, Sirotci), was and remained indeed the official name of Žižka's soldiers after his death. Could the mourning for a beloved leader be expressed with greater simplicity and force? Žižka's soldiers never ceased to be Žižka's children as long as they fought his good fight for the Law of God.

Two priests conducted the body to its resting place: Ambrose of Hradec, one of his oldest and closest friends, faithful to Žižka and his religious and political legacy till his own end in 1439; and Prokop the Lesser, a man whom we meet in connection with Žižka only at this late hour but who was also, historically speaking, one of the executors of his will. In 1427, succeeding Kuneš of Bělovice, he became the main commander of the Orphans' field army, and leading this army in the great and tragic battle of Lipany he died a hero's death in 1434.

That Žižka was buried in Hradec Králové is so well established by various sources that it seems difficult to doubt it. *The very pretty chronicle* even says with some emphasis: "And there he lies."[16] We can also be very sure that later his remains rested in Čáslav, in the Church of SS. Peter and Paul where he must have worshiped often in his life and which had served as the meeting place for the great national assembly of June 1421. His tomb was seen there, and described in detail, by visitors in the sixteenth and the beginning of the seventeenth century.[17] There is one later source which claims that he was

[13] See Šimák, *Český časopis historický*, 1912, pp. 16, 17.

[14] Chapter 47, p. 99. [15] P. 21 in Novotný's edition. [16] *ibid.*

[17] Theobald, in his *Hussiten-Krieg*, written shortly before the outbreak of the Thirty Years' War, describes not only the tomb itself but quotes completely the considerable number of inscriptions, most of them in Latin verse (Part 1, 228, 229). On the top of the grave was a sculpture of Žižka with the simple inscription: "Anno 1424 Die Jovis ante festum Galli vita functus Johannes Ziska a calice, rector Rerum publicarum laborantium in nomine & pro nomine Dei, hoc templo conditus est." While the verse inscriptions are probably quite late, the one quoted above may date from the time of the burial at Čáslav. The description of Žižka as the

immediately buried at Čáslav, and that the body buried at Hradec Králové was not Žižka's but that of a German supplanted by the Čáslavians.[18] What the Old Annalist reports is far more likely: that some time after his death he was disinterred at Hradec Králové and reburied at Čáslav. And we can also accept the theory[19] that the reasons for moving the body were political. In 1437 Hradec Králové, till then dominated by Priest Ambrose, was besieged and finally overcome by the very man who had lost the city to Žižka fourteen years earlier: by Diviš Bořek of Miletínek. It seems that the new, conservative regime did not like the view of Žižka's tomb occupying the most prominent place of the city's main church. At Čáslav, a town where Žižka's old comrade in arms Roháč of Dubá had long been captain and where his friends were still in a majority, his body was welcome.

But even there a further turn of history disturbed his sleep: after the battle of the White Mountain which, in 1620, destroyed the political and religious freedom of Bohemia, the servants of the victorious Habsburgs did not overlook the grave of the man who, two hundred years earlier, had done so much to gain this freedom. It was a mint master of Kutná Hora, William of Vřesovice, a worthy successor to Nicholas Divoký, who in 1622 ordered the tomb to be completely razed and demolished.[20] In view of the frightful catastrophe which overwhelmed Bohemia at this time the disappearance of Žižka's tomb was a minor loss, but it had its symbolic significance. And if a last item told about Žižka's personal history should be true,[21] then his mortal remains were dug up and reburied for a third time, now under the gallows. Thus he would have shared the fate of Wiclif and Cromwell—two great ones of Western history between whom Žižka, though living in another land, was something like the connecting link.

As Žižka's tomb was visible and accessible to thousands of people for almost two centuries, it seems strange enough that a very different

---

"director of the communities working (i.e. fighting) in and for the name of God" corresponds closely to the titles used later in the war by the Hussite leaders. The Church of SS. Peter and Paul, dominating the city of Čáslav, appears clearly in the center of Merian's engraving (Fig. 4).

18 See about this Čáslavian tradition Tomek, *Žižka*, pp. 206, 207, in n. 31.

19 Pekař (II, 109) formulates this supposition in general agreement with Tomek (*Žižka*, pp. 204, 210). Czech historiography has, especially at the time of the five hundredth anniversary of Žižka's death, devoted considerable attention to this question. See e.g. Šimák in *Český časopis historický*, 1912, pp. 7ff., and 1923, pp. 200ff. Urbánek, *Žižka v památkách . . .*, pp. 21ff., Bartoš, *Sporné otázky*, in *Žižkova doba*, IX, 18ff., and Pekař, II, 109, 245, 268. The issue seems too involved and too specialized to be discussed in the frame of this book.

20 Paměti Dačického as quoted by Tomek, *Žižka*, p. 218, n. 50.

21 *ibid.*

story about the fate of his body was told and widely believed. Against the fact that Žižka was buried twice it set the claim that he was never buried at all. The author of this legend—or at least the author in whose work we find it printed first and from whom it was copied by numerous later writers—was Aeneas Sylvius.[22] His admiring account on the brilliant career of the great general had perforce to be balanced by a final turn through which the great heretic would disclose himself as a man of sinister, devilish powers and designs: "Struck by the plague he expired, the detestable, cruel, horrible and savage monster. Whom no mortal hand could destroy, the finger of God extinguished him. When asked in his illness where, after his death, he wanted to be buried, he commanded that his body be flayed, the flesh thrown to the birds and beasts, and a drum be made from his skin. With this drum in the lead they should go to war. The enemies would turn to flight as soon as they heard its voice."

The story of Žižka's drum became very popular. It somehow helped to explain, in a simple magical way, the later successes of the Hussite armies, and in the end this was one of the few things which were generally "known" about Žižka.[23] In the eighteenth century the drum—some drum with real human skin—was actually exhibited in the armory of the fortress of Glatz, and from there it was taken, as a trophy of war, by Frederick the Great when he conquered Silesia and the County of Glatz in the War of the Austrian Succession.[24]

In a way, of course, even this morbidly fantastic story shows in what awe successive generations stood before the striking phenomenon of the invincible heretic. And the legend of Žižka's drum has its counterpart in another legend which was not put out by the hero's enemies but by his admirers. We have read it at the beginning of this book in *The very pretty chronicle*, the earliest biography written about Žižka. "And the people of Hradec Králové," so it says, "ordered Žižka to be painted on their banner, mounted on a white horse, in knightly armor, holding his battle club, as he looked when he was alive. And whenever the people of Hradec Králové went into battle under this banner, they were invincible." Žižka's spirit, in both those legends, was not dead. He still wielded magic power, still led his troops from victory to vic-

[22] P. 98.

[23] More than once this author has had the experience that when he mentioned Žižka's name in the presence of fairly well-read Europeans, their reaction was: "Oh, he was the man who had a drum made out of his skin, wasn't he?"

[24] A. Caha in *Svědomím českých dějin*, v, Brno 1924, nos. 11-16, pp. 91-93.

tory. And in the sense that men live on in their works this was surely true. Žižka's successors in command of the two field armies, Taborite and Orphan, especially the two Prokops, were remarkable and perhaps great men in their own right. But they started from a national strength which he had built, and used the weapons that he had forged.

# CHAPTER 29

## "A MAN MOST BRAVE"

THE understanding of Žižka's personality has formed a major issue in modern Czech historiography. The fact that his historical role is separated from our time by some five hundred years has not made for much emotional distance. There is, on one side, an almost official portrait presented by a majority of Czech historians, all of them more or less following V. V. Tomek, the author of the monumental *History of Prague* and of the first modern biography of Žižka.[1] This Žižka was essentially a national unifier, seeking to establish a strong, disciplined state under a Slavonic king, a man standing above the party struggle, a builder far more than a destroyer, almost a conservative at heart and a revolutionary only in his rebellion against Sigismund; in short what might be called a George Washington of the Czech revolution.

A radically different picture was drawn by a great twentieth century historian, Josef Pekař, in what is to date the most elaborate work on Žižka and his time.[2] A rabid revolutionary, ever driven by his religious fanaticism, rarely accessible to the voice of reason or of constructive patriotism, personally bloodthirsty and vindictive and on occasion deceitful, even treacherous, his Žižka, though not without greatness, is essentially a destructive force whose role in Bohemia's history was predominantly damaging.[3]

[1] Tomek's works, volume IV of his history of Prague and his *Žižka,* have been amply quoted above. His interpretation of Žižka's life and work has in general been followed by Prokeš (*Jan Žižka z Trocnova,* Prague 1920), Urbánek (*Žižka,* Prague 1925), as well as the many monographs (quoted earlier) by F. M. Bartoš and some popularizations like J. F. Čečetka, *Jan Žižka,* Prague 1925.

[2] No other work has made such wide and thorough use of all sources pertaining to Žižka's personal history, to its ideological background and to the way in which Žižka's personality was reflected in contemporary and later opinions. But the work was clearly begun with a political bias—Pekař fought against Masaryk's utterance: "Tabor, that is also our program"—and his book is polemical to an extent which, even in historical writing, is unusual and almost never permits a detached view. Yet part of his "debunking" activity has surely been useful.

[3] See Pekař, III, 304ff. His contention is very clearly and impressively refuted by K. Krofta in his little book *Žižka a husitská revoluce,* Prague 1937, pp. 116-126. This book is a very careful and very friendly criticism of Pekař's work, going quite far in supporting his general interpretation of Žižka's personality but still critical of some of Pekař's most obvious exaggerations

Both views, while containing some elements of truth, seem to me to misinterpret Žižka's character and historical role by partial overemphases of one set of facts and by a one-sided understanding of Žižka's tenets and actions. Žižka was capable of both a fanatical drive for the destruction of those people and institutions which he considered hateful in the eyes of God, and of acts of constructive statesmanship. If this implies contradictions and conflicts, then they existed rather outside than inside Žižka the man. Aside from the struggle between friends and foes of the Chalice the Hussite camp itself was split between conservatives and radicals, and even the radicals between the Pikharts and the believers in transubstantiation. Žižka's actions and reactions were those of a man holding strong, simple, unambiguous views, forced to defend and implement them in a world full of highly complex, at times almost chaotic trends and developments. But perhaps it is best to survey, in a last summary, the main results of our study of Žižka's few but eventful years as leader of the Hussite revolution and especially of the sparse but expressive heritage left to us in his letters and messages.

Nothing could be more clearly documented—and incidentally less contested by any serious historical writer—than that Žižka, in all his actions, was completely dominated by his religious ideas. There was for him no escape from this all-pervading and all-embracing thought: whatever he did had to be in the service of God. True, this was a religiously excited time, following a long period in which religion had always been a matter of high importance. Yet one has only to compare Žižka's letters with those of other contemporary writers, even inside Bohemia,[4] to realize the exceptional intensity of his religious feelings. The long and seemingly cumbersome greetings and benedictions at the beginning and ending of his letters, referring to God, Christ or the Holy Trinity, seem never to be empty phrases. And in his later letters his very name—John Žižka of the Chalice—became an expression of his religious devotion. The choice of this name shows also the extent to which the Holy Eucharist dominated his religious thinking. His almost equal hatred for the Romanist clergy and the Pikharts is based

---

and oversimplifications. For other criticisms of Pekař's work see E. Chalupný, *Husitství, Taboři a prof. Pekař*, Prague 1928 (a rather rude counteroffensive in favor of Tomek's views), several articles by F. M. Bartoš, especially in *Jihočeský sborník historický*, VI, part 3, finally Slavík, *Husitská revoluce*, pp. 10ff.

[4] See e.g. the above quoted letters and messages exchanged between Prague and Poland, Korybut's letter to Rosenberg, the latter's correspondance with Sigismund as preserved in the *Archiv český*, etc.

upon it. The Catholic priests were those who, haughtily disregarding the needs of the people for salvation, kept the beneficence of the blood of Christ for themselves; the Pikharts those heretics who, by denying the real presence of Christ in the act of the Communion, blocked the way to salvation just as wickedly and dangerously as the orthodox Catholics.

I have earlier suggested that this preoccupation with the role of the Chalice for salvation led Žižka to look up with special respect to Jacobellus of Stříbro, the restorer of the Communion in the two kinds. There is only indirect evidence to support this assumption, but as such I believe it to be quite strong. Jacobellus, for instance, had early insisted on the Communion for children right from baptism. In the later official version of the Four Articles as adopted by the First diet of Čáslav the Communion for children was approved, but only in general terms.[5] In the special version, on the other hand, in which Žižka's Military Ordinance adopted the Four Articles, Jacobellus' old demand is inserted in very specific terms. The Body and Blood of Christ is to be taken by all, "the old and the young, children right upon baptism and after that throughout their childhood."[6] Žižka could hardly have been unaware that he was, in this instance, directly following the precept of the famous master. In addition it seems that several of Žižka's actions or attitudes—his silence at the disputation in the house of Zmrzlík, his vote against John Želivský at the meeting of the arbitrators (at a time when Želivský's main adversary was Jacobellus) and his attitude in the issue of the vestments, are fully understandable only on the basis of Jacobellus' influence upon him. His cooperation with Želivský during the first phase of the revolution does not contradict this assumption, as the antagonism between the two great clerics of Prague did not develop, or at least did not come into the open, until the time that Žižka's cooperation with Želivský also ceased.

This assumption that Jacobellus and not one of the "radicals" was the determining religious influence upon Žižka does not imply that the old squire was willing and able to follow the nice intricacies of those dogmatic struggles, which could only be fought with the weapons of theological erudition. On the contrary we have every reason to think of him as an unsophisticated mind, a man who tended to see things in clear, simplified terms. But just because his creed was as simple and straight as it was strong, he could and did rely on the commands of his religion as an unfailing guide for action, especially of course in his

[5] "To all true Christians old and young." See the manifesto in *Archiv český*, III, 226ff.
[6] See Appendix, x.

judgment of other people. It was his religion which established his scale of values. Thus, even though he consciously accepted and kept the traditional social order, his religious evaluation of people transcended and implicitly superseded the scale of traditional ranks.[7]

Žižka's own self-evalution, too, was based on this theocratic scale of values. He had no preconceived notions of personal greatness, was no "man of destiny" in his own eyes. He simply felt that his services to God were greater, that he was fighting for His Law more strenuously and more successfully than others. For this reason alone he placed himself, without any false modesty, at the head of the new community of God's warriors which received the law of their holy war from his Military Ordinance. And this conviction emanated from him so forcefully that some of the greatest lords of the kingdom were not ashamed to put themselves under Žižka's command.

Yet for all this religiously determined self-assurance and even self-righteousness he was, in other ways, genuinely humble. There is true humility in his personal puritanism and it would be difficult to imagine him in the semi-royal role of a lord protector. He never laid claim to any higher title than to be the knight of the Chalice and the military "director of all communities of the Land of Bohemia which adhere to and fulfill the Law of God." But then, of course, no title of nobility or even royalty could have greater weight, or higher rank, in his scale of values.

On the negative side of his scale of values were, of course, all the enemies of God and His Law, and there were only too many of them, "first among them . . . the Hungarian King Sigismund, that heretical King, him that has betrayed our Lord God and His sacred word, the violator of virgins and women, the murderer and incendiary who seeks to destroy our Czech nation."[8] With Sigismund, Žižka was utterly irreconcilable. His conviction that the King wanted to destroy all Bohemians was shared by the leaders of Prague and apparently confirmed by many of Sigismund's utterances and actions. It is characteristic that the final compromise with Sigismund reached in 1436 was resisted to the last by those men who, like Roháč of Dubá, had been especially close to Žižka.

But if Žižka reserved an especially intense hatred for this one man we

[7] If, for example, the lords in the Pilsen Landfrieden were enemies of the Law of God, then it was right to shake off their rule over the federation. For Žižka's letter to the Landfrieden, see Appendix, III.

[8] *ibid.*

find him less implacable toward people who had served Sigismund at one time but were now ready to follow the Law of God by accepting the Four Articles and might thus save their souls. On this basis he concluded his truce with Rosenberg, and accepted Bohuslav of Švamberg, at the beginning one of his staunchest enemies, as his friend and cocaptain. On this basis he assented to the generous armistice for Pilsen and to forgiveness for Čeněk of Wartenberg. At times, at least, he was ready to forgive those who trespassed against him as he hoped for forgiveness from God.[9]

Laymen, indeed, might be given a chance to save their souls. They had, very likely, been seduced, confused by wrong teachings, led astray by false priests. But in no case could the seducers, the false teachers and devilish priests themselves be forgiven, nor would they ever have a chance to save their souls. All that mattered was to render them impotent and innocuous, to prevent them forever from increasing still further the number of their victims. Thus there could be no question of pardon for those priests and monks who, by preaching and living against the Law of God as expressed in the Four Articles, or preaching against the real presence of Christ in the Eucharist, had become the servants of Antichrist and of the powers of Hell. The hundreds of priests and monks who lost their lives as victims of Žižka's harsh creed are sad witnesses to the cruelty which the belief in the danger of heresy brought out in some of the most deeply religious minds. They were among the first of an endless chain of victims, Protestants and Catholics alike, who were to lose their lives in those waves of religious wars and persecutions lasting well into the seventeenth century. Even in Žižka's own time there were people whom this frightful slaughter filled with horror and the longing for a more humane, more tolerant way toward religious reform, and Bohemia, Žižka's own country, had the honor of first establishing a regime approaching true tolerance, still in the Hussite century, in 1485.[10]

Do we have to assume, then, that there was a highly developed sadistic streak in Žižka's character? It is a question which could perhaps better be answered by a schooled psychologist. Perhaps he would say that, without a strongly aggressive element in Žižka's character, he would, for all his hard and fast beliefs, have grown tired of killing people, even those people whom he deemed the enemies of God. This may well be. Yet we must not forget that Žižka, in thinking little of the value of hu-

[9] For the declaration for Korybut, see Appendix, VII.

[10] The Statutes of Kutná Hora. See above, Chapter 27, n. 14.

man lives on this earth and all the more of the need to save souls, was the child of his time. In extirpating "heretics" and especially those likely to spread and increase heresy, Žižka acted quite fully in accordance with the basic attitude of the medieval Church, differing from it only in determining who was to be regarded as a heretic. And in trying to judge Žižka's character as expressed in his cruel persecution of the "enemies of God," we should also have to look at his behavior toward other people before deciding that he was a bloodthirsty monster. And there we come to very different impressions. We have seen that, as far as possible, he strictly enforced the saving of women and children, in striking contrast to the behavior of the crusading armies in their invasions of Bohemia. We know that he took the young sons of an enemy lord under his personal protection, making sure that they were united with their father. We saw him take the trouble to write in behalf of a woman who was, in all probability, the widow of a fallen foe, just to make sure she would not lose some rather trifling possessions. In this sense Žižka's "good heart" was acknowledged even by his bitterest critic.[11]

Our judgment on Žižka's character could be more securely established if his contemporaries had left us with more detailed accounts of the impression he made upon them. This, however, was not the fashion of the time, and there are few personal utterances which might help us.[12] The one contemporary chronicler whom we can be sure knew Žižka personally, Březová, has nothing but admiration and praise for him, though he was highly critical of, sometimes openly hostile to, the Taborite movement and such of its leaders as Nicholas of Hus.

But to some extent at least we can base our judgment on the types of men whom Žižka could call his friends. They reached through all spheres of society—from the royal prince down to the lowliest peasant soldiers, including many great lords and many members of the lower nobility. The popularity which he enjoyed among the people of Prague —it was probably matched by those of the Orebite cities like Hradec

[11] Pekař, III, 295.

[12] By and large, only the German chroniclers such as Ludolf of Sagan and Windecke showed any hostility toward Žižka, while some bias seems to emerge from the expression "Žižka with his accomplices" often used by Bartošek of Drahonice, a man who was, after all, one of Sigismund's soldiers. A somewhat strange expression of dislike is to be found in that part of the *Chronicon veteris Collegiati* which reports Žižka's death. There, amidst the Latin text, are to be found two Czech words with the approximate meaning of "that wicked traitor." It seems very doubtful whether these are really the chronicler's words. A later interpolation by a scribe (only one manuscript survived) seems at least very likely, even though Pekař has rejected this possibility.

Králové or Čáslav—is well described by Březová; his attraction for the rural population is manifest from the large number of peasants who flocked to his standards; and the feelings of his soldiers toward this stern disciplinarian are sufficiently expressed in their assuming, after his death, the name Orphans.

From the beginning Žižka had, even in the Hussite camp, the greatest difficulties in getting along with the priests. His relationship to the two great radicals of the Hussite clergy, Koranda and John Želivský, close as it may have been at the beginning, was soon marred by dissent and ended, in both cases, in a definite break. Among the instances where we find Žižka losing his self-control in a fierce outbreak of wrath, two are concerned with priests: the beating up of Antoch of Tabor who had tried to sabotage, by a call to mutiny, Žižka's policy of help for Prague—and later, after the battle of Strachův Dvůr, the killing of the priest of Prague who had carried the host. There seemed to be two main sources for those frictions: the leadership claims of the clergy, especially at Tabor, which were bound to clash with Žižka's own claims and with his understanding of the third of the Four Articles; and the apparent danger, again among the Taborites, of heretic innovations or teachings, especially regarding the Eucharist. Yet among the priests, too, he had his friends. It is interesting to note that none of the well-known masters of Prague University, as far as our records go, ever included Žižka in their often violent criticism of Taborite creeds and practices,[13] and that he found nothing but the most willing and active support among the Orebite clergy, men like Ambrose of Hradec and Prokop the Lesser who were his followers and his last companions on his way from Přibyslav to his resting place.

In the religious field we have come to regard Žižka as a man of simple and strong beliefs, but at the same time rigid and unyielding. There is nothing in his utterances that would suggest any original creativeness of religious thought, and the faithfulness with which he clung to those beliefs that, at an advanced age, he had made his own did not render him any less dependent on the spiritual leadership of other men, especially of Jacobellus. He was the very opposite in his own element, the art of war. As a soldier he was neither rigid nor dependent on others, but as original and creative as it was possible to be at his time.

What seems most impressive about his military achievements is the

[13] Only Rokycana seems, just before the battle of Malešov, to have publicly agitated against Žižka, but made up for it by winning Žižka for the Peace of Libeň. See Pekař, IV, 161.

complete freedom from fixed traditions and the very full use he made of all potentialities which an unfettered intelligence could perceive. He profited from his early experiences in the guerilla type of warfare which naturally set a special premium upon resourcefulness. It is characteristic that he returned to a similar style of fighting in his harrowing war later fought against Rosenberg and the Pilsen Landfrieden.

We have pointed before to the ways in which Žižka used new weapons so as to be able to employ the manpower of his peasants, from the simple battle flails to the battle wagons as carriers of fire weapons, serving as the first field artillery used for the tactical offense, and as basic units of a mobile fortress for the defense. We have found him equally ingenious in the often amazing use he made of the terrain. We have seen him achieve tactical surprise by swift decisions and speedy moves. We have seen him, contrary to the usage of the time, relentlessly pursue a beaten enemy so as to make victory as complete as possible.

Žižka's greatness as a soldier thus appears in almost every conceivable field of warfare: in the organization of his troops, in the way he equipped them with unusual weapons or put known weapons to a new use; in the way he trained his troops in the use of these weapons and for this purpose formed them into disciplined tactical bodies; finally and most impressively, in the tactical leadership during the battle itself. Scores of conquered towns and castles show his ability to overcome the resistance of strong fortifications. But on the other hand, at least according to Aeneas Sylvius, who should have been well informed about this, he was also a fortress builder of high rank.

It is somewhat less easy to evaluate Žižka's performance as a strategist. Strategy in the modern sense of the word was as yet very little developed at Žižka's time. People did not think of it then, as we do now, as a special field of military art or science. The narrow limitations of strategic thought in the early fifteenth century are shown, for instance, by the often astonishing failure to exploit even a great victory. It is also shown by the large degree in which personal motives—either loyalty to a threatened friend or rancor toward a hated enemy—would interfere with what the modern military critic would consider sound strategy. Traces of this attitude are clearly to be found also in some of Žižka's strategic decisions.[14] And we must certainly beware lest we read too much strategic thought of the modern, refined type into his often very simple and straightforward moves.[15] On the other hand, there

[14] See some examples in Chapter 17.

[15] This is done, partly in what seems to me a rather primitive way, by Kamil Holý in his book *Žižka strateg* (*Spisy vojenského archivu RČS*, 1, 2), Prague 1928.

is no reason to suppose that his rational, highly astute mind, capable of exceptional tactical decisions, should have failed in decisions of strategic importance. And there are certainly some large moves which can stand as sound and effective strategy even before the critical modern eye. His defense of Prague against Sigismund's first crusade showed a brilliant ability to anticipate the enemy's strategic intentions. There is a tendency, observable in several of his campaigns, to strike against and occupy castles or towns flanking or even covering the rear of his enemy's main position. Thus he operated, for instance, in his campaigns against the Pilsen Landfrieden. His conduct of the campaign in January 1422—when he forced Sigismund to evacuate Kutná Hora even before the main battle had been fought—was strategically perfect in that it achieved, with a somewhat inferior army and largely through strategic surprise, results as far-reaching as he could possibly strive for. Undoubtedly he was a master of the "strategic retreat"—that is, in his case, retreat to a point where his tactical mastery could be fully used. It is rather ironical that what has often been considered his most ingenious retreat, the one from Hungary, actually never took place. The best examples of Žižka's planned retreat are the moves leading up to the battles of the Vladař and of Malešov. And these two battles are also among his most brilliant tactical achievements, equaled or exceeded perhaps only by the way in which, before Christmas 1421, he extricated himself from the iron ring into which he had been forced by the betrayal of the Kutnohorians.

The new forms of warfare which he created and developed—there were but few tactical changes in Hussite warfare after his death—had an enormous influence upon the development of armies, weapons, and tactics in the fifteenth and sixteenth centuries, especially in central and eastern Europe. It was essentially the use of Žižka's art of war which enabled the great Hungarian, John Hunyadi, to gain his victories over the Turks. His son, Mathias Corvinus, perhaps Hungary's greatest king, recruited his famous crack forces, the "Black Troop," mainly from Czechs reared in Hussite war traditions. Farther west the German armies of the fifteenth and early sixteenth century also followed the Hussite example.[16] It seems likely that this influence went further in both directions than has as yet been recognized, and thus contributed

[16] Toman, in his *Husitské válečnictví* (pp. 402-461) publishes a large number of German military ordinances from 1428-1480 mainly concerned with the "Wagenburgen" (mobile wagon fortress) and also otherwise showing the strong influence of the Hussite art of war. See also Urbánek, *Husitské válečnictví a cizina,* in the symposium *Co dali naše země Evropě a lidstvu*, Prague 1940.

very considerably to the growth, all over Europe, of mercenary infantry and artillery as an instrument which put an end to the feudal structure of society to the advantage of princely power.

Žižka's greatness as a soldier had never been questioned. There is far less agreement on his political achievements, on his role as a statesman and conscious leader of his nation. We cannot, of course, think of Žižka's national feeling as something independent of his religion. It was, on the contrary, in his own eyes one and the same. God had revealed His Truth, at this great moment, to the Czechs, and it was up to that nation to prove itself worthy of this special grace and fight for it with all its strength. Žižka's understanding of the Czech nation as different from all other nations (though less different from Slav nations such as the Poles) is very clearly expressed in his correspondence: in his letter to Pilsen where he calls himself and his followers "truly Czech people in the hope of God"; in his great letter to Domažlice where he reminds the people of that town of "the old Czechs who . . . defended not only God's cause but also their own" and then admonishes them to stand and fight bravely against the Germans, the "enemies and destroyers of the Czech land"; finally in his Military Ordinance where he declares that "all faithful Czechs" must join in the good fight, and promises, in the name of the whole Orebite brotherhood and field army, to help "all the faithful, especially in the Czech and Slav nation." (The word used for nation is, characteristically, the same as that for language, "jazyk," rather than the more general "národ.")

The common task by which the Czech people was distinguished among all other nations was the fight for the freedom of God's Law. Pursued without any regard for political reality this overpowering religious idea could well lead toward a primitive and politically impractical theocratic orientation, especially as long as it was electrified by a mood of chiliastic expectations. This, indeed, was clearly the tendency of the early Taborite movement. And as long as Žižka could be fully identified with this movement he could hardly be expected to think and act as a responsible national leader.

But at the latest by the beginning of 1421 this identification was no longer valid. Žižka had then begun to think in different, more truly national terms and had thereby got into conflict with at least an influential part of Tabor. There was, first of all, the alliance with Prague. Žižka was realist enough to understand that, in view of the weakness of the young movement and the strength of its enemies, such an alliance was indispensable for survival of both his religion and his nation. There was the question of finding a new national king. Again Žižka was realist enough to see that monarchical leadership would strengthen the commonwealth and effectively keep Sigismund from the throne of Bohemia. And in speaking out and acting for the Polish-Lithuanian candidature he was very likely also influenced by his Slav feelings. But on both issues he collided with the Taborite implacables—with Nicholas of Hus, with Priest Antoch, with Koranda. And on the question of the choice of the king he very likely also collided with John Želivský.

Žižka's final turn against Želivský has been discussed in detail. It was a highly important and somewhat fateful step. It sealed or at least helped to seal Želivský's fate, and in the outcome strengthened elements —the group around Hašek of Waldstein—with whom Žižka was bound to collide because they tried to reestablish the rule of the baronial caste with little regard to religious differences. It was the policy which later led to the civil war, was temporarily victorious at the St. Gall diet, and lost out at Malešov.

The final development of Žižka's policy shows, I think, both the strength and the limits of Žižka's statecraft. It took him a long time to see and fully understand the socio-political implications of the great struggle, as he had looked at events and people so exclusively in religious terms. But once he had understood them he embarked, with great energy and clarity of purpose, upon what from his point of view was the only correct and effective policy. He, the old squire from the rural south, based his plan for the Hussite reconstruction of Bohemia on the cities of the Kingdom, upon the spiritually, economically and militarily strongest supporters of the Chalice. His campaigns in 1424 are no longer defensive, nor are they any longer much influenced by such considerations as the punishment of an individual lord. They are conducted in the service of a great overall policy and go very far in realizing its basic aims.

The Peace of Libeň is the last but only one of many instances which show that in his political development Žižka was no blind fanatic, that he was ready to change his mind and that he was open to compromise if he believed that it might work. If his decision in the Peace of Libeň can be criticized—in the terms, of course, of the specific logic of his own policy—it would be not for blind perseverance in a line once chosen but for the opposite: that he was not as persistent as he should have been. But we hardly know enough of his motives at this grave moment to pass a fair judgment.

Only one fact can be ascertained, once more with great certainty, from Žižka's readiness to compromise again with the Prague of Korybut: that he was not ambitious in the ordinary sense, not thirsty for power for its own sake. This could also be seen much earlier, in January 1422, when returning to Prague from Německý Brod as the confirmed head of a strong all-Hussite army and supported by the prestige of his greatest and most consequential series of victories over Sigismund, he did not try to turn this strength into permanent political power. At Libeň, in 1424, a truly ambitious man, so near the goal of national dictatorship, would not have compromised. Not even the golden tongue of a Rokycana would have persuaded him to desist. But if he had been ambitious enough to stick to his plan out of a longing for personal power—then he might have been something like Bohemia's Caesar, or like an earlier Cromwell or Napoleon, but he would not have been John Žižka of the Chalice.

In one way, however, he was like those other great soldiers. He, too, was strong enough never to lose faith in his mission, never to be discouraged in adversity. In Žižka's case this appears in a rather strange form. It is as if Fate had said to him at his cradle: "Thou must do all things twice!" Twice he began his fight for the Chalice in the service of a great city: first in Prague, then in Pilsen. Twice he had to organize his own fighting brotherhood: first at Tabor, then in the Orebite community. Twice he saved Prague from impending ruin, and twice, in January 1422 and in September 1424, he almost achieved a position of national rulership. Twice, instead of grasping at this prize, he lent his support to the Prince from Lithuania. Twice he began the conquest of Moravia, and at the second attempt he died. But it could almost be said that he died twice: in 1424, at Přibyslav, and ten years later at Lipany, when the Taborite and Orebite field armies which he had created, having finally succeeded in forcing Rome and the Empire to a policy of compromise, eventually succumbed to a coalition of the conservatives led by Žižka's old disciple and foe: Diviš Bořek of Miletínek. And thus, having died twice as a force in the great revolution, he was twice buried, and twice disinterred, thus proving his great symbolic significance for the fate of Hussite and Protestant Bohemia through the history of two centuries.

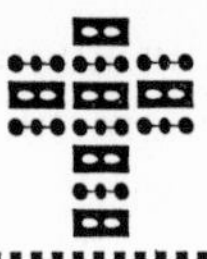

CHAPTER 30

# THE HUSSITE REVOLUTION AFTER ŽIŽKA

WITH Žižka's death the supreme command of the Hussite armies on their Moravian campaign fell to Prince Korybut.[1] As commander of the Orebite field army—the Orphans—he appointed Nicholas Sokol of Lamberg, the son of Žižka's protector of earlier days. But when late in fall the Orphans returned from Moravia, they elected their own captain general: Žižka's friend, Kuneš of Bělovice. The Taborites, on the other hand, called on Hvězda to take over the leadership of their field army. Had Žižka lived, it would have been quite likely that the two brotherhoods and their armies would eventually have reunited under his leadership. His disappearance from the Bohemian scene perpetuated the split between them, just as it tended to perpetuate the uneasy relationship between both brotherhoods and the capital. Yet the frictions which recurred sporadically between the Orphans and Tabor were insignificant for the political and military development inside Bohemia. They redivided their respective "zones of influence," with the result that the Orphans limited themselves again to eastern Bohemia and that the original power of the Older Tabor, in geographic as well as in military terms, was fully restored. The brotherhoods remained different in their ritual, but the social structure and with it the political interest of the two communities was largely parallel and facilitated a fairly permanent understanding and cooperation.

Not so the relationship between the two brotherhoods on the one hand and Prague on the other. Žižka had been right when he had expressed his doubts whether the Peace of Libeň would last very long. As early as February 1425 the civil war between the two sides flamed up again. In its course Prague lost still more of the towns which she had

[1] As this chapter, in its narrative part, only contains a rapid summary of the most important events, there is no point in further documentation. The sources are generally the same as those used previously, with the "Documenta" of the council of Basel (especially vol. I) added. Among modern treatments the most detailed is still Tomek's *Dějepis*, IV, 307-716. Most valuable as a monograph on the later phases of the Hussite wars up to the battle of Lipany is Urbánek's *Lipany a konec polních vojsk* (Lipany and the end of the field armies), Prague 1934. For treatments in English see Creighton's *History of the Papacy* and Lützow's *The Hussite War.*

governed. Some were conquered by the field armies of the brotherhoods, others acceded to them of their own will. Only in October 1425, one year after Žižka's death, was peace restored between the Hussites by the treaty of Vožice which was guaranteed by all the responsible Hussite leaders of both parties. This time it proved to be much more stable.

The situation following that agreement was basically this: Prague, though deprived of its direct overlordship over most of the royal towns of Bohemia, retained its position as the political and spiritual center of Hussitism. Its political head was still Korybut, with William Kostka and Hynek of Kolstein wielding considerable influence. The University however, as the highest religious authority, was ever more distinctly divided along religious and political lines. The conservative wing, under the leadership of John Příbram, constantly tried to push things back toward increasing agreement with the Roman dogma and ritual. Příbram was strongly resisted by the men who held with Jacobellus of Stříbro. Jacobellus had lost much of his personal strength and vigor in these years—he died in 1429—but his role was taken over most effectively by his young friend and disciple John Rokycana. Furthest left among the masters stood Peter Payne, the "Master English," who eventually threw in his lot with the brotherhoods. At Tabor itself the leadership changed twice within a short time. Soon after the Peace of Vožice, Hvězda died from a wound he had received in one of the last encounters of the civil war. In his stead Bohuslav of Švamberg, long the leading baron of the Taborite brotherhood, was officially appointed as its captain general. He led the Taborites when another all-Hussite campaign under Korybut's leadership was launched late in October 1425 against Sigismund's and Albert's forces in Moravia. It was more successful than the campaign of the previous year which had yielded only the possession of a couple of small towns and the destruction of some castles. But in the course of this campaign Švamberg, too, was killed. Thereby the way was opened for the man who, in many ways, can be regarded as Žižka's true successor during the following seven or eight years, from 1426 to 1434: Prokop the Bald.[2]

We have met with Prokop before. Born around 1380 as the son of a well-to-do family of Prague citizens, he had at an early time joined the Taborite movement but, under Želivský's patronage, had temporarily

[2] The one modern biography of Prokop is A. Neubauer's *Kněz Prokop Holý* in *Č.Č.H.*, 1910, pp. 28ff. See also the second part (*Prokop Holý a Lipany*) in Urbánek, *op.cit.*, pp. 83-160.

held a preacher's position in the capital. There he had come under suspicion of Pikhartism, had been arrested but was soon released, and had rejoined the Taborites. At Konopiště in spring 1423 he had shown his sense for the really important issues by trying to reduce the friction over the vestments: he, the Taborite priest, had celebrated mass in the ornate way of the Praguers. Later stories claiming that he had been Žižka's special favorite[3] are not supported by contemporary sources. They seem unlikely in view of Prokop's religious views, which were more in line with those of Koranda and Nicholas of Pelhřimov and surely less orthodox on the subject of the Eucharist than Žižka's.[4] Nor would Žižka have approved of a priest taking over the supreme military and political direction of the Taborite brotherhood. This arrangement, however, which had worked rather badly in the case of John Želivský, proved highly successful and became even more the rule when his namesake, the Orebite priest Prokop the Lesser (or the Short)[5] soon afterwards became the main leader of the field army of the Orphans.

There were some qualities which Prokop and Žižka had in common: both were unusually gifted military leaders, both showed in critical situations a striking sense for the essential, and both were remarkably free of traditional limitations. But they were different in almost everything else, and even their similarities expressed themselves in rather different forms. Prokop, Žižka's junior by at least twenty years, had still an open mind on issues on which Žižka's judgment had become final and rigid. As a townsman and priest he had, of course, a higher erudition than the squire of Trocnov. He was one of the first among the Taborite clergy to make use of the sanction, by that community, of priest marriage. He was surely superior to Žižka as a diplomat. Where Žižka would never have set eyes on King Sigismund except as an enemy in battle, Prokop met the King personally and would have been prepared to accept him as Bohemia's ruler if Sigismund had been ready to underwrite the Four Articles. In the early negotiations with the Council of Basel, especially those conducted at Cheb in spring 1432, he showed a combination of firmness and versatility which contributed much to the success there achieved by the Hussites. But if, in these ways, he was more brilliant and more versatile than Žižka he lacked the

[3] Aeneas Sylvius, chapter 44, and later authors copying from him.

[4] On Prokop's religious attitudes see Urbánek, *op.cit.*, pp. 87, 88, 216.

[5] In Czech Prokůpek, in Latin Procopius Parvus. He was called this, because of his short stature, long before the people began to call the other one "Procopius Magnus," Prokop the Great.

older man's iron strength and resilience. If the word discouragement did not figure in Žižka's vocabulary it did in Prokop's, and his shaken self-reliance in the fall and winter 1433-1434 contributed to certain weaknesses and mistakes culminating in his tragic end at Lipany.

As a military leader Prokop could very largely rely on the organization, the weapons, and the tactics developed by Žižka. But throughout most of his career he handled them splendidly, and his most important contribution to the final success of Bohemian arms lay in the field of overall strategy. Unlike Žižka, and despite the protests coming from part of the Taborite clergy, he did not feel bound by the religious principle that the war for the freedom of the Law of God had to be conducted by merely defending the soil of Bohemia. (It is, of course, possible that Žižka, too, had he lived long enough, would eventually have adopted a more offensive strategy against the foreign enemies, to which his enterprises against Moravia might well have served as preludes.)

By the time Prokop took over the direction of Tabor's forces the war had lasted for seven years. It was then rather obvious that the foreign enemies had only a very remote chance of ever destroying Hussitism by force of arms. But this did not mean peace or recognition for the Chalice. In 1426 neither the Church nor the Empire were any more ready for compromise with the heretics than they had been at any time before. There was only one way in which to change their mind: by carrying the war, so far exclusively fought on Bohemia's soil, into their own lands. It was Prokop who first understood or at least acted according to this simple but essential truth. And with this resolve, with Hussite Bohemia's armies going over to the offensive against her aggressive neighbors, the war did, indeed, enter an entirely new phase.

It was by no means easy for Prokop to get this new strategy approved by the majority of the Hussite communities. The year 1426 stood, in the main, still in the sign of national defense. In June of that year the town of Ústí, on the Elbe in the north of Bohemia, was besieged by Hussite forces. The town had been pledged, as had some other Bohemian towns, by Sigismund to the dukes of Saxony in return for money. The desire of the Saxon rulers to safeguard Ústí led to the greatest invasion which Bohemia had as yet experienced from the north (though the claim that the Saxons had 70,000 men can hardly have been true). The Saxons were opposed by a Hussite army under the command of Prince Korybut, with the brothers of Poděbrady and Hynek of Kolstein among his lieutenants, and with a strong Taborite force under Prokop's command. The German army, despite its superiority, suffered a catastrophic defeat, losing supposedly 15,000 men in dead alone. It was immediately after this battle that Prokop first proposed following up the victory by an invasion of Saxony, but he was overruled by strong opposition on the side of Korybut and of Hynek of Poděbrady who, by this time, had become one of the Prince's followers. The issue actually led to an outbreak of limited fighting between the Taborites and Hynek in the course of which he fell in battle. His brother Victorin, perhaps Žižka's closest friend, remained with the brotherhood of the Orphans but died a natural death at the beginning of 1427, leaving as his heir a young boy, George, the future king.

Despite these initial difficulties the policy of invading the countries of the enemy was actually adopted before the end of the year. In October 1426 the Orphans marched into Silesia, conquering and burning the town of Landshut. In November Prokop, who with his Taborites had achieved considerable successes in Moravia, followed this up by a minor invasion of Austria. It was repeated in a much larger way a few months later, in March 1427. At Zwettl, about forty miles northeast of Linz, a strong Austrian army was routed by Prokop's Taborites, leaving thousands of dead on the battlefield. It was the first great victory achieved by Hussite arms on foreign soil. This success went far in establishing Prokop's position as the foremost among Hussite leaders. It was strengthened even further by political developments inside Prague.

The capital, all through this time, had been under the rule of Korybut. The Prince still had his adherents among both the nobility and the citizenry, but his position in the country at large had not grown stronger since the Peace of Vožice, not even after the victory of Ústí of which he had made little use. Lately he had taken some part in the acrimonious struggles between the conservative masters led by John Příbram and their adversaries at the University, lending his help to the former group and in turn receiving their support. It may have been upon Příbram's suggestion that he eventually decided to try his hand in a rather daring diplomatic game. He began secret negotiations with the Holy See, promising Pope Martin V that with the help of the conservative elements he would lead the Czechs to complete reconciliation with the Church, based on full recognition of the rights of the Pope to pass final judgment on all outstanding issues. It was a return to the idea that, if he "delivered the goods," the curia would be ready to drop its support for King Sigismund's claims and acknowledge Korybut's Bohemian kingship, and that under those conditions he would also gain forgiveness and renewed support from his royal uncles in Poland and Lithuania. But the Prince badly overrated his strength. It would never have been sufficient to bring off a maneuver which all except the arch-conservatives among the Hussites were bound to regard as treason to their most sacred principles. Exposed by the alert Rokycana and not even defended by men like Kostka, he was seized on April 17, 1427, and for some time held captive and incommunicado at the castle of Waldstein. In the following year he was allowed to go back to Poland, while his accomplices in the plan, Příbram and the other conservative masters, were exiled from Prague.

Korybut's second regency, if we may call it that, was largely a failure and fell far short of the expectations put in him on the basis of his performance in 1422. But it has to be acknowledged that his situation, through no fault of his, was precarious from the beginning, as he had lost the support from Poland and as neither of the two brotherhoods recognized his regency after 1424, as Žižka had done in 1422. It is to Korybut's credit that he did not bear any prolonged grudge against Hussite Bohemia. He remained a vigorous advocate of Polish-Bohemian cooperation and alliance and in 1431, no longer as claimant to a regency or kingship but merely as an ally, he once more led Polish troops south to help the Hussites defeat the fifth and last crusade in the battle of Domažlice. He eventually went back to Lithuania and there died in one of the bitter dynastic feuds arising after the death of Grand Duke Witold.[6]

The politically and religiously less conservative groups that gained power in Prague after Korybut's removal—we find among them, even in the Old Town, former friends of John Želivský—made close cooperation between the capital and the two brotherhoods much easier. In particular Rokycana and Prokop, though not always in agreement, got along fairly well with one another. Prokop could thus devote his attention even more wholeheartedly to the pursuit of the war outside Bohemia. The spring of 1427 saw Hussite armies again in Lusatia and Silesia. But the main event of 1427 was the Fourth Crusade which, after having been postponed again and again, finally got under way in that summer. The Pope had made enormous efforts to secure a vast participation from all over the Empire, and as his personal representative appeared Henry Beaufort, Bishop of Winchester, a half-brother of the

[6] See on Korybut's later history the various references in Goll, *Čechy a Prusy*.

late King Henry IV of England. The German troops which, in August 1427, first laid siege to the town of Stříbro supposedly numbered between 160,000 and 200,000 men. Their numbers, however, really mattered little. Even if they had been less than a quarter of that strength they should have had a chance against the Hussites who—about 18,000 men under Prokop's command—marched against them. Actually the crusaders fled even before the Czechs had arrived, and they suffered heavy losses only when the Hussite pursuers caught up with them near Tachov. Cardinal Henry, in furious contempt, tore the imperial standard into pieces, but he, too, had to flee to avoid being taken prisoner.

For the next four years no major attempt was made by the Catholic world to invade or conquer Bohemia, whereas the Hussites now took the initiative in grand style and ranged far and wide through northern, central and southern Germany, Austria and occasionally Hungary. There were few real battles as the fear of the Hussites was such that the German troops mostly fled long before they had even heard or seen their enemies. Occasionally when their leaders succeeded in enforcing a stand the result was invariably a total defeat. Again and again the Hussites returned with rich booty, and many German towns tried and often succeeded in buying safety by considerable money payments.

Those invasions, now almost constant, of one German territory or another were highly effective in more than one way. While they relieved some of the burden which the maintenance of the Hussite field armies had long meant for Bohemia they put an even greater burden on the German principalities and cities and evoked among all classes of people an impatient demand that an end be put to this misery, if need be by yielding to the demands of the Czechs. But even more effective, and from the point of view of the Church of Rome a far more dangerous result of the Hussite campaigns, was their impact upon the religious morale of the people in the invaded regions. Why, so they were bound to ask themselves, did God permit the Hussites to obtain victory after victory? Was He not, perhaps, really on their side? The Hussites, and especially Tabor, tried hard to support this trend of thought by sending out thousands of pamphlets presenting their case, some of which penetrated as far as the Netherlands, France, and even Spain. This "psychological warfare" was of course severely limited by the need to copy by hand every one of those pamphlets. Perhaps it is permissible to speculate that the Hussite reformation might have spread effectively far beyond the limits of Bohemia if Gutenberg's invention had been made and developed just three or four decades earlier.

Even so there was a good deal of ferment in some parts of Germany, enough to strengthen materially the longing for peace on the side of the German rulers.

But this longing was not one-sided. In Bohemia, too, ten years of war and troubles, of bloodshed and destruction, of reduced trade and production and corresponding inflation, had caused frightful hardships and with it a strong wish for it all to end. On the spiritual plane it was not easy for a proud people which for five centuries had held an honorable place in the community of Western Christendom to face a prolonged isolation from the rest of Europe, which gave Bohemia the position of a religious outcast. Even though the overwhelming majority of the Hussites had little doubt about being in the right, about being those who least deserved the ignominious name "heretics," they wished their honor and innocence finally vindicated before Christianity at large. This was true not only for the adherents of the Calixtine High Church but even for many people in the Taborite and Orphan brotherhoods. There the chiliastic fervor had long cooled off, and the somewhat naïve hopes for a quick conversion of all good Christians, though they had not altogether disappeared, had become far less confident. It was also with some uneasiness that the people perceived a slow change in the composition and character of the Taborite and Orphan field armies. They had begun to attract many men, from Bohemia as well as from outside, even Germans, for whom the defense of the Law of God meant little, who really looked just for the chance of living a carefree life and partaking in the rich booty made during the "work in the field," that is the permanent service with the army, as opposed to the militia type.[7]

The history of the negotiations between the Hussites and the Church which finally led to the Basel Compacts is so complex that even an outline would go far beyond the frame of this book. We can only point out some of the main stages. In April 1429 Prokop and Payne followed an invitation to see Sigismund at Bratislava, but their suggestion that the King accept the Four Articles only met with a harsh refusal. Soon afterwards a Bohemian diet discussed the question whether the Hussites would be ready to participate in a future church council. They declared their readiness to do so if the Eastern Church (where Communion was taken in both kinds) were represented as well. This stipu-

[7] The expression "working in the field" (e.g. exercitus Taboritorum in campis pro nomine dei laborantes) occurs frequently. See Urbánek, *op.cit.*, p. 193, n. 69.

lation was not upheld when, after enormous difficulties, Pope Martin's resistance against a new council was finally overcome and the great assembly called to Basel for March 1431. Yet the Hussites showed great and justified caution before committing themselves to participate. A first series of preliminary negotiations, conducted at Cheb early in 1431, broke down. Cardinal Giuliano Cesarini, whom Pope Martin had appointed as his legate for the Empire and as his representative at the council, thereupon decided once more to appeal to arms, and upon his demand an imperial diet at Nürnberg decided on a Fifth Crusade. It was to be the last one. The great army—the lowest estimates know of 130,000 men—this time penetrated somewhat deeper into Bohemia. The Hussite countermeasures, completely directed by Prokop, were prompt and effective, and the Czech army was less inferior to those of the Germans than many times before. It approached the Germans in the region of Domažlice, and again their stampede began before there had really been a clash of arms, the Hussite cavalry pursuing the Germans far into the wooded valleys of the Šumava (Böhmerwald) and cutting down thousands of them. Cesarini, as before him Beaufort, barely saved his life. God had once more denied the help for which He had been so solemnly invoked. The invincibility of Hussite arms was established beyond any further challenge. The glowing joy of the Czech patriots over this achievement is strongly expressed in Lawrence of Březová's great poem.[8]

Yet these same people, now without doubt the military masters of all of Central Europe, kept remarkably free from any boastful arrogance. And when now Cesarini, one of the best men the Church could provide for this job, urged upon the Council the speedy beginning of true peace negotiations, the Hussites were not averse to it.

Another series of preliminary talks took place, beginning at Cheb in May 1432. The main issue was the form of the safe conduct to be issued to the Czechs so as to preclude a repetition of the events that seventeen years earlier had occurred at Constance, and the role in which the Hussite delegates would appear at the Council. In those prolonged negotiations Prokop wisely held out against the demand for an armistice. This, he felt, would immediately take that pressure from the Council which had operated most strongly in favor of concessions to Bohemia. Eventually the Hussite demands were almost completely accepted: the personal safety of all delegates was guaranteed beyond any doubt. They would have the right freely to express their opinions, to criticize abuses within

[8] Vavřinec z Březové, *Piseň o vítězství u Domažlic*, ed. Hrdina and Ryba, Prague 1951.

the Church, to defend the Four Articles, in short they were not to appear as accused but as equals, and would occupy seats in accordance with this honorable standing. Even the interdict upon towns through which they passed was to be left unenforced, and at Basel they would have the freedom to worship in their way and to give the Communion in the two kinds.

On January 4, 1433, the Bohemian embassy arrived at Basel, received with great friendliness and full honors. It was led by Prokop the Bald and William Kostka of Postupice. Among the other delegates most prominent were John Rokycana as representative of the Prague Calixtines, Nicholas of Pelhřimov for the Taborites, and Peter Payne, this time representing the Orphans. There were long disputations on the Four Articles, first in plenary sessions, later in more intimate talks between the Hussites and the leaders of the council of whom, besides Cesarini, the papal auditor Juan Palomar, a Spaniard, played the most prominent role. Progress was slow, and it was decided that the Hussites, accompanied by Catholic representatives of the Council, should return to Prague where, in June, a diet was to be held. One of the most difficult issues arose out of the Hussite demand that the Communion in both kinds should be obligatory in all of Bohemia and Moravia. Its acceptance would have meant that the Council would have to command the Bohemian Catholics, especially in the Pilsen region, to adhere to the Hussite forms of worship. It was, indeed, hard for the Council to go that far, but both Prokop and Rokycana insisted on it, the latter emphasizing that the coexistence of the two forms of Communion in the country would perpetuate the internal strife. This issue now also began to influence the conduct of military operations, which had never been completely suspended.

The summer of 1433 witnessed one of the most spectacular campaigns of the Hussite war. The relationship between Poland and Bohemia during the last phase of the war had again much improved. We have mentioned earlier the presence of Polish auxiliaries under Korybut at the battle of Domažlice. In 1432 war broke out again between Poland and the Prussian Order. Thereupon a solemn alliance against the Germans was signed in July 1432 between Poland and Hussite Bohemia, and in the following year Hussite troops—an Orphan army with strong cavalry under the command of John Čapek of Sány—came to the help of the Poles. Marching through the Neumark into West Prussia they conquered several castles and towns, among them the strongly fortified city of Tczew (Dirschau) on the Vistula. Eventually, not far from the mouth of that river, they reached the Baltic and there staged a victory celebration, having proved that nothing but the wide sea had been able to stop their advance. Their campaign greatly helped in compelling the Order, soon afterwards, to sue for peace.

Historically far more important, however, were the military events inside Bohemia, which, in turn, were largely influenced by the political development of the country. Since 1428 there had been less strife between the Hussites than during the earlier phases of the revolution. True there had been considerable friction inside Prague, especially between the Old and the New Town, largely based on the old social and religious conflicts; and whereas the Old Town was still closely allied with some of the great barons, the New Town had developed a rather intimate cooperation with the Orphan brotherhood. But the increased emphasis on the war outside the Kingdom, and the strengthened national leadership of Prokop the Bald, had prevented any dangerous outbreaks of internecine strife, to the extent that even the struggle with the Catholic elements within the Kingdom became secondary in comparison with the foreign wars. Nevertheless the tasks imposed by the peace negotiations seemed to make the establishment of a firm national government increasingly desirable. In February 1432 a diet in Prague, representing the barons, Prague, and the two brotherhoods, elected a regency council which, as nine years earlier, consisted of twelve members. But as before, it proved to be rather weak and ineffective as soon as real trouble developed.

The issue which now came into the foreground was connected with the Hussite demand for enforced uniformity of religion throughout the Kingdom. The main bulwark of the Catholics inside Bohemia was still Pilsen. Feeling that a conquest of this city, and therewith the subjection of the Pilsen Landfrieden, would go far in solving this problem, Prokop began to besiege the city in August 1433, a few weeks after his return from Basel. But the resumption of major military operations inside Bohemia met with much stronger resistance even among the Hussites than Prokop had anticipated. The usual forcible methods of supplying the army with food and other necessaries from the country had scarcely bothered Bohemia during the last few years as the war had been mostly conducted on foreign soil. The renewal of these hardships inside the country came as an unpleasant surprise, and especially the nobility bitterly resented it.

Prokop's siege army—mainly his own Taborites, but with Orphans and also some Prague troops added—could not stop provisioning, but to mitigate the consequences for Bohemia he sent Taborite contingents, some 2,000 men with about a hundred wagons, from Domažlice across the border into Bavaria to requisition cattle and other food from the German peasants. There, at the village of Wintersried near Waldmünchen, they were surprised by an army consisting mostly of Germans, but reinforced and led by one of the lords of the Pilsen Landfrieden. The Hussite troops had no time to reach the safety of their wagon fortress and lost 1,200 men in dead and 300 in prisoners—about three quarters of their total strength. This first defeat of Hussite arms outside the country, though in comparison with the Hussite victories it seemed but a small matter, nevertheless had serious repercussions, especially on the morale of both sides. In the Taborite camp before Pilsen it led to an outbreak of mutiny against Prokop, who, following the fierce agitation of one of his subaltern officers, was seized and kept under arrest for a few days. This personal humiliation deeply depressed the Taborite leader, and upon his release he refused to let himself be reinstated and left the army, taking residence in the New Town of Prague.

Prokop's resignation from the political and military leadership of Tabor badly harmed the national (and probably also the international) prestige of the two brotherhoods and their field armies. In particular it restored some of the confidence and the hopes of the high nobility whose role in the leadership of the nation during the last few years had been less in evidence than ever before. They now felt that the time had come to regain much, if not all, of their lost influence. At a diet held in December 1433 they managed to replace the weak regency council of twelve by a single regent for Bohemia and Moravia: Aleš of Riesenburg, once a founding member of Žižka's Lesser Tabor and even later a friend of the Orphan brotherhood. Prokop the Bald in his self-chosen retirement did not object to this measure. But it soon became clear that Aleš, though a good Hussite, intended fully to safeguard the interests of his own caste in the name of domestic peace, order, and efficient government.

The siege of Pilsen, maintained by both Taborites and Orphans under the command of Prokop the Lesser, became more and more a bone of contention. After some time the situation of the city grew critical; yet not only the Germans and the Catholics of the Landfrieden but even Hussite adversaries of the brotherhood made attempts, some of them successful, to send food through to the besieged people. The

Taborite troops, on the other hand, continued to requisition and confiscate food for themselves, and refused to permit negotiations for an armistice which the regent tried to conduct. In March 1434 a group of noblemen, led by Meinhart of Jindřichův Hradec (cousin of the late Ulrich Vavák, who had once been Žižka's prisoner and had later gone over to the Hussite side) and Diviš Bořek of Miletínek, concluded a league and covenant in which they obliged themselves to uphold, if need be by force, domestic peace and order in obedience to the regent against anyone trying to disrupt it. The group was joined by a majority of the Czech nobility, especially by most of the barons. Also the Old Town of Prague (and with it the Small Side which, having been partly rebuilt, had again taken its place as the third borough) adhered to the league, whereas the New Town, still closely allied with the Orphans, remained aloof.

In the following weeks the members of the league made extensive military preparations for the showdown with the brotherhoods whose field armies were hampered in their countermeasures by the continuing siege of Pilsen. The councilors of the New Town, alarmed by these threatening measures, strengthened and garrisoned their walls and gates against the Old Town. But on May 5 the army of the lords entered the Old Town, and they together with the councilors of the Old Town delivered an ultimatum to the New Town to join the League against the brotherhoods as the disturbers of the peace. When the New Town refused, the allies stormed and conquered it. The entering soldiers were permitted to take all the spoils they wanted, the councilors and other popular leaders who did not escape in time were arrested and the city put under the government of the Old Town.

Among those who managed to escape was Prokop the Bald. The league's offensive shook him out of his lethargy. He immediately wrote to Prokop the Lesser, telling him that "with divine permission the false lords, together with the Praguers of the Old Town, have overcome by surprise attack our dear brethren, the citizens of the New Town. Therefore it seems to us that you ought to leave all else and move from Pilsen to Sedlčany. Čapek [of Sány, general of the Orphans] is already collecting many troops, and we of Tabor, as we hope, will do likewise. For it is better for us to die than not to revenge the innocent blood of our dearest brethren which was shed so treacherously."[9]

Prokop the Lesser immediately complied. On both sides the preparations continued with the utmost energy. On May 30, 1434, the two

[9] The Latin text in Urbánek, *op.cit.*, p. 261.

armies stood opposite each other in the plain between Kouřim and Český Brod, near the village of Lipany. The army of the League had in its ranks most of the barons and many of the knights with their retainers, including troops from the Pilsen Landfrieden, from Ulrich of Rosenberg and from other Catholics, further the forces of Prague, including troops from the town of Mělník. Though the regent, Aleš of Riesenburg, was with them, the supreme command had been given to Diviš Bořek of Miletínek. He had, altogether, 25,000 men under him. On the other side stood the troops of the brotherhoods, that is the two field armies and militias from most of the Hussite cities except Prague and Mělník. Their strength was somewhere between 12,000 and 18,000.[10] Prokop the Bald was in overall command. Among his lieutenants were Prokop the Lesser, Čapek of Sány who led the cavalry, and only four lords, among them Roháč of Dubá and Sezema of Kunštat, both formerly members of Žižka's Lesser Tabor.

Diviš of Miletínek now had his great chance. He could show himself, as a soldier, a worthy pupil of Žižka's by winning a decisive battle against Žižka's heirs, thus avenging after a decade his defeat and that of his friends at Strachův Dvůr and Malešov. He succeeded by using a clever maneuver: Attacking first but beaten back, he ordered his infantry to retreat fast. When his enemies, believing that the army of the league was really in full flight, left their encampment in pursuit he had them charged by concealed cavalry. Before the Taborites could regain the safety of their wagon fortress the troops of the League had penetrated into it. The situation of the brotherhood army became quite hopeless when Čapek of Sány, despairing of victory, fled from the battlefield with his cavalry. The brotherhoods lost several thousands in dead and an equally large numbers of prisoners.[11] About a thousand of these, mostly old soldiers of the Taborite field army, were herded into several barns and pitilessly burned to death. The two Prokops fell in the heat of the battle, whereas the few lords fighting with them were taken prisoners and subsequently released. Later the saga spread among the people of Bohemia that the Taborite fighters who had fallen at Lipany were not really dead. They had mysteriously disappeared into a great cave in the mountain Blaník, whence they would one day emerge to free Bohemia from her oppressors.

[10] On the contradicting sources, see *ibid.*, pp. 248ff.

[11] The number of dead usually given (13,000) is certainly an enormous exaggeration. See again Urbánek, *op.cit.*, pp. 156, 256.

The Hussite Revolution, it could be said, had not one but two Thermidors. The first was the end of John Želivský and of his party's rule over Prague. It was in the main due to Žižka that the process of further weakening of the popular or, as Palacký would have said, democratic forces was checked, that they could organize themselves in the great alliance between the brotherhoods and the cities and that thus arose among the religious, political, and social forces, something like a precarious equilibrium which lasted for ten more years. During the last of these, Prokop's powerful personality tended to shift the center of political gravity even farther toward the left, to a point where even he himself was no longer able to control the unruly forces under his command, too many of them no longer "warriors of God" but uprooted people who had turned into hungry and greedy mercenaries. It was not surprising that eventually a second reaction set in, that it gained quick support from all those who stood to lose by a continuation of revolution and war, and that it thus prevailed in the short, brisk, and bloody struggle which culminated in the battle of Lipany.

In reading the contemporary records, of which we have had room to quote just part of one—Prokop's letter to his namesake—it is difficult not to feel sympathy and compassion for this great man, surely the most tragic figure, in the Greek meaning of the word, of all the important actors in this vast drama. But at the same time we ought to preserve a good deal of caution in trying to evaluate the significance of this event. On the side of the brotherhoods there perished at Lipany some of the noblest, most clearly idealistic representatives of the reform movements, as well as the great brotherhoods which they had led. With them also disappeared the field armies, at least as autonomous organizations, as states within the state. Created by Žižka as militant theocracies of tremendous striking power, they had fulfilled their historical role, had forced Church and Empire to recognize, if ever so grudgingly, the right of the Bohemian Reformation to live and develop within a Christian Europe. But by completing this task they had also outlived that role. In the long run they were bound to divide the nation more than they could strengthen it. It was probably this insight which induced men of sincere devotion to the principles of the Reformation and to the well-being of their nation, men such as William Kostka and Beneš of Mokrovousy, to join the League of the Lords and the Old Town, even though this meant for the moment to side also with people with whom they had really very little in common, especially with some of the most selfish reactionaries among the great barons, and with some of the leaders of the Catholic minority inside Bohemia.

It is understandable that the news of the destruction of the field armies was received with the greatest satisfaction by the Council of Basel. There was a widespread hope among the Catholics that the leadership of the Czech nation had now passed into the hands of people who, like John Příbram, had almost entirely abandoned the program of reform. This, however, soon proved to be a miscalculation. Even though the most conservative among the masters, with Příbram, Christian of Prachatice, and Prokop of Pilsen, could no longer be eliminated from the further negotiations with the Council, the leading role in these talks remained in the hands of Rokycana who was backed wholeheartedly by the great majority of the Hussites. The basis for the eventual compromise had indeed been laid before the battle of Lipany, when early in 1434 those articles were drafted which have gone into history as the Basel Compacts. In their final form in which they were accepted by the Hussites in July 1436 and ratified early in 1437 by the Council they were still based on the Four Articles, though watered down in important respects.

The first of the Articles, concerned with the Eucharist, declared that the Communion is to be given freely to Christians in Bohemia and Moravia and elsewhere to adherents of the Hussite form of worship, but it fell short of the original Hussite demands in that it did not exclude the Communion in one kind from being practiced in the Kingdom. The second and third article of the Compacts generally corresponded to the fourth and first of the Articles of Prague as they had been officially accepted and pronounced by the University and the first diet of Čáslav. It goes without saying that the punishment and extirpation of mortal sins was reserved to those "whose office it is." More significant was the limitation of the free preaching of the Word of God, which was to be done "by the priests of the Lord and by worthy deacons." The fourth article of the compacts, concerned with the role of the priests, was worded in a way which the Church could accept without fear for its economic and political position (which, in Bohemia, of course, had already sustained irreparable losses). Priests, so it said, shall in the time of the law of grace claim no ownership of worldly possessions such as hereditary estates, and shall administer faithfully the property of the Church.

The true scope of the Hussite concession to the Council are even today subject to varying interpretations, and the history of the endless and extremely intricate negotiations would demand a very special study to be rendered understandable. On the other hand there is no doubt that many of the leading churchmen regarded the Compacts as a Hussite success going far beyond what should by right have been conceded and that they were, together with the whole peace settlement, finally accepted only because the Emperor Sigismund—he had finally acquired this dignity through being crowned by the Pope—exerted strong pressure and at the same time played an extremely skillful diplomatic game.

Sigismund was now an old man. Ever since 1419 he had waited for the moment when he would be able to take possession of his Bohemian inheritance. Now, that things had taken a turn where his hopes seemed so much nearer fulfillment, he grew understandably impatient. That he would now be recognized as lord of the land was, after Lipany, hardly questioned by anybody. A diet called by the regent in July 1434 decided to send a delegation to Ratisbon, consisting of representatives of all parties and groups, including the defeated brotherhoods, which would discuss with the Emperor the conditions under which he would be asked to take over the kingship of the country. Sigismund showed his most conciliatory side, and the negotiations, though not immediately conclusive, proceeded under good auspices. There was, however, one difficulty which held up agreement between the Hussites and the Council. The Czech representatives, with the diet almost constantly in session, demanded the right for the estates to elect the Archbishop of Prague and his suffragans. Whereas the Emperor agreed to this the Council kept stalling, as the recognition of an Utraquist priest as archbishop would give too strong a sanction to a religious group which had so recently been branded as heretic. Sigismund personally promised the Czech negotiators that he would recognize anyone they elected. Thereupon, in September 1435, the estates unanimously elected Master John Rokycana as Archbishop of Prague. The Council, however, refused to ratify this election, and a new crisis arose. But the Emperor, clever and quick with double dealings as always, managed to convince the Bohemian estates that he would eventually obtain this sanction from the Church while simultaneously, but secretly assuring the Council that this was an ecclesiastical matter in which he was not going to meddle. The scheme worked: The Bohemians, trusting the Emperor's promise, honored their part of the deal without waiting for the ratification of Rokycana's election. It was never granted.

On July 5, 1436, at a solemn diet of the estates of Bohemia and Moravia held at Jihlava, in the presence of the Emperor and the representatives of the Council, the Compacts were signed and the excommunication against Bohemia was repealed. Two weeks later Sigismund signed the documents guaranteeing all the freedoms and privileges of the Bohemian estates which opened the way for his assumption of the crown. On August 16 he solemnly pronounced the restoration of peace between Bohemia and the Christian world, thereby ending seventeen years of war. A week later he entered the capital for whose possession he had fought so desperately during the earlier years of the revolution. He only left the city fifteen months later, a dying man, trying in vain to reach Hungary before death overtook him.

The short-lived restoration of the House of Luxemburg on the Bohemian throne and the acceptance of the Compacts by the Hussites and the Council of Basel put an end to war and revolution. But it did not end the struggle, did not restore the former unity of the Roman Church. For the Czech nation as represented by its estates, the Compacts remained the sacred basis of their religious constitution, and they defended them vigorously all through the fifteenth and the early sixteenth century, till the wider Reformation in Germany, Switzerland, and the rest of northern and northwestern Europe changed the whole religious climate and map of the continent. The Popes, however, never recognized the Compacts, and in 1462 Pius II, the former Aeneas Sylvius, solemnly abrogated any obligations of the Church to abide by them. The man who then bore the Crown of St. Wenceslas—after the two short rules of Sigismund and his son-in-law Albert, each to be counted in months rather than years, and the virtual interregnum prevailing during the minority of Albert's posthumous son Ladislas—was one whom the Hussite estates had elected from their own ranks: Victorin of Kunštat's son and, so it seems, Žižka's godson, George of Poděbrady. Only during the two decades of his rule, first as regent (1452-1457), then as king, did Bohemia fully recover domestic stability. But his attempts to gain recognition for the Compacts from the Holy See were in vain. On the contrary Pope Pius' successor Paul II excommunicated the King and even succeeded in subjecting Bohemia to new invasions, again using a Hungarian ruler, Mathias Corvinus, as his instrument. As once before, the Hussite majority of the Czech people rallied to the defense of their faith and their country. When in 1471 George died (almost at the same time as his main religious adviser, the elected archbishop and administrator of the Utraquist Church, John Rokycana), the old plan of the election of a Polish prince was finally carried out, and with Vladislav II the Jagiellone dynasty mounted the throne of Bohemia. Vladislav promised to accept and defend the Basel Compacts before his coronation, but though a Catholic himself he could not prevail upon the Curia to recognize it.

Under these circumstances the Utraquist Church of Bohemia, though still bound to the Church Catholic by seeking to obtain ordination of its priests from Roman bishops, developed ever more clearly into an independent, national religious body.[12] It had its own administration which, while it was never recognized by Rome, was not dependent on her either. It not only continued in the practice of the Chalice for the laity but challenged in its teaching the Papal supremacy as well as the claim that Rome alone represented the true succession and representation of Christ on earth. And while, in matters of dogma, it soon developed its own orthodoxy, which was not too far removed from the older faith, its moral conduct and its general attitude were still dominated by the reforming principles of Hus who was always regarded as a sacred martyr and whose day—July 6, the anniversary of his death—was celebrated as a religious and national holiday. The memory, on the other hand, of the bitterness and destructiveness of the Hussite wars led the Hussite majority of Bohemia to adopt an attitude of tolerance toward the Catholic minority, which found its most remarkable expression in the statutes passed by the diet of Kutná Hora in 1485. Basically more progressive than the Peace of Augsburg and perhaps even the Edict of Nantes, the statutes of Kutná Hora permitted the free choice of religious services, Utraquist or Catholic, by everyone, even to subject persons without regard to the religion of their lords. The statutes, originally limited to thirty-one years, were in 1512 newly confirmed and declared valid for all times.

It would probably have been too much to expect that this tolerance should have been extended also to the more radical religious reformers who remained outside the Utraquist Church, never recognized the Compacts and, in 1459, established their own organization without any regard to the continuity of priest ordination: the Unity of Brethren or, as they were known later, the Bohemian and Moravian Brethren.[13] Their origins have been much disputed, and we cannot here discuss

[12] See on this development Krofta, *Duchovní odkaz husitství*, Prague 1949, pp. 206ff.

[13] See the great works by Gindely (*Geschichte der Böhmischen Brüder*) and Goll (*Quellen und Untersuchungen zur Geschichte der Böhmischen Brüder*).

the question of their relation to the Waldensians with whom they had much in common. They themselves later denied any connection with Tabor, yet they were in many ways the religious heirs of the Taborite brotherhood, just as their spiritual father, Peter Chelčický, was in close contact with some of the leaders of the Taborite sect. This was true even though he as well as the later Brethren sharply opposed any militant defense of religious convictions. Their steady growth all through the fifteenth century, unchecked by the persecution to which they were subjected under George of Poděbrady and Vladislav II, testifies to the intensity and independence with which the idea of evangelical reform was still sustained by the masses of the Czech people, slowly but effectively penetrating beyond the borders of Bohemia and there preparing the way for Luther and Calvin. Their thoughts had considerable part in shaping, together with the Lutherans, the Confessio Bohemica of 1575, and they found final recognition in the Letter of Majesty granted by Rudolph II in 1609, this truly great document of religious freedom and tolerance for whose defense, ten years later, Bohemia rose against the counterreformatory zeal of the Habsburgs only to lose her religious and national freedom in the holocaust of the Thirty Years' War.

One of the important historical conclusions which, I believe, can be drawn from a study of the Hussite Wars is that the Bohemian Reformation was not, like Waldensianism or Lollardism, a "forerunner" of the later Reformation but an integral part of it, its first and by no means least important phase. In other words, the birth of Protestantism as a movement of decisive importance for the shaping of modern, Western man did not originally take place in Germany at the beginning of the sixteenth century but a hundred years earlier in Bohemia. There ought to be two main criteria for the justification of this thesis: first the degree to which the Hussite movement and the religious organizations developing from it contained the main elements of what we call Protestantism and preserved them till they were freed from their original, national isolation by the arrival, on the historical scene, of Luther and Calvin; second the degree to which Hussitism, in the later fifteenth and beginning sixteenth century, directly or indirectly helped to bring about the movement generally called "the" Reformation. As far as the first criterion goes this book has, I hope, submitted some valid material in support of our thesis. The second criterion goes way beyond its scope. The question of the direct influence of Hus and Hussitism upon the German and Swiss Reformation can probably only be answered fully after a good deal more work has been done in the field.[14] We can, in this context, only point to some indirect connections which nevertheless seem of great significance. One is the strengthening, as a result of the Hussite revolt, of the tendency toward more national independence in other countries. The Pragmatic Sanctions of Bourges and Mainz (1438-1439) for instance might never have come about if the Hussite revolt and its exhaustive discussion at the Council of Basel had not given the cue to the partisans of increased independence from Papal centralization, and the frantic efforts of the Holy See to recover the lost power eventually contributed to an even sharper reaction in all those countries that eventually cut their ties with Rome. But more important appears a psychological element. It was nothing new for the Church to deal with heretical movements, and it had always done this so effectively that those movements were either completely destroyed or driven underground where they ceased to be an open challenge to the universal rule of the Church. The Hussite Reformation and Revolution presents the first case in history where this challenge remained unsuppressed, undefeated, where it was supported by the prestige of an ancient crown (as this word was understood at the time) and by the passionate and effective support of a whole nation. But by fighting the heresy before the eyes of an amazed Europe, by suffering defeat after defeat, by having to give way if ever so grudgingly, and even more by the later insistence that the Hussite Church was, after all, still an illegitimate and heretical organization, Rome blunted its strongest weapons and accustomed the people of Europe to the spectacle of an irremovable heresy. After a second unsuccessful attempt at suppression by force of arms the Curia may have hoped, in 1471, that the return of Catholic kings upon the Bohemian throne would put an end to it. Instead it was presented with the fact of a Catholic king guaranteeing the Compacts and putting up with the Statutes of Kutná Hora. This whole process was bound greatly to diminish the fear, quite apart from the horror and shame, which the reproach of heresy had always aroused in the minds of medieval man. The great reformers of the early sixteenth century still showed an admirable courage, but the masses of their followers no longer needed quite the self-sacrificing heroism

[14] See on this Krofta, *Nesmrtelný národ* (Immortal Nation), Prague 1940, pp. 269ff., and short bibliography in footnote on p. 270. On the special problem of Hussite influence on Luther, see the important article by S. Harrison Thomson, "Luther and Bohemia," *Archiv für Reformationsgeschichte*, vol. 44, 1953, pp. 160-181, with bibliography.

with which untold thousands of Czech people had braved defamation and death for the sake of their reformed faith. In this sense, then, the Bohemian Reformation was more than just a harbinger of things to come: it had already changed the religious climate of Europe when Luther stood before the Reichstag of Worms. And perhaps the simplest proof for this fact is that Charles V, quite consciously, refused to act like Sigismund, and that Luther left unscathed.

The religious issues and motives in Hussitism were of such overwhelming strength and significance that they still overshadow everything else. To think of them as anything like an "ideological superstructure" must appear quite absurd to anyone who has ever exposed himself with an open mind to the voices of men like Hus, Jerome, Jacobellus of Stříbro, Žižka, Prokop, or Rokycana. But by giving full acknowledgment to the original, self-supporting strength of the religious element as a great motive force we do not deny the significance of the social and political forces which, though sometimes obscured, constantly played their role in the history of those decades of upheaval, often tending to change directions, to accelerate or retard the movement.[15]

Far from underrating the role of those forces we have claimed for the Hussite movement, in the beginning of this study, a great historical significance aside from the fact that it was the beginning of the Protestant Reformation. We called it the first in the great chain of European revolutions which helped to shape the character of modern, Western society. This again implies a considerable difference between the Hussite Revolution and earlier movements of political and social revolt in Europe, and an essential likeness with later events such as the Dutch Revolution, the Puritan Revolution in England, the American Revolution and the Great French Revolution. (This is no place to explain why I do not think the Russian revolutions quite belong in this "chain," except perhaps for suggesting that the social structure of Russia has never been fully European.)

The proof that none of the earlier revolts of the Middle Ages "qualify" for the role which, I believe, can be claimed for Hussitism does not seem too hard to deliver. All of them without exception were isolated movements carried by one social group, in some cases the peasants, in others the "lower middle class" of the cities represented by the

[15] On the comparative role of religious and social forces in the Hussite revolution, see Krofta's arguments against Slavík in *Žižka a husitská revoluce*, Prague 1937, pp. 97ff.

craft guilds. Just because they were thus isolated they were invariably defeated without, in most cases, notably changing the structure of their society. This was still true, in the main, of the great social upheavals contemporary with the German Reformation. The revolt of the knights preceded that of the peasants; neither of them found sufficient support from the urban middle class which had been one of the main carriers of the religious reform movement, and thus both revolts suffered a quick and thorough defeat.

It was the characteristic mark of the great "successful" revolutions that they involved the whole of society even though their truly active protagonists were never more than a large minority of the nation. It is equally characteristic for them that, while they mostly ended in some form of restoration which on the surface seemed a complete return to the "ancient regime," they really left in their wake a profoundly changed society.

How far, then, was this true for the Hussite Revolution? We hardly need to repeat those facts which show that it really involved, very fully, the whole of Bohemian society of the time. We have seen it develop toward increasing radicalism, have seen the two-fold occurrence of a "Thermidor," and have seen it ending with the return of the Luxemburg dynasty, like that of the Stuarts and Bourbons, for a last short lease of life.

We may further remind the reader of the many significant and consequential "firsts" which could be observed during the course of the revolution. There are the great military renovations, most of them inaugurated by Žižka, of whom the increasing tactical strength of the infantry and the new fully mobile use of fire weapons were the most lasting ones. They were carried across Bohemia's borders especially when many of the officers and soldiers of the Taborite and Orphan field armies, after the defeat of the brotherhoods, sought and found employment in foreign service. There were the governmental experiments, early and immature but significant attempts to create, on a representative basis, instruments for resolving party struggles and for making political majority consent the basis of executive government. There were the strong, often enthusiastic expressions of an effective and unifying spirit of nationalism. There was, at the same time, the lead given to the nation by the urban middle classes, especially in Prague but later also in other cities, a leadership so far unheard of in a great commonwealth (though not in the city state structures of

Italy and to some extent Germany).[16] All this we have witnessed while following, in considerable detail, the political development during the early years of the Hussite Revolution. There remains the question to what extent these changes left more permanent traces in the social and political structure of Bohemia.

Let us remember that the social structure of every European country at the time depended on the distribution of the land. Around 1400 the Church had owned about one half of the land. The revolution deprived her of most of this enormous property which had made her the true ruling power of the country. The Hussite wars thus can be regarded as the beginning of the long process of the secularization of land which went on, in varying forms, almost all over Europe until the French Revolution and the Napoleonic wars in the main finished this job. In the seventeenth and early eighteenth century the Church in Bohemia regained part of this lost property, but never recovered anything like her previous economic status.

The corresponding gain was made by the upper strata of lay society. The great barons probably received the lion's share, no matter whether they were Hussite or Catholic. Indeed the baronial house of Rosenberg was perhaps the greatest single winner. But as a class the knights and squires, at least relatively speaking, gained even more than the lords, economically as well as politically. Rather weak, often impoverished and politically without influence in the fourteenth century, they now held and maintained the strong position which they had conquered through their vigorous leadership in the revolution, representing the main body of the free landowners throughout the fifteenth, sixteenth, and early seventeenth centuries and all the time exerting a strong influence through their representation in the diets.

Somewhat less simple are the effects the revolution had upon the towns. The zenith of their strength and power was reached while the revolution was still in full motion, and the defeat of Lipany not only doomed the brotherhoods but also weakened the cities allied with them. Yet they, too, profited from the secularization of the Church property and politically continued playing an important role through their curia in the diet to the end of the fifteenth century. During the second half of the Jagiellone period, however, an alliance of barons and knights, not effectively checked by the Jagiellone kings who too

[16] The developments in France (Grande Ordonnance) and Spain which, in the fourteenth century, tended toward this goal were checked before reaching it.

often were absent from Prague, residing in their second kingdom, Hungary, brought a political weakening of the towns which continued, more in favor of the crown than of the nobility, under the Habsburgs.

It has often been said that the real victims of the Hussite wars were the peasants.[17] And this seems to be true in a double sense. Though they had, especially during the early phases of the war, played a more active role than ever before in Bohemian history, and though individual peasants had unusual opportunities as soldiers in the field armies of the brotherhoods, they were as a class more hopelessly and defenselessly exposed to the ravages and horrors of the war than any other group of people, and their expectations that they would achieve full social and economic equality in the brotherhoods was disappointed at an early stage. But even beyond those temporary losses their position deteriorated in the decades after the Hussite Revolution. Already during the times of George of Poděbrady legislation was passed which limited their freedom of movement, and under the Jagiellone kings, especially by fugitive laws passed by the diet in 1487, they definitely became serfs, a status which lasted for nearly three centuries, up to the reforms of Joseph II. There have been disputes on whether this deterioration of the lot of the peasants was a consequence of the Hussite wars.[18] It can be argued that the decrease of population which the war brought about heightened the interest of the landowners in keeping their peasants tied to the soil. But this is probably too simple an explanation. The introduction of serfdom was no isolated development in Bohemia but took place equally in all neighboring countries. Rather can it be said that even under serfdom the situation of Bohemia's peasants never grew quite as appalling as for instance in Poland or Hungary.

We have earlier stressed the wave of national consciousness and enthusiasm which, though closely allied with the religious uprising, appears as a strong motive force in the Czech fight against Sigismund and his crusading armies. This, certainly, remained as a permanent heritage. The war itself, as we have seen, had resulted in the thorough Czechization of the overwhelming majority of Bohemia's towns, and the losses suffered by the Church very largely were also losses suffered by Germans. After the war a return movement of Germans

[17] See on this Krofta's *Dějiny selského stavu*.

[18] See Pekař, *Žižka*, I, 197, and against him Krofta, *Žižka a husitská revoluce*, p. 141.

began, first slow, later increasing. But they could no longer claim a privileged position. On the contrary, the Czech character of the country was very clearly established, perhaps most of all by the dominant role then achieved by the Czech language. Hand in hand with this increased political strength of the Czech nation there went a tremendous growth in national self-confidence. Where, during the war itself, it had largely been based upon the almost mystical feeling of a special task given to the Czechs by God, it later also derived from the knowledge that this people had been able to do deeds of valor not surpassed by any nation on earth. In the sixteenth century the coming of Lutheranism tended to weaken for a while the specific anti-German character of this nationalism, but left the sentiment itself unimpaired.

A word should be said about the cultural consequences of the Hussite Revolution. They present, on an earlier and more primitive level, a surprising similarity with the English development in the seventeenth century. The great flowering of Humanism and early Renaissance in the Bohemia of Charles IV and Wenceslas IV was, of course, cut short not only by the ravages of the war but also by the fierce puritanism of the strict Hussites who saw in all forms of art (with the exception of religious music) nothing but the expression of idolatry and wanton pride. Just as in England the period of Puritan strictness was followed, though after a somewhat longer time, by something like a restoration mentality, especially among the nobility, expressed for instance by the erotic poetry of Duke Ignatius of Münsterberg, one of the sons of King George. But the late fifteenth century also restored very largely the vigor and creativity of Bohemian art; and though Vladislav II is not remembered as a great king his time, at least, has left the heritage of a great and in its character unique architectural style, the so-called Vladislav Gothic which was really an indigenous Bohemian form of early Renaissance.

For the general rhythm of the Hussite Revolution we can perhaps, as for all great western revolutions, employ the image of the "jumping procession" of Echternach: It went two steps forward, and one back. And the net result, the one step forward that remained, would still be most important in its contribution toward religious reform, toward the rise of Protestantism. This statement, of course, contains something like a value judgment. The Catholic historian, even if he acknowledges the specific vigor with which Protestantism has sustained the development of an individualist, competitive, and economically productive society, can argue that the price paid for it in terms of religious strife and cultural disintegration has been too high. But quite aside from this problem, and certainly without any reference to the deeper questions of religious dogma, it can hardly be denied that (with the exception of Germany) modern democracy has struck deeper roots in those countries where the Church of Rome was sooner or later subject to the Protestant challenge than in those where this challenge has never been known. And this brings us back, once more, to the permanent effects of the Hussite Revolution upon Bohemia and its successor, modern Czechoslovakia, the only country in Central Europe to develop, in the period between the two world wars, a vigorous and stable democracy.

Here, however, we are immediately faced with the objection: how is it possible to talk of the permanence of any effects of the Hussite Revolution, in view of the prolonged loss of Bohemia's national independence and the thorough suppression of Bohemian Protestantism after 1620? But it is always wrong to underrate the tenacity and resilience with which a great national and libertarian tradition can survive harsh and oppressive governmental policies even for generations. During the darkest days of vindictive Habsburg oppression, in the second half of the seventeenth century, Czech national pride speaks with a clear and unmuffled voice through a man who was supposed to serve only the Church of Rome: the Bohemian Jesuit historian Balbinus. It is he whom we have to thank for the preservation of the two most important pieces of Žižka's literary heritage: the so-called Military Ordinance and the resounding letter of encouragement to the people of Domažlice. And Protestantism did not really die in Bohemia. When, after one hundred and sixty years of forcible suppression, Joseph II in 1781 issued his Tolerance Edict, tens of thousands of people professed to have secretly worshiped in the Protestant way. Though the great majority of the Czech people in pre-war Czechoslovakia belonged to the Catholic Church, with Protestants (including the neo-Hussite "Czechoslovak Church") amounting only to about one sixth of all Czechs in Bohemia and Moravia, the role of the Protestants in the spiritual life and the political leadership of the Czech people has consistently been out of all proportion to this relatively modest share. This is particularly in evidence in the case of František Palacký, the founder of modern Czech historiography and not only one of the greatest historians of all times but also the most highly respected political leader of the Czech nation in the third quarter of the nineteenth century. Palacký, in a way, was a living example of the permanence of the Hussite tradition in Bohemia's life, himself descending from a family that had belonged to the Church of the Brethren and revealed their faith after the Tolerance Edict had made this possible. Palacký's work, especially his great History of the Bohemian People, has not only influenced his contemporaries but—for all the corrections that more modern research and changed viewpoints necessitated—has educated generations of Czech historians, Protestants and Catholics alike. The resurgence of Hussite traditions which he brought about leads, in a direct line, to the historical philosophy of Thomas Masaryk and to his evaluation of Hus and Chelčický as well as of Žižka and Tabor.[19]

These traditions are all essentially Western traditions. The great role of this small nation was its role within Western Christianity. It was within this Western community that the Czechs tried to organize their religious and national freedom, even though they sometimes looked toward the East where the Holy Communion was always given in the two kinds. It was to the West that they gave their heritage of religious freedom. Yet the West has betrayed them again and again. In 1620 King James of England refused all help to his son-in-law, Frederick, the last king of a free Bohemia, elected by the Protestant estates to protect them against the determined attack of Ferdinand of Habsburg. In 1938 Chamberlain, to justify the betrayal of Munich, explained that the English could not go to war in defense of democratic Czechoslovakia—a far away people of whom they knew nothing. And after the Second World War Czechoslovakia became once more the victim of a foreign totalitarianism largely because the West let her go by default. Perhaps all this would never have happened in quite so cruel and senseless a way—if the people in the West had known a little more about this "far away people" and of the role they once played in the shaping of our civilization. And what could have been more important, more enlightening and inspiring to know than the history of this great Hussite movement; of the preachers and their sermons; the great diets and their resolutions; and in their defense, the brotherhoods and their armies, with the blind old Žižka in the lead, soldiers of freedom, soldiers of faith, God's own soldiers.

[19] See e.g. K. Čapek, *Hovory s T. G. Masarykem* (Masaryk tells his story), reprint by Arts, Inc., New York 1951, pp. 252ff.

# APPENDIX

# THE LETTERS AND MESSAGES OF JOHN ŽIŽKA

## I

## ARMISTICE WITH ULRICH OF ROSENBERG

[Písek, November 18, 1420]

We, Jan called Žižka of Trocnov, Chval of Machovice, Zbyněk of Buchov, Pavlík of Mutice and the community of Písek, as guarantors, publicly acknowledge by this before all who may hear of it by way of the spoken or written word, that by the power of this letter we have entered and will remain in a right Christian armistice, up to the beginning of Lent, including the whole of Shrove Tuesday, with the noble Lord Ulrich of Rosenberg and with all those belonging to him. And we promise to keep him this safe armistice upon our good Christian faith, also including all our communities, and under the caution of ten thousand threescores of pennies [groše] in good Prague silver coinage. And we, the before named guarantors, as well as the captains, the judge, the burgomaster, the councilors, and the whole community of the town of Písek, promise individually and collectively, with one indivisible signature, to keep the aforesaid agreement under the penalty of ten thousand.

On the other hand the aforesaid noble Lord Ulrich of Rosenberg has undertaken, under this agreement with us, to keep on all his dominions and manors the following articles: one, that the word of God be preached freely; second, that the Body of God and His Holy Blood be given regularly to all faithful, no person excepted; third, that the riches of the clergy be done away with; and fourth, that on all his dominions he put an end, as far as he can possibly do so, to all deadly sins. And hereto he commits himself under the same penalty as mentioned before.

If, however, we should fail to keep the aforesaid armistice, which God forbid, then it is our duty and we promise to deliver, within one month after being reminded, the aforesaid caution at Krumlov or Nový Hrad, wherever our creditors demand. If we should not have delivered the aforesaid caution within one month, then we give full power to the aforesaid

[1] Original of this letter preserved in the Archives (originally of the Rosenberg administration) at Třeboň. First published by M. Millauer, *Diplomatisch-historische Aufsätze über Johannes Žižka*, Prague 1824, then in *Archiv český*, III, 239.

noble Lord Ulrich of Rosenberg or his burgraves, that they may reprimand, curse, arrest, imprison, and lay under contribution ourselves and all our people as long as we have not delivered the aforesaid caution. And to confirm this whole agreement we have affixed our seals to this letter.

Given in the year one thousand four hundred and twenty after the birth of God, this Monday of the octave of Saint Martin.

## II

## TO TABOR'S SOUTHERN NEIGHBORS[2]

[Prachatice, November 22, 1420]

Our Lord Jesus Christ, who for us has sadly shed his blood, be with us and with you, all. Amen.

Dear brethren and neighbors:

We give you this message: If you hear it said by some lords that we have become your enemies, we vow and we beseech you as our dear neighbors that you should not believe that; but you shall know whose enemies we are: that is of all evil priests and laymen, who write and stand against the holy evangel. Furthermore we want you to know that we also hate all false Christians for the sake of Four Articles; the first: that the word of God be preached everywhere, and all through Christendom, which is not being done; the second: that the true Body of our Lord and His Holy Blood be communicated to all true Christians, young and old; the third: that the rule of priests, from the highest, even the Pope himself, to the commonest and lowest, not be tolerated, neither be their owning estates or collecting tithes, and that the aforesaid rule of the ecclesiastical lords, exerted with the help of the secular lords, be done away with; the fourth: that all manifest sins be driven out, be it of kings or lords, of squires or priests, of people ecclesiastical or secular.

Therefore we trust you well as our dear brethren that you will accept the truth and will, for its sake, help us against all false and unbelieving Christians, ecclesiastical and secular, who stand against this holy truth. So now do answer this our letter in writing. But if you should fail to do so, then we would know that you were willing to be the enemies of God and of all Taborite brethren.

Given at Prachatice, on Friday before Saint Catherine.
Jan Žižka, Chval, commanders and directors of the Taborite people.
Jeník, captain at Prachatice.

[2] Original not preserved, doubtful whether it was in Czech or German. Translation into English here directly from the German of Windecke, *Denkwürdigkeiten zur Geschichte des Zeitalters Kaiser Sigmunds*, ed. Altman, Berlin 1893, p. 148. Dating in accord with Pekař.

## III

## TO THE LOWER ESTATES OF THE LANDFRIEDEN OF PILSEN[3]

[In the field, February 1421]

We, Jan Žižka and Chval of Machovice, commanders and directors of the people of Tabor, truly Czech people in the hope of God, admonish you all, for the martyrdom of our Lord, you the knights and squires, the townsmen and peasants, of the Landfrieden of Pilsen: Oppose no longer the Lord God and His sacred law, nor the salutary Four Articles. It is for these that we fight with God's help. And you oppose them and try to keep us from this goodness and from the salvation of our souls. The first of these is the freedom to listen to God's word. The second is the receiving of God's Body and God's Blood: yourselves you will not receive it, and us and other faithful men you seek to keep from receiving it. Third is the richess and luxury of the priests: this, as a heresy, you should have destroyed, yet against the Lord God you defend it and are willing to die for it and to suffer the frightful peril of death in heresy. The Fourth Article: Those guilty of deadly sins you should have confounded and cast out; yet, alas, you support them.

First among them you help the Hungarian King Sigismund, that heretical King, him that has betrayed our Lord God and His sacred word, the violator of virgins and women, that murderer and incendiary, who seeks to destroy our Czech nation. With him there are the Lord of Švamberg, the Lords of Švihov, Henry of Elsterberg and the Lords of Kolovraty. Those men you have helped to oppose the Lord God, to prevent the reading of His word and the establishment of God's order in the land as He wills it. And their will is to seduce you to lose your souls as well as your estates, and they seek to earn the King's praise and honor for making you humbly serve him and work for him and thus lose your souls and all else. And we are not astounded that whoever keepeth not faith with God will not keep faith with man either.

And thus we needs must warn you to beware of them lest they betray you even more so your souls be lost. And likewise they would fain do to us if it were not for the help of God. But we trust our Lord God that He will save us from their cunning designs. And may the Lord God grant you that you, too, escape from the snares of His enemies and that you seek and find the way to Him who gave you body and soul. And you would that we burn not your houses and leave your land destroyed. Why, then, have you not given freedom to the word of God, and to the salutary Four Articles *ut supra* of which you were among the first to hear? And have you not

[3] Original not preserved. Copied, but perhaps not completely, by Jafet in his "Hlas strážny," ca. 1600. First published by F. M. Bartoš in his collection of Žižka's letters in *Žižkův duch, jeho povaha a listy*, Prague 1924.

spoken to us, that you are willing to give that freedom to the Articles, and agreed, that this was good and right? And thus you spoke lies before the face of God and before us.

## IV

## TO THE PEOPLE OF DOMAŽLICE (1)[4]

[Orlík Castle, September 12, 1421]

God give that you may acquire again the state of original grace, and be the first to achieve worthy things!

Dear brethren in God:

I ask you for the sake of the Lord God to remain in the fear of God, as His most beloved sons, and not to complain when you are exposed to His chastisement. But remember Him who wrought the strong foundations of our creed, the Lord Jesus Christ, defend yourself bravely against the misdeeds which those Germans commit against you, follow the example of the old Czechs who, their pikes firmly propped,[5] defended not only God's cause but also their own. And we, dear brethren, seeking the law of God and the common good, will do the very best that is in our power so that anyone who can swing a club and hurl a stone should be up in arms.

And therefore, dear brethren, be it known to you that we are drafting men from all sides against such enemies and destroyers of the Czech land. Therefore you, too, order your priests to arouse the people to arms against such forces of Antichrist. Also call the people together in the market place, so that all men, even the youngest and oldest, who are strong enough, may be up in arms at every hour of the day.

And we, God willing, will soon come to you. Hold ready bread, beer, fodder for the horses, and all weapons of war. For now is the time to fight against the foreign enemies at least as hard as against those inside our country. Remember your first fight when, little men against the great of the land, few against many, unarmored against men in iron, you fought bravely and successfully. As yet the arm of God has not grown shorter. Therefore let your hope rest in God and be prepared. May the Lord God strengthen you!

Given at Orlík Castle on Friday after the birth of the Virgin Mary, Jan Žižka of the Chalice, director of the Taborite people.

[4] Original not preserved, but early copy in National Museum in Prague. First discovered by Žalanský and mentioned by Balbin, first published by R. Ungar, "Žižka's militärische Briefe und Verordnungen," *Abhandlungen der Böhmischen Gesellschaft der Wissenschaften*, II, F.I.B., 375. As for the dating (in which I agree with Pekař as against F. M. Bartoš) see above the detailed justification in Chapter 17, n. 22.

[5] This passage, "zatknuce klanici za škorni," is especially difficult to translate. There may be a better way of rendering the meaning, but I have not been able to find it.

To the stalwart captains and the community of the town of Domažlice, my dear brethren.

## V

## TO THE PEOPLE OF TŘEBOŇ[6]

[Before Německý Brod, January 10, 1422]

May our Lord the Almighty God be with you and with us in His holy grace.

Brethren in God:

Jan Žižka of the castle of Chalice, director of all communities of the Land of Bohemia which adhere to and fulfill the Law of God, in the hope of God: to the judges, the burgomaster, the councilors, and the community of the town Třeboň. I am sending to you Rybka of Lužnice who will present to you this letter and who is well informed about my intentions. And I beg you to trust him in everything that he is going to discuss with you now to the same extent as if I personally were present to talk with you.

Given on this Saturday in the field before Německý Brod.

## VI

## TO THE PEOPLE OF DOMAŽLICE (II)[7]

[In the field, probably Spring 1422]

Greetings to you in the name of God Father and our Lord Jesus Christ, who sacrificed himself for our sins and died not only for us but for all the world so that he might free us from the evils of this world.
Praise be to Him in eternity, Amen!

My best wishes to you, dear brethren in God:

I want you to know that I was informed by the widow of Kučtajn of Dvorec, that she has left all her bedding and clothes in your town in the care of one man by the name of Šproch. Therefore I beg you to permit her to recover what is hers.

Jan Žižka of the Chalice, director of the Taborite people in the hope of God. To the captains and the whole community of the town of Domažlice.

[6] Original in Třeboň Archives. First published by Millauer, *op.cit.*, then in *Archiv český*, III, 280.

[7] Original in the Archives of the town museum of Domažlice. First published by Joseph Dobrovský, *Geschichte der böhmischen Sprache und ältern Litteratur*, Prague 1818, p. 406, then in *Archiv český*, III, 301.

# VII

## PUBLIC PROCLAMATION IN SUPPORT OF PRINCE KORYBUT[8]

[Čáslav, June 11, 1422]

With the help of God, Amen!

Please take cognizance, lords and brethren, that whereas we with the brethren of Tabor; the cities of Domažlice, Klatovy, Sušice and Písek; also other lords, knights, squires and other communities; further the towns of Prachatice and Horažd'ovice; all those who of their free will are followers of myself and of Chval and Buchovec and have trusted their fate to our guidance; we all have accepted His Highness the Prince as our helper and as the supreme regent of this country. And we will gladly obey His Highness and will faithfully help him and council him in all things that are good and right, so help us God. And we also ask all of you that you obey His Highness as you have promised before the Lord God.

Furthermore we ask you also that from this day onward you all, in harmony, faithfully and permanently forgive all annoyances, struggles, and bitter feelings which you have had toward one another either from the beginning or in the last year or just recently; so you may, with a righteous conscience, pray your pater noster and may say: "Forgive us our trespasses as we forgive those who trespass against us."

If, however, you should not do so, but should want to arouse, after this day, any riots or any calumnies and quarrels, forming factions among your communities, then we, with the help of God, and in common with His Highness the Prince, with the lord-councilors [of Prague], and with the other lords, knights, squires, and with all the faithful communities, shall interfere and punish such deeds, whoever may have perpetrated them, no person excepted. Will you then promise to help us in those measures?

And if someone should have trouble with someone else, whether it be over merchandise or other things, then he should, without causing any riots, go before the burgomasters, the councilors and judges and claim justice before them in an orderly way. And they should honor their elders such as burgomasters, councilors, officials, and judges. And they should love one another like brothers.

And thus the Lord God and His sacred grace will be with us, and He will give us success for all that is good and right.

[8] Original not preserved. Early copy in memorial book of the Old Town (Prague) library, called "Primus liber vetustissimus privilegiorum, statutorum et decretorum Veteri urbis Pragensis," containing copies of documents dating 1366 to 1540. First published by F. M. Pelcl, *Předmluva v Příhodám Václava Vratislava z Mitrovic*, Prague 1777. Also in *Archiv český*, III, 301. As for the dating, especially in regard to Čáslav, see above Chapter 20, n. 39.

## VIII

## TO THE BROTHERS OF VALEČOV[9]

[Vilémov, March 26, 1423]

May the Grace of the Holy Spirit dwell with you and with us, and enlighten our hearts and our minds to fulfill the will of the Almighty Son.

Dearest brethren in the name of our Lord God!

I want you to know that I am now at Vilémov, and I beg you that one of you come to join me so that together we may discuss the things to be done for the honor and pleasure of our Lord God the Almighty. And also I want you to know that I have remained in complete agreement with the people of Tabor. And they have, of their own free will, declared that they will follow my orders as at any time before. I have ordered them to gather their forces for the fight, and they have made ready for it. I am also sending messages to your towns so that all the leaders of the faithful appear now on the Wednesday or latest on Thursday of Easter at Německý Brod, so that we may do penance there where we have sinned, and stay there in the council of God united as one man, according to His Holy Law, and in the council of the poor and rich prepare ourselves in the truth of our father the Lord Almighty for the fight against the faithless deceivers at home and abroad.

I also give you the news that the Prince[10] has now left our country. And do not conclude an armistice with Lord Čeněk, unless you can do it with all other neighbors also. This question we shall, so God will, discuss when we meet.

Given at Vilémov, on the Friday after the annunciation of the blessed Virgin Mary.

Jan Žižka of the Chalice.

To the honorable, stalwart brothers in the hope of God, Bartoš and Bernard of Valečov, members of the Lesser Tabor.

## IX

## TO THE PEOPLE OF SKALICE AND NÁCHOD[11]

[Vilémov, April 1, 1423]

With God's help Jan Žižka of the Chalice, humble servant in the hope of God. May the Grace of the Holy Spirit dwell with you and with us, and

[9] Original preserved in Archives of National Museum in Prague. First published by Millauer, *op.cit.*, also *Archiv český*, III, 302.

[10] Prince Korybut of Lithuania.

[11] Original not preserved. Oldest copy in the Osek manuscript of the Old Annalists. First published by H. Toman in his edition of Žižka's letters in *Literární památky, duch a povaha Žižkova*, Prague 1893.

enlighten the hearts and the minds of ourselves and of all the faithful who have dedicated their lives to the truth of our Lord the Almighty God. To each and all, no one excepted, in the towns of Skalice and Náchod, and to all others dwelling in the country of Bohemia who adhere to the truth of our Lord the Almighty God: my humble greetings and wishes for our well-being!

Dearest brethren!

I wish to remind you of the benefactions of the Lord our Almighty God, who has given us much help and has freed us from powerful enemies, as He did at Německý Brod, where, overpowering his enemies, He Himself deigned to fight for us. We however, did not receive this help with due gratitude, nor did we at that place give due praise to His gracious favor. Instead we indulged in greed, pillage, haughty wantonness and betrayal, and thus we made our Lord God angry, and ever since there has not been much good that we have achieved. And the Lord God rightly punishes us for our sins.

Also for God's martyrdom and for the liberation of His sacred truths I admonish all leaders to gather together so that the cause of the faithful in the Holy Church may prosper, and that the evil ones and the faithless heretics may be destroyed. And may those gathered with God's help all now come, on Wednesday of Easter, to Německý Brod.

There, at the very place where we have sinned, we will do penance and repent our sins; then we will thank the Lord God for his great and immeasurable gift which was bestowed on us, unworthy ones, by our most gracious Father to whom praise be given eternally, Amen!

Furthermore we will then at the same place, under the guidance of the Lord God and His Sacred Law, consult and resolve with all who are faithful to Him, with the council of the poor and the rich, and stay united as one man against all faithless deceivers at home and abroad. And we will fight with the help of the Holy Trinity, of our one Lord, who makes free all who trust in Him.

Given at Vilémov on the Great Thursday of the year 1423 of the birth of God.

## X

## THE STATUTES AND MILITARY ORDINANCE OF ŽIŽKA'S NEW BROTHERHOOD[12]

[Probably drafted and signed in July 1423]

Whereas, by the grace and the gift of our Father and Lord God the Almighty,

[12] Original not preserved. An early copy exists in the Archives of the National Museum of

we believe in and have received the enlightening of the certain, enduring, revealed and proved Truth and Law of God:

First, that they give freedom to the Word of God, by preaching it everywhere, no one place being excepted, and that they receive it in their hearts with love, that they really fulfill and hold it, and that after that they lead others toward it and teach them too.

Second, that we all take the Body and the Blood of our Lord Jesus Christ, the Almighty God, in awe, devotion, and reverence, we the old and the young, children right upon baptism and after that throughout their childhood, everybody, no persons excepted; and that we induce and urge them to do this, at least every week on Sunday.

Third, that we lead and direct the clergy toward the life of the Son of God, the Lord Jesus Christ, and to the life of the Apostles, and stop and do away with their enrichment and simony, with the help of God.

Fourth, that we stop, suppress, and destroy all sins, mortal and venial, first of all in ourselves; after that in the kings, the princes and lords, the townsmen, the craftsmen, the peasants and all people, of male or female sex, no persons excepted, neither old nor young, and always with the help of the Lord God the Almighty.

And anyone who would not want to keep and truly fulfill the above written pieces and articles, and would not want to help protect and defend them; such a one, without regard to person, we will not suffer amongst us and in this army fighting with God's help, nor on the castles and in the fortresses, nor in the cities and in the towns, walled or open, nor in the villages and hamlets, no place excepted or exempted. But all persons we will everywhere admonish, advise, push, and urge toward this goodness with the help of our Lord God.

And whereas we are moved by a goodly spirit, knowing and understanding that all things of this world are destined to fall and pass away, but that the Truth of our Lord Jesus Christ, the Almighty God, endures through the Ages, therefore:

We, John Brother Žižka of the Chalice, John Roháč of Dubá, Aleš of Riesenburg and Vřešťov, John of Potštain at Žampach, Boček of Kunštat and of Jevišovice; Bartoš and Bernard, brothers of Valečov, Bartoš, John and Martin, brothers of Vysoká;

We, the burgomasters, councilors and the whole communities of the towns of Hradec on the Elbe and of Čáslav;

---

Prague. First discovered and mentioned by Balbin, first published by R. Ungar, *loc.cit.* Since then repeated publications, such as that by H. Toman in his *Husitské válečnictví* (Prague 1898) where it is carefully compared with other similar statutes; last in F. Svejkovský, *Staročeske vojenské řády*, Prague 1952. An incomplete and not very precise translation into English is to be found in Lützow's *The Hussite War*, London 1914. As for the dating, see above Chapter 23, n. 2.

We, Beneš of Mokrovousy, Jaroslav of the Chalice, Wenceslas Horyna of Honbice, Christian of Žernoseky, Francis of Litožnice, George of Řečice, John of Studená;

And we, burgomaster, councilors and the whole community of the town of Jaroměř,

We, Zdislav the squire, Lawrence of Paňov the Pole, Blažek of Kralupy, Jacob of Březová, Peter Kralovec of Příbram, John of Domažlice, John of Tehov, Martin of Borovnice, Gallus the Orebite;

And we, burgomaster, councilors and the whole community of the town of Dvůr;

And we, Chústník of Košov, Andrew of Studená, Sárka of Slavné, Kříž the captain, Beneš the captain, Mikát Brada Odraný, Aleš of Hostačov, Polévka of Hoštka, Nicholas the Orebite, Veta of Chlumčany, Litobor of Trubeč, Linhart of Sleza, Beneš of Horošovice, John Baštín, Mařík Velek, Šeňk, Jíra, Roh, Nicholas Brada; the captains, lords, knights, squires, burgomasters, councilors, and all the communities of the lords, the knights, the squires, the townsmen, no one being excepted or exempted:

We all rightly demand, request, and command all of you that there be orderly obedience. For through disobedience and disorderly excesses we have undergone great losses both in the lives of brethren and in our possessions, and have often suffered shame from those who are the enemies of God and of ourselves.

Henceforth, with the help of God and of you and of all the faithful we mean to beware of such happenings by the following measures:

1. When we want to leave some town or move away from some place where we have encamped in the field, no one shall ride in advance to the next town or walk or drive there to secure quarters or lodgings, nor shall any one encamp in the field without the permission or order of his older captain or the several captains who will be specially appointed for this. And if someone should encamp or march or post himself somewhere else without order from these elders, we want him and such a one to receive retribution and punishment by taking his goods and his life as being a disobedient man, whoever he may be, and to whatever rank he may belong, with no person excepted.

2. When they want to move on from the place where they have encamped in the field with the permission and command of the appointed elders, they shall march on till they arrive at a place that is likely and proper and there wait till the whole army has moved out from the encampment.

3. No one shall light a fire or set anything else on fire on the march or while lying encamped, except those who will be specially selected and appointed to do so, and this under great penalty, that no others may do so.

4. Then, when they move out from some place and before they undertake or order some enterprise in the war, they shall first make a prayer to the

Lord God, and kneeling down before the Body of God and before the Face of God, at the time when they want to leave an encampment or a town, pray that Lord God the Almighty deign to give His help, that they thus may wage His sacred war for the praise of His sacred name and for the enhancement of this beneficence, and for salvation and help to the faithful.

5. After that the people shall form in proper order, each troop under its own standard. Then the watchword shall be given out. After that, without delay, they shall proceed on the march. And thus shall they march with the troop leading which for that day was ordered to march on first under its standard. And others shall not mingle with them nor get in their way or take a different route. And once they have been assigned to a troop or formed under one standard, they shall march in good order together in that troop, and no troop shall mingle with another. And they shall march with proper care, having regard to protect the van, the rear, and the flanks of their troops, as each will be ordered by their elders.

6. And if God should not protect us so that we suffer some damage through the carelessness or neglect on the part of those captains in the army, either on watchtowers or in the field or at the outposts which will be committed or entrusted to them by the commanders and by the community, then the commanders and the whole community intend and are resolved to find those responsible and to punish them with the loss of their lives and their possessions, whether they be a prince, a lord, or anyone else, no person being excepted or exempted.

7. But when and wherever the Lord God grants us to overcome and defeat our enemies and to conquer towns, fortresses or castles, and thus to make booty, either while moving in the field or operating from some encampment, then shall all things captured and all booty be carried and assembled at a place chosen and pointed out by the elders, be it much or little. And herefor elders shall be chosen from all communities, those of the lords, the knights, the townsmen, and the peasants, that they faithfully administer these things to the poor and the rich, and that the things be justly distributed and divided among them as is proper. And no one take anything for himself or keep it. But if someone takes anything for himself or keeps it and is convicted of this by good testimony, such a one, whoever he be without exception shall they punish by loss of his head and his possessions as one who has robbed God and the Commonwealth, just as it happened to Achan for the cap and the cloak of the king's daughters; or by some other death, be he a prince, lord, knight or squire, townsman, craftsman, or peasant. Without excuse for any man or without looking at his person shall they, with God's help, wreak vengeance upon him.

8. No quarrels, brawls, or riots shall be suffered in our army or between our people.

9. If someone should strike, wound, maim, or slay someone else, retribution shall be wrought upon him according to God's law, as the Lord God permits, no one being excepted and without regard for his person.

10. Further let it be known that if anyone should slink away, walk, ride, or drive away from us in the army while we march in the field or are encamped, without the permission of the elders mentioned above, and should not have the true password, whether he be a prince, a lord, a knight, a squire, a townsman, a craftsman, or a peasant, or any other man whatsoever; he shall, when he is seized, be punished with the loss of his head and his goods as a faithless thief who slinks away from God's fight and from the faithful brethren of our army, wherever the army marches or is encamped.

11. Also we do not want to suffer among us faithless men, disobedient ones, liars, thieves, gamblers, robbers, plunderers, drunkards, blasphemers, lechers, adulterers, whores, adulteresses, or any other manifest sinners, men or women; all these will we banish and chase away, or punish them with the help of the Holy Trinity according to the Law of God.

12. Also Brother Žižka and the other lords, captains, knights, squires, townsmen, craftsmen, and peasants named above, and all their communities, with the help of God and of the Commonwealth, will punish all such crimes by flogging, banishment, clubbing, decapitation, hanging, drowning, burning, and by all other retributions which fit the crime according to God's Law, excepting no one from whichever rank and sex.

And thus, if we observe, keep and fulfill the salutary articles written above, the Lord God will be with us with His grace and His help. For thus it behooves us to act in the fight for God: to live a good, Christian life in the love of His order and in the fear of God, and to put our trust for all our demands, our needs and our hopes in the Lord God without any doubt, expecting from Him eternal reward.

And we beg you, dear communities, of all regions, of the princes, the lords, the knights, the squires, the townsmen, the craftsmen, the peasants, the laborers, men of all estates, and first of all especially of all faithful Czechs, to join in this good fight and to give us readily your counsel and your help. And we on our side will keep, fulfill and recompense this to you for our dear Lord God and His Holy martyrdom, for the liberation of the truth of God's Law, for the Saints and their glorification, to help all the faithful everywhere in the Holy Church and especially in the Czech and Slav nation, also in all Christianity, for the elevation of the faithful and the shame of the obstinate ones and the manifest heretics and the hypocrites and evildoers.

Thus may Lord God the Almighty deign to give His help to us and to you so that we gain victory over His enemies and ours, and fight for us and with you with His might, and not withhold from us His Holy grace. Amen!

May the Lord God be with us and with you wherever you are and wherever it pleases the Holy Trinity. And for better testimony, confirmation and certainty of this, and to prove our greater zeal, together with the clergy, in rising above the wretched reasoning of this world, we, the above-named, do hereby, with good and conscious deliberation and good will, testify our agreement with this declaration and writing, and we vow truly to keep, preserve, and defend it with the help of the uncreated and eternally blessed Holy Trinity. Amen.
May the Lord God grant this!

## XI

## ŽIŽKA'S BATTLE SONG[13]

(Kdož jsú boží bojovnici)

You who are the warriors of God
And of His Law,
Pray for God's help
And believe in Him
So you will with Him always remain victorious.

Christ will reward you for what you lose,
He promises you a hundred times more.
Whoever gives his life for Him
Will gain life eternal.
Blessed everyone who stands by the truth.

This our Lord bids us not to fear
The destroyers of the flesh
If you want to win the life
For the love of your nearest.

Therefore archers and lancers
Of knightly rank,
Pikesmen and flailsmen
Of the common people,
Do all keep in mind the generous Lord.

Never fear the enemies,
Do not mind their great numbers,
Keep your Lord in your hearts,

[13] There are several versions of this song, and the critical evaluation of them has become both a historical and philological issue of some importance, discussed at length in Nejedlý, *Dějiny husitského zpěvu*, II, Prague 1913, and in A. Kraus, *Husitství ve literatuře*, Prague 1914/27. I have followed both these authors in what they have considered the authentic form of the song. The translation is strictly literal, as any attempt to re-create the rhythm of its harsh poetry could only succeed if a large part of the original diction were sacrificed. But it is the original diction rather than the poetic value which can serve as an indirect source of Žižka's thought.

Fight for him and with him
And do not ever retreat before your enemies!

Long the Czechs have said
And have had a proverb,
That under a good lord
There is good riding.

You all must remember the password
As it was given to you.
Always obey your captains.
Each shall help and protect the other.
Each shall look for and stay with his own battalion.

You baggage boys and grooms,
Keep it in mind
That you forfeit not your lives
By theft or robbery,
And let yourselves never be tempted by spoil.

And thus joyously shout:
"At them, hurray, at them!"
Feel the pride of the weapons in your hands,
Attack with the cry: God is our Lord!

# BIBLIOGRAPHY

## I. BIBLIOGRAPHIC PUBLICATIONS

(Besides the titles listed below the *Český časopis historický,* the most important historical journal in Czech, publishes periodical bibliographic supplements under the heading *Bibliografie české historie.* The journal is quoted in this bibliography as *Č.Č.H.* in accord with Czech usage.)

Bartoš, F. M. *Literární činnost M. Jakoubka ze Stříbra* (The literary activity of Master Jacobellus of Stříbro). Prague 1925.

———. *Literární činnost M. Jana Rokycany, M. Jana Příbrama, M. Petra Engliše,* Prague 1928.

Kraus, A. *Husitství ve literatuře, zejmena německé* (Hussitism in literature with special regard to German writings), 3 vols., Prague 1914-1927.

Krofta, K. *Novější bádání o Husovi a hnutí husitském* (Recent research on Hus and the Hussite movement), *Č.Č.H.*, vol. 21.

Lützow, Count F. *Lectures on the Historians of Bohemia,* London 1905.

Palacký, F. *Würdigung der alten böhmischen Geschichtschreiber,* Prague 1830.

Zíbrt, Čeněk. *Bibliografie české historie,* Prague 1900-1912.

## II. SOURCE MATERIAL

Aeneas Sylvius, *Historia Bohemica,* many editions. (Edition used here published by J. G. Steck, Frankfurt 1687.)

Andreas von Regensburg (Andrew of Ratisbon). *Sämtliche Werke,* ed. Leidinger, in *Quellen und Untersuchungen zur bayrischen und deutschen Geschichte,* Neue Folge 1, Munich 1903.

Bartoš, F. M. *Manifesty města Prahy z doby husitské* (Manifestos of the city of Prague from Hussite times), Prague 1933.

Březan, V. ed., "Rosenberské kroniky krátký výtah" (Excerpts from the Rosenberg Chronicle), *Časopis musea českého,* 1828.

Caro, J. ed., "Liber cancellarii Stanislai Ciolek," *Archiv für österreichische Geschichte,* vols. 45 and 52.

Cochlaeus, J. *Historia Hussitarum,* Mainz 1548.

*Deutsche Reichstagsakten,* Munich, J. G. Cotta, 1867-1935, vol. VIII.

Dlugosz, Joannes. *Historia Polonica,* in *Opera omnia,* ed. A. Przezdiecki, Cracow 1877, vol. XIII.

Ebendorfer of Hasselbach, Thomas. *Chronicon Austriacum*, in *Scriptores Rerum Austriacarum*, ed. Pez, vol. II, Leipzig 1725.

Goll, J. ed., *Fontes Rerum Bohemicarum*, vol. V, Prague 1893, containing, among others, the chronicles of Lawrence of Březová and Bartošek of Drahonice, Prague 1893.

Grünhagen, C. ed., *Geschichtsquellen der Hussitenkriege*, in *Scriptores Rerum Silesicarum*, Breslau 1871.

Hegel, C. ed., *Magdeburger Schöppenchronik*, in *Chroniken deutscher Städte*, vol. VII, I.

Höfler, K. ed., *Geschichtschreiber der husitischen Bewegung in Böhmen*, containing among others the Taborite Chronicle of Nicholas of Pelhřimov and the *Chronicon veteris Collegiati* Pragensis, in *Fontes Rerum Austriacarum*, Abt. I, vols. 2, 6, 7.

Jecht, R. ed., *Codex diplomaticus Lusatiae superioris*, vol. II, Görlitz 1899.

Ludolf of Sagan, "Tractatus de longevo schismate," ed. Loserth, *Archiv für österreichische Geschichte*, vol. 60, Vienna 1880.

Mareš, F. ed., *Popravčí knihy pánu z Rosenberka* (The court-books of the lords of Rosenberg), *Abhandlungen der böhmischen Gesellschaft der Wissenschaften*, Prague 1878.

Neumann, A. *Nové prameny k dějinám husitství na Moravě* (New sources to the history of Hussitism in Moravia), Olomouc 1930.

Novotný, V. ed., *Kronika velmi pěkna o Janovi Žižkovi* (The very pretty chronicle on Žižka), Prague 1923.

Palacký, F. ed., *Staři letopisové čeští od r. 1378 do 1527* (Old Czech Annalists), *Scriptores Rerum Bohemicarum*, III, Prague 1829.

———. *Archiv český*, the early volumes of this great collection of historical documents in Czech, especially vols. I, III, and VI.

———. *Urkundliche Beiträge zur Geschichte des Hussitenkrieges* (Documents in other languages, mainly Latin and German), Prague 1873.

Příbram, Jan. "Život kněží taborských" (The life of the Taborite priests), *Časopis katolického duchovenstva*, 1863.

Prochaska, A. ed., *Codex Epistolaris Vitoldi*, Cracow 1882.

Raczyński, R. ed., *Codex diplomaticus Lithuaniae*, Breslau 1845.

Rynešová, R. ed., *Listař a listinař Oldřicha z Rožmberka* (Collection of letters and documents of Ulrich of Rosenberg), Prague 1929.

Siegel, K. "Briefe und Urkunden zur Geschichte des Hussitenkrieges," *Zeitschrift des Vereins für die Geschichte Mährens und Schlesiens*, XXII, 1918.

Svejkovský, F. ed., *Staročeské vojenské řády* (Old-Czech military ordinances, including Žižka's), Prague 1952.

Theobald, Zacharias. *Hussiten-Krieg*, Nuremberg 1621.

Vavřinec z Březové (Lawrence of Březová), *Piseň o vítězství u Domažlic* (Poem on the victory of Domažlice), ed. Hrdina and Ryba, Prague 1951.

Windecke, Eberhart. *Denkwürdigkeiten zur Geschichte des Zeitalters Kaiser Sigmunds*, ed. Altmann, Berlin 1893.

## III. GENERAL HISTORIES WITH SIGNIFICANT TREATMENT OF HUSSITISM

Bachmann, A. *Geschichte Böhmens*, 2 vols., 1899-1905.

Bartoš, F. M. *Čechy v době Husově* (Bohemia in the time of Hus), part II, vol. 6 of the great standard work on Bohemian history, ed. by Novotný and Krofta, Prague 1947. Unfortunately the continuation, treating the period of the Hussite Revolution, has not yet been published.

Bretholz, B. *Geschichte Böhmens und Mährens*, 4 vols., Reichenberg 1921-1925.

*Československá vlastivěda* (General knowledge of Czechoslovakia) vol. IV, History, especially the parts by Odložilík (1273-1418) and Urbánek (1419-1526), Prague 1934.

Dvořák, R., *Dějiny Moravy* (History of Moravia), vol. III, Brno 1899.

Eisenmann, L. *La Tchécoslovaquie*, Paris 1921.

Krofta, K. *Dějiny československé* (Czechoslovak history), Prague 1946.

Lindner, Th. *Deutsche Geschichte unter den Habsburgern und Luxemburgern, 1273-1437*, Stuttgart 1893.

Lützow, F. *Bohemia, An Historical Sketch*, revised ed., London 1939.

Odložilík, O. *Nástin československých dějin* (Survey of Czechoslovak history), 6th ed., Prague 1947.

Palacký, F. *Geschichte von Böhmen*, 10 volumes in German and Czech, 1830-1869.

Seton-Watson, R. *A History of the Czechs and Slovaks*, London 1944.

Thomson, S. Harrison. *Czechoslovakia in European History*, second edition, Princeton 1954.

## IV. THE HUSSITE MOVEMENT: RELIGION

Histories of the Church in Bohemia, among them those by A. Frind (1864-1878), F. Vacek (1890), V. Naegle (1921) and J. Ráček (1940). No attempt has been made here to list the considerable monographic literature on Hus as a religious figure, on other leaders of the religious reform movement and on the purely religious aspects of this movement, except where these works have some direct bearing on the revolution 1419-1436.

Bartoš, F. M. *Do čtyř artykulu* (To the Four Articles), Prague 1926.

———. *Husitství a cizina* (Hussitism and the foreign world), Prague 1931.

———. *Bojovníci a mučedníci; obrazky z dějin české reformace* (Fighters and martyrs, sketches from the history of the Bohemian reformation), Prague 1939.

———. *Světci a kacíři* (Witnesses and heretics), Prague 1949.

Borecký, F. *Mistr Jakoubek ze Stříbra*, Prague 1945.

Goll, J. *Quellen und Untersuchungen zur Geschichte der böhmischen Brüder*, Prague 1878, 1882.

Haupt, H. *Die religiösen Sekten in Franken vor der Reformation*, Würzburg 1882.

Hofman, L. *Husité a concilium Basilejské* (The Hussites and the Council of Basel), *Č.Č.H.*, vol. 7.

Holinka, R. *Sektářství v Čechách před revoluci husitskou* (Sectarianism in Bohemia before the Hussite Revolution), Prague 1929.

Hrejsa, F. *Dějiny Křesťanství v Československu* (History of Christianity in Czechoslovakia), Prague 1947.

Kestenberg, R. "Hussitentum und Judentum," *Jahrbuch der Gesellschaft für Geschichte der Juden in der Č.S.R.*, VIII, Prague 1936.

Krofta, K. "Kurie a cirkevní správa zemí českých v době předhusitské (The Curia and the Church administration of the Czech countries in pre-Hussite times), *Č.Č.H.*, vols. 10 and 12.

Krummel, L. *Geschichte der böhmischen Reformation*, Gotha 1866.

———. *Utraquisten und Taboriten*, Gotha 1871.

Martinu, J. *Die Waldensier und die hussitische Reformation in Böhmen*, Vienna 1910.

Neumann, A. *České sekty ve stol. XIV a XV* (Czech sects in the 14th and 15th centuries), Prague 1920.

Odložilík, *Wiclif and Bohemia*, Prague 1937.

Smend, J. *Kelchspendung und Kelchversagung in der abendländischen Kirche*, Göttingen 1898.

Spinka, M. *John Hus and the Czech Reform*, Chicago 1941.

———. *Advocates of Reform*, Philadelphia 1953.

Stein, E. *Želivský jako nábožensk̄a osobnost* (Želivský as religious personality), *Věstník královské české společností nauk*, Prague 1947.

Thomson, S. Harrison, "Luther and Bohemia," *Archiv für Reformationsgeschichte*, vol. 44, 1953, pp. 160-181, with bibliography.

Uhlirz, M. *Die Genesis der vier Prager Artikel, Sitzungsberichte der K. Akademie der Wissenschaften*, 175, 3, Vienna 1914.

## V. THE HUSSITE MOVEMENT AND DEVELOPMENTS LEADING TO IT: SOCIAL AND ECONOMIC PROBLEMS

Chaloupecký, V. *Selská otázka v Husitství* (The peasant problem in Hussitism), Bratislava 1926.

Grauss, G. *Městská chudina v době předhusitské* (The poor classes in the cities in pre-Hussite times), Prague 1949.

Heymann, F. G. "The Role of the Towns in the Bohemia of the Later Middle Ages," *Journal of World History*, vol. II, 1955.

Hrubý, F. "Z hospodářských převratu českých v stol. XV a XVI" (On the great economic changes in Bohemia in the 15th and 16th centuries), *Č.Č.H.*, 1924.

Kapras, J. *Právní dějiny zemí koruny české* (Legal history of the lands of the Bohemian crown), Prague 1913-1920.

———. *Přehled právních dějin zemí koruny české* (An outline of the legal history . . . ), 5th ed., Prague 1935.

———. *Narodnostní poměry v české koruně před válkami husitskými* (Nationality conditions in Bohemia before the Hussite Wars), Prague 1911.

———. *Narodnostní poměry v české koruně od valek husitských do bitvy bělohorské* (same, from the Hussite Wars to the Battle of the White Mountain), Prague 1912.

Krofta, K. *Dějiny selského stavu* (History of the peasant class), 2nd ed., Prague 1949.

Lippert, J. *Social-Geschichte Böhmens in vorhussitischer Zeit*, Prague and Vienna 1896.

Mendl, B. "Hospodářské a sociální poměry v městech Pražských v letech 1378-1434" (The economic and social conditions in the Prague towns in the years 1378-1434), *Č.Č.H.*, 1915-1916.

———. "Sociální krise a zápasy ve městech čtrnáctého věku" (The social crisis and the struggles in the cities of the 14th century), *Č.Č.H.*, 1924-1927.

———. *Z hospodářských dějin středověké Prahy* (On the economic history of medieval Prague), Prague 1925.

———. "Počátky našich cech" (The beginnings of our guilds), *Č.Č.H.*, 1927.

Prokeš, J. "Sociální proudy v hnutí husitském" (Social currents in the Hussite movement), *Nové Čechy*, III, 1919-1920.

Vacek, F. *Socialní dějiny české doby starší* (Social history of Bohemia in the older times), *Vzdělavací knihovna katolická*, vol. 39, 1905.

Werunsky, E. "Böhmens sozialpolitische Entwickelung in vorhussitischer Zeit," *Neue Jahrbücher für das klassische Altertum, Geschichte und deutsche Litteratur*, vol. 4, 1901.

Winter, Z. *Dějiny řemesel a obchodu v Čechách v XIV a v XV století* (History of crafts and commerce in Bohemia in the 14th and 15th centuries), Prague 1906.

## VI. THE HUSSITE WARS: MILITARY PROBLEMS AND DEVELOPMENTS

Frankenberger, O. *Naše veliká armáda* (Our great army), Prague 1921.

Hoch, K. "Husité a válka" (The Hussites and War), *Česká Mysl* 1907.

Kuffner, H. *Husitské vojny v obrazech* (Hussite campaigns in pictures), Vinohrady 1908.

Neumann, A. "K válečnictví za doby husitské" (Warfare in Hussite times) *Hlidka*, XXXVII, 1920.

Toman, H. *Husitské válečnictví za doby Žižkovy a Prokopovy* (Hussite Warfare in the times of Žižka and Prokop), Prague 1898.

Urbánek, R. *Lipany a konec polních vojsk* (Lipany and the end of the field armies), Prague 1934.

Wagner, E. *Jak válčili Husité* (How the Hussites waged war), Prague 1946.

Wulf, M. v. *Die Hussitische Wagenburg*, Berlin 1889.

———. "Hussitisches Kriegswesen," *Preussische Jahrbücher*, vol. 69, 1892.

———. "Zahlen der hussitischen Heere," *Mitteilungen des Vereins für Geschichte der Deutschen in Böhmen*, 1893.

(See also the main works on the history of war in the Middle Ages, such as those by Delbrück, Köhler, Oman, and especially F. Lot, *L'art militaire et les armées au Moyen Age*, Paris 1946. Almost all of them, however, are hampered by their lack of knowledge of Czech and of most of the source material.)

## VII. HUSSITES: THEIR FOREIGN RELATIONS, ESPECIALLY TO POLAND-LITHUANIA

Brückner, A. "Zur Geschichte des Hussitentums in Polen," *Archiv für slavische Geschichte*, vol. 15, 1893.

Goll, J. *Čechy a Prusy ve středověku* (Bohemia and Prussia in the Middle Ages), Prague 1896.

———. "König Sigmund und Polen 1419-1436," *Mitteilungen des Instituts für österreichische Geschichtsforschung*, vol. 15, 1896.

Heinl, E. *Witold von Litauen in seinem Verhältnis zum Deutschen Orden in Preussen*, Berlin 1925.

Kochanowski, J. *Witold, wielki książę litewski*, Lwów 1900.

Kolankowski, L. *Dzieje wielkiego księstwa Litewskiego za Jagiellonów* (History of the Grand Duchy of Lithuania under the Jagiellones), vol. 1, Warsaw 1930.

———. *Polska Jagiellonów, Dzieje polityczne* (Jagiellone Poland, political history) Lwów 1936.

Kopetzky, F. "Die Gefangennahme der hussitischen Gesandten in Ratibor," *Zeitschrift des Vereins für Geschichte und Alterthum Schlesiens*, Breslau 1869.

Krofta, K. "Die historischen Beziehungen zwischen Polen und Čechen," *Slavische Rundschau*, vol. 4, Prague 1932.

Lewicki, A. "Ein Blick in die Politik König Sigmunds gegen Polen in Bezug auf die Hussitenkriege," *Archiv für österreichische Geschichte*, Vienna 1886.

———. "Król Zygmunt Luksemburski a Polska 1420-1436" (König Sigismund and Poland), *Kwartalnik historyczny*, Lwów 1896.

Lohmeyer, K. "Witowd, Grossfürst von Littauen," in *Zur altpreussischen Geschichte*, Gotha 1907.

Łowmianski, H. *Witold, wielki książę litewski*, Wilna 1930.

Pfitzner, J. *Grossfürst Witold von Litauen als Staatsmann*, Brno 1930.

Popiolek, K. *Śląsk i Polska w okresie wojen husyckich* (Silesia and Poland in connection with the Hussite Wars), *Polski Śląsk*, Katovice 1937.

Prochaska, A. *Polska a Czechy w czasach husyckich aż do odwotania Korybuta z Czech* (Poland and Bohemia in Hussite times up to the recall of Korybut from Bohemia), *Rozprawy Wydzialu Hist. Filoz. Akademii Umiejetności*, Cracow 1878.

———. *Dzieje Witolda, w. księcia Litwy* (History of Witold, Grand Duke of Lithuania), Wilna 1914.

Sherbowitz-Wetzor, O. P. *The Polish foreign policy under King Władysław Jagiello in relation with the Hussite movement in Bohemia*, Harvard dissertation, 1933.

## VIII. LITERATURE ON ŽIŽKA

Bartoš, F. M. *Z Žižkových mladých let* (Of Žižka's young years), Prague 1922.

———. *Jan Žižka z Trocnova*, Prague 1924.

———. *Žižkův duch, jeho povaha a listy* (revised edition of Toman's work, listed below), Prague 1924.

———. Several articles on Žižka in *Jihočeský sborník historický*, VI, 3.

———. *Listy a řád vojenský Jana Žižky* (Letters and military ordinance), Prague 1935.

Čečetka, J. F. *Jan Žižka*, Prague 1925.

Čermák, K. *Listy Jana Žižky z Trocnova a jeho vojenský řád* (Žižka's letters and his military ordinance), Čáslav 1912.

Chaloupecký, V. *Byl Žižka slepý?* (Was Žižka blind?) *Věstník české akademie věd a umění*, LX, 1951, no. 6.

Chalupný, E. *Žižka*, Prague 1924.

Císařová-Kolářová, A. and Daňhelka, J. ed., *Listy dvou Janu* ("Letters of two Johns," Hus and Žižka), with a postscript by F. M. Bartoš, Prague 1949.

Hauner, V. J. "Žižkova taktika v dějinách válečnictví" (Žižka's tactics in the history of warfare), *Vojenské rozhledy*, Prague 1924.

Herben, J. *Jan Žižka z Trocnova*, Prague 1921.

Holý, K. *Žižka strateg* (Žižka as strategist), *Spisy vojenského archivu RČS*, I, 2, Prague 1928.

Krofta, K. *Žižka a husitská revoluce*, Prague 1937.

Mareš, F. "Bratr Žižkův Jaroslav z Trocnova" (Žižka's brother Jaroslav), *Časopis musea českého*, 1899.

Millauer, M. *Diplomatisch-historische Aufsätze über Joh. Žižka*, Prague 1824.

Pekař, J. *Žižka a jeho doba* (Žižka and his time), 4 vols., Prague 1927-1933.

Prokeš, J. *Jan Žižka z Trocnova a jeho doba* (Žižka and his time), Prague 1920.

Sand, George. *Jean Zyska*, Paris and Brussels, several editions beginning with 1843.

Sedláček, A. "Doklady k otázce o Žižkově staří" (Documents referring to the question of Žižka's age), *Č.Č.H.*, vol. 19.

Šimák, J. V. "Byl-li Žižka v Litoměřicku v 1422?" (Was Žižka near Litoměřice in 1422?), *Č.Č.H.*, vol. 19.

Škorpil, V. M. ed., *Na množství nehleďte* ("Never mind their numbers"), documents relating to Žižka, Prague 1946.

Šusta, J. *K otázce staří Žižkova* (To the question of Žižka's age), *Přehled* 1911 and reprint in *Úvahy a drobné spisy*, vol. 1, Prague 1934.

Terebelský, J. *Život Jana Žižky z Trocnova* (The Life of Žižka), Olomouc 1850.

Titz, K. *O původu jména Žižka* (On the origin of the name Žižka), Brno 1924.

Toman, H. *Literární památky, duch a povaha Žižkova* (The literary heritage, spirit and character of Žižka), Prague 1893.

Tomek, V. V. "O rodu a počatcích Jana Žižky" (On the family and early life of Žižka), *Časopis musea českého*, 1876.

———. *Jan Žižka*, Prague 1879 (also in German translation).

———. "Oprava a doplňek k životopisu Žižkovu" (Correction and supplement to the biography of Žižka), *Časopis musea českého*, 1892.

Ungar, R. *Žižka's militärische Briefe und Verordnungen*, *Abhandlungen der böhmischen Gesellschaft der Wissenschaften*, II, F.I.B., 375.

Urbánek, R. *Žižka v památkách a úctě lidu českého* (Žižka in the memories and reverence of the Czech people), Brno 1924.

———. "Žižka the Hussite," *Slavonic Review*, vol. III, 1924.

———. ed., *Sborník Žižkův 1424-1924.* (A collection of major articles on Žižka on occasion of the quincentenary of his death), Prague 1924.

———. *Jan Žižka*, Prague 1925.

*Žižkova doba* (Žižka's time), a series of lectures published by the Památník odboje, Prague 1924.

## IX. OTHER PUBLICATIONS REFERRING TO THE HUSSITE REVOLUTION

Aschbach, H. *Geschichte Kaiser Sigmunds*, Hamburg 1844 and later.

Auštecká, B. "Jan Želivský jako politik" (Želivský as politician), *Husitský archiv*, II, 1925.

Baker, J. *A Forgotten Great Englishman: The Life and Work of Peter Payne*, London 1894.

Bernhardt, R. *Die Inanspruchnahme des Deutschen Reiches durch die Hussitenfrage*, Halle 1901.

Bezold, F. v. *König Sigmund und die Reichskriege gegen die Hussiten*, Munich 1874.

Binder, P. S. *Die Hegemonie der Prager im Hussitenkriege*, 2 vols., Prague 1901, 1903.

Denis, E. *Hus et la guerre des Hussites*, Paris 1878.

Dobrovský, J. *Geschichte der böhmischen Pikarden und Adamiten*, *Abhandlungen der böhmischen Gesellschaft der Wissenschaften*, 1788.

Droysen, J. G. *Geschichte der Preussischen Politik*, Leipzig 1855, vol. I.

———. "Eberhard Windecke," *Abhandlungen der k. sächsischen Gesellschaft der Wissenschaften*, II, 1857.

Grünhagen, C. *Die Hussitenkampfe der Schlesier*, Breslau 1872.

Haupt, H. "Hussitische Propaganda in Deutschland," *Raumers Historisches Jahrbuch*, Leipzig 1886.

Herben, J. *John Hus and his followers*, London 1926.

Heymann, F. G. "The National Assembly of Čáslav," *Medievalia et Humanistica*, Fasc. VIII, 1954.

Jecht, R. "Der Oberlausitzer Hussitenkrieg," *Neues Lausitzer Magazin*, vol. 87, Görlitz 1911.

Juritsch, F. *Der dritte Kreuzzug gegen die Hussiten*, Prague 1900.

Krofta, K. *Nesmrtelní národ* (Immortal Nation), Prague 1940.

———. *Duchovní odkaz husitstvi* (The spiritual heritage of Hussitism), Prague 1946.

Kroker, E. "Sachsen und die Hussitenkriege," *Neues Archiv für sächsische Geschichte*, XXI, 1900.

Lenfant, J. *Histoire de la guerre des Hussites et du Concile de Basle*, Amsterdam 1731.

Lützow, F. *The Hussite Wars*, London 1914.

Macek, J. *Husitské revoluční hnutí* (The Hussite revolutionary movement), Prague 1952.

Mathesius ed. *Co dali naše země Evropě a lidstvu* (What our lands gave to Europe and humanity), Prague 1940.

Nejedlý, Z. *Dějiny husitského zpěvu* (History of the Hussite Song), vol. II, Prague 1913.

———. *Spor o smysl českých dějin* (The struggle over the sense of Czech History), Prague 1914.

Neumann, A. *K dějinám husitství na Moravě*, Olomouc 1939.

Odložilík, O. "Z počátku husitství na Moravě" (On the beginnings of Hussitism in Moravia), *Časopis matice moravské* 1925 and special book edition.

Pekař, J. *Smysl českých dějin* (The Sense of Czech History), Prague 1912.

Schmidt, K. G. *Beiträge zur Geschichte der Hussitenkriege*, in *Forschungen zur deutschen Geschichte*, Göttingen 1866.

Sedláček, A. *Hrady, zamky a tvrze království českého* (Castles of Bohemia, with histories of the baronial families), 15 vols. 1882-1927.

Sello, G. "Die Einfälle der Hussiten in die Mark Brandenburg," *Preussische Jahrbücher*, XIX, 1882.

Slavík, J. *Husitská revoluce*, Prague 1934.

Tomek, V. V. *Dějepis města Prahy* (History of the city of Prague), vol. IV, 2nd ed. Prague 1898, also separately as *Dějiny válek husitských* (History of the Hussite wars).

Urbánek, R. "K historii husitské Moravy," *Časopis matice moravské*, 1940.

Voigt, G. *Enea Silvio de' Piccolomini*, Berlin 1862.

# INDEX

NOTE: Members of the nobility are listed under the place (usually castle) after which they normally called themselves, except where they used another "second" name in preference (such as Žižka, Hvězda, Sokol, Vavák, Zmrzlík). Other people such as priests are listed under their first names, except where, as in the case of Příbram, Rokycana, and Želivský, the name of origin has become the generally accepted identification.